The
Devil's
Music
Master

The Devil's Music Master

The Controversial Life and Career of Wilhelm Furtwängler

Sam H. Shirakawa

OXFORD UNIVERSITY PRESS

New York | Oxford | 1992

Oxford University Press

Oxford   New York   Toronto
Delhi   Bombay   Calcutta   Madras   Karachi
Kuala Lumpur   Singapore   Hong Kong   Tokyo
Nairobi   Dar es Salaam   Cape Town
Melbourne   Auckland

and associated companies in
Berlin   Ibadan

Copyright © 1992 by Sam H. Shirakawa.

Published by Oxford University Press, Inc.,
200 Madison Avenue, New York, New York 10016

Oxford is a registered trademark of Oxford University Press.

Library of Congress Cataloging-in-Publication Data
Shirakawa, Sam H.
The devil's music master : the controversial life and career of Wilhelm
Furtwängler / Sam H. Shirakawa.
p. cm.   Includes index.
ISBN 0-19-506508-5
1. Furtwängler, Wilhelm, 1886–1954.   2. Conductors (Music)—
Germany—Biography.   I. Title.
ML422.F92S53   1992
784.2'092—dc20
[B]   91-25994

The following page is regarded as an extension of the copyright page.

9 8 7 6 5 4 3 2 1

Printed in the United States of America
on acid-free paper

The author gratefully acknowledges considerations granted by the following sources:

Elisabeth Furtwängler for permission to quote excerpts from her late husband's writings and to quote from her own memoir, *Über Wilhelm Furtwängler*, third edition, Brockhaus Verlag, Wiesbaden, 1986.

The I.H.T. Corporation, Washington, for permission to quote excerpts from reviews by Lawrence Gilman in the *New York Herald-Tribune*, 5 and 24 January 1925 and 11 February 1927. All rights reserved.

Quartet Books Ltd., London, for permission to quote excerpts from *Notebooks*, by Wilhelm Furtwängler, translated by Shaun Whiteside, 1990.

S. Fischer Verlag, GmbH, Frankfurt-am-Main, for permission to quote an unpublished letter by Thomas Mann, 1 July 1947; excerpts from an unpublished lecture, "Germany and the Germans," delivered at the Library of Congress on 29 May 1945; and excerpts from *Briefe, 1894–1962*, by Bruno Walter, 1969.

The New York Times Company, New York, for permission to quote passages from reviews and articles from 1925, 1926, 1927, 1931, 1936, and 1937.

The Bruno Walter Foundation for permission to quote portions of unpublished letters by Bruno Walter from 1946 and 1948.

Farrar, Strauss, & Giroux, Inc., New York, for permission to quote excerpts from *Hilter's Secret Conversations*, translated by Norman Cameron and R. H. Stevens, 1953.

Edition Spanenberg, München, for permission to quote a letter by Erika Mann, 31 May 1947.

Doubleday, New York, for permission to quote an excerpt from *Cellist*, by Gregor Piatigorsky, 1965.

Herbert A. Strauss and the Smithsonian Institution Press, Washington, for permission to quote an excerpt from *The Muses Free Hilter*, 1983.

Alfred A. Knopf, Inc., New York, for permission to quote excerpts from *Theme and Variations*, by Bruno Walter, translated by James A. Galston, 1946; and from *Understanding Toscanini*, by Joseph Horowitz, 1986.

HarperCollins Publishers, New York, for permission to quote excerpts from *Heritage of Fire*, by Friedelind Wagner and Page Cooper, 1945.

Lippincott, Philadelphia, and Harper Row, New York, for permission to quote excerpts from *Unheard Witness*, by Ernst Hanfstängl, 1957.

The Metropolitan Opera Association, New York, for permission to quote excerpts of letters by Rudolf Bing, 1952.

In memory of my parents

Preface

He was perhaps the greatest conductor this century has produced. Almost forty years after his death, however, Wilhelm Furtwängler remains one of the most controversial figures in any field, his memory and reputation clouded by misinformation and lies. Several books and numerous articles have been written about this extraordinary and enigmatic figure, but no work has yet sought to view Furtwängler's life within the broad range of his career as a musician, work as a composer, and the complexities of his politics and personal life.

While better-publicized musicians may be more famous, Furtwängler is no mere cult figure. Any musician living or dead who has had his recordings available in every format on 40 different commercial labels for over thirty years throughout the world must be reaching more than a lunatic fringe of the record-buying public. Decades after his death he not only holds his audience but steadily acquires new listeners who were born too recently to have heard him "live." This, despite quantum leaps in the quality of sound recording and expensive publicity campaigns selling a variety of other over-recorded conductors. The vast corpus of his recording output is gaining yet another life on compact discs, and dedicated pirate recording efforts have scrupulously cleaned up the sound on an enormous number of his live performances and put them out again on one label after another. Unscrupulous entrepreneurs have also made a lucrative living over the years selling so-called Furtwängler recordings that he never made.

Only in the United States is he unfamiliar despite his persistent and growing presence in record shops since his death. There are good reasons why he is not better known to the American public, and I am getting into all that later. The fact that he rarely performed in North America has little, if anything, to do with why he is not as well known as, say, Toscanini or Karajan. But *why* Furtwängler appeared in the United States only three seasons during his 32-year career as conductor of the Berlin and Vienna Philharmonic orchestras has almost everything to do with the hostility that still so frequently attends his name in the United States.

Poorly informed critics frequently berate Furtwängler for ignoring modern and contemporary works and preferring instead to perform an unchanging regimen of 18th and 19th century masters. They fail to recognize that Furtwängler was a vociferous and active champion of new music among his generation in the 1920s and 1930s, even though his personal preferences abjured the trend toward atonality. The halcyon culture of the Weimar Republic (1918–1933) would have been far less lustrous had it not been for his pioneering and imaginative contributions to the musical life of Berlin and Vienna during those years. In this period, he not only presented more than his share of new works, but brought the breadth of the Homeric epic and the passion and awe of classical tragedy to his interpretations of the German masters.

When thousands of intellectuals and artists joined the exodus of Jews from Germany after the Nazis seized power, Furtwängler remained behind with the naive but overwhelming conviction that he could save the culture that produced Bach, Beethoven, Brahms, and other great composers from annihilation by the Third Reich. Despite his well-documented and astonishingly successful efforts to keep Jews a part of German cultural life in the early part of the Nazi era and his manifold endeavors to assist *anyone* who asked him for help throughout the Third Reich, saving hundreds of them from certain death, he was all but branded a war criminal and nearly framed at his denazification trial at the end of the war. This, even though Furtwängler never joined the Nazi Party and openly acted against the regime until its fall.

Finally returning to public life in 1947, after a forced hiatus, he entered a new phase of musical development both as a conductor and composer. But even as he achieved new heights of insight in his postwar studio recordings and live performances, he began finally to buckle under the pressure of having stood up to the Nazis, to those in his own profession who had used the evil regime to undermine him, and to the hatred he now encountered from some of those he had sacrificed his career and endangered his life to help. Ultimately his health broke, and with it, his will. Wilhelm Furtwängler died in 1954 at the relatively early age of 68.

The present book seeks to view Furtwängler's life within the turbulent times in which he lived, but the events in his life do not proceed cohesively in a single arching line. Furtwängler led many lives, frequently all at the same time. He was a musician, a musical essayist and thinker, an incorrigible womanizer as well as loyal friend to women, and in spite of himself a complicated but deeply committed political figure whose significance has yet to be assessed properly. What is more, his non-musical lives are every bit as central to the man as his music. The reader who expects merely a musical biography is in for a bit of a surprise.

This book is about the development of a musician, and a great one at that, but it is also about a man who becomes a tragic figure in the classical sense of that word. Wilhelm Furtwängler was a creature whose overweening confidence in his own capacity to make a difference against one of the most malevolent forces the world has known catapulted him far beyond the confines of his profession. That peculiar spark of hubris drove him into resistance, rebellion, and sedition in defense of a culture being annihilated. In striving to salvage what he felt was the "true Germany," he bartered his great gift, his prestige, and his honor, and he became a leading figure in the resistance inside Germany despite later efforts to prove otherwise. Even today, however, many remain convinced that Furtwängler at best compromised and at worst simply sold out. For them, Wilhelm Furtwängler will forever be the Devil's music master. They will probably stay unmoved by the central portion of this book, which examines his deadly relationship with the Third Reich. On the other hand, those who know Furtwängler only from fragmentary evidence, declarations, or hearsay may find this book helpful in coming to their own conclusions about a unique musician who was also one of the most compelling personalities of our time.

Much as I would like to say I have done it all alone, battling in solitary persistence unspeakably hostile forces and rude people, I have encountered very few who were reluctant or unable to speak with me. Most gave generously and tirelessly of themselves by submitting patiently to my interviews, many of which were carried out over a long period: Sir Yehudi Menuhin, Sir Reginald Goodall, Carl F. Flesch, Albert and Paula Catell, Claudio Abbado, Elisabeth Legge-Schwarzkopf, Leonie Rysanek, Wolfgang Schneiderhan, Friedelind Wagner, Ernst Drucker, Klaus Lang, Rudolf Schwarz, Martha Mödl, Wolfgang Stresemann, Professor Raymond Klibansky, Werner Thärichen, Egon

Hanfstängl, Rudolf Schwarz, Joanna Graudan, Suzanne Bloch-Smith, Anthony Griffith, Dagmar Bella-Sturli, Dorothea and Dr. Andreas Furtwängler, and Elisabeth Furtwängler, whose implicit trust and indefatigable assistance enabled me to prepare for writing this book in a manner that I hope will be worthy of its subject.

Countless people, some of whom I never had the privilege of thanking personally, assisted me with unflagging interest in my project at the following institutions: the staff of the Music and Periodical Divisions at the Library of Congress, the personnel at the Library for the Performing Arts at Lincoln Center, the executors of the Bruno Walter Foundation, New York; the staff of the Music Department, Free Library of Philadelphia; Brenda Nelson-Strauss and her colleagues at the Archives of the Chicago Symphony Orchestra, Chicago; Dr. Günther Birkner and Frau Dr. Mireille Geering and staff of the Musikabteilung, Zentralbibliothek, Zürich; Mme. D'Amour of the Bibliothèque Nationale and the Library of the Paris Opéra, Stéphane Topakian and Philippe Jacquard, Société Wilhelm Furtwängler, Paris; Frau Liselotte Homering of the Theater Collection, Reissmuseum, Mannheim; the staff of the Mannheim Staatarchiv; Dr. Michael Kuschnia, Axel Schröder, and Frau Scharmacher of the Staatsoper Unter den Linden, Berlin; Curt Roesler and the staff of the Deutsche Oper Berlin, Dr. Clement Hilsberg and Otto Strasser of the Vienna Philharmonic, Vienna; the staff of the Musikabteilung, Staatarchiv, Berlin; the staff of the Musikabteilung, Albertina, Nationalbibliothek, Vienna, the staff of the Archives, New York Philharmonic, Dr. Saupe and the staff of the Staatarchiv and Bayerschen Staatarchiv, Munich; Mr. David Marwell and the staff of the Berlin Document Center, Dr. Wolfgang Trautwein and the staff of the Archives, Akademie der Künste, Berlin; the staff of the Bundesarchiv, Koblenz; the staff of the Archives, Boston Symphony; Brigitte Grabner of the Vienna Staatsoper, Dr. Helge Grünewald and the staff of the Berliner Philharmoniker and the staff of the Archives, Berlin Philharmonisches Orchester.

I am especially grateful to Judith and Fred K. Prieberg for their friendship and hospitality and for Fred's tireless help with sources, details, and facts. I am also indebted to Professor Daniel Gillis for his encouragement and sage critical suggestions as the manuscript evolved; to Raymond Donnell for his encyclopedic knowledge, his unflagging vigor in looking through my manuscript, and for helping me connect with countless sources of information; and to Sheldon Meyer, my editor at Oxford University Press, whose patience, good sense, and relentless insistence on saving me from myself are behind whatever worth this book may ultimately have. I also wish to thank his colleagues in the editorial department—Leona Capeless, Karen

Wolny, and Scott Lenz—for their generous assistance in preparing the manuscript for publication.

Some of the following names are more recognizable than others, but their owners are all equally distinguished human beings, and what you are about to read could not have been possible without their kind graces: Nora Aponte, Merle Hubbard, Illtyd Harrington, Tom Currie, Anthony Staffieri, Rose Ganguzza, John David Riva, Robert Sandla, Peter and Monique Wolrich, Robert Plotczyk, Markus Kiesel, Christopher Downes, Joseph Green, Bonnie and Major General Fred Haynes (U.S. Marines, ret.), Siegfried Schoenbohm, Robert T. Levine, Judith Sullivan, Dame Ruth King, Alan Carrier, Michael McMahon, Gary Allabach, Phyllis Melhado, Christabel Bielenberg, Donn Teal, Cryder Bankus, Tom Clear, Steven Wakeman, Erik Canel, Robert Kozovsky, Les Robbins, Bouy Nunnally, Vincent Urwand, Steven Shirakawa, Dieter Senft, Ingo Wackenhut, Elisabeth Arlt, and many others whose forebearance I must ask for forgetting to include them here.

This book was completed without grants and the customary forms of charity to which endeavors of its sort are heir. Nonetheless, I could not have written it without having gainful employment, and through much of its gestation, I had the good fortune of meeting and working with some extraordinary individuals. Among them: Bill Applegate, Walter Liss, Henry Florsheim, David Friend, Mariane Scheer, Larry Goodman, Phil Tucker, Gloria McDonnough, Chauncey Howell, Joel Franklin, Kaity Tong, Greg Hurst, Jay Scott, Rolanda Watts, Roz Abrams, Joel Siegel, Tappy Philips, Diana Williams, John Johnson, David Novarro, Tim Fleischer, Kay Kusuda, Art McFarland, Kathy Wolff, Carlos Granda, Doug Johnson, Marc Stevens, Sarah Wallace, Jay Adlersberg, Sam Champion, Susan Roesgen, Scott Clark, Corey McPherrin, Lawrence Balter, N. J. Burkett, Tim Minton, Bill Evans, Celeste Ford, Pat Dawson, Jim Dolan, Bill Beutel, Marvin Montgomery, Eugene Young, Connie Green, Kathy Green, Al Romero, Ana Maria Braga, Tom Busby, Fred Chieco, Todd Ehrlich, Mitch Fields, Mark Noble, Betty Capellan, Iris Dudman, Lisa Ellen, Steve Hochbrunn, Suzanne Bergerac, Jill Adams, Grace Anorve, Rocco Garramone, Barbara Ann Linton, John Chow, Jim Doran, Al Giardelli, Kevin Pultz, Daniela Royes, Elissa Rubin, Maura Sweeney, Jodi Fleisig, Richard Regan, Sandy Lechner, Ilene Rosen, Howard Price, Graciela Rogerio, Glen Steinfast, Rebecca Lipkin, Judy Hernandez, Vicki Metz, Peggy Payne, Elaine Peake, Jeff Greene, David Chan, Angelo Pernicone, Walter Dawless, Ron E. Bell, John Cook, Don Dotson, Ed Rickerts, Hal Feldman, Kathleen Jalbert, John Kooistra, Al Webber, Linda Roennau, Marian Tuazon, Linda Wintermute, Jim Devenney, Herb Aust, Fred Cosman, Mike Bencivenga, Joe Butler, Bob Caccamese, Gerardo Lago, Bill Lind, Angelo Martin, Glenn Mayrose, Ishmael Meir, David Mulsewski, Bob Strauss, Mark Fettner, Susan Greenstein, Esperanza Martinez, Tom McCann, Peter Menkes, Ken Plotnik, Mel Francis, Bill Carey, and the rest of the Eyewitness News team at WABC-TV. Without them I would have been just another starving writer. Television, especially local television news, is not known for breeding professional generosity. But to my grateful astonishment, Bill Carey defined time and again the nature of selfless friendship. He and most others at Eyewitness News are indeed possessed of a quality of mercy borne with no constraints.

Mannheim   S.H.S.
25 January 1992

Contents

The
Devil's
Music
Master

1

~

With Music
Empowered

He was born Gustav Heinrich Ernst Martin Wilhelm Furtwängler in Berlin on 25 January 1886. His father, Adolf Furtwängler, was a well-known classical archaeologist and his mother, Adelheid (Wendt), was a painter. The Furtwänglers eventually had three more children—Walter (1887–1967), Marthe Edith (1891–1974), and Anna (1900–1974)—but Wilhelm turned out to be the only musician in the family.[1] His father's family traced its beginnings to the Black Forest Region of south Germany where they thrived as farmers. Wilhelm's grandfather (also named Wilhelm) became the first intellectual in the family. He led a successful career as a teacher and headmaster at a school in Freiburg.

In the year of Wilhelm's birth, two of the most important pianists of the coming century also were born: Edwin Fischer and Arthur Rubinstein. Both would later figure importantly in Furtwängler's career; Fischer positively, Rubinstein otherwise. It was also the year Franz Liszt died, having outlived his son-in-law Richard Wagner by

---

1. In 1940 the Nazi Propaganda Ministry "allowed" Friedrich Herzfeld, who was partly (one-quarter) Jewish, to write a biography of Furtwängler (*Wilhelm Furtwängler: Weg und Wesen*). In it he tries to find other musicians in his ancestry, but he is not successful in tracing a genetic musical connection. No mention, by the way, is made of any of the many Jewish composers he had performed. Herzfeld also wrote anti-Semitic tirades to keep himself out of difficulties, at least until his ancestry was discovered and publicized in 1942. See Chapter 18.

four years. In that year, Anton Bruckner finished the first version of his *Te Deum*, and Saint-Saëns completed his "Organ" Symphony. Nietzsche wrote *Of Good and Evil* and Rimbaud published *Les Illuminations*.[2]

By the time Wilhelm was eight, Arturo Toscanini (b. 1867) was 27 years old and making a name for himself, creating *La Wally* by Catalani in Lucca (1892), as well as conducting premieres of other verismo operas. Richard Strauss had succeeded Hans von Bülow as director of the Berlin Philharmonic (1893), and the 28-year-old Artur Nikisch had just been appointed music director at the Budapest Opera (1893). Verdi had completed *Otello* (1887), Mahler his First Symphony (1888), and Tchaikovsky had finished his last two symphonies (1888, 1893), conducted the New York Philharmonic at the opening of Carnegie Hall (1891), and died of cholera in 1893.

Adolf Furtwängler quit his post as director of the Museum of Antiquities in Berlin in 1894, and the Furtwänglers moved to Munich where Adolf was appointed Professor of Archaeology at the University of Munich. His mother, whose father had been a friend of Brahms, came from the house of Dohrn in northern Germany. Her uncle was the zoologist Anton Dohrn, who established the famous zoological park in Naples, which his friend Hans von Marees furnished with a striking set of frescoes.

Munich was a Bavarian and Catholic city, and its intellectual roots formed a curious mixture of easy-going liberalism and religious conservatism. It was an appropriate environment for the classical education Wilhelm was to receive, for the liberal disposition of the city coincided with the ideals of the Greeks and Romans of antiquity. Both parents had a strong command of English, and his mother encouraged him to translate books into and from English. They did not concern themselves much about nationalism, national boundaries, or national politics, but they knew they were German, though they, like most other Germans, would probably have had a difficult time defining exactly what it meant to be German.

Virtually from infancy, Furtwängler took an intense interest in nature, and he showed musicality at the age of four. But his native intelligence alienated him from most other children his age, and he found a fitful contentment in his isolation. Wilhelm was frequently on the receiving end of that infantile cruelty with which children frequently relate to each other, and these experiences gave a deep-seated suspicion of others. As he grew older, his wary nature grew into a more complicated matrix of wholesale suspicion that became a mild

2. See Gérard Gefen, *Furtwängler: Une Biographie par le Disque*, (Paris) 1986. Hereafter referred to as Gefen.

form of paranoia. He became a compulsive walker, and he used the exercise as a kind of meditative experience nearly every day to the end of his life. He was also athletically inclined, but he preferred solitary sports like hiking and mountain climbing to combative games such as soccer. Which is not to say that he was disinclined to be competitive. To the very end, he was always ready to take part in an argument, and the more intellectually challenging, the more appealing the fight.[3]

He was aptly conditioned for such eristic inclinations early in his life. Wilhelm was a relatively happy child, extremely intelligent and quick-witted, but he did poorly in school. Waiting for less gifted children to catch up bred disinterest, and he formed antagonistic relationships with many of his teachers, some of whom were probably no match for his Brahmin endowment. Both Wilhelm's parents soon realized they had borne an intellectual thoroughbred and decided that conventional schooling was not appropriate for him. So they took him out of his local elementary school and had him educated almost entirely at home, where he progressed with amazing rapidity. His tutors included the archaeologist Ludwig Curtius (1874–1954), the art historian and musicologist Walter Riezler (1878–1965), and the sculptor Adolf Hildebrand (1847–1921). Curtius and Riezler were both assistants to the elder Furtwängler at the University of Munich. All of them later remarked at Wilhelm's lively mind and the sureness of his instincts. He developed enormous self-reliance very early in his life, for the swiftness of his mind kept him ahead of several of his tutors. His intellectual precocity also prompted him to challenge authorities—such as teachers—who had power over him. The need to take on figures who had something—anything—over or on him later developed into virtually a pathological streak of contentiousness, and that pugnacity ultimately would not serve him well.

When he was about 15, Furtwängler formed a passionate affection for Adolf Hildebrand's daughter, Bertl. She was the youngest of the sculptor's daughters, and apparently the most vivacious. Although they were almost married a few years later, the marriage was canceled for some reason. In one of his letters to her, he compares her to the scherzo of Beethoven's Seventh Symphony, which probably was the highest compliment he could pay at the time. Bertl was the first of literally hundreds of women whom Furtwängler loved, but theirs was an idealized affection, one of the few platonic relationships with women he was to have.

While his interest in girls developed almost as prodigiously as his

3. See H. H. Stuckenschmidt, "Wilhelm Furtwängler," *Der Monat*, November 1955, p. 70. This article is scheduled to appear in English in a volume of commemorative essays on Furtwängler, edited by Daniel Gillis.

musical talents, it was a passive interest rather than the sort of wolfish adolescent hankering to which boys of 15 are typically prone. Wilhelm was one of those blessed boys to whom girls readily flocked, forever making themselves available to him. He had grown into a gangly young man well over six feet tall, blazing blue eyes under hooded bushy brows, topped off with a shock of burnished blond hair that turned white in the summer. For all the feminine distractions that came so easily, Wilhelm remained serious and aloof—a somewhat moody, Nordic Byronic figure replete with a scar that creased the right side of his face. The scar aroused lascivious fantasies in many of the women who came to know him. Some thought it was a birthmark that indicated a touch of cruelty. Others thought it was an emblem of machismo gained from a fencing match. Actually, it resulted from an accident when he was ten. He was lost to the world reading a book in the family library when the housekeeper called him for dinner. Not hearing her, he continued reading. Finally she came up and snatched the book from under his eyes and vanished through the French doors of the library. Livid at the interruption, Wilhelm charged into a glass pane in the door. A shard of glass ripped deeply into his cheek from the right side of his mouth.[4] Both the mark and the incendiary temperament that caused it remained with him for the rest of his life.

Wilhelm became acutely aware of his instinctual and imaginative powers early on. Combined with his inordinate capacity to articulate, he frequently could be obstinate in defending his ideas and conclusions. In his youth, he took several trips to Italy and Greece, and his early years were filled with the specters of classical heroes, demigods, and gods standing naked before the world to project the inevitability and rightness of what they represented. The influence not only of the classics and the tragic world-view fostered by the ancient Greeks, but also the tragedies of Shakespeare and the romantic world-view of the supreme German writers—especially Goethe—all were to haunt Wilhelm in more ways than he could perceive at his young age.

Elisabeth Furtwängler, who became his second wife in 1943, recalls his intense interest in drama in her biography of Furtwängler:

> In the dramas of Shakespeare, *King Lear* was without question above all the other tragedies for Furtwängler. He spoke only with greatest respect and love for the work. He also told me how deeply moved he had been with this powerful drama, and how dumbfounded he was that his sister did not want to read it.

4. The lighting in numerous portrait photographs of Furtwängler darken the right side of his face.

He was fairly cool on Schiller because for Furtwängler, Schiller clearly was not capable of Shakespeare's pathos. When I tried to defend Schiller in comparison to Goethe, he merely laughed about my reasoning and said, "You know, I am no professor of literature, but if I may be allowed to make a completely subjective assessment of a work—only for myself," and added in a conciliatory tone, "for ourselves."

Über Wilhelm Furtwängler, pp. 106–107

He studied piano first with his mother and then with his aunt, Minna Furtwängler, at four, and he was composing by age seven.[5] His first surviving composition is entitled "A Little Piece about Animals" for voice and piano. Although it did not exude Mozartean brilliance, his musical talent did not go unnoticed, and his parents fostered and encouraged it. Before the end of the year, he had completed 24 short pieces, most of them for piano.[6] Everyone who knew young Furtwängler was aware of his musical ability. When he was ten, he composed a Sonata for Violin and Piano, a Trio for Piano, Violin and Cello, a string quartet and a set of six piano sonatas. He also composed some short pieces during 1896 and sent them to his grandmother Christiane and his aunt Minna Furtwängler in Mannheim with a greeting:[7]

Here I am sending you my latest work—the Rondo in D flat—which I am dedicating just to you both. It should arrive just in time for Christmas. I like it best of all, so I am sending it to you . . . *Munich, 17 December 1896*

He began his formal studies in composition with Anton Beer-Walbrunn, and started a course in advanced counterpoint in 1900 with Josef Rheinberger, who was the leading authority on the subject in Munich at the time and was himself a prolific composer of comic operas, symphonies and organ music. Rheinberger gave Wilhelm an intensive survey of Beethoven's string quartets. These chamber works were a revelation to him and inspired several works he completed in the next two years: a string Quartet and Sextet, the Trio in E Major for Violin, Cello and Piano, a Fantasy for the same instruments, and a pair

5. Curt Riess, *Furtwängler: Musik und Politik,* (Bern) 1953, says Furtwängler began his piano studies with his aunt after his mother explained the keyboard to him, p. 24. Note: An abridged form of this extremely helpful biography was published in England (Frederick Muller, 1955), translated by Margaret Goldsmith. Unless otherwise noted, all citations hereafter refer to the German text, not the English, and will be listed as Riess. Hans Hubert Schönzeler in *Furtwängler,* (London) 1990 (hereafter referred to as Schönzeler), says he received his first piano lessons from his mother.
6. Listing Nr. 1a in the catalogue of the Zentralbibliothek, Zürich. The items in this group were compiled by Furtwängler's mother. The pieces include four sonatas, a form that became a fixation for Furtwängler for the rest of his life.
7. *Briefe,* (Wiesbaden), p. 16.

of Fantasies for piano. These works are notable primarily for their formal clarity and sincerity of intention. They bear some evidence of the intensity that became a hallmark of his mature works, but they are more apt to strive for the sublime than actually achieve it.

Furtwängler's work with Rheinberger was cut short by the latter's death from incurable lung disease in 1901. Max von Schillings took over Furtwängler's education in composition. It was Schillings whom Furtwängler later credited as the first to recognize his potential for a big career in music. His work with all of them made him acutely aware of the problems of interpretation, and he was fascinated with those questions throughout his life. There was no doubt in young Wilhelm's mind that he would grow up to be a composer.

For all his prodigious musicality, Furtwängler toyed with the idea of following his father into archaeology. But two incidents from these early years show how music decisively claimed his full interests. When he was fourteen, his father took him to Greece. He always carried a pocket score of Beethoven's string quartets. On another occasion, he visited Florence with his tutor Ludwig Curtius. When they came to the chapel of the Medicis in the Church of San Lorenzo, Wilhelm was so overcome by Michelangelo's architectural design and sculptures that he went off to a corner and recorded his thoughts—in little musical notations. These jottings ultimately became his *Te Deum* (1909).

Incidents such as these also demonstrate two other burgeoning characteristics in his personality. On the one hand, the empirical world for Furtwängler was a network of interconnections. Art, history, archeology, literature, and culture in general were all part and parcel of a larger unity demanding expression and offering redemption. He ultimately found he best expressed that unity through music, and in it lay fulfillment.

In these incidents he also exhibited a duality in his sensibility that later would cause him indescribable difficulties. While music became a means of redemption for him, it also became a vehicle for escape. As a consequence, he shuttled constantly between the real and ideal, between the way things are and the way he wanted them to be. Such pendulations quickly became a fixed way of life for him, and they eventually had a corrosive effect on his decision-making faculties in dealing with certain practical matters. While it was perfectly natural for him to shift from one section of music to another, from one set of ideas to another, and from the world of musical ideas to the reality of actualizing those concepts, that extraordinary gift for transition in his music making also produced a a maddening sort of vacillation in everyday life. Later, at a critical point in his life, that tendency became liberating in his work but enslaving in the way he led his personal affairs.

No composer reflected his musical ideals more than Beethoven, and no composer so preoccupied him for the rest of his life. Beethoven both illuminated and, in some ways, tyrannized him. Furtwängler not only adored Beethoven's music but identified with his struggle against the limitations of his deafness and his uncompromising fight for personal independence. The late works of Beethoven opened up a world quite apart from the reality of everyday life. In the last quartets and sonatas, Furtwängler perceived an eerie, even frightening region of consciousness in whose beauty also resided a sublime concreteness of form. By the time he was 12, Furtwängler had memorized virtually all of Beethoven's works, and he could play any of these on the piano— note perfect. His phenomenal memory and his capacity to make instant reconstructions of any orchestral or ensemble work by Beethoven became legendary. Otto Strasser, for example, who was a second violinist with the Vienna Philharmonic for forty years, recalls an incident showing Furtwängler's extraordinary capacity to marshal a perfect rendition of a quintet.

> I frequently played chamber music with Furtwängler. I remember once during the war, we went to his rooms here in Vienna to play Brahms' Quintet, Opus 34. Then he took the violin part—just the violin part—of Brahms' Quartet opus 67 and put it on the piano stand. He proceeded to play the whole quartet on the piano note perfect! He knew it all from memory. Another time, he played the last movement of the Beethoven Quartet Opus 131 on the piano entirely from memory.[8]

Furtwängler's passion for Beethoven eventually prompted him to write one of his earliest surviving essays. In it, he points out the immediacy of the composer even in his last great period where critics usually find him becoming increasingly "abstract:"

> And yet, [Beethoven] is not "abstract," as many believe, even in his last period. To the contrary, the inner glow is much more direct, whose force inspires him toward a Totality, which keeps him from pursuing the individual possibilities of the instruments and thereby allows himself to be inspired by them. Thus, in part, he does not exploit instrumental possibilities; in part, he demands too much of them.   *Ton und Wort, p. 11*[9]

8. Personal conversation with author, Vienna, 9 April 1990.
9. This article appeared in the *Neue Badische Landes Zeitung*, 15 March 1918.

But the power Beethoven had upon him was really secondary to what lay behind Furtwängler's growing obsession with music in general. He became convinced that music at its best and highest was a world unto itself, a universe far richer and infinitely more satisfactory than anything mere reality with its enslavement to chance and vicissitude could make possible. To this extent, Furtwängler was a romantic in the literary sense of the word:

> The artist forces us—each of us—to encounter his creation, forces us to wrestle with him as he is wrestling with us; it is surrender he wants, not mastery. Where the historian is the man of discerning intelligence, the artist is the man of love.   *Concerning Music, p. 74.*

For Furtwängler, then, music not only illuminated the real world and vivified it, but it could at moments become the real world. He resolved to be worthy of entering that universe, of being one of the great composers of the ages.

One of his peers of this world, however, did not support his view of himself. In 1899, he met the famous violinist for whom Brahms had composed his Violin Concerto. Joachim was impressed with Wilhelm, but he did not think of him as a gifted genius. But Wilhelm was not deterred. In 1903 his first Symphony in D was performed in Breslau.[10] It was a fiasco, though the surviving fragments reveal a sophisticated command of orchestral color and instrumental balance. The influences of Brahms and Bruckner are unmistakable, but a restless sense of individuality emerges from these pages.[11] Possibly the orchestra was under-rehearsed; possibly the audience and critics expected something other than what they got. We may never know.

While Furtwängler was disappointed at the reception of his debut as a symphonist, he resolved not to give up composition. Nonetheless, the experience reinforced his feeling that he could not make a living at it. If Mozart, Wagner, Schubert and so many others had lived in such penury, how could he be an exception? Unlike these composers, Wilhelm came from comfortable and sheltered beginnings, and he was never able to see himself living the lifestyle of a Bohemian. When he returned to Breslau two years later in 1905, it was to take a job as rehearsal pianist, one of the two routes by which aspiring conductors learned their craft.[12]

---

10. In recent years, this work has been called Symphony 0 or Null because Furtwängler completed a large-scale orchestral work in 1941 that he called his First Symphony.

11. Listing Nr. 23b, 24a, in the catalogue of the Zentralbibliothek, Zürich.

12. The other means of developing as a conductor was to join an orchestra and play through music with a variety of experienced conductors.

It was not a promising beginning. As the junior-most staff member, he was obliged to conduct off-stage bands and prompt singers. Furtwängler was never given a chance to conduct a full performance of a major opera, but his fortunes were improving even if he didn't know it. He made the acquaintance of Frau Lilli Dieckmann, a patronne of the arts. She immediately recognized something special in the personality of this young man, and she made sure that he was invited to family gatherings where he met other well-known people in the arts. From childhood, Furtwängler was shy and socially awkward, but he felt comfortable in the Dieckmanns' home.[13]

Frau Ida Boy-Ed was another patronne of the arts, who liked Furtwängler, sensed the depth of his musical gifts, and introduced him to the Wolff family, who ran Wolff and Sachs, one of the most powerful concert agencies in Europe until the Nazis shut them down. He was a frequent visitor to their home, and there met influential personages. It would be many years before such phenomena as the international competition would provide entry points for young musicians, and Furtwängler was typical of his generation in gaining opportunities through personal introductions and the connections they produced. A member of the Wolff family would eventually prove most helpful with his professional advancement.

In 1906 Furtwängler moved to Zürich, where he was engaged as third conductor at the Opera House. The Swiss city was a monetary mecca if not a major cultural capital, and it offered Furtwängler an attractive credential as well as a springboard for widening his experience elsewhere in his free time. For his part, Furtwängler saw himself as a composer first and everything else was subsumed to that ambition, so his work at the opera house was far more a necessary inconvenience than a way station to a position as General Music Director at a major opera house or orchestra. Unlike Nikisch, who regarded himself a conductor first and a composer second, Furtwängler never had any intention of becoming a conductor, but he knew it was a good way to introduce his own works. What is more, he needed to make a good living. After his father died at 54 in 1907 Furtwängler became the breadwinner of the family, and he had to support his widowed mother, his brother, two sisters and himself. While his family was never indigent, his father did not leave adequate provisions for his family.

His professional life here was no easier than it had been in Breslau, for he found himself in much the same position as the one in which he

13. Riess offers the most thorough review of Furtwängler's childhood and early years. He quotes frequently from Dieckmann's diary, to which he evidently had access. See also Schönzeler.

had been trapped as a schoolboy, a position far beneath the scope of his raw talents. During a performance of *The Merry Widow*, he lost his concentration during the last scene of this new hit (and a plum conducting assignment) where the orchestra softly plays the main theme under the dialogue. The singers spoke the cue three times for Furtwängler to begin the orchestra. Finally, the tenor walked off the stage in a huff. Furtwängler did what he could to save the night, but it was a unique finale, and one that might have given Franz Lehar some pause.

It was the last performance Furtwängler conducted that year. The management allowed him to continue his "private interests" until the end of the season, which meant that he could use the time to find another job. He was not surprised when his contract was not renewed. Operetta, as the general manager of the opera house had pointed out, was not his métier.

Furtwängler took advantage of his free time during this year by conducting his first full concert program with the Kaim Orchestra in Munich, which his father helped to arrange for him.[14] The major work on the program was Bruckner's Ninth Symphony, the most complex and demanding of all of this composer's works. The orchestra members were skeptical that this novice would be able to bring it off. But he immediately established a natural rapport with the musicians from the very outset of rehearsals, and the performance was enthusiastically received. Everyone who knew the demands of the work were surprised that a musician with so little experience could elicit such passion and depth of feeling from relative strangers.

His success in Munich enabled him to take a position there at the Royal Opera in the summer of 1907. He received an income of 500 marks a week as an assistant conductor, a decent though not extravagant living for the time.[15] Munich became his home again and in this major musical center the Royal Opera exposed him to first-class singers and conductors. They in turn were also impressed with him. Zdenka Fassbender, for example, was one of Munich's finest sopranos of the time, and she was preparing the title role for the local premiere of Strauss' *Elektra.* She was astounded at Furtwängler's facility in sight-reading the difficult score on the piano.

But the most formidable figure in his new job was Felix Mottl

14. The Kaim Orchestra took the name of its founder Franz Kaim, the son of the piano manufacturer. He organized the "Kaim Konzerte" with this new ensemble in 1893 in Munich and built a concert hall to house it. Siegmund von Hausegger and Felix Weingartner were among its principal conductors. The Kaim was one of the most important orchestras in Munich until 1908 when it was replaced by a new Concert Society Orchestra, a precursor of the present-day Munich Philharmonic.
15. Contract reposited at Munich Hauptstaatsarchiv.

(1856–1911). He spent two more years in Munich learning the basic operatic repertoire under this great conductor of the old school and observed how he deployed his manifold talents in running the artistic affairs of a major opera house. Mottl was a gifted stage director, music editor, and composer, and was also a competent organizer and administrator, a rare set of qualities in one musician. He had been a stage conductor at the original performances of Wagner's *Ring* at Bayreuth in 1876, and he had conducted the Metropolitan Opera premiere of *Parsifal* in 1903, the first time the work had ever been performed outside Bayreuth.[16] He loathed routine and strove to endow every performance he conducted with a sense of discovery. It was a habit Furtwängler cultivated assiduously.

In 1909 a position opened up at Strasbourg—still a part of Germany at the time—and he was named third conductor of the Municipal Opera. Here he came under the tutelage of yet another formidable musician.

Hans Pfitzner was both a fine conductor and one of the best-known living composers in Germany at that time. He was 17 years older than Furtwängler, and he possessed the kind of professional breadth from which Furtwängler could draw copiously. As a composer, Pfitzner was preoccupied with two themes concerning all German intellectuals at the time, not the least of whom was Furtwängler. First, he was intensely concerned with the relationship between an artist and his work and the place this relationship has in the world at large. He was working out his ideas on these matters in his most enduring work, *Palestrina*, during the time Furtwängler was paying his dues at Strasbourg.[17] Second, he was obsessed, like many artists and intellectuals who had sprung from the preoccupations of German Romanticism of the 19th century, with the nature of the German identity. He cast this fixation in a vast cantata entitled, appropriately enough, *Von deutscher Seele (Of the German Soul)*, completed in 1922 and set to poems by Joseph von Eichendorff—who also wrote "Im Abendrot," which Richard Strauss set in his valedictory *Four Last Songs*.[18]

While some writers have viewed Furtwängler's relationship with Pfitzner as something akin to a father-son relationship, a more accurate description of their association might be one of ugly sister–pretty

16. Mottl was General Music Director at Munich from 1907 until his death in 1911.

17. *Palestrina* was completed in 1917.

18. *Four Last Songs* was completed in 1948 shortly before Strauss' death. Furtwängler conducted the world premiere with Kirsten Flagstad as soloist on 22 May 1950 in London.

sister. There is no doubt that Furtwängler, as the junior member of this relationship, admired Pfitzner and continued to remain on friendly terms with him and his wife until Pfitzner's death in 1949. But Pfitzner saw how easily his younger colleague attracted admiring women, and he resented him deeply for it.[19] For Furtwängler's way with women was something like perfect pitch. You either have it or you don't. Furtwängler had it to spare. Pfitzner's grizzled demeanor and crotchety personality hardly made him a beau of the boudoir. Elisabeth Furtwängler recalls:

> Joseph Keilberth [the conductor] told me why Pfitzner said bad things about Furtwängler. He hated the fact that Furtwängler had hundreds of women throwing themselves at his feet. Pfitzner loved women, but they were not attracted to him. He had a wonderful wife and a lovely daughter who committed suicide. He was a genius, but he was very complicated. Of course, it is not easy to live with genius because they can be exhausting—always something to do. But the other side of that is they give so much. But Pfitzner was a bit of a curmudgeon. He saw women throwing themselves at Furtwängler, but none of them threw themselves at him. He could have played Alberich with the Rhine maidens to perfection.
>
> In any event, a friend of our family named Helmut Grohe[20] who was an excellent musician and good friends with both Pfitzner and my husband once told me he was sitting with Pfitzner and several other people in the main restaurant at the Adlon Hotel in Berlin. Pfitzner was in a particularly sour mood, but the other people at the table tried to involve him in their conversation anyway. But he had a stunting effect on the table talk. So they started talking about a new planet that just had been discovered—Uranus. Our friend turned to him and said, "Meister, what do you think of this new star that's been discovered?" Pfitzner looked into his soup and growled, "And what is the name of this star? Maybe 'Furtwängler'?"[21]

Strasbourg was an important musical center at the time, made all the more so by Pfitzner's presence there, and it was an excellent place for a rising conductor to be observed by influential people. Soon

19. Peter Heyworth adumbrates Pfitzner's attitude toward Furtwängler in his biography of Otto Klemperer, who was one of Furtwängler's successors at Strasbourg. Pfitzner had a far more abrasive relationship with Klemperer. In fact, Klemperer was imputed to have manoeuvred Pfitzner out of his position in 1916, a canard he hotly denied. For a lively survey of the backstage backbiting surrounding their relationship in Strasbourg, see Heyworth's excellent *Otto Klemperer: His Life and Times*, Vol. I, (Cambridge) 1983, pp. 99–119. The second volume is scheduled for publication in 1992.

20. Grohe contributed perhaps the most comprehensive essay on Furtwängler's years in Mannheim in *Wilhelm Furtwängler: Im Urteil seiner Zeit*, edited by Martin Hürlimann in collaboration with Elisabeth Furtwängler, (Zürich) 1955, pp. 149–165.

21. Personal conversation with the author, Clarens, 4 April 1990.

enough, Furtwängler also caught the attention of Bruno Walter—nine years his senior and well on his way to international fame as one of Germany's brightest conductors. Walter, who had succeeded Felix Mottl at Munich in 1911 after a brilliant success at the Vienna Court Opera, became something of a friend and advisor to Furtwängler, a fact Furtwängler always acknowledged despite some unfortunate changes in their relationship later.

In Strasbourg, Furtwängler got his first chance at building a repertoire as an opera conductor, though the works were minor and the critical reception anything but sensational. He prepared and rehearsed a wide variety of operas and operettas for Pfitzner and the other senior conductors. The range of works he prepared included Gilbert and Sullivan's *The Mikado.*[22] The operas for which he was entirely responsible (rehearsals through performances) were Maillart's *Das Glöcken des Eremiten,* von Flotow's *Martha,* Messager's *Die kleinen Michu's,* all sung in German of course. About *Die kleinen Michu's,* said the critic for *Journal d'Alsace Lorraine:*

Furtwängler conducted with all the grace of a young elephant.[23]

On his *Martha,* the *Strassburger Post* was barely more enthusiastic:

The musical direction left much to be desired, primarily caused by the excessive agitation of the young conductor Wilhelm Furtwängler.[24]

Furtwängler was not even mentioned in a review of *Rigoletto.*[25] While such notices would have offered Pfitzner a perfect chance to get rid of Furtwängler, he encouraged him to continue conducting, and Furtwängler followed his advice.

During this period, he also finished his *Te Deum* in 1910. Thus the jottings he started in the chapel of the Medicis came to completion. A large, somewhat sprawling work for chorus and four soloists, it was first performed by his uncle Georg Dohrn in Breslau in November of that year. It was not a huge success, but Furtwängler took it to Strasbourg the following year and conducted it himself. The perfor-

---

22. *Centenaire W. Furtwängler,* Société Wilhelm Furtwängler, (Paris) 1986, p. 4. The playbill states Richard Fried conducted the actual performances, but Gefen, p. 26, writes that Furtwängler conducted. Possibly Furtwängler replaced Fried at the last minute. It would have been a most fascinating event to witness.
23. 1 January 1911.
24. 28 October 1910.
25. *Elsässer,* 13 March 1911.

mance received mixed reviews, but the Strassburger *Neueste Nachrichten* was the most enthusiastic:

> ... The *Te Deum* reveals a young musician full of talent: Wilhelm Furtwängler, who has appeared occasionally as conductor at the Municipal Theater ... The work which demands a great deal from the chorus and orchestra, is constructed in an audacious fashion and is animated by the force of indomitable youthfulness.[26]

It received several other performances, notably under Hermann Abendroth at Essen in 1914 and under Karl Straube at Leipzig the following year. The *Te Deum* was the last of Furtwängler's compositions to be performed for more than 20 years to come. He continued to compose in the next two decades, but it would be 1937 before he would be satisfied enough to allow another of his works to be performed in public.[27]

Through Pfitzner's recommendation and the suggestion of both Frau Lilli Dieckmann and Ida Boy-Ed, Furtwängler applied for an appointment to succeed Hermann Abendroth (1883–1956) as music director in Lübeck in the spring of 1911. He almost did not get the job. An experienced conductor named Rudolf Siegel had long been lined up for the position, but custom dictated that there should be a competition among four contestants anyway. When Ernst Wendel, one of the contestants, dropped out because he learned that the contest was "fixed" in favor of Siegel, Furtwängler applied to take his place.[28]

Since he was an unknown and relatively inexperienced, the orchestra committee saw no threat in having him fill in for the withdrawn applicant and arranged for him to conduct both the choir and the orchestra. At the chorus rehearsal, the committee sat facing him at the rear of the choir. Their presence made Furtwängler self-conscious and hampered his performance. At the orchestra rehearsal, though, the committee sat behind him. As soon as the music began, he became so absorbed that he completely forgot they were watching him. At the break, an impromptu delegation from the orchestra approached the committee and all but demanded that Furtwängler be hired. His engagement was the first phase of a meteoric flight toward becoming the leading conductor in Germany, for it was unusual in

26. 7 December 1911.
27. A number of biographical entries suggest that Furtwängler gave up composing altogether in those years. Even a cursory glance at the material in the Furtwängler archives in the Zentralbibliothek, Zürich, proves quite the contrary.
28. Riess, p. 42–43, and Schönzeler, p. 18.

those days that a musician so young would be given the post of Music Director of any orchestra. Furtwängler was only 26.

While most young conductors would leap at taking on the fruits of such good fortune, Furtwängler almost turned the job down. The streak of vacillation that was increasingly to corrode his decision-making faculties overtook him. He was not experienced enough to handle such responsibilities. His repertoire was not large enough. He knew nothing about administration. He recited the litany of his limitations over and over. Only after Frau Boy-Ed laboriously massaged his confidence and patiently countered his arguments against himself did he finally accept the position.

For once, though, most of his doubts were well-founded. He *was* inexperienced. He did need to enlarge his repertoire. But once he arrived in Lübeck, he resolved to rectify each of those limitations. Among the works he conducted for the first time were Tchaikovsky's Fifth Symphony and Bruckner's Eighth Symphony. He also set about mastering Beethoven's symphonic literature. He conducted the Ninth Symphony for the first time, and performed the *Eroica* on several programs. Since his predecessor in the post, Hermann Abendroth, had left him a good orchestra with a high standard of playing, Furtwängler concentrated on enlarging the scope of its repertoire. He was committed to conducting eight subscription concerts during the season and several choral concerts. He also was obliged to conduct a popular series, a chore he hardly relished but was determined to fashion to his liking. Since his reputation as an up-and-coming conductor spread quickly, audiences flocked to his concerts no matter what he played. As a result, the cheap cafe music usually played in the popular series soon made way for a healthy diet of Brahms and Wagner interspersed with quality light music. To make his busy schedule even more hectic, the Municipal Opera invited him to conduct, and he seized the opportunity in order to expand his own operatic repertoire. During his four seasons at Lübeck, his audiences heard his first performances of *Die Meistersinger*, *Merry Wives of Windsor*, and *Fidelio*.

But perhaps the most important experience of his stay in Lübeck was his meeting with the man who was to become the most significant influence in his life: Artur Nikisch (1855–1922). To say that Nikisch was something of a legend is merely to demean the esteem in which he was universally held by both the public and by his contemporaries. By 1900, he not only had become Germany's leading music director, but quite possibly the first conductor ever to became famous on a grand international scale. More than 30 years older than Furtwängler, his career foreshadowed Furtwängler's in many ways.

Born to a bookkeeper in Lebenyi Szant Miklos, Hungary, he showed signs of musical gifts at the age of three, and started playing the violin at five. At eleven, he entered the Vienna Conservatory where he studied piano with Hellmesberger, Schenner, and Dessof. His memory was so acute that he could make piano reductions of Rossini overtures after hearing them only once. In 1872 he was among the first violins in the consecration ceremony of Wagner's new Festival Theater (Festspielhaus) in Bayreuth and performed Beethoven's Ninth under Wagner's direction. He was also a competent composer and conducted his own First Symphony with the Vienna Conservatory Orchestra in the following year. His ambition had always had been to become a composer/conductor, and he had to decide which of the two options open to an aspiring conductor of that time was best for him: to become a rehearsal assistant at an opera house or to join an orchestra. He chose the latter and became a first violinist in the Vienna Court Orchestra in 1874. He learned his craft literally at the feet of the great masters of the 19th century: Wagner, Brahms, Liszt, and Anton Rubinstein were among the guests who conducted the orchestra during the three years he was a member.

In 1878 he received his first appointment as conductor at the Leipzig Opera. In the following decade, he made Leipzig an opera center to be reckoned with, mounting new productions of neglected masterpieces and presenting premieres of contemporary operas. He also began a career as a symphonic conductor, astounding audiences and his colleagues by conducting without a score—an unusual feat at the time. By 1889 he was famous throughout Europe. That year, he accepted the musical directorship of the Boston Symphony and spent the next four years building it into America's best orchestra and touring America.

He now was the world's best-known conductor, and he returned to his native Hungary in 1893 for a brief tenure as first conductor of the Budapest Opera. Two years later, he succeeded Reinecke as conductor of one of Europe's oldest orchestras, the Gewandhaus in Leipzig—an ensemble whose tradition went back to Mendelssohn and Beethoven. Here he took a great orchestra to even greater heights by honing its beauty of tone, expanding its virtuosity, and enlarging its repertoire. But there was still more to come, and Artur Nikisch achieved the pinnacle of his career when he took over the Berlin Philharmonic in 1897 in addition to his directorship at the Gewandhaus. From then until his death in 1922, Nikisch was a household word, even to those who never attended his concerts. In an age when recording was still in its infancy, Nikisch—without record sales, publicity

mills, backstage dramas, or podium gymnastics—became the prototype of the modern superstar conductor.

With the simplest movements of his hands and arms, he created a
Svengali-like spell over the orchestra and the audience alike, conjuring sounds of unearthly beauty and unbearable excitement. Listeners
invariably went wild at the conclusion of his performances, especially
of the large-scale romantic works. Emerging conductors of that time
later scorned many of the maestros of their youth, but one conductor
upon whose greatness they all agreed was Nikisch. Even Toscanini
begrudgingly mentioned him when he talked about conductors he
admired. One of the leading violinists of the century, Carl Flesch, who
later would figure importantly in Furtwängler's career and performed
with him on a number of occasions, recalled in his memoirs:

> To me [Nikisch] was a revelation . . . I was still used to the unimaginative
> stick wagger who, strictly according to the compass, beat ¼ in the four car-
> dinal points. Now for the first time, I saw a musician who, impression-
> istically, described in the air not simply the bare metrical structure, but
> above all, the dynamic and agogical nuances as well as the indefinable
> mysterious feeling that lies between the notes; his beat was utterly per-
> sonal and original. With Nikisch began a new era of conducting. I could
> not judge whether he continued what [his predecessor] Bülow had pre-
> pared, for I had never heard Bülow conduct. In any case, Nikisch's tech-
> nique itself seemed unprecedented and completely individual, in no wise
> thought out, but experienced, felt—an instinctive expression of his per-
> sonality. He was the first conductor to beat in advance, i.e. to give the note
> value a fraction of a second early, a style that was later adopted, and some-
> what exaggerated, by Furtwängler.[29]

Lilli Dieckmann took Furtwängler to hear Nikisch conduct in
Hamburg in 1912. He was so overcome during this concert that he
could not utter a word to the maestro when he was introduced to him
after the concert. Although he had been exposed to the daily rough and
tumble of meeting and working with difficult artists and dealing with
strangers both professionally and privately, Furtwängler at 27 was
still extremely shy and awkward in social circumstances. When
Nikisch invited him to dine with his friends, he resolutely refused.
Later, after he had recovered from the experience, Furtwängler confided to his friend Werner Wolff that he wanted to be Nikisch's successor. Wolff was a member of that family who ran the concert agency
of Wolff and Sachs. Its matriarch was Louise Wolff, Werner's mother,

29. *The Memoirs of Carl Flesch*, (London), p. 148.

who all but ruled musical life in Germany from her office in Berlin. She was so powerful that she was called "Queen Louise." Wolff eventually related the confidence to his mother. But while Furtwängler revered Nikisch and now set himself to qualify as a successor if Nikisch ever decided to move on from Berlin or Leipzig, the thought of trying to undermine Nikisch's position or elbow him out of the way was inconceivable to him. He always regarded the elder conductor as a mentor in whom he found the music he heard in his mind's ear brought gloriously to life.

While Nikisch's style gave Furtwängler a practical model through which he could develop his sense of musical form, he needed a foundation on which to build it. During his stay in Lübeck Furtwängler discovered, almost by accident, a book written by the noted Viennese theorist Heinrich Schenker (1868–1935). He had heard of Schenker but did not know he had written anything. Reading it immediately, he found Schenker's exegesis titled *Beethoven's Ninth Symphony* (1911) entirely compelling. Years later, he recalled his first encounter with Schenker's monograph:

> If I did not agree with everything he said, even if his polemical attitude in many cases disagreed with me, the way the questions were phrased and the conviction and insight with which he handled them were so unusual and so different from the usual run of musical criticism at the time, that I felt deeply moved. Here for the first time were direct and objective questions about what was inherent in the Ninth Symphony rather than mere explanation.
>
> *Ton und Wort, p. 199*

It would be almost ten years before he would meet and strike up a lasting working relationship with Schenker, but it is no understatement to say that Furtwängler's interpretive development would have taken a very different route had he not been so "deeply moved" by both Schenker's approach to musical theory nor so receptive to the heuristic impulses he awakened.[30]

30. With the possible exception of Nadia Boulanger (Schenker's junior by 19 years), Schenker is one of the most influential forces in the fundamental *attitude* composers, performers, and teachers of the first half of this century have manifested toward music. Musical figures as diverse as the violinist Carl Flesch and the Broadway composer Maury Yeston (*Nine, Grand Hotel*) not only have encountered (in Yeston's case indirectly) this frequently overlooked genius but have been moved to pay tribute to him both in their writings and their respective arts. Schenker's most revolutionary concept centered upon using the music itself as a starting point for interpretive and other kinds of analysis rather than achieving those objectives by imposing preconceived theories on it. But for Furtwängler, Schenker opened his imagination to approaching a masterwork with a view toward "re-creating" it rather than merely reporting it or dotingly following its instructions.

Furtwängler remained for four seasons at Lübeck and became not only musically experienced but increasingly passionate about what he believed to be the special nature of music. While he was not given to tantrums, his highly charged personality could make him violent when provoked. He had a scar on his face to prove it. Consequently, his tenure there was not without incident: A house tenor became upset when Furtwängler asked him to repeat a passage he had sung incorrectly during a rehearsal of *Fidelio*, so Furtwängler jumped up on stage and punched him.[31]

His pugilistic tenacity paid off. The house tenor was replaced with Carl Günther, a well-known guest singer from Hamburg, at a performance of *Fidelio* he conducted on 23 March 1915. That event was attended by a five-member search committee from Mannheim headed by its General Music Director, Artur Bodanzky, who was resigning as Mannheim's leading conductor to accept Giulio Gatti-Casazza's invitation to head the German wing at the Metropolitan Opera in New York.[32] This development left the music director's job at Mannheim open. By the time the performance was over, Bodanzky and his associates had decided that Furtwängler would be his successor. Furtwängler must have made an extraordinary impression—he had only three operas in his repertoire at this time, there were numerous other conductors who easily dwarfed his experience as an orchestra conductor, and the performance was pockmarked with mistakes.[33] In any case, that flawed *Fidelio* proved to be a major turning point in the life and career of Wilhelm Furtwängler.

31. Riess, p. 61.

32. Artur Bodanzky began his career in 1896 as a violinist in the Imperial Court Opera in Vienna. He later became chief conductor following an apprenticeship under Mahler. Seven years after his move to Mannheim, he gained international attention by conducting the London premiere of *Parsifal* in 1914. The following year, he went to New York where he remained at the Metropolitan until shortly before his death.

33. Riess, p. 62. The review of the performance indicated dissatisfaction with both lead singers. Günther sang Florestan correctly but with a "cool reserve" that did not match well with the "warmth of the orchestral sound." A certain Frau von Pander, did not possess the "sunny warmth" in her voice or the "intense temperament in her acting" demanded by the title role. J. Hennings, *Lübeckische Blätter*, pp. 203–204, 1915. I am indebted to M. René Tremin for information on various segments of Furtwängler's conducting career. His chronology of Furtwängler's professional activities is scheduled to be published in 1992.

2

Mannheim

Since the 18th century Mannheim had been graced with a tradition of uninterrupted excellence, and Artur Bodanzky brought those standards to a new peak after he became the General Music Director *(Generalmusikdirector)* of the Court Opera in 1907. His predecessors in the post included some of the most significant personalities in German music since 1870, among them Felix Weingartner, Ernst Nicholas von Reznicek, and Willibald Kaehler. Bodanzky himself was no slouch as a conductor and is probably the most underrated Wagnerian of this century, but he is best remembered for his uncanny instinct at picking talent. Despite an increasingly abrasive personality during his later years that frequently lashed out at his musicians, his unfailing nose for quality proved right time and again. Furtwängler and—much later—Kirsten Flagstad were only two of his famous "discoveries."[1]

Again, Furtwängler almost missed out on the opportunity Bodanzky was handing him, but this time it was not out of self-doubt or vacillation. Germany was now engaged in a war that she would ultimately lose, and Furtwängler at age 29 was still eligible to be called up for military duty. Furtwängler had suffered pulmonary difficulties

1. Flagstad was little known even in Europe when Bodanzky auditioned her for the Metropolitan Opera in the summer of 1934. He awarded her a contract over a better-known singer—Elisabeth Delius—who auditioned at the same time.

since childhood, but he was prepared to enlist.[2] His friend Frau Ida Boy-Ed, the patronne of the arts who had introduced him to many important people, used her influence to have him exempted, and the authorities ultimately granted an indefinite exemption. Despite the bitter consequences of the war on Germany—economically, politically, and above all, socially—cultural life went on more or less unhampered. But the impulses driving that culture were undergoing a radical transformation whose characteristics would become fully recognizable only after the collapse of the Second Reich following World War I.

Once he arrived in Mannheim in late summer 1915, it did not take long for Furtwängler to see that the city offered him a kind of musical and cultural environment unusual even in Germany. As one of Germany's leading cultural centers, Mannheim competed more than favorably with Berlin, Leipzig and Munich in its active musical life. The city had always been conscious of its fame as the place where the ideals of orchestral performing practices were born. During the reign of Duke Carl Theodor (1743–1778), himself a trained musician, the Czech virtuoso violinist Jan Václav Stamitz took charge of the court orchestra and created unheard of standards in orchestral playing, especially among the violins. His pupil and successor Christian Cinnabich enlarged the orchestra and cultivated what came to be known as the "symphonic style" of performance. Its unique characteristics— perfect ensemble playing, exciting and expressive execution, uniform bowing among the strings, thrilling dynamics and unerring phrasing—quickly became the very qualities demanded of all ensembles as they rapidly grew into the institution known as the symphony orchestra.

Mannheim's orchestra was called an army of generals, even in Mozart's time, and now, in the second decade of the 20th century, this ensemble prided itself on maintaining the standards that Stamitz and Cinnabich first developed through it. For the first time Furtwängler had a first-class orchestra at his disposal, and he had no problem taking command of it. His reputation as a musician of the first order started to take hold across Europe during his stay in Mannheim, and well-known musicians began to attend his concerts.

One of them was Leopold Stokowski, who had taken over the Philadelphia Orchestra in 1912. He had first heard Furtwängler in Lübeck and later remarked that he was greatly impressed with both the Mann-

---

2. Furtwängler suffered several bouts of bacterial pneumonia throughout his life. Ultimately, it was the illness that would kill him.

heim orchestra and Furtwängler's way with music. Stokowski's intense preoccupation with sonic color and brilliance that were later to become the hallmarks of "the Philadelphia sound" may well have been influenced by the concerts he attended at Mannheim. Throughout his long life, Stokowski mentioned only three conductors whom he considered truly great: Artur Nikisch, Hans Richter, and Wilhelm Furtwängler.[3] Since Furtwängler was the only one of these three who was his contemporary and *younger* to boot—Stokowski was born in 1882—this was high praise indeed.

Furtwängler's responsibilities at Mannheim fell into two broad areas, the opera and the *Akademiekonzerte*—a series of eight subscription orchestral concerts whose personnel largely came from the opera orchestra. (By the end of the 19th century, Stamitz' original court orchestra had become one and the same as the orchestra at the Royal Opera.) At the opera, he was solely in charge of choosing repertoire, casting, and assigning conductors, and consulting with the Intendant (General Manager) on the selection of new productions, designers and other details on production. Of course he had to do his share of conducting the staple repertoire from night to night. The opera shared the house with the resident National Theater, so the performances were divided roughly 40 percent for plays and theater pieces and 60 percent for opera. Most of the productions were directed and produced by the Intendant, Carl Hagemann, or one of the house producers. The singers were usually provincial "house" artists. For the *Akademiekonzerte* he chose the repertoire, invited and scheduled soloists and guest conductors.

Furtwängler found that he had two important assets at the opera: a strong, highly disciplined orchestra and a competent chorus, both of which had been drilled to precision by Bodanzky and his chorus master Karl Klaus. Such dependable forces freed him to conduct more performances than he might otherwise have been able to do. During his first season alone, he conducted 14 operas, 12 of them for the first time. Taking no chances, he made his debut in the pit on 7 September 1915 with *Fidelio*, one of the three operas he already had in his repertoire and a work Bodanzky had frequently conducted. The cast included Hermine Rabl as Leonore, Walter Günther-Braun as Florestan, Gertrud Runge as Marzelline, and Max Felmy as Jaquino. He programmed the *Third Leonore Overture* for the interlude preceding the final scene. The specter of Bodanzky was omnipresent in the reviews, but by and large, the critics found the young new music director a worthy if very different successor. Karl Eschmann wrote the verdict in the *Neue Badische Landes Zeitung:*

3. Abram Chasins, *Leopold Stokowski: A Profile,* (New York) 1979, p. 22.

Bodanzky conducted *Fidelio* on no less than five series of revivals while he was here, and each time it was a real pleasure for both musicians and devotees to attend his performances.

What Mr. Furtwängler offered last night gives a pleasant feeling of what his future work here may produce. He seems to be an artist of real individuality, who never lapses into spiritless or businesslike routine. He is a personality with superior artistic gifts and possessed of idealistic longings.

He interpreted Beethoven's music out of the deepest wells of his feelings, giving his individuality and style to the incomparable greatness and soulful profundity of this music.[4]

Furtwängler's performance must have been persuasive indeed, for even at this point in his career his approach to the opera was a far cry from the martinet-like exactitude demanded—and gotten—by Bodanzky, who was revered by the local critics and far more inclined toward the musical attitude most closely associated with Toscanini.

Nonetheless, another critic from one of Mannheim's five daily newspapers at the time was impressed with the new music director but had mixed feelings about Furtwängler's approach. Arthur Blass— who also had the title of Kapellmeister—felt that Furtwängler performed a miraculous account of the *Leonore Overture* but may have expended too much attention to the orchestra:

> Herr Furtwängler, so to speak, "symphonized" the entire opera. The special features of his tempi (its enormous flexibility) stems from this concept. This approach tended to separate the musical elements from the dramatic and led to some loss of effectiveness in the vocalism, for it was only natural that the singers developed some difficulties.
>
> Nonetheless, Herr Furtwängler was warmly received, especially after the [Leonore] Overture, and the applause left no doubt that the new Kappelmeister has made a generally favorable impression.[5]

In the following months, he went on to conduct his first performances of six of the major Wagner operas in quick succession, beginning with *Fliegende Holländer* (3 October 1915), *Die Walküre* (7 November), and continuing with *Tristan und Isolde* (23 January 1916), and finally, the rest of the *Ring* operas in separate performances throughout the season, capped off by a complete cycle between 11 and 19 March 1916.[6] He also conducted two operas with which he would

---

4. 8 September 1915.
5. *Neue Mannheimer Zeitung*, Nr. 435, 8 September 1915.
6. Furtwängler conducted all the major Wagner operas except *Lohengrin* during his tenure as music director in Mannheim. However, he conducted the opera for the first time ever on 15 September 1929 when he returned to Mannheim as guest conductor for a gala performance that included Margarete Teschemacher as Elsa, Gertrude Bindernagel as Ortrud, and Adolf Loeltgens in the eponymous role.

become closely identified late in his career: *Der Freischütz* (5 December 1915) and *Don Giovanni* (20 February 1916). He paid his respects to his composition teacher Max von Schillings by mounting two of his operas within a month [*Mona Lisa* (28 November 1915) and *Hans Heiling* (19 December)], and conducted several performances of *Die Fledermaus* during the year, a work he apparently found rewarding, even though it was far removed from the kind of repertoire that later became associated with him.

The singers in the first casts for virtually all the heavier operas Furtwängler conducted during his first season were nearly the same. Hermine Rabl, for example, was the house-brand Isolde, Senta, and Brünnhilde.[7] Walther Günther-Braun took the tenor leads in almost everything. Hans Bahling, Joachim Kromer, and Matthieu Frank usually sang Wotan, Alberich, and Fafner respectively and easily slipped into other roles for their ranges. Occasionally big-name guest artists of the time such as Michael Bohnen (Mephistopheles), Helene Wildbrun (Isolde), and Fritz Vogelstrom (Siegfried) appeared for special engagements at inflated admission prices, but subscription audiences were usually treated to the same singers over and over again. Several went on to make significant careers for themselves elsewhere, but only Gertrud Runge and Dorothea Mansky achieved a significant degree of lasting fame.[8] While the level of ensemble among the resident singers was highly disciplined, the general quality of voices Furtwängler had at his disposal was typical of most provincial houses: middling to awful. One critic frequently offered variations on: "the singers were not all in their best form last night, yet that was but little hindrance to the overall felicitous impression."[9]

7. Hermine Rabl née Kristen apparently made most of her career exclusively in Germany. She was married to Dr. Walter Rabl, who was first Kapellmeister at the Stadttheater in Magdeburg from 1915 to 1924. She later became actively involved in the N-S Frauenschaft, which means she almost certainly was a member of the Nazi Party. So active was her involvement in the Party and the Women's Corps that she committed suicide in 1945 when all hope for a Nazi victory over its foes was lost. (I am deeply indebted for this information to Frau Liselotte Homering and her predecessor Wilhelm Hermann at the Theater Collection of the Reiss Museum in Mannheim.)

8. Gertrud Runge (1880–1948) became a well-known coloratura in Germany, though she had no international career to speak of. Nonetheless, she left an inordinate amount of recordings for a singer with career of such limited scope. She is not to be confused with Gertrude Rünger (1899–1965), a singer of astonishing range who sang contralto parts as well as the *Fidelio* Leonore with gripping intensity and dark beauty of tone.

The German-American Dorothea Mansky (1891–1967) became a comprimaria singer at the Metropolitan Opera in 1927, after singing Isolde and other heavy roles under Furtwängler in Mannheim between 1917 and 1920, and going on to successes as a leading dramatic soprano at Stuttgart, Berlin, Salzburg, and Vienna. She ultimately became a highly respected singing teacher at Indiana University.

9. Karl Eschmann, Review of *Tristan*, *Neue Badische Landes Zeitung*, 24 January 1916.

About Furtwängler, though, the remarks usually were complimentary. On *Mona Lisa* (28 November 1915):

> The most difficult part of the work—the musical preparation—fell upon Herr Furtwängler. He delivered a very conscientious and highly successful reading; the orchestra played its demanding and extremely complicated parts very impressively.[10]

On his first *Tristan* (23 January 1916), two of the reviews indicated the enthusiastic consensus of all the local newspapers. *Neue Badische Landes Zeitung:*

> [Furtwängler] had been scheduled to conduct the first performance on October 24th and had begun rehearsals on it, but had [to cancel] because of illness. Now that he has taken the production to completion, the results show us his scrupulousness as our leading opera director. His well known capabilities also worked to the benefit of last night's *Tristan* performance in a gratifying way, by infusing the presentation of this masterpiece with the vivid strength of its varied outbursts and intense spiritualization.[11]

Neue Mannheimer Zeitung:

> Herr Furtwängler conducted Tristan for the first time with reserve and calm. His epic-monumental tempi recalled the great age of Hans von Bülow. We have no way of determining if Furtwängler is aware of this style or if he somehow recovered it by way of some means. But he certainly sought to enliven Wagner anew with a profound love for this music, and he endowed the total form with a new content through subjective feeling—first in the Prelude and even more so in the second act.[12]

On his first complete *Ring* cycle (11–19 March 1916):[13]

> *Rheingold:* The orchestra playing was substantially high, and Herr Furtwängler knew how to inspire it with dramatic life. He took the animated tempos very quickly, but elsewhere they stretched into expressive breadth.
> *Götterdämmerung:* Herr Furtwängler brought breadth and expression to the scene with the men's chorus and the oath scene [of Act II] . . . He showed how brilliantly he has mastered his task. An accident here and

10. *Neue Badische Landes Zeitung,* 29 November 1915.
11. 24 January 1916.
12. Blass, 24 January 1916.
13. Several dates are given for Furtwängler's first performances of the *Ring.* His first complete cycle took place in March 1916 not later as frequently and erroneously suggested.

there in the brass section may be excused, for all the musicians have had a very hectic week.[14]

But not all the reviews were glowing. While Furtwängler quickly managed to persuade audiences and critics that he was a legitimate alternative to Bodanzky and not merely his successor, there were occasions throughout his whole career when the magic simply did not materialize. His debut with *Don Giovanni* (20 February 1916) is a case in point. Eschmann seized the opportunity of a "lackluster" performance to invoke the spirit of Furtwängler's predecessor:

> Herr Furtwängler has taken on the work in a praiseworthy way. He produced Mozart's wonderful music in the orchestra with fluency and energy, and a good sense of rhythm, especially in his account of the overture. A number of the arias were exceptionally decent and expressively accompanied, and yet the excitement of the performance as a whole— which was always elicited under Bodanzky—failed, because Bodanzky strikingly distributed the shades of light and dark in the dynamics, because he also brought somewhat more variety to his tempos. Therefore, the performance remained somewhat lackluster.[15]

Furtwängler shared his conducting load with several associate Kapellmeisters, usually Victor Schwarz or Felix Lederer. Lederer, in fact, stepped in for Furtwängler when he became ill during rehearsals for his first *Tristan* and took on an ever increasing workload as Furtwängler neared the end of his Mannheim stint in 1920. Furtwängler never forgot the goodwill of this colleague, as we shall see a bit later.

Of all the works he performed for the first time in Mannheim, none was more challenging than the *Ring*, and the acclaim he received for his debut in a complete cycle led to an invitation to take the production of the four operas for a gala guest engagement in nearby Baden-Baden in September 1917. He succeeded sufficiently with it on both occasions to warrant a repetition of a complete cycle at the beginning of his third year in Mannheim. Wagner was an acquired taste for Furtwängler, and he had come to admire him only during his adolescence. But once he was convinced of Wagner's genius, he gave him a good deal of thought throughout his life, putting many of his ideas and conclusions on paper. During the summer of 1917, Furtwängler wrote an essay on the *Ring* that was published in the *Neue Badische Landes Zeitung* while he was conducting the complete cycle for the second time in his life. In it, he calls the tetralogy the most "controver-

14. *Neue Badische Landes Zeitung,* 20 March 1916.
15. *Neue Badische Landes Zeitung,* 21 February 1916.

sial" of Wagner's works, the focal point of the intense adulation as well as the rabid opposition the composer engenders. Wagner's detractors, according to Furtwängler, deride him for constructing his mature works out of bits and pieces that add up to "decoration" essentially unrelated to music, rather than forging an unique aesthetic core out of purely musical values. Furtwängler finds Wagner's gift for description and for relating music to gesture and dramatic values so persuasive in its overwhelming sensuousness that it constitutes for him a new kind of power all its own:

> Certainly, the totality [of the *Ring*] is more surface than core. But how voluptuously that surface takes shape! What astounding power these visions possess in the scenes of Valhalla, the Ride of the Valkyries, the Fire Music. Whatever is lacking in weight and unity in the music and poetic intuition is compensated by the inspired effect of the moment. Would the monumental greatness, the awesome strides of *Walküre*, the liberating spirit of *Siegfried*, the colossal dimensions of *Götterdämmerung* be possible without the musically descriptive foundations of a mythic world which evokes and supports these superhuman figures?

Furtwängler finds the confusion stemming from what is meant by Wagner's philosophy of the Total Art Work (*Gesamtkunstwerk*) can lead to bad performances.[16] For every factor contributing to the totality of the work—especially the singers, or the musicians, or the stage director—has a tendency to overshadow the other components. The frequent results of such conflicts only give fuel to the anti-Wagnerites. Thus, it is easy to lose sight of what, according to Furtwängler, is at the heart and soul of such a work as the *Ring:*

> Only the music can give the guiding principles for [a truly correct] performance. It pulls all the elements inside the totality of the work cohesively together; it is also the ultimate and most specialized tool of the poet, for he speaks most clearly though it. It is actually the stylistic catalyst of the whole work. Every gesture emerges from it and dissolves back into it. Therefore, the musician is the true executor of the poet's will.[17]

16. Wagner's mature works result from his philosophy of lyric theater as an homogenized amalgamation of all the arts: poetry, music, gesture (dance), painting, etc; a philosophy he outlined in such prose writings as his articles "The Art Work of the Future" (1850), and "Art and Revolution" (1851), and his treatise *Opera and Drama* (1850). This in spite of evidence that Wagner did not express his theories very clearly and did not know much about subjects outside music and poetry. According to the tenets of what can be deciphered from his extremely convoluted theoretical expositions, music serves several functions in such works as the *Ring, Tristan,* and *Parsifal:* descriptive, narrative, decorative, hortatory, and so on. But as far as Furtwängler is concerned, it also serves its original function as pure music. It is from this point of view that he sagely derives his conclusions about music as the chief and driving priority of the *Ring.*
17. 19 September 1917.

Furtwängler might well have written these words today, when so much of opera has degenerated into the producer's or director's medium. But what is remarkable about this article is the breadth of background it displays in Furtwängler's reading and knowledge, not only of Wagner, but of Lessing, Nietzsche, Hegel, and other German writers relevant to the complex (and rambling) aesthetic dialectic Wagner developed.[18] It would have been difficult if not impossible to write with such clarity about his views unless he had thoroughly familiarized himself with these Germanic intellectual Titans of the 19th century. But while the brilliance of this rich intellectual brocade illuminated Furtwängler's developing attitudes toward music and culture in general, the inviolable past it represented would also come to immobilize him and ultimately destroy him.

But all that was far into the future. While Furtwängler was busily expanding his operatic repertoire during his first year at Mannheim, he also had to make sure the eight *Akademie* subscription concerts continued to keep up the high standards to which his illustrious predecessors had brought to them. Since his orchestral repertoire was hardly encyclopedic, he kept himself busy brushing up on the extensive number of scores he already knew but never had performed, as well as learning new ones, sometimes studying several at the same time. While the repertoire he chose fully justified the accusations of conservatism that were to haunt him for the rest of his life, he also programmed the local premiere of Strauss' *Alpine Symphony* and scheduled an all-Reger concert to be conducted by the composer himself.

Max Reger was the first of two guest conductors on the prospectus; the other was Felix Weingartner, whose wife Lucille also appeared as vocal soloist. The other soloists scheduled for 1915–1916 were two violinists, Carl Flesch and Arnold Rosé, who was the veteran first concertmaster of the Vienna Philharmonic and Gustav Mahler's brother-in-law; two pianists, Artur Schnabel and Alfred Höhn; and one celebrity vocalist, Julia Culp. The season was to be capped off with Beethoven's Ninth Symphony with Mansky, Johanna Lippe, Günther-Braun, and Wilhelm Fenton.

For his first program on 19 October Furtwängler again took no chances, and yet took a great risk at the same time. The first half of the evening was given over entirely to Julia Culp (1880–1970), the Dutch

18. Even as devout a Wagnerite as Ernest Newman was impatient with Wagner's voluminous prose: "There are few of us who would not give three-fourths of the prose works for another opera from his pen; and he would have had time to write half a dozen if had abstained from all this prose." *Wagner as Man and Artist* (1924), (New York) 1960, p. 226.

soprano, who was an eminent recitalist at the time. Rather than performing with the orchestra, she simply lent her prestige to Furtwängler's debut with the orchestra by singing a selection of songs by Schubert, Mahler, and Brahms, assisted on the piano by her longtime accompanist Coenraad von Bos. Furtwängler and the orchestra performed Haydn's "Military" Symphony and Beethoven's Fifth Symphony. That meant Furtwängler could devote nearly all his restricted time to Beethoven, but it also meant that the critical evaluation of Mannheim's new Court Kapellmeister would be based entirely on his interpretation of that trap-laden symphony. Furtwängler had the presence of mind to know his career would not be made or broken by even the harshest reception to his account of Haydn's "Military." Nonetheless, the critic for the *Neue Mannheimer Zeitung* paid more attention to Furtwängler's Haydn than Beethoven's Fifth:

> The performance gave felicitous evidence that Herr Furtwängler possesses a full understanding of the beauty in Haydn's naive music. He gave us Haydn simply and truthfully and without pretensions. If the signs are not deceiving, we have gained a conductor of spirit, taste, and soul in our new Kapellmeister.[19]

Eschmann began his review in the *Neue Badische Landes Zeitung,* with cautious cordiality:

> Herr Furtwängler will conduct these concerts from now on and will be giving the stamp of his individuality to them. One cannot know yet how his style of conducting will reveal itself or how it will develop and form musically. We can tell already that Furtwängler has something individual to say, that the orchestra under his leadership can preserve the reputation it has achieved in recent years. He is a musician of talent and taste, he works with energy and artistic scrupulousness, and his efforts have had justifiable success.

Eschmann proceeded to give a fairly detailed description of Furtwängler's account of each movement in the Beethoven and concluded that Furtwängler demonstrated "a profound understanding of the musical drama in each movement." He especially liked some portions of the final movement but made a point of recounting a few gaffes made by the orchestra:

> In the final movement, [Furtwängler] surprised us suddenly with a very sensitive rhythmic and dynamic articulation, as well as with a fleet,

19. Friedrich Mack, 20 October 1915.

sprightly tempo. Small imperfections in the orchestra are simply to be excused under the circumstances, for the orchestra deserves much praise in acclimating itself to its new music director.[20]

By the end of the season, Furtwängler had established himself as a worthy successor to Bodanzky, though his reviewers would continue to find comparisons anything but odious during the rest of his five year stay in Mannheim. In a post-season round-up, Eschmann declared:

> Furtwängler has grasped the gravity of his artistic task surprisingly quickly and also has emerged brilliantly as Artur Bodanzky's successor, which is to the great benefit of the whole musical life in Mannheim.[21]

Eschmann tempered his compliment by complaining that Furtwängler's programming for his debut season had not been characterized by the variety his predecessor infused into his own concerts. Indeed, Furtwängler's traversal of major orchestral music amounted to little more than staple works from the 19th century: one Beethoven symphony (the Fifth), Liszt's *Faust Symphony*, the Bruckner Fourth, and the Brahms First. Strauss' *Alpine Symphony* was about the only new and major orchestral work of that season. Furtwängler had removed a scheduled performance of Beethoven's Ninth to make way for its local premiere, and Eschmann described Furtwängler's account as a carefully wrought and "superior" performance of the work.[22] Originally, the premiere was supposed to take place earlier in the season, but practical complications delayed it until the final concert of the year.[23] Furtwängler planned the Ninth two more times in later seasons, but for various reasons—most notably a fear of being inadequate to the demands of the work, even though he already had performed the work in Lübeck—he did not actually perform it in Mannheim until 1 April 1919 with Elfriede Müller, Lippe, Max Lipmann, and Fenton.[24]

A month after this concert, Furtwängler made the personal

---

20. 20 October 1915.
21. *Neue Badische Landes Zeitung*, 29 March 1916.
22. *Neue Badische Landes Zeitung*, 29 March 1916.
23. The extra personnel required for this outsize work must have taxed Mannheim's resources to the limit. It is scored, for example, for 20 horns, each of whom must be of virtuoso calibre. Since it was a premiere, Furtwängler also had to teach the music to the musicians after learning it himself.
24. Furtwängler expressed his fears in a letter to Bruno Walter 2 September 1918. Source: Library of the Performing Arts, Lincoln Center, New York. He conducted the Ninth for the first time in April 1913 in Lübeck. The exact date is not clear.

acquaintance of Heinrich Schenker. He had known about this brilliant Viennese musical theorist since 1912 when he read Schenker's monograph on Beethoven's Ninth, but he had not yet met him.[25] A mutual friend invited them both to dinner during one of Furtwängler's trips to Vienna, and Furtwängler impressed Schenker with his knowledge of Schenker's writings.[26] A few months later, Schenker attended one of Furtwängler's concerts with the Tonkünstlerorchester. While he quibbled with details in Furtwängler's performance of Beethoven's Fifth ("some fermatas or pauses were exaggerated in the expressive sense . . ."), his verdict was high praise indeed:

> The last movement was as good on the whole as it was in its separate parts. Without doubt, the young conductor's interpretation is superior to Weingartner, Nikisch, and Strauss. It is a only a pity that he is not more deeply involved in the work.[27]

Furtwängler not only became Schenker's pupil but also his long-standing friend. Despite Schenker's prestige and fame, derived primarily from his numerous books, articles and monographs, he never held a teaching position at a conservatory or a university. His "tutorials" were held in his home or in various cafes he frequented around Vienna. In the years to come, Furtwängler studied and re-studied many scores—especially Beethoven—with Schenker and took every opportunity to see him whenever he came to Vienna.[28] It is not clear whether Schenker charged fees for his services, but Furtwängler, as we will see later, became one of his most significant benefactors.[29]

In his later seasons at Mannheim, Furtwängler conducted a wide variety of operas including, *Meistersinger, Tannhäuser, Parsifal, Ariadne auf Naxos, Salome, Magic Flute, The Marriage of Figaro, Abduction from the Seraglio, The Barber of Seville, Orpheus and Eurydice, Carmen, Aida,* and *Otello,* all in German and all for the first time. He also performed his share of contemporary works: *Herr Dandolo* by Rudolf Siegel, his competitor at Lübeck, *Violanta* and *Der Ring des*

25. See Chapter 1.
26. Schenker's *Diaries,* 4 May 1919.
27. *Diaries,* 4 November 1919.
28. Furtwängler sent many notes to Schenker asking for appointments or requesting changes of dates. Several of them are to be found in the Oster Collection at the Library of the Performing Arts, Lincoln Center, New York, and in the Oswald Jonas Collection at the University of California at Riverside. Despite the heights Furtwängler scaled over the years, he usually demonstrated his respect for Schenker by writing out his messages in his own hand rather than relegating them to a secretary to be typed. The tenor of these brief notes was consistently and appropriately precative.
29. See Chapter 5.

Polykrates by Erich Maria Korngold (on a double bill), *Schahrazade* by Bernard Sekles, and three operas by his old mentor at Strasbourg, Hans Pfitzner: *Der arme Heinrich, Christelflein,* and *Palestrina.* He also conducted one ballet: *Klein Idas Blume* by Paul von Klenau (6 December 1916), based on Hans Christian Andersen's story "Lille Idas Blomster." It was described as a "Tanzspiel" and paired with another Klenau bijou called *Olga.* The reviewer admitted he could not bear sitting through a Tanzspiel after enduring *Olga,* made worse by depressing news he read that day from the war front, but he promised to return to look at it later. He kept his word, praised Furtwängler, and said precious little about the quality of the dancing.[30] Furtwängler's association with Klenau, who also studied with Heinrich Schenker, came into fuller bloom when he conducted the world premiere of another gem by this Danish composer-conductor called *Kjartan und Gutrun,* this one a full-length opera and his most important work for the lyric stage (4 April 1918). It was favorably received, but it appears to have been quickly forgotten.

Furtwängler expanded his repertoire during succeeding seasons with the *Akademie* concerts, but restricted that expansion primarily to the large romantic works of the 19th century. In the 1917–1918 season, for example, he repeated Beethoven's Fifth and added the First and Seventh. He also performed Bruckner's Eighth, *Dante* by Liszt, and Schubert's Eighth ("Unfinished") and Ninth ("Great"). The contemporary works he chose were very much in the tonal tradition: *Variations and Fugue on a Theme by Mozart,* op. 132, by Max Reger and another set of *Variations* by a certain pianist-composer, Georg Szell.[31] His soloists included a balanced mix of established artists and up-and-comers of that period: Felix Gerber (violin), Eva Brun (soprano), Wera Schapira (piano), Adolf Busch (violin), Carl Müller (cello), Waldemar Stegemann (baritone), and Edwin Fischer (piano).

Furtwängler assiduously avoided one area of music throughout the years of the First World War. While he was frequently invited to conduct military bands and concerts supporting Germany's involvement in the war, he steadfastly refused such invitations. Music, for him, had nothing to do with politics, especially war, and he was not about to allow himself or the musical forces under his direction to participate in political events. In fact, he effectively shielded both the opera house and the *Akademie* Concerts from playing for the war

---

30. 7 December 1916 and 18 December 1916, *Neue Badische Landes Zeitung.*
   31. Who, of course, later became music director of the Cleveland Orchestra (1946–1970).

effort and even refused to bow to the Kaiser's box when the monarch attended one of his concerts.

During his Mannheim years, Furtwängler presided over two gala events that solidified his professional ties to two of the most important musical personalities of the time. In the spring of his first season, Artur Nikisch made a guest appearance at the Mannheim Court Opera to conduct *Carmen* and *Fledermaus.* Nothing has yet surfaced about how he got along with Germany's leading conductor of the time, but Furtwängler had by this time surely overcome speechless awe for his idol to converse intelligently and cordially with him. The rapport they engendered enabled Furtwängler to make his debut with the Berlin Philharmonic eighteen months later. This, in spite of disaster hovering over the performance of *Carmen* at Nikisch's first night (16 May 1916). Illnesses in the cast forced last-minute substitutions. The changes evidently created infelicities in the performance that could be noticed even by the hearing-impaired.[32]

During the following season, Furtwängler presided over a Richard Strauss Festival at which the composer himself appeared to supervise performances of *Salome, Rosenkavalier, Ariadne,* and an orchestral concert consisting of his own works. It was a gala and highly successful series of events that climaxed in a visit of the Court Opera to Zürich under Strauss' direction. Strauss already had entrusted Furtwängler with the local premiere of his *Alpine Symphony* at the end of the previous season. But when Strauss came to the first orchestra rehearsal for the revised version of *Ariadne,*[33] he disliked Furtwängler's tempo in the overture and mentioned it in a letter to his librettist Hugo von Hofmannsthal:

> The Overture was botched completely at the most heavy-footed pace by F[urtwängler], otherwise a very gifted conductor, and put right by me for Switzerland in three rehearsals: it's odd how difficult it is for even the most gifted people to get into the new style.[34]

But Furtwängler established an agreeable relationship with the composer-conductor, and it was no coincidence that Strauss' basically positive disposition toward him paved the way for Furtwängler to suc-

32. *Neue Badische Landes Zeitung*, 17 May 1916.

33. Strauss' original version was completed in 1912. The revised version usually performed today was finished in 1916 and produced in Vienna with Lotte Lehmann as the composer and Maria Jeritza as Ariadne.

34. 7 February 1917. Quoted from *A Working Friendship: The Correspondence Between Richard Strauss and Hugo von Hofmannsthal,* translated by Hanns Hammelmann and Ewald Osers, (New York) 1974, p. 265.

ceed him as Music Director of the Berlin Staatsoper Orchestra concerts in 1920.[35] Their relationship remained constant with an ebb here and there until Strauss' death in 1949.

Ovations at Furtwängler's concerts were now commonplace, but even as his name became increasingly familiar to musical circles throughout Germany, he had no real close circle of friends. Such was a quirk of his personality that would beset him for good or ill throughout his whole life. He was a familiar sight around the wooded outskirts of Mannheim, where he took long walks with a brisk gait almost daily, humming and singing scores he was learning while bobbing his head and gesticulating with his hands in time to his music-making. With more than a dozen operas to learn during his first season alone, of course, he had little time for social life, and his letters during this period to Toni Ketels, a piano teacher in Hamburg, make it clear that all work and virtually no recreation did not sit entirely well with him:

> I am really beginning to be a good conductor. That truly is my only pleasure right now. My health is not really brilliant, but it is astonishingly good under these circumstances.[36]

When the pace had not let up more than a year later, he looked forward to Frau Ketels' visit to his mother's house in Tegernsee where he had gone for a rest. He sent her a note describing her forthcoming arrival as a "welcome respite" from his busy activities.[37]

But his solitary nature did not stop him from having affairs with an endless file of women who fell into his arms the moment he opened his dressing room door after every concert and opera performance. Furtwängler was not "sexy" in the movie-star mode, nor did he present the requisite picture for endorsing hair lotion (he was losing it rapidly by this time), but he exuded what women time and again called an "aura" that was irresistible. It is not certain whether Frau Ketels was among his paramours, but one of his affairs during his tenure in Mannheim led to an illegitimate child—Wilhelm (b. 1916)—whom Furtwängler later adopted.

Not all his admirers, of course, were women. And not all of them

---

35. Distinctions between institutions here are complicated but important. Furtwängler became director of the Staatsoper Orchestra in 1920, not the Staatsoper itself. The concerts of the Staatsoper Orchestra were managed separately from Staatsoper operatic performances, even though most of the same personnel played for both orchestras. Furtwängler did not conduct opera at the Staatsoper until 1931. He did not become Music Director of the Staatsoper until 1933. By then, he had long given up his activity with the Staatsoper Orchestra concerts.
36. 26 December 1915.
37. *Briefe*, Nr. 33, p. 51.

stampeded his dressing room after a concert. Perhaps his most innocent fan was a bright schoolboy who would soon become a student of
architecture. For one crucial moment many years later, this gifted
Mannheimer, who fell under the conductor's musical spell, would
become the best friend Furtwängler ever had. His name: Albert
Speer.[38]

Furtwängler's success in Mannheim also owed a lot to the fact that
he was no stranger to the city. His grandmother lived there, and he
knew many of its prominent families. The Geissmars were among
them. The senior Geissmar was an influential attorney with a great
love of music. He was an amateur violinist and had an enormous collection of fine instruments, including the Vieuxtemps Stradivarius.
He frequently held musicales and parties for the constant stream of
musicians and artists who passed through Mannheim, and a dinner
party at the Geissmar house always boasted at least one representative
of the finest in European artistic life. Furtwängler met many of them
at the Geissmars' house, and he struck up a close friendship with
Geissmar's daughter Berta that lasted until her death in 1948. Berta
eventually became his personal assistant, and there were rumors that
they might marry. She had all the qualities that Furtwängler needed
except one. She was painfully plain. Nevertheless, she was bright,
intellectual, organized, highly personable and could be offensively
aggressive if the occasion warranted. But while Furtwängler had
gained himself a reputation as a ladies' man almost from the time he
first started functioning sexually, he apparently never physically
turned his abiding respect and affection for Berta into an actual love
affair. Ultimately, Berta eventually all but ran Furtwängler's life. She
became well known for the quiet efficiency with which she managed
all his professional and private affairs, and there was not a conductor
or even top-level executive in Germany who did not envy Furtwängler
for his luck in having such an exemplary secretary.

He also began to widen his reputation as well as his repertoire by
guest conducting while he was based in Mannheim, but his remarkable development during this period had its ironies, for it took place
against a background of ever-increasing hardship for Germany. On
one hand, the Emperor and the aristocracy in the military were prone
to acting out delusions of machismo. Such proclivities prompted
them to charge into the Great War as something of a body-building
exercise, a purposeful means of avoiding flabbiness from the boredom
of everyday life. On the other, Germany convinced herself she was the

38. Speer became Hitler's leading architect shortly after 1933 and later was
appointed his munitions expert.

victim of jealousies among foreign powers envious of her commercial successes. To defend and maintain her honor, she needed power. When war came, following the assassination of Archduke Ferdinand of Austria, Germany appeared to be prepared militarily for a long, painful war, but it had neither the materiel, morale, nor the political resolve to remain mired indefinitely in trenches in order to outlast and vanquish its enemy. For trench warfare was not merely a new phenomenon of the battlefield. It also created a siege mentality that made people regard the extreme deprivation they were enduring as noble sacrifice, but few were really fooled.[39] By the time Furtwängler was preparing for his first *Meistersinger* in Mannheim on the eve of the Armistice in November 1918, Germany had deteriorated from a glorious if somewhat anachronistic empire into a physical quadriplegic and a spiritual cripple. Immobility fueled by despair had her teetering on the brink of nothing short of suicidal rebellion. Such depredations would soon create an impulse for Armageddon that would simmer over the next fourteen years and incubate a monster to bring it about. Furtwängler left no record that he consciously aspired to become a wound-healer in this period, but the contributions he was to make to the cultural life of Germany during those turbulent years after the Great War would ultimately help counteract this demon.

Furtwängler resigned his post in Mannheim at the end of the 1919–1920 season because he wanted to expand the sphere of his career without being tied to a demanding position that involved administrative as well as musical duties. He became something of an itinerant conductor, making guest appearances in various cities throughout Germany and Austria. Nonetheless, he maintained his job as Music Director for the subscription series of the Frankfurt Museum Concerts, which he held from 1920 to 1922. It was far less time-consuming than Mannheim, and Furtwängler had added the job to his widening list of activities after Willem Mengelberg resigned as conductor of the Frankfurt Opera Orchestra concerts—known as the Museum Concerts—in 1920 to pursue his career abroad.[40]

The Museum Concerts were a prestigious if not especially exciting assignment, for the orchestra had a long tradition of historic associations. Brahms was soloist in a performance of his own Second Piano Concerto in 1882, and he also conducted his Third and Fourth Symphonies with the orchestra in 1884 and 1886. Tchaikovsky, Richard

---

39. Modris Eksteins details how the concept of trench warfare profoundly affected European culture after World War I in *The Rites of Spring*, (New York) 1989.

40. Willem Mengelberg (1871–1951) was Music Director of the Concertgebouw Orchestra from 1895 to 1945. He also had a successful career in the United States, principally with the New York Philharmonic.

Strauss, Dvořák, Grieg and others had also presented their own works at the Museum Concerts. Furtwängler saw his job as a torch bearer of this noble tradition. Between 1918 and 1922 Furtwängler conducted 17 separate programs at Frankfurt, first as a guest conductor in 1918 and later as its chief conductor. They reflect little of the swirl of experimentalism that was going on at the time, but several works by Schönberg (*Transfigured Night* and *Pelleas und Melisande*) and a work each by Braunfels, Sekles, and Erdmann appeared here and there throughout his tenure. At his first concert in Frankfurt, Furtwängler accompanied Leonid Kreutzer in Rachmaninoff's Second Piano Concerto on 15 September 1918. The rest of the program was filled out with Strauss' *Don Juan* and Brahms' First Symphony. For some reason, most of the reviewers for the major papers in Frankfurt stayed away from all his concerts until he took over as Music Director in 1920.

Unlike most conductors making their careers later in the 20th century, Furtwängler established himself firmly as a conductor to be reckoned with through a relatively small number of guest appearances. Between 1915 and 1922 he made his debut in only six major cities outside Mannheim: Vienna in 1915 (with the Konzertvereinsorchester and in 1919 with the Vienna Tonkünstlerorchester), Berlin (Berlin Philharmonic) in 1917, Frankfurt in 1918, Hamburg in 1919, Stockholm (Stockholm Philharmonic) in 1919—his professional foreign debut, and Leipzig (Leipzig Gewandhaus Orchestra) in 1921. While the number of his engagements outside Mannheim were minuscule by present-day standards, the cities in which he appeared were the most important for any conductor coming along at that time. What is more, Furtwängler scored big successes in these cities despite the fact that some of the programs he conducted were hardly designed to bring attention to him. The most significant of these engagements, of course, were Berlin and Leipzig, for the orchestras in these cities were led by Artur Nikisch, which perforce made them the most important in Germany at this time. The frenetic audience reaction, the enthusiastic reviews, and most especially—the opinions of the musicians—inevitably came to Nikisch's attention.

Furtwängler's Berlin debut was one of those "sleeper" events that keep music lovers returning to concert halls and opera houses to endure dozens upon hundreds of mediocre performances, especially today. On paper, the likelihood of any attention falling on Furtwängler on the evening of 14 December 1917 was remote indeed. The celebrity soloists on that night were Heinrich Hensel and Fritz Feinhals, two of the reigning Wagner singers of their day. Furtwängler was hired primarily as a musical traffic cop to make sure the orchestra did not get in the way of the singers. The program consisted of six "bleeding chunks" of Wagner and two Strauss pieces.[41] The purely orchestral portions of the concert were limited to the Overture to *Tannhäuser* and to *Don Juan*. But these two samplings of Furtwängler's way with the music were enough for the audience to go wild and for the critics to all but ignore the singers in their reviews and rave about Furtwängler. Wilhelm Klatte of the *Berliner Lokal-Anzeiger* did not ignore the celebrated vocalists, but he mentioned their presence at the concert as something of an afterthought:

> One discerns in [Furtwängler] not only a real temperament, but a keenness of spiritual superiority, in whom indifference and routine must be eliminated. Besides leading Don Juan with great success, he also led the Tannhäuser Overture as a purely orchestral piece. For the rest of the program, he led the orchestral accompaniment for the vocal soloists Heinrich Hensel and Fritz Feinhals, who offered richly colorful selections of Wagner and Strauss and received a great deal of applause. They both showed their well-known gifts in a favorable light.[42]

Furtwängler's success was all the more astonishing under the circumstances, for Richard Strauss himself had led *Don Juan* at the Staatsoper Concerts only a few days earlier. The concert proved to be something of a turning point for him, for nothing cultural in Germany really happened until it happened in Berlin, both then as now, and Furtwängler had now irrefutably happened. He returned two more times to conduct the Berlin Philharmonic during that season and scored a big success with his performance of Bruckner's Fourth on January 18th.

Less than two years later, Furtwängler gained his first solid footing in Berlin. Strauss was about to resign his post as Music Director of the Berlin State Opera Concerts, and Furtwängler seemed the most likely candidate to succeed him. During Holy Week in 1920 he led the Staatsoper Orchestra in three concerts of two programs. The first took place on Good Friday, 2 April, at noon; a program of Wagner (the Prelude to *Parsifal*), Bach (Suite No. 3 in D Major), and Beethoven (the *Eroica*). The next afternoon and evening, he conducted a Concerto Grosso by Handel and Beethoven's Ninth with probably the strongest group of vocal soloists he had yet had at his disposal: Ethel Hansa,[43] Karin Bran-

41. George Bernard Shaw is the author of this aptly descriptive phrase.
42. 17 December 1917 (Evening Edition).
43. Little is known about Hansa, but she was extremely successful during her 11-year career at the Berlin Staatsoper, a phenomenon made somewhat more astonishing by the fact that she was an American. She was born in Philadelphia, studied in Paris with Marchesi and later with Albert Loesch in Berlin. She made her German debut in Elberfeld (now part of Wuppertal) in 1911, and went to Berlin in 1913 as a light soprano with the Kurfürstin Oper. She joined the Berlin Staatsoper a year later and remained with the

zell, Josef Mann, and Karl Armster. Several days later, Klatte contributed his part to the chorus of approval:

> And the fact [that there was a meeting of minds between conductor and the musical forces before him] showed clearly, palpably, and comprehensibly in the specters and waves of great masses of sound. It gave proof that a positive, essential, and instinctive contact had set off a desire for a mutually satisfying collaboration between conductor and orchestra. If no way can be found to keep Richard Strauss as head of the Staatsoper Concerts, then Furtwängler's estimable gifts should be secured.[44]

Secured they were, and his appointment at the Berlin Staatsoper Concerts assured his position as one of Germany's leading conductors.

Furtwängler's career was now moving along at an ever accelerating clip. At the end of the following summer, he made his debut with the "other" orchestra Nikisch directed, the Leipzig Gewandhaus. It took place on 30 August 1921, and the occasion was a bit more auspicious for him than his first appearance with the Berlin Philharmonic. The event inaugurated both the opening concert of the season and the launching of the city's annual Autumn Fair. By present-day standards the event could be described as a mini-monster concert: Weber's Overture to *Freischütz*, Schumann's Fourth Symphony, Strauss' *Till Eulenspiegel*, and both the *Hungarian Fantasia* and the First Piano Concerto by Liszt played by the Italian virtuoso Telemache Lambrino. By this time, Furtwängler's reputation had preceded him, and the critics were impressed. Said one review, "The audience witnessed a great musical event."[45]

But Furtwängler's biggest opportunity came when Artur Nikisch died suddenly of influenza on 23 January 1922, at the age of 66, leaving vacant the music directorships of both the Berlin Philharmonic and the Leipzig Gewandhaus Orchestra. Nikisch was undisputed king of conductors in Germany—some would have said even the world and his only serious rival for that title on the international music scene at the time was Toscanini. Those who spoke of him as "irreplaceable" intoned that word with absolute seriousness. Unlike some extremely powerful musical figures later in the century, he was loved as much as he was respected, and the thought of musical life without

company as its house soubrette until 1925. She enjoyed successes as Zerbinetta and Olympia and made guest appearances in Holland and Scandinavia. She apparently disappeared after she left the Staatsoper.

44. *Berliner Lokal-Anzeiger*, 6 April 1920.

45. Cited from Philippe Jacquard, *Furtwängler à Leipzig*, (Paris) 1988, p. 3. Hereafter referred to as Jacquard.

Nikisch, especially a Nikisch who had departed from this life with such suddenness, was simply unimaginable.

Being the resilient community it has always been under any circumstances, however, Berlin initiated its delectable sweepstakes of Pick The Successor even while draping itself in mourning. Nikisch's body was barely cold before the murmur of names dripped from veiled lips into bold print. And without exception the race for the podium was among thoroughbreds: Richard Strauss, Bruno Walter, Erich Kleiber, Otto Klemperer, and Felix Weingartner were the favorites; Willem Mengelberg, Fritz Busch, Siegmund von Hausegger, and Carl Schuricht were the contenders. Every day, a new winner was rumored. Each day, there was no announcement.[46] The dark horse in this derby was Furtwängler, but the gossip mill largely dismissed him because he already had a tight contract as the Music Director of the Staatsoper Orchestra Concerts. While men of great knowledge, insight, or simply wishful thought passed the days following Nikisch's death arguing vociferously among themselves in cafes on Potsdamerplatz, in green rooms of theaters and concert halls, or flexed their influential opinions in the newspapers, the ultimate decision of The Successor was left to a woman.

46. Wolfgang Stresemann, . . . *Und Abends in die Philharmonie*, (Munich) 1981, pp. 9–19, offers a fascinating reminiscence of the transition between Nikisch and Furtwängler from a schoolboy's point of view. He later became Intendant of the Berlin Philharmonic. Hereafter referred to as Stresemann.

3

Berlin

And Louise Wolff had an impressive field to choose from. As directress of Wolff and Sachs, Germany's most powerful concert agency, her stable of artists included many of the top performers not only of that day but of the entire century. They included (to name only a few of the hundreds) Edwin Fischer, Adolf Busch, Sigrid Onegin, Georg Kulenkampf, Karl Muck, Felix Weingartner, Teresa and Artur Schnabel, Emmi Leisner, Karin Branzell, Jascha and Tossy Spivakovsky, Claire Dux, and Carl Flesch. The newspaper advertisements heralding performances of her clients were usually the largest in the Sunday editions and were set off with a thick black border running around all sides, crowned with discreet little boxes midway along the top and bottom lines, the top box containing the agency's name in miniscule letters and the bottom one touting Bote und Bock as its primary ticket outlet.[1] She was known as Queen Louise in musical circles throughout Europe, and far more respect than sarcasm attended her title. She had taken over the successful agency founded by her husband Hermann after he died in 1902 and made it grow in prosperity by holding on to established talents while nurturing promising new ones. Her gift for picking talent was every bit as bright as the best musical talent among

---

1. Bote und Bock were also publishers and music retailers who later brought out a biography of Hermann (the founder of the agency) and Louise Wolff by their daughter Edith Stargardt-Wolff: *Wegbereiter grosser Musiker*, (Berlin and Wiesbaden) 1954. Hereafter referred to as Wolff.

the clients she selected. Much of the respect accorded her also stemmed from her reputation as an even-handed dealer with entrepreneurs and promoters, in spite of commanding a deck that obviously was loaded.

Perhaps the biggest of Louise Wolff's clients was the Berlin Philharmonic. Though it was far from the wealthiest of them, it was the first orchestra of Berlin, the bearer of that city's musical franchise. One of the primary considerations she would have to keep in mind in promoting a successor to Nikisch was the power of that conductor both as a box-office draw and as Steward of musical life in Berlin, and for that matter, of all Germany. But a choice based on these considerations alone was all but impossible, since every contender had a large and loyal following in Berlin and was fully qualified in musical pedigree, talent, and experience. Bruno Walter, Otto Klemperer, and others all had their own well-attended subscription series with the Berlin Philharmonic, but the most important and prestigious of the concerts given by the orchestra were those under the leadership of the Music Director.

As the hours after Nikisch's death passed into days, and the date of the memorial concert approached, Louise Wolff still had made no firm decision. Furtwängler, meanwhile, had gone to Leipzig to conduct a guest engagement with the Gewandhaus Orchestra scheduled for January 26th. It was clear that the event would have to serve as a memorial concert, even though Nikisch's family for some reason requested it be canceled. The program consisted of only three works. It began with Beethoven's *Coriolanus Overture*, an appropriate procession to the fallen king. Sigrid Onegin sang Brahms' *Four Serious Songs* accompanied by Michael Raucheisen at the piano, an utterance of mournful contemplation. The orchestra finished the concert with the slow movement from the *Eroica* while the audience stood. The selection was both a eulogy to a true hero taken before his time and a recessional from the rite of mourning.

After the concert, Furtwängler returned directly to Berlin, made an unexpected visit to Louise Wolff's office, and got straight to the point. He told her he wanted to be Nikisch's successor at the Berlin Philharmonic. The idea startled Frau Wolff because Furtwängler was firmly ensconced as Music Director of the Staatsoper Concerts, and it was a very good post indeed. Did Furtwängler want more rehearsal time at the Staatsoper? Did he prefer the superior acoustics of the Philharmonie—the concert hall that was the home of the Berlin Philharmonic? Did, perhaps, he really want to take on the Philharmonic post in addition to his present job to make sure that he would not be threatened by a new rival at either the Staatsoper or at the helm of the city's premiere orchestra?[2] Louise Wolff knew full well that the environs of the Staatsoper, even though Furtwängler conducted only the orchestra concerts and no operas there, had one advantage that the Berlin Philharmonic simply could not offer. It had a resplendent bevy of pretty choristers and dancers on tap to keep his libido massaged. The Berlin Philharmonic consisted entirely of men.

Whatever motives may be deduced for Furtwängler wanting to leave a cushy job in an establishment that had a large guaranteed subsidy, a clear and simple fact remained: ever since he became aware of his superior talents as a conductor he wanted to be Germany's first conductor. Now that Nikisch was gone, he was merely placing himself before the right person at what he undoubtedly knew was the right place and time. For her part, Frau Wolff was galvanized by the proposal. The passing of Nikisch at age 66 represented the passing of an era, an age in which the values and traditions of the 19th century had come into their fullest bloom. What the orchestra needed now was a personality who could develop those traditions further in a new and modern way, who could reconcile music from the past with the experiments and trends that now appeared to be taking it into a variety of different directions. In essence, the Berlin Philharmonic needed new blood, a younger image, a fresh personality.

Shortly after this meeting, the details of the memorial concert for Nikisch appeared, and the announcement sent shivers of excitement through Berlin's musical gossip mill while curdling the cream in the coffee cups of numerous aspirants to the throne. Furtwängler would preside over the major portions of the program set for February 6th, which included conducting the entire *Eroica* and accompanying at the piano the baritone Julius von Raatz-Brockmann in Brahms' *Four Serious Songs*. The rest of the program would consist of Brahms' *Nänie* and the chorale "*O Welt, ich muss dich lassen . . .*" sung by the Bruno Kittel Choir with Walter Fischer at the organ.

Once Furtwängler's name on the announcement of the memorial concert appeared, the odds on Nikisch's successor changed dramatically, and the dark horse charged ahead, although staunch supporters of Walter, Klemperer, Weingartner and others kept insisting that their man would ultimately win out. Actually, Walter looked as though he would emerge as the victor, for he already had a subscrip-

---

2. Wolff, pp. 236–237. It is not clear whether Frau Wolff actually considered these motives during this conference or whether Frau Stargardt-Wolff is simply imputing them to Furtwängler.

tion series of six concerts per season in addition to his duties as Music Director of the Nationaltheater in Munich. Only Nikisch had had more—10 concerts—in his own series.[3]

To say that Louise Wolff had pulled strings in favor of Furtwängler would hardly overstate the matter. By late March, she was able to secure the agreement of both the board and membership of the Philharmonic, and Furtwängler got out of his contract with the Staatsoper Orchestra amicably, promising to conduct regularly throughout the remainder of his contract, a pledge he rigorously kept. Frau Wolff paved the way for him to succeed Nikisch at both Berlin and Leipzig, and he was on his way to becoming the foremost German conductor of his time. Indeed, Furtwängler was fulfilling his great promise. He was 36, and published reports already had hailed him as a miracle—"*Das Wunder Furtwängler.*" The phrase would be used again seventeen years later—and used against him at that time, but for now, almost nothing hurtful seemed possible in this hour of triumph.

Furtwängler's arrival in Berlin as Music Director of the Philharmonic coincided with one of the most important phases of that city's cultural history. Germany was now four years into what came to be known as the Weimar Republic, and Berlin had long been its undisputed cultural capital. Furtwängler's appointment was among the numerous phenomena that contributed to making Berlin even greater as the center of Europe's cultural universe from 1922 to 1933. Paris may have had its writers and painters, and London may have had its novelists and poets, but for sheer variety, energy, and importance of the work being produced in that period, there was nothing quite like Berlin during Weimar.

Despite political instability that created galloping inflation, starvation, and seething social unrest in the general populace, Germany of the Weimar Republic was an exuberant center teeming with cultural activity, and Berlin was its vortex and zenith. Here, far more than any other city in Germany, the cultural life at once reflected the unrest and anxiety of the society from which it grew, and articulated time and again the longing for "wholeness," for a coherent if not entirely unified vision of existence. Toward that end, Berlin alone provided 43 legitimate theaters, four opera houses, and more than 20 orchestras. In one week, a music lover could choose among Furtwängler, Walter, Klemperer, and Kleiber conducting various ensembles. Their concerts sometimes would compete with recitals by Sergei Rachmaninoff, Emmanuel Feuermann, Moritz Rosenthal, Paul Hindemith, or Elly

---

3. See Peter Muck, *Einhundert Jahre Berliner philharmonisches Orchester*, (Berlin) 1982, Vol. II, pp. 507–508. Hereafter referred to as Muck.

Ney given on the same evening. Max Reinhardt, Leopold Jessner, Karl-heinz Martin, Gerhardt Hauptmann, and Bertholt Brecht are but five of the recognizable names in a galaxy of theatrical luminaries who were active in Berlin during this time. Berlin was also home to visual artists such as Klee, Kandinsky, and Kokoschka and was the capital of the Expressionist movement. Döblin and Zweig, Mann and Hermann Hesse; Werfel, Kafka, and Hofmannsthal all enlivened Weimar Berlin with their writings even if they did not all live there. Einstein and other scientists who produced important and far-reaching research did live and work there. Even mere "entertainment" frequently tran-scended the mere; the Berlin of Weimar fostered a relatively new genre: the Kabarett, smoke-filled rathskellers and cafes whose sedi-tious music and rhymes, scraping out raspy syncopations and gro-tesque ironies, challenged the spirit with grim humor. Caustic satire and a spirit of cynicism at first caused infectious mirth, but ironically perhaps, the very cautery of their satire ultimately infected and dis-eased the cultural organism to which they were essential.[4]

And it would soon infect every facet of life in Germany. The three areas this virus would eventually infect most significantly and in a multitude of ways were the burgeoning German film industry, Ger-man publishing, and journalism. Berlin had 120 newspapers, every one of them purveying a slightly different angle on perceived realities and each of them thriving on a loyal following.[5] While it was certainly not the most literary city of this century, only New York and Paris of the '20s came close to approaching the Berlin of Weimar in the variety and cosmopolitanism of its ideas. In all, Berlin evolved rapidly into the crossroad where venerable old trafficked boldly with swaggering new, the intersection at which shocking contradiction and blasphe-mous experiment aggressively bisected inviolable tradition.[6]

While Furtwängler performed some dazzling concerts and was

4. Peter Sloterdijk in Part IV of *Kritik der zynischen Vernuft,* translated as *Critique of Cynical Reason* by Michael Eldred, (Minneapolis) 1987, offers a radical but incisive survey of the cynicism pervading Weimar and how it not only contributed to its destruc-tion but still infects the marrow of post-modern German culture.

5. Newspapers of that period usually contained only a few leaves per edition. Except for Sunday, the dailies rarely ran more than 16 or 20 pages, but many of them were published in three different editions. Theater and music reviews almost invariably appeared in the afternoon.

6. Perhaps the concert most symbolic of the meeting between old and new in Wei-mar Berlin took place on 21 November 1927 when Oskar Fried conducted a program of the Berlin Philharmonic starting with Stravinsky's *Rite of Spring* and concluding with Beethoven's Ninth, separated, of course, by an intermission. His soloists for the finale included the immortal Emmy Land, the unforgettable Jenny Sonnenberg, the redoubt-able Eugen Transky, and last but at least a recognizable name from that period, Wilhelm Guttman.

dazzled at finding himself in the very crucible of both German Kultur and European culture, his first season was not without its problems. In fact, it started off poorly. The opening concert of the season took place on 9 October. The program was strange in choice and peculiar in sequence; for some reason, Furtwängler turned the usual order of items upside down.[7] To start the concert, he picked Bruckner's brooding Seventh Symphony, almost invariably the closing work of a program. It was also a distasteful choice to many in the audience, for Nikisch had presented its premiere in Berlin and was closely identified with it. Furtwängler often made it a practice to conduct works that had been performed by other conductors in the same season or even in the same week, presumably to show how the piece really should go. He had been fortunate at his debut with the Berlin Philharmonic in 1917, for he succeeded in beating Strauss at his own composition when he conducted *Don Juan* only a few days after the Meister had conducted it himself. But the lather-raising cadencies of *Don Juan* are but an inebriated revival meeting beside the apocalyptic meditations from which the Bruckner Seventh is wrought. While Furtwängler was to prove time and again that he could perform countless works to greater effect than other conductors, this performance of Bruckner's monumental symphony was not one of those occasions. Nikisch was a devoted and devout Brucknerite, and he had persuaded Berliners during his tenure that his pious but epic-proportioned view of the work was the way to perform it, at least for their time. It looked as though the new Music Director was trying to appropriate it. At best, both critics and audiences were likely to view such puerility with disdain. At worst, they would loathe it.

And the critics, at least, detested it. Walter Schrenk of the *Berliner Deutsche Allgemeine Zeitung* found Furtwängler guilty of the "vanity of podium virtuosos" in trying to search for "lovely effects" rather than maintaining Nikisch's humility. The *Berliner Tageblatt* appreciated Furtwängler's sincerity but found his interpretation "weak." Max Marschalk of the *Vossische Zeitung* concurred but was ultimately optimistic:

> Whether [Furtwängler] has a personality strong enough to dissipate the memory of Nikisch and maintain the superiority of the orchestra remains to be seen . . . That he began his first program with Bruckner may be an acknowledgment of that intention, but perhaps a little superstition was

7. Open public rehearsal was held the day before—a practice that prevailed in those days in Europe and continues in Germany and Austria to this day.

involved here, for he had his first big success in Berlin with Bruckner.[8] The most appealing side of his character so far appears to be his capacity for ecstasy, and we always had the impression that he comes alive and achieves greatness only in the ecstasy of working with an orchestra. That he was somewhat feeble this time, that he did not reveal Bruckner as boldly and glowingly, as richly contrasted in the mists of color as we had hoped, should not disturb us very much.[9]

After the intermission, the well-known pianist Josef Pembaur played Franck's *Symphonic Variations*, followed by Liszt's *Dance of Death*. Furtwängler and the orchestra closed the lengthy evening with the Overture to *Die Meistersinger*. That Pembaur played well was duly recorded. Just how well may never be known. The critics barely mentioned this part of the program.

Furtwängler's first concert as Music Director was indeed a manifesto of sorts, for he continued to challenge both his critics and his audiences throughout his inaugural season. The next pair of concerts, on October 22–23, brought mixed reviews. The program included Brahms' Second Symphony, the Schumann Piano Concerto played by Carl Friedberg, and a novelty for the Philharmonic: Scriabin's *Poem of Ecstasy*. Schrenk praised Furtwängler's "superior" conducting technique and "phenomenal power of feeling" but admitted "other commitments" prevented him from hearing the Brahms. Leopold Schmidt of the *Berliner Tageblatt* heard the Brahms and castigated Furtwängler for "preciously stretched tempos" that "Brahms himself never had taken." He sealed his judgment with first-hand authority: "I can testify to that." Schmidt was born in 1860, and was among many music lovers who could still make that statement in 1922.[10]

The critical verdicts and the audience reaction became more favorable over the next two concerts, which included the Berlin premiere of Max Reger's *Variations on a Theme by Beethoven*, but the fifth subscription concerts on December 10–11 brought Furtwängler's name to the lips of more Berliners than would ever attend his concerts. What is more it blew up into a scandal that made Furtwängler a mentionable commodity on the international musical stock market. The program began respectably enough with the Overture to *Ruler of the Spirits* by Weber, and proceeded to the Glazunov Violin Concerto played by Alexander Schmuller. But the dissonances of Schönberg's

8. Not entirely true. Furtwängler performed Bruckner's Fourth to great acclaim on 25 January 1918 (his birthday), but his first success was with Richard Strauss' *Don Juan* at his debut a month earlier.
9. 13 October 1922.
10. 24 September 1922. Brahms completed the symphony in 1877.

Five Pieces for Orchestra, op. 16, induced whistling and catcalls from the audience—a relatively rare occurrence at Philharmonic concerts. Furtwängler was presenting the Berlin premiere of the revised version of this work, and several reviewers credited him for showing great courage in programing such a controversial piece during his first season.[11] Schrenk—the most kindly disposed of the critics toward the avant-garde—was impressed both by the work and Furtwängler's interpretation. Marschalk, however, was not overwhelmed, but he advised Furtwängler:

> . . . not to close the Philharmonic's [window] to the morning air. The interest in modern music is growing gradually, and it must be perceived as meritorious, for it is exerting an influence on the shape of our musical life.[12]

Leopold Schmidt at the *Deutsche Allgemeine Zeitung* waxed sarcastic:

> I do not begrudge those finding pleasure in these arithmetic calculations for fulfillment in life and art . . . poor youth![13]

At this concert, Furtwängler first gave notice to the Berlin public that the new music director of its Philharmonic was a figure to be reckoned with. With it, the era of Nikisch had come to an end. Wolfgang Stresemann, son of the president of the Weimar Republic, still recalls that season, even though he was a schoolboy at the time: "During his last years, audiences got a little restless with Nikisch. It was always the same beautiful sound; but he wasn't really recreating the spirit of the music anymore. Now Furtwängler at the beginning could be a little exaggerated, but he had a new approach to music, and he was a new personality, and people were ready for a change."[14]

Despite objections from the audience and grumbling among the critics, Berlin quickly accepted the kind of change Furtwängler was bringing about. Furtwängler saw it as part of his responsibility to introduce his audiences to new music, even though he made it all too clear that it was not to his taste either. While he gave more than his share of performances of new music throughout his entire career, he was never to gain a well-deserved reputation for being a "champion"

11. Stresemann, p. 28. Furtwängler had presented the world premiere of the new version of the *Five Pieces for Orchestra* with the Leipzig Gewandhaus a few days earlier on 6–7 December.
12. *Vossische Zeitung,* 13 December 1922.
13. 12 December 1922.
14. Personal conversation with the author, Berlin, 10 October 1990.

of the avant-garde, for he did not perform music with atonal leanings as frequently as, say, Hermann Scherchen or Oskar Fried. Nor did he become identified as an experimentalist in the way Otto Klemperer and Erich Kleiber earned such tags. But a look at his first season alone demonstrates how ill-founded is the charge of inadventurous programming, for it was heavily skewed in favor of contemporary music: six works by living composers within ten pairs of concerts. In addition to the premieres of the works by Reger and Schönberg, he also performed Max Trapp's Second Symphony for the first time in Berlin (28–29 January) and programmed Strauss' *Till Eulenspiegel* (also on 28–29 January) and Sibelius' *En Saga* (4–5 March), which were both relatively new works at the time.

Bruno Walter and George Schneevoigt, on the other hand, performed no premieres and no contemporary works in their respective subscription series that year. But other conductors and artists were clamoring to perform new music with the Philharmonic, and Furtwängler as Music Director gave them ample opportunities in various series organized by the orchestra's management such as the Popular Concerts, the Austrian Music Week Festival, and the three-concert series sponsored by the International Society for Contemporary Music. Some of the works receiving their world premieres or their Berlin debuts during this season alone under various conductors were Nielsen's Violin Concerto (30 September) led by the composer and played by Emil Telmanyi, Respighi's *Concerto Gregoriano for Violin* (27 October) performed by Armida Senatra, *The Firebird* (2 November) by Stravinsky conducted by Furtwängler's colleague at the Leipzig Opera Gustav Brecher, the Orchestral Suite from Hindemith's opera *Nuschi-Nuschi* (26 January), *Passacaglia and Hymnus* by Kurt Weill and Rachmaninoff's Third Piano Concerto in D Minor played by Nicolai Orloff (both on 12 March) under Alexander Selo, Webern's *Passacaglia* (5 June), Schönberg's *Gurrelieder* (7 June), and Busoni's *Two Ballads* for baritone and orchestra (27 April) sung by Wilhelm Guttmann.[15]

As the season progressed, Furtwängler, the audience, and the critics rapidly became acclimated to one another, and by the end of the season, most doubts had been removed about the worthiness of Nikisch's successor. But on two aspects of his conducting, the critics remained resistant. The older critics like Schmidt continued to harp on the fluctuations in his tempos, especially in Beethoven and Brahms. Nearly all the critics looked askance at his broad, romantic view of

15. This by no means is a complete list of premieres during the 1922–1923 season. See Muck, Vol. III, pp. 201–207.

Bach and Handel. Furtwängler was extremely touchy about criticism, and he frequently contacted his critics, especially after reading a negative comment, to argue over their reviews. Occasionally such conversations devolved into shouting matches, for Furtwängler always enjoyed a good fight, especially with individuals he considered his intellectual equals. No doubt, such calls were eagerly anticipated by dissenting critics.

"Obviously, I was never personally involved in such incidents," says Stresemann, who was Intendant of the Berlin Philharmonic from 1959 to 1978, "but I happen to know that Furtwängler could become furious about negative criticism. He was known to go to the editors of the paper and threaten never to conduct again if a critic became too hostile in his estimation. He could be extremely insecure."[16]

On the upstage side of his podium, Furtwängler also had his difficulties during his first season. His peculiar baton technique gave the musicians some difficulty at the outset of the year, for they were used to the crystalline clarity of Nikisch's beat and his imperturbable calm on the podium. Furtwängler swayed and shuddered, danced and wriggled, and it was anybody's guess where his baton would finally stop wavering, thus indicating the inflection of the beat.[17] His notorious downbeat engendered numerous jokes over the years. Question: How do you know when to strike the first chord of the *Eroica?* Answer: When Furtwängler's baton reaches the third stud on his shirt. Question: How do you know when to start the murmuring semiquavers at the beginning of Beethoven's Ninth? Answer: As soon as Furtwängler enters the platform, we all walk around our chairs three times, sit down, count to 10, and play. Alternate answer: When we lose patience.

Actually, Furtwängler's baton technique could be as clear as, say, Fritz Reiner's or even Nikisch's, but his fuzziness of beat was purposefully calculated to a great extent; constant, absolute unison of ensemble was not necessarily his primary objective. The clarity and depth of the tonal mass was usually of far greater importance than mere lucidity of beat. Thus, bold chords, such as those starting the *Eroica,* frequently took on a slightly arpeggiated quality under his direction while still maintaining their lightning rhythmic impact. Those weaned on the spit-bang rigors of certain other conductors such as Toscanini would always find such an approach utterly incomprehensible. But the legions who would come to understand it would also learn to feel its rightness. Among those who came to understand and

16. Personal conversation, 10 October 1990.
17. Stresemann, p. 22.

admire this view of producing sound were the members of the Berlin Philharmonic. The first season was an extensive period of adjustment for both conductor and his musicians, and by the end of it, a feeling of mutual trust and confidence materialized.

Leipzig was another matter. Contention characterized his relationship with the venerable organization from the moment Nikisch died. The directors of the Gewandhaus, led by Max Brockhaus, one of Germany's leading publishers, wanted Furtwängler to sign a five-year contract.[18] The idea of committing himself for such a long period all but rattled Furtwängler, for he always was obsessed with freedom in the broadest possible sense. He also was not satisfied with the balance of power in determining artistic and organizational policy. As far as he was concerned, the board had too much power and the music director had too little. This problem had also nettled his great predecessor, and Furtwängler was determined not to be trapped in the same way. On one point he was resolved to have his way: touring. For some reason, the board of the Gewandhaus had no ambitions for widening the reputation of the orchestra by the most obvious means. It was quite comfortable with the laurels it had accrued over two centuries of survival under the likes of Bach and Mendelssohn.[19] Furtwängler won assurances about power over artistic policy, but the matter of touring remained vague.

He was about to sign his contract when certain members of the orchestra published a petition to the directors complaining that their first choice for Nikisch's successor—Hermann Abendroth—was not even considered. The publication deeply wounded Furtwängler, and he almost withdrew. But Karl Straube, long a friend of Furtwängler and director of the Thomaskirche Choir in Leipzig, prevailed upon Furtwängler to change his mind. He, of course, had his own reasons for persuading Furtwängler to take the post: he wanted Furtwängler to use his choir for big choral events. To appease Furtwängler, the board guaranteed him the right to participate in selecting guest conductors, and they also prevailed upon the orchestra to publish a declaration approving Furtwängler's selection as General Music Director. On 12 October 1922, Furtwängler opened the Leipzig Gewandhaus season with another concert dedicated to the memory of Artur Nikisch. The program contained only two works, Beethoven's *Third Leonore Over-*

18. Brockhaus Verlag, once one of Germany's leading publishers, was based in Leipzig at the time. Since 1945, it has had its headquarters in Wiesbaden and Mannheim and the firm has been sold to a conglomerate.
19. Bach conducted the first concerts of the Leipzig orchestra in 1743. Mendelssohn was chief conductor from 1835 to 1843.

ture and Bruckner's Seventh Symphony. Its brooding Adagio was a fit homage to a great conductor.

All at Leipzig, at least on the surface, was now smoothed over.[20] Furtwängler's uneasy relationship with Leipzig never really improved during his tenure, partly because he continued to widen his reputation by touring with the Berlin Philharmonic and taking guest engagements in Vienna and Milan, where he made his debut at La Scala on 19 June 1923 conducting its orchestra in a pair of concerts.[21]

He was no less busy trying to form some semblance of a domestic life for himself. Having suddenly been thrust into the limelight, he wasted no time in assembling the accoutrements of the social standing in which he found himself. While he never was vain or ostentatious about his physical appearance, he could never shun his basically bourgeois upbringing by ignoring the social standards he was now expected to set. He needed a house, so he bought one in St. Moritz in Switzerland—long the rest haven of Europe's famous, elite, and wealthy. He also needed a wife.

"Wilhelm suddenly decided he didn't want to be a bachelor," says Elisabeth Furtwängler, his second wife whom he married in 1943. "He already had three illegitimate children by women he never had intended to marry.[22] He acknowledged all his children and two of them took his surname—Wilhelm and Frederika.

"The women by whom he had children were all over thirty, and they all knew exactly what to do—you understand what I mean. But Wilhelm never had the slightest intention of marrying them, even though he always remained on good terms with them."

Zitla Lund was also over 30—exactly the same age as Furtwängler—36—when he met her in Berlin. She was Danish and exceptionally beautiful and on her second marriage when she met Furtwängler. She had married a millionaire industrialist, but Furtwängler's extraordinary charm was sufficient to make her divorce her husband instantly and marry him.

Elisabeth Furtwängler recalled to me, "Zitla once said that she would be so wealthy if she had stayed with her second husband, and she must have wondered why she left him for Wilhelm."[23]

The marriage was hardly made in heaven. They were joined in a civil ceremony on 22 May 1923 (Wagner's birthday) after knowing each other for only three months. It was not long before they discov-

20. Jacquard, pp. 1–18, presents a superb discussion of Furtwängler's turbulent relationship with the Leipzig Gewandhaus. See also Chapter 5.

21. Furtwängler did not conduct opera at La Scala until 1950. See Chapter 19.

22. Wilhelm (1916), Dagmar (1920), Fredericka (1921).

23. Personal conversation with the author, Clarens, 4 December 1989.

ered that whatever they may have found attractive in each other was no longer appealing. They also soon discovered that Furtwängler had sired yet another illegitimate child. Iva was born three months after his marriage. Shortly, the couple started leading separate lives and were legally separated in 1931. During this time, they both had numerous affairs, and Furtwängler eventually had at least one more illegitimate daughter two years after their separation—Almut in 1934. Presumably, this was the last child born out of wedlock, but Furtwängler's reputation as an incorrigible philanderer bred rumors persisting to this day that the total number of posthumous claims is at least thirteen. (*"Man spricht von dreizehn . . ."* ["they talk about 13"] was the phrase occasionally used.)

By this time, Furtwängler was nearly bald, and his face had developed into striking though not especially handsome proportions. It was his eyes, however, that became the most appealing aspect of the powerful aura he exuded. With merely a glance at the brass, he could conjure wall-trembling climaxes. A soulful scan across the violin section brought ravishing pianissimi. The same eyes could just as easily bring even the most shrewish of women swooning into his arms, and he was all too pleased to oblige.

Furtwängler never permitted his marital unhappiness nor his quantum extramarital affairs to mar his work, and he made sure that the Berlin Philharmonic's fame would be recognized by all Europe. He also increased its wealth as a private "limited liability" organization by taking the orchestra on tours through Switzerland, England, Scandinavia, and Hungary. He was not nearly as successful in making the Leipzig Gewandhaus Orchestra a more progressive institution. In fact he failed miserably. Furtwängler won his demand about touring with the Gewandhaus, but it was a marginal victory. Its board was reluctant to let it leave home, and the orchestra made only one tour (through Switzerland) during Furtwängler's tenure there.

What was worse, his conflicts with Leipzig became a public issue in 1925. The eminent musicologist Alfred Heuss viewed himself, perhaps rightly, as the guardian of the Gewandhaus tradition. It was bad enough that Furtwängler wanted to spend less time in Leipzig, and it was barely to be tolerated that the opera was using the orchestra so much as to cut down on rehearsal time for concerts. But Heuss felt the limit had been lapidated when the board announced that another orchestra—the Dresden Staatskapelle—would "stand-in" for the Gewandhaus at two subscription events. When Heuss talked, people throughout Germany listened, for he not only was a respected musicologist and critic, but he also edited the *Zeitschrift für Musik*, the internationally renowned music journal based in Leipzig. Along its nearly century-old history, its illustrious contributors included Richard Wagner. By the end of World War I, though, its influence derived more from the dry intensity of its earnestness rather than the heuristic profundity of its insights. It galled Heuss that Leipzig, with a superior orchestra, was depending on Dresden to fill out its principal concert series. As far as he was concerned, any kind of change in structuring the subscription series was unacceptable, especially one that involved importing an orchestra from outside to complete the magic number 10. Invoking one of the greatest musicians connected with the history of the Gewandhaus, Heuss ranted forth:

> . . . Mendelssohn created a tradition in the first three years of his exclusive commitment to Leipzig in which many succeeding conductors, who were not as eminent, could work over many decades. In sharp contrast to Furt-wängler, Mendelssohn had proven he was not only a brilliant technician with individual gifts, but a far-sighted strategist. What absentmindedness we have today![24]

This was published in July. In December, Furtwängler's reply to Heuss appeared. The lengthy missive argued the question of who had the best interests of the Gewandhaus at heart, and Furtwängler, of course, felt that he did. But:

> With respect to the musical life of Leipzig, if an old honorable tradition is going to be sacrificed to the petty self-interest of a "prima donna conductor," one is of the opinion that someone who can put his talents in greater quantity at the service of the Gewandhaus might be better in this position—and one cannot really conclude otherwise from my course of action. So one might say quite openly: I will be the first who, if it furthers the interests of the Gewandhaus, is ready and willing to give up my position.[25]

Here Furtwängler was again playing out a behavioral pattern he repeated throughout his life. From childhood he always enjoyed a good fight, and the forum for his altercations was frequently the media. His word crossing with Heuss, however, was but a scrimmage for the nastiest brawl of his life. But that was almost a decade into the future. For now, Heuss countered with further complaints about Furt-wängler's increasingly lengthy absences from Leipzig, and insisted again and again that the integrity of the Gewandhaus tradition remain

24. p. 463.
25. p. 722.

intact. In the end, however, Dresden and Fritz Busch came to Leipzig, and Furtwängler's relationship with the Gewandhaus continued to deteriorate.

In the meantime, of course, he was doing exactly what Leipzig resented so much: enlarging his field of activity. In 1922 he conducted the Vienna Philharmonic for the first time. Otto Strasser was a young substitute player who was playing one of his first concerts with the orchestra in the violin section on the evening of March 27th. "I remember it well," he says. "The occasion was a concert honoring the 25th anniversary of Brahms' death.[26] For some reason, Furtwängler programmed Mahler's Third Symphony, but the impression was overwhelming."[27]

The following year, Furtwängler made a successful debut with the Scala Orchestra in Milan with two programs in the space of four days.[28] In 1924 he traveled to England for the first time and conducted the Royal Philharmonic and the London Philharmonic. His debut in London was an unusual event both for him and for London, for he shared the podium of the Royal Philharmonic at Queen's Hall with Ralph Vaughan Williams, who conducted the premiere of the orchestral version of *On Wenlock Edge*.[29] It is possible that Vaughan Williams' presence was arranged to guarantee a fuller house, but the more likely reasoning behind the arrangement was Furtwängler's eagerness to include music native to the country in which he was conducting. In his visit to Sweden in 1920, for example, he programmed several works by Ture Rangström and Oskar Lindberg. In Milan, he concluded both concerts with works by contemporary Italians. But the engagement in London was one of the few occasions in which he shared the podium with anyone else. In any event, the critical reception at his first concert with the RPO on 24 January was largely enthusiastic:

> . . . His performances of Strauss' Don Juan and Brahms' First must have made their mark, for his control of his players is masterly, his knowledge

26. Brahms died 3 April 1897.

27. Personal conversation with the author, Vienna, 9 April 1990. The program in the Archives of the Vienna Philharmonic, however, does not show a corrected sequence change. The penny-plain sheet states the evening consisted of the *St. Anthony Variations*, the *Song of Destiny* with the Singverein, and the Fourth Symphony.

28. Programs: 19 June 1923, Beethoven: Seventh Symphony. Wagner: *Meistersinger* Prelude Act I. Strauss: *Tod und Verklärung*. Santoliquido: *Acquarelli*. 23 June 1923, Schumann: Fourth Symphony. Reger: Beethoven Variations. Beethoven: *Egmont Overture*. Wagner: Magic Fire Music from *Walküre*. Marinuzzi: *Elegia*.

29. The program included: Handel: Concerto Grosso in D Minor. Strauss: *Don Juan*. Brahms: Symphony No. 1.

of and care for every detail is complete, and he can spur his forces to a climax which takes the breath away.[30]

Despite a quibble or two, the venerable critic Ernest Newman was also impressed:

> Although he is plainly a bundle of nerves, his conducting is outwardly very quiet, and none the less masterful for that. In this respect, he may be taken as a model by one or two of our young native conductors.[31]

Furtwängler must have objected to Newman's quibbles (". . . If he could not find [opportunities for expression] he created them . . ."), for Newman rarely ever paid him another compliment.

At home, Furtwängler also enlarged the repertoires of both the Berlin Philharmonic and the Leipzig Gewandhaus Orchestra. Besides the Berlin premiere of Arnold Schönberg's *Five Pieces for Orchestra,* op. 16. (10–11 December 1922), he programmed other important new works his first seasons. He conducted Stravinsky's Piano Concerto with the composer as soloist (7–8 December 1924), as well as *Rite of Spring* (6–7 January 1924).[32] Bartók's Dance Suite (4–5 October 1925), Max Reger's *Variations and Fugue on a Merry Theme by Hiller,* op. 100 (6–7 December 1925), his own arrangement of Two Chorale Preludes by Bach (8–9 March 1925), and the *Concerto for Orchestra* by Paul Hindemith (20–21 December 1925).[33] Wolfgang Stresemann attended most of these premieres. "He did the modern pieces because he felt it was his duty to do them. This was expected of him as a young conductor. In doing these new and important pieces, he enriched the musical life of Berlin and Germany in a way that Nikisch no longer did."[34]

While Furtwängler's later critics derided him for conservatism in his programs, it would have been both irresponsible as well as a practical impossibility for him to conduct more of the high quality new music being produced in the 1920s, even if he wanted to. As the leader not only of the Berlin Philharmonic but of musical life in Berlin, he viewed himself as the Steward of Germany's musical culture. His responsibility, in his own view, was to preserve a balance between old

30. Unsigned, *London Times,* 25 January 1924.
31. *London Sunday Times,* 27 January 1924, p. 6.
32. The local premiere was given two years earlier by Ernest Ansermet, on 20 November 1922, and not by Furtwängler as sometimes cited.
33. These premieres all were included in Furtwängler's series of subscription concerts. Besides touring with the orchestra, Furtwängler also conducted in bonus concerts and in the Popular Concerts Series.
34. Personal conversation with the author, Berlin, 10 October 1990.

and new music in his own subscriptions series.[35] Nonetheless, the new music Furtwängler chose for his own programs in that first heady decade of his leadership says much about the sagacity of his taste. Of Stravinsky's works, for example, he also performed *Petrushka*, *Firebird*, the First Suite for Small Orchestra, *Fireworks*, and *Scherzo fantastique* in addition to *Rite of Spring* and the Piano Concerto.

The critical reception for *Rite* reflected the collision of old and new, or rather, the passing of senior music critics and the arrival of junior ones. Even though the work was over ten years old when Furtwängler first conducted it in Berlin, it was one of the most controversial works produced before World War I. It had caused a riot at its premiere in Paris under Pierre Monteux in 1913, and it was regarded as scandalous almost everywhere it was performed for many years thereafter. But by the middle of the 1920s, the reaction to it said more about the generation of the listener than about the work itself. At the *Berliner Tageblatt*, the aging Leopold Schmidt had pronounced *Rite* a "destructive work" and a "passing fad" at its Berlin premiere in 1922. By 1930 he had been replaced by the young and talented musicologist Alfred Einstein, who said it could no longer be regarded as a revolutionary work.

But numerous compositions that were undeniably revolutionary were being produced at this time, and Berlin was the locus where they established their international importance under many conductors. Erich Kleiber, for example, conducted the premiere of Alban Berg's *Wozzeck* at the Staatsoper in 1925. This work was at the forefront of a radical approach to composition that fell under the rubric of 12-tone music, but the composer in this genre who caused the greatest furor everywhere was its founder and leader, Arnold Schönberg.

The most significant of Furtwängler's collaborations with Schönberg took place on 2–3 December 1928, when he opened the program with the world premiere of *Variations for Orchestra*, a revolutionary, 25-minute piece in which Schönberg's theories on 12-tone music achieved full fruition.[36] Furtwängler already had given the premiere of Schönberg's *Five Pieces for Orchestra* in its revised version in 1924, and their collaboration dated back to 1919 when Furtwängler performed *Verklärte Nacht* in Mannheim. During his final season there, Furtwängler invited Schönberg to conduct his *Pelleas und Melisande* and was so eager to have Schönberg make a personal appearance that he rehearsed and prepared the orchestra himself so that the composer

35. See *New York Times*, 26 January 1926, p. 16. A substantial part of the interview in which he airs his view as Music Director appears in Chapter 4.

36. For a fuller discussion of Furtwängler's attitude toward Schönberg and atonality, see Chapter 8.

would need only two rehearsals before the performance set for 2–3 March 1920. Furtwängler knew Schönberg suffered from severe respiratory problems (a condition to which he was vulnerable himself) and took on the role of assistant conductor to ease the inevitable strain on the composer's health. Such a gesture was quite a compliment from any first Kapellmeister, and it was only one of hundreds of courtesies Furtwängler extended to colleagues throughout his life despite severe bouts of insecurity regarding any conductor who came near his podium. In the end, Schönberg canceled, and Furtwängler conducted the work himself to a polite acknowledgment from both public and press.[37]

The debacle that broke out in Berlin at the end of the *Variations* was probably exceeded only by the riot that erupted at the close of the premiere of Stravinsky's *Rite of Spring* 15 years earlier in Paris. Whistling, catcalls, and rattling of house keys punctuated the applause, and it was a good quarter-hour before the program could continue. The soloist of the evening was none less than the great Wagnerian baritone Friedrich Schorr, but his rendition of Lysiart's aria from Weber's *Euryanthe* passed all but unnoticed. There was also another premiere that evening: *Lethe*, a Scene for Baritone and Orchestra by Hans Pfitzner. But nobody seemed to hear that one either.

Wolfgang Stresemann was there. "People rattled their keys and hooted," he recalls. "He, of course, did not have enough rehearsal time, and he himself said to me that he was not sure at the time that he was quite clear about what the composer wanted. But the important issue here is that he was doing his duty as Berlin's first conductor, and his contribution to the expansion of the orchestral repertoire with important new works cannot be overestimated."

While *Variations for Orchestra* marked the culmination of Schönberg's 12-tone system, the scandal erupting at its premiere also transformed the composer into an evil totem among cultural arch-reactionaries. For this faceless but increasingly powerful interest group, Schönberg now stood for all that was un-German and became the living symptom of the rootless age into which Germany had fallen. Nonetheless, one of the senior music critics of Berlin's dailies, Max Marschalk of the *Vossische Zeitung*, threw his support behind the work:

37. It is not clear whether ill-health or a rail strike in Germany at the time forced Schönberg to cancel. Schönberg's biographer says the concerts in Mannheim were "planned" for 3 March and mentions the rail strike only in connection with a series of concerts in Holland Schönberg was prevented from conducting during that month. See H. H. Stuckenschmidt, *Arnold Schönberg, His Life and Work*, (New York) 1977, p. 245.

Schönberg convinces us with the Variations that he has succeeded in discovering new vistas in music in which we can feel comfortably at home ... The music he presents in the Variations is without precedent . . .[38]

While radical compositions, toward which Furtwängler felt at best uneasy but performed anyway, got him a measure of notoriety, he also gave Berlin and Leipzig first hearings of many other works. Furtwängler encompassed the cross-currents—both great and mediocre—in the music flowing through the Weimar period. A sampling of these compositions gives evidence of Furtwängler's breadth of interest as well as his instinct for proportion in creating programs:[39]

HANS PFITZNER: Piano Concerto in E flat Major, op. 31. Soloist: Walter Gieseking; 28–29 October 1923.

BERNHARD SEKLES: *Gesichte: Fantastic Miniatures for Small Orchestra.* 11–12 November 1923.

PFITZNER: Violin Concerto in B Minor, op. 34. Soloist: Alma Moody; 19–20 October 1924.

WALTHER BRAUNFELS: *Don Juan.* 16–17 November 1924.

GEORG SCHUMANN: *Variations and Gigue on a Theme by Handel.* 22–23 February 1925.

BACH/SCHÖNBERG: Two Chorale Preludes. 8–9 March 1925.

BÉLA BARTÓK: Dance Suite. 4–5 October 1925.

OTTORINO RESPIGHI: *The Pines of Rome.* 18–19 October 1925.

RICHARD STRAUSS: *Parergon on Symphonia domestica for Piano Left Hand and Orchestra.* Soloist: Paul Wittgenstein; 1–2 November 1925.

PAUL HINDEMITH: *Concerto for Orchestra,* op. 38. 21–22 December 1925.

ARTHUR HONEGGER: *Song of Joy.* 10–11 October 1926.

PHILIPP JARNACH: *Morgenklangspiel.* 7–8 November 1926.

ALFREDO CASELLA: *Partita for Piano and Orchestra.* Soloist: Casella; 19–20 December 1926.

SERGE PROKOFIEV: Suite from the Ballet *Le Chout.* 9–10 October 1927.

KAROL RATHAUS: *Overture for Large Orchestra,* op 22. 4–5 March 1928.

CLAUDE DEBUSSY: *La Mer.* 16–17 December 1928.

---

38. 5 December 1928.
39. These performances include world premieres, Berlin premieres, and first performances by the Berlin Philharmonic.

PAUL HINDEMITH: *Concerto for Organ and Chamber Orchestra,* op. 46, Nr. 2. Soloist: Fritz Heitmann; 24–25 February 1929.

GÜNTHER RAPHAEL: *Theme, Variations, and Rondo for Orchestra,* op. 19. 24–25 March 1929.

BACH/SCHÖNBERG: Prelude and Fugue in E flat Major. 10–11 November 1929.

OTTORINO RESPIGHI: *Roman Festivals.* 8–9 December 1929.

PAUL KLETZKI: *Variations for Orchestra.* 19–20 January 1930.

GEORG SCHUMANN: *Variations,* op. 74. 2–3 February 1930.

PAUL HINDEMITH: *Concerto for Viola and Large Chamber Orchestra,* op. 36, Nr. 4. Soloist: Hindemith; 30–31 March 1930.

PAUL HINDEMITH: Overture to *News of the Day.* 19–20 October 1930.

KARL MARZ: *Concerto for 2 Violins and Orchestra,* op. 5. Soloists: Henry Holst, Szymon Goldberg; 30 November–1 December 1930.

HANS PFITZNER: *The Dark Kingdom.* 24 November 1930.

MAX TRAPP: Symphony No. 4. 14–15 December 1930.

ZOLTÁN KODÁLY: *Summer Evening.* 25–26 January 1931.

ERNST TOCH: *Little Theater Suite,* op. 54. 8–9 February 1931.

SERGEI I. TANEJEW: Violin Concerto. Soloist: Georg Kulenkampff; 15–16 March 1931.

VLADIMIR VOGEL: *Two Studies for Orchestra.* 25–26 October 1931.

CLAUDE DEBUSSY: *Three Nocturnes* (final version). 15–16 November 1931.

IGOR STRAVINSKY: *Scherzo fantastique.* 6–7 December 1931.

MAURICE RAVEL: Piano Concerto. Soloist: Marguerite Long, Ravel conducting; 14–15 April 1932.

MAX EDGINGER: *Old English Suite.* op. 30; 3–4 April 1932.[40]

Perhaps Furtwängler sensed by his tenth year that the so-called Golden Age to which he had contributed more than his fair portion could not go on without interruption forever. What no one of this age could imagine or prepare for was the lethal progression that dimly sensed interruption would take. Wittingly or not, two concerts in 1932 provided a glowing sunset to a tumultuous decade and cast the last light before the long night to come. In April, he presented the premiere of Hindemith's *Philharmonic Concerto, Variations for Orchestra,* which the composer had dedicated to the Philharmonic in honor

40. See Muck, Vol. II.

of its 50th birthday. It was one of several works by Hindemith that
outlasted their collaboration. Later, on 30–31 October Hindemith
appeared in a program featuring Berlioz' *Harold in Italy* and the world
premiere of Prokofiev's Fifth Piano Concerto. Hindemith, who was
professor at the famous Hochschule für Musik in Berlin, played the
viola solo in the Berlioz. The soloist in Prokofiev's Piano Concerto
was the composer himself.

Within the first three years of his tenure, Furtwängler had indisputably become Germany's leading conductor and was well on his
meteoric way to solidifying his international fame. But one triumph
still remained to be achieved during his first decade as Germany's
foremost conductor. Its locus lay at the far end of a shark-infested
stretch of water, and it was a relatively brief victory, filled with
intrigue.

4

America

When Furtwängler arrived in New York with his wife Zitla and his secretary Berta Geissmar over the Christmas holidays of 1924, all America was in the midst of defining the Roaring '20s.[1] New York was the undisputed capital of this new cultural ferment. Nothing quite like it had ever happened before, for a type of culture quite different from European high culture was frenetically coming into its own. New York of the 1920s was the cradle of popular and mass culture, where entertainment was valued as highly if not preferred to mere enlightenment. It was not just the crossroads where the underworld met the elite but the junction where technology forked into art to form an avenue paved with gold and profit. Radio was the new invention of the age, and there was even talk of something called television that the American Telephone and Telegraph Company was promising would soon be available. There were over 70 legitimate theaters on Broadway, and silent movies and vaudeville enlarged the potential audience for entertainment from thousands to millions. The hit musicals on Broadway that season were "Big Boy" with Al Jolson and "Sunny" starring Marilyn Miller. George Kelly won the Pulitzer Prize

---

1. Daniel Gillis, *Furtwängler and America*, (Palo Alto) 1970, presents a vivid and frequently chilling account of Furtwängler's turbulent relationship with the entire American musical scene from 1925 to his death. I am extremely indebted to this account and to Gillis' generous personal assistance in locating much of the information I present here. Hereafter referred to as Gillis.

that year with the now-forgotten "Craig's Wife." Noël Coward's scandalous first play, called "The Vortex," also received its New York premiere during this season. Among other topics, it dealt openly with drug addiction and turned out to be one of his most serious and underrated plays. It did not, however, cause the kind of furor that it raised in London, where the Lord Chamberlain closed it and forced its move to a private theater club in Hampstead. Eugene O'Neill's "The Fountain" had only a brief run, but it was one of his better seasons on Broadway: "Desire Under the Elms" and "The Emperor Jones" were playing around the corner from each other.

On the music scene, Stravinsky arrived in New York about the same time as Furtwängler to make his conducting debuts with both the Philharmonic and the New York Symphony. Rachmaninoff, Pablo Casals, Fritz Busch, and many other musical luminaries were also in town, and Janáček's opera *Jenůfa* made its first appearance on the Metropolitan Opera's schedule on 3 January, the night of Furtwängler's debut with the Philharmonic. The cast included Maria Jeritza and Margarete Matzenauer. It was sung in German and conducted by Artur Bodanzky, Furtwängler's predecessor at Mannheim. The opera was not heard again after that season until 1974.

Furtwängler's first appearance with the New York Philharmonic was part of the management's grand plan to beef up the orchestra: engaging top conductors, increasing its size to 110 musicians, widening the scope of its audiences to include educational and children's programs, and simply beating out competing orchestras.[2] The organization also was undergoing an extended period of transition, one that had started in 1922 when Willem Mengelberg succeeded Josef Stransky as chief conductor.[3] Under the guidance of its energetic Chairman of the Board Charles Mackay, the Philharmonic was not only attempting to become New York's premier orchestra but one that would serve the whole community and have the support of a broad public. It ultimately would win that war, but not before a number of crucial and costly battles were fought and won.

To that end, Mackay had already proven himself a master tactician. Before coming to the Philharmonic in 1921, he had been President of the National Symphony of New York, a good orchestra and

2. For more on Furtwängler and the circumstances of orchestral life in New York at the time, see Howard Shanet, *Philharmonic: A History of New York's Orchestra*, (New York) 1975. Hereafter referred to as Shanet.

3. The title "Music Director" was not used by the New York Philharmonic-Symphony Society until 1943 when Artur Rodzinski was so appointed. Toscanini occasionally referred it to himself during his tenure as chief or master conductor (1927–1936), but no such position existed at the New York Philharmonic before it was created for Rodzinski. See Shanet, p. 296.

tough competitor for the Philharmonic. He engineered a merger between the National and the Philharmonic and had himself named Chairman of the Board of the combined orchestras. He effectively took charge of the new organization and called all the shots. He quickly brought in Frederic A. Juilliard as an "associate" to the Philharmonic's President, Henry E. Cooper. A year later, Cooper was elbowed out (retired), and Juilliard, the guardian of the 20-million-dollar Juilliard Music Fund, moved up to become President.[4]

Mackay still had stiff competition on his hands from another big rival ensemble, the New York Symphony Society. He was determined to beat it out at all costs. And it cost plenty. The conducting roster of the Philharmonic for the 1924–1925 season, for example, consisted of three stellar and expensive names: Igor Stravinsky, Mengelberg, and Furtwängler. Stravinsky was no conductor, but he had become a big-name composer in recent years, and the Philharmonic was all too glad to have him do a star turn on the podium. Mengelberg may have been chief conductor but Mackay had the real power. Mackay was not specifically dissatisfied with Mengelberg, but he needed a star conductor who would make the Philharmonic indisputably first among New York's orchestras, a personality that would bring the public steadily to the box office, preferably in hordes. To make the New York Philharmonic profitable, he needed a musician who had both musical and personal magnetism. Mengelberg had the musical magnetism, for he had drilled the orchestra into a well-honed troop of soldiers—disciplined, responsive, and highly flexible. But he did not possess the high-voltage personality Mackay had to have to capture the imagination of a diverse and demanding audience. Nor did Mengelberg have a cohesive artistic policy. Worse, he was unwilling to exert the time and energy required for tours, administrative work, and the day-to-day grind that was expected of him. Mackay had all but decided that Mengelberg's days as chief conductor of the New York Philharmonic were numbered.

Into these genteel proceedings strode Wilhelm Furtwängler. At his first rehearsal with the Philharmonic in Carnegie Hall, Furtwängler was surprised to see that so many of the musicians were Europeans—a convocation of artists from virtually every country on the Continent and Russia was assembled before him—and it excited him to feel them responding to him warmly. A few of the players had been with the orchestra since the days when Gustav Mahler was its Chief conductor between 1909 and 1911.

4. Shanet, p. 245.

Furtwängler's debut on 3 January 1925 was a resounding success; he mesmerized both the audience and the orchestra in the same way he was conquering Europe at home. He was truly coming into his own. Before the end of the month, he would be 39 years old. Pablo Casals, who remained Furtwängler's admirer throughout his life, was soloist at Furtwängler's first concert in a program that included the Haydn Cello Concerto, Richard Strauss' *Don Juan*, and Brahms' First Symphony. Both he and Furtwängler received mostly rapturous notices, and Mackay soon talked privately with Furtwängler about becoming the Philharmonic's Chief conductor for the 1925–1926 season.[5]

The most important of the critics, Olin Downes of the *New York Times*, started out rather liking Furtwängler:

> Not all the performances were to be accepted without reservation, but they invariably revealed the stature of a true musician, and the performance of the Brahms C Minor Symphony was perhaps the most thrilling in the writer's experiences . . . It was high time that such an interpretation should take place here.[6]

Two of the other important critics gave him even better notices. Lawrence Gilman:

> Mr. Furtwängler is one of those rare conductors who possess the great style . . . He has that largeness of style, that sweep of vision, that intensifying and vitalizing power which are necessary to the communicating of music that is conceived in the passionate and heroic vein of the great Romantics . . . He has warmth and fire (they do not always dwell in the same breast), a broad and encompassing vision, an enlarging imagination.[7]

W. J. Henderson praised Furtwängler's sense of balancing the choirs of the orchestra and clarity in articulating rhythm, but he sensed his best asset:

> . . . Mr. Furtwängler proved himself to be an ardent searcher after the melodic line. No matter how crisp the enunciation, the lyric flow was never lost. All of which relates to the technical means by which a conductor constructs a reading.[8]

5. Shanet, p. 252.
6. *New York Times*, 4 January 1925, p. 31.
7. *New York Herald-Tribune*, 5 January 1925, p. 14.
8. *The New York Sun*, 5 January 1925, p. 22.

Pitts Sanborn at the *New York Telegram and Evening Mail* described his reaction to Furtwängler's interpretation of the Brahms First in terms that other admirers would use in years to come:[9]

> The performance of the C minor symphony—a work played almost, it seems at times, *ad nauseam*—was genuinely a re-creation—an experience like hearing and completely grasping a master work for the first time.

Sanborn was obviously well aware of Mackay's search for a new chief conductor, and he rounded out his review by putting Furtwängler's hat in the ring:

> A "Guest" conductor who ought to be made permanent.[10]

In other sections of the papers that reported Furtwängler's debut, news of a development in Italy that seemingly had nothing to do with his future in America was also printed. On 3 January 1925 Benito Mussolini suspended democratic guarantees in Italy. It was a decisive moment in the history of modern Fascism, but it would be two years hence before the consequences of this event would impinge upon the life of Wilhelm Furtwängler.

The reviews had hardly hit the newsstands before Furtwängler discovered how politics can influence music. Since he had grown up in a world where princes, rulers, and governments paid for the performing arts as part of their responsibilities, private sponsorship was something altogether new to him. In America of that time, it was not merely society that raised money to maintain institutions like the New York Philharmonic and the Metropolitan Opera, but *high* society. Such organizations provided a means of social legitimacy for two major types of wealthy contributors. On the one hand, they gave New York's Old Money a respectable and useful way of carrying out the demands of *noblesse oblige.* It was the duty of Old Money with its banners of pedigree and comfortable fortunes to keep culture alive, and well-heeled descendants of the Pilgrims, the Revolution, and emigrant European nobility used cultural functions as settings for entertaining each other and displaying themselves as pillars of society. New Money also found these institutions an attractive way to "get in," to move among the same circles as the highest members of high society. These *arrivistes* had recently made their booty or were on their way to accruing even more money. They needed to legitimize

9. This review was among the notices translated and published in German newspapers a few days after Furtwängler's debut.
10. 5 January 1925, p. 8.

their social standing by rubbing shoulders with each other and with Old Money who maintained these institutions as clubs for themselves.

For both groups of contributors, the acquaintance of artists, who represented Old World culture, brought prestige and palpable evidence of social validation. Most European artists coming to America adapted to being trotted out like exotic circus animals at elite gatherings and elegant dinner parties. Their motivations for adapting to this peculiarly American social more ranged from mere courtesy, to curiosity, to social ambitions of their own. Even if the atmosphere at these parties was usually frivolous and the intellectual depth of conversation puddle-deep, the symbiotic nature of such gatherings was well understood by most visiting artists. There was something in such occasions for everybody, not the least of which was good public relations for artists trying to make a career in America. Furtwängler, of course, was neither prepared nor willing to sing for his supper at the homes of the Philharmonic's high and mighty. He had always been socially awkward and feeble at the sort of party talk which passed for musical discussion at such gatherings, his English was weak, and he loathed the idea of "selling" himself to people with whom he felt he had nothing in common.

While his failure to make an effort at social intercourse proved a serious liability, his success at sexual intercourse came as naturally to him as it had at home. The queues of adoring women whom he happily obliged were just as long as they had been everywhere else. But his willingness to oblige them eventually caused him trouble in ways he could not have anticipated.

The most important event for Furtwängler during that first season was the premiere at the New York Philharmonic of Stravinsky's *Rite of Spring (Le Sacre du printemps)*. That Furtwängler would even consider conducting such a difficult work with an orchestra that not only had never played it, but with one he never had faced before was a clear example of his naive enthusiasm on the one hand and that bald but requisite ego on the other. Those close to him always maintained that enthusiasm far exceeded mere ego as his ruling force, but to those farther away the outrageous risks he took in every aspect of his life were purely the by-products of overblown self-esteem. Nonetheless, he never thought twice about conducting *Rite*, even though Stravinsky who was scheduled to conduct the premiere had backed out.

The reason for the composer's cancellation put the gossip mill to quick work. It instantly circulated the story that Stravinsky withdrew because he knew he did not have the technique to conduct it properly. On later occasions when he did conduct it, the rumors of his technical limitations in this monstrously difficult work proved true. By then, however, the orchestras he conducted knew the work thoroughly. The idea of stepping in for the composer also gave Furtwängler an added impetus to take on the work with the Philharmonic, even though it would provoke disaster.

What made the idea of Furtwängler conducting such a work with a strange orchestra especially disaster-provoking was his own unusual conducting technique. Although he was perfectly capable of rapping out sixteenths and thirty-second notes with his baton, he generally conducted in phrases and paragraphs of melody. For *Rite*, however, Furtwängler's beat had to be as precise as a computer. He already had had a tremendous success with it leading his own orchestra a year earlier, and he presented the work at Carnegie Hall on 22 January 1925, after attempting to teach the orchestra this music in only two rehearsals.[11]

The critical reception of the premiere by the major dailies was mixed, but on one point all the critics agreed: Furtwängler did not have enough time or rehearsals to make it an unqualified success. Olin Downes gave him grudging credit for a flawed performance whose imperfections were not owing to deficiencies on Furtwängler's part:

> . . . It is said that Mr. [Serge] Koussevitsky did not wish to conduct "Sacre" here with less than six rehearsals. He was prudent. The "Sacre du Printemps" is a test of any orchestra and of any conductor under any circumstances. It is no doubt testimony to the remarkable authority, control, and self-possession of Mr. Furtwängler that he secured the performance that he did. A second one might better reflect his intentions.[12]

I.W. at the *New York Evening Journal*, however, took the opportunity of an under-rehearsed performance to barrel into Furtwängler:

> But the chief reason, apparently, why the music failed to make a proper impression was Mr. Furtwängler.
> He customarily conducts the classics without a score, which permits him freely to do his conductorial calisthenics all over the podium; for the "Sacre," however, he had the notes in front of him and he kept his eyes

---

11. To clarify some confusion over Furtwängler's performances of this work, he did not present either the Berlin or the New York premieres of the work. He conducted only the first performances by the New York Philharmonic. Leopold Stokowski conducted the American premiere in Philadelphia on 3 March 1922. Serge Koussevitsky presented it for the first time in New York later that year with the Boston Symphony. The first performances of *Rite* in Berlin were conducted by Ernest Ansermet on 19–20 November 1922. Furtwängler conducted it with the Gewandhaus in Leipzig on 1 November 1923 and later with the Berlin Philharmonic on 7 January 1924.

12. *New York Times*, 23 January 1925, p. 22.

glued to them. This, in any case, kept him stationary, but it was not greatly helpful to Stravinsky.[13]

Lawrence Gilman at the *Herald-Tribune* seemed to give with one hand while taking away with the other:

> We have heard more impressive performances of the score than that which Mr. Furtwängler gave last night with the Philharmonic. Perhaps he is not wholly in sympathy with its imaginative world; but the music under his baton missed fire at more than one point—particularly in the second part, which was almost an anti-climax. Nor did the orchestra seem to have mastered completely the heart-breaking, nerve-wracking task that Stravinsky sets it. Yet there were thrilling moments in the earlier portions of the work, and Mr. Furtwängler worked up the "Danse de la terre" to a climax of frenetic power.[14]

The audience, in any event, did not remain to make a judgment on its worth. Nearly all the critics remarked that the Philharmonic subscription audience fled in droves throughout the performance.[15]

In the meantime, Furtwängler rode high on the crest of his public popularity during the rest of his month-long debut season with the New York Philharmonic. His negotiations to take over from Mengelberg the following season fell through because he was fully committed during the period he would have to spend in the United States. But he accepted a longer engagement for the next season—11 February through 2 April 1926—including a brief tour of the mid-Atlantic states. Furtwängler did not quite bring off the roaring triumph he might have hoped for during his first American season, but he returned to Europe feeling that he had conquered New York.

Meanwhile, though, his marked ineptitude at mingling with those socialites who contributed to his fees began a process of alienation from the Philharmonic's board. His increasingly "personal" way with musical interpretation, which later was to become the hallmark of his art, also was to cause him an unexpected about-turn in critical

13. 23 January 1925, p. 24.
14. 23 January 1925, p. 12.
15. Toscanini, incidentally, never attempted *Rite*. Winthrop Sargeant, a violinist in the New York Philharmonic before he became music critic for *The New Yorker*, suggested to Joseph Horowitz in *Understanding Toscanini* that Toscanini had difficulty in beating out complicated rhythms and that may have been one of the reasons why he shied away from most modern music:
> There were passages even in Strauss' *Till Eulenspiegel* that taxed his sense of rhythmic orientation. He never attempted Stravinsky's Sacre du Printemps, and I am sure that if he had it would have proved an almost impossible ordeal for him.
> p. 133

appraisal by the time he returned for his second season. Until then, his critics had carped parenthetically at his so-called subjectivity, but they always duly noted that audiences went wild over his performances.

He simply continued to ignore or forget after his first direct encounter with the Americans that popular success with the Philharmonic audiences or with the musicians of the orchestra meant little as far as his "success" with the "public imagination" in the United States was concerned. Furtwängler not only offended the benefactors of the New York Philharmonic by avoiding their parties, but by flagrantly opting instead to slip away after concerts with a pretty admirer. The benefactors who had been stood up were neither amused by his snub nor sympathetic toward the apparently "modern" arrangement he had with his wife Zitla, who was left to her own devising throughout most of their stay in New York.

Part of Furtwängler's difficulties with the social set that supported the Philharmonic also stemmed from his life-long problems in dealing with *any* representatives of authority, a development that began in childhood when he created adversaries of teachers and other adults wielding power over him because he felt they were not as intelligent as he. He never was especially respectful to public officials and never thought twice about making his attitude clear.[16] It probably is not far-fetched to speculate that he timed his trysts to show the all-powerful board members exactly what he thought of them.

Most of Furtwängler's peccadillos were arranged and orchestrated by his faithful secretary Berta Geissmar. She had long since become his special assistant, and there was nothing about his professional or private life to which she was not privy. Officially she was an employee of the Berlin Philharmonic, but anything to do with Furtwängler was part of her job. She took care of his voluminous correspondence, she negotiated contracts with artists and their agents, she single-handedly arranged every detail of the Berlin Philharmonic tours, and she made sure Furtwängler's various residences in Berlin, Leipzig, Vienna, and St. Moritz were kept in order. She screened and even subtly importuned attractive young ladies on Furtwängler's behalf. In effect, she all but ran the Berlin Philharmonic from day to day, and she certainly managed the life of the awkward, unkempt genius who was its chief conductor.

Perhaps it was somewhat remiss of Geissmar not to direct Furtwängler's social life in America with more circumspection. After all, she knew the importance of the socialites in the cultural arena even if he did not. But by 1925 she had taken over his entire life. All his needs

16. As mentioned earlier, he once even refused to salute the Kaiser from the podium at one of his concerts because he felt it undignified. Gillis, p. 13.

were her domain, and she was as anxious to have them addressed as he was. Their relationship was entirely platonic, but there is no doubt that Geissmar loved Furtwängler and largely lived that love vicariously through his endless stream of affairs.

Early in the following year, Furtwängler returned to the Philharmonic and encountered the same adoring audiences after each concert. The newspapers reflected the anticipation attendant upon his arrival, and the *Times* published portions of an interview conducted in Berlin in which he spoke candidly about American orchestras in comparison to their European counterparts:

> "America is in a position to assemble the best orchestral talent that money can obtain," he said. "In the orchestras that I have heard or directed, each man is a soloist of the first quality, whether he plays a string, reed, or brass instrument. The fact that the symphony orchestras are not required to do double duty in opera and on the concert stage as is almost invariably the case in Europe makes possible a specialization of symphony music such as is to be found nowhere else except possibly Berlin.
>
> "On the other hand, most American orchestras are still too young to be welded together as they are, for instance, in Vienna, where all the brasses or the strings may all come practically from the same school. But this is coming rapidly in America."[17]

He went on to give some surprisingly acute perceptions about popular music and American audiences:

> Herr Furtwängler believes that New York, Berlin, and Vienna are the world's greatest music centers today.
>
> "But," he added, "the audience of the new world is less satiated than those of the old. The American listener is especially more alive to anything sensational in the realm of music.
>
> "Jazz undoubtedly will give symphonic composition more marked rhythm,. Beginning with Richard Wagner and for a long period after him rhythm was rather neglected. The marked rhythm of jazz is finding symphonic interpretation in the works of men like Stravinsky and Hindemith.
>
> "Jazz, however, does not lend itself to composition in the sense in which the waltz, for instance, does. The original thing about jazz is the improvisation.[18] In a jazz band the various members [who] work out new and original ideas all the time as they play, [also] play the same tune. Take

---

17. News report, no by-line, 11 January 1926, p. 32.

18. Furtwängler was not nearly as diplomatic about jazz several years later when he wrote a somewhat vituperative article entitled "Was ist Jazz?" Admitting at the very outset of the piece that he had no idea what jazz is, he proceeded to call it "a bad dream" from which musicians would eventually awaken. *Neue Freie Presse*, Wien, 23 October 1929.

improvisation away from jazz and try to fasten it down to fixed forms, such as a symphony, and most of its originality is lost. Jazz in this respect is much like the improvised music of the Gypsies."[19]

While his statements were basically complimentary to the American music scene, Furtwängler was privately troubled by the craving he saw in American audiences for what he called "the sensational": big effects and self-conscious drama in performing, and he regarded the popularity of jazz as an element of it.[20]

As he entered the stage in Carnegie Hall on the night of 11 February 1926, a sold-out house braved the bitter cold (almost zero Fahrenheit) to greet him. The orchestra also rose as he reached the podium and applauded him before a note was played.[21] His notices were as warm as they had been the previous year, but the management appeared a bit cooler. If Furtwängler wondered what kind of game was being played on him, he could easily have surmised what was up simply by looking for a new name on the conducting roster. It was typically the custom for the Philharmonic management to ease out any unwanted member by introducing an "associate" on the roster. After a season or two, the unwanted individual would disappear.[22] The new name on the conducting roster for 1926–1927 was Arturo Toscanini.

Among the press, it was Olin Downes at the *New York Times* who ultimately took the lead in trashing Furtwängler, but he was by no means his most virulent opponent.[23] Downes started carping about Furtwängler's "personal leanings," and his reviews quickly turned to frontal attacks. One of his volleys against Furtwängler had nothing to do with music making, but it had everything to do with the crux of his festering antipathy toward Furtwängler. Downes chided Furtwängler on his insistence that there be no applause between movements of a symphony:

The conductor signalled for no applause after each of the movements. This practice has been referred to on several occasions in these columns,

19. News report, no by-line, 11 January, p. 32.
20. Elisabeth Furtwängler recalls her husband finding jazz not to his taste, but she never heard him explain why. Personal conversation, 4 April 1990, Clarens.
21. Pitts Sanborn, *New York Telegram*, 12 February 1926, p. 8, led his review with a report on the enthusiasm greeting Furtwängler on the night of his return to the Philharmonic.
22. Shanet, op. cit., p. 246. Though it was hardly an unusual tactic, it had been used effectively in replacing Stransky with Mengelberg, and supplanting Henry E. Cooper with Frederic A. Juilliard as the Philharmonic's President in 1922.
23. Pitts Sanborn at the *Telegram* attacked Furtwängler far more frequently than did Downes in his last two seasons as we shall see later in this chapter.

with the remark that it often detracts from the effect of the music and the audience's enjoyment of it. Certainly it is hard to believe that Mozart would have written in the lighter vein, for no more purpose than that of pleasure and entertainment. Why an audience should sit through such a performance as seriously and silently as if it were Bach's B Minor Mass is a question that will obtrude itself, even on the auspicious occasion of Mr. Furtwängler's opening American concert of the year 1926 . . .[24]

Furtwängler had almost as little respect for critics as he had for public officials, and he chose to ignore Downes—at least for the moment. The audience, in fact, appeared to be siding with him, grateful to be taught the superior manners of European concertgoing.[25] But Downes' carping about Furtwängler's impromptu lesson in concertgoing etiquette dramatized a thorny issue that had long nettled American cultural life, especially in the performing arts. His ire undoubtedly betrayed an inferiority complex common to most Americans of the time at being in the presence of someone who undoubtedly represented cultural legitimacy—*Old World* cultural legitimacy—in his approach to performing.

In the years following World War I, the United States entered into its first full stage of becoming "cultured." The defining characteristic of this notion of culture was sophistication in the realm of matters artistic.[26] But it was not "culture" in the European sense wherein a cultural heritage grew out of each nation's ethnic, social, and political history. For Americans, it was a frame of mind that could be acquired like any other commodity in a laissez faire economic and, for the most part, social environment. What is more, it was a frame of mind that did not remain the exclusive property of the best and brightest individuals in American society—the intellectuals. Cultural sophistication became the virtual birthright of anyone who sought to have it. High culture could be made accessible to the vast unwashed, and it became a social trend both to have access to it and to make it accessible. To this day, television commercials offering 100 Immortal Classics for $19.95 post-paid continue this notion of culture now, culture affordable, culture-as-commodity. At the same time, the attitude toward high culture after World War I remained suspicious. As Joseph Horowitz points out:

24. 12 February 1926, p. 16.
25. Gillis, pp. 20–21, quotes several letters to the *Times* in support of Furtwängler.
26. Joseph Horowitz, *Understanding Toscanini*, (New York) 1987, gives an excellent account of the crosscurrents of cultural life in America and how they influenced the rage for Toscanini and informed the rivalry between Toscanini and Furtwängler. Hereafter referred to as Horowitz.

More than Europeans, Americans abhor elitism and apply democratic values with broad strokes. In the realm of music, the nineteenth century rise of the public concert and commercialization of opera here proceeded without court or state subsidies—a circumstance favoring both personal enterprise and marketplace exigencies.[27]

Horowitz cites Dwight MacDonald and his 1960 essay "Masscult and Midcult" as one of the most illuminating on the topic. MacDonald gets squarely to the point: "Midcult pretends to respect the standards of high culture while in fact it waters them down and vulgarizes them."[28]

In his disparaging remarks about Furtwängler's lesson in concert-going etiquette, Downes clearly placed himself in the role of a midcult missionary in the presence of an unacceptable Apostle. Furtwängler and his toffee-nosed applause shushing, girded with his undeniable brilliance as an exponent of music—*European* music—made him in Downes' eyes both an oddball to be watched carefully and a representative of those venerable Old World cultural values that made red-blooded Americans such as Downes feel like country cousins. Furtwängler certainly satisfied the American public's craving for a big personality, a regal musician. But what Downes interpreted as Furtwängler's petulance with the noisy masses signalled an unforgivable deficiency: Furtwängler did not have the common touch. And nobody among American critics appeared to be more touchy about that than Olin Downes.

Furtwängler returned for his third consecutive season with the Philharmonic in January 1927, amid reports that he might be named chief conductor.[29] Toscanini had just finished his extended engagement under gales of fervent praise by Downes and Lawrence Gilman leading the press corps and making him an act that would be impossible to follow. But Furtwängler made a bad start even worse by speaking frankly in an interview taken in Berlin just before he sailed. He discussed his hesitance to program new contemporary music. It is a bit long, but worth quoting in substantial part:

27. Horowitz, p. 7

28. To clarify the context in which Horowitz and I use this statement, MacDonald is referring to a specific kind of attitude among certain American magazines that he finds "mid-cult" because he believes they demean high culture while paying lip-service to it. His pronouncement, as I at least understand it, can also be applied to the very insititutions that profess to belong to high culture, especially in the performing arts. The quote appears in *Against the American Grain: Essays on the Effects of Mass Culture*, (New York) 1962, p. 37. MacDonald's provocative and ultimately distressing piece was expanded from several earlier versions published between 1944 and 1960 in various magazines. Its final version first emerged in *Partisan Review*, Spring and Fall, 1960, pp. 203–233 and pp. 589–631.

29. *New York Times*, 20 January 1927.

It has become the fashion to demand that each conductor's program contain at least one premiere presentation of a contemporaneous composer's work. I agree, of course, that the fate of contemporaneous music should be one of the conductor's prime concerns. But he should produce modern composers because of the intrinsic value of their work and not merely to fill up a program with a novelty. I protest against sensationalism as an end and object.

There are those who believe that it is better to offer a first production of a poor composition than a repetition of a good one. I disagree. I would rather conduct a good second performance than a bad first. Besides, I think it is a conductor's duty not only to produce modern things, but to give modern life to old.

The musical director is, after all, the trustee of the musical possessions accumulated throughout the ages. It is his duty to maintain the highest standards by choosing from this accumulation of immortality, including the most modern if it has innate value.[30]

Here was Furtwängler's child-like naivete revealing itself in all its unaffected candor, heartfelt sincerity, and embarrassing disregard for the probable consequences of such statements. Without knowing it, he was clearly drawing the lines, serving notice to proponents of new music, and all but begging for trouble that would long outlive him.

By this time, Downes was well aware that Mackay was ardently courting Toscanini for the Philharmonic, so he waxed all the more surly when he found a Furtwängler concert not to his liking. Furtwängler was vaguely aware of these backstage shenanigans, but he played out his contractual obligations while putting on the face of a good sport and a team player. Perhaps the most notable evidence of his willingness to get involved in New York's cultural life during a period of no little duress was his participation in a gala concert at the Metropolitan Opera House in honor of Walter Damrosch and benefiting the National Music League. The event brought together the entire forces of both the New York Philharmonic and the New York Symphony. "Over 200 Musicians!" cried the advertisements. What is more, this aggregation would be conducted not only by Damrosch but by Fritz Busch and Furtwängler. Furtwängler hardly knew Damrosch, but he was on good terms with Busch, contrary to claims later made by Busch's widow.[31]

The soloists of the evening included Florence Easton, Ernestine Schumann-Heink, George Meader, Walter Kirschhoff, and Clarence

30. Unsigned report, Dateline: Berlin, 25 January, *New York Times*, 26 January 1927, p. 16.
31. Grete Busch, *Fritz Busch, Dirigent*, (Frankfurt) 1970, p. 65. Fritz Busch was Music Director in Dresden from 1922 to 1933, and he was responsible for bringing that city's musical life to a level second only to Berlin during the 1920's.

Whitehill singing beefy portions of Wagner under Damrosch's direction. Furtwängler's contribution consisted of two excerpts from Berlioz' *Damnation of Faust* and the Overture to *Tannhäuser*. Since the concert was a benefit, it was not reviewed.

Meanwhile, Downes learned that Furtwängler had tried to have him removed from reviewing his concerts. Not *Furtwängler* exactly. In fact, Furtwängler may not have been aware of the strings that were being pulled in his name, for Geissmar frequently acted alone in Furtwängler's professional as well as private affairs. According to Suzanne Bloch, daughter of composer Ernest Bloch, it was Geissmar who tried to have Downes removed from reviewing his concerts. "During Furtwängler's first visit to the United States," she recalls, "Geissmar became a good friend of the Warburg family. The family was among New York's wealthiest financiers and they dealt frequently with Geissmar's relatives in Mannheim, who were also lawyers and bankers. Gerald Warburg, the fifth son of Irwin Warburg, was a musician and devoted admirer of Furtwängler. The Warburgs and the Ochs family, who owned the *New York Times*, were related through marriage. Geissmar persuaded Gerald to talk to Ochs about removing Downes. At least, that is what Gerald told me, and he had no reason to lie."[32]

The scheme was preposterous, but Warburg wanted to help Furtwängler in any way he could. He apparently went to the *Times* and had a chat with his uncle. Nothing came of it, but word of the conversation eventually crept along the *Times* grapevine. Forked tongues transformed the incident into a personal demand by Furtwängler to have Downes dismissed. By the time the viper reached Downes, enough vinegar had been pressed to garnish all the copy he would write about Furtwängler for the rest of his career. If Geissmar's part in Downes' antipathy toward Furtwängler bears any truth at all, it is safe to say she fueled the destruction of her boss' career in America. If Furtwängler indeed consented to such a ploy, he clearly had destroyed any chance of making a rapprochement with Downes. Several years later, for example, Downes visited Suzanne Bloch and saw Furtwängler's autographed photograph on her piano. He exclaimed, "Take that swine away from there!"[33]

While Furtwängler returned to Europe perplexed and saddened that the board of the Philharmonic had chosen Toscanini over him, he had no idea that their decision was an agglomerate of circumstances that had been set into motion long before he ever went to America.

---

32. Conversation with the author, New York, 16 April 1990.
33. Conversation with the author, New York, 16 April 1990. Also Gillis, p. 27.

But the exact time Toscanini finally looked back toward New York after an absence of almost 11 years probably occurred on the same date as Furtwängler's Philharmonic debut—January 3, 1925. For on that day Mussolini abrogated democratic guarantees in Italy. Toscanini was no admirer of Mussolini and is reported to have told *Il Duce* as much in a face-to-face confrontation.[34] In any event, Italy was no longer a viable base for the aging conductor, and the Philharmonic's elaborate blandishments of courtship eventually convinced him to return to New York. Board Chairman Charles Mackay had finally succeeded in making the New York Philharmonic the best orchestra in New York.

But he had not done it alone.

Olin Downes of the *New York Times* had become an ardent admirer of Toscanini during the conductor's fabled reign at the Metropolitan Opera in the early years of the century. After feuding with the Metropolitan's true franchise, Enrico Caruso, according to several histories of the Metropolitan, Toscanini forced General Manager Giulio Gatti-Casazza to choose between them. Other accounts, however, maintain that Toscanini was tiring of the hectic rough-and-tumble of daily life at the Met, and wanted to lead an easier life. He was also finding it increasingly frustrating to keep up performance standards in a repertory house with limited facilities and rehearsal time. In any event, Caruso remained; Toscanini returned to Italy.

The Metropolitan certainly survived without Toscanini, but it might not have fared so well had he not left his mark in the first place. Born in Parma on 25 March 1867, Toscanini studied cello in his home town and in Milan. When he was 19, he was playing in the pit of the Opera in Rio de Janeiro. During a performance of *Aida*, the original conductor of the evening stalked out. Toscanini took over the podium. His phenomenal memory, clear stick technique, and telepathic rapport with the singers gained him a triumph. By the time he reached the Metropolitan in 1908, he had given the world premieres of *Pagliacci* (1892), *La Bohème* (1896), and the Italian premieres of operas as diverse as *Götterdämmerung, Pelléas et Mélisande,* and *Eugene Onegin*. He also began a life-long but fitful relationship with La Scala when he became Music Director there in 1898.

At the Metropolitan, Toscanini not only improved standards in the Italian wing, but also distinguished himself in Wagner. This, at a time when Gustav Mahler was still in the house. During his tenure, he gave America its first hearing of Puccini's *Le Villi*, Catalani's *La*

---

34. Toscanini was originally a supporter of the fascists and won a candidacy under the party banner in a minor local election in 1919.

Wally, Franchetti's *Germania*, Dukas' *Ariane et Barbe-Bleue*, Wolf-Ferrari's *Le Donne curiose*, Mussorgsky's *Boris Godunov*, Montemezzi's *L'Amore dei tre re*, and Giordano's *Madame Sans-Gêne*. He also led the first Metropolitan production of Gluck's *Armide*, and the world premiere of *La Fanciulla del West*. It was Toscanini in fact who transformed the Metropolitan into a predominantly Italian opera house, veering it gradually away from the German repertoire prevailing there since the 1890s.

Nonetheless, Toscanini was no stranger to German music. Besides conducting Wagner at the Met, he also had begun making orchestral appearances in Italy around 1900 and quickly established a reputation for superlative performances of Brahms and Beethoven. But his debut as an orchestral conductor in the United States, for some reason, did not take place until 13 April 1913 at the Metropolitan Opera House. The program consisted of an all-German evening capped off with a performance of the Beethoven Ninth. The singers were an international mix: Frieda Hempel and Karl Jörn (German), Louise Homer and Putnam Griswold (American). The concert electrified audiences and critics, and brought his career and his art to full maturity.[35]

But Toscanini's relentless search for perfection, coupled with a nasty temper that prompted him to abuse virtually everyone with whom he worked—singers, chorus, orchestra, and especially the General Manager Gatti-Casazza—eventually wore the company down. Whatever the final straw may have been, he left the company in a rage at the end of the 1915 season after seven years, shrieking that he would never return. And he never did.[36]

But he did return to the United States. His first visit to the America after his stormy exit from the Metropolitan was in 1920, when he took the orchestra of La Scala Milan on a cross-country tour. Downes' ecstatic memories of Toscanini's performances at the Met were revived when he heard the revered Italian maestro lead the Scala Orchestra in New York. After these concerts, Downes became Toscanini's leading advocate in the American media. When he learned that Toscanini might be coming back to stay, there was no doubt in his mind with whom the Philharmonic should be identified.

On the surface, at least, no two conductors could have been more dissimilar in their approaches to music than Toscanini and Furtwäng-

35. A thousand people were turned away from the box office on the first day tickets went on sale. Even Caruso had to take standing room.
36. For years, the Metropolitan tried to entice him back, but he only sneered. He was heard to rant, "I'll conduct on the ashes of the Metropolitan!"

ler. According to simplistic pundits, Toscanini was the great objectiv-
ist; Furtwängler the ardent subjectivist. Any generalization may have
some measure of truth to it, but the complexity of their respective
approaches severely limits the usefulness of this one. Nonetheless,
popular criticism leaped at this convenient syzygy, and they have been
compared with it ever since. Downes' support for Toscanini was
clearly racist:

> In listening to operatic and orchestral interpretations of Toscanini it has
> often seemed that after all the statement holds true of the quality of the
> Italian mind, the racial mind that has the finest facture of any in the
> world; the genius which, at its height, combines marvelously the qualities
> of analysis and perception, the objectivity of form, and the consuming fire
> of creative passion.[37]

However meretricious this line of reasoning may be, Toscanini's
magic was indisputable. He returned to New York and remained for
eight seasons, giving the Philharmonic a sonic profile and technical
solidity that made it one of the great orchestras of the world. He also
consistently induced a steady stream of *thrill* in his audiences. He
knew instinctively how to wow his audiences, and they never were
disappointed. But the thrill never was produced by showy, crowd-
pleasing antics. Toscanini's art drew its inspiration from white-heat
energy and a zealous conviction that only his way with any work he
approached truly vivified the composer's intentions. While he occasionally made changes in the score to realize those intentions, his critics and audiences cheerfully overlooked them and found his art irresistible. He also made the New York Philharmonic popular through
recordings, tours and live radio broadcasts. What is more, he was the
very picture of the self-made, sensible artist, a picture that conformed
to the average American's image of himself or herself.

   Furtwängler's impact on his own audiences was no less powerful,
but his art was grounded in a conviction that the conductor's job was
to re-create the work, to imbue every performance with a sense of
what he misleadingly called "improvisation." For Furtwängler the
conductor at his best should be a fulcrum of a divine will, drawn not
only from the composer but from the ages. If Furtwängler had had
more opportunities to purvey this view to Americans, he may well
have disaffected them as much as he alienated some of his critics.

   As it turned out, he eventually became something of a cult figure
in the United States, known and appreciated by a large, cultivated

37. *New York Times*, VII, 10 January 1926, p. 6.

minority. Following the announcement that Furtwängler was not returning for the 1927–1928 season, one letter to the *Times* articulated the view of a substantial portion of the audience:

> It is a deplorable fact that leaders striving for popularity frequently sacrifice the artistic principals in their art to please the modern tendency of the sensational and the superficial. Mr. Furtwängler is different. He is possessed of that inexplicable something akin to Beethoven both without and within popular only to the element who understand and value his exceptional qualities and artistic merits.[38]

Before long, however, it would become seditious even to speak of him. In the meantime, the bulk of his listeners were almost exclusively European, and relatively few Americans ever had the opportunity to compare the two Titans side by side.[39] As Toscanini's ties with America strengthened, the musical forest became dominated by only one giant. Europeans, on the other hand, frequently heard Toscanini and Furtwängler, and the musical Prometheus in Europe was, in more ways than one, Furtwängler.

Furtwängler's final performance in America was in the same hall where Toscanini had first taken leave of his American audiences twelve years before: the Metropolitan Opera House. Originally, Furtwängler was scheduled to conduct Beethoven's Ninth Symphony. But professional politics again intervened. Toscanini wanted to lead the Ninth that season, and he reportedly feigned illness and implied cancellation to get his way. The Philharmonic was vigorously pursuing Toscanini to become chief conductor at this point, so they prevailed upon Furtwängler to change his last performance to Brahms.[40] On 3 April 1927 he made his last appearance in a performance of Brahms' *German Requiem* with the New York Philharmonic and Louise Lerch and Fraser Gange as the vocal soloists.[41] Though he did not know it at the time, the incident was a turning point for both Furtwängler and Toscanini. By giving in to Toscanini's wishes and letting him have his way, Furtwängler also tacitly backed down from ever conducting in America again; Toscanini would reign supreme in America, Furtwängler in Europe.

38. Signed Olga Paulson; VI, 17 April 1927, p. 6.
39. Toscanini and Furtwängler appeared with the Philharmonic during the same season in 1925–1926 and 1926–1927. They both also appeared in Salzburg in 1937.
40. Gillis, p. 19. See Harvey Sachs, *Toscanini*, (New York) 1978, pp. 184–185, for a different view of this incident.
41. Elisabeth Rethberg sang the soprano part two days earlier at the first performance of these concerts at Carnegie Hall. In those days, the New York Philharmonic played a series of subscription concerts (usually Sundays) at the Metropolitan.

In bringing Toscanini to the New York Philharmonic, Mackay finally played his winning trump against the New York Symphony. In spring 1928 Mackay formalized the merger of the Philharmonic and the Symphony Society. Toscanini now had the best players from three of New York's leading orchestras: the National Symphony, the New York Symphony, and the New York Philharmonic.[42] As the New York Philharmonic-Symphony Society, it not only became New York's best orchestra, but its newly aggregated strength endowed it with the potential to become the finest orchestra in America, *pace* Philadelphia and Boston.

Furtwängler may have lost the sweepstakes to become the chief conductor of this potentially incomparable organization, but his contribution toward honing the future New York Philharmonic into a greater ensemble in a relatively short space of time cannot be underestimated. Nor can the energy he invested in adapting himself to the rigors and practical realities of American concert life be overlooked. During his three seasons with the Philharmonic, Furtwängler conducted over 70 concerts of 51 programs in New York, Philadelphia, Harrisburg, Reading, Pittsburgh, Baltimore, and Washington. In New York alone, he appeared with the Philharmonic at Carnegie Hall (in subscription concerts, galas, and children's concerts), the Metropolitan Opera House, the Brooklyn Academy of Music and in a private concert of light music in the grand ballroom of the Waldorf-Astoria Hotel.

Although his programs consisted primarily of the larger romantic orchestral works, he also performed Max Bruch's *Kol Nidrei* and Leo Schulz's *Berceuse*, both with Schulz as cello soloist, the original version of Stravinsky's *Rite of Spring*, the American composer Ernest Schelling's *Suite fantastique* with the composer performing at the piano, Giuseppe Valentini's *Suite for Cello and Orchestra* with Hans Kindler as soloist, and orchestral excerpts from Richard Strauss' latest opera of the time, *Intermezzo* (1923–1924). Even a cursory glance over American concert programs during the years immediately following World War I reveal that Furtwängler not only conducted balanced programs of old and new music but was comparatively progressive in his program choices. What is more, he made it a point to perform works by emigrant contemporary and American composers Valentini, Schulz, and Schelling, an American composer who was a crusader in concerts for children and students at the Philharmonic.

His departure from America, however, did not go entirely unobserved. As soon as the Philharmonic issued a lame statement on 4

---

42. The merger officially took place on 8 June 1928.

March, saying Furtwängler would not return for the 1927–1928 season almost at the same time that it announced Toscanini for an extended engagement during that period, a scandal erupted. Furious letters poured into the *New York Times*. One of them smelled a cabal against Furtwängler:

> Is there a conspiracy against Wilhelm Furtwängler? . . . Why all of a sudden, when Toscanini conducts, forget everyone, and knock Furtwängler especially? It isn't fair play, and it is with profound regret that I look upon the absence of this sincere artist who consistently refuses to prostitute his art for applause and the favor of critics.[43]

On the same day as this letter appeared, Olin Downes defended his views on Furtwängler in a lengthy article on the front page of the *Times'* Sunday Arts Section and made numerous statements of opinion which he asserted as "facts":

> A consensus of critical opinion, coming from different quarters, without the slightest prejudice or collusion, has rated Mr. Furtwängler's performances less highly than those of either of his colleagues, Messers, Mengelberg and Toscanini of the Philharmonic this season.

What precisely was the "critical consensus?" The implication in Downes' article against Furtwängler indicated that Furtwängler's performances were in general less critically well received than Toscanini's. The critics indeed had raved about Toscanini during his first two seasons beginning in 1926. But the critics had also been favorable to Furtwängler during *his* first two seasons too, and the reviews during his third season disclose a consensus that is anything but unfavorable. Downes himself, in fact, liked far more concerts by Furtwängler in his last two seasons than he disliked. Henderson almost invariably appreciated Furtwängler. Curiously, Pitts Sanborn was much more consistent in his antipathy during Furtwängler's last American season, for he had been the most vocal of Furtwängler's champions during his first season.

Gilman, on the other hand, had come out as an ardent Toscanini supporter following his last concert at the end of his 1926 engagement with the Philharmonic. He greatly praised him in the Sunday section of the *Tribune*.[44] Once he announced his verdict on Toscanini, Gilman rarely attended Furtwängler's concerts during the last two of Furtwängler's American seasons. In 1926 he was busy writing reams about

43. 27 March 1927, p. 8.
44. 7 February 1926, p. 1.

the Metropolitan's Wagner cycle which was going on during Furtwängler's New York appearances. In 1927 he was simply elsewhere much of the time, but he attended Furtwängler's first concert of that season and disliked it:

> We did not find [Furtwängler's] reading of ["Ein Heldenleben"] altogether satisfying. The heroic opening pages lacked weight and impact; the fires of the love scene did not blaze as high as we are certain that they can . . . But Mr. Furtwängler played most of the battle scene with admirable intensity and furor and happily chosen tempi . . .
>
> Mr. Furtwängler too has given a better account of himself than he did in "The Freischútz" Overture, which was at times mannered and heavy-handed.[45]

The palpable negativity in the review of this and several other concerts of the 1927 season conveyed a *general* condescension on his part toward Furtwängler that in turn could prompt readers to generalize against him. It was precisely this sort of suggestiveness that gave Downes' prattle about "critical consensus" against Furtwängler the resonance of God's-honest-Truth. Gilman based his arguments exclusively on his own concepts of musical values, and he never suggested that Toscanini was superior to Furtwängler because he was Italian. Most of the other reviews of Furtwängler's concerts in the *Herald-Tribune* that year were unsigned, which does not necessarily indicate that someone else wrote them.

Downes crept further along in his protracted article to carp about the general quality of Furtwängler's concerts, when—with a quibble here and there—he manifestly had complimentary things to say about most of them:

> Mr. Furtwängler has not maintained during the season anything like the technical and artistic level of his opening and historic performance of Brahms's *First Symphony*. This is not opinion but fact. There are and there have been many minor divergences of opinion concerning this or that Furtwängler performance.

The "minor divergences of opinion" to which Downes refers usually concerned the measure of excellence rather than the degree of deficiency in a Furtwängler performance. In any event, Downes offers no data for his "fact," and reviews in other periodicals do not support it. He goes on to say that Furtwängler concerts were not well attended, certainly not to the capacity he had enjoyed in his first two seasons.

45. *New York Herald-Tribune*, 11 February 1927.

His "failure" at the box office was still another reason why the Philharmonic board made a good decision in letting him go:

> It is a fact that may be ascertained by the curious fact that the public, which originally greeted Mr. Furtwängler with warm and spontaneous acclaim, has given its silent verdict upon his performances by patronizing them in lesser degree than it patronized the performances of his fellow-conductors. This is a matter which must and should count with a great orchestral organization.

This was but one of numerous gambits that brought an avalanche of mail to the *Times* and brought the scandal into the open. One reader questioned Downes' line of reasoning:

> Aren't you establishing a standard of quantity rather than quality? If Mr. Babe Ruth were to lead the Philharmonic he would probably draw larger audiences than Messers. Furtwängler, Mengelberg, and Toscanini put together. Would that mean that the public would therefore benefit, musically, more by Mr. Ruth's conducting?[46]

And finally, Downes pointed with finger-wagging concern to Furtwängler's "limited" international experience, and the effect such deficiencies might have on his choice of repertoire:

> Like many other German conductors lacking wide experience outside their own country, his repertory has been limited, particularly in his first two seasons, and when he ventured outside the stock German repertory, it was not always with happy results. German conductors as a class, when they come to America, have to outgrow certain nationalistic musical leanings. It is astonishing and sometimes unwelcome to them to discover that American audiences are accustomed to a broad and catholic repertory; that American standards of performance are considerably higher—not lower, but higher than those which obtain today in Europe . . .

This gaggle of unfounded statements eventually caught on as inviolable truth and later became all but tattooed on Furtwängler's chest. Furtwängler, in fact, had conducted in England, France, Switzerland, Italy, Hungary, Denmark, and Sweden by the time he finished his third American season. His repertoire with the Philharmonic alone included Berlioz, Bruch, Dvořák, Franck, Miaskovsky, Prokofiev, Ravel, Respighi, Saint-Saëns, Sibelius, Stravinsky, Tchaikovsky, Valentini, and Ernest Schelling. But few people of influence knew enough about him to stand up for him and take on Downes. No one among

---

46. Harold Freeman, VIII, 3 April 1927, p. 8.

those who did know took action because it simply was too risky for their own futures.

For all the cant Downes spewed about Furtwängler's alleged shortcomings, the whole controversy reflected much more basic issues. By 1927 Furtwängler no longer was the current rage. He was yesterday's news. The fickle New York public had gorged itself on the exotic, gangly German for two years in a row, far longer than it usually feasted on a novelty. It now needed a change of diet, a new cultural fix. Furtwängler's diffidence toward perpetuating the sensation he had created in 1925, his disinterest in chasing the bright lights and hoopla, and his peculiarly un-American ascetic modesty ultimately fused into an albatross around his baton. He was not playing the American Game, and through that abstention he was communicating his disapproval of it—a transgression that Americans audiences as a crowd could not allow. The people who did come to his concerts could not have cared less, but they amounted to little more than a cult. They were neither large enough nor sufficiently influential to insure the only recognized barometer of success in America: sold out houses. The public now was flocking to what the critics were telling them was the high-wire walker of all time: Toscanini.

The superficial crux of Downes' appraisal in the article was, as one reader pointed out, simply that he was siding with the Philharmonic board for Toscanini and against Furtwängler.[47] But what made his argument so subtly potent and so insidiously vicious was its appeal to the ethnocentric, anti-German bias to which many Americans were prone in the years following World War I. Downes' article is a remarkable document of an ethnically influenced career assassination in action, disguised as informed critical assessment and earnest journalistic objectivity. While it may also be argued that Furtwängler was too ascetic, too precious, or too special ever to have had a big American career, Downes' saprogenic brew of complaints poisoned Furtwängler's chances for any future American career at all.

On one point, though, Downes was absolutely right. The technical standards of the best American orchestras of that time were higher than most European ensembles, perhaps even surpassing Berlin and Vienna, and Furtwängler was vitally aware of it. A few years later, his memories of working with the New York Philharmonic produced an extensive entry in his *Notebooks:*[48]

47. 10 April 1927, VII, p. 8.
48. Translated by Shaun Whiteside, edited by Michael Tanner, (London) 1989. Note: This excellent contribution in English to knowledge of Furtwängler appeared during the writing of this book. I use the designation *Notebooks* where I quote Mr. Whiteside's translation. Elsewhere, I use the original German title *Aufzeichnungen* when I quote with my own translation.

The ways and extent to which the American method is superior to our own became immediately clear to me when I visited America as conductor of the New York Philharmonic Orchestra. There, thanks to the money behind it (and that is always privately raised), it is possible to assemble the best forces from the whole world. So, for example, the woodwind players from France, the brass players from Germany . . . etc. The technical virtuosity, lightness, elegance and natural beauty of tone of such an orchestra are extraordinary.   *1929, p. 33*

But Furtwängler saw a negative side to this phenomenon. His experience in America made him sharply conscious of some problems inherent in musicians from diverse backgrounds playing together in one ensemble. One of the first difficulties he encountered was in making these musicians from diverse national backgrounds play as a cohesive unit with a unified concept of the music:

This puts one in mind of the artist, who, in order to create Venus, assembled, from various models, the most beautiful nose, the most beautiful eyes, arms, legs, etc., in the opinion that he could thus not fail to assemble the most beautiful figure.   *p. 34*

For Furtwängler, the discrepancies of tone resulting from musicians schooled in different national styles and techniques also led to inconsistencies in "feeling" the music:

An orchestra with this uniform tonal character in all its sections, with a naturally unified way of feeling, with such roundness and homogeneity of tone in the tutti passages, produced of its own accord and not by being externally and artificially smoothed off, like that of the Vienna Philharmonic, cannot be found in America.   *p. 34*

Most important to Furtwängler, though, the paucity of an internal, *natural* unity in feeling among orchestra players also led to a weakening of the improvisational element in performing in general:

. . . That imperceptible variability of tempo and color, can in no way be achieved mechanically by means of rehearsals. In the end the conductor is often faced with the decision of either having to exaggerate or of completely neglecting his intentions in this regard. Either without a natural structure in the beat or with studied intentional "nuances"—a situation then, which also to a high degree corresponds to contemporary reality.
                    p. 35

Both the substance and the final point of his discourse here are among the more astonishing and prescient statements he makes in his

Notebooks. Furtwängler had no problem listening to German orchestras play Italian music, or Italian orchestras performing Debussy and so on, and neither the thrust nor the substance of his contention ever argues for the superiority of one national style over another. To the contrary, he felt the unified musical identity of any group of players enabled a valid statement to be made about any work regardless of its origin. What troubled him was how a nationally mixed orchestra would affect interpretation. The absence of a common cultural background, he felt, would lead to imitating an interpretation or compromising that interpretation into something satisfying no one, instead of producing an emotionally cohesive expression of that work. That cohesion, as far as Furtwängler was concerned, could be better informed by the common cultural background of its players. But he saw clearly that American players would eventually evolve their music making into a distinct and formidable national style.[49] As far as he could see at the time, though, that development was far in the future.

The Toscanini faction won far more, of course, than mere employment for an aging maestro at the New York Philharmonic. Its victory created a turning point in the history of orchestral performing that was to have far-reaching consequences right to the last decade of the century. For all his depth as a conductor of the great classics from Mozart through Richard Strauss, what made Toscanini's art singular was his gift for galvanizing the high-gloss discipline and technical sheen of the Philharmonic that Mengelberg, and Mengelberg alone, had hammered into the New York Philharmonic.[50]

Toscanini refined the organization Mengelberg (the real loser in this struggle) had strengthened into a mechanism of matchless flexibility, stamina, and—above all—precision. Except for Stokowski and the Philadelphia Orchestra, and perhaps Koussevitsky and his Bostonians, Toscanini had no real rivals in the United States, and the mammoth public relations machine behind him in both the press and at the Philharmonic developed what became the myth of Toscanini-as-Superconductor. At least two generations of conductors would stand in awe of him and try to emulate him. Three generations of listeners would deify his lapidary interpretations as the final and divine word on "how to do it."

49. See above p. 20f. Also *New York Times*, 11 January 1926, p. 32.
50. For evidence of how the New York Philharmonic sounded under Mengelberg, listen to the recording he made of *Ein Heldenleben* (which Strauss dedicated to Mengelberg and the Concertgebouw of Amsterdam) that has been re-mastered and issued on both long-play records and compact discs.

In Europe, Furtwängler continued to seek his own way, searching above all for the spirit and heart of every work he performed, allowing matters of ensemble unison to take care of themselves—which occurred, with occasional disastrous exceptions, with inexplicable regularity. Furtwängler's concerts in Europe and especially in Berlin became all but religious services. "The awe the man induced in his concerts was really quite incredible," recalls Elisabeth Schwarzkopf, who started attending Furtwängler's concerts when she was a school-girl in the 1930s. "Listening to his concerts was almost like being in church."[51] While a few conductors came close to achieving the kind of mystical rapture he created at his concerts, there were no aspiring imitators except one: a music student in Vienna whose laser blue eyes were targeted on every podium on which Furtwängler stood. But it would be almost a decade before his blazing ambition would materialize into a menace. In the meantime, certain critics continued to forge a polarity between the approaches of Toscanini and Furtwängler, concluding that one or the other was far superior. But the differences between them were neutralized more often than not by what they shared in common: an unforgettable impact on their audiences.

51. Conversation with the author, 2 April 1990, Zumikon.

5

Successes and Conquests

While Furtwängler was bewildered about what had happened in America, he had no time to worry about it. There were enough difficulties at home. Throughout the three years of his American seasons, his energies in Europe were fully taken up with shuttling among Berlin, Leipzig, and Vienna and taking the Berlin Philharmonic on several tours. In 1926 he entered a brave new world that would both frustrate and immortalize him. He made his first gramophone recordings for Polydor (later to become Deutsche Grammophon) with the Berlin Philharmonic. Furtwängler's life-long antipathy toward the recording studio is well known, but some listeners have concluded that he was not interested in recording at all. To the contrary, he saw the value of recordings as a way to bring music to more people than ever before:

> The practical significance of radio and recordings cannot be overestimated. Their time has come. For music, they possess the possibility of popularizing music enormously. They also have further importance as teaching aids. *Ton und Wort, p. 34*

But the medium discomfited him personally and interfered with his own concept of performing as a continuous flow. He loathed being forced to record a piece or a movement lasting, say, 12 minutes in three spurts of four-minute takes—the maximum length of a shellac 78-rpm record. One of the stipulations in his recording contracts allowed him to have the flexibility of making records with any company that would enable him to record in longer takes.[1] The realization of the long-play format was still two decades in the future when he entered the first phase of his recording career, but experiments for that format were going on even as he signed with Polydor. His first two records consisted of Weber's overture to *Freischütz* and Beethoven's Fifth Symphony complete.[2]

It is no surprise that Furtwängler chose *Freischütz* for his first recording. He revered the opera as possibly the greatest expression of German lyric theater, and it is short enough to fit comfortably on two sides of a shellac disc. His affection for the work shows through the impassioned playing he draws from the orchestra. The strings are full and buoyant, but there is relatively little portamenti—the practice of sliding from one note to the other—that was both accepted and encouraged at the time. Although he later got a reputation for taking slow tempos, this sprightly reading gives no presentiment of it. He drives the orchestra propulsively here without worrying it. The unity of ensemble may not have quite the bloom that imbues, say, Stokowski's recordings with the Philadelphia Orchestra of that period, but that facility in connecting phrases and effecting transitions that marked Furtwängler's work throughout his career is fully evident here.

Furtwängler's first recording of the Beethoven Fifth is another matter, and quite a problematic one. He made three studio recordings of it during his career and performed it more times than any other work in his repertoire.[3] This first account presents a portrait of Furtwängler in this period that runs contrary to the evidence clearly in abundance on later recordings. It also belies published and informed eyewitness reports about his concert performances in this period.[4] For the most part, it is turgid and inflexible, lacking scale and lyricism. It is a disappointing recording, and it amounts to little more than a reading of the work rather than emerging as a performance of it. Perhaps he knew it was not up to his standard: he did not make another recording of any piece until three years later in 1929.

His relationship with the Berlin Philharmonic in the 1920s was blossoming into a marriage that would last until the end of his life. But

1. See "Furtwängler et l'Enregistrements," Société Wilhelm Furtwängler Newsletter, March 1988, for an extensive discussion of Furtwängler's recording activities.
2. I will deal with all of Furtwängler's recordings separately in later chapters, but these two recordings may be worth surveying here because they are the earliest known example of Furtwängler conducting and presumably give at least a faint shadow of his musical approach in the 1920s.
3. I will discuss it at length later in Chapter 26.
4. See Chapter 23.

his liaison with the Leipzig Gewandhaus Orchestra was presenting him with as many difficulties as his marriage to Zitla. On one hand, he gave the Gewandhaus premieres of works by Ambrosius, Atterberg, Casella, Gal, Graener, Hindemith, Honegger, Kletzki, Kopsch, Marx, Reger, Respighi, Schoeck, Scriabin, Sibelius, Strässer, Stravinsky, and Vaughan Williams. He also conducted the world premieres of works by Braunfels, Graener, Kempff, Raphael, Schönberg, Toch, and Trapp.

The soloists and conductors Furtwängler brought to the podium of the Gewandhaus for their debuts in Leipzig included Volkmar Andreae, Gustav Brecher, Edwin Fischer, Erich Kleiber, Otto Klemperer, Carl Schuricht, Bruno Walter, Felix Weingartner, and Ernst Wendel. He was no less perceptive in picking future conductors as he was in choosing players for his orchestra. For example, he selected the future music director of the Boston Symphony, Charles Münch, as his first concertmaster in 1925 and Rudolf Kempe was an oboist. Instrumental and vocal soloists new to Leipzig included Gieseking, Alexander Borovsky, Dusolina Giannini, Vladimir Horowitz, Lubka Kolessa, Georg Kulenkampff, Mia Peltenberg. and Joseph Szigeti. A glance over these names gives some indication of why Furtwängler wanted to be guaranteed more say about the artists invited to Leipzig. While many of the names ultimately became legendary, nearly all of them already were well known before Furtwängler invited them. Some inexplicable reason, perhaps the parochial tastes of the selection committee, kept them away before Furtwängler invited them.

On the other hand, Furtwängler succeeded in taking the orchestra on only one tour through four cities in Switzerland. Quite apart from the board's parochial aversion to instituting new ideas, the big obstacle in touring was the orchestra's commitment to playing for the Leipzig Opera. In spite of an economic crisis in Germany that threatened to liquidate the whole nation, opera became more popular in the post-World War I period than ever before, and performances at the Opera House became more frequent. Consequently, the orchestra had to remain within hailing distance of Leipzig most of the time.[5] A concert tour of the United States in 1925 was simply out of the question. Contention over the orchestra's priorities quickly became a sore point between Furtwängler and the music director of the opera, Gustav Brecher.

What irritated Furtwängler most, however, was losing the grabbing match for the orchestra's rehearsal time. He always insisted on at

5. Vienna faced a similar problem but solved it simply by enlarging the orchestra, so that part of it could tour as the Vienna Philharmonic, while the other part played opera.

least two rehearsals and a final general rehearsal at which a paying audience was admitted (a practice still in effect in Europe) prior to the concert itself. As the activity of the orchestra at the Opera became more demanding, he found himself losing rehearsal time that he had assumed was his a matter of course. As early as 1923, Leipzig became more of a problem than it was worth. According to Max Brockhaus, Furtwängler's secretary Berta Geissmar started requesting a release from his contract as soon as he married Zitla Lund in May of that year.[6] He had also gotten into an open argument about orchestral policy with Alfred Heuss (1877–1934), critic for the *Zeitschrift für Musik,* and publicly offered his resignation as early as 1925.[7] Furtwängler was now becoming increasingly famous, and his fights at Leipzig prompted him to lose interest in continuing his relationship with the Gewandhaus.

Something of a godsend came to him in 1927, when Felix Weingartner resigned as regular (ständige) conductor of the Vienna Philharmonic.[8] The orchestra nominated Furtwängler to be his successor, and he readily accepted. The Directors of the Gewandhaus tried to extend his contract, offering a compromise on the time he would spend in Leipzig. He politely but flatly refused and he sent an open letter of resignation to Max Brockhaus, the head of the renowned publishing firm and Chairman of the Gewandhaus Orchestra. It was published in the *Neue Leipziger Zeitung:*

> The necessity to limit my activities presents me with an inexorable problem . . . I am convinced that a limited activity on my part—eventually as you propose—that I conduct half the concerts, and that other conductors lead the other half is not acceptable. The interests of the institution necessitates in my humble opinion, that as much as possible, one person should take charge of the concerts and all the responsibilities that go with them.[9]

He relinquished his directorship of the Leipzig Gewandhaus Orchestra on 28 March 1928 with a performance of Beethoven's Ninth Symphony. For a year, he had been not only Europe's leading conductor but its most ubiquitous. He was music director or principal conductor of the three most important orchestras in Europe: Berlin, Vienna, and Leipzig. But his contentious experience at Leipzig unnerved him and left a permanent scar on his psyche. Instead of

6. Jacquard, p. 10.

7. See Chapter 3 for a fuller discussion of the Furtwängler-Heuss controversy.

8. The Vienna Philharmonic did not have a music director at that or at any time to this day. A regular or chief conductor was nominated (or re-nominated) every year by a committee comprised of players.

9. 30 January 1928.

teaching him a lesson in wariness, an unfortunate streak of paranoia surfaced around this time. From childhood he was never really secure in his knowledge of himself, and to the end of his life, he was prone to bouts of obsessive suspicion. Although many, if not most, of these instances of extreme apprehension were anything but delusional, he never really learned to distinguish between those who did not act with his welfare in mind and those whom he was convinced were out to do him in.

After leaving Leipzig, he shifted his energies to refining the Vienna Philharmonic and making the Berlin Philharmonic an even greater orchestra than the one he inherited from Nikisch. Spending more time in Vienna also enabled him to devote more time to studying with the Viennese musical theorist Heinrich Schenker. Furtwängler first read Schenker's monograph on Beethoven's Ninth in 1912 while he was Kapellmeister in Lübeck. He later struck up a personal acquaintance with Schenker in Vienna and began studying with him in 1919. Schenker's approach to music was derived from a lifelong study of the great masterworks of the German masters—Bach, Handel, Mozart, Beethoven, Wagner, and so on. He believed the proper method of musical analysis was to see it as a totality, a form—a Gestalt—rather than as the sum of many parts. The Schenker approach contradicted the older method of splitting up a piece into sections and examining them without necessarily putting them back together again.

Schenker's influence on Furtwängler's musical vision frequently has been overlooked and usually underestimated. Furtwängler constantly was trying to put what he learned from Schenker into practice, and he occasionally mentioned him during rehearsals.[10] Quite apart from an appreciative essay he wrote on Schenker[11] in 1947, the characteristics of interpretation that have come to be associated with Furtwängler—the sense of a work's entire canvass in every played note, the grasp of a work's totality, the mastery in achieving seamless chains of transitions culminating in an organic unity—are the very objectives Schenker strove to elucidate in teaching his brand of analysis. The number of times Furtwängler uses the multifarious word *Ganz* (whole, totality) and its variants in his writings suggests an almost pathological preoccupation with the concepts the word arouses in

10. In his reminiscence of *"Furtwänglers geistige Welt"* ("Furtwängler's Spiritual World"), the art historian Walter Riezler (and one of Furtwängler's tutors) recalls the fascination Schenker's writings and thinking exerted on the young conductor. See *Wilhelm Furtwängler im Urteil seiner Zeit*, (Zurich) 1955, pp. 84–85. The essay has also been reprinted in *Ein Mass, dass Heute fehlt* (A Standard Missing Today), (Vienna) 1986.

11. *Ton und Wort*, pp. 198–204.

German, and there can be little doubt that it was Schenker who cultivated it in Furtwängler.

By the end of the 1920s Schenker had become a world renowned
figure in music. He had published several more monographs on Beethoven's symphonies, two important books on theory *(Kontrapunkt,
Der Tonwille)*, and was about to complete his multi-volume thesis
Das Meisterwerk der Musik. But this project almost ran aground
because a world monetary crisis wracked by the Wall Street crash of
October 1929 had made his publishers unwilling to produce these
tomes whose appeal was at best esoteric. The work was finished by
1930 but appeared to be stillborn. Furtwängler, who never worried
about his personal finances even in the midst of such economic unrest,
stepped into the breach and helped finance the publication of the third
volume himself with a contribution of 3,000 marks.[12]

Furtwängler's hectic professional schedule did not prevent him
from leading an equally vigorous personal life. His marriage to Zitla
had become an "arrangement" by this time, and Geissmar had her
hands full running Furtwängler's professional and private affairs, and
doing the day-to-day chores of the Berlin Philharmonic.

One of the women who witnessed how Geissmar orchestrated
Furtwängler's affairs was the young Suzanne Bloch, a lutenist and
musical lecturer, who was a daughter of the Swiss-American composer Ernest Bloch.

"I heard Furtwängler conducting the Berlin Philharmonic for the
first time in Paris," she recalled to me during a series of conversations
in spring 1990. "It was while I had gone there to study composition
with Nadia Boulanger. I almost didn't go to the concert because I had
no idea who this man was, but someone had given me a ticket, so I
didn't want to waste it.

"I believe it was the first time Furtwängler had taken the Berlin
Philharmonic to Paris. I was late, and I had to wait in the foyer. But as I

12. The transaction was made through the Deutsche Bank in Mannheim on 1 June
1931. The receipt for the cash transfer is reposited in the Oster Collection at the Library
for the Performing Arts, New York. Item 54/298. No provisions were attached to the
contribution; Furtwängler neither demanded nor wanted any share in whatever profits
the book might accrue. A note on Schenker's papers: When he died in 1935, leaving his
entire estate to his widow Jeanette, she divided his personal papers and gave some of
them to Schenker's disciple Oswald Jonas and the rest to Oswald's pupil Ernst Oster
(1908–1977) because she justifiably feared the Nazis might destroy his effects if they
took over Austria, which of course, they did in 1938. Both Jonas and Oster fled and took
their respective allotment of Schenker's papers with them to the United States. Jonas'
portion of these papers was left to the University of California at Riverside. Jeanette
perished at Theresienstadt shortly before that death camp was liberated by Allied Forces
in 1945.

listened, I got goose flesh. Such a sound coming through the closed doors! The music was Handel. And the audience at the end went crazy. He got right to the heart of the music. At the end of the whole concert, the reception of the audience was something to see. I went home, and I told my mother, 'You would not believe the concert I just heard!'"

The concert Bloch attended took place on 11 May 1928.[13] It was indeed the first time the Berlin Philharmonic had played in Paris since 1908 under Richard Strauss. The French were reluctant to allow a foreign orchestra and conductor whose reputation had not recently been proven on French soil to perform at the Opéra. So the concert was held at the Salle Pleyel.[14] When the reviews appeared, however, *Le Monde Musical* called Furtwängler a "consummate magician"[15] and *Le Figaro* said:

> The imperceptible and mysterious manner through which Furtwängler inspired his orchestra . . . is worthy of the highest praise.[16]

The Berlin Philharmonic never again had a problem about the hall in which they played in Paris. Future concerts were always held at the Opéra or the Théâtre des Champs Élysées.

Bloch's mother encouraged her going to Berlin to meet Furtwängler and in December 1928 she went. She kept a diary of her trip, which she saved over the years and showed me in 1990, explaining and illuminating the entries as she turned the leaves. As the entries in the diary accumulate, it reveals how far Berta Geissmar had gone by this time in running Furtwängler's life and how bold she was in attempting to capture people she found useful to him. The trip started off happily enough:

> Berlin—1929—January 19—Sneak into Berlin Philharmonic rehearsal at Philharmonie—Kreisler the soloist. American woman sees me and asks me if I am Suzanne Bloch. She tells me Berta Geissmar mentioned that she lost my address, and she is trying to find me! She brings me to meet Geissmar who takes me to meet F. at the end of rehearsal. He keeps talking to me, asking me about my father. I am later told he kept Mrs. Kreisler waiting outside while talking at length with me.

13. Friday at 9 p.m. Program: Handel: Concerto Grosso No. 10, op. 6, No. 4. Beethoven: Fifth Symphony. Strauss: *Till Eulenspiegel*. Wagner: *Meistersinger* Prelude Act I.
14. See Geissmar, *Two Worlds of Music*, (London and New York) 1949. Hereafter referred to as Geissmar.
15. Fred Goldbeck, Nr. 5, 1928.
16. R. Brussel, 14 May 1928.

"Geissmar was very intelligent and very efficient, but she was one of the ugliest persons I have ever met," she recalled over 60 years later. "When she took me to Furtwängler, I remember he stood up very tall and just looked at me. I will never forget those eyes. I was fascinated by them. He started talking to me, but I have no idea what he said because I was hypnotized by those eyes. His manner was very quiet and softspoken, and it all gave him a kind of aura. I've met many far more handsome men, and he was not physically beautiful by any means—that long neck of his—my God! But some people have an aura, and some people just don't. Furtwängler had a great one, and I could feel it the moment I walked into the room.

"I went home and told Mother about it, and she thought it was terrific. Immediately, she said, 'Now he will play more of Father's music!'"

Bloch eventually learned that Geissmar was priming her for an affair with her boss. He recently had fallen in love with a young Swiss woman, and it was not working out very well. Geissmar evidently thought Bloch would make a good replacement in Furtwängler's bed.

"But strangely, I had no desire to go to bed with him. He was very attractive to me, but I had witnessed all my father's love affairs and how miserable they made him and everybody around him. I was determined not to fall into that trap, even though it was all right there for me to take."

> February 2—G. calls in p.m. and says F. would like to see me later and invites me to bring along my lute to her place. When I arrive, she tells me to wait because he is at his house composing. We wait for him to call.
> We go to his apartment—decorated by Zitla. Too feminine for my taste. A lot of kitsch. We have discussions about music. I sing and play the lute for him—troubadour songs. He suggests I take singing lessons so I could maybe sing with the orchestra.

Furtwängler followed up the next day with a different ploy.

> February 3 [1929]—G. phones me and tells me Furtwängler has programmed Father's *Schelomo* for a concert with the Berlin Philharmonic in Hamburg on February 5th.
> February 4— I go with Mother to the rehearsal for Schelomo in Berlin. Graudan the cello soloist . . .[17] Geissmar tells me at the break that

17. Nicolai Graudan was co-principal cellist with Gregor Piatigorsky and Schuster at the time. "Sometimes, when Piatigorsky saw me from the platform at rehearsals," says Suzanne Bloch, "he would put his cello across his lap and strum it like a lute for me."

tickets, train, and hotel accommodations will be provided for us in Hamburg compliments of the Berlin Philharmonic.

"So the plot thickened. The concert was to be a program consisting entirely of Jewish composers. A Mendelssohn overture, Father's *Schelomo*, and Mahler's First Symphony. I don't know if it had been planned all in advance, but the news of the program surprised me. Geissmar told me our rooms would adjoin Furtwängler's suite, and I quickly told her we wanted separate accommodations. I was not about to do anything like that. My mother at first was not impressed with Furtwängler at the rehearsal. Then he went back over the work and started shaping the dynamics and the structure. Then my mother realized he knew what he was doing. You could see the proportions growing. It was like a miraculous picture coming into focus.

"After the rehearsal, I remember walking back with him to the hotel in the bitter cold. It was hard for me to keep up with his long legs taking those big strides. We talked about Mahler, and I said I didn't like the work. At that time, I thought it sounded stupid. He just said, 'When you are older, you will understand this music.' As he was talking to me, an old woman came over and gave him a little bouquet of flowers. He gave them to me and I pressed them inside my score of the Mahler. I think it's still there.

"The night of the concert, my mother and I had separate seats. She was seated in the parkett—the orchestra stalls. I was placed all by myself at the front of the organ loft above the orchestra—facing Furtwängler! At the intermission everybody was buzzing about that girl in the organ loft. Somebody sitting next to my mother said I looked like Kundry[18] because I had long dark hair over my shoulders. My mother said I was her daughter. When she was not believed, she took out my passport and showed them my picture.

"Anyway, the concert was a wonderful success. I never forgot the way Furtwängler began the *Midsummer Night's Dream*, just by holding his hands in front of him and trembling his fingers."

Neither Furtwängler nor Geissmar could wait forever, and when Bloch continued to side-step the opportunities Geissmar threw at her for a tryst, Geissmar lost patience. Nonetheless, Bloch and Furtwängler continued to be friendly. One night, after a performance of the *St. Matthew Passion* in Berlin, Bloch got a glimpse of the sad state of Furtwängler's personal affairs. "Backstage afterwards, you would never

---

18. The enigmatic, multi-faceted seductress in Wagner's *Parsifal*, at once wild and wily, creative and destructive.

have thought there had been such an incredibly beautiful concert. I saw Zitla, and she looked as though she had been crying. He looked just awful—very different from the beatific way he looked on stage only a few minutes before.''

Even while he carried on such personal involvements—or attempts at them—Furtwängler meticulously kept up a full schedule conducting throughout Europe. Nothing, not even a monstrous libido, kept him from carrying out what he perceived as his first duty; music. He made his debut at the Vienna Staatsoper conducting *Rheingold* on 17 October 1928, took the Berlin Philharmonic on annual tours of central Europe and England, and continued developing his immensely satisfying relationship with the Vienna Philharmonic. During this year, he also received an honorary doctorate from the University of Heidelberg. In late spring of the following year, he made his operatic debut in Berlin with a special festival performance of *The Marriage of Figaro* with the Berlin Municipal Opera (Städtische Oper) at the Schauspielhaus on 13 June.

Furtwängler's operatic debut in Berlin was indeed a long-awaited event, and he presented himself under the best circumstances: first-class singers, a quality production, and festival conditions. But there may well have been other reasons why he waited for five years before giving Berlin his operatic credentials. In the first place, Berlin's operatic scene was a cesspool of internecine politics and the setting for a nobly conceived but wretchedly executed experiment in making this intrinsically aristocratic art form more democratic.

The father of this experiment was Leo Kestenberg, the Referent for music in the Prussian Ministry of Culture since 1918. Kestenberg was probably the most powerful bureaucrat in the Weimar Republic, and his influence on all the performing arts during this period cannot be overlooked.[19] But the sphere of his greatest achievements—and failures—was not merely opera but opera in Berlin. Berlin had always had a poor reputation as a city of opera, and part of Kestenberg's scheme was to raise artistic standards at its two principal opera houses: the Staatsoper on Unter den Linden and what became the Städtische Oper in Charlottenburg. But Kestenberg was also a socialist, and his grand objective was to popularize opera among the proletariat and, in doing so, elevate middle class and blue-collar cultural tastes. Such objectives aroused the ire of the right, which wanted to

---

19. Kestenberg's domain was specifically music, while Ludwig Seelig had responsibility for spoken theater, but eventually Kestenberg took the leading role in both areas.

preserve the so-called old German values, even though that is precisely what Kestenberg was actually trying to do in his own way. His dreams were realized for a fleeting but blazing moment with the establishment in 1924 of the Kroll, which became Berlin's third major opera house and was transformed three years later into a symbol of Weimar's progressive energy when the company came under Otto Klemperer's direction from 1927 to 1931.[20] But it took Kestenberg six years from 1918 to get the new opera house going, and another three years before he had the good fortune of bringing Klemperer to it. Along the way, he encountered one nest of hornets after another in attempting to liberalize opera in Berlin.[21]

One of his thorniest obstacles was Max von Schillings, a renowned composer who had been appointed Intendant at the Staatsoper in 1919. Schillings was a conservative, and he was constantly at loggerheads with Kestenberg and the rest of the Prussian Ministry of Culture, although he was by no means a self-styled villain in such matters. Like any other opera house, the Staatsoper demanded the whip-cracking authority of a tiger trainer and the diplomatic skills of Machiavelli. Schillings was deficient in both qualities, although he was liked and respected by the members of his company. His real gift was on the podium, and he kept the performance level of the Staatsoper at international standards throughout his tenure. He also started a monthly magazine to improve communication between the opera house and its subscribers and formed a press office, both headed by the company's versatile archivist Julius Kapp. But he hated those who counted beans at the Ministry and made no secret of viewing Kestenberg as an adversary rather than the source of support he might have won from him had he played his cards more skillfully. Worst of all, he refused to endorse or cooperate with Kestenberg and the Prussian Ministry of Culture in furthering the idea of a third opera house, primarily because he knew he would be made responsible for it, and he had his hands full already.

Furtwängler steered clear of these troubled waters and with good reason. Schillings had been one of his composition teachers in Munich when Furtwängler was still in his teens, and he was not about to compete with him now that he had achieved renown and influence. Furtwängler was also on good terms with Kestenberg, but he was not sym-

20. See Peter Heyworth, *Otto Klemperer: His Life and Times*, (London) 1983, pp. 234–373, for a detailed and vigorous examination of Klemperer's activity at the Kroll.
21. See John Sargent Rockwell, *The Prussian Ministry of Culture and the Berlin State Opera, 1918–1931*, Doctoral Dissertation, University of California, Berkeley, 1972, for a superb survey of opera politics in the Weimar Republic.

pathetic with his politics or his attempts to politicize opera.[22] Probably at Geissmar's prompting, he realized that he needed a very special showcase for his operatic debut in Berlin, and the current conditions of petty backbiting and epic territorial imperatives simply could not provide that backdrop.

Kestenberg finally forced Schillings to resign in 1924, after Leo Blech, the Staatsoper's leading conductor, had gone to the less prestigious Städtische Oper. Blech's resignation was just the excuse Kestenberg needed to mount an attack on Schillings' competence. His case was advanced when Schillings refused to offer Blech's position to Bruno Walter, Otto Klemperer, or Blech's gifted right-hand man Fritz Stiedry, giving it instead to Erich Kleiber. Kestenberg could not fail to notice that the contenders were all Jews, while Kleiber was not—or at least less Jewish.[23] He replaced him with Heinz Tietjen, who previously had headed the Städtische Oper. Tietjen was one of the most mysterious and yet phenomenally influential individuals in the history of opera performance in Germany in this century, and he was later to have a significant role in Furtwängler's career. He was precisely the man Kestenberg needed, for Tietjen was a gifted administrator, a talented producer, and a competent conductor who could cope with the daily grind of running an amorphous institution, keep an eye on costs, and manipulate budgets to keep the quality of productions up to the standard expected of Germany's cultural capital. The appointment as Intendant of the Staatsoper was the turning point in Tietjen's long and checkered career, but it hardly seemed so at the time. Within three years he would become Intendant of all Prussian Theaters.[24]

Schillings' dismissal intensified the attacks on Kestenberg from the right, and thus the ousted Intendant was turned into the symbol of martyred *völkisch* genius, the fallen hero of noble German art at the hands of Bolshevik (i.e., Jewish) barbarians.[25] The event also

22. See Kestenberg, *Bewegte Zeiten*, (Wiesbaden) 1961, p. 58. This memoir is not especially revealing, but no evidence has surfaced to contradict Kestenberg's warm memories of Furtwängler.

23. Kleiber was evidently partly Jewish.

24. Tietjen tried to set up a system in which Berlin's three opera major houses could combine their sets and casts to be interchangeable, a plan monstrous costs have forced present-day opera houses into adopting. Tietjen's plan worked for a while, but it ultimately failed because the Staatsoper and the Kroll belonged to the Prussian State, while the Städtische Oper belonged to the city. City and State did not want to cooperate. See Rockwell, pp. 196f.

25. See Rockwell, pp. 167–174, who rightly points out that Schillings' Nazi biographer harped upon the Brownshirt view of Schillings as a martyr to the deleterious influence of socialism on German culture. See Wilhelm Raupp, *Max von Schillings: Der Kampf eines deutschen Künstlers*, Hanseatische Verlagsanstalt, (Hamburg) 1935.

prompted a raucous debate in the Reichstag on 14 December 1925, in which the far right lambasted Kestenberg. By some metaphysical coincidence, the Staatsoper was suddenly vaulted out of its torpor that night into the very forefront of progressive contemporary opera with the world premiere of Alban Berg's *Wozzeck* under Erich Kleiber. It was clearly the most important lyric premiere in Berlin of the Weimar period and possibly of the century, but it did not cause quite the furor that accrued to it over the next few years. Most of the arch-conservatives simply stayed away, preferring instead to attend a recital given by Barbara Kemp, who by now had become Schillings' wife.

Meanwhile, anticipation of Furtwängler's operatic debut was becoming an issue in Berlin's cultural politics, and he wanted more than ever to wait for the right time and appropriate setting. While Furtwängler was on good terms with Klemperer, the press attempted to create a rivalry between the two conductors because their approaches to music were so dissimilar. Furtwängler was paranoid about the mere thought of such rivalries, and he had no desire to aggravate competition unless he knew he could win. Klemperer had a large and loyal following, so Furtwängler also had no desire to take him on by trying to compete with him in his own domain. Nor did he have any appetite for identifying himself with a company that was so singularly politicized by both reputation and admission. Consequently, he delayed his operatic debut in Berlin until 1929, when the event—a brilliant production of *The Marriage of Figaro* at the Schauspielhaus—could highlight the gala atmosphere of the Berlin Festival and take place on politically neutral territory. While the production and singers were mostly from the Städtische Oper, the Schauspielhaus was a theater for spoken drama whose connections with the Staatsoper, the Städtische Oper, and the Kroll were at best tenuous. This house was one of celebrated director Max Reinhardt's several theatrical homes, each of them famous as a hothouse of exciting and provocative productions whose innovative concepts derived from Reinhardt's artistic vision rather than from his political outlook. In an environment such as the Schauspielhaus, located in the Gendarmenmarkt—the great square behind the Staatsoper, Furtwängler had sufficient rehearsal time with superior singers whose frame of mind would be elevated above the attitude they might have toward a mere repertory performance.

His cast for *Figaro* included Hans Reinmar as the Count, Nelly Merz-Gehrke as the Countess, Lotte Schöne as Susanna, Margaret Pfahl as Cherubino, and none less than Alexander Kipnis as Figaro. Otto Schrenk of the *Deutsche Allgemeine Zeitung*, Berlin, left no doubt over how he felt about the performance:

The immense richness of the score streamed felicitously from Furtwängler's hands, and Mozart's melodies took on a magical life under his direction.[26]

Schrenk also reported that Furtwängler was called out for a solo
bow after the second act by a "highly enthusiastic" audience.[27] A few
days later, on June 18th, he made his house debut with the company
in Charlottenburg with *Tristan und Isolde*. He probably had the finest
cast any opera house could buy at the time. The performance marked
the first time Lauritz Melchior sang the title role in Berlin. His Isolde
was Frida Leider. Others in the cast included Friedrich Schorr and Sigrid Onegin.

Furtwängler returned to the Vienna Staatsoper in the following
autumn to conduct two performances of *Tristan* with a different but
no less stellar cast: Helene Wildbrün was the Isolde, Gunnar Graarud
her Tristan, Emil Schipper as Kurwenal, and Rosette Anday as Brangaene.[28] But for reasons we may never know, he did not conduct opera
in Austria again until 1935.

Suzanne Bloch went back to Paris in March 1929, but neither Furtwängler nor Geissmar forgot her. A few weeks later, Geissmar went
to Paris to arrange another engagement of the Berlin Philharmonic set
for 29 and 30 April. The dates were the only opportunity the orchestra
could play in Paris during their spring tour, but the Opéra was already
booked for performances. The Philharmonic would play this time
at the Théâtre des Champs Élysées. Geissmar found time to seek
out Suzanne Bloch, and they met for lunch. She got right to the
point.

"She told me again that Furtwängler was having great problems
with his marital situation. She mentioned a mistress in Vienna, but
she did not say who it was, and I did not ask. It turned out to be a certain Belline Fleischmann. That news hurt me a little because—even
though I was only a friend, for now I knew he had other women, and
many of them."

Bloch returned to the United States in June 1929. Upon her
return, she began a turbulent phase of her life, beginning her career as
a musician and meeting the man whom she would later marry in a
short-lived union. During the summer, she corresponded with Geissmar and Furtwängler. They both wrote to her in English, and their letters reveal a great deal about their respective personalities. Geissmar

26. 15 June 1929.
27. *Deutsche Allgemeine Zeitung*, Berlin, 15 June 1929, Nr. 270–271.
28. The cast remained the same for both performances: 6 and 14 November.

was direct and unobtrusively flattering; a little encouragement, a little chitchat, a little news:

From Geissmar: Mannheim July 10th, 1929

My Dear Suzanne,

Your letter of June 27th reached me today, as well as your last letter (April), and I'll answer at once so that you won't think that your friends have forgotten you. How quick you are to decide anything about your life. How sharp are your instincts, for what is safe and what is not. I can only *read* and say nothing. I am sure you will do everything right and good in life. Furtwängler had a marvellous season, the tour was splendid and so were the operas in Berlin. He just left our house here a week ago, and is somewhere hidden in the mountains where nothing can reach him. But he telephoned yesterday and I gave him your news. He has still your letter with his papers and will write to you soon and he will also answer the sweet letter your father wrote to him. [Here are] our plans for the summer. I will remain retired from everything, I think, until the middle of August. At any rate, [Furtwängler] will begin his season here in Mannheim September 10th and we shall all be back in Berlin Sept. 16th.—You [could] best, as his addresses over the summer are so uncertain, write to him [care of] me [in] Mannheim. I'll always be happy to hear from you and please do write whenever you feel like.

Love from your,

Berta Geissmar

For some reason, however, she did not mention that one of the highlights of the season for Furtwängler was his induction into what might be the German equivalent to the Order of Merit in the British Empire. In June 1929 he became one of three distinguished Germans awarded the medal *Pour le Mérite*.[29] The other two recipients were the graphic artist Käthe Kollwitz and the philosopher Karl Stumpf. Nor did she mention that Furtwängler was returning to Mannheim in order to make an important addition to his repertoire. He had conducted all the major Wagner operas there except *Lohengrin* during his tenure as first Kapellmeister. He was now going back to complete the cycle. The first and only performance in Mannheim was a gala event taking place on 15 September with a stellar cast that included Margarete Teschemacher, Gertrud Bindernagel, Adolf Loeltgen in the title role, and Hans Bahling as Telramund.

Dr. S. Kaiser of the *Neue Mannheimer Zeitung* was duly impressed:

29. For some reason, the title of the medal was French, even though it was conferred by the German government.

Furtwängler outlined the structure of the first act with the full resources of his intuition. As he phrased Lohengrin's arrival, he revealed the most profound impulse of this music.[30]

But Furtwängler already was on his way back to Berlin by the time the notice appeared, preparing several concerts, a revival of *Tristan* on 20 September, and a new production of *Lohengrin* at the Municipal Opera (Städtische Oper) with Hans Fidesser, Maria Müller, Barbara Kemp, Gotthold Ditter, and Alexander Kipnis set for 9 October. Heinz Tietjen produced and Emil Preetorius designed the sets. Two days after the revival of *Tristan*, he dropped a handwritten note to Suzanne Bloch:

22 September '29

It would be so difficult for me to write in English. I [would have] answered your letters often. Because I had always a great pleasure with your letters and it was a real Freude [joy] for me to hear from you. These many things you have suffered[31] in your young life in the last year I have felt with you, and I hope for you that your new life in New York will be for you always better and better, and that you will have soon the possibility to come to Europe. But first, I hope you will write from New York, about people and life there and about music and concerts. I hope you will have the possibility to hear Toscanini and other concerts often—and from yourself, your lute playing and other things you must write.

With very many many best wishes,
and herrlichsten Grüsse—

Yours,

Wilhelm Furtwängler

Despite his mounting antagonism toward Toscanini's approach to music, he nonetheless encouraged Bloch to attend Toscanini's concerts. He also wanted to communicate effectively in a language foreign to him.

The new production of *Lohengrin* proved highly successful, and it was the first of many collaborations with Tietjen and Preetorius. Furtwängler's dealings with the latter proved satisfying time and again throughout their careers, but if his initial encounter with Tietjen was a happy one, it was, as we shall see later, probably the last, for they would literally run into each other frequently throughout the rest of their lives.

Bloch returned to Europe during the winter to study the lute in

30. 16 September 1929.
31. Bloch was undergoing a divorce from her first marriage at the time.

Vienna. Furtwängler was in the hospital when she arrived in early January 1930.

"Furtwängler was suffering from pneumonia, and he was very, very sick. But when I finally went to his room, he took my hand and said, 'Oh, your hands are so cold!' He then placed my hand on his stomach under the bed sheets. I knew plenty about men by that time, but that shocked me a bit.

"Zitla came in after a while. She went right over to the mirror without even saying anything to Furtwängler or kissing him and adjusted her wide-brimmed hat. Then she came over and was very nice to me."

Eventually, Bloch met Furtwängler's mistress and found her charming, cordial, and woefully unhappy about her affair with Furtwängler. Bloch also nearly found herself caught in the middle of a nasty domestic affair. Although Zitla was unhappy with Furtwängler, she had no desire for a divorce and was determined to keep him.

In the meantime, Belline Fleischmann poured out her heart to Bloch. "She told me how she first met Furtwängler as a girl of 12 in Switzerland. When he went to America she was already there. She went to one of his concerts at Carnegie Hall dressed to kill and that's exactly what happened. Gerald Warburg told me much later that Furtwängler slipped away with her after a concert one night when he was supposed to be going to a big party given by the New York Philharmonic's board of directors.

"Belline said she followed him back to Europe and went to Vienna where she became his weekend mistress. He came to Vienna two or three weekends a month from Berlin or Leipzig, and she stayed with him at his hotel. She had to sneak out in the morning. She had given up her entire life just to have these dirty weekends with Furtwängler, and she was really terribly unhappy. She had lived with him for one month in St. Moritz, but she complained to me that he was always composing. She used to call him 'Furtie.' She had her own money, but she didn't know what to do with herself. I suppose he had no reason to tell her about me because I never slept with him. But I said I probably knew more about him than she did because all he did was come to sleep with her.

"According to Geissmar, who told me this much later, Furtwängler wanted to divorce Zitla, and he was all set to do it, but at the last moment he could not bring himself to do it. Zitla had a terrible breakdown and had internal hemorrhaging. He simply couldn't leave her.

"Belline told me, 'One day Zitla came to see me, and to beg me to leave her husband. I told her, you have no chance because I am young, and you are getting old. It's me he wants.' She fainted in the elevator when she left. Belline told me that. Belline could be very cruel.

"I told her she was wasting her time. She should find a job and a new life for herself. She soon found a job teaching English. And that was the end of it. It seemed like a torrid affair at the time, but his second wife later told me that Belline was not at all important compared to some of his other affairs."

And Bloch's own feelings about Furtwängler?

"Yes, I loved Furtwängler, too, but I was not *in* love with him. I did not lust after him. It may have been an instinct for self-preservation that kept our relationship Platonic. Nor do I regret not having had a physical relationship with Furtwängler. Not at all! I felt I could do something to give something to this man without asking anything from him. To know him was simply an enrichment for me. I didn't want anything else."

The affair with Fleischmann eventually came to an end, and Furtwängler returned to Zitla and countless further conquests, women ever hovering around him in Berlin, in Vienna, on tour. Ultimately, they separated the following year in 1931. Except for a gaffe here and there, Geissmar scheduled all Furtwängler's dalliances with all the alacrity of a master taxi dispatcher. Furtwängler was to have many intense affairs both physical and spiritual in the future, but few of them would be as well remembered as his friendship with Suzanne Bloch.

Bloch continued to correspond with both Furtwängler and Geissmar after returning to the United States. Geissmar found her a useful contact for gaining information and gossip on artists:

7 July 1930 Mannheim

Dear Suzanne,

Thank you very much for your last letter. I had not at all the feeling that you had not written to me as Furtwängler had your news and told me about you.

We are all here over holidays just now and have left Berlin since a week. This year was really too much and we felt in many ways. Let us hope the best it'll change!

Mischa Elman will be soloist with F. next season. How do you find him?

I am very sorry to hear that you are not well though I absolutely can't find what ails you. The word is so "mysteriously" written.

I got the spiral pad in Paris all right. And bought a lot.

When is your father coming and whereto is he going? You best write here, while F. is travelling his mail will be forwarded from here. Mrs. F. will be in Berlin around the 20th and he will join her at latest middle of August. I'll be at Pontresina from July 27th–Sept—ish.

I would be very interested if you could find out very discretely without mentioning me why Merovitch, the manager of the pianist Gabrilowitsch who was made vice-president of the Judson office (Steinway Hall) a year ago, is already out again. Whose fault it was?

The address you want is Villa Mourep. 131 Route de Lausanne, Genève.

But please *never* mention me in any letter any connection and tear this letter at once. Let me hear soon.

With love,

Yours,

Bertel Geissmar

Furtwängler also continued to remain warm in his letters—written for the most part in English—and enigmatically seductive:

From Berlin 10 June 1930

My Dear Suzanne;

It is long ago I had written, but I think that you have not done the same. Your letters were a great pleasure for me every time. I had always the feeling of your vitality, despite you are so far from here. I have not understood you—will you come to Bayreuth this year? Because next year is no Bayreuth (the next is 1933); but it is not so important that you come here to Bayreuth. But I hope to see you if you come over. Surely you are more changed than from what you were—with your many lovers. Your father, is he satisfied with you?—But surely, it was necessary for you, as woman and as human being. But I know you are a very seductive woman, and sometimes it was not easy for me . . .

I am sorry this is so difficult for me to write in English, I cannot say what I mean, but I understand every word you have written. I don't know whether I come to New York once more. It is in the last years so interesting for me in Europe, not only in Germany, but in France, Switzerland, etc. that I cannot einsehen [understand] why I should go to Amerika with its stupid publicity, etc. With my orchestra, I'm very content.

I did see your sister in Paris. She looked very well and very nice. Now I will write to your father too. It is only so difficult for me because I had not answered his kind, long letter two years ago. I am very sorry that I cannot bring something of his works in my concerts during the next season. But I have a new concerto by Ravel, and something new by Stravinsky, etc.—and so I have no place for more étrangers.

I hope you will write soon to me again. You give me a real joy. And tell me something about your job—and your lovers too. I am sure many people will think it was a big Dummheit von mir not geworden zu sein [to have been] the first. But it was better so, And we are the best of friends.

Much love—Your

Wilhelm Furtwängler

6

Decisions

While Furtwängler seemed to have no problem juggling ephemeral affairs of the heart, he found his relationship with the orchestras in Berlin and in Vienna similar to a bigamist who has two demanding wives he loves deeply. The double responsibility of keeping up standards in two musical capitals eventually proved to be too much for him. By 1930 he realized the time had come to choose between Berlin and Vienna. Weeks of uncertainty over which city and which orchestra and which country he would choose made front-page headlines throughout Europe and kept the gossip mills in both cities hard at it.

His loyalty to the Berliners ultimately won out and he was named General Music Director of Berlin. Of course, there was a measure of pressure brought to bear on Furtwängler to remain exclusively with the Berlin Philharmonic. The Berlin Municipal Authority gave (as it does to this day) its orchestra an annual stipend to make up its inevitable yearly deficit. The Authority now made it clear that it was not prepared to continue its sponsorship of the orchestra until Furtwängler devoted his services as chief conductor exclusively to the Berlin Philharmonic. Furtwängler clearly understood the Authority's position and was not about to endanger the orchestra for the sake of his own career. But one condition at the Berlin Philharmonic appealed to Furtwängler enormously: the orchestra did not have to do double duty as an opera house band. Only two years before, he had declined the tempting offer to become chief of the Vienna Staatsoper despite his success there and the chance to accrue even more power. He saw the futility of lusting after power—the message of *Das Rheingold*, the first opera he ever conducted there—and for all the accusations to the contrary that rained upon him in the dark years to come, he was determined to avoid its trap.

His decision to give up Vienna was especially disappointing to its Philharmonic, which had grown into a world-class orchestra in the three short years Furtwängler led them as chief conductor. Furtwängler did not have the heart to inform them face-to-face that he was choosing Berlin. After a triumphant visit to England with the orchestra in May, Furtwängler returned to Berlin and shortly after sent the management of the Philharmonic a telegram informing them of his decision to give up Vienna. The Board of Directors was so shocked that they kept the telegram a secret. Alexander Wunderer, the orchestra's Executive Director, traveled from Vienna all the way to Heidelberg where Furtwängler had gone for a respite at the home of his mother. There, he tried to persuade Furtwängler to change his mind. His trip was in vain. Furtwängler promised that he would come to Vienna as often as possible as a guest conductor, but his first loyalty now was to Berlin. In a gesture of goodwill, he pledged to return every year to conduct the annual Nicolai concert—the Vienna Philharmonic's prestigious annual concert named after the composer and former Music Director of the orchestra. What is more, he would conduct without fee.[1]

Furtwängler's commitment to Berlin paid off for both conductor and orchestra, and he rapidly became known as the music director of Europe's leading orchestra—Vienna notwithstanding. Furtwängler also solidified his reputation as a musician of the first rank throughout the rest of Europe. He returned to England for a second time in 1927, taking the Berlin Philharmonic with him for three concerts—two in London and one in Manchester.[2] On this tour he again encountered Ernest Newman, the august critic for the London *Sunday Times*. Three years earlier, Furtwängler gave several concerts for the first time in England and Newman had rather liked his first concert but had decidedly mixed feelings about the second:

---

1. Otto Strasser, *Und dafür wird Man noch bezahlt*, (Munich) 1978, pp. 75f. Hereafter referred to as Strasser.
2. London, 2 December, Queens Hall. Weber: Overture to *Freischütz*. Brahms: Second Symphony. Strauss: *Till Eulenspiegel*. Wagner: *Tannhäuser* Overture. Manchester, 3 December, London, 4 December, Royal Albert Hall. Beethoven: First Symphony. Vaughan Williams: *Tallis Fantasia*. Tchaikovsky: Fifth Symphony.

We began to suspect that Furtwängler is a mannerist who has just one set of formulae, which he unconsciously imposes upon all the music he plays, what ever its period or whatever its genre.[3]

If Furtwängler followed his pattern of arguing over negative criticism, he almost certainly must have had a row with Newman. A year later, Newman happened to be in New York at the time Furtwängler made his debut with the New York Philharmonic. His dispatch to his paper on American orchestras sneered at Furtwängler's success while deprecating the American audiences who gave it to him:

> Of visiting conductors, I heard only Vladimir Golschmann . . . and Furtwängler, who, in his three or four concerts with the Philharmonic, had a great popular success. As he is the Apotheosis of the Obvious, the perfect example of the German Machine, this is readily understandable.[4]

And now, in 1927, Newman seemed to be doing an about-turn by going to extravagant lengths praising the Berlin Philharmonic in his column. While he felt the Berliners were no match for the orchestras he had heard recently in Philadelphia, Boston, and New York, he used the visiting Germans as a whip against local performance standards:

> When some of us used to keep reiterating that the best orchestral playing we now hear in London is no more than a good second-rate, we were frowned upon as unpatriotic disturbers of the public peace. Now at last the London public knows; and everyone who heard the Berlin people will henceforth judge the local playing by a new standard.[5]

He also used the shameful light the Berlin Philharmonic concerts put on British orchestras to advocate the formation of a permanent year-round symphonic ensemble—a vigorous and protracted campaign that ultimately produced the BBC Symphony Orchestra. But nowhere in Newman's lofty paeans to the Berliners was Furtwängler's name to be found.[6]

However hostile Newman's attitude toward Furtwängler may have been, and it remained consistently negative for the rest of his life,

3. 10 February 1924, p. 5.
4. 15 March 1925, p. 7.
5. 11 December 1927, p. 7.
6. Furtwängler returned to England with the Berlin Philharmonic almost every year until 1938 when he also took the Vienna Philharmonic on their first tour of Britain. The latter also became welcome visitors after the war, but Newman and other critics sometimes carped about a certain rhythmic vagueness with the Viennese when they played there under Furtwängler's direction.

his claims for the embarrassingly high standards purveyed by the visiting Germans were not exaggerated. On the night of the Berlin Philharmonic's first London appearance, a young man out of curiosity bought a ticket for their performance in Queen's Hall. His life was changed by Furtwängler's performance. Many years later, Sir Reginald Goodall (1901–1990) recalled, "The string playing! The way British string players went about it was a bit like this," he said, jerking his right hand rigidly back and forth across the strings of an unseen cello. "Very stiff and wooden. But Furtwängler made that string section— he made that whole *orchestra*—sound like nothing I had ever heard before."[7] Goodall was later to become one of the century's premier Wagner conductors and observed Furtwängler carefully over the years to prepare for his chance to show what he had learned from him. He did not get his first real opportunity until he was on the threshold of old age when he conducted *Die Meistersinger* with the Sadler's Wells Opera Company at the age of 67 in 1968.

Berlin was now rolling into the 1930s on the crest of a cultural wave never known before in Germany or, for that matter, Europe. These years were the cultural heyday of the Weimar Republic, and in a few short seasons Furtwängler had molded the orchestral gem he had inherited from Nikisch into the crowning jewel of the city's cultural coffers. Berlin and Paris were Europe's leading cities at the time, but Berlin possessed a musical life rivaled by no other metropolis. The entire Continent seemed to be attending an epic cotillion, and in both high and bourgeois culture German music provided the tunes and tempo for that ball. Few people had the slightest inkling that it all was soon to end.

For those few, however, the febrile creativity of Weimar was also charged with anxiety and an impending sense of doom. That insidious fear was articulated in many of the most significant works to emerge from this period. What is more, the men and women who made Weimar culture—intellectuals, academicians, even merchants and industrialists—were what historian Peter Gay has called "outsiders."[8] Poised precariously between the old monarchy they rejected and the new republic they regarded (and were regarded by) with suspicion, this group individually and collectively had influence but almost no real power. Worse, their influence was strongest outside Germany:

7. Conversation with the author, London, 27 September 1979. See also Shirakawa, "Reginald Goodall: Opera's Oldest Wunderkind," *Ovation*, 1981.
8. See Peter Gay, *Weimar Culture*, (New York) 1968; and *Freud, Jews, and Other Germans*, (New York) 1978.

Their influence was . . . more pervasive after than during the Weimar Republic. For while these men may have been at the heart of the Weimar spirit, they were not at the heart of public affairs; they met, cultivated, and sometimes influenced insiders without really becoming insiders themselves.[9]

Some of these outsiders gravitated toward the center of the most important developments in music during the inter-war period, and most of them were German or Austro-Hungarian. Since the turn of the century, all Europe had witnessed enormous changes in musical composition, but Germany and Austria hosted the widest and most radical of those progressions. Some composers, such as Richard Strauss, were determined to continue and amplify the traditions of romanticism that had flowered throughout the 19th century while others—Brahms, for example—sought to revive the character of music prevalent during and before the 18th century. Furtwängler as composer counted himself among the latter. Still others, like Béla Bartók, Ralph Vaughan Williams, and Carl Orff were preoccupied with integrating national and folk themes into their works. And yet another group of forward-looking composers found all existing forms of music either exhausted in their potential or too limiting for the sonic possibilities they now were hearing within their minds' ears.

The emergence of atonal music was perhaps the most significant and far-reaching of all these crosscurrents. It grew primarily out of German post-romanticism of the late 19th century. The music of this last great burst of tonality was characterized by huge splashes of rich, elaborate harmonies best exemplified by such works as Wagner's *Tristan* and Debussy's *La Mer*. The harmonic complexity of these works and those like them were already pointing toward a kind of music which avoided all the materials (harmony, rhythm, key, form, etc.) from which music had been shaped up to this time. While such music side-stepped traditional materials and tools, it did not altogether exclude them.

The father of this new branch of music was Arnold Schönberg (1874–1951). He preferred the more accurate term *pantonal* rather than *atonal* to describe his music, for while the school of music he was developing at the turn of the century avoided a so-called tonal center, he still used the 12 notes of the scale as the foundation of all his music. The manner in which he arranged those notes led listeners to describe it as "dissonant," the most frequently used term applied to this kind of form. Schönberg progressed from tonality to his evolving dodeca-

9. *Weimar Culture*, p. 43.

phonic system around 1902 and fully turned his back on tonality by 1908 in a series of piano pieces (op. 11) and the 15 songs he set to Stefan George's texts from *The Book of the Hanging Gardens*, op. 15.

The following year he composed a monodrama for soprano and large orchestra to a text by Marie Pappenheim and called it *Erwartung (Expectation)*. In it, he gave a theatrical and musical articulation of what the rubric Expressionism was all about. A woman meanders through a forest and is filled with grave forebodings about her lover. Before long, she finds that her worst apprehensions have come true, as she discovers his corpse along the path. But anxiety confirmed is not the end of her nightmare. Could she have killed him? Nothing in the synopsis nor the music is resolved. Even as the curtain falls, the situation has not been clarified. Neither has anything in the score; no repetitions, no thematic developments, none of the structural mechanisms that might give the listener-spectator some clue to resolution, to certainty, to catharsis. Although he completed the score—which lasts about 30 minutes—in 16 days, it was not produced until 1924 in Prague.

Furtwängler respected Schönberg's music and also championed many other "progressive" composers such as Hindemith, even though he felt their compositional bearings were based on technique rather than an intrinsic vitality and were leading them toward a cul-de-sac:

> Previously, technique was something positive, because it only ran parallel to what it had to express. Since it has become an end in itself, since it has become learnable, something—mind you—which was not the case before, since then it has moved further and further away from its meaning. In this Hindemith continues on from Strauss. The real problem of our time is therefore how to reunite it with content. Brahms pioneering in this. And now it becomes apparent that there is yet another technique of which today's world is no longer aware, which is infinitely more difficult. The difference between these two concepts of technique contains everything of any importance that today's world should and does not know.
>
> *Notebooks, 1929, p. 30*

Late in his life, Furtwängler used the same metaphor of the forest developed in *Erwartung* to describe his view of the difference between tonal and atonal music. It appears in a transcript of conversations with the musicologist Walter Abendroth published in English as *Concerning Music*:[10]

---

10. Translation by L. J. Lawrence, (London) 1953. Originally published as *Gespräche über Musik*, (Zürich) 1948.

> . . . if we let ourselves be guided by the atonal musician we walk as it were through a dense forest. The strangest flowers and plants attract our attention by the side of the path. But we do not know where we are going nor whence we have come. The listener is seized by a feeling of being lost, of being at the mercy of the forces of primeval existence. It seems as though the atonal musician had not paid attention to the listener as an independent personality: the listener is faced with an all-powerful world of chaos. But of course it must be admitted that this strikes a chord in the apprehensions of modern man! *p. 90*

Here, of course, Furtwängler is also describing the very nature of Expressionism. The term was first used in connection with painting, but it worked well enough to refer to most of the works of art in Europe between the world wars. While art works described as *impressionistic* strove to articulate the fragility of existence through showing people, objects and scenes caught in an inkling of time, Expressionism delved into the inner world, communicating the twilight area of experience. The essence of Expressionism is man adrift in a rootless world, alienated, and defenseless before potentially hostile forces. Such an individual is prone to psychological conflict, trauma, anxiety. He or she is at the mercy of both internal and external irrational drives and conditions. Such persons can feel instinctively suspicious of societal mores and even behave defiantly against them. Furtwängler intuitively understood the nature of this kind of music, but he had little time to ponder how its implications might affect him personally. It was all just as well perhaps. Before long, he too would come to experience in nightmarish proportions the very problems besetting this tormented alienated individual to which Expressionism came to give a voice and idiom.

Furtwängler divided his time in Berlin between the Philharmonic and the Staatsoper, making his operatic debut there on 12 November 1931, conducting the Berlin premiere of *Das Herz* by Hans Pfitzner, his old boss during his apprenticeship at Strasbourg. His appearance at Berlin's first opera house came four months after a long and virulent internecine battle shrank the number of major opera houses in Berlin from three to two. The Kroll was Berlin's progressive opera house and closed after a brief but glorious life under the musical leadership of Otto Klemperer.[11] The battle pitted the Kroll against the Prussian

---

11. See Heyworth, *Otto Klemperer: His Life and Times,* for an excellent account of Klemperer's stormy but dazzling career at the Kroll, pp. 234–378. Rockwell also gives an heuristic survey of the politics that conspired to destroy the Kroll: pp. 248f. Hans J. Reichardt's . . . *Bei Kroll 1844 bis 1957,* (Berlin) 1988, pp. 85–116, offers an informative survey of the Kroll's greatest period—1927–1931—and contains handsomely produced visual material.

Ministry of Culture. Growing reactionary forces within that body discerned the very embodiment of un-German evil in the Kroll, its "modern" productions and works, and its largely left-leaning Jewish staff. But the Kroll was not merely the victim of overwhelming attacks from the right. It failed because the Ministry could not implement its progressive policies with the required combination of skilled management, aggressive education, and disciplined administration. Ultimately, the Kroll's budget was reduced and finally cut, and the company ceased operating on 3 July 1931 with a performance of *Figaro* under Fritz Zweig in which the benign sadness of the work overwhelmed the performance.[12]

For once, Furtwängler was not at the center of a raging controversy. His debut at the Staatsoper, in fact, was a comparatively tepid affair. Pfitzner staged the work himself in an unremarkable production designed by Lothar Schenck von Trapp.[13] The cast included a stellar assembly: Delia Reinhardt, Walther Grossmann, Fritz Soot, Charles Kullman, and in a small part a new mezzo-soprano named Margarete Klose, who would work time and again with Furtwängler to the end of his life. The conservative, tonal, and heartless work was received coolly, but Furtwängler garnered unanimous praise for making it more than the sum of its parts. Among the Berlin critics, Alfred Einstein, the eminent musicologist who was music critic of the *Berliner Tageblatt* at the time (1927–1935), singled out Furtwängler's enhancement of a largely lackluster evening:[14]

12. The last year of the Kroll was especially bitter for Klemperer. He found himself the target of an investigation for corruption and had to defend himself before a committee at the Prussian Ministry of Culture. As pressure mounted to close the Kroll, he found that Tietjen, who by now was building his empire as Intendant of all Prussian theaters, would not support him. That neither surprised nor fazed him. But he thought he could count on Leo Kestenberg. Kestenberg not only diminished his own role in getting the Kroll started during his testimony, but even denied that he tried to advance modern music during his tenure as referent. (See Rockwell, p. 228.) This episode of bald prevarication set a rift between Klemperer and Kestenberg that was to last until long after World War II. Klemperer, who was over 6' 4" and no weakling, was severely beaten up by Nazi Brownshirts in broad daylight while he was walking through the Tiergarten near the Kroll early in 1932. After the Nazi takeover the following year, he fled to Paris and later to the United States. Kestenberg "retired" under severe pressure in December 1932. By May 1933 he was in Prague. He later became General Manager of the Palestine Philharmonic, the precursor of the Israel Philharmonic.

13. *Das Herz* was eagerly awaited as the first stage work he composed after his enormously successful *Palestrina* in 1917. In fact, Pfitzner was possibly the most revered contemporary composer in Germany after Richard Strauss at the time. The work was given a double world premiere. It was presented for the first time on the same night in both Berlin and Munich. Pfitzner attended the Munich premiere, conducted by Hans Knappertsbusch with Heinrich Rehkemper in the leading role. This performance also received unenthusiastic responses from the audience and critics.

14. Einstein emigrated to America after the Nazis took power. He led a successful career as a musicologist, publishing several books in English.

He drew a dramatic impact from the score with the orchestra, a transparent beauty at once palpable but fantastic; he discovered color itself amidst the gray.[15]

The critic for the *Berliner Morgenpost* was equally enthusiastic about Furtwängler:

The musical part of the evening was supervised by Wilhelm Furtwängler; no one knows how to make this music so clear and bold, so intense and warm, as he can.[16]

Furtwängler may have been gone from America, but he was not entirely forgotten.[17] Geraldine de Courcy, the German correspondent for *Musical America*, concluded:

A further element of element of distinction surrounding this performance was the presence of Furtwängler at the conductor's desk—his first appearance in this opera house. Pfitzner might have sought to the proverbial four winds to have found a more inspired and sympathetic interpreter of his work . . . Musically, this was a gorgeous production.[18]

Furtwängler's successful debut promised greater involvement with the Staatsoper, an affiliation that gave every promise of a great future at the Weimar Republic's leading opera house. While he grew from strength to strength in performing the great romantic German works of Wagner, Mendelssohn, Schumann, and his beloved Beethoven, he also conducted Berlioz, Tchaikovsky, Franck, Ravel, Prokofiev, Miaskovsky, Sibelius, and the American composer Ernest Schelling. He was realizing his potential as a musician while becoming at the same time the embodiment of the "German way" of performing music. Though he hardly knew it, Furtwängler was now the maestro who would open Germany's ears to the music of the world. But more importantly, he would open Germany's ears in the years to come to her innermost being.

His way with music, however, did not enrapture some of his eminent colleagues the way it hypnotized his audiences. The great cellist Gregor Piatigorsky was Furtwängler's first principal cellist at Berlin until 1929. Furtwängler discovered him playing in a cafe and imme-

---

15. 13 November 1931.
16. 13 November 1931.
17. Herbert Peyser covered the opening for the *New York Times*, carrying on a lengthy survey of the work. But for some reason he mentioned neither Furtwängler nor the singers in his story; 29 November 1931, VII, p. 9.
18. 10 December 1931.

diately offered him a job. In his memoirs, he recalls Furtwängler's
encounter with Sergei Rachmaninoff during the rehearsals for the Berlin premiere of the great virtuoso composer's Third Piano Concerto in
1929. Rachmaninoff had been sitting in the front row of the hall while
Furtwängler rehearsed an orchestral piece . . .

> [Rachmaninoff] rose. Lean and very tall, he walked to the stage. Not pay-
> ing attention to Furtwängler, who was rehearsing a symphony, Rachma-
> ninoff sat down at the piano, looked at his watch, and thunderously
> struck a few chords. Perplexed, Furtwängler stopped. He looked at Rach-
> maninoff, who showed his watch and said, "My rehearsal time was ten-
> thirty."
> With no further exchange the rehearsal of the concerto commenced.
> After five minutes or so, Rachmaninoff walked to the conductor's stand
> and began to conduct. The orchestra had two conductors—Furtwängler,
> bewildered, and Rachmaninoff, swearing in Russian. Even after he
> returned to the piano the tension held on until the end of the long and
> unpleasant rehearsal. Still at odds at the concert, the two extraordinary
> artists nevertheless brought forth an exciting performance of a peculiar
> unity.[19]

But a peculiar disunity and bitterness in another area of Furtwängler's ever burgeoning career was more immediately at hand. In 1930
Furtwängler was appointed Music Director of the Bayreuth Festival.
Ever since 1876, when Richard Wagner opened the Festival in a small
north Bavarian town as a shrine to his works and himself, it had been
a citadel of German culture. With the exception of the years during
World War I, Wagner's descendants presented a festival of Wagner's
works nearly every summer, frequently at great personal sacrifice and
hardship.[20] For years, Karl Muck was the reigning conductor of the
Festival, though Siegfried Wagner—the composer's only son—was
its musical director. Muck's relationship with Winifred Wagner,
Wagner's daughter-in-law and executrix of the Festival, began to deteriorate when she invited Toscanini to conduct there.

Matters worsened when Cosima Wagner, the infirm widow of
Wagner, died in April of 1930. In August, Siegfried collapsed and died
during a rehearsal of *Die Götterdämmerung*, leaving his widow with
a debt-laden Festival, a white elephant of an opera house, and two egomaniacal conductors who regarded each other with all the amiability
of rabid pit bulls. Possibly in a move to placate Muck, Winifred sought
to bring Furtwängler to Bayreuth as its new music director. Muck and

19. *Cellist*, (New York) 1965, p. 151.
20. See Friedelind Wagner and Page Cooper, *Heritage of Fire*, (New York) 1945, for
a personal account of the hard times the Wagner family underwent before 1933.

Furtwängler got along well. While Muck hated Toscanini, Furtwängler at least respected Toscanini. While he had by no means forgotten
his humiliating encounter with the Toscanini faction in New York
three years earlier, and found his approach to music inimical to his
own, he never—at least up to that point—bore any personal enmity
toward the old man. Winifred felt that surely Furtwängler would be a
welcome ameliorating influence. Among the blandishments she
offered him for his services were a car and chauffeur (though this may
have been a safety measure because Furtwängler was a dangerously
bad driver), and a saddle horse with its own stable boy.[21] The ploy
failed. Muck resigned at the end of the Festival in 1930, after learning
that Toscanini had been invited to return. And Toscanini did return,
at least for a moment.

While Furtwängler and Toscanini are frequently said to have
detested each other, that is not quite the case. They were both strong
personalities with their own ways of going about making music. It
was only after 1936 that Toscanini took a personal dislike to Furtwängler, and we will see why a bit later. Throughout his life, though,
Toscanini begrudgingly admitted the only living conductor worthy of
competing with him was Furtwängler. Furtwängler, on the other
hand, did not care for Toscanini on purely musical grounds. He had
heard Toscanini on a number of occasions in New York, Milan, and
Zurich, and in 1930, after a series of concerts Toscanini gave with the
New York Philharmonic in Berlin, he wrote a protracted meditation
on Toscanini's art in his *Notebooks*. He makes a fairly surgical analysis of the way Toscanini performed each piece, and ultimately comes
to some devastating but acutely perceptive conclusions:

> In contrast to, say Nikisch, [Toscanini] has no innate manual talent, and
> what he does have has been fought for and worked upon. But certain strik-
> ing shortcomings have remained; above all the enormous waste of space
> in the forte. The size of his beat in the f is such that it makes any differ-
> entiation impossible. As a result, these tuttis are all the same, they sound
> noisy and are always the same volume, and the conductor's ability to
> bring out differences within the forte, in the lower or middle range or
> even in important major parts, is quite minimal.
>
> I do not hold with taking the conductor all too seriously as a person.
> It is of no consequence whether or not he is disciplined, whether or not
> he looks good. But I must acknowledge his importance, not because he is
> playing such a role today, but because the lives of many masterpieces
> absolutely depend on him.
>
> Toscanini believes what he says, that he plays, as far as possible, lit-

---

21. Op. cit., p. 62.

erally and in a disciplined manner—not superior and not rational—but still himself and the orchestra.

His greatness lies in his character. This helps him in the eyes of the world, but it does not, unfortunately, help art. One can say with certainty that if he were a greater artist, if he had deeper insights, a livelier imagination, greater warmth and devotion to the work, he would not have become so disciplined. And this is why his success is disastrous.

Those of us who hold great music close to our hearts can never replace true artists with prima donnas and others who are just as disciplined, even if they appear in the sheep's clothing of literal rendering. The view, previously held unconsciously in Germany, that inspiration and understanding in art are more important than discipline and autocratic behavior, is still correct. *Notebooks, pp. 45–46*

The manner in which Furtwängler arrived at the little municipality of Bayreuth about 60 miles west of the Czechoslovakian border turned out to be an omen of his fortunes there. He had taken up flying during the 1920s and was quite an able pilot. He decided to fly to Bayreuth from Berlin, but the plane developed engine trouble, and he narrowly escaped with his life. He arrived at the first rehearsal late. The fact was delectably reported in all the newspapers, for the tardiness of Bayreuth's new music director at his first rehearsal carried as much news value to Germans as news of the Pope being late for Easter Morning mass surely would carry anywhere else.

The Festival repertory for 1931 consisted of the annual cycles of the *Ring* conducted by Karl Elmendorff, *Tannhäuser* led by Toscanini, and *Tristan und Isolde* under Furtwängler. As rehearsals for the six operas wore on, Furtwängler found Bayreuth an entrenched and difficult place to explore his own ideas about how the Wagnerian tradition should be carried on. In fact, he found its artistic standards Baroque and its politics Byzantine. Much of the latter was fanned by Heinz Tietjen, who was fast becoming perhaps the most powerful man in the performing arts in Germany.

Tietjen was virtually the emperor of theater and music in northern Germany from 1928 until the mid-1950s. By 1930 he was artistic and business director of all the Prussian State Theaters. He was also the Intendant of the Berlin Staatsoper. While any theatrical professional—actor, singer, stage director, lighting designer, set decorator and most musicians—might be able to work in Berlin or in Prussia without his approval, no one in any of these professions could perform anywhere in northern Germany if Tietjen expressed his disapproval. Only a few individuals like Furtwängler were beyond his grip, and even Furtwängler was to have his share of difficulties caused by Tietjen.

Born in Tangier to British and German parents, Tietjen grew up in Turkey, England, Africa, India, and South America. Clever and extremely skilled at diplomacy, the duplicitous world of the performing arts—especially opera—suited him perfectly. He started off his career in Berlin on the business and policy-making side of the footlights and dabbled in music criticism. In the 1920s, he began to stage operas. After 1930 he added opera conducting to his vast array of talents. He was a jack of every conceivable trade and a supreme master at anything devious. Some light on this enigmatic and brilliantly capable figure has been cast by none less than Wagner's granddaughter Friedelind:

> This small, dark little man with the thick spectacles was one of the most sinister and astonishing of all the creatures who scrambled to hold their power . . . He never appeared in public. Indeed, if he had he was so insignificant looking that he wouldn't have been noticed. His fellow artists paraphrased the title of a book then popular in Germany, Did Christ Ever Live? and asked each other "Did Tietjen Ever Live?" In my opinion, his business abilities far outstripped his conductorship.[22]

Following the death of Siegfried Wagner, Tietjen became indispensable to his vulnerable widow, and Friedelind developed a marked distaste both for him and for Furtwängler:

> In no time at all Tietjen had Mother in his pocket and the entire staff of the festival by the ears. Furtwängler was an easy prey because the conductor was weak and indecisive; he listened to the advice of everybody, distrusted everybody including himself and fell prey to every intrigue. Temperamentally, he was an irritant to Mother who was a forthright person and couldn't understand people with devious personalities.
>
> "He's like a sponge," she once said. "Whenever you try to get a firm hold of him he can squeeze himself in a dozen different directions."
>
> Tietjen fanned this dislike into guerrilla warfare by telling Mother Furtwängler's remarks about her and carrying Mother's comments to Furtwängler. Each had perfect confidence in Tietjen and considered him a true friend and adviser. Furtwängler who was always sulking, hesitant and difficult, became suspicious of Mother and convinced that she disliked him violently. As a consequence there was anything but a happy atmosphere about them.[23]

22. Wagner and Cooper, *Heritage of Fire*, (New York) 1945, p. 63. This highly controversial book was also published in England under the title *The Royal Family of Bayreuth.* Its contents so infuriated the Wagner family that its sale was forbidden in Bayreuth. Hereafter referred to as F. Wagner. All citations refer to the American version *Heritage of Fire.*
23. F. Wagner, p. 64.

Tietjen evidently did not stop there. He fanned the natural distrust between Toscanini and Furtwängler too. But Toscanini in turn loathed Tietjen, and this unctuous creature had less luck in manipulating him.

Furtwängler opened this festival of discontent, making a dazzling debut with *Tristan und Isolde* on 23 July. On paper at least, the cast was one of the finest available at the time: the famed Swedish soprano Nanny Larsen-Todsen as Isolde, Lauritz Melchior and Gotthelf Pistor alternating as Tristan, Anny Helm singing Brangaene, Joseph Manowarda as King Mark, and Kurwenal sung by Rudolf Bockelmann. The event was covered by the international press, and Herbert F. Peyser reviewed it for the *New York Times* and referred to Furtwängler in glowing terms:

> But if Furtwängler's first act was great and if his third act was greater, it was even more by his second that his performance enscrolled itself on Baireuth's [sic] records in characters of flame. I recall no presentation of this act—neither Hertz's nor Mahler's nor Toscanini's nor Muck's—which has excelled the present one in soaring ecstasy of lyric mood, in majesty of far-flung line and in the progressive luxuriance of its unfoldment . . . In the utmost trait of subtlety was always implicit the vast imperative sweep of Wagner's architecture, and an unfailing rectitude in the relation of the part to the whole.

Peyser and other critics were not nearly as pleased with the singers. Larsen-Todsen's voice was in a state of precipitous decline at this point in her career, and the press exerted no effort ignoring the fact.[24] Peyser was also diffident about Melchior:

> The Tristan of the occasion was Mr. Melchior about whose enamored knight it hardly behooves me to particularize at this juncture. That he was better in the last act than in the first or second is neither here nor there.[25]

Melchior was used to singing under Toscanini, who fussed obsessively over singers, and he felt neglected by Furtwängler, who, he felt, paid too much attention to orchestral details at his expense.[26] Furtwängler, on the other hand, felt Melchior paid too much attention to

24. Larsen Todsen began her career as a principal singer in 1906 and started taking on Wagner roles around 1922. She sang successfully at the Metropolitan Opera between 1925 and 1927. She never sang at Bayreuth again after 1931.

25. 1 August 1931.

26. Shirlee Emmons, *Tristanissimo*, (New York) 1990, pp. 109–111. See note below.

himself and not enough to the music.[27] He could not abide Melchior's frequent lapses of attention when the Danish Bear sang with knuckle-whitening disregard for pitch (more often flat than sharp) and all but made up the music as he went along.[28] There were even reports that Melchior demanded and got certain cuts in the score that were sanctioned in some other opera houses—notably the Metropolitan—but unheard of at Wagner's shrine. To this day, those unfounded rumors have been taken as fact, though Friedelind Wagner scoffs at the idea.[29]

Melchior's biggest dissatisfaction, however, was not with Furt-wängler but with the management of Bayreuth.[30] The Festival had changed radically for him in the year since the death of Cosima and Siegfried, and he felt oddly out of place. He had been singing at Bay-reuth since 1924, and he had always been adored and coddled by Sieg-fried, but Wagner's only son was gone now. It was time for him to move on, and 1931 turned out to be his last year there. To make his summer especially vexing, a nasty anti-Melchior faction was starting to fester, replete with the preposterous ethnic slur that the Viking tenor was non-Aryan.[31] In actual fact, though, Melchior simply did not need Bayreuth anymore. He had scored an enormous success as Tristan at the Metropolitan in 1929, and he realized now that he would never look back. Tempting offers at ever-increasing fees were pouring in from around the world. Although he never had the kind of warm rapport with Furtwängler that he had with Toscanini, Melchior sang with him again on several notable occasions after his departure from Bayreuth.

Excerpts from the opening night performance of *Tristan und Isolde* were broadcast and recorded, but they have presumably been lost. Fragments of Act I from a later performance with Gotthelf Pistor singing Tristan, however, give a faint but tantalizing clue to what Furtwängler's interpretation was like at that point in his career.[32]

27. Elisabeth Furtwängler, personal conversation with the author, 4 December 1989.

28. Some broadcasts and pirated recordings of Melchior at the Metropolitan during the 1930s and '40s give shudder-provoking evidence of these habits.

29. Emmons has been among the credible writers to further this rumor in her "authorized" biography of Melchior *Tristanissimo!* p. 111. However, she acknowledges some critics find the report of an abbreviated *Tristan* at that or any Bayreuth Festival unlikely. In fact, it is nothing short of sheer rubbish as far as the German critic Wolf Rosenberg is concerned: "Such absurd claims should be cited only if the case has been researched and proof can be produced." See "Widerrede aus gegebene Anlass." *N-Z für Musik,* June 1987, p. 9. Hereafter referred to as Rosenberg. Perhaps the final word on the subject comes from Friedelind Wagner, who attended those performances. "The whole business of cuts for that *Tristan* is nonsense. Nobody ever got a cut at Bayreuth. If by some chance Melchior got one, everybody—*everybody* would have heard about it." Personal conversation with the author, Mainz, 6 October 1990.

30. Geissmar, p. 50.

31. Rosenberg, p. 9.

These bits and pieces also constitute the earliest known evidence of Furtwängler in live performance. The tempo is about the same as his Berlin performances in 1947, though a tad slower than the studio recording he was to make for HMV in 1952. The orchestral rush at Kurvenal's announcement of land sighted hints at the "imperative sweep" Peyser reported in his review. Larsen-Todsen's voice is indeed in precarious estate. She husbands her resources in the Narrative and Curse and appears uncertain of pitch in her recriminatory exchange with Tristan, wedging from beneath into notes at the top of the staff (above F).

Amid the Byzantine political atmosphere of back-biting and duplicity infecting the Festival, a special memorial concert for Siegfried Wagner was scheduled for August 4th. Furtwängler and Toscanini were to share the program, Toscanini opening the evening with Liszt's *A Faust Overture*, and Furtwängler closing the concert with the *Eroica*.[33] With good reason, Toscanini felt that Furtwängler was getting the lion's share of the program, and that perception kept fueling Toscanini's discontent all summer. Ever since he arrived for the Festival, Toscanini had been brooding, angry about the way Winifred was handling its affairs and taking no measures to conceal his loathing for the unctuous Tietjen. He respected Furtwängler and their relations at this time appear to have been cordial. But what he felt about Berta Geissmar's innovative weekly press conferences for Furtwängler may never be known.[34] He was also in excruciating pain.

"Toscanini was suffering the horrors of the damned that summer," recalls Friedelind Wagner. "He had a terrible case of bursitis in his right shoulder. When the pain got too much for him, he began conducting with his left hand. The torture made him all the more irritable, and I remember him being almost in tears with pain. Everything annoyed him—*everything*."[35]

His fury eventually came to a head at the first rehearsal for the memorial concert. In the middle of it, he began shouting in Italian, broke his baton, and left. He was livid because he had expected to rehearse the orchestra with no visitors sitting in the hall. Instead, the house was filled with singers, chorus, and staff members. Furtwängler sent Berta Geissmar after him, but the maestro was gone, never to return to Bayreuth. The incident was especially embarrassing for the Festival. Furtwängler finished the rehearsal and conducted Toscani-

32. Excerpts from Act I, recorded 18 August 1931. LP transfer: Danacord DACO 131–3 (1983).
33. F. Wagner, p. 65f.
34. Nor are Furtwängler's reactions recorded.
35. Personal conversation with the author, Mainz, 6 October 1990.

ni's portion of the concert in addition to the *Eroica*. Friedelind recalls the evening:

> In spite of the absence of Toscanini the concert was memorable. Furt-wängler outdid himself and the women in the audience fairly swooned with ecstasy; even Daniela [Cosima's daughter from her first marriage to the conductor Hans von Bülow] was swept away by the warmth and color of his conducting and Daniela fought her way to the podium to congrat-ulate him. Later at supper, when he came down the stairs from the bal-cony, his head on top of the long neck darting this way and that, one could hear a sigh sweep over the place and a rustling as the women gathered about him, thick as bees at a honeycomb.[36]

For all the adulation and ballyhoo Bayreuth-style, Furtwängler ulti-mately got fed up too, especially with Winifred's incessant interfer-ence on musical and artistic matters he felt to be his province. Tietjen fueled the disagreements although neither Winifred nor Furtwängler realized how he was manipulating them; Winifred because she was completely captivated with Tietjen, Furtwängler because he was beset with paranoia about Winifred and too naive to see through Tietjen. It was widely reported that Winifred and Tietjen became lovers. At the end of the summer Furtwängler resigned as music director, leaving the way open for Tietjen to accrue even more power. But it was not the last time he would see Bayreuth. Nor would it be the last time he would have cause to regret conducting there.

While the Weimar period was a heady time for artists, there was also a good deal of mediocrity and dross—certainly as much as there was in any other "golden" age. What is more, not all Germans were san-guine about the most enduring developments in the arts at that time. There were riots after performances of many plays, notably Kurt Weill's *Mahagonny*, and even such time-honored older works as *Dan-ton's Death* by Georg Büchner had to be removed from repertories of leading theater companies in the interests of public safety. The rise of German chauvinism which had proliferated steadily since the end of the Great War brought about a straight-laced moral consciousness in the face of increasingly relaxed social and sexual mores. The Ger-man public flocked to mindless epics about heroes of the German past such as Frederick the Great. Much of the new music was labeled "dec-adent," and hostility toward modern music and its atonal proclivities grew to hysterical proportions as Weimar careened toward its collapse in 1932. Furtwängler was personally leery about the direction new

36. F. Wagner, p. 67.

music was taking, but he played his contemporaries' works frequently all the same.

> [The conductor] carries on his shoulders a greater burden of responsibility than ever before; for there is no longer the great creator who shapes the style of the age, but the conductor who must shape the style of individual works from within themselves, from within these alien works. He is not carried by the age, rather he must generally help to carry the age. This explains how important the conductor is, and also how rare he is today. Indeed these two things are necessarily connected. It also explains the malformations: the boundless vanity, the innumerable desperate attempts to create effects through charlatanism.
>
> *Notebooks, 1925, p. 25*

Charlatanism, of course, was only a cultural skin disease. He was far more worried about the cultural blood disease in which performing music was becoming mere entertainment:

> Where production ceases to be reflected unambiguously and compellingly as the focus of musical life of the age, otherwise unimportant things take on significance. Here then is the source of today's ridiculous personality cult, of conductors of "genius," who turn up as supermen of the conductor's desk, either "obsessed" or "suggestive" or "objective," either as animal tamers and trainers or as male cocottes, who in any case appear infinitely important to themselves and the audience.
>
> *Notebooks, 1929, p. 25*

Someone had to make an effective example as a viable alternative to these trends, and he was determined to embody the principles against them:

> In music in Germany, we have to defend the greatest concert tradition that a people ever possessed. We have more important things to do than take part in ridiculous sports competitions.   *Notebooks, 1929, p. 26*

Furtwängler here was not speaking as an effete aesthete, for he was a decent sportsman himself. Rather, he was making a distinction between two kinds of cultural strength. For him, the maintenance of Germany's artistic achievements was infinitely more important than its vain spectacles of athletic machismo.

Two years later, in an essay entitled "The Power of Music," he worried whether music would "survive as a necessity, as an unquestionable need, as a natural expression of modern man."[37] He worried

---

37. Published in *Ton und Wort*, 10th ed., (Wiesbaden) 1982, pp. 33–39.

equally as much that the question "has been discussed endlessly in such a way that it may as well be about politics rather than art."[38] But it did not stop him from finding technology as yet another force contributing to this sinister erosion:

> That our concert life is dangerously vulnerable cannot be denied. One could indeed say that at the present time all the branches of cultural life are exposed to the same shrinking process, one in which music is being especially threatened through mechanical music reproduction, through recordings and radio. One does not know if it is more the cause or the consequence of the general and considerable deterioration of musical interest and understanding. But this erosion, this weakening of musical experience and integration is our most pressing concern, not the threat of mechanical music.
> *Notebooks, p. 34*

Furtwängler was hardly religious in a conventional sense, but if there was a God, His kingdom lay in the realm of music. And the conservation and, more importantly, the communication of music and the musical tradition Furtwängler had inherited from the Titans before him became his tacit holy mission, now and for the rest of his life. He had been blessed with musical gifts, and he had decided to become a composer, a creator, an artist who would bring a greater and more recondite reality into being from that realm. But as the practicalities of living in an industrialized civilization pushed him into conducting, he quickly grasped that it, too, was a creative activity. So, he was twice blessed. But be it through composition or conducting, there was a price to pay for that Promethean instinct, for that need to bring the fires of aural imagination from unearthly regions to the here-and-now. If he saw himself as the child of Prometheus, though, he had yet no notion what would be exacted from him for warming humanity with that fire during the cold cruel days to come. And if he fancied himself as a son of Orpheus—the progenitor of all communicators, no imagination could possibly conjure up the savagery of the monsters he soon would attempt to soothe.

---

38. *Ton und Wort*, p. 33.

7

Weimar and the Third Reich

The doomsayers say it was inevitable. Others insist the National Socialist movement was a grotesque aberration of German and world history that could have been avoided. Some saw it coming and left Germany. Most remained and flowed with the tide. Some chose either not to see it coming or were not able to see the specter of Nazism looming ever more menacingly across the German landscape in the decade that followed World War I. When it did come, naive as that may seem in retrospect, a few of those who remained behind dared to try as they might to do something about it.

Until 1932 the National Socialists were not taken seriously if they were noticed at all. But the fringes of political lunacy had come into the open throughout the 1920s largely because Germans had been embittered by the punitive terms of the Treaty of Versailles at the end of World War I. Most Germans felt they had never lost the war on the battlefield, and they were convinced, perhaps rightly, that the war was lost at the hands of their own duplicitous politicians. Rightly or wrongly, they were in a bellicose mood. Throughout the 1920s their bitterness was exacerbated by an unstable economy and an ever widening belief that the Jews were at the root of all their woes. The decade was also the most radical period in Germany's shift from an authoritarian form of government in the 19th century to a democratic one in the 20th. In the absence of a paternal figure to provide leadership and continuity, the concept of the Fatherland, a Führer—leader—and a

Germany free of pollutive "impurities" loomed ever larger in the national imagination. It was an idea Hitler and the six other original members of the National Socialist Party seized upon from their very beginnings in 1920, and they worked assiduously throughout the decade to become the political embodiment of that concept.[1]

Their method was fairly simple. They sowed dissent at every level of the social structure, especially among the poor, the dispossessed, the young and the intellectuals at universities. Their efforts were speeded up by the Wall Street crash of 1929, which had devastating consequences throughout the world. The effects of the world-wide Depression were not immediately as shattering to Germany as they were to America, but the impact of this severe economic downturn eventually was more dramatic. Between the autumns of 1929 and

1. I make no pretense at defining the myriad complexities of Germany as it fell heir to the hell that possessed it from 1933 to 1945. I am merely trying to provide a framework for the situation in which Furtwängler and other artists and intellectuals found themselves at that time. It may be useful, however, to note here that historians tend to approach the Third Reich from two broad and differing perspectives as this period slips further into the distance. Those who see the Third Reich as the outcome of conflicting crosscurrents in German politics, culture, and social development fall into one group. To borrow a term normally applied to grammar, these scholars take a "diachronic" view of this period. Their approach casts Hitler within a broad historical panorama wherein his importance varies in significance—depending on the scholar. Generally, however, Hitler is considered less crucial than the swirl of circumstances and the combined impact of other key figures during this period. The other group regards Hitler as the progenitor and nucleus of what became the Third Reich. To use the corresponding term usually applied to grammar, these historians have a "synchronic" outlook on the Nazis. To oversimplify, Hitler was the Third Reich as far as these scholars are concerned. They interpret *Mein Kampf* not as a mere manifesto but as a blueprint for the rise and establishment of the Nazi dictatorship. Some even see in this book the road map of Hitler's downfall. Both views are the subject of intense ongoing debate, and many historians try to merge the two approaches. It is not my purpose to discuss the merits or flaws of their views, much less to take sides. Both views are singularly disturbing: the diachronic view because it posits a grand and determinist scheme of events in which a peculiar logic, perhaps of divine origin, appears to play a crucial part; the synchronic view because it imputes to the collective human psyche a perverse tolerance, even a grotesque need, to confer divine mystique on a monster capable of compelling millions to enact his heinous will through that mystique. I am particularly indebted for the compressed view of Germany I am presenting here to several superb works on Germany in the first half of the 20th century. Among them: Richard Grunberger, *The Twelve-Year Reich*, (New York) 1971, hereafter referred to as Grunberger; Walter Laqueur, *Weimar: A Cultural History*, (New York) 1974; Peter Gay, *Weimar Culture: The Outsider as Insider*, (New York) 1968; S. William Halprin, *Germany Tried Democracy: A Political History of the Reich from 1918 to 1933*, (New York) 1946 and 1965; Alex de Jonge, *The Weimar Chronicle: Prelude to Hitler*, (London and New York) 1978; Henry Pachter, *Weimar Etudes*, (New York) 1982; Fred K. Prieberg, *Musik und Politik im N-S Staat*, (Frankfurt) 1982; Josef Wulf, *Kultur im dritten Reich*, five volumes, (Frankfurt & Berlin) 1989; *Musik und Musikpolitik im faschistischen Deutschland*, Hanns-Werner Heister and Hans Günther Klein, eds., (Frankfurt) 1984; Michael Meyer, *Politics and Music in the Third Reich*, (Bern) 1991; George L. Mosse, *The Crisis of German Ideology*, (New York) 1964 and 1981, *Nazi Culture*, (New York) 1966 and 1981, and *Fallen Soldiers*, (New York) 1990.

1932, unemployment skyrocketed from 1.3 million to 5.1 million. The pervasive lack of jobs, cash, and long-term credit was aggravated by the constant presence of inflation and the nerve-shattering apparition of a giant industrial machine grinding to a virtual standstill.

This fatal combination of circumstances quickly enabled the Nazi propaganda machine to sell its promise of a productive, autonomous Germany free of decadent and seditious influences. In 1930 one year after the Wall Street crash, Nazi representation in the Reichstag—the German parliament—zoomed from 12 to 107. While the anti-Semitic rantings the Nazis used to rally the populace might have gone ignored in other times or places, a large and powerful body of the electorate was now listening to what they had to say. They consisted of middle- and lower-middle-class people, the *petit bourgeois* for whom home, hearth, and security were the only objectives of life. With their savings—the means to achieving their life goals—wiped out by inflation, they were now panic-stricken. Worst of all, jobless white-collar workers who still had some savings seized vacancies that had previously been held by lower-class workers. The "common man's" resentment at being cut off from his access to a livelihood reached seething proportions. A mood of *Endsituation* (final situation) prevailed. The nation was on the brink of either total chaos or some kind of conversion, and the likes of either could not be imagined. *Das Volk*, as Hitler engagingly called those fellow Germans whose problems he so cared about, were ready for a change, and it was the latchword he used over and over to capture the imagination of Germans who were out of work, out of money, and out of patience.

The idea of the German people as a separate and pure entity—*a Volk*—was and even today remains a leitmotif as persistent and inexorable as the Fate motif in Wagner's *Ring*, and Wagner harped on it throughout his "Volk" masterpiece *Die Meistersinger von Nürnberg* (1868). When the concept came into being may never be known, but it was Johann Gottfried Herder (1744–1803) who not merely radicalized the so-called German "Folk Soul" *(Volkseele)* as an absolute value, unceasing and unchanging, but cast it as a concept always in danger of being destroyed or altered beyond recognition by outside, alien, non-German forces.[2]

The characters in all of Wagner's major works, for example, are constantly seeking some form of identity or some means of validating identity in the midst of a hostile and chaotic universe. In *Die Wal-*

2. Mosse gives an excellent account of the development of Volkish thought in several books, most notably *Nazi Culture*, (New York) 1970, and *Germans and Jews*, (Detroit) 1987.

küre, both the dramatic and musical thrust of Act I seethe with the drive toward certainty of identity, even though the achievement of that identity has tragic consequences, as Siegmund and Sieglinde fall into each other's arms when they discover they are of the same race and blood. Similarly, in *Meistersinger,* Walter von Stolzing wins Eva's hand only after he proves not only who he is but demonstrates he understands what it takes to be a worthy Volk artist. In fact, it is his successful traversal of the Prize Song in the final scene that both affirms his identity and proves that he is a German of the Volk. The man who coaches and nurtures Stolzing is Hans Sachs, benevolent custodian of Nürnberg's sacred lyric tradition, yet another word for identity. To make sure Stolzing does not miss the point of his accomplishment, Sachs lectures him sternly on safeguarding that tradition/ identity against forces that would destroy it in a finger-wagging peroration replete with sinister tremolos in the strings:

> Beware! Evil forces threaten us,
> If we fall prey to false and alien influences,
> No prince will be able to communicate with his subjects . . .

"Evil forces" were internal more often than foreign, and this passage comes about as close as Wagner ever came in his operas to hammering upon a theme he and many other German intellectuals before and after him, such as Herder, Justus Möser, and Oswald Spengler pursued relentlessly in their prose.[3] The evil to which Sachs refers is, of course, the Jewish presence in Germany. The Jew had been used for centuries throughout German history as the force against which the sanctity of things truly German must guard itself. But Wagner was the first to set the idea to intoxicating harmony, and Hitler, a devout Wagnerite from childhood, became ever more inebriated under its spell as he grew older. Small wonder that *Meistersinger* was the Führer's favorite opera, and he fully grasped the potency of Sachs' final message, using its essentials brilliantly to gather the tide that was bringing him to power. In fact, he may well have viewed himself as something of a Hans Sachs, that self-effacing arbiter of social and cultural order in the Elysium of medieval Nürnberg, however preposterous the thought may seem in hindsight. Nonetheless, he learned his lessons from Der Meister well, and his own brand of Das Volk kindled the imagination of an ever-growing number of Germans.

---

3. Herder, *Von deutscher Art und Kunst,* (Hamburg) 1773; Möser, *Deutsche Geschichte,* 1773. Cited in Mosse, *Germans and Jews,* p. 15.

Between the elections of 1928 and July 1932, the Nazi vote climbed from 800,000 to 13,750,000 or up from 2.16 percent of the popular vote to 37.3 percent.

In the years immediately preceding Hitler's seizure of power in 1933, Germany became the only country in modern history to undergo a broad political transformation in the middle of an economic downturn. After the election of November 1932, Hitler wasted no time in restoring economic order. With support from leading businesses and the coincidental narrowing of the trade gap, numerous public works projects and an all-out job procurement program put millions of people back to work almost instantly. Within a year, the Nazi regime cut unemployment from a staggering six million to 3.6 million. The dramatic recovery did not go unnoticed by the trade unions, who quickly offered their help in the spring of 1933, and big industry was all too glad to back someone who was protecting their profits from the dreaded predatory hands of the communists. The non-Marxist political parties, academic faculties, the churches of all denominations, and professional organizations quickly followed suit. After all, Hitler had performed a miracle: he had brought Germany back from the very brink of the abyss. In doing so, he gained the image of the phoenix rising from a Germany in ashes. That abyss had been especially terrifying to average Germans of that time, for they had been conditioned by their history to believe that economic failure was nothing short of existential devastation. It was a living nightmare perhaps only Germans who lived through that time truly could understand. At any rate, they would neither soon forget it nor refrain from any measure that might prevent it from happening again.

The "measure" Germans finally took to prevent chaos from threatening them again was National Socialism. Expressionism may have given all Europeans a cultural idiom for their anxiety and helplessness against a hostile universe, but Nazism now provided Germans, at least, with a political answer, an insurance plan, a way out of chaos, and a gateway into their justifiable craving for order. The election returns proved that Germans were herding themselves through that door at the rate of a stampede. The Nazis readily accepted all the support they got—except from the trade unions, which they brutally rejected because unionism was inimical to Nazi doctrine; the Party was the only union. The rush to join the Party became a delirious national compulsion. Civil servants and school teachers could not join the membership lines fast enough. In a few short months, Germany went from the threshold of unequivocal chaos to a paradox. She now was in the middle of revolution and unification at the same time. Rather than further confusing inflation-weary and humiliated German patriots, the paradox galvanized them. They now experienced the thrill of revolution (which Alexis de Tocqueville a century earlier had said would be impossible in Germany because the police would not allow it) with the support of police protection at the same time.[4]

But in January 1933 Hitler still had no overwhelming support. He was merely slipping by. On 30 January he simply seized control of the government. Whatever might have stopped him was paralyzed by its disarray. So Germans now had the best of two seemingly irreconcilable concepts. On the one hand, they had a Leader in the all-pervading sense that the word *Führer* carries within it. He had charisma and rendered the illusion of embodying not just the best and highest of things German, but the deepest and most profound yearnings of his people. Hitler's investiture at the hands of none other than old Chancellor Hindenburg unimpeachably legitimated both him and the yearnings he represented. On the other hand, they had chosen their authoritarian figure through the democratic process—though Hitler ultimately hurried the process along. These elections validated him in the modern 20th-century way. Even Germans who had not voted for him could now feel proud that they finally had a leader gained through a procedure belonging to the present, and they showed their gratitude to their savior by allowing him whatever he wanted. For what Hitler wanted was what "true" Germans thought they really desired: a unified sense of reality in which the Volk would emerge from the shadows and regain that golden time when "nothing mattered but the honor of the nation."[5] A dictatorship may not have been inevitable at this point, but it was now a probable certainty.

Hitler as the Führer was now becoming the arbiter of civil as well as martial law, so the general populace saw nothing unusual about his willingness to take pre-emptive and warlike measures during peacetime. In 1932 alone, Germany had held five national and local elections. Half the country—51 percent—voted Nazi in the March 1933 elections. This was the half of the nation given to unleash the anger they felt at being victimized by history. It had now essentially vanquished the other presumably more moderate half. When it was all over and the Nazis were in power, playwright and author Gerhardt Hauptmann was heard to moan, "If only Germans could be spared making any more decisions."[6]

4. Grunberger, pp. 18–20.
5. Mosse, *Germans and Jews*, p. 9.
6. Grunberger, p. 23.

This remark was not an isolated sentiment. Having come to the democratic process later than other nations, Germans still subscribed at heart to the authoritarian principle of kings and princes as the rightful rulers of their nation. What is more, the authoritarian principle permeated every aspect of their lives. By and large, Germans overwhelmingly craved being led, and, concomitantly, being told what to do. Decision-making in any broad sense was something relatively new. It took on the feeling of an existential, unpleasant, and even traumatic activity.

This deeply ingrained obedience syndrome may partially account for why the Nazis were greeted so hysterically in most of the elections in 1932 and 1933. Hitler had all the answers the majority of Germans needed at the time, and he looked like he could carry them through. What is more, he appealed to the darker, angry side of his supporters. He gambled losing everything in a possible scandal when he used his power as party leader to get five storm troopers acquitted of sadistically murdering a communist in August, 1932. When no audible alarm was raised in the wake of his abusive use of power, he knew the dawn of the Third Reich was virtually on the horizon.

There was, of course, dissent. But the opposition had no focus, no clear alternative to the concrete, overwhelmingly attractive blandishments the Nazis offered. To their immense relief, Germans really had only one unequivocal choice, and they ran to the polls to voice their approval and heave a sigh of relief that they were at last being delivered from so many years of unending doubt, humbug, and futile choices.

The Nazis went on in rapid course to pre-empt rival political parties, the press, the civil service, teaching, and the professions. Their methods were frequently brutal, and usually unlawful. Ultimately the arts were taken over by the regime too. Thousands of artists in literature, graphic and performing arts left Germany. Perhaps literature lost the most. Following the housecleaning at the Prussian Academy of Poetry, Nobel Laureate Thomas Mann and his brother Heinrich left Germany.[7]

Thomas Mann, of course, had difficulties with the Nazis even before the takeover. In 1932 they were grimly displeased with a lecture he delivered in Brussels on the 50th anniversary of Wagner's death. It was later published under the title "The Sufferings and Greatness of Richard Wagner." The rest of the world recognized the

---

7. For a fuller account of the exodus of artists and intellectuals from Nazi Germany, see *The Muses Flee Hitler*, edited by Jarrell C. Jackman and Carla M. Borden, (Washington) 1983.

piece as one of the most penetrating essays on the composer that had ever been written. To the Nazis, however, it was not good enough. As was his wont, Mann analyzed and considered the inner workings of Wagner's thought and the forces that culminated in his genius, rather than babbling breathless praise as the Nazis would have preferred. Hitler's media organ *Völkischer Beobachter* dubbed the author of *The Magic Mountain* and the future *Doctor Faustus* a "semi-Bolshevik," a curse in the Nazi cultural lexicon just below "decadent" and "Bolshevik" with no ameliorating qualifier. A group of "approved" Nazi artists signed an open letter hauling Mann over the coals. Richard Strauss was among them.

While Mann may have had his difficulties with the Nazis, and was hostile to some of their policies, his response was rather mild until he himself found that exile was his best alternative. While he lamented the loss of Jews as a tempering force in German culture in his diary of March 1933, he was prone to bouts of semi-anti-Semitism in April. When, for example, the critic Alfred Kerr was ousted early that year soon after the takeover *(Machtübernahme)*, Mann rejoiced that the dismissal of this "Nietzsche-baiting" Jew was ultimately "no misfortune." His antipathy toward Kerr was purely a matter of personal loathing rather than ethnic hate, but in virtually the same breath, this future anti-Nazi crusader (from a safe distance abroad) hailed the de-Judification of the German legal system.[8]

Mann knew his life in Germany had come to an end—for now, maybe forever. His decision to leave was redolent with anger and inner conflict, and he wrote a letter to Albert Einstein articulating the misgivings of his choice with a sadness he rarely permitted himself even in the most melancholy passages of his best fiction:

> Not so natural is the position in which I now find myself; at bottom I am much too good a German not to be heavily oppressed by the thought of permanent exile. The break with my country, a break which is almost inevitable, weighs on me and frightens me—a sign that my action does not fit my character, which is shaped by elements of a tradition going back to Goethe and is not truly suited to martyrdom. To force this role on me, things false and evil had to happen. False and evil is the entire "German Revolution," according to my deepest conviction. It lacks all those traits which have won the sympathy of the world for true revolutions, however bloody. Its essence is not "exultation," whatever its supporters say or bellow, but hatred, revenge, common killer-instinct, puny chicanery of the

8. *Thomas Manns Tagebücher*, (Frankfurt) 1977, 10 April 1933, p. 46. Mann also railed against Jews on 15 July 1934, calling them pathbreakers for the anti-liberal turn Germany had taken, pp. 473–474.

soul. Nothing good can come of it, never will I believe it, neither for Germany nor for the world. To have uttered to the best of our ability a warning against the moral and mental misery which these forces have brought about—that will some day earn us a degree of honor, even though we may perish in the meantime.[9]

Here Mann probably spoke for all Germans who were leaving. Today, when political situations shift from year to year and international travel is a matter of minutes and hours rather than weeks and months, it may be difficult to understand the psychological impact that the thought of sheer physical distance thrust on any traveler in those days. For a prospective exile, someone confronted with that distance as unchanging and eternal, the trauma could be shattering. More to the point, Mann and other Germans forced into exile were abandoning their *homeland*—a place in reality and a nexus of the heart none of them took lightly—and turning their backs on their country with full awareness that returning might never be possible. At the philosophical level, as far as Mann was concerned, Germany was sliding into evil and chaos; the only viable option was emigration. At the practical, realistic level, however, Mann was simply being shoved out despite later attempts to portray him sweeping out of Germany draped in anti-fascist purple. He left Germany because he had little choice in the matter.[10] And for those German artists like Mann whose lives were inextricably entwined with the feel, flux, and tow of being German, exile required reserves of the soul that might never be tapped under any other circumstance.

The purge also ousted Alfred Döblin, Leonhard Frank, Georg Kaiser, Jakob Wasserman, Franz Werfel and hundreds of other "degenerates and undesirables." German literature alone lost an estimated 2,500 writers before 1938. In the theater, such legendary directors as Max Reinhardt, Leopold Jessner, and Erwin Piscator were forced to leave. Playwrights such as Bruno Frank, Bertolt Brecht, and Franz Unruh soon followed. Leading actors such as Paul Wegener, Albert Basserman, Alexander Moissi, and Ernst Deutsch were branded "undesirable" or, worse, "Jewish," and forced out of work. Some

9. May 15, 1933.
10. At the exhibition of "Degenerate Art" in Los Angeles and Chicago in 1991, which admirably recreated the Nazis' infamous exhibition of art, literature, and music "unacceptable" to the Third Reich, a larger-than-life poster of Mann was the first introductory artifact seen by a visitor upon entering the exhibition. His ambivalent attitude toward the political situation in Germany prior to his ouster was not displayed. Nonetheless, the catalogue to the exhibit is highly informative and clearly arranged. The essay on "Degenerate Music" by Michael Meyer is helpful. *Degenerate Art*, Susan Caroselli, ed., (Los Angeles) 1991. Also see Chapter 16.

actors, such as Marlene Dietrich, who had already gone abroad out of career necessities, simply did not return.[11]

In music, the list of expelled artists was especially distinguished. Arnold Schönberg, Alban Berg, Ernst Krenek, Kurt Weill, Carl Ebert, Fritz and Adolf Busch, Artur Schnabel, Alfred Einstein, Bruno Walter, Otto Klemperer, Erich Kleiber, Richard Tauber and hundreds of others, not the least of whom was Paul Hindemith, left Germany.

All these artists were being replaced by individuals not nearly as well known, and for the most part, for good reasons. Names on the qualitative order of Werner Beumelburg, Hans Grimm, and Hans Friedrich Blunck were appointed to the Prussian Academy of Poetry, and Cesar Bresgen and Heinrich Spitha became state-sponsored composers of the first order. Despite the purges, however, a good many artists of outstanding quality remained in Germany, much to the undying gall of the émigrés. The works of Frank Wedekind and Gerhardt Hauptmann were eventually appropriated by the Nazis despite their dissident grumbling. Werner Krauss, Käthe Dorsch, Heinrich George, Albert Basserman, Gustav Gründgens, Jürgen Fehling, and Heinz Hilpert were among the better-known names in the theater to work throughout the Nazi regime. Richard Strauss, Carl Orff, and Werner Egk willingly accepted Nazi commissions for compositions. Many other internationally well-known musical performers such as Walter Gieseking, Gerhard Hüsch, and Margarete Teschemacher enjoyed prominent careers throughout the regime. The Heldentenor Helge Roswänge was a Dane by birth but a German by choice. Hitler is reported to have regarded him a greater singer than his Belgian rival Marcel Wittrisch—who worked especially hard to put himself in the good graces of the regime. This indubitably great singer of a vast repertoire even gave posterity a heartfelt recording of a hymn entitled, "God Bless Our Führer."[12] The bass Ludwig Hofmann, who was making an estimable career for himself at the Metropolitan Opera for several seasons, bought a full-page advertisement on the front cover of a widely read German music magazine announcing he had "returned to Germany following a call from the Führer."[13]

Richard Strauss, now in his seventies, was appointed President of the newly formed Reichsmusikkammer. It was basically an honorary title in an organization that really amounted to the state-run musi-

---

11. Goebbels' attempts to lure her back were in vain. Eventually, he secured a Swedish singer-actress, Zarah Leander, in the late 1930s who became perhaps an even greater idol.

12. Telefunken A 1550.

13. *Signale*, Nr. 15/16, 17 April 1940, front leaf advertisement.

cians' union. His signature appeared on the notice of exclusion sent to undesirable musicians, including Arnold Schönberg. He did not, as we soon will learn, keep the position for very long.

The Nazis indeed were freeing Germany, but they were making Germans free at the expense of everything that they felt was un-German. In return for reviving their identity as Germans and the much craved self-respect so essential to that identity, the Nazi regime demanded total, absolute, and undeviating loyalty. Sacrifice, specifically *self*-sacrifice, became a venerated theme pervading every aspect of life in Nazi Germany. As Hitler's propaganda minister, Joseph Goebbels adroitly manoeuvered these themes into the public's mentality through the tremendous media resources he had at his disposal, whipping all Germany into a frenzy of psychotic self-abrogation. Germans were all too willing to give up the autonomy they, for some inexplicable reason, always had mixed feelings about. This ambivalence probably prevented shock from being expressed at the construction of concentration camps for "re-educating" alien scoundrels almost immediately after the Nazis seized power.

In their pursuit to possess Germany's mind and heart, the Nazis swiftly adapted all the great figures of Germany's cultural past and put them into service. Beethoven's music introduced radio speeches by Nazi leaders. Hitler's visits to the shrine of Richard Wagner at Bayreuth became an official annual rite, somewhat akin to the Queen of England opening the Chelsea Flower Show. Goethe's beloved oak tree outside Weimar stood at the very center of a concentration camp to be built a few years later. An air of ancient Greece—the Golden Age of cultural perfection—was consciously purveyed as government buildings such as the Reichs Chancellery were built in the mock-classical style.

Much, if not all, of the epic pomp, Byzantine atmosphere, flamboyant neoclassicism, and seemingly euphonious public attitude of Nazi Germany was shaped personally by Joseph Goebbels, Hitler's Minister of Propaganda.[14] Born on October 29, 1897, in Rheydt in the lower Rhine region to a factory bookkeeper and his wife, the infant Franz Joseph Goebbels came into the world with a club foot, which not only undermined his self-confidence but probably gave him the impetus to find both concrete and imaginary compensations throughout his life. Reared as a Catholic, the young Goebbels was deeply impressed with the ceremonial panoply of the mass with its resplen-

14. I owe the details of Goebbels' background I am presenting here primarily to two of his biographers: Helmut Heiber, *Goebbels*, (New York) 1972; and Curt Riess, *Joseph Goebbels*, (New York) 1948.

dent display of power, an impression he would later transmute into epic pageantry for more secular purposes at such places as Nuremberg and the Berlin Sportspalast. Although he was highly intelligent and received his doctorate in German literature at Heidelberg in 1922, Goebbels was typical of many disenfranchised, tormented, and angry Germans who gravitated toward National Socialism and its charismatic leader in the early 1920s. His deformity prevented him from joining the army during the Great War, and his literary aspirations— he wanted to be a novelist—were vitiated when his novel *Michael* was rejected by every publisher to whom he sent it.

Both his dissertation and his failed novel present something of a road map to the directions his aspirations were taking. He is less revealing in his thesis "Wilhelm Schütz as Dramatist: A Contribution to the History of the Romantic School," but his biographer Helmut Heiber has pointed out several telling details. At one point, for example, Goebbels speaks of "all these people of little or no significance" who long for a leader "but who find no great man to take them in his arms." The author of this observation was certainly one of those insignificant tormented people. "It is the individual alone," he writes later, "who shapes the cry from the depths of his longing." He also introduces his dissertation with a quotation from *The Possessed* by Dostoyevsky:

> Reason and Knowledge have always played a secondary, subordinate, auxiliary role in the life of peoples, and this will always be so. A people is shaped and driven forward by an entirely different kind of force, one which commands and coerces them and the origins of which is obscure and inexplicable despite the reality of its presence.

A little more than a decade later, reason and knowledge would virtually disappear from the German lexicon, and Goebbels will have been the chief philologist in charge of replacing them with dogma and cant.

"When the upper and lower classes are one, only then will the world be ours," is perhaps the most revealing line in his novel *Michael*.[15] It was a credo that Goebbels hungrily espoused all his life, and its implications of Total Conformity *(Gleichschaltung)* were soon to become reality. His capacity to believe and convince others to believe, "Credo, ergo sum" (I believe therefore I am) put the kind of twist on familiar phrases that became the intoxicating "gift" he soon

15. An English translation by Joachim Neugroschel has been published, (New York) 1987. This outburst appears under the chapter heading 16 January, p. 73. Hereafter referred to as *Michael*.

was to foist on the German people. The story of *Michael* recounts the life-journey of the eponymous hero, who vainly seeks God in "dead books" and fruitless intellectual discussions. Michael Voorman finally finds paradise living among simple men and setting an example for all as a diligent worker. Midway through the narrative, Michael is seen wandering into a political meeting, quickly to be enthralled by the oratory powers of a thinly disguised Hitler.[16] He becomes part of the mass psychosis ("I am no longer a man, I am a Titan, a God!") the author later was so brilliantly able to induce in real life, and he schools himself to be a confirmed anti-Semite ("For me the Jew is physically nauseating. I want to vomit at the sight of him.").[17]

Such passages of purple gargle or pure offensiveness struck Goebbels as the gold of genius. In the instances where his intelligence prevailed, he wrote some worthwhile passages ("The idea of a United States of Europe is the smartest idea that anyone has thought up in decades").[18] Where his innermost self came to the fore, the results were sententious ("Being complimented by a Jew is the worst punishment that a German can endure") and ridiculous ("Christ cannot have been a Jew"),[19] but he could never look at his work critically. His prospective publishers, some of whom were Jewish, were all too adept at sharpening their red pencils on such manuscripts. Ultimately, he published it after many revisions as a serial in his own newspaper shortly after the Nazis came to power.

Goebbels in the 1920s could not even get a steady job as a hack journalist. One paper returned over 50 articles to him. The fact that many of these papers were owned or managed by Jews riled and obsessed him. He failed to recall that Aryan editors had also refused his work. But his exclusion from the profession he had thought his calling was making him believe that it was an effort on the part of Jews to keep the profession for themselves. Goebbels never was, like Hitler, an instinctive anti-Semite. But he became a catechistic Jew-hater through a bitter process of elimination. As his biographer Helmut Heiber has perceptively noted:

Fundamentally, he was a prototype of the intellectual whose intellect cannot come to grips with even the most superficial facets of being. In Goebbels nature created a kind of grotesque: a rigorously logical man whose mental capacities became even keener while his personality remained mired in puberty.[20]

16. *Michael*, 27 April, pp. 82–83.
17. *Michael*, 9 August, pp. 44–45.
18. *Michael*, 18 October, p. 61.
19. *Michael*, 9 August, p. 45.
20. Heiber, *Goebbels*, p. 77.

Such was the nature of the man who was ultimately to make the press into "sort of a piano" on which the tunes composed by his Propaganda Ministry would be played. Such was the shunned aspirant to Berlin's formidable literati who in short order would take control of German radio, the German film industry, German publishing, and almost all theatrical establishments and enterprises except the Prussian State Theaters. The theaters that eventually came under Goebbels' control included the People's Stage, a number of "Reichs Theaters," the Theater on Nollendorfplatz, the Metropole and the Admiralspalast in Berlin, the German Theater in Wiesbaden, and (after 1938) the Reichs Theater in Vienna.

While Goebbels' theatrical kingdom was extensive, it was provincial compared to the Prussian State Theaters which Hermann Göring requested from Hitler and promptly got after the Nazis came to power in 1933. Göring ruled these theaters—which included the Staatsoper on Unter den Linden—at lavish and prodigal expense. After the invasion of Austria, Göring installed Baldur von Schirach as his deputy in Vienna, a slight Goebbels smarted from, and, we will soon learn, was determined to do something about. But what he did over the years to get more of Göring's pie was halfhearted because he took scant interest in theater and only pragmatic interest in music. Goebbels had little time for the small and local demographics of theaters and concert halls. He craved access to the millions who listened to the radio or read newspapers or attended the cinema, and he had them firmly under his thumb. At one point, he scoffed at the relatively tiny number of people Furtwängler commanded at his concerts—usually no more than 2,500:

> What do I care about Furtwängler and his puny thousands? What we need are the millions, and we are getting them through the radio.[21]

Nonetheless, Goebbels also assumed control of the symphony orchestras in Germany eventually, and the Berlin Philharmonic was no exception. Now that he was in command of the German mind, he gave himself a mandate to put that mind into the service of the Thousand Year Reich. Goebbels was able to finance that mandate because the Propaganda Ministry—or ProMi as it usually was called—was

---

21. The composer-conductor Werner Egk mentions hearing this remark in his memoir *Die Zeit wartet nicht,* (Munich) 1981, p. 318. Goebbels had just finished handing out awards at the Reichs Music Days festival in 1939 to several musicians, one of whom was the concertmaster of the Berlin Philharmonic, Siegfried Borries. A small gathering including Borries and Egk clustered around Goebbels when he pointedly made the remark. Egk fondly recalls Goebbels as "restless, suspicious, and insolent."

also the wealthiest of the fiefdoms in the Third Reich. Even during the war, Goebbels had one of the largest budgets of any Minister in the Reich. Estimates of the money at his disposal range from 20 to 375 million RM (Reichsmarks) annually.

But the very people who could make Goebbels' fief even wealthier were being expelled or leaving of their own volition. At the rate Jews and other undesirables were departing Germany or simply going adrift, enormous gaps in the rosters of virtually every cultural organization in Germany began to appear. In opera alone, singers who were accorded star treatment only a few months past were suddenly let go. Rose Adler, Gitta Alpar, Irene Eisinger, Melitta Heim, Fritzi Jokl, Sabine Kalter, Lotte Leonhard, Fritzi Massary, Delia Reinhardt, Lotte Schöne, Vera Schwarz, Emanuel List, Benno Zeigler, Joseph Schmidt,[22] Richard Tauber were only a few of them.[23] Even artists married to Jews or half-Jews were in jeopardy. But there were two notable exceptions among this group of "undesirables." One was Max Lorenz. Although he was quite clearly Aryan, his wife was Jewish. He also made little attempt to hide his preference for keeping the company of attractive young men. Nazi zealots tried to have him removed, but they never got very far. His biggest fan was Adolf Hitler, who made sure his choice of wife and friends was simply overlooked. Lorenz also owed his survival to Winifred Wagner, who told Hitler flatly that the Wagner festival at Bayreuth could not continue without him. The other notable exception was Frida Leider, whose husband was Jewish. While the Nazis made life as miserable for them as possible, Furtwängler's intervention kept her working both in Germany and abroad.[24] What is most astonishing about Germany's performing arts scene after the purges was that it actually survived, and survived in relatively robust condition. The great days of the Weimar period were over forever, but theatrical and musical life kept going. For all the signs pointing to a cultural wasteland, the performing arts, at least, continued to flourish. The mainstay of their activities, however, was the past: works from the great masters of German tradition. Virtually no new works of substance were to be created and performed as the Nazis strengthened their power.

22. Schmidt was an immensely popular tenor who gained his following through numerous radio appearances and films. He won safe passage to the United States in 1937 and was making a name for himself in America when he decided, against pleas from his friends, to return to Europe. He died in a detention camp in Switzerland on 16 November 1942, after crossing the border illegally.

23. See Prieberg, *Musik im N-S Staat*, (Frankfurt) 1982, pp. 45f., for a sobering list of expelled artists from the musical professions. Hereafter referred to as *Musik im N-S Staat*.

24. Both Lorenz and Leider survived the war with their spouses unmolested.

Wilhelm Furtwängler also had a number of significant and generous opportunities to leave, and he almost did. But while he rarely read the newspaper and adamantly insisted on the separation of music and politics, he was soon drawn into paying the consequences for his refusal to connect one with the other. The results of the regime's anti-Semitic policies started hounding him almost immediately after the decisive elections of 1932. Jewish musicians or artists related to Jews lined up to beg him to intercede for them in obtaining exit visas. He could have joined their exodus, but he remained behind.

Why?

ABOVE: Wilhelm was the oldest of Adolf Furtwängler's four children. This photograph was taken about 1889 when Wilhelm was three and his brother Walter was almost two. BELOW: Wilhelm had few friends. His exceptional intelligence got him into trouble with schoolmates and teachers. His father finally educated him with private tutors. (*Wilhelm Furtwängler Private Archives, Clarens*)

ABOVE LEFT: About 1902. Wilhelm was sixteen, his sister Anna was two. ABOVE RIGHT: Furtwängler's apprenticeship took him to Munich in 1907 where he became an assistant conductor to Felix Mottl at the Court Opera. He was still sporting a healthy crop of hair and a moustache. BELOW: Furtwängler in a bucolic setting with the daughters of a woman he was seeing, about 1913. *(Wilhelm Furtwängler Private Archives, Clarens)*

Mannheim was home at various times to both Mozart and Schiller. The opera house had superb acoustics and offered subscribers music and drama. Furtwängler conducted his first *Ring* in this house in 1916. It was destroyed in Allied air bombing in 1943. *(Theater Collection, Reiss Museum, Mannheim)*

ABOVE: Same roles different destinies. Hermine Rabl and Dorothea Manski sang the big dramatic parts during Furtwängler's stay in Mannheim. Manski later took secondary roles at the Metropolitan Opera and became a well-known teacher. Rabl became active in the Women's Corps of the NSDAP after she retired from the stage. *(Theater Collection, Reiss Museum, Mannheim)*

Two giants. Furtwängler was tall, but Otto Klemperer was taller. 1928. *(Wilhelm Furtwängler Private Archives, Clarens)*

FACING PAGE LEFT: By 1920, Furtwängler was ready to leave Mannheim where he had widened his orchestral and operatic repertoire. An air brush was used on this photograph to conceal a scar on the right side of his face from a childhood accident. FACING PAGE RIGHT: Suzanne Bloch, daughter of Swiss-American composer Ernest Bloch, first met Furtwängler in Berlin in the 1920s and had a lifelong friendship with him. "Yes, I loved him," she recalls. "But I was not *in* love with Furtwängler." *(Courtesy of Suzanne Bloch)*

LEFT: Through no fault of his own, Furtwängler gained a reputation for avoiding contemporary composers. He conducted the world premiere of Schönberg's Variations for Orchestra in 1928. He also introduced *The Rite of Spring* by Stravinsky (left) to the New York Philharmonic.

BELOW: An informal performance of Haydn's "Toy" Symphony around 1928 featured some distinguished performers. Furtwängler's secretary Berta Geissmar, pianist Edwin Fischer, violinist Georg Kulenkampff, and Paul Hindemith. *(Wilhelm Furtwängler Private Archives, Clarens)*

ABOVE: Furtwängler and Lauritz Melchior at Bayreuth in 1931. They did not care for each other. BELOW: Facing off. Furtwängler at Bayreuth with Heinz Tietjen and Winifred Wagner in 1931. Furtwängler left Bayreuth after quarreling with Frau Wagner over final say on artistic matters. He later tangled with Tietjen who accrued the most power in the performing arts in Germany before and during the Third Reich. He survived unscathed, according to Wagner's granddaughter Friedelind, "because he was too clever to join the Nazi party." (*Wilhelm Furtwängler Private Archives, Clarens*)

ABOVE: Happier moments. No one, least of all Szymon Goldberg and Nicolai Graudan, could have guessed what would happen to them when this photograph was taken in 1931. Goldberg was the youngest concertmaster ever to hold that position in the Berlin Philharmonic. Nicolai Graudan was a principal cellist. *(Courtesy of Joanna Graudan)* BELOW: Shortly after the Nazis seized power in Germany, they tried to give their regime respectability by giving out titles and forming commissions in the arts. Furtwängler and Strauss were named President and Vice-President of the Reichsmusikkammer. They both resigned their positions within a few months of being named.

ABOVE: Fateful day in Mannheim. A rehearsal of the Berlin Philharmonic and Mannheim orchestras, 27 April 1933. The Nazis demanded putting Jewish first-desk string players in the rear and replacing them with Party members of the Mannheim Orchestra. Furtwängler refused. After the concert, he vowed never again to conduct in Mannheim, a promise kept until shortly before his death. Note Szymon Goldberg at the concertmaster's stand. *(Theater Collection, Reiss Museum, Mannheim)* BELOW: Photographers were positioned to catch Furtwängler bowing after a concert that Hitler, Goebbels, and Göring attended. The photograph was used, especially in America, as "proof" that Furtwängler was bowing before the Nazis in every respect. *(Wilhelm Furtwängler Private Archives, Clarens)*

DEUTSCHE STAATSOPER
ADMIRALSPALAST / BERLIN / FRIEDRICHSTRASSE 101/102

Donnerstag, den 2. Oktober 1947, 19 Uhr

Wohltätigkeitskonzert

zum Besten der Jüdischen Gemeinde Berlins

Dirigent:
WILHELM FURTWÄNGLER
JEHUDI MENUHIN
(Violine)

DIE STAATSKAPELLE

Ouvertüre zu › Alceste ‹ . . . . *Chr. W. Gluck*

Sonate für Violine C-dur . . . . *Joh. Seb. Bach*
        Adagio
        Fuga
        Largo
        Allegro assai

Violinkonzert D-dur op. 61 . . . . . . *Ludwig van Beethoven*
        Allegro ma non troppo
        Largetto
        Rondo

Vorspiel und Liebestod aus › Tristan und Isolde ‹ . *Richard Wagner*

ABOVE LEFT: Furtwängler was harassed mercilessly at his denazification trial in 1947. During a break, he muttered: "I should have left Germany in 1934." He emerged spotless, but the report of the trial was perversely distorted in American newspapers. *(Kreusch Ullstein)* ABOVE RIGHT AND BELOW: Yehudi Menuhin and Furtwängler gave a charity concert for the Jewish community after the war. Menuhin was Furtwängler's staunchest defender when a smear campaign in America was mounted against him. *(Photograph: Wilhelm Furtwängler Private Archives, Clarens; program: Berliner Staatsoper Archives)*

ABOVE: Elisabeth Albert Ackermann became Furtwängler's second wife in 1943 and bore him a son the following year. Andreas became a classical archaeologist like his paternal grandfather. *(Wilhelm Furtwängler Private Archives, Clarens)* BELOW: Furtwängler conducted opera for the first time after the war in Berlin. His cast included Erna Schlüter, Margarete Kose, and Ludwig Suthaus. Frida Leider was the producer. *(Berliner Staatsoper Archives)*

ABOVE: Furtwängler became increasingly involved with the Vienna Philharmonic immediately after the war. This photograph was taken at the Royal Albert Hall in London in 1949. Note television camera in foreground. (*Vienna Philharmonic Archives*) BELOW: Max Lorenz sang Siegfried to Kirsten Flagstad's Brunnhilde at La Scala in 1950. Furtwängler also conducted *Parsifal, Orpheus and Eurydice,* and *Die Meistersinger* there over the next two years. (*Wilhelm Furtwängler Private Archives, Clarens*)

ABOVE: Bayreuth, 1951. Furtwängler rehearsing the orchestra in the restaurant of the Festspielhaus. His performance of Beethoven's Ninth Symphony re-consecrated the house after the war. BELOW: Furtwängler with his wife Elisabeth. In his last years, Furtwängler's great solace was his family. *(Wilhelm Furtwängler Private Archives, Clarens)*

ABOVE: Rehearsing *Don Giovanni* at Salzburg in 1954. Paul Czinner made a film of the production. BELOW: Furtwängler was interred on 2 December 1954 by his mother's side in the family plot at Bergfriedhof in Heidelberg. Following Deacon Dr. Hermann Maas in the funeral cortege, Furtwängler's oldest son Wilhelm, one of Furtwängler's five known illegitimate children; Elisabeth Furtwängler, his second wife; Andreas Furtwängler; and Thomas Ackermann, one of Elisabeth Furtwängler's four children by a previous marriage. *(William Furtwängler Private Archives, Clarens)*

WILHELM FURTWÄNGLER
25 January 1886–30 November 1954

Inscribed along the border of the grave stone: "Meanwhile, these three: Faith, Hope, and Love abide with us, but the greatest of these is Love." From First Corinthians 13:13. *(William Furtwängler Private Archives, Clarens)*

8

Nazimania

After the Nazis took power in early 1933, the Prussian State Theaters and Berlin's leading lyric theater—the Staatsoper or the State Opera—fell under Hermann Göring's supervision.[1] Furtwängler had signed a contract with the Staatsoper in the last days of the Weimar Republic and saw no reason why he should not honor it, since he felt Göring really had nothing to do with him. When Göring tried to void it because he wanted to give the Music Director's post to Fritz Busch, Furtwängler forced him to honor it and prevailed.[2]

The orchestras, including the Berlin Philharmonic, the Städtische Opera or the Municipal Opera, all the non-Prussian theaters, and the media were taken up by the Propaganda Minister, Joseph Goebbels. For the rest of the twelve dark years that lay ahead, Germany's cul-

---

1. While I usually refer to as many German institutions as possible with an English equivalent, there are a number of exceptions, and Berlin's two leading opera houses are among them. The Berlin State Opera will be referred to as the Berlin Staatsoper or the Staatsoper, and the Berlin Municipal Opera as Städtische Oper. It should be noted at this point that the Berliner Staatsoper Unter den Linden has been known by that name or by simply Lindenoper or Staatsoper since 1918. The Städtische Oper underwent several switches in names. It originally was called the Deutsche Oper or German Opera. In 1925 it became the Städtische Oper or Municipal Opera. It went back to being called Deutsche Oper in 1933, the name it has at present. Throughout its history—at least until the 1950s—the opera house has been referred to as the Charlottenburg Opera because of its location on the Bismarckstrasse in the Charlottenburg section of Berlin. Note also that I refer to Vienna's principal lyric theater as the Vienna Staatsoper.
2. See Riess, p, 160.

tural life—especially opera—would be a battleground on which these two men would fight bitterly for power, and the most important squabbling point was the Prussian State Theaters.

There always was a question as to which man really controlled them. Göring staked his claim by forming a theater committee within the Ministry of Culture in March 1933. To head this committee, he appointed Hans Hinkel who was State Commissar in the Ministry of Culture. This committee nominally took charge of all the theaters in the Reich except the Prussian State Theaters. This select group of theaters included those in Berlin, and chief among them was the Staatsoper. These theaters Göring absorbed into his own domain at the Ministry of Interior where he was chief. All Göring really cared about, however, was the Staatsoper. Over at the Propaganda Ministry or ProMi, Goebbels viewed these developments with dismay. Sharing was never one of Goebbels' virtues, and he was very disturbed at the thought that the most prestigious vessels of the performing arts in Germany belonged to his rival.

To redress this humiliating state of affairs, he formed the Reichskulturkammer (RKK) in November, which was intended to become an umbrella over the Ministry of Culture and the various departments within it that controlled the Prussian State Theaters. But Göring did not relinquish his control and shifted them from their former position as a sort of department within the Ministry of Interior into his own office, the Office of Minister President. Goebbels followed suit by serving notice to all other government ministries and their departments in March 1934 that he alone was the highest authority in the Prussian State Theaters. Göring retorted no! He alone was the highest authority in the Prussian State Theaters. What is more, the Führer backed him. Ultimately, Goebbels won, but it would be 1944 before he could claim a Pyrrhic and short-lived victory.[3]

Furtwängler was now beholden to the two most powerful men in the Third Reich, but the idea never intimidated him, as both Goebbels and Göring were soon to learn. Whenever possible, he tried to exploit their enmity and use their common need for him to subvert their attempts to co-opt and destroy German musical culture.

Göring was a different sort from the rude, ignorant breed constituting most of the senior level of Nazi officials, but he was not entirely

3. See Boguslaw Drewniak, *Theater im N-S Staat*, (Düsseldorf) 1983, Jutta Wardetzky, *Theaterpolitik im faschistischen Deutschland*, (Berlin) 1983, Fred K. Prieberg, *Musik im N-S Staat*, (Frankfurt) 1982, and Henry Bair, "Lenkung der Berliner Opernhäusern," in *Musik und Musikpolitik in faschistischen Deutschland*, (Frankfurt) 1984, pp. 83–89. They each present comprehensive surveys of the complexities of backstage politics during the Third Reich.

atypical.[4] He was just as arrogant as most of the riffraff that were taking over important positions, but his family was connected to pedigree, even though it really could not lay claim to any blue blood itself. Born Hermann Wilhelm Göring on January 12, 1893, at Rosenheim in Bavaria, his father, Heinrich Göring, was a Prussian military careerist and his mother came from a nondescript peasant background. Fanny Göring was Heinrich's second wife, and she bore him five children of whom Hermann was the second of her two sons. The elder Göring had fought in Bismarck's campaigns and eventually joined the diplomatic corps. At the time of Göring's birth, he was consul-general in Haiti and 64 years old. The family was typical of that social class which straddled the aristocracy and the middle classes. Their life was the very embodiment of genteel poverty, for their position forced them to keep up appearances without the financial foundations to support those pretensions. The ruling force in a family like the one young Hermann was born into was duty; duty reinforced by intense patriotism and a shrewd sense for accruing influence. That orientation became increasingly threatened during Hermann's formative years, as the rising middle class spawned by late 19th century industrialism brazenly began to co-opt the service class to which the Görings belonged.

Having been born to a Prussian father with Spartan northern German sentiments and living his seminal years in Bavaria and its romantic southern German mentality, Göring grew up as something of an outsider. He lived in a castle at Veldenstein near Nuremberg, surrounded by an odd sort of medieval pageantry. The accommodations were provided by the lover of Göring's mother, an Austrian nobleman named Hermann von Epenstein. Epenstein was an Austrian Jew and a wealthy physician, who purchased his title and the ostentatious estate that went with it. He was little Hermann's godfather and namesake, a fact of which Göring was all too aware as he grew up. During these years in Bavaria, Hermann immersed himself in the romantic brand of "German-ness" that was fermenting into the spirit of National Socialism. The potent forces of Bavarian romanticism and Prussian rigor set against Göring's isolation and restlessness—a result of belonging completely to neither world—fashioned him into prime material for enlistment into the Nazi movement. The class from which he and other ambitious conservative men came was becoming obsolete, and only Nazism seemed to offer a concrete, viable alternative.

Although he was a poor student in conventional subjects, he dis-

---

4. Several excellent biographies of Göring have been published, but the author found two of them most useful for this sketch: R. J. Overy, *Göring: The Iron Man*, (London) 1984, and R. Manvell and H. Fraenkel, *Göring*, (London) 1962.

tinguished himself in training at the military college at Lichterfelde. He willingly followed his father into military service, and he proved more than adequate in displaying bravery in battle during the first World War. He received many honors, but the medal *Pour le Mérite* was the most distinguished and well deserved of them. Göring returned to civilian life in a defeated Germany with a multiple sense of betrayal. His fiancee broke off their engagement because he was penniless through no fault of his own. The socialists and the conservatives had both "stabbed Germany in the back"—a rallying cry of the Nazis that later seized the angry and hungry Germans in the 1920s.[5] He was an ex-soldier who resisted the restoration of the old system but felt alienated from the present cosmos of Weimar. Worst of all, he realized he was the product of an extinct class, that nameless social domain that had teetered between the elite and middle classes. The old Reich had protected this feeble estate for its own political ends, but it now had become a discarded, ghost-filled realm.

Göring was among the coming generation in Germany who felt something had to be done about this unbearable state of affairs. The conventional political parties were running amok, and he saw the desperate need for a new and radical political movement to speak for the disaffected millions who no longer were content to let the conservatives represent them. He found the answer in National Socialism and especially in its articulate and charismatic leader. What magnetized Göring and many other young shiftless men to Hitler was that the Führer-to-be could express in words what they could not. Hitler gave resounding voice to their overwhelming sense of alienation and helplessness. What is more, Hitler had concrete answers and explanations about what had gone wrong, and he offered alternatives, options, and *hope*.

Throughout the 1920s, Göring's relationship with Hitler went through a number of changes, not all of them amicable. Nonetheless, he became what they later called one of "the old fighters," and he was elected to the Reichstag as a Nazi deputy just before the Seizure of Power in 1933. By then, he had sworn undying fealty to Hitler, and the two became akin to blood brothers, though Göring never ingratiated himself into the Führer's inner circle of close associates. Throughout the heady days before the takeover, Hitler remained somewhat doubtful of Göring's abilities. But he finally gave him the post of Minister of the Interior, an ambivalent position that Göring himself proceeded to make important. In accepting the position gratefully, Göring also

5. The belief that Germany had lost the war at the hands of politicians was held by most Germans, though the Nazis were most successful in exploiting the bitter resentment behind it.

requested charge of all the Prussian State Theaters as part of his domain. Although Goebbels was nominally head of all German entertainment, Hitler granted Göring control of these theaters, which included the crown jewel of German opera houses—the Staatsoper Unter den Linden. Thus, Göring, the future chief of the Luftwaffe and second in command to the almighty Führer, became Wilhelm Furtwängler's "other" boss.

Furtwängler ignored these developments even though he had some idea of what was going on. He took a certain degree of pride in rarely reading the newspapers, apparently bearing out his view that if an artist is to remain apart from politics, he or she must be ignorant of it too. That he was painfully naive in many respects rapidly became self-evident. That he was politically ignorant in a willful way became a commonplace that eventually challenged credulity. Nobody, went the line of uninformed thought, could be that politically feeble-minded and still be a great musician, an artist, an intellectual. Those who did not know him also read sinister motives into his incredible public behavior after the Nazis came into power. Instead of arousing admiration, his ensuing conduct precipitated a legend of gossip, misinformation, and lies which eventually caused him great anguish. In the meantime, however, the enormity of the fabrications about him mushroomed throughout the world. Since he was about to live in a totalitarian state, it took him a while before he realized that he had only a vague idea of what was being said about him abroad. But it would not be long before he became all too aware that his image abroad was to be viciously manipulated by the powers coming to be.

Furtwängler left Germany shortly after the day Hitler came to power. He was embarking on a brief European tour with the Berlin Philharmonic. When he returned, his first taste of the new regime was served as Nazi spies boarded the train bearing the Philharmonic members home from The Hague. They eavesdropped on Furtwängler joking about the high rate of taxes with his secretary Berta Geissmar.[6] They duly reported the incident to the Gestapo. A concert they were to give in Bielefeld was almost canceled when Brownshirts threatened violence at the concert hall, branding the whole Philharmonic "national criminals." Not content to stop at that, Hitler's aides gave him a memorandum indicating that Furtwängler's Jewish secretary had deposited his concert fees abroad while members of the orchestra went for months without salaries. The contrary, of course, was the case. In the last chaotic months of Weimar, Furtwängler refused his salary so that the orchestra could be paid.

6. Geissmar, p. 59.

It was not long before the racial policies of the Nazis were put into effect, and Jews began losing their jobs at cultural and educational posts on all levels throughout Germany. Letters such as these began to be sent from Headquarters of the State Commissar in Berlin:

Herr Stefan Auber:

Since you have been eliminated from the Reichsmusikkammer, your teaching permit has expired. I request that you return the permit certificate to me within three days. You no longer are permitted to engage in teaching Aryan children.[7]

Auber's expulsion ultimately came to a happy ending. He had been a cellist and organized a radio concert orchestra in Königsberg which was led by one of the foremost German conductors of the time, Hermann Scherchen. After his proscription from playing professionally and the confiscation of his teaching certificate, he emigrated to America. There he married a wealthy woman and lived comfortably in New York until his death in 1987. Countless others were not nearly as lucky.

Some better-known Jewish musicians received the Nazi message more directly. Bruno Walter received a telephone call from his agent Eric Sachs of Louise Wolff's agency informing him he had received word from the Propaganda Ministry (ProMi) that if Walter conducted his next scheduled concert with the Berlin Philharmonic, the Nazis would burn the hall down. The message came from Walter Funk, the future president of the Reichsbank. The threat, as Walter later learned, was part of a ploy organized by Hans Hinkel, the new expert at ProMi on musical matters, to put fear and trembling in the hearts of undesirable musicians. Hinkel had gained favor with Hitler's inner circle as editor of *Miesbacher Anzeiger*, one of the oldest Nazi newspapers. He now was acting out the anti-Semitic fantasies he had published for years in his rag sheet.

The ploy worked. Walter canceled and left Berlin immediately, and Richard Strauss, with a spirit of The-Show-Must-Go-On, stepped in to conduct the concert. The incident sent shock waves through the musical world, for the Nazis had garnered a decisive victory in their racial policies and had Germany's greatest living composer put his stamp on it. Strauss' motivation for allowing himself to be used in such a manner is unclear, but his behavior in the future demonstrates

7. Wulf, *Musik im dritten Reich*, (Berlin) 1965, pp. 405–406. This book is part of Wulf's five volume history in documents of the Third Reich first published separately and re-issued under the umbrella title *Kultur im dritten Reich*, (Frankfurt & Berlin) 1989. *Musik im dritten Reich* will hereafter be referred to as Wulf.

that it was not entirely self-serving; he really thought, however incredible it may seem in hindsight, that he was saving the show.[8]

The unimpugned lootings of Jewish-owned property and businesses had already begun, and the move to examine everybody's family tree for signs of Jewish blood became the deadly Trivial Pursuit of the time. Furtwängler had no intention of firing the Jewish members of the orchestra, and he made his views clear. There were five members of the orchestra who were Jews or half Jewish. Szymon Goldberg, was a Polish violinist who was the quintessence of the child prodigy. A pupil of Carl Flesch, he became first concertmaster of the Dresden Staatskapelle Orchester when he was 15. Four years later, he became the youngest concertmaster in the history of the Berlin Philharmonic, a record unbroken to this day. He joined the Philharmonic in 1929. The others were principal cellists Nicolai Graudan and Joseph Schuster, and two other permanent members of the violin section who were half Jewish.[9] For reasons that some later attributed to collusion between Furtwängler and the regime, the Nazis left the Berlin Philharmonic alone—at least for the time being. Nor did they protest Berta Geissmar sitting in her customary box at the State Opera on Unter den Linden for a gala performance of *Die Meistersinger* on the inaugural of the Third Reich on March 21, 1933.

Nonetheless, the harassment of Jews and other "undesirables" persisted and grew in vitriolic strength. Finally, less than a month after the Nazis were officially installed as Germany's leaders, Furtwängler wrote an open letter to Goebbels which was published in the *Vossische Zeitung* on 11 April 1933:

Quotas cannot be placed on music, as they can for bread or potatoes. If nothing worth hearing is given in concerts, the public will just stay away. For this reason, the quality of music is not merely a matter of ideology. It is a matter of survival. If the fight against Jewry is focussed upon those artists who are rootless and destructive, if it is waged against those who would profit through rubbish and empty virtuosity, the fight is justified. The struggle against such individuals and the spirit they personify—and this spirit has its German adherents too—cannot be waged vigorously and thoroughly enough. But if this attack is directed against real artists, too, it is not in the best interests of our culture. Real artists are very rare

8. Walter himself gives a chillingly understated account of this incident in his memoir: *Theme and Variations*, (New York) 1946, pp. 298–300. Louise Wolff's daughter Edith Stargardt-Wolff recounts a similar version of these events in her biography of her parents, *Wegbereiter grosser Musiker*, (Berlin) 1954, pp. 275–278. Hereafter referred to as Stargardt-Wolff.

9. See Chapters 15 and 18, for a list of Jewish and Jewish-related members of the Berlin Philharmonic.

. . . and no country can afford to renounce their service without enormous harm to its culture.

Plainly, it must be said that men like Walter, Klemperer and Reinhardt and others must be enabled in the future to practice their art in Germany. I repeat again, let our fight be against the reckless, destructive, shallow, harmful spirit, but not against the real artist who is always creative and constructive in his own way, regardless of how his art may be appraised.

In this spirit, I appeal to you in the name of German art before events take place that may never be put right.

Goebbels issued a clever reply to Furtwängler's letter in the *Berliner Lokal-Anzeiger* on the same date. He identified the creators of the Third Reich with all great artists. He went on to say that art "cannot be merely good or bad, but racially conditioned." Furthermore, he conceded, "real artists are rare. But," he added, taking it back, "they have to be genuine artists." He later clarified what he meant by real and genuine, resting the crux of his argument against the Jews on his contention that "many German musicians have been condemned to silence over the past 14 years by their Jewish rivals."[10]

Goebbels allowed Furtwängler's letter to be published with his rejoinder to demonstrate his tolerance of dialogue and varied opinions, but he was buying himself time to consider how to handle this prickly but potentially useful errant. He made his point. The exchange was published all over the world and momentarily mitigated the demonic image the Nazis had gained in the eyes of the rest of the world.

Furtwängler received hundreds of telegrams and letters congratulating him from abroad. In America especially, the public at large was eagerly waiting to see how others in Germany would react. Furtwängler, too, hoped that his colleagues might join him. A few came up with endorsements or tepid objections, but there were no further protests of a major order from figures of Furtwängler's stature. The published protest of 12 April was only the beginning of countless arguments and discussions Furtwängler had with Nazi officials, but few of them were ever heard outside Germany. Most of them took place in correspondence, telephone calls, and innumerable personal visits Furtwängler made to the offices of top officials and petty bureaucrats where he frequently was made to wait for hours, hat in hand, before some parvenu petty official deigned to see him.

If making an adversary of Goebbels was not enough, Furtwäng-

10. Furtwängler's letter and the summary of Goebbels' reply are cited in Geissmar, pp. 71–72, and Riess, pp. 142–145. The full texts of both letters appear in Wulf, pp. 86–88.

ler's impolitic way of dealing with the roustabouts who had seized the government earned him another important enemy. When a physician who was a good friend of Furtwängler was arrested on vague charges, Furtwängler learned that the man who was at the top of the police force was a gentleman named Heinrich Himmler. Furtwängler did not have a clue as to who this person was and could not have cared less. He rang him up and demanded the immediate release of his physician friend. Himmler was not about to be told what to do by a musician, even if the musician was Furtwängler, and a shouting match ensued. Ultimately, they both slammed down the receiver. Later, of course, Furtwängler knew all too well who the dreaded Gestapo chief was, but he completely forgot the identity of the person with whom he had argued.

Himmler never forgot. Nor did he forgive. He immediately ordered a file opened on Furtwängler and patiently began collecting information on him.

In the meantime, Furtwängler personally replied to every plea for help in the sheaves of mail he was beginning to receive.[11] He took numerous appeals personally to the authorities, and spoke with Goebbels far more frequently than the latter would have preferred. The help he was to offer ultimately took up more of his time, energy, and finances than the work to which he had devoted his life. Furtwängler usually approached the Nazis on racial matters from a public relations angle. He tried to impress Goebbels with the embarrassment the latest expulsion or dismissal might have on Germany's image abroad. An instance of this approach surfaces in a letter he wrote to Cultural Minister Rust on 4 July 1933:

> Arnold Schönberg is considered by the Jewish International as the most significant musician of the present. It must be recommended that he not be made a martyr. And if he is suspended now—I would not indeed consider this right—to treat the question of indemnity with generosity.[12]

Furtwängler played devil's advocate in this letter. He admired Schönberg despite the canyon separating their points of view on the direction of music, but he cautioned Rust about mistreating the composer on the basis of his significance as a Jew. Many years later, the letter would be used against him in a most perverse way.[13]

While his enemies created the impression that Furtwängler helped

11. See Chapter 15 for a discussion of Furtwängler's assistance to persecuted individuals.

12. This letter was read into the proceedings at Furtwängler's denazification trial in Berlin, 17 December 1946.

13. See Chapter 18.

only those who could help him professionally in some way, he helped everybody who asked him, even if they were complete strangers.[14] For all his fist hammering about keeping music and politics apart, however, Furtwängler could not deny that he was throwing acid into the eyes of the Nazis by helping political undesirables and Jews. The immediate backlash was a new phenomenon for Furtwängler: half-empty houses at his concerts. The Nazis did not come out of principle, for the orchestra had not been Aryanized. Pride prevented the Jews from attending, even though the new racial laws permitted them to go to public entertainments. That left a sizable but hardly overwhelming group of fans who were devoted to Furtwängler and the Philharmonic.

Nazimania spread through Germany like a raging opportunistic disease, but Furtwängler was determined to prevent it from infecting cultural life in Germany. Exactly two weeks after the open letter had been published, Furtwängler and the Philharmonic went to Mannheim for a joint concert with the Mannheim Orchestra on 26 April. The concert had been arranged the previous year before the Nazis seized power and was intended to commemorate the 50th anniversary of Wagner's death.[15] A few weeks prior to the concert, the Mannheim Orchestra Committee demanded that Furtwängler replace Philharmonic concertmaster Szymon Goldberg with their own leader. Furtwängler knew that the Mannheim concertmaster was an inferior musician and knew that he was a Nazi. He refused and threatened to cancel the concert if it did not go according to the original plans. Even at the rehearsal on the afternoon of the concert, Furtwängler refused to be moved. Possibly to add a streak of perversity to the proceedings, Furtwängler opened the program leading the combined orchestra through the Third Symphony of Wagner's musical antipode Johannes Brahms. Following the interval, the full complement of 170 players traversed the Prelude to Act I of *Lohengrin*, followed by the Bacchanal from *Tannhäuser*, and rounding off the evening with the Overture to *The Flying Dutchman*. Throughout the evening, Goldberg remained at his appointed stand. After the sold-out event, the committee appeared in Furtwängler's dressing room and roundly berated him for his lack of patriotism. Hurling a score at their feet, he left the concert hall and returned to the house of Berta Geissmar's mother, where he usually stayed when he was conducting in Mannheim. All night, the committee telephoned to beg him to come to the banquet that was in progress. Furtwängler finally shouted his refusal into the phone, vow-

14. See Chapter 15 for a fuller discussion of Furtwängler's assistance to individual Jews and other threatened people in the Third Reich.
15. Wagner died 13 February 1883.

ing he would never conduct in Mannheim again, and slammed the receiver down.

Although Berta Geissmar in her memoir *Two Worlds of Music* and Curt Riess in *Furtwängler: Musik und Politik* (English version: *Furtwängler*) both recount this incident at length, Goldberg told me in January 1989 that he had no recollection of such an episode. "If something like that had happened—which is quite possible—I think I would somehow have heard about it," he said, making it clear that he had no wish to explore that painful period with me. "But I don't remember anything like that happening."[16]

Furtwängler, however, was not about to forget the incident, and he wrote several furious letters to the authorities on the subject. The first missive was fired off to the Board of Directors of the National Orchestra Mannheim. Furtwängler repeated the reasons for putting the (Jewish) string players at the front of the Mannheim orchestra and accused members of the orchestra of lodging their protest out of mere professional jealousy:

Karlsruhe, 29 April 1933

To the Board of Directors of the National Orchestra Mannheim.

Att. z. Hd. von Herrn Sanders

Gentlemen:

At the end [of the concert], the concert master informed me that he was so disturbed by the seating order, that he had called a meeting of the Kampfbund. I remained firm: they are fully aware of the artistic and financial advantages of concerts under my direction . . .

I doubt very much if it is in the mind of the national socialist regime that your well considered political line of thought will be manipulated and misused to the satisfaction of small vanities. As long as such a mood prevails it will be impossible for me to continue artistic activity with you.

I must protest . . . that what it means to be German is for the individual to decide, and that in an orchestra which represents the highest order of German orchestral art, not only in Germany, but in the entire world, the first line of the capability principle must be measured and maintained. The great German masterworks spring as a consequence from this principle, and not from what is offered by mediocre music.[17]

16. Personal conversation with the author, Philadelphia, 15 January 1989. During our conversation, Goldberg also flatly stated to me that he never appeared together with Henry Holst, his immediate predecessor as the Berlin Philharmonic's first concertmaster. The programs of the orchestra show, however, that they played the Berlin premiere of the Concerto for Two Violins, Opus 5, by Karl Marx on 30 November and 1 December 1930. Nonetheless, his recollections of other events concerning his participation with the Berlin Philharmonic were astoundingly accurate.

17. Source: Bundesarchiv, Koblenz, R55/1138, pp. 105f.

When he wrote to Goebbels the next day from Baden-Baden, he minced no words about his concern over the corrosive impact such incidents would inevitably have on Germany's cultural well-being:

> My impressions of the provinces (Cologne, Frankfurt, Essen, Mannheim, etc.) are, as far as native concert life is concerned, extremely pessimistic. I fear that the maintenance of the basic and "German" art of our people— I mean above all—pure "absolute" music and its originality—will suffer more than any other spiritual area as a consequence of the present revolution. If free competition is not established immediately, and if the public is not calmed down and allowed again to make its own judgment, the slave revolt of the masses, which is carried out many times over in musical life today very successfully, will vitiate Germany's place in the world as the land of music.[18]

Such a mood of incipient terrorism did prevail, for the Brownshirts had a strong following in Mannheim and elsewhere in Germany, but Furtwängler was determined to prevent the music of the German masters from being destroyed as a consequence of the revolution. By comparison, the individuality if not always the superiority Germany could boast in some of the other arts before 1933—literature, the visual and plastic arts, film, and theater—all declined precipitously over the next twelve years because there was no one concomitant to Furtwängler in those areas. And while Germans capitulated all too soon to the vicious notions the Nazis sold them of what it meant to be German, Furtwängler's tenacity in remaining true to his own idea of "German-ness" led him toward a destiny that was to be tragic in the plangent and fearsome sense with which the Greeks used that word. All the while, he stood firmly by his tenebrous vow to Mannheim. He did not conduct there again until 1953.

Around the end of 1933, Szymon Goldberg decided to leave the orchestra. Quite apart from the vicious psychological pressure being brought to bear on him and the other Jewish members of the Philharmonic, he had long wanted to pursue a concert career exclusively. He had informed Furtwängler of his intention to resign in late 1932, a few months before the Nazis had taken over. "I had a long talk with Furtwängler, and during the course of it, he asked me to stay," he recalled. "He was afraid that the other Jews in the orchestra—there were about five of us—would be in danger from the Nazis if they took power. I agreed to stay for another year, providing that I performed only for

---

18. Source: Bundesarchiv, Koblenz, R55/1138, p. 102–103. See also Fred K. Prieberg, *Kraftprobe: Wilhelm Furtwängler im dritten Reich*, pp. 92–93. Hereafter referred to as *Kraftprobe*.

the concerts Furtwängler conducted. We agreed on that arrangement, but I finally did resign at the beginning of 1934."[19]

It was not so easy. Goldberg's passport was confiscated, and an ugly scene involving the authorities, Goldberg's wife, and himself developed at the police station when the return of their documents was refused. Finally, the Berlin Philharmonic's new Kommissar business manager, Rudolf von Schmidtseck—a Nazi—secured the passports for them.[20] Goldberg first went to his native Poland and then to Italy. On a concert tour of Java in 1942, when the Japanese occupied the island, he was placed in an internment camp for the duration of the war.

19. Personal conversation with the author, Philadelphia, 15 January 1989.

20. Schmidtseck may have been a Nazi, but he was a man of some qualities. Born in 1901, he became a musician and conductor who also possessed formidable diplomatic talent. He acted skillfully as a go-between for Furtwängler and the Berlin Philharmonic in their dealings with the new government. Schmidtseck remained with the orchestra for only a brief time, however, appearing out of nowhere in March 1933 and disappearing after December 1935 when Furtwängler had resigned all his official positions. See *Kraftprobe*, pp. 73–74.

9

Prometheus
Agonistes

The Mannheim scandal sent shock waves through the bureaucratic corridors of the Third Reich. Furtwängler's unconscionable lack of patriotism in refusing to remove his Jewish first-desk string principals, his absence from the post-concert banquet, and his taking lodgings with Jews made the Mannheim officials bristle with rage. They wasted no time in reporting Furtwängler's behavior to Berlin and to the Party officials at Karlsruhe and Baden-Baden, where the Philharmonic was scheduled to play next. The Party seats in the front rows of the hall at both concerts were conspicuously empty.

A few days later, Furtwängler took the orchestra to Paris, Marseille, and Lyon between 2 and 7 May. At first, the orchestra and Furtwängler were met with demonstrations and newspaper editorials objecting to a "Nazi orchestra" coming to France. A rumor was also put into circulation that Furtwängler had written the public letter to Goebbels as a self-serving publicity stunt. But word quickly got around that Furtwängler was no Nazi and had not Aryanized the orchestra. Both series of concerts played to tense but sold-out houses. A week later, the critic for *Le Courrier Musical* intoned the sentiments of nearly all his colleagues at other periodicals:

Wilhelm Furtwängler: what a splendid animator! On the podium, he appears possessed by the demon of music. He embodies the very gesture of incantation, almost like a magician exercising his spell.[1]

Furtwängler remained in France to conduct *Tristan* and *Walküre* at the Paris Opéra. He had met with enormous success performing *Tristan* a year earlier, and Jacques Rouché, the venerable Intendant of the Opéra, persuaded him to return with virtually the same cast. Lauritz Melchior starred with Frida Leider, who took the leading distaff role. Herbert Janssen, Alexander Kipnis, and Sabine Kalter appeared respectively as Kurwenal, King Marke, and Brangaene. Louis Laloy confirmed the impression he had received the year before:

Wilhelm Furtwängler is a musician for whom the music is made of sound rather than mere notes. The abstract sense of a melody or a geometric combination of lines interests him less than the total sound mass and harmonious accent. The *Tristan* he gave us is an earthy *Tristan*. There is nothing metaphysical in its fiery impetus, it always returns to that pain, that joy coupled with guilt, that dark despair . . .[2]

Walküre was no less successful, and his cast was again perhaps the finest of its day. In addition to Melchior, Leider, and Kalter, Lotte Lehmann sang Sieglinde, and Friedrich Schorr made one of his last appearances in Europe as Wotan before emigrating to America and a great career at the Metropolitan and other American opera houses.

While Furtwängler triumphed on artistic grounds, his recent experiences in Mannheim and France gave him a taste of his embattled future in Germany. On the one hand, he was becoming a pariah in his homeland for standing up to the Nazis; on the other, he was being vilified elsewhere for what his unwillingness to leave Nazi Germany implied.

Despite the vise that was tightening around him, he continued to believe that he could persuade the Nazis that their racial policies would kill German culture instead of vitalizing it. He neither knew nor imagined at this point that this indeed might be the very objective of his country's new leaders. He held numerous interviews with Goebbels and other Nazi officials on the importance of keeping Jews as part of the nation's artistic life, and he became obsessed with obtaining a personal interview with Hitler, a wish that took two months to accomplish. In the meantime, Goebbels and other top gov-

1. 15 May 1933.
2. *Le Monde Musical*, No. 5, 1933.

ernment officials always treated him with deference and respect, fervently promising change or continued freedom, and he interpreted their obsequies as sincere and fortified his belief that he, because of his prestige and achievements, could make a difference in the mad world in which he now found himself. Throughout all of it, he continued to believe his efforts were not futile. In the summer of 1933 he told Friedelind Wagner, "I feel it is my duty to stick it out here and save whatever can be saved artistically at a time when the country is headed for ruin and destruction."[3]

He soon found that the promises of top-ranking Nazis were empty, but not always because their commands directly contradicted their promises to Furtwängler. The New Order was rife with envious and power-hungry petty bureaucrats who took no small delight in hampering, delaying, or thwarting directives from the top. Furtwängler unwittingly aggravated this situation by circumventing these troublesome middlemen and going straight to Goebbels, Göring, or Hitler, sometimes all three in quick succession. The officials he bypassed took every available opportunity to make anything relating to Furtwängler maddeningly difficult. He worsened his problems in refusing to conduct mediocre compositions by subsidized composers who were active members of the Party. Politics, he insisted, would not intrude upon any art that he had anything to do with.

If Furtwängler was ready to give up at this point, he had neither the time nor the opportunity. A new problem now jangled his fraying nerves: the very survival of the Berlin Philharmonic. The orchestra had always been a "limited liability" enterprise, autonomous and self-governing ever since it was established in 1882. While it had been a world-class orchestra from the start, it continually maintained close ties with the Berlin community. It could welcome the likes of Rachmaninoff presenting the local premiere of his latest concerto on one evening, only to play a program of light music at reduced prices on the following night. Since conductors were directly responsible for paying the orchestra on a per concert basis, anyone who could afford to pay the orchestra could conduct the Berlin Philharmonic. Between generally sold-out performances and extensive tours, the orchestra always kept itself in business, but an annual deficit was inevitable. This was invariably cancelled by a subsidy from the City of Berlin. The First Mayor of Berlin had long been chairman of the Philharmonic board and always made sure that the orchestra was protected. With the arrival of the new regime, however, all payments had ceased. Dr.

3. Friedelind Wagner, "Nazis or Non-Nazis . . ." *Musical Courier*, 15 March 1946, No. 3128, p. 7.

Friedrich Lange, the current mayor at the time, made it clear to Furtwängler that he could not guarantee protection for the orchestra.[4]

Goebbels kept promising that the subsidy would be paid, but
nothing had arrived by June 1933. The Prussian Minister of Finance
simply stopped all payments to the Philharmonic. The Reich radio
network declared its agreement with the orchestra void. Göring
referred the matter back to Goebbels; the matter went around and
around.

Meanwhile, the orchestra grew restive. Some of its musicians
seized on the notion that all their problems would be solved if the Jews
in and connected with the orchestra quit. At a meeting held among the
musicians, they voted to oust a Jewish board member and remove the
Philharmonic offices from the suite presided over by Berta Geissmar.
When he returned to Berlin from his triumphant engagement at the
Paris Opéra, Furtwängler put a stop to these proceedings and forced a
meeting with Goebbels, who had been avoiding him assiduously.
Furtwängler's enormous success in France was success for Germany,
and Goebbels could not help but see its propaganda value. So a meeting was arranged. The upshot of the conference resulted in two developments, and they both appeared to be a break-through for Furtwängler. First, Goebbels threw a bone at Furtwängler. He had telegrams
sent to the Prussian State Theaters under his charge, instructing them
in so many words to allow general concert licenses to all applicants,
namely Jews.

In effect, he was reversing, at least temporarily, the ban on Jewish
performing artists.[5] The measure, of course, was a stop-gap effort.
Walter, Klemperer, and other top Jewish musicians were already
gone, but it was the only viable way of stanching the loss of talent
among those who still were left in Germany.[6] But when Furtwängler
invited Fritz Kreisler to appear with the Berlin Philharmonic following the announcement, he politely declined, saying only a recall of artists like Walter and Klemperer "could demonstrably clarify at home
and abroad the cause which is as dear to me as it is to you . . ."[7] He also
expressed skepticism about the measure to the newspapers:

> I would rather appear, if at all, at the end of the season after having seen it
> demonstrated that Commissioner Hinkel's words have been translated

4. Geissmar, p. 90.

5. They were dated 6 July 1933 and sent to five political provinces of the Reich
including: Lippe, Oldenburg, Anhalt, Lübeck, and Sachsen. Source: Bundesarchiv,
Koblenz.

6. Prieberg gives a full account of Furtwängler's role in this frequently ignored
development. *Kraftprobe*, pp. 119–121.

7. Quoted in Louis Lochner, *Fritz Kreisler*, (New York) 1950, p. 281.

into action. Art is international and I oppose chauvinism in art wherever I encounter it.[8]

Goebbels' decree became known as the Capability Principle; or *Leistungsprinzip*, because Furtwängler convinced him that Germany could not do without the capabilities of those being ousted.[9] This development also coincided with the creation of the The German-Jewish Cultural Alliance (Kulturbund der deutscher Juden). Jewish artists who could not or would not emigrate formed their own troupes and were now begrudgingly given special dispensation for public performances. Furtwängler had no direct connection with the musical elements of the Alliance, but he kept in touch with many musicians for whom this organization was the only means of making a meager income, and he freely gave them advice and material help to anyone who came to him.[10] This, at a time when it was becoming increasingly dangerous to speak even casually to Jews. The musical elements of the Alliance included choruses and several orchestras throughout the Reich comprised entirely of Jewish musicians. The largest of these ensembles were located in Frankfurt and Berlin. Wilhelm (later William) Steinberg was the first conductor of the Frankfurt orchestra. Joseph Rosenstock and Michael Taube started the orchestra in Berlin. Later, Julius Prüwer, Rudolf Schwarz,[11] and various others led both orchestras.[12] These groups continued to perform legally in public until 11 September 1941 when the Final Solution of the "Jewish Question" was formulated at the Wannsee Conference and swiftly put into effect.[13]

Despite the doubts expressed by Kreisler and others, Furtwängler kept holding tenaciously to his belief that he could effect some sort of return to normalcy, and he set out to plan the 1933–34 season of the

8. Lochner, *Kreisler*, pp. 281–282.

9. *Kraftprobe*, p. 120. Also see p. 443, note 30.

10. See Chapter 15 for a fuller discussion of Furtwängler's help to Jews and other persecuted individuals.

11. See Chapter 15.

12. The Frankfurt orchestra also toured. Aside from periodic harassment and severe financial pressures, the ensemble also had to adjust constantly to attrition, for all members who could emigrate left immediately, sometimes without notice. I am grateful to Ernst Drucker, one of the original concertmasters in the Frankfurt orchestra under Steinberg for generously illuminating for me this fascinating and neglected area of Jewish culture under the Nazis. Drucker also played for a few months in the Berlin Jüdischer Kulturbund orchestra before he emigrated to the United States in 1938. Personal conversation with the author, New York, 25 December 1990.

13. For a fuller discussion of this crucial episode in Jewish cultural life under the Nazis, see Prieberg, *Musik im N-S Staat*, pp. 81–105. Also, a frequently poignant illustrated and documented chronology of the Kulturbund is to be found in *Fritz Wisten: Drei Leben für das Theater*, ed. Akademie der Künste, (Berlin) 1990. This book was published in connection with an exhibit bearing the title of the book at the Akademie in autumn 1990.

Berlin Philharmonic. This, he reasoned, would be the test case season for his convictions, the season in which first-class artists from all over the world could come to Germany and lend their support to the principle of art free from political incursions. He got the Reich Chancellery to agree to the list of artists he wanted to invite for that season, even though they clearly saw what he was up to. He sent personal invitations to Artur Schnabel, Pablo Casals, Alfred Cortot, Fritz Kreisler, Josef Hofmann, Bronislaw Hubermann, Jacques Thibaud, Gregor Piatigorsky, and Yehudi Menuhin. In each invitation, Furtwängler repeated his argument that art and politics had to be kept separate. Only by activating that principle through public appearances, he maintained, could that principle be upheld. All these artists sent back basically the same reply. Furtwängler, they unanimously concurred, was a brave, lone soldier in the fight to keep this separation sacrosanct. But politics, whether or not he liked or knew it, already had intruded into art in Germany. None of them could accept the special privileges in the new Germany simply because they were famous or famous and Jewish. Only Cortot later changed his mind.

Furtwängler wrote again to Bronislaw Hubermann, the great violinist of the '20s and '30s. They had known each other for many years, and Furtwängler now besought him to reconsider, to help "break down the wall that separates true artists" from each other and the rest of the world. Hubermann sent a copy of his lengthy second reply to the press. At heart, he said:

> . . . it is not a question of violin concertos nor even merely of the Jews; the issue is retention of those things that our fathers achieved by blood and sacrifice, of the elementary essentials of our European culture, the freedom of personality and its unconditional responsibility to itself unhampered by the chains of caste and race.
>
> Whether these achievements will again be reflected depends not upon the individual who is "the first to break through the wall that separates, " but, as in the past, upon the collective urge that rouses the conscience of all artists in unison that, once roused will break through the sources of tyranny like a force of nature, destroying them as it would a paper wall.
>
> I cannot close this letter without expressing my deep regret at the conditions that keep me separated for the moment from Germany. And nothing would make me happier than observing a change outside the realm of concert life which would free me from the compulsion of conscience striking at my very heartstrings to renounce Germany.[14]

In the meantime, Goebbels also offered Furtwängler a so-called reorganization of the Philharmonic administration. All it meant,

14. Vienna, 31 August 1933.

however, was that Furtwängler alone would be responsible to the government on Philharmonic matters.

The "re-organization" turned out to be a hopeless arrangement. Goebbels, for example, tortured Furtwängler by calling board meetings without appearing at them. Furtwängler tried again and again to appeal to Hitler, but he finally was told the Führer had gone to Berchtesgaden on his way to Bayreuth for the Wagner Festival. By the beginning of July, the Berlin Philharmonic faced bankruptcy. Ultimately, an intermediary agreed to talk with Hitler.

The emissary was Rudolf Schmidtseck, the Nazi Kommissar in the orchestra who had known Hitler for a long time.[15] The Führer saw him immediately. Furious at what Schmidtseck told him, he sent at once for Goebbels, who sat nervously as the litany of the Philharmonic's woes was repeated to Hitler. Fully aware that his lieutenant had sabotaged him, Hitler demanded immediate remedies. The premier orchestra of the Reich could not go bankrupt, and Goebbels was to take immediate action to make sure it would survive. Hitler again repeated his admiration for Furtwängler to Schmidtseck and requested that Furtwängler come to see him at Obersalzburg.[16]

Furtwängler arrived at Obersalzberg in August, armed with an enormous portfolio detailing the orchestra's problems. He was astute enough to know that simply telling Hitler he was dead wrong about the new racial laws was foolish, so he took a backhanded approach to the delicate issue, acknowledging the "Jewish question" as a problem that had to be dealt with, but treated in a more sophisticated manner:

> Insofar as the Jew is a spiritual enemy, we must deal with him with spiritual weapons. Only through you (Hitler) can it happen—for the Jewish controversy to be handled appropriately. Laws alone will not be effective because it all depends upon how the matter is handled . . . If we attack innocent people, it gives ammunition for negative propaganda abroad . . . And I must say: much of what has happened in our cultural life is thoroughly unnecessary; the expulsion of the intelligentsia is much too excessive; we cannot solve spiritual problems merely through biological means.[17]

Furtwängler wrote this memorandum in preparation for the meeting, and he also sketched out his approach for convincing Hitler to keep the Berlin Philharmonic independent of state interference:

---

15. See Chapter Eight for more on Schmidtseck.
16. See Geissmar, pp. 91–94, and *Kraftprobe*, pp. 136–155.
17. Memorandum, "Conversation with the Führer," pp. 3–4, August 1933; Wilhelm Furtwängler Archives, Zürich.

Allowance for an exception [for retaining Jewish members of the orchestra—six full Jews and two half-Jews] must be made. The Berlin Philharmonic is the only cultural export still in demand abroad at the moment.[18]

For all his careful preparation, Furtwängler was not prepared for Hitler himself. The meeting turned into a shouting match. Furtwängler angrily denounced the catastrophic effects of the Party's racial policies on German culture and the negative impact they were having on Germany's image abroad. Hitler retorted, "When the Nazis were only seven members, three were for the Jews and four were against." The government's anti-Semitic policy, he continued, was now a "wagon rolling down a hill," with an irreversible momentum.[19] But while Furtwängler could appreciate Hitler's base, even atavistic, appeal to the masses, he failed to realize how base and atavistic Hitler himself was. Few among the top-ranking Nazis were substantially educated, and Furtwängler had problems enough communicating with those with whom he had nothing in common. Furtwängler's highly cultivated background had long fostered his penchant for expounding. Hitler was a poor listener, but just as given to rambling. Furtwängler also forfeited what he might have gained by charm or humor because he was vulnerable to a nervous spirit and a bad temper. In matters of conviction, he could lose all control. Hitler, on the other hand, was a master at appearing to lose control while making his convictions hit their mark with unerring impact. Furtwängler had met his match. Hitler finally shouted that he could do nothing for the Jews, shrieking that intervention was impossible and politically "incorrect." The anti-Semitic policy had been cast during the earliest days of the Party, and it had become—in that phrase the Nazis used over and over to sanctify their dogma—*the will of the people.*[20]

Furtwängler telephoned Geissmar in Berlin and told her of the meeting. "Hitler is not just the enemy of Jews," he said despondently. "He is the enemy of the spirit." The conversation was, of course, overheard by the Gestapo. But it didn't stop Furtwängler from saying exactly what he thought again and often.[21]

In spite of Furtwängler's seditious attitude, the Berlin Philharmonic was taken under the patronage of the Reich on 26 October 1933. It was exempt from the Aryan law, the musicians were guaran-

18. Memorandum, "Conversation with the Führer," p. 8.
19. Riess, p. 163.
20. Furtwängler also planned to discuss education and the press with Hitler, but we may never know if he got that far in this encounter. *Kraftprobe,* p. 146.
21. I am indebted to Riess, pp. 162–164, and *Kraftprobe,* pp. 144–146, for this account of the meeting.

teed salaries, and the Philharmonic office remained where it was. Furt-wängler had scored a major victory for the Philharmonic, for music, and for his contention that art and politics have nothing to do with each other. But it was a Pyrrhic victory, for the Jews left in the Berlin Philharmonic would shortly emigrate of their own accord.

10

Staatsrat

Opera was a natural pastime for members of Feldmarschall Hermann Göring's class, and the future chief of the Luftwaffe (German Air Force) had long nurtured a passion for the lyric theater. When the Nazis seized power, Göring began receiving many official titles that eventually added up to making him the second most powerful figure in the Third Reich. In the first months of the new regime, he was appointed Minister of the Interior and Minister President of Prussia.[1] He asked for control of the Staatsoper (State Opera) in Berlin—which was both the capital of Prussia as well as of Germany—and got it. The opera house in Unter den Linden was the foremost lyric stage in Berlin and one of the major musical organizations in the world. It had all the attributes he needed to embellish his ambitions: prestige, elegance, tradition, and high artistic standards. Here Göring could infuse the inveterate distinction of the opera house with his own adornments for the purpose of impressing foreign dignitaries and flattering himself. To this end, he needed a link within the musical establishment that would give credence to his image as a cultivated master of the Reich.

1. Göring was also named Chief of Police during the first months of the regime, a department that underwent a rapid and sinister evolution. In response to the dreaded threat of a communist uprising, Göring worked with SS *(Schutzstaffel)* chief Heinrich Himmler and SD *(Sicherheitsdienst)* director Reinhard Heydrich in establishing the first concentration camps for political enemies of the new Reich. He was later appointed head of the Luftwaffe (German Air Force) in 1935.

Since Furtwängler already had signed his contract[2] to become Music Director of the Staatsoper—a position created specifically for him in the previous year before the Nazis took over—Göring arrived at his new post with Germany's finest conductor already in place, even though he really wanted Fritz Busch to have the position.[3] One Sunday morning in summer 1933, Göring had an inspiration. "Quick! Let's make Furtwängler a State Councilor!" he shouted to one of his adjutants. After the war, Furtwängler recalled to his biographer Curt Riess: "One day, shortly after Göring ratified the contract I had signed before the Nazis came to power, I received a telegram from him. 'You are named a Prussian State Councilor.' I had no idea what that meant."[4] He ultimately would learn that it meant far more trouble than either he or the Nazis could ever have imagined, but for the moment, it simply meant a flattering blandishment that he had no choice in accepting because it simply was conferred.[5]

Essentially, the State Councilor (Staatsrat) was a newly created honorific title whose purpose was to give bolstered prestige to established public figures favored by the Nazis and to give themselves an air of legitimacy and propriety at a time when Germany had no credibility to the world or to its own intellectual and military classes. The title was brought into law on 8 July 1933. The details of the new position were outlined in five paragraphs of the amendment:

> 1. The Staatsrat advises the state ministry in conducting state affairs.
> 2. The State Council consists of: The President of the Ministry and the State Ministers. A total of 50 persons can be nominated [to the State Council] by the Ministry President.
> 3. The members of the State Council carry the official title: Prussian State Councilor.
> 9. State Councilors are obliged to participate in all meetings unless they are excused by the Ministry President.

2. Exact details of Furtwängler's engagement at the Staatsoper are not known. The contract has been lost.

3. Riess says Göring asked Busch to be patient while he "showed Furtwängler to the door" because he was under the impression that he was not bound to a contract Furtwängler had signed with the previous regime, p. 160. Furtwängler recounted Göring's annoyance at realizing he could not give the job to Busch in a letter to former Berlin Philharmonic member Gilbert Back dated 12 March 1949. See Chapter 19.

4. The telegram was dated 18 July 1933. Riess, p. 156.

5. As late as 1991, Furtwängler was portrayed as eagerly accepting the title, a charge for which evidence has yet to surface. See Albrecht Duemling, "Nationalism as Racism: Nazi Policies Towards Music," *Entartete Musik: Banned by the Nazis*, Los Angeles Philharmonic Association Program booklet, (Los Angeles) 1991, pp. 5–6. Duemling also says Furtwängler grabbed the title of Staatsrat after he got involved in defending Paul Hindemith. Furtwängler was named Staatsrat in July 1933. The Hindemith Scandal erupted in November 1934.

14. The office of the State Councilor is an honorary position. State Councilors receive free train fare and an honorarium [6000 RM per annum] from the State Ministry. A waiver of the honorarium is not permissible.[6]

Nor, as Furtwängler was to find, could the title be refused or renounced. It was a title for life. Except for an elaborate and highly publicized opening session on 15 September, inaugurated with colorful flourish by Göring, the State Council never met again. Nor did the title carry any substantive influence, except perhaps in making hotel or restaurant reservations. While Furtwängler was always referred to as Staatsrat in the newspapers and in official documents and correspondence relating to him, he never used the title himself. By appointing him to this meaningless but high-sounding post, Göring was literally cementing Furtwängler's feet in the bedrock of his personal empire. What is more, he was using the honorific title to cast him as a Nazi, even though Furtwängler had firmly refused to join the Party and was bridling openly at the new cultural policies. He was also using the title to make Furtwängler feel as though he had power, a ploy that resulted more from coincidence than from manipulative guile. There, Göring achieved his objective, even though Furtwängler actually had more tacit power probably than any other musician in Europe at the time.

For his part, Furtwängler thought the new title would indeed give him the authority to keep the Nazis at bay on musical matters, and he found Göring quite flexible in the Aryan policy. The young thugs who were constantly on the prowl in the name of the State rarely harassed him—at least in Berlin.[7] To many both at home and abroad, Furtwängler's decision to honor his contract at the Staatsoper was reason enough to condemn him as a Nazi. Foreign reports of his new position as music director left most readers to assume he had negotiated his contract with Göring, not the previous administration, and the Nazis were not about to disabuse anyone of that notion.

But there were also purely practical reasons for establishing his presence at the Staatsoper. Max von Schillings had died suddenly on 24 July 1933, shortly after he had been selected to take charge of the Städtische Oper, Berlin's "other" opera house in Charlottenburg. Schillings had been one of Furtwängler's composition teachers and the composer of several successful operas in the post-Wagnerian vein

6. These paragraphs of the State Councilor Amendment are cited by Riess, p. 157.
7. On more than one occasion, Göring shouted, "I will be the one who decides who is Aryan and who is not around here!" See Geissmar, p. 122.

including *Mona Lisa.* Furtwängler admired his work and believed in the conservative tradition in German composition that Schillings had staunchly represented. But Furtwängler also clearly saw disruption festering in the wake of Schillings' death, for his passing left a gap at the top of the opera house administration, leaving Berlin's second most important opera house vulnerable to the depredations of politics in artistic and day-to-day matters.

Furtwängler saw that disruption being led by a politically connected opera singer who wanted the job. Wilhelm Rode had long been one of Germany's outstanding and most popular dramatic baritones, and he now was making trouble for Heinz Tietjen, who was General Intendant for all the Prussian theaters, including the Staatsoper Unter den Linden and the Bayreuth Festival. Rode's legion of fans included a very special opera lover: Adolf Hitler. Schillings' death opened an opportunity for him to try to run an opera house, and he had no compunctions about exploiting his political ties to get the job. In fact, Rode took Tietjen on, even before Schillings died, writing a nasty letter to Tietjen in the spring of 1933, denouncing him for hiring too many Jewish performers in the Prussian State Theaters.[8] Tietjen was almost fired because he already was in big trouble with the Nazis for permitting a modernistic production of *Tannhäuser* to be staged at the Staatsoper, but Furtwängler intervened to save him, a gesture of sincere goodwill he would later regret.

Rode got the job at the Städtische Oper, which was under Goebbels' control, and Tietjen remained in charge of the Staatsoper, which belonged to Göring. But Rode now had a wily and dangerous enemy. Always mindful of his debts, Tietjen gave Rode a long rope to do with as he might. A year later, Rode began to feel pressure around his collar. Colleagues who only a few months earlier had signed petitions to Hinkel, urging him to select Rode as their new boss, now were writing poison pen letters about this towering Wotan for trying to organize a drag ball for the last birthday Ernst Roehm (chief of the SA—*Sturmabteilung*) was to celebrate before his untimely demise.[9] The musical portion of the festivities was to include a transvestite (men as women, of course) orchestra.[10] The accusation proved groundless, but the investigation it prompted cast Rode's file into a pinkish leather binder.

8. 25 April 1933. Source: Berlin Document Center, RKK. Tietjen, Vol. 1, p. 105.

9. Roehm was arrested and summarily executed after a conspiracy in the Nazi hierarchy successfully plotted his undoing. See Chapter 11.

10. Memorandum from Schlösser, 22 August 1935. Source: Bundesarchiv, Koblenz, R 55/970, pp. 102–106. Cited also by Henry Bair, "Lenkung der Berliner Opernhäuser," in *Musik und Musikpolitik im faschistischen Deutschland,* ed. H.-W. Heister and H.-G. Klein, (Frankfurt) 1984, p. 85.

Such was the Byzantine atmosphere surrounding Furtwängler at Berlin's two premier opera houses.[11] Despite the infighting backstage, the egomaniacal way Göring ran the company on Unter den Linden, and the ongoing power ploys Goebbels was always organizing against Göring, Furtwängler discovered his move to the Staatsoper was something of a godsend, for Göring's personal order of priorities maintained the Staatsoper as the gilt-edged symbol of his pretensions, and he managed by and large to get away with it. For once in operatic history, personal vanity actually worked to the benefit of an opera house: Göring owed most of his success there to keeping the repertoire and production values relatively free of ideological intrusions. Later, he took progressively less interest in his opera house, gradually handing over virtually complete control to Heinz Tietjen, who steered it through the war with devious but dexterous skill.[12]

Meanwhile, Goebbels tried with limited success to make the rival Städtische Oper a model Nazi opera house and kept eyeing Göring's Staatsoper greedily for his own domain.[13] But for all his ongoing attempts to bring music under Total Conformity *(Gleichschaltung)*, the cultural apparatus of the Nazi Party never really came up with a clearly defined and enforceable policy spelling out what was Naziesque music and what was not.[14] While they constantly used or attempted to use past and recently composed music for certain short-term political ends, they had no precise philosophy about what constituted acceptable contemporary, newly created music. As a result, the greater part of the repertoire at the Staatsoper remained devoted to the masterworks of the 18th and 19th century, just as it had under Schillings, and far fewer new works from mediocre Nazi-approved composers surfaced on Unter den Linden throughout the Third Reich. Ironically, its record for presenting better contemporary German opera outstripped the Städtische Oper. Nonetheless, the policy

11. The Kroll Opera, once Berlin's third major opera house, had a short and noble existence on the Platz der Republik beginning in 1925 and ascended to legendary heights under Otto Klemperer's direction after 1927, but it succumbed to internecine politics and the economic woes plaguing Germany in 1931. See Chapters 5 and 6.
12. Göring officially gave Tietjen full control of his domain on the eve of the war in a letter (1 September 1939) to the Prussian Ministry of Finance. Geheimes Staatsarchiv, Rep. 151, Nr. 197, pp. 31–32.
13. The fruits of Goebbels' objectives in producing acceptable contemporary lyric works at the Städtische Oper included such enduring staples as *Black Peter* by Norbert Schultze (1938), *Katerina* (with Elisabeth Schwarzkopf in a small role) by Arthur Kusterer (1938), and *Boccaccio* (with Elisabeth Schwarzkopf in a leading role) by Walter Lutze (1940). See Detlef Meyer zu Heringdorf, *Das Charlottenburger Opernhaus*, (Berlin) 1988, pp. 356–425, and Prieberg, *Musik im N-S Staat*, for a fuller discussion of Schultze (pp. 335–340) and Lutze (p. 60).
14. Goebbels organized a Reichs Music Days festival in 1938 to redress the problem of an amorphous policy toward music. See Chapter 16.

toward older established works at both houses also become subject to political shifts in Germany's affairs as time passed. But again, the policy was quirky and full of exceptions: French composers were banned after 1940 upon the Nazi occupation of France, but Bizet's *Carmen* remained simply because it was so popular. This even though many Germans believed Bizet was Jewish (he did marry a Jewess, Geneviève Halévy). Polish and Russian composers were removed from the repertoire after Germany widened its eastern front in 1941, but Chopin remained an exception.[15]

Of the new works that managed both to pass muster as Aryan music and receive popular acclaim were *Rembrandt von Rijn* by the resident Danish composer Paul von Klenau and *Peer Gynt* by Werner Egk.[16] Klenau's opera was an especially surprising choice because it dealt sympathetically with the Dutch painter, who was Jewish. Göring never was fully conscious of this discrepancy with Nazi philosophy, simply because he was bereft of the intellect required to take notice of it. But Furtwängler instinctively realized Göring's ineptitude at such details. That awareness prompted him to follow his irascible nature, and he set about looking for ways to test how far that breach could be widened. This was an enterprise that would take a little time.

For now, Furtwängler was content to embark on his new post at the Staatsoper with relatively conservative projects. Limitations on his hectic schedule also constricted the range of operas he chose. For someone holding the position of Music Director at the Staatsoper, he conducted relatively infrequently.[17] Between his debut there in November 1931 with Pfitzner's *Das Herz* and the end of the 1932–

15. I am deeply grateful for much background on this period to Henry Bair, Lewis and Clark College, for access to his highly informative unpublished paper "Opera Goes to War: The Berlin Opera Houses, 1939–1942."

16. The world premiere of *Rembrandt van Rijn* took place on 23 January 1937. *Peer Gynt* received its first performance on 24 November 1938. The casts included the best singers available at the time: Marcel Wittrisch, Rudolf Bockelmann and Käte Heidersbach in the former, Matthieu Ahlersmeyer, Hilde Scheppan and Benno Arnold in the latter. These works turned out to be the major operatic achievements of the Third Reich, indicating how miserably the Nazis failed in inspiring operatic composition. Between 1933 and 1942, little more than a half-dozen operas by contemporary German composers were produced at the Staatsoper. Werner Egk also had premieres of *Zaubergeige* (1935) and his ballet *Joan und Zarissa* (1940). Other contemporary works receiving premieres at the Staatsoper included another opera from the resident Dane Paul von Klenau: *Die Königen* (1940); and an opera each from Paul Graener: *Schirin und Gertrud* (1937, completed in 1920) and Fried Walter: *Andreas Wolfius* (1940). The Staatsoper gave other premieres, but the operas mentioned here constituted the bulk of new works by contemporary composers. See Julius Kapp, *Geschichte der Staatsoper*, (Berlin) 1942, pp. 197–251.

17. Furtwängler's immediate superior at the Staatsoper was Heinz Tietjen, and their relationship, as we shall see, was anything but felicitous.

1933 season, he led only 24 performances of three other operas: *Elektra* (4), *Tristan* (5), and *Meistersinger* (15). Nonetheless, he conducted more opera during this period than at any time since he had left Mannheim in 1920. Broadcast recordings of these performances have been lost, and while reviews were uniformly glowing, only a faint impression of what they must have been like can be inferred from cast lists.

Some of these performances must have been grand indeed. Furtwängler's Elektra, for example, was Rose Pauly-Dreesen, one of the finest and best-known dramatic sopranos of her time. Elektra became something of a signature role for Pauly-Dreesen, and she sang it with enormous success later at Salzburg and in New York.[18] With possibly one exception, her colleagues in Berlin were fully her equal in temperament and vocal competence. They included Margarete Klose (Klytämnestra), Viorica Ursuleac (Chrysothemis), Walter Grossman (Orest), and Marcel Wittrisch (Aegisth).[19] In *Tristan*, Furtwängler had Gotthelf Pistor and Lauritz Melchior alternating in the title part with Leider as Isolde, Herbert Janssen and Rudolf Bockelmann sharing Kurwenal, Karin Branzell occasionally replacing Klose, and Alexander Kipnis usually playing King Marke. For *Meistersinger*, Furtwängler had Lotte Lehmann, Käte Heidersbach, Bockelmann, Friedrich Schorr, Emanuel List, Kipnis, Max Lorenz, and Fritz Wolff at his disposal. To say these were "dream casts" is no hyperbole. Such combinations of vocal talent were hard to come by and rarely put together anywhere else in the world at the time, though Furtwängler took most of the *Tristan* cast to Paris for his operatic debut on 7 June 1932. He also returned later with his casts from Berlin for *Meistersinger* in 1935. The recorded evidence left by these singers attests to their vocal gifts. What they must have sounded like under Furtwängler in the white heat of an inspired performance we can only imagine.

For all these operatic triumphs, Furtwängler's real home and affections lay with the Berlin Philharmonic. In the ten years he had been its leader, this ensemble had become an extension of his whole being and reflected what he most cared about in an invariably spontaneous and exciting way. He had developed a special, almost mystic rapport with his musicians over the years that he could never really cultivate at the State Opera with its myriad production details, ever-changing casts, stagehands, and production technicians.

While Goebbels had given Furtwängler what he wanted at the

18. The intensity and vocal strength Pauly-Dreesen brought to the part emerges through the wretched sound reproduction on a recording of excerpts from a concert performance in New York in 1937 under Artur Rodzinski. UROC 322.
19. The exception was Viorica Ursuleac. She was married to the conductor Clemens Krauss and received many opportunities well above the standard of her vocalism.

Philharmonic, only because Hitler ordered him to do so, neither Furtwängler nor the orchestra had heard the last of him. For a brief time,
the Brownshirts left the Philharmonic and its concerts alone, but
marauding Nazi youths continued to step up their harassment of Jews
at every available opportunity. Their efforts were not always on target. One evening, for instance, they arrived at a concert hall to disrupt
a recital given by a Jewish singer. The artist performing that evening
happened to be the famed pianist, Edwin Fischer, a *tragbar*, or
"approved," artist. Meanwhile, the Jewish singer performing in the
hall next door completed his program unmolested.[20]

In something of a diversionary move, Goebbels' plans to appropriate all German culture took a new and devastating direction. He
already had absorbed the authority of Department VII into his Propaganda Ministry. This Department was the cultural affairs sector of
the Foreign Office which had always been responsible for German cultural interests outside Germany. No art exhibition or artistic activity
could properly be executed abroad without their help. They also facilitated paperwork for artists coming to Germany, and frequently
assisted the Philharmonic in providing smooth passage for guest performers. Once Goebbels appropriated Department VII into his Propaganda Ministry—ProMi—doing artistic business outside Germany
became increasingly difficult. Most of the officials in the Department
who actually had looked after Germany's cultural image were
replaced by coarse, incompetent bureaucrats. This new group of petty
bureaucrats quickly destroyed the delicate lines of communication
that previously had eased the exportation of German culture to the
rest of the world.

In winter 1934 Furtwängler took the Philharmonic on a tour of
England, Holland, and Belgium. Despite threats of disruption, the
tour went successfully. In London, Furtwängler was photographed
with the Austrian Ambassador, Baron Franckenstein, and rumors
flared that Furtwängler was resigning from the Berlin Philharmonic to
go back to Vienna immediately. Sir Thomas Beecham, who was the
most powerful figure in British musical circles at the time, had long
been an admirer of Furtwängler and personally made sure that neither
he nor his secretary Berta Geissmar were disturbed. By taking a direct
hand in making them feel comfortable, he also observed Geissmar
closely and was greatly impressed with her deftness in handling all of
Furtwängler's affairs. In Brussels, anti-German demonstrations outside the concert hall almost forced a cancellation, but Furtwängler
would not hear of it. In Antwerp, a stink bomb exploded during the

20. Geissmar, p. 98.

concert, but the orchestra finished the performance. Afterwards, police escorted Furtwängler from the hall.[21]

Now that Department VII was under his control, making it impossible for the Berlin Philharmonic or Furtwängler to go abroad without his permission, Goebbels made another attempt at exerting more influence over the orchestra by sending an auditor to review the Philharmonic's books. Of course, the auditor's report put the orchestra in a very bad light, recommending that culprits such as Geissmar and other Jews in the orchestra should be fired. Furtwängler immediately wrote a lengthy time-consuming counter-report and repeated yet again his view of the consequences for taking such unwarranted action.[22]

Even before Furtwängler finished his counter-report, Goebbels' Ministry sent two unemployed non-entities to the orchestra offices with letters demanding that they had to be put on the payroll. Philharmonic finances already were stretched to the limit, but Geissmar delicately rearranged the budget so that the Berlin Philharmonic could participate in Hitler's massive job procurement project.

Goebbels' next move was made against Geissmar. He was the grand master in the Nazi technique of pushing to see how much the quarry could endure before making some kind of counter-move, and he relished the challenge of removing the strongest barrier between Furtwängler and the rest of the world. Actually, Goebbels grudgingly admired Geissmar and made no secret of it, for she was the perfect factota. In fact, he told Friedelind Wagner, "It's too bad Geissmar is Jewish. Otherwise, I'd force her to become my secretary."[23] At first, she received a gentle warning that she should not spend so much time with Furtwängler. Then she was told to keep away from the orchestra offices. Finally she was told to stay away from Philharmonic concerts if she did not wish to endanger Furtwängler's life. She complied and said nothing to him. He quickly learned why she was becoming so distant, and he threatened to resign if he and all his working collaborators were not left alone. Goebbels backed off, again for the moment.

But Goebbels' feline pursuit turned deadly when Geissmar performed a diplomatic coup that earned her top-billing on his blacklist. The Italian Ambassador, Benito Cerutti, besought her on behalf of Mussolini to include Italy on the orchestra's approaching spring tour. She promised to try to rearrange the orchestra's schedule so that they

21. Geissmar, p. 101.
22. Geissmar, p. 102.
23. Personal conversation with the author, 6 October 1990.

could accept his invitation, but she soon let him know there would be a stiff price for her trouble. Mussolini at this time was considered a protector of persecuted German intellectuals, and Geissmar told Cerutti that the least he could do was to arrange a meeting between Furtwängler and *Il Duce*. The brief tour of Italy was a triumph. Furtwängler was duly received by Mussolini at his palace early in May 1934, and the fact was reported all over the world.

Goebbels was livid, for a swiney Jewish secretary whose skills he made no secret of envying had managed to garner a diplomatic relations victory with neither the help nor approval of his Ministry. He went to Hitler and demanded her immediate dismissal. Göring saw the situation as an opportunity to do Furtwängler a favor and at the same time thwart his rival Goebbels. He sought an audience with Hitler, who had promised Göring that Furtwängler's secretary would remain protected, and made sure Geissmar was retained.[24]

In the autumn, Goebbels tried again to bring Furtwängler to heel. This time, Furtwängler received an invitation "at the wish of the Führer" to conduct at the Nürnberg Rally. Nazi officials waited eagerly to see how he would deal with this dilemma, for they deeply resented his refusal to become "one of the boys" and loathed the prestige he enjoyed abroad that had enabled him to get away with his apostasy unscathed. For them, the invitation was the long awaited litmus test. Surely his appearance at the rally would be inevitable. Furtwängler knew all too well that if he conducted at any political function, especially a carnival of this order, he would forever abrogate his belief in the separation of art and politics. He conveyed to Hitler his disinclination to conduct at the rally.

Surprisingly, Hitler was sympathetic. He may well have been forewarned by his "musical adviser" and director of foreign press relations Ernst "Putzi" Hanfstängl (who greatly admired Furtwängler both as a musician and person) not to make an issue of Furtwängler's reluctance to perform. Whatever the reason, Hitler claimed vehemently that he never had known about the invitation. Of course, Furtwängler should be excused![25]

The importance of Hanfstängl's influence over Hitler in artistic matters is usually overlooked, since he has invariably been dismissed as a mere court jester to Hitler. If Hanfstängl's memoirs bear any credibility, he was the only person who had a special channel of access to Hitler, quite unlike all his other cronies prior to 1940.[26] Born in

24. See Geissmar, p. 111, and Riess, p. 172.
25. Riess, p. 172.
26. Ernst Hanfstängl, *Unheard Witness*, (Philadelphia and New York) 1957.

Bavaria in 1887 to partially American forebears (his maternal grand-father was General William Heine who was on General Dix's staff in the Army of the Potomac during the Civil War), his family were noted purveyors of art replicas. Hanfstängl attended Harvard and graduated in 1909. His classmates in Boston included Franklin Delano Roosevelt, and he attended stag parties in the White House basement while Franklin's grandfather Theodore was President. Hanfstängl returned to Europe to take the customary Grand Tour of the Continent common to young men of his class. He went back to America and served as the manager of the family's New York store until World War I when the Custodian of Enemy Property appropriated it. With the help of his powerful cronies from Harvard, he remained in New York and opened the Academy Art Store opposite Carnegie Hall. He had married an American by this time, and they decided to live in Munich. Around 1923, Hanfstängl encountered a brash, brilliant orator who seemed to articulate Germany's problems perfectly, and he at once fell under Adolf Hitler's spell. He and his American wife instantly recognized in Hitler a diamond-in-the-rough, and they took the unemployed house painter under their wing. The Hanfstängls opened up a world for young Hitler that he never had seen. They introduced him to the cream of Bavarian society and trained him to be sophisticated in dress and artistically knowledgeable.

What drew Hitler to Hanfstängl especially, though, was the latter's extraordinary musical skill. Hanfstängl had studied piano with Bernhard Stavenhagen, Liszt's last pupil, and he was an amateur in the positive sense of the word—one of those gifted musicians who never took up a concert career, even though he had the mastery for one. Hitler, too, was an amateur, but he had neither the discipline nor perhaps the requisite capability to make a life of music. He had already developed an obsession with music during his formative years in Austria, and he knew the operas of Wagner by heart. When it came to these music dramas, he evidently could be very perceptive. As Hitler's political fortunes began to rise in the late 1920s, Hanfstängl frequently played Wagner on the piano for him late in the evening. Hanfstängl discovered that Hitler's mood palpably calmed after such brief recitals, and he used these opportunities to try and temper the increasingly radical views Hitler was developing—particularly against the Jews. In fact, he, like many conservatives around Hitler, naively kept believing until it was far too late that he could eventually normalize the Führer.

Hanfstängl's unique connection to Hitler was obsessively resented by others who were closest to the Führer. Whenever Hanfstängl accompanied Hitler to Goebbels' house, for example, the Minister of Propaganda would have the radio blaring so that Hanfstängl could not play the piano. Goebbels also played recordings—sometimes by Furtwängler—so that a piano recital could be avoided.

Furtwängler managed to extricate himself from taking part in the official portions of the Nürnberg event in 1934, but the Nazis were ready for him the following year. If they could not get him to perform in the official part of the rally, they obliged him to conduct a gala performance of *Die Meistersinger* at the Nürnberg Opera on the eve of the rally. A performance by Furtwängler anywhere within hailing distance of a Nazi Party function was a major coup for the regime, and the fact was duly reported in the international press.

Was the great Furtwängler finally buckling under?

All the while, Goebbels continued to exert pressure on Furtwängler through the Music Department of the Reichskulturkammer, which had become the state's official concert booking agency. No artist, foreign or German, could appear in Germany without the permission of this agency, and its mandate was to further the careers of *tragbar* or "acceptable" artists, many of whom had suddenly risen from well-deserved obscurity.[27] Since most of the finest foreign artists now refused to appear in Germany, Furtwängler had endless arguments with the agency in booking the best that were still available. His efforts were further frustrated by corruption within the Reichskulturkammer and their efforts to undo Geissmar's bookings, which she continued to make without going through them.

The real challenge to Furtwängler that the rank-and-file Nazis had hoped for was soon to come, and the gauntlet would be thrown not by the Party but by Furtwängler himself.

27. A notable exception to the ban was the creation of the German-Jewish Cultural Alliance (Kulturbund der deutscher Juden). See Chapter 9.

11

The Hindemith Scandal

Before the summer of 1934 was over, another turn of events sent world history further down a course fated to last for more than a decade. Chancellor Paul von Hindenburg died on 2 August. Although the old man wanted a simple small funeral, Hitler would have none of it. He ordered an ostentatious memorial rite that gave the Nazis another opportunity for an epic panoply of bombast and pomp. Goebbels tried to invite Furtwängler to conduct the funeral music, but Furtwängler left Berlin before he could be asked, and did not return until the funeral was long over.

Hitler now became both Chancellor and President of the Third Reich. In attaining the highest power he had so long awaited, the gigantic machine he had built over the years was poised to achieve even more power and glory. No one could have taken these ambitions less seriously than Furtwängler; the only concept of power he could understand was in the realm of music. Cannier men instantly became aware of the rampant violence in the streets and what it signified, but if he was aware of it at all, Furtwängler felt it would somehow soon blow over.

Furtwängler continued to arrange the Philharmonic's programs as though nothing had happened on the political scene, and thus, Mendelssohn—now a banned composer—was performed several times during the autumn. About this time, Furtwängler read and liked parts of an opera Paul Hindemith was composing called *Mathis der Maler,* based on the life of the great German painter, Mathias Grünewald. Hindemith was a professor at the High School of Music in Berlin at the time, and he had gained considerable notoriety throughout the 1920s for his severe expressionist compositions. Leading conductors of the period such as Otto Klemperer and Hermann Scherchen championed his works, which were associated with a feature of German Expressionism known as the New Reality (*Neue Sachlichkeit*). Furtwängler had been looking for a work to test how far he could push the Nazis' murky, inconsistent policies on musical matters, and he found the perfect goad in Hindemith's new opera. He programmed it for the new season at the Staatsoper.

What he did not realize—nor care about—was that Hitler hated Hindemith's music. The Führer had attended the premiere of the composer's opera *Neues vom Tage* in 1929 and loathed it, dubbing it with the worst artistic epithet the Nazis could hurl on a work that did not conform to Party ideals: degenerate. Furtwängler also had no idea that Goebbels loathed Hindemith personally because the latter had dismissed the Jews as a menace to Germany when he told a reporter from the Nazi newspaper *Völkischer Beobachter*, "Worry about the Jews? I wish I had only such big problems to worry about."[1] Even though Hindemith was the most qualified composer to represent Germany music at that time and was an Aryan to boot, his "bolshevist" approach to composition, his impolitic remarks to the press, and his failure to please Hitler conspired to earn him a special place on the Nazis' blacklist, not to mention his Jewish wife. While the Nazis' chief ideologue Alfred Rosenberg castigated Hindemith for fouling German music, Göring summarily removed *Mathis der Maler* from the production schedule at the Staatsoper. Furtwängler protested vigorously. Göring explained that only Hitler could give the approval to perform this opera. Furtwängler was furious that his authority over musical matters was being challenged and demanded an audience with the Führer.[2]

While he was waiting for the interview, Furtwängler programmed a symphonic synthesis of the opera with the Berlin Philharmonic for a pair of subscription concerts. The Nazis were still jockeying for strength as a regime, and Furtwängler capitalized on their insecurity by going ahead, convinced that he could somehow persuade Hitler to approve the premiere of the opera after the public heard the suite and once he talked with him face-to-face. When Furtwängler actually conducted it on 11 and 12 March 1934 the public took the performance as an open protest and seized the event to vent their sympathy. Wild

1. Quoted in Riess, p. 177.
2. See Geissmar, pp. 129–134.

applause greeted the music, and Party officials who were present interpreted the ovation as outright sedition, but they could not arrest the entire audience. Nor were they willing to gamble on arresting an internationally revered figure like Furtwängler. The Nazi press had a field day condemning Hindemith, his degenerate music, and Furtwängler. Rant as they might, however, the Nazis were hard-put to stop him and Furtwängler knew it. The experience also taught him that there was a significant number of people in his audiences who were opposed to the Nazis but powerless to act against them.

While the controversy brewed into an odiferous stew, Furtwängler had little time to brood over it, though he bridled every time another attack was published in the state-run newspapers. Having conducted earlier in the season the Berlin premiere of Strauss' latest opera, *Arabella*,[3] to enormous acclaim with a cast including Viorica Ursuleac in the title part, Käte Heidersbach as her sister, and Jaro Prohaska as her patient suitor, he now busied himself with a new production of *Der Freischütz* at the State Opera set for five performances beginning 20 March 1934. As usual, Furtwängler's immediate superior Heinz Tietjen produced it, assembling a heavyweight cast featuring Maria Müller, Marcel Wittrisch, Herbert Janssen, and Michael Bohnen. He also took the Berlin Philharmonic on a tour through the German provinces, France, Switzerland, and Austria. As the Hindemith controversy continued to simmer, he took his first casts of *Tristan* and *Meistersinger* in late May and June to Paris for a pair of performances of each opera.[4]

If Furtwängler or anyone else in Germany thought at this time that the Nazi regime would be short-lived, the night of 30 June 1934 put these hopes seriously in doubt. It became known as "The Night of the Long Knives"; the Nazi hierarchy writhed in lethal convulsions. A major segment of the SA *(Sturmabteilung)* was wiped out, and its leader General Ernst Roehm was arrested. The SA had been the Nazi movement's muscle in its early days, and their aim was to intimidate and crush opposition to the Party. Roehm was one of Hitler's oldest and closest allies during the Nazis' formative struggles, but he turned out to be the big loser in the grab for power within the Nazi organization after the regime was solidified. His enemies—notably Himmler and Göring—convinced Hitler that Roehm was hatching a plot to overthrow him and was planning to use the SA to do it. Hitler saw that

3. Furtwängler gave the premiere at the Staatsoper on 12 October 1933, a few weeks after Fritz Busch conducted the world premiere in Dresden. The date of the premiere occasionally has been given incorrectly as 21 October.

4. Melchior, Leider, Janssen, Kipnis, and Gertrude Runger appeared in *Tristan*. Lehmann, Lorenz, and Bockelmann took the principal parts in *Meistersinger*.

Roehm and his SA were indeed becoming more powerful even as his need for his old ally was diminishing. What is more, Roehm's flagrant homosexuality was becoming an embarrassment to the machismo image the Nazis took every opportunity to portray. Roehm had to go. Hitler boasted later that he arrested Roehm himself as his friend of bygone days was cavorting in bed with a recent SA recruit.[5] In any event, Roehm was taken away and summarily shot. As his executioners aimed to fire, he shrieked, "Heil Hitler!" The surviving predators closed ranks, Himmler's SS *(Schutzstaffel)* became the elite security force within the regime, and Hitler continued to consolidate his power.

In midsummer, while Furtwängler was vacationing at his house in St. Moritz, the Nazis expanded their crusade of violence by blowing up a railway bridge near Salzburg, making the annual summer Festival there a dangerous place to visit. On 25 July Engelbert Dollfuss, the Chancellor of Austria, was assassinated. That the Nazis had their acquisitive eyes on their German-speaking neighbor was clear even to someone as politically myopic as Furtwängler. When the news reached Hitler, he was in the official box at Bayreuth listening to a performance. Friedelind Wagner was sitting next to him when Goebbels softly entered the box, bent his head between Hitler and Friedelind, and whispered the news loud enough so that Friedelind could hear. "Hitler's lips curled into a smile," she recalls. "'Now we must make a good show of our grief.'"[6]

The Jewish members of the Berlin Philharmonic read these developments clearly. Furtwängler begged them to stay and face down the intimidation these events portended, but the pressure undeniably had become too much for them. One by one, the full Jews Goldberg (first concertmaster), Joseph Schuster (cello), and Gilbert Back (violin) left the orchestra and emigrated. Only Nicolai Graudan (cello) remained until the end of 1935.[7] Several other members of the orchestra were half Jewish or were married to Jews. Furtwängler obtained special permits for them to remain with the orchestra and made sure their spouses were never harmed.[8]

But Furtwängler himself was not about to be intimidated—at

---

5. A well-circulated riddle at the time: How do you describe the perfect Nazi? He is as blond as Hitler, as slender as Göring, as tall and strong as Goebbels, and as heterosexual as Roehm.

6. Personal conversation with the author, Mainz, 6 October 1990.

7. See Chapter 15 for an account of Graudan's departure from Berlin.

8. The amount of Jewish blood flowing through the veins was a crucial issue for the status of Jews in the grim light of the racial laws. With numerous exceptions, the future of full and half-Jews became gravely endangered. Quarter-Jews generally were left unharmed. See Chapter 15 for a fuller discussion of Furtwängler's assistance to Jews and other persecuted individuals.

least not yet. He also felt he had to set an example, since virtually no one else inside Germany was speaking out against the Nazis.⁹ Increasingly he had grown angry about ongoing attacks against him in the press following the Hindemith Scandal, and over the summer, he wrote a lengthy article entitled "The Hindemith Case." This was published on the front page of the first Sunday edition of the *Deutsche Allgemeine Zeitung* on 25 November 1934. The editor, Fritz Klein, telephoned Furtwängler to make him aware of the risk to his own safety, but Furtwängler told him to go ahead and publish it. The first edition sold out instantly. A further printing had to be issued. From start to finish the piece enraged the Nazis, but two assertions especially made them apoplectic. First, he compared Hindemith's controversial musical nature with the venerated Nazi-sanctioned composer Richard Strauss, recalling the furor that had accompanied the latter's 1909 premiere of Salome, based on the lurid closet drama by Oscar Wilde. For Furtwängler it was an apt comparison. They were both "approved" racially, and they both were committed to promulgating the German spirit in music. For the Nazis, such comparisons were akin to likening Satan with God. Secondly, he concluded his piece with this assertion:

> It is certain that no one of the younger generation has done more for the international prestige of German music than Paul Hindemith. What is more, it is impossible to predict what importance in the future his work may have. But that is beside the point. We are concerned with more essential matters, and we should clearly understand that there are very few real musicians in the world today, and we cannot afford to deprive ourselves of a man like Hindemith.

The shock waves the article created even took the jaded citizenry of Berlin by surprise. Furtwängler rarely conducted twice in one day, but on that Sunday, he supervised an open rehearsal with the Philharmonic in the morning and conducted *Tristan* at the Staatsoper in the evening. The general rehearsal in the morning was jammed with spectators. "All hell broke loose," recalls Hans Schwieger, who was an assistant to Erich Kleiber at the time—later to become conductor of the Kansas City Symphony. "Everybody in Berlin was talking about the article, and the Philharmonie was as tense as it was sold out. Nobody thought anyone would do what Furtwängler did."¹⁰

When Furtwängler appeared, thunderous applause broke out. The

9. At a safe distance outside Germany, of course, the chorus led by Thomas Mann and other notable non-Jewish émigrés was vociferous and usually in perfect unison.

10. Personal telephone conversation with the author, 5 May 1990. Furtwängler later helped Schwieger when he got into trouble with the Nazis for being married to a Jew. See Chapter 15.

reception lasted several minutes, prompting reports to the authorities that it had amounted to a demonstration in support of the article. The generous program included a new work by Heinrich Kaminsky, two violin concertos performed by Zino Francescatti, and the Brahms First.[11] But few noticed what was being played; the occasion was the main event. In the evening, a similar ovation met Furtwängler as he stepped into the pit of the Staatsoper.

Göring was seated with friends in his box and heard the gales of approval himself. When the applause continued unabated, he shouted that "such things cannot be tolerated!" He phoned Hitler after the performance and told him Furtwängler was "endangering the authority of the government."[12] The Nazi music magazines were exercised. One of them howled:

> We reject the accusation that the attack against Hindemith is the result of political considerations. We reject Furtwängler's attempt to discredit our objective disapproval of Hindemith. The fact that Hindemith had displayed a consciously un-German attitude before the Third Reich already excludes him from the Party's cultural affairs.[13]

Hindemith's career as the Great White Hope (he was an Aryan despite efforts to prove otherwise) of German music and his career in his homeland were effectively finished. He soon left with his wife for Turkey and eventually secured passage to America. The Staatsoper premiere of *Mathis der Maler* never took place.[14]

Göring remained impassive as Furtwängler told him that he would resign unless the attacks against him ceased, but he really was not enthusiastic about quitting. That would mean he had given up to the Nazis. He offered to continue working in Germany as long as he was not required to hold any political office. Göring took the offer to Hitler who rejected it immediately.

Furtwängler drafted his resignation from the Staatsoper, the Philharmonic, the Reichsmusikkammer, of which he was vice-president, and the State Council. Göring saw him a week later and tried to bargain. He would accept his resignation from the Staatsoper, but he could continue as music director of the Philharmonic. Furtwängler

11. Kaminsky's work was a short tonal work called *Dorische Musik*. It has never since been performed again by the Berlin Philharmonic. Francescatti played Bach's Concerto in D minor and Paganini's Concerto in D Major.

12. Riess, p. 182. See also *Kraftprobe*, pp. 186–188.

13. *Die Musik*, December 1934, p. 215.

14. The premiere ultimately took place on 28 May 1938 in Zürich and was revived the following year. The Nazi press ignored both. During that interval, it was given a concert performance over the BBC in England.

declined the arrangement, arguing that the two posts were a unit. Finally, Göring let him go free of all his duties except State Councilor. "That is not a position but a title," he argued. "It cannot be given up by anyone on whom it has been conferred. Only I, Göring, can remove this title if someone has committed treason or a civil crime. If, for example," he suggested leering, "you were caught stealing silver spoons . . ."[15]

Of all the musicians still in Germany, only Erich Kleiber—a highly regarded staff conductor at the Staatsoper—openly supported Furtwängler after his resignation. When Kleiber entered the pit at the Staatsoper to conduct *Otello*, he was greeted with scattered hisses from Nazis planted throughout the house. Kleiber read these extra-musical disturbances as the sign of a situation he had neither the temperament nor the fortitude to keep resisting. Göring tried to prevent him from quitting, but Kleiber refused, saying he could not conduct in a country where racial discrimination was a government policy.

Göring was furious at being backed against the wall by two employees, but he was not to be undone by them. He resourcefully engaged Clemens Krauss from the Vienna State Opera as music director. Krauss was an inveterate Nazi, a close friend of Richard Strauss and had influence with excellent artists in Austria. Berlin, however, did not find his performances exceptional and he eventually resigned. In the meantime, Göring began searching for a trump card that would prevent him from being vulnerable to the troublesome likes of Furtwängler and Kleiber. Germany's leading opera house still boasted great vocal talent such as Max Lorenz, Frida Leider, Helge Roswänge, Gerhard Hüsch, Heinrich Schlusnus, Margarete Teschemacher and many others, but major new talent of any race was becoming increasingly rare all over Germany. It would be a while before Göring could find a conducting personality sufficient to fill the gaping breach left by Furtwängler and Kleiber. But his wait would ultimately be rewarded.

Meanwhile, the Nazis' chief ideologue and "high priest of the master race" also entered the fray.[16] Among his various duties at the top of the Nazi hierarchy, Alfred Rosenberg was editor-in-chief of the main Nazi newspaper, the *Völkischer Beobachter*, and he used it to promulgate the racial theories that eventually would give substance to the extermination of millions of non-Aryan people. In a scathing editorial entitled "Aesthetics or Peoples' Struggle?" he cast Furtwängler

---

15. Riess, p. 184.
16. This accurate epithet was pronounced by Justice Robert H. Jackson in his concluding remarks on Rosenberg's culpability in the extermination of Jews, Asiatics, and other ethnic groups deemed undesirable by the Nazis.

as a man of yesterday, an anachronism literally out of tune with the times:

> It is unfortunate that a great artist like Furtwängler intervened and identi-
> fied himself with Hindemith. He regrettably went so far as to label the
> criticism against Hindemith as a political denunciation when it had been
> entirely based on facts gathered by the National Socialist *Cultural Com-
> munity* . . . When Furtwängler persisted in his 19th century mode of
> thought, and clearly had no sensitivity to the great national struggle of
> our time, he had to take the consequences.[17]

Goebbels easily out-ranted Rosenberg on 6 December 1934, the same day Rosenberg's article appeared, when he gave a two hour address to the assembled masses at the Berlin Sportpalast. Toward the end of his tirade, he took on Furtwängler, his article, and Hindemith, all at the same time without actually referring by name to any of them:

> . . . we vigorously refrain from allowing this type of artist to be consid-
> ered of pure German origin, and the fact that he is, by blood, of purely
> German origin only emphasizes how radically our own people have been
> infected with Jewish intellectual principles. Discussing this influence has
> nothing whatever to do with political denunciations. We are loftily above
> any suspicions of desiring to thwart real and true art with petty and
> annoying regulations. We only wish to see National Socialist character
> and philosophy preserved. No one, no matter how distinguished he may
> be in his own profession, has the right to limit the political field or to
> exclude these ideals from art.
>   In view of the incredible lack of real and productive artists in the
> world today, we cannot afford to reject a real artist. But he must be a genu-
> ine artist and not a noise maker of no musical talent.[18]

While the speech was rife with Nazi humbug, one line in it was deadly serious in both content and delivery: "No one . . . has the right to limit the political field or to exclude these ideals from art." Few realized, as winter approached in 1934, that this was about as concise an articulation of Nazi cultural policy as would ever be uttered. Fewer

17. *Völkischer Beobachter*, (Berlin Edition) 6 December 1934, p. 5. Note: The *Völkischer Beobachter* was published once daily in three separate but frequently inter-locking regional editions: The Berlin edition was considered its flagship. The North German Edition and the South German Edition carried additional news and information pertinent to their respective areas. As head ideologue for the regime, Rosenberg was editor-in-chief of the whole newspaper, and his articles usually ran in all editions. After the war, Rosenberg was charged with war crimes at the Nürnberg Trials and was sentenced to death. He was executed on 16 October 1946.
18. Riess quotes most of the speech, pp. 189f. The *Völkischer Beobachter* (Berlin Edition) quoted it on 7 December 1934, pp. 6–7.

still, Furtwängler least of all, had any idea how viciously this state-ment would be carried out as the Thousand Year Reich fell under the spell of its all-pervasive psychosis.

The speech was capped with the arrival of a "telegram" from Rich-ard Strauss, who was in Holland at the time. Goebbels read aloud the wire containing Strauss' congratulations for "removing undesirable elements." The assembled legions of carefully rehearsed claques took their cue and roared. Strauss made no objections then but later denied writing the telegram. One report eventually indicated that his son had sent it after its contents had been dictated by one of Goebbels' assis-tants. Nonetheless, Strauss did not deny the telegram at the time. He also made no bones about his awareness that there were more opera houses in Germany prepared and willing to produce his works than there were anywhere else in the world.

At worst, Richard Strauss was indifferent to the Nazis. He lived only for his royalties so that he could keep his henpecking wife Pau-line happy. A professional musician in the modern sense, he energeti-cally sought the best possible showcases for his works and appears to have had no specific political inclinations. Strauss was willing to accept flattery from anyone who could keep him in the lifestyle to which his wife Pauline had become accustomed.

However, he nearly shortened his life by 15 years when he sent a letter belittling the Nazis to his collaborator Stefan Zweig. The letter Zweig wrote to Strauss that provoked Strauss' reply has never been found, but it was clear that Zweig was feeling uncomfortable about his collaboration with the composer. The Nazis had made no secret of their displeasure about the Third Reich's leading composer taking on a Jewish librettist. Strauss at first tried to persuade Zweig to be a "silent" collaborator on *Die schweigsame Frau*. Zweig resisted and finally refused and apparently decided to confront Strauss about his pandering attitude toward the Nazis. Evidently, he broached two sen-sitive topics in his letter to Strauss. First, he pointed out Strauss' will-ingness to fill in for Bruno Walter after the Nazis had hounded him into cancelling a performance. Second, he must also have referred to Strauss substituting for Toscanini when the latter refused to return to Bayreuth in 1933 in protest against the regime's cultural policies, for Strauss responded:

> Who told you I have exposed myself politically? Because I have conducted a concert in place of Bruno Walter? That I did for the sake of the orchestra. Because I substituted for Toscanini? I did that for the sake of Bayreuth. All that has nothing to do with politics. It is none of my business how the boulevard press interprets what I do, and it should not matter to you

either. Because I parody the president of the Reichsmusikkammer? I do that only for good intentions and to prevent greater disasters! I would have accepted this bothersome honorary office under any government, but neither Kaiser Wilhelm nor Herr Rathenau [the Foreign Affairs Minister in the Weimar Republic who was Jewish] offered it to me. So be a good boy, forget Moses and the other apostles for a few weeks and work on your two one-act plays.[19]

Two officials from the Gestapo appeared at Strauss' home on July 6th, and held out the offending letter, duly marked in red pencil. They demanded his immediate resignation as President of the Reichsmusikkammer on grounds "of ill-health." Only his international reputation saved him from arrest and worse. He appealed to all the top Nazi officials and wrote an obsequious humble pie letter to Hitler, groveling for pardon:

> My Führer! My entire life belongs to German music and to a tireless effort to uplift German culture. I have never been politically active nor even expressed myself in politics. I believe therefore that I will find understanding from you, the great architect of German social life, especially I assure you with deep emotion and deep respect that even after my dismissal as president of the Reichsmusikkammer, I will devote the few years left to me only to the purest and most ideal goals.
>
> Confident of your high sense of justice, I beg you, my Führer, most humbly to receive me for a personal discussion, to give me the opportunity to justify myself in person.[20]

The letter was never answered, and, of course, the audience never took place. Strauss knew two things now, once and for all. First, the Nazis were not to be trifled with. Second, his collaboration with Stefan Zweig, the beloved collaborator of his old age, was over. Zweig left Germany shortly afterward and went to America after divorcing his first wife, Fredericka, and remarrying. The gifted poet and writer produced a number of significant works during his exile—notably the posthumously published novella *The Royal Game* (1943) and his memories of a Germany gone forever *The World of Yesterday* (1943). But writing in exile proved to be as depressing as it was cathartic. The horrible events taking place throughout the world crushed him beyond endurance. He and his second wife, Lotte, committed suicide in Petropolis, Brazil, in February 1942.

Strauss receded into relative obscurity, although he continued to compose. For the 1936 Olympiad in Berlin, he contributed a hymn,

19. 17 June 1935.
20. 13 July 1935.

and in 1940 he composed a *Japanische Festmusik* to honor the Japanese royal family. He had some reason to be as cooperative with the regime as he was. His daughter-in-law Alice was Jewish. Consequently, his grandchildren, whom he kept at his villa in Garmisch, were also considered Jewish. So was his publisher Adolph Fürstner. Strauss continued to pay lip service to the regime, and they in turn never harmed him or his family. His prestige value was simply too great for them to make trouble.

Furtwängler's value for Nazi public relations was second only to Strauss', but he was not nearly as cooperative, and so he was not nearly as fortunate. Following his resignation, the Nazis "sent him to Coventry," and he found himself isolated and snubbed. No one dared to approach him or have anything to do with him. Actually, they had no reason to keep up contact with him. He had lost his two principal bases of power inside Germany—the Philharmonic and the Staatsoper. These developments were bad enough, but others were also suffering the consequences of his idealism. Fritz Klein, who had published many anti-Nazi articles in the *Deutsche Allgemeine Zeitung*, died shortly after the Hindemith article appeared, reportedly from a horse-riding accident. The Berlin Philharmonic took a severe financial blow when subscribers to Furtwängler concerts demanded their money back, and the box office was obliged to return about 180,000 RM ($143,000).[21]

Worst of all, he finally had to face up to the reality he had been denying for so long. Politics and music are not mutually exclusive. Music was not sacrosanct and an end unto itself. Hubermann was right. All the great artists who had rejected his invitation to stand with him against tyranny were right. Music *could* be corrupted by evil men, and they were around him everywhere.

But the voice within him was right, too.

If he had harbored Promethean longings, Furtwängler now was bereft of his torch. As 1934 came to a close, he also found himself an alien in his own country, a non-entity in his profession, a pariah in his calling. His last performance in Berlin following his resignation took place on 12 December at the Staatsoper. The opera was *Tristan*. He wanted only to get away from Berlin. He was about to visit friends in Egypt when Hitler sent an urgent message to him "requesting" that he remain in Germany until the Hindemith Scandal quieted down. Furtwängler was now obliged to remain in Germany anyway because his passport could not be stamped until the Führer personally approved

21. Muck, p. 116.

it. If he identified himself with Orpheus, however, there was still one instrument the Nazis could not take away from him.

It had been a long time since he had composed, and he spent the early part of 1935 in Bavaria trying to rectify his neglect.[22] During his walks in the woods, the prospect of having to leave Germany haunted him. His destiny was to be a composer, and he realized that the Fates had brought him to this low ebb to remind him of his real mission. And looking about him in the woods, he now understood as he never had before, that he was, for better or worse, a German and a German composer. He resolved not to give in and returned to Berlin.

A new set of proposals in hand, he tried to contact Goebbels to discuss them. Smelling desperation, Goebbels evaded Furtwängler. Failing to grasp the war of nerves the Minister of Propaganda was waging against him, Furtwängler vainly kept after an appointment. But Goebbels also made an error in judging character. He thought Furtwängler now craved his orchestra and his adoring audiences like an addict his narcotics. He was right about the first; wrong about the second. Furtwängler did indeed miss his musicians, but he would do without them if he must. While he appreciated his audiences, he did not need them to survive. Music itself was his only passion. All time stopped for him as he read through his scores. Page after page, the music resounded from the chains of black and white dots and crotchets assembled along the parallel vertical lines to form what ultimately became the *Second Sonata for Violin and Piano* and the *Symphonie Concertante for Piano and Orchestra*.

The proposals Furtwängler eventually presented to Goebbels contained nothing new. Essentially, they were the same as the ones Hitler himself had rejected previously. This time, however, Goebbels took an interest, for he now had given some thought to how Furtwängler would fit into his plans for creating a massive cultural program for the Third Reich. The object, he concluded, was to co-opt Germany's foremost conductor and mold him into a symbol of the highest and best in the new Germany. He drafted a declaration in which Furtwängler would formally accept Hitler's cultural policy. Furtwängler read the document and flatly refused to put his name to it. It was because of the cultural policy that he had resigned in the first place. Goebbels appealed to Furtwängler's devotion to the German public. Sensing his bluff being called, Furtwängler crisply stated that he did not need Germany. He had attractive offers from all over the world. Goebbels came

22. Riess gives a richly detailed account of this troubled segment of Furtwängler's life, and the present account is based on it: pp. 192–211.

directly to the point. "You can leave Germany, if you want, but you must keep one thing in mind: as long as we are in power, which we expect to be the case for a long time to come, you never will be allowed to return under any circumstances to your home."

"The only criterion for art is the truth which art alone can produce," retorted Furtwängler. "This cultural policy is impossible."

"I know all there is to know about art and artists," answered Goebbels coolly. "We have no intention of interfering with your purely musical affairs, but some Germans would construe the independence you want as open revolt. Within our province, we demand complete support even from great artists. Consequently, you must declare your recognition that Hitler and the Ministers he appoints are entirely and solely responsible for cultural policy. You can say this with no misgivings about the truth of this statement because it is already a fact, and everybody everywhere knows it."[23]

Furtwängler left the meeting with two conclusions. He saw that recognizing Hitler as the supreme power over all matters, cultural or otherwise, was already a fact. Stating it would only be acknowledging the obvious. While the Nazis were in power, there was nothing to be done about that, and refusing to understand it would be as useless as resisting it longer. But Furtwängler also reasoned that if he acknowledged Hitler's power over cultural matters above and independently of anyone who purveyed German culture, he could not be held jointly responsible for the damage they would inevitably wreak. He could then go about his own business as a conductor, undisturbed by the government and free of the bad conscience that had moved him to resign all his posts. Open resistance, he finally learned, was not the way to deal with these thugs and criminals. He would have to find other means of safeguarding German music.

For the price of acknowledging Hitler and his supreme mastery on policy, Furtwängler requested only permission to keep working in Germany as a free-lance conductor. He would give up a steady salary and be paid only for the performances he conducted—2,000 marks per appearance. He would also forego all pensions and other perquisites he had long received in the years prior to the Nazi takeover. He would not be obliged to accept any official position and be free from performing at state functions.

He also made one further demand: all the conditions pertaining to the resumption of his musical activities would be published in full.

"We leave it to you how you will work with us," purred Goebbels.

23. Riess, pp. 200–201.

"I am satisfied that you should serve music as you see fit, and I give you my promise that you may remain a non-political musician. I am sure the Führer will confirm everything I have said."[24]

Goebbels issued an announcement ending the impasse. It was a paragon of factual manipulation:

> Suffice it to say that Furtwängler underestimated the consequences of the issues he raised in his article. He believed that a musical problem, in which Hindemith was the focal point of the debate, could be solved strictly as an artistic matter and forgot that no issue can exist independently of the National Socialist State. He overlooked the totality of our approach that is an essential component of National Socialism. It is to his credit that he has recognized through his own declaration the limitations to which everyone—even the greatest artists—are bound.[25]

Goebbels had indeed kept his word—or at least part of it. The conditions under which Furtwängler would remain and work in Germany were clear: He had seen the light of Nazi doctrine and acknowledged the error of his ways in the Hindemith Scandal. In doing so, he not only rendered unto the state that which now belonged to it anyway, but he also subscribed to the abrogation of free thought it demanded. The statement contained no mention of Goebbels' promise that Furtwängler would be allowed to remain in Germany as a non-political musician.

Goebbels' carefully crafted news release had its desired effect. Inside Germany, all were now duly informed that Furtwängler had reached a reconciliation with the authorities. Outside Germany, especially in America and England, Furtwängler had merely capitulated.[26] Furtwängler was furious that his friends and public all over the world construed his arrangement with the Nazis as a "deal," and he tried to get Goebbels to publish the part of the agreement that allowed his professional independence. Goebbels scoffed contemptuously. Furtwängler decided to go to Hitler. He had to see him anyway to obtain

24. After the war, Riess asked Furtwängler how he would have reacted if Goebbels had simply told him there could be no such person as a free artist in the Third Reich. Furtwängler replied without hesitation, "Then I would have had no choice but to leave Germany. As difficult as it would have been, I would have left, for I could never give up my stand on my view that art and politics should have nothing to do with each other" (p. 206).

25. Riess, pp. 201–202. The provenance of this statement is unclear. It was not published with the statement of reconciliation which appeared in many German newspapers on 1 March 1935.

26. "Whether conductor Wilhelm Furtwängler swallowed his artistic conscience or whether Nazi Germany suddenly decided it could dispense with him no longer, no one was willing to say . . ." *Time*, 6 May 1935.

permission to leave Germany for a conducting engagement in Austria. The meeting was set for 10 April 1935, the day he was scheduled to leave Berlin for Vienna.

The major event of that day, of course, was Göring's marriage to the actress Emmy Sonnemann. It was the State's social event of the year, and the Reich outdid itself for the occasion. The day started off auspiciously on something of a musical note: two people were executed by decapitation at dawn for murdering Horst Wessel, a national martyr and composer of the New Germany's unofficial national anthem.[27] As the sun rose over the eastern part of Berlin, the entire length of Unter den Linden was cordoned off and garlanded with early pine twigs. Elaborate formations of the SS and the SA, Hitler Youth and BDM Girls started moving early in the morning to their positions on the bridal way. Flags were hoisted along the route, and schools, shops, factories and other businesses were closed to celebrate the nuptials. At 1:30 in the afternoon, the bridal motorcade passed through the Brandenburg Gate and proceeded up Unter den Linden toward the Cathedral (Berliner Dom). Hitler's car led the procession. Göring followed in an open limousine. He was accompanied by his sister-in-law Countess Rose from Sweden. The bride sat in the third car decked with white roses.[28]

Furtwängler was probably the only person in Berlin who had no idea what a great state occasion was taking place on this day. He drove his car to the Chancellery with the expectation that he would have no trouble getting there. By the time he passed through the innumerable security barriers, Hitler had already left for the wedding. After much telephoning between the Chancellery and the Cathedral, another appointment was set up a half hour before Furtwängler's train for Vienna was due to leave Anhalter Station.

Hitler began the meeting auspiciously: "I don't have much time." Furtwängler quickly received confirmation that he would be allowed to pursue his career without having to assume political positions, but Hitler bridled when Furtwängler told him that he would like the entire agreement—including the part averring his non-political status—published in the newspapers.

"No," he declared. "It would be detrimental to the honor of the state to print more than we already have published on the matter." With a wave of his hand, Hitler ordered his aides to phone Anhalter to hold the train until Furtwängler arrived.[29]

---

27. The next day, the report of the execution shared space with details on Göring's wedding on the front page of the *Völkischer Beobachter*, 11 April 1935 (Berlin edition).

28. Riess, pp. 203–205.

29. Riess, pp. 205–206, and *Kraftprobe*, p. 231.

Furtwängler was whisked away to Anhalter Station by an escort. As he stepped into his compartment, the train left the station. He sank into the armchair relieved that he had at least won half the argument. He would be allowed to remain in Germany as an independent, non-political person. For the time being.

12

Another Scandal

Furtwängler returned from Vienna in late April 1935 to conduct the Berlin Philharmonic in a Winter Assistance (*Winterhilfe*) charity program set for the 25th. These annual concerts raised money for clothing for the poor during the winter months and had been a tradition at the Philharmonic long before the Nazis came to power.[1] The concert was sold out a few hours after the tickets went on sale. Furtwängler's first appearance in Berlin since the Hindemith Scandal put to rest rumors that he had remained in Austria, sought asylum in Switzerland, had gone to America, or was in a concentration camp.[2] The occasion had all the ornaments of a state occasion. Top ranking members of the government were present. The diplomatic corps from most of the embassies were also there.

The crowd cheered wildly when he appeared. Furtwängler bowed appreciatively to the crowd, but did not give the now obligatory Nazi salute. He turned to the orchestra and began an all-Beethoven program consisting of the Fifth and Sixth Symphonies introduced by the Overture to Goethe's *Egmont*. At the end of the concert, the ovation lasted for almost an hour, and Furtwängler was recalled 17 times.

A week later, the Winter Assistance program was repeated. At the last moment, Hitler announced that he was coming. Furtwängler was

---

1. After the war, the Allies attempted at Furtwängler's denazification trial to cast the Winterhilfe Concerts as political events. See Chapter 18.
2. *New York Times*, 8 December 1934, p. 18.

so enraged that he ripped the wooden covering off the radiator in his dressing room, but there was nothing he could do to prevent Hitler from attending a non-political concert. Furtwängler was, after all, conducting as a private individual, and Hitler was attending as part of the audience. The Nazi salute was now an issue. "I don't have to acknowledge him at all," he kept saying, as though its repetition would provide a solution. But Furtwängler knew better. If the leader of the Reich, whom Furtwängler now acknowledged as the lord of cultural matters, was present, he might be obliged to give the salute.

Franz Jastrau, the orchestra's handyman, finally came up with a solution. "Why not enter with your baton in your hand? If you gave the salute, it would look as though you were trying to strike Hitler." Furtwängler gratefully took the suggestion. He mounted the podium with his baton in his right hand, bowed quickly to the audience, and turned to the orchestra. The musicians struck the ominous chords that begin the Overture to *Egmont* while the applause was still ringing full tilt. A gasp went through the hall. Would Hitler make some sort of retaliatory demonstration? Would his ministers stop the concert? Hitler sat through the entire concert, joining the rest of the audience in its ovation of every piece. At the end of the concert, Furtwängler received his customary reception. A photographer caught him in mid-bow as Hitler and other officials applauded in the foreground. The photograph was published around the world; its implications needed no explanations. Furtwängler was a Nazi conductor.

Several months later, he conducted three performances of Beethoven's Ninth Symphony in Berlin to benefit the Bruno Kittel Choir, which frequently performed with the orchestra.[3] At the last moment, Hitler decided to attend again. Furtwängler followed the same baton-in-hand procedure of the previous concert: a quick nod to the audience as he spun around to begin the hushed opening of the work. At the end of the performance, the soloists in the last movement gave the Nazi salute as they each took their calls; Furtwängler did not. This time, Hitler leapt to his feet, approached the platform, and extended his hand to Furtwängler, who had little choice but to grasp it. Again, the photographers were poised for the historic moment. The next day, the world had proof that art and politics can indeed join hands. Goebbels immediately took advantage of the new rapprochement by organizing a tour of England for Furtwängler and the Berlin Philharmonic. When Furtwängler heard that it was to be a state-sponsored journey, he abruptly canceled. To the end of the regime, the orchestra never

3. 27, 28, 30 October 1935. The soloists were Käte Heidersbach, Gertrude Pitzinger, Walter Ludwig, and Rudolf Watzke.

officially represented the Nazis when it performed with Furtwängler and always financed their own tours as a private company.[4]

Furtwängler now realized that his pact with Goebbels and Hitler meant nothing. He did not have to be a Party member or subscribe to the cultural policy; the Nazis would use him as they pleased to further their cause. There was little he could do about it immediately, but he was hurriedly solidifying or re-establishing his ties abroad. In May, he had conducted his first *Tristan* in London with Leider and Melchior and had taken them to Paris in June for a performance each of *Tristan* and *Walküre* at the Paris Opéra.[5] Earlier in October, he returned to the Vienna Staatsoper for three performances of *Tannhäuser.*

Bits and pieces of these performances were recorded and pre- served, and despite sound quality that can only be described as pollut- ive, they offer a glimpse of the kind of energy and excitement he brought to this opera at that time. The orchestra sounds well rehearsed and glows at moments with the burnished "spin" on the string tone that Furtwängler conjured with particular mastery from the Vienna Philharmonic. Esther Bathy is a radiant Elizabeth in her first aria, and Alexander Sved is a warm and ardent Wolfram, a singer deserving of a far bigger career than he had. Kersten Thorborg and Ludwig Hoffman respectively sang Venus and the Landgrave.[6]

In the meantime, another foe appeared on the scene to menace Furtwängler. Hans Hinkel had been appointed Administrator of Cul- tural Affairs, and he was reputed to be one of the most hateful men in the Third Reich.[7] He had already driven Bruno Walter and innumera- ble other luminaries in the arts from Germany, and it was his avoca- tion to make life as miserable as possible for Jews in the performing arts. Since so many Jews distinguished German culture, he was rarely idle. Now he set his target on Furtwängler's Jewish secretary Berta Geissmar. Since Geissmar was so crucial to Furtwängler, Hinkel and his superiors reasoned that eliminating her would almost certainly cripple his capacity to function. By far the most unnerving tactic he used was to confiscate her passport, put her through tortuous bureau-

---

4. This was an issue clarified at the denazification proceedings. See Chapter 18.

5. In London, there were two performances of *Tristan* on 20 and 24 May. Bee- cham's orchestra, the London Philharmonic, played in the pit of the Royal Opera House Covent Garden. At the Opéra in Paris, the house orchestra played on 1 and 4 June.

6. The surviving excerpts can be heard—pitched properly—on Belvedere Teldec 6.43333 AG. Gothelf Pistor sang *Tannhäuser* in the first two performances (13 and 15 October) and Josef Kalemberg replaced him on 18 October. Sadly, neither of them are presented on this disc. The excerpts on the Belvedere disc includes a "Dir Töne Lob!" sung by Max Lorenz from a performance on 9 January 1936.

7. "One of the most evil officials of the Third Reich" is how Louise Wolff's daugh- ter fondly describes Hinkel in her memoir. Stargardt-Wolff, p. 276.

cratic procedures to get it back, return it, only to confiscate it again. Furtwängler's appeals to obtain a special work permit for her were of no avail.

Geissmar finally decided she had no choice but to leave Germany. Hinkel begrudgingly gave her permission to remain in Germany for a few weeks in order to complete unfinished matters for Furtwängler, but her work was hampered because the Gestapo stepped up their cruel game of alternately giving and taking away her passport. Furtwängler finally protested to Göring, and she left Germany immediately. Ultimately, she went to work for Sir Thomas Beecham in London after a brief stay in the United States. In a way, Furtwängler was relieved that she was going. For all her loyalty and efficiency, Berta Geissmar had so completely taken over his life that he must have felt in somewhat the same position as the characters Harold Pinter was to create many years later in his play *The Caretaker:* enslaved by his retainer.

For her part, Geissmar had no idea how fortunate she was in escaping Germany with her life. Nor did it ever cross her mind that Furtwängler was beginning to feel stifled by her control. She later told Hitler's ousted press chief, Ernst "Putzi" Hanfstängl, that Furtwängler had not tried hard enough to keep her with him. Hanfstängl also was living in London with his family at the time. Long afterward, Hanfstängl's son Egon informed me:

> Frau Geissmar came to visit my father [in London in 1938], whom she had known before his flight from Germany. She complained bitterly about being "dropped" and "betrayed" by Furtwängler after all her years of faithful service, merely because she was Jewish. Could he not, with all his prestige and connections, have arranged a *Sonderstatus* [special exemption] for her? My father strove to calm her and explained that it took immense power to circumvent the Nürnberg race laws.[8]

Contrary to some persistent allegations from envious colleagues, however, Furtwängler did not fire Geissmar. He merely did not run lengths he could have to keep her, and we may never know if he would have been successful in any case.[9] Nonetheless, she continued to

8. Letter to the author, Munich, 25 April 1990.
9. In Grete Busch's reminiscence of her late husband, the conductor Fritz Busch, she claims Furtwängler fired Geissmar. See *Fritz Busch, Dirigent*, (Frankfurt) 1970, p. 282. No documentation has been found to support this assertion. But the Busch family was living in England during this period when Busch was music director of the Glyndebourne Festival), and Geissmar probably also told Frau Busch that Furtwängler had "dropped" her, as she evidently had told Ernst Hanfstängl. Frau Busch may in turn have taken that to mean he fired her. In any event, no trace of Geissmar's indignation reported in Egon Hanfstängl's letter to me appears in her memoir, for by that time, she must have realized that her departure from Germany—whatever the circumstances— was a blessing in disguise. Also see *Kraftprobe*, pp. 209–210.

remain loyal to him from abroad, helping him in whatever way she could whenever he came to London. According to some witnesses who knew them both at the time, she was most useful in arranging assignations for him during his tours to Britain.[10]

While the Nazis thought they finally had gotten rid of Geissmar, by no means had they seen the last of her.

Furtwängler began to cancel concerts. He excused himself on reasons of illness, but he actually was exhausted from the pressures the Nazis were putting on him, and from his efforts to resist, circumvent, or simply wait them out. On one occasion he tried to argue with Bernhard Rust, the Minister of Culture, about Rust's contention that a musician's greatness could be measured by the contours of his skull. Rust was full of Hans Günther's theories about Aryan superiority and answered Furtwängler with dogma from Günther's vituperative but highly influential books on the matter extoling the "Nordic creative spirit" and deriding the dullness of Semitic races. Even Furtwängler's capacity to argue endlessly on any matter he felt passionate about was no contest for Rust and his instant and relentless recitation of Günther's dogma.

On 25 January 1936 Furtwängler celebrated his 50th birthday. He conducted a special concert in his honor which included Beethoven's Fifth Symphony as the major work. At the rehearsal, the musicians of the Philharmonic gave him an autograph facsimile of the score. A few moments after the rehearsal started, the players made mistakes in a critical passage. Enraged, he threw the facsimile on the floor and bellowed, "It would be worth more if you played it better." Goebbels sent him a silver baton, and Hitler flattered Furtwängler with a framed autographed photo of himself.

Now that he had his passport returned to him, he was free to travel again. Shortly after his 50th birthday concert, he left Germany to stay with friends in Egypt while he rested and thought about what he would do. His hosts on this trip included authors John Knittel and Robert Hichens who had long been friends with Furtwängler and his family. Although he had resolved to remain a German and stay in Germany, the Nazis were making life increasingly miserable for him. At this point, a way out of his misery suddenly revealed itself.

By 1936 Toscanini had come to the end of his tenure with the New York Philharmonic, and the board of directors was looking for a suc-

10. During one of his visits, according to Friedelind Wagner, Geissmar reportedly created a furor by introducing a very mature 17-year-old girl to Furtwängler. The infatuation was apparently immediate and reciprocal. The liaison ended abruptly when the girl's grandmother, who was one of Queen Mary's Ladies-in-Waiting, got wind of the affair. Personal conversation with the author, Mainz, 6 October 1990.

cessor. Furtwängler had been approached, and after some negotiation he accepted. By the time he received the cable informing him of the appointment, the New York papers had already leaked the information. The reports, however, failed to mention two crucial points. First, Toscanini had declared Furtwängler the only conductor worthy of following him. Second, one of the conditions of his engagement in New York would be his complete abstinence from accepting any permanent post in Germany, even though it was agreed that he could keep Germany as his domicile where he would spend his vacations. Since he already was a free-lance conductor anyway, the condition seemed to present no problem.

When Göring heard the reports, he became diastrophic. Furtwängler had turned down every top musical position in Germany—including the directorship of the Staatsoper—but had accepted an appointment in America. Göring then made sure that another announcement was planted in the American papers. It made the front page of the *New York Times:*

> The complete professional rehabilitation of Wilhelm Furtwängler . . . was forecast today in an official announcement that he would shortly resume his activities as "guest conductor of the Berlin State Operas."[11]

The announcement made its desired point, for it implied that Furtwängler was officially joining the Nazis. And if he was indeed to resume his ties with the Nazis, he was perhaps too controversial for an orchestra with many Jewish subscribers.[12] W. J. Henderson of the *New York Sun* put the sentiment right even though he got the premise for it wrong:

> Mr. Furtwängler is a prominent and active Nazi; at least one half of the patrons of the Philharmonic-Symphony concerts are of the race which the Nazi government of Germany has singled out for severity of treatment . . .
> There is no musical enterprise of any kind whatever that can prosper in this great Jewish city without the support of the Jews.[13]

Prospects for Furtwängler's future in New York all but vanished when a department store executive and former Philharmonic board

11. 1 March 1936.
12. Daniel Gillis offers a full account of this episode in *Furtwängler and America,* pp. 51–58.
13. 7 March 1936.

member named Ira Hirschmann organized a committee to boycott Furtwängler and enlisted unions, home-front groups, and such personalities as Mayor Fiorello La Guardia to back it.[14] Among the groups that gladly fell in line with Hirschmann's efforts was the New York–based German-American Alliance (Deutsch-Amerikanische Bund), a Nazi-sponsored organization dedicated to cultivating racism, anti-Semitism, and other unsavory ideals.[15]

When the New York Philharmonic cabled him about the report of his reinstatement at the Staatsoper, Furtwängler cabled back:

> I am not chief of Berlin Opera but conduct as guest. My job is only music.[16]

If ever a message fell on deaf ears, this was it. What Furtwängler failed to understand was that Americans, especially many of the subscribers to the New York Philharmonic, were in no mood to make hairline distinctions between a "guest" status with an opera house run by the Nazis and full reinstatement. The Philharmonic board tried to clarify the matter by releasing a statement with Furtwängler's cable dissociating him from the Nazis:

> . . . Mr. Furtwängler risked and sacrificed his prominent position in Germany by waging single-handed, earnestly and persistently, a contest for tolerance and broad-mindedness toward musicians as well as composers.

But the antagonism against Furtwängler was growing out of control. A number of Jewish publications protested vigorously. The *American Hebrew* blasted the appointment by presenting some astonishing information:

> Two years before Hitler's rise to power, Furtwängler was promised the post of general music director of Germany if and when the day should arrive. In this position he has given tacit approval to the grotesque artistic creed promulgated by the Kultur Kammer in the Spring of 1933. That esthetic monstrosity has flagrantly denounced not only music by Jews but also all music of an original or experimental nature; and, despite his own

14. Hirschmann boasts about his efforts to keep Furtwängler out of New York in *Obligatto* [sic] (196?), a sort of memoir in manuscript form on deposit at the Library of the Performing Arts, New York Public Library. As late as 1983, he was promising to present irrefutable proof that Furtwängler was a bona fide Nazi who fired Jewish musicians (*New York Times*, 21 September).

15. See *Kraftprobe*, pp. 257–258.

16. The statement appeared in various stories across the country on 7 March 1936. The *New York American* put it in bold print.

sham squawks, Furtwängler permitted the wholesale dismissal of Jewish musicians from his own orchestra, the Berlin Philharmonic.[17]

The *Jewish Times* was more accurate in its facts, a good deal less hysterical, and got right to the heart of the issue. It minced no words in reminding the Philharmonic board where most of its financial support came from and pointed out that:

> This disregard of Jewish sensibilities is inexcusable. It is a direct slap in the face of all the liberal elements in this country who have time and again emphatically protested against Nazi barbarism . . .

But attacks on Furtwängler were by no means limited to the Jewish popular press. The *coup de grâce* on the issue came from *Commonweal*, the independent and intellectually up-scale Catholic-based magazine, when it brought a somewhat ecumenical slant on the controversy:

> Can one look upon the appointment as anything short of an endorsement of Nazi attacks upon what after all we may term Christian culture?[18]

After the story about his supposed reinstatement at the Staatsoper was further investigated, reporters learned that the information had been leaked by Göring, and he, they felt, ought to know what he was talking about. Göring indeed knew exactly what he was talking about, but Furtwängler had no idea that Göring had engineered the whole mendacious mess. He simply regarded the attacks on him as part of a general antagonism by Americans against Germany. That hostility was growing through the weekly arrival of new refugees and highly publicized boycotts of German products. What little sympathy may have been rallied for Furtwängler evaporated when Hitler's armies marched into the Rhineland on 7 March 1936. Neither inclined nor physically able to engage in another political debate with the Americans at this low ebb in his energies, Furtwängler threw in the towel a week later with a crossly worded cable to the New York Philharmonic:

> I am not a politician, but an exponent of German music, which belongs to all mankind and is independent of politics. I suggest, in the interests of the Philharmonic Company, that I postpone my appearances in the U.S.A.

17. 6 March 1936, pp. 443–444. While the author of these statements is not known, Ira Hirschmann used almost the same words fifty years later accusing Furtwängler of firing his musicians in a letter to the *New York Times*, 30 September 1983.
18. 13 March 1936, p. 535.

until the public realizes that music and politics have nothing to do with each other.[19]

Time mocked his petulance by quoting the entire telegram in block capital letters under the headline "Nazi Stays Home."[20] To make matters worse for himself, he seemed to be blaming his withdrawal on the willful blindness of "the public." For the second time in a fortnight, Furtwängler made the front page of the *New York Times* and received what amounted to good riddance in an editorial:

> . . . Mr. Furtwängler's decision has relieved a situation that would speedily have become full of danger to the continuance of [the New York Philharmonic], or to its most satisfactory functioning, and saved himself much trouble.[21]

Furtwängler retained his composure, at least outwardly, but he now had boxed himself into a position where had become the very embodiment of a political individual in spite of himself, and it caused him grief that was to be unending. In America, an ever-growing population who had fled Germany with no options saw no reason why he should be allowed to have it both ways when they could not. The *American Jewish World* articulated the view of thousands for whom emigration and emigration alone was now the sole criterion for who was and who was not a Nazi. The editorial may have put it sneeringly, but it could not have drawn more precisely the corner they saw Furtwängler painting himself into:

> Yes, Herr Furtwängler! we want to keep politics out of music. It is precisely for this reason that we opposed the appointment of a musical conductor who is bound hand in hand with the Nazis.[22]

In view of the icon Furtwängler embodied to countless people who thought of themselves as German first before anything else, many refugees undoubtedly longed for him to join them in exodus and felt viciously traduced when he remained behind, whatever and however noble his reasons may have been. One Jewish émigré recalled his reaction to the New York Philharmonic scandal:

> My wife and I knew Furtwängler was no Nazi, but we wanted him to share our plight at that time. We wanted him to be with us, so to speak. It

19. 15 March 1936.
20. 23 March 1936, p. 51.
21. 16 March 1936, p. 16.
22. 20 March 1936, p. 8.

may sound stupid and selfish, but we could not help it. Furtwängler meant so much to us both even though neither one of us ever met him, and we had lost so much . . . everything. Were we to lose Furtwängler to the Nazis too? We needed him here, not over there . . . But if he was to be here, he could not be there in Germany too. What the hell was he doing with those [Nazi] *Schweinerei?* No. We stopped talking about it because it would just end with us both crying. I could understand why he stayed, but my wife could not.[23]

And whatever may have been the driving force behind it, resentment against Furtwängler indeed festered among many of the exiled as the months of grim chance in an alien land passed into fitful habitation and eventually into survival, as the years brought charred rationales to heap upon what they viewed as his betrayal.

Ultimately, John Barbirolli, a brilliant but relatively inexperienced conductor from England, was chosen as Toscanini's successor. But Barbirolli could not compete with the ghost of his predecessor who was still in town with the NBC Symphony, an orchestra formed especially for him in 1939. Barbirolli eventually was driven out and went back to England.

When Furtwängler returned to Berlin from Egypt, he learned for himself that Göring was behind the whole New York Philharmonic scandal. But it was all over now, and there was nothing he could do about it. The photograph of Hitler attending Furtwängler's concert by now had become more than a propaganda ploy. It was a picture of the "truth," at least as far as the world was concerned, and it became the icon of Goebbels' ambition to co-opt all the arts, beginning with Germany's most venerated conductor.[24]

To make matters even more uncomfortable for Furtwängler, the Nazis held a plebiscite on 29 March 1936 and solicited endorsements from artists. The Reich Culture Senate (Reichskultursenat) perforce issued a declaration of solidarity, and Furtwängler reportedly cabled his support for that proclamation, an act his critics pounced upon as proof that he had sold out to the Nazis. The supposed telegram was summarized in the Nazi press, but it never was quoted directly, and no evidence of such a cable has ever been found.[25] If Furtwängler really sent such a wire, it was surely inconsistent. If he did try to play up to

23. Personal conversation with the author, 15 May 1991. The speaker requested his name withheld.
24. The photograph appears on the dust jacket of Boguslaw Drewniak's *Das Theater in N-S Staat*, (Düsseldorf) 1983, even though it primarily concerns the legitimate theater in the Third Reich.
25. The "telegram" was summarized in the *Berliner Lokal-Anzeiger*, Nr. 72, 24 March 1936. The incident is discussed and part of the newspaper report summarizing the cable is cited in *Kraftprobe*, p. 260.

the regime with it, Hitler promptly rewarded him by summarily cancelling his guest contract at the Berlin Staatsoper and postponing a new one for more than a year, thereby depriving him of any kind of portfolio and exerting further pressure to heel.

One line of resistance remained open to Furtwängler. He took a year's sabbatical in order to devote more time to composing. In short course, the foreign press insisted that Hitler, Göring, and Goebbels had forced him into taking time off. Actually, both Göring and Goebbels tried to keep him from taking leave because they knew exactly how his departure from the scene would be interpreted outside Germany.

Furtwängler took the time to embark on a series of compositions that reflected his opposition to totalitarianism. He set to work on two pieces for which he had taken notes for a long time. They were the *Sonata for Violin and Piano* in D Minor and the *Symphonie Concertante for Piano and Orchestra* in B Minor. Both of them were long, difficult, and tragic works, the expression of a man reflecting upon a painful condition. The sonata took almost an hour to perform and contained as much demanding music for the piano as it did for the violin. The concerto was indeed more a symphony than a work for piano solo and orchestra. When it was premiered in Leipzig, the critics all described it as a "confession." Furtwängler could hardly quarrel with them. In it, he had given musical expression to his innermost sorrow and torment at being in a situation from which there was no escape, no happy ending. In every measure, the clarity of structure reaffirmed his faith that goodness and meaning still had a place and value in the world so rampantly gone mad. Aside from two tours with the Berlin Philharmonic, a recording session,[26] and a few opera performances in Vienna,[27] Paris,[28] and Bayreuth,[29] where he had patched up his differences with Winifred Wagner, Furtwängler severely curtailed his performing schedule from the end of 1935 to the middle of 1937 so that he could devote his time to composition.

Before he knew it, however, the period of his quasi-sabbatical was

26. For Polydor: Overture to *The Barber of Seville*, Overtures to Act I and III, *Freischütz*.

27. In Vienna, Furtwängler conducted *Tannhäuser* (9 January and 15 June with Lorenz in the title role. Maria Müller took the role of Elisabeth in January, Lotte Lehmann in June), and *Walküre* (13, 15 and 17 February 1936 with Anni Konetzni as Brünnhilde, Franz Völker and Maria Müller as the Wälsung twins, and Walter Grossmann as Wotan).

28. Two performances of *Meistersinger* on 19 and 28 May at the Opéra with Müller, Lorenz, and Prohaska as Eva, Walter, and Sachs respectively.

29. *Lohengrin* (Völker, Müller, Klose, and Manowarda), *Parsifal* (Helge Roswänge, Marta Fuchs, Ivar Andressen, and Herbert Janssen), and one cycle of the *Ring* (with Leider Völker, Lorenz, Müller, and Bockelmann as Wotan).

over, and he returned to Berlin. His political battles and his prolonged absence from concert life had made him a glamorous, mysterious figure, and he was now receiving far more offers than he could accept. During 1937, he conducted two complete *Rings* in Berlin and in London. The London *Ring* was a new production in honor of the Coronation of George VI and featured Frida Leider in one cycle and Kirsten Flagstad in the other. These performances were organized by Beecham's enterprising associate, a young producer named Walter Legge. No one could have imagined it at the time, least of Furtwängler, but far into the future Legge would have a strong hand in directing Furtwängler's destiny. Their protracted relationship began auspiciously. The event was a triumph for Furtwängler. The two cycles also signified the end of one era and the beginning of another. Leider was coming to the end of a long and brilliant singing career. Although Flagstad had been singing professionally even longer than Leider, only now was she coming into her own as the world's leading Wagner singer.[30]

HMV made experimental recordings of these performances using the optical method, and purloined segments of *Walküre* (Act III complete—26 May) and *Götterdämmerung* (excerpts—1 June) with Flagstad as Brünnhilde have gained wide circulation in recent years. Aside from Flagstad's thrilling vocalism at this point in her career (capped by a glorious sustained high C at the end of the Prologue in *Götterdämmerung*), Furtwängler draws a restrained but tense line from the London Philharmonic and white heat from the rest of the cast which includes Melchior, Maria Müller, Rudolf Bockelmann, and Herbert Janssen. Furtwängler all but fell in love with Flagstad's voice, and as we will see later, this Coronation *Ring* was the first of several important collaborations which culminated 15 years later in one of the finest recordings produced in this century.[31] The surviving fragments of this *Ring* offer a tantalizing sketch of Furtwängler's view of the work at the time and give evidence of the kind of intimate but strongly detailed scale and sweep that prompted the *Times* to conclude:

> Dr. Furtwängler's steady exposition of the three preceding dramas gathers cumulative momentum, so that the long finale seems actually to move speedily to the dissolution, and his reading as a whole last night was more impulsive without any loss of breadth or proportion.[32]

30. Flagstad was born in 1895 and made her debut in Oslo in 1913. Leider was seven years her senior, and she made her debut in Halle in 1915, working first as a bank clerk to finance her vocal studies with Otto Schwarz in Berlin.
31. See Chapter 24.
32. 2 June 1937, p. 14.

But Furtwängler had his detractors in the London press, Ernest Newman undoubtedly the most formidable:

> Furtwängler and the orchestra gave us some exquisitely polished playing, but neither have the greatest imaginative heights of the score been scaled nor the profoundest depths been plumbed.[33]

During his stay in London, Furtwängler also conducted several concerts, including two performances of Beethoven's Ninth with different orchestras but with the same choir and vocal soloists. On 25 March he took the London Philharmonic through the work at Royal Albert Hall. On 1 May, he performed it with the Berlin Philharmonic at Queens Hall. Both concerts of the Ninth were hugely successful, but they were not without incident. At Queens Hall, the secretary of the London Philharmonic Choir, Ritson Smith, tried to explain that since the Ninth—lasting almost an hour and a half—was the only work to be performed on the program, they were planning to insert an intermission between the second the third movements. Furtwängler's spoken English was extremely competent, but he had no idea of what the man was talking about. Ritson enlisted Victoria Spenser Wilkinson—a member of the choir who later became its chairman—to explain the situation to Furtwängler. He still could not understand why this, the most transcendental of Beethoven's symphonies, should be ruined with the insertion of an intermission. Ritson did not enhance his position by stating that the intermission was necessary so that the bar could be opened for business.

"Is the Ninth to be ruined for bar profits?" cried Furtwängler. "If I am to conduct the Ninth, there will be no interval! The bar can go to hell."

Which is where the bar went on that night. The Ninth was performed without interruption.[34]

This performance of the Ninth carries several statistical distinctions. The concert was broadcast over the BBC and acetates from that relay have been made into a commercial recording. It is also the first surviving example of a complete live performance by Furtwängler and the earliest full documentation we have of ten live performances of this symphony preserved from various periods in his career.[35] It was

---

33. *Sunday Times*, 23 May, p. 7.
34. Summarized from an anecdote in *The Furtwängler Sound*, 2d ed., (London) 1985, p. 13.
35. See Chapters 20–26 for a fuller discussion of this and other recordings by Furtwängler.

an important performance for Furtwängler because he was bringing one of the holies of German music to a foreign country performed by Germany's premier orchestra and sung by a quartet of German vocalists whose caliber would have been hard to surpass anywhere at that time: Erna Berger, Gertrude Pitzinger, Walter Ludwig, and Rudolf Watzke. The *Musical Times* noted the extreme tension in the performance and found it accounted for its "great eloquence."[36] A listener hearing it more than 50 years later may find its eloquence all the more moving, for the performance represents everything Furtwängler stood for, especially at that time. Now more than ever, an observation he made two years earlier was becoming a traumatic reality:

> Currently, when *Brüder! überm Sternzelt and Seid umschlungen, Millionen* by the Germans, Schiller and Beethoven are being rejected from the *racial standpoint*, it is the very *best* of Germanness that is being rejected.[37]   *Notebooks, p. 72*

Throughout his stay in London, many well-known personalities were also performing as part of the Coronation Season, and Furtwängler's performances at Covent Garden frequently competed with them. One night, for example, Friedelind Wagner attended the first act of *Götterdämmerung* at Covent Garden at 6 o'clock. She then rushed to Queens Hall for a concert by the newly formed BBC Symphony under Toscanini, raced back for the final act of *Götterdämmerung*, and finally took a taxi to have a late supper with Toscanini and his family. All that after being dropped off by Toscanini in his limousine earlier in the day for a rehearsal at Covent Garden under Furtwängler. "Toscanini offered to drop me off, and he knew exactly whose rehearsal it was," she recalls. "Actually, Toscanini was quite curious about my impressions of Furtwängler's performance, which were very high. He never once said a word against him. Later, when I visited with Furtwängler, he asked what I thought about Toscanini's concert. He asked questions but never said anything about Toscanini, one way or the other. Toscanini's statements about Furtwängler and the Nazis were for the benefit of the press. They respected each other apart from politics."[38] Neither Furtwängler nor Toscanini apparently made public statements about each other during this period, and the press made no

---

36. April 1937.
37. The quotation, of course, comes from Schiller's text to the vocal portions of the fourth movement: Brothers! above the star-lit canopy / a loving father must dwell there . . . I embrace all you millions . . . Here, Furtwängler finds the quintessence of what he perceived to be the gift Beethoven and Schiller offered the world in this expression of faith in unity of all mankind under a benevolent God.
38. Personal conversation with the author, Mainz, 6 October 1990.

effort to compare them or play them off each other, although a few of them surely must have been tempted. The reason was quite simple: the Coronation Season was a celebration for Britain's new monarchs, George VI and his consort Queen Elizabeth. Nothing was to cheapen or detract from their ascendancy to the throne, and the press carefully observed its sanctity.

Between performances in London Furtwängler returned to Berlin for a *Ring* cycle at the Staatsoper and a further performance of Beethoven's Ninth with the same vocalists he had used in London. There, he saw all too clearly how the Nazis were "rejecting" Beethoven and Schiller by distorting their intentions. By coincidence, the open rehearsal and concert took place just before Hitler's birthday, but the Nazi press portrayed it as part of the celebrations:

> Beethoven's Ninth yesterday gave nothing short of a symbolic acknowledgment of the Führer's birthday with its strengths and struggles, conquests and happy victories.[39]

It became customary in the press for all reflections on artistic matters to be subordinated to political humbug. Such considerations were required to "acknowledge" and assist the political appropriation of art and artists.[40] Two months later, one of Goebbels's administrators at ProMi sent Furtwängler a missive all but commanding him to conduct at the forthcoming Nürnberg Rally in September:

> The Cultural Celebration at this year's Party Day will take place on 7 September at the Opera House in Nürnberg. I request that you take the leading part with the Berlin Philharmonic in setting the stage for the Führer's speech on culture during the Celebration denoted above. Furthermore, I request that you submit suggestions for the program as soon as possible.[41]

39. Erich Roeder, *Der Anzeiger*, 22 April 1937. Cited in *Kraftprobe*, p. 276.

40. Ibid., p. 276. After the war, a reporter in the New York–based German language newspaper *Aufbau*, claimed that as a GI, he saw a telegram while he was in Berlin in which Furtwängler sent Hitler a birthday greeting. While the text of the telegram was quoted in full—"20 April 1937, Adolf Hitler. Best wishes to you and for your work on this day. General Music Director Wilhelm Furtwängler. Prussian Staatsrat"—the telegram itself has never been located: Nor, according to Prieberg (*Kraftprobe*, p. 276–277), are there any notations in his calendar around that time to send such a message. Furtwängler was also busy with preparations to depart from Berlin on 21 April for another tour with the Berlin Philharmonic that would take him back to London for the Coronation season. Despite assiduous efforts by the Allies, no other similar or delectably incriminating greeting from Furtwängler to Hitler was found after the war. There is no doubt Furtwängler occasionally played up to Hitler when he needed concessions on professional matters, but stomach-turning hypocrisies such as sending birthday notes to his adversaries were never part of his make-up.

41. Gutterer, ProMi, 11 June 1937. Source: Wilhelm Furtwängler Archives, Zürich, and Berlin Document Center.

Furtwängler fired off a reply as soon as he received the "invitation":

> I cannot conduct in Nürnberg since I have already accepted other engagements for that time period.[42]

In fact, Furtwängler was scheduled to perform the Ninth with the Berlin Philharmonic at the World's Fair in Paris on the 7th and begin a *Ring* cycle at the Staatsoper in Berlin the next day. ProMi must have known about it, but harassing Furtwängler was now standard operating procedure at the Ministry.

About this time, Furtwängler regained contact with Berta Geissmar, who had gone to work for Beecham in London after a short and unhappy stay in the United States. Beecham was quite fond of this painfully plain, but extremely sharp woman who had been the mainstay of the Berlin Philharmonic before the Nazis had taken over. But he also knew that she longed to return to Germany, and he soon gave her that opportunity. When Hitler ordered von Ribbentrop to arrange a tour of Germany by Beecham's orchestra—the London Philharmonic—Beecham readily consented on one condition: Geissmar must supervise all the arrangements and accompany him and the orchestra during the tour. Ribbentrop smiled maliciously as he accepted. "Miss Geissmar will be most welcome. She has many friends in Germany."

Geissmar was dispatched to Germany, where she was not only allowed to travel freely but was treated like an Aryan by silently furious Nazis who had to kowtow to her because she had come back at Hitler's invitation.[43] Many of them chatted amiably with her as though nothing had happened, as though the monstrous treatment she had received before her departure had never occurred. But Goebbels got even with Beecham and used him for the aggrandizement of the Nazi government. Shortly after the tour, Beecham was shown a photograph in which he was seated with Hitler in the Führer's box at the Philharmonie Hall. The shot was a fruit of Goebbels' experiments with photomontage. Beecham actually met Hitler, but at the Chan-

---

42. 14 June 1937. Source: Wilhelm Furtwängler Archives, Zürich.
43. In her memoir (p. 174), Geissmar says she was "diffident" about the trip, but Egon Hanfstängl, son of Hitler's foreign Press Secretary Ernst Hanfstängl, who was living in London at the time, recalls that she not only was eager to return to Germany but anxious to find a way to stay there. Letter to the author, 25 April 1990. See Chapter 13. Impressions of Geissmar's relationship with Hanfstängl are conflicting. In her book, she loathes him, blaming him for manipulating her ouster from Germany, and she outlines her distaste for him on pp. 272–273. Nonetheless, Egon Hanfstängl's letter to me suggests that she was on good enough terms with his father to be frank about her bitterness over the way she felt treated by Furtwängler.

cellery, not in a theater box. After that meeting, he told friends, "Now I know what's wrong with Germany."[44]

For all the triumphs in England, Austria, and Paris where he conducted *Tristan* and *Walküre* at the Opéra and concert tours with the Berlin Philharmonic, Furtwängler was anything but happy. Nonetheless, he was fully immersed in his abiding passion. In the summer of 1937 he returned to Germany to conduct *Lohengrin* at Bayreuth, where he was again enthusiastically received. From there he made the relatively short journey to Salzburg in Austria, to make his debut at the famous summer Festival. He was relieved that he was no longer at the center of political arguments he abhorred. But his relief was to be short-lived.

44. Beecham spent part of his trip to Germany in the Electrola (HMV) studios committing *The Magic Flute* to record with the Berlin Philharmonic and principals largely drawn from the Berlin Staatsoper.

13

A Meeting
of Minds

Before World War II, Bayreuth and Salzburg were the most prestigious summer festivals in Europe. In his memoirs, Bruno Walter aptly
summarized the essential philosophical differences between them. If
Bayreuth was the citadel of tradition and the past in German music in
the 1930s, Salzburg was the Mecca of the new, the cosmopolitan.[1] The
Salzburg Festival was originated in 1920 by Max Reinhardt and Hugo
von Hofmannsthal as a center for theatrical experimentation on a
grand scale. Reinhardt's production of Everyman was performed
every year in the cathedral square and gained world-wide fame.[2] Mozart's birthplace had become equally well known over the years for its
lively and innovative musical programs, begun by Bernhard Paumgartner in 1921 and soon made internationally important by Bruno
Walter and Arturo Toscanini. In fact, Salzburg became something of a
summer home to Toscanini's musical activities after he had left Bayreuth in 1931.

Austria had not yet come under Nazi domination in the summer
of 1937, and Salzburg became a haven for artists who either could not

---

1. Walter gives an affecting lively account of his experiences at Salzburg in the
shadow of the Nazi expansion in *Theme and Variations*, pp. 306–322.
2. Several excellent accounts of the Festival's history have been published, but the
most informative in English is Stephen Gallup, *Salzburg Festival*, (London and Tops-
field) 1987. For data and chronology, especially in the inter-war years, I found Josef
Kaut's *Salzburger Festspiele: 1920–1981*, (Salzburg and Vienna) 1982, most useful.

work in Germany or refused to do so. Many German artists appeared at Salzburg, but Goebbels eventually refused them permission because he had no desire to contribute to the Festival's prestige. When the Festival administration invited Furtwängler to make his debut there conducting Beethoven's Ninth, Toscanini was livid. He telephoned the Minister of Education, who was responsible for the Festival, from Milan and shouted "Walter or I could have done the Ninth. You can do without me altogether!" He then slammed down the receiver. The Minister immediately asked Walter to cool the old man down.

Bruno Walter drove from Sils Maria where he had gone for a rest to Milan. Toscanini's rages were usually like summer thunder storms—violent but brief and quickly forgotten—but when he vowed never to conduct at the Metropolitan Opera and Bayreuth after fights with the managements at both institutions, he had kept his word. Neither Walter nor the Austrian authorities wanted Toscanini to add Salzburg to his hate list. Toscanini loathed nearly all his contemporaries and later called Walter a "sentimental fool," but he was susceptible to being charmed by almost anyone. And Walter's charm was exceeded only by the enormity of his musical gifts. Without forcing the issue, Walter and Toscanini conversed about music in general, Wagner, and Bayreuth. Toscanini cooled down and showed Walter his collection of Wagner's letters and other memorabilia he happened to have with him. When they parted, Walter said simply, "I hope to see you soon." Salzburg had never been mentioned during the meeting, but Toscanini understood what he meant. The next morning, Toscanini arrived in Salzburg to begin rehearsals for a hectic series of operas and concerts. Before beginning, however, he immediately made it plain that he did not want to conduct in the same place where Furtwängler was also performing.

Only a year earlier, Furtwängler had been Toscanini's only nominee to succeed him as Music Director of the New York Philharmonic, but Toscanini had witnessed too many expulsions from Germany in the following months to remain loyal to someone who evidently embraced the regime. The devastation the Nazis had wrought on Germany's cultural life became depressingly clear to him when he went to Palestine in 1936 to conduct a new orchestra founded by Bronislaw Hubermann. He was shocked and deeply moved to find so many German émigrés assembled before him. The members of the nascent Israel Philharmonic (originally called the Palestine Symphony Orchestra) must have given him vivid accounts of the expulsions and purges, which, at that point, were only gearing up steam. There is no evidence, however, that any of them criticized Furtwängler to Toscanini or accused him of ill-treating them. And this certainly was their opportunity to do so.

Albert Catell, who was principal cellist for the Palestine Symphony from its beginnings until 1953, recalled that members of the orchestra were divided in their reaction to Furtwängler's decision to remain in Germany after the Nazis came to power.

> Some of them thought he should leave because they feared for his safety. Nearly all of us understood what he was doing by staying behind. It is hard to explain or categorize a specific reason like protecting German culture. We all respected that because most of us came from that culture and understood that safeguarding it was important—a mission. A few agreed with Toscanini's way of thinking and thought Furtwängler should leave, but I think we all would have admitted that if we had the chance to go back before 1942, we would have returned. I think that all of us felt that way deep in our hearts. There was nothing like Germany—especially Berlin—before those bastards took over, believe me. Even though I was born in Russia, I felt very much a part of German culture. It all went with the Nazis *vom Wind Verweht*—Gone with the Wind—but how were any of us to know that before the war? How was Furtwängler to know? There was disagreement on whether he made the right decision. But everybody in the Palestine Symphony understood why, and we sympathized with him openly or secretly. At least, I know I did.[3]

Catell had his first contact with Furtwängler when he was chosen from students at the Leipzig Conservatory to play in the Leipzig Gewandhaus Orchestra during the 1926–1927 season. Each season one pair of seats in each of the string section was set aside for the brightest students from the Conservatory. Catell was fourteen and studying with Julius Klengel, the principal cellist of the Gewandhaus and a renowned concert soloist, who chose him and one other student to play with the Gewandhaus that year. "Furtwängler was marvelous, a revelation. But I was so young, and I thought everybody conducted like that. I soon found out that was not always so."

Toscanini also had personally suffered the vicious side of Fascism on 14 May 1931 when he was attacked in Bologna by pro-Mussolini thugs after he refused to perform the Fascist anthem and had publicly denounced *Il Duce*. Having been an early admirer of Mussolini and a Fascist Party candidate in Milan in 1919, this attack sealed a dramatic turning point both in his political views and the manner in which he would express them for the rest of his life.[4] He was to return to Pales-

3. Personal conversation with the author, New York, 3 March 1989.
4. See Harvey Sachs. *Toscanini*, (London) 1978, pp. 139–140, and *Music in Fascist Italy*, (New York) 1987, p. 208.

tine again, even though the weather made him ill. These journeys were his way of expressing his conviction that music and politics are inextricably connected. Toscanini's economically poor background had forced him to become "street smart" at an early age. Life had prepared him for the rough-and-tumble of professional advancement in a highly competitive profession, and he had learned his lessons early and well. Despite a volcanic temper that made him many enemies—among them Enrico Caruso—he was always the clear-eyed and shrewd careerist. For all his pragmatism and ego, he frequently showed almost saintly kindness to those who needed his help. As the dark days of the late 1930s descended, there would be many indeed who would be in need of his compassion. He plainly saw what was coming down the international road and how that grim machine would separate the whole world into two inexorably opposed groups. He saw nothing unnatural about declaring exactly where he stood.

Toscanini agreed to fulfill his contract at Salzburg, providing that Furtwängler would not be engaged again. He also made it clear that he was not to be invited to any social or official functions attended by Furtwängler. If secrets have always travelled fast in musical circles, openly available information becomes general knowledge instantly. Furtwängler heard about Toscanini's arrangement with the Festival management, and he decided to confront him. One version of the story has it that Furtwängler went to Toscanini's dressing room after a concert in the large Festival Theater. Toscanini was curt. "Go away. I don't want to have anything to do with you."

"Why?" asked Furtwängler.

"Because you are a Nazi."

"That is a lie!"

"That is no lie. I am well aware that you do not belong to the Party. I also know you have helped your Jewish friends. You even meet them outside Germany. But all that is unimportant after the fact that you work for Hitler. Now get out."[5]

Another version had them meeting by accident at a banquet following a performance of *Meistersinger* conducted by Toscanini. When Furtwängler congratulated him, Toscanini was supposed to have replied:

> I wish I could say the same about your performance of the Ninth, but I have always thought that a man who approves a system which persecutes anyone who thinks independently cannot honestly interpret Beethoven's symphonies. You Nazis have suppressed the spirit, and admit nothing by

5. Cited in Riess, p. 225.

forced rhythms and boastful spectacles of physical force. You reflected this attitude the other day when you conducted Beethoven's Ninth Symphony. You suppressed everything noble in it, you overemphasized the loud passages, which you probably called "dynamic." But remember, my dear sir, the Ninth is a Symphony of brotherly love. And don't forget, it was a German who wrote the words, "be embraced all you Millions," and a German who set them to music. How can anyone continue to be Nazi who conducts this great work?[6]

This statement comes from a memoir published in 1941 by the German-Jewish émigré Otto Zarek, an observer and occasional participant in theatrical circles before he fled to England in 1938. His compelling "eyewitness" evocation of the cultural and political atmosphere in Germany and Austria during the 1920s an '30s gave the quote he imputes to Toscanini the stamp of authenticity, and it later became a beacon in the Toscanini-as-anti-Fascist legend. But his account of the controversy actually sheds more light on his bias than on anything relating to Furtwängler's encounter with Toscanini.[7] In the first place, Furtwängler did not attend the enormous reception given by the Governor of the province, Franz Rehrl, in honor of the artists participating in the Festival on 15 August.[8] In the second place, Furtwängler's performance of the Ninth took place on 27 August, long *after* the banquet at which the remark was supposedly made. In the third place, eyewitness accounts by individuals who were present in Salzburg in 1937 say Toscanini never attended Furtwängler's performance of the Ninth.[9] Zarek added spitefully that Furtwängler was all but run out of town after his performance of the Ninth and "never came back to Salzburg again." Neither assertion is true.[10]

As far as Furtwängler was concerned, there was indeed an encounter with Toscanini, but it took place accidentally on the street and did

6. Otto Zarek, *Splendor and Shame*, (Indianapolis and New York) 1941, p. 228.
7. The statement also portrays the usually taciturn Toscanini spouting musical philosophy. Such a habit was uncharacteristic. Some contemporaries of Hugo Burghauser find his memoir *Philharmonische Begegnungen*, (Zürich) 1979, as roseate in some of its contents as it undeniably is colorful in narrative. As General Manager of the Vienna Philharmonic at that time, he was in close contact with both conductors and he clearly preferred Toscanini to Furtwängler. In any event, he avers that there were no witnesses to the exchange between Furtwängler and Toscanini (p. 91).
8. *Neue Freie Presse*, 16 August 1937, p. 3; *Salzburger Chronik*, 17 August 1937. The press noted that Toscanini, Hans Knappertsbusch, and Bruno Walter were among those flanking the founder of the Festival, Max Reinhardt. The Guest of Honor on this evening was none less than the Chancellor of Austria, Kurt von Schuschnigg. Virtually the entire guest list—which was impressive indeed—was recited cooingly by the local and national papers, but Furtwängler's name was absent from it.
9. See Otto Strasser's statement to the author below.
10. Furtwängler appeared in Salzburg again in 1938. Zarek's book was published in 1941.

not concern the Ninth. According to the recollection Furtwängler gave his biographer Curt Riess, Toscanini approached him smiling and twirling his walking stick. "In the world of today," said Toscanini, "it is impossible for a musician who conducts in an enslaved country to do so in a free country. If you conduct in Bayreuth, you should not conduct in Salzburg."

"I am the same man I was six months ago when you reproached me for not accepting your invitation to come to New York," replied Furtwängler.[11]

"Those were different times. Today, there is only either—or."

"I should be quite willing to give up coming to Salzburg, if that meant your activities here would continue. Personally, I believe that for musicians there are no enslaved and free countries. Human beings are free wherever Wagner and Beethoven are played, and if they are not free at first, they are freed while listening to these works. Music transports them to regions where the Gestapo can do them no harm."

Toscanini made no reply.

"If I conduct great music in a country which is, by chance, ruled by Hitler, must I therefore represent him? Does not great music, on the contrary make me one of his antagonists? For is great music not utterly opposed to the soullessness of Nazism?"

The old man shook his head. "Everyone who conducts in the Third Reich is a Nazi!"

"By that," replied Furtwängler, "you imply that art and music are merely propaganda, a false front, as it were, for any government which happens to be in power. If a Nazi government is in power, then, as a conductor, I am a Nazi; under the communists, I would be a communist; under the democrats, a democrat. No, a thousand times, no! Music belongs to a different world, and it is above chance political events."

Toscanini again shook his head. "I disagree." He walked on. The conversation lasted only a few moments.[12]

What remains constant about these versions is that both men believed in the sanctity of music and its capacity to serve as an instrument of social conscience, of a greater good, of a divine voice. Toscanini's view was the more pragmatic of the two. For him, musicians were the instruments through which music is performed. They should

11. The form of "reproach" is not known. Toscanini apparently did not write to Furtwängler. In any event, Toscanini was always the clear-eyed pragmatist in such matters and gave little heed to the complications and circumstances surrounding Furtwängler's withdrawal from the New York Philharmonic.

12. This account is derived from Riess, pp. 224–227. See also Horowitz, *Understanding Toscanini*, pp. 319–320.

deny performing it before those who would use it (and the musicians who play it) for evil purposes. Furtwängler believed in music as a beacon to guide the soul home, as a source of hope to those subjected to suppression. Only by performing it before such listeners trapped within a totalitarian society and reminding them that there *is* a world of freedom and joy would there be any hope of deliverance from enslavement. If the artist was to remain the sole fulcrum of this hope, then he, too must remain above politics. Right or wrong, this was Furtwängler's unshakable and tragic conviction, and no one could persuade him to think otherwise.

Those who visited Salzburg in the summer of 1937 had a unique opportunity to compare the two conductors, for they each gave a concert with the Vienna Philharmonic within the space of four days. Otto Strasser was associate leader of the second violins at both concerts. "On the 24th of August," he recalled, "Toscanini conducted the *Pastorale* Symphony.[13] On the 27th, Furtwängler the Ninth. Furtwängler went to hear the *Pastorale,* and I could see him in the audience. He told me after the concert, 'It was very good, but it was not my Pastorale,' meaning that he admired Toscanini, but his interpretation was not to his taste. Furtwängler conducted the Ninth with Ria Ginster, Rosette Anday, Helge Roswänge, and Herbert Alsen and that was a very special occasion for us. The first rehearsal took place on the morning after Toscanini's concert, and Furtwängler discussed and rehearsed everything in greater detail than was customary for him. Toscanini did not attend the concert."[14]

Even though it took place at 11 in the morning, the concert was a gala occasion. Members of the Austrian government, the former German Crown Prince, and the Crown Princess of Italy were there. It was a great success with the public and most of the critics. Herbert F. Peyser reporting for the *New York Times,* seems to have relished the privilege of reviewing the concert:

> Mr. Furtwängler has at one time or another been an eloquent interpreter of the Ninth symphony, but this morning's performance was one of the poorest the present reviewer can recall. On different occasions during the last few years it has been evident the conductor's talents have undergone, for this reason or that, a kind of spiritual deterioration, and today's Beethoven only gave fresh evidence of this decline.

13. This concert was broadcast live to all parts of Britain, non-Nazi Europe, and by trans-Atlantic relay to the United States. WJZ in New York aired it at 12 noon, EST. Toscanini and the musicians donated their fees to the Festival's building fund.

14. Personal conversation with the author, Vienna, 9 April 1990. See also Strasser's memoir *Und dafür wird Man noch bezahlt,* (Vienna) 1974, pp. 112–113, for an eyewitness account of both concerts.

The symphony's first three movements, for the great part monumentally dull, were extraordinarily deficient in emotion and dramatic feeling.

Peyser found the strings at the opening "quite inaudible" (sic), the second movement "joyless and rigid," the adagio "wooden," and the finale "hysterical, exaggerated." But his appraisal waxed rhapsodic in its parting caress:

> One thing should not pass unnoticed—Mr. Furtwängler's spasmodic and convulsive mannerisms in conducting, if they have not become any better, have not grown any worse.[15]

The shrapnel from Furtwängler's argument with Toscanini kept flying as the months passed. In early September, the Austrian papers—still a free press—took great delight in publicizing the controversy. On 1 September the *Neue Freie Presse* in Vienna published a brief but catty article mentioning a "letter to a Viennese Friend" from Furtwängler. The recipient's identity was not imparted, but the missive was said to express Furtwängler's concern over the controversy and his hope that it would soon be settled. The real news value of the article, however, was the disclosure that Furtwängler was postponing his forthcoming engagement to conduct the Vienna Philharmonic's annual Nicolai Concert. Why? Because Toscanini apparently wanted that date for his own concert with the orchestra. The unsigned article concluded with an expression of regret about the controversy taking place in a neutral country like Austria, leaving the impression that Toscanini had demanded Furtwängler's pre-emption.[16] The next day, Hugo Burghauser, the General Manager of the Vienna Philharmonic, issued a statement to the press, making it clear that both Furtwängler and Toscanini would conduct the Philharmonic in the coming months. He explained that Furtwängler had agreed to postpone his engagement with the Philharmonic so that Toscanini could conduct the second of his two subscription concerts on a date that originally was set for Furtwängler. In November and December, said Burghauser, Furtwängler would conduct several concerts including the annual Nicolai Concert and the gala performance celebrating the 125th anni-

15. 28 August 1937, p. 8. Peyser also pointed out near the beginning of his report that one of the vocal soloists had been refused permission by the Nazis to perform in the Verdi *Requiem* under Toscanini a few days earlier because one of the other soloists was Jewish. Ria Ginster, in fact, was replaced at the last minute in Toscanini's performance on 11 August by Zinka Kunz. The "offensive" member of the quartet was Alexander Kipnis.
16. p. 8.

versary of the venerable Society for the Friends of Music (Gesellschaft der Musikfreunde).[17]

The news made Furtwängler's value to the orchestra unmistakable—at least for Europeans following the controversy. Few conductors in the orchestra's history had ever been granted the honor of two such prestigious concerts in one season. But the gossip persisted, and Furtwängler finally wrote a letter to the *Neue Freie Presse* reiterating his view:

> If I conduct today at Bayreuth and tomorrow at Salzburg, it has nothing to do with politics. Those who appear to assume that Bayreuth and Salzburg are being used for other means than for art are to blame for the accusation that art is being turned to political ends. What would be left for us if we artists also lost sight of the supernational significance of our great masters?[18]

In the meantime, the *New York Times* reported that Furtwängler had *withdrawn* from his engagement, saying nothing about a postponement. It also relayed speculations that Furtwängler did not want to follow Toscanini's engagement with the Vienna Philharmonic because he was too humiliated at the tongue-lashing Toscanini supposedly gave him in Salzburg. What is more, clucked the *Times:*

> Another cause for his decision is the possibility that the ticket sale for Dr. Furtwängler's event might be adversely affected by the Vienneses' [sic] willingness to pay any price for Toscanini concerts, thus furnishing another ground for unflattering contrasts.[19]

Nor did the baiting stop there. When the prospectus for the next Salzburg Festival was released in November, the *Times* chortled that it featured Toscanini's name but not Furtwängler's, a clear sign that Toscanini and the anti-Nazis were prevailing in Salzburg. Just before Christmas, the *Times* kept up with the story in true holiday spirit with a surprising report that Hugo Burghauser, General Manager of the Vienna Philharmonic Orchestra Committee, had denied ever receiving an "ultimatum" from Toscanini about Furtwängler.[20] In that supposed ultimatum, Toscanini told Burghauser that he would not participate in the Salzburg Festival if Furtwängler was included on the roster. Such news must have startled American readers because

17. *Neue Freie Presse*, 2 September 1927, p. 10.
18. 7 September 1937.
19. 3 September 1937, p. 15.
20. Burghauser was also a bassoonist in the Vienna Philharmonic. His wife was Jewish, and Furtwängler tried to help him. See Chapter 15.

they already were under the impression that Furtwängler was a past issue, and no report about an ultimatum had been published before. The *Times* also reported Burghauser declaring that the Austrian government would in any case refuse Furtwängler permission to conduct in Salzburg in 1938—again a bewildering disclosure since Furtwängler would have no reason to attempt conducting at a Festival that did not feature him.[21]

Had Furtwängler hoped it would all soon be settled, he could not have bargained for the way it came about. On 18 February 1938 Toscanini suddenly canceled his engagement at Salzburg, throwing the Festival management into a panic that was both an artistic as well as political crisis.[22] Toscanini's repertoire for that year would have included five operas[23] and several concerts, no mean feat for a man who had just turned 70. A top-of-the-line conductor had to be found to replace him immediately. On 11 March Germany annexed Austria, shortening the short list of possible racially acceptable replacements critically.

Furtwängler, of course, was leery of becoming involved in another political contretemps and had no enthusiasm for going back to Salzburg. Nonetheless, he reluctantly agreed to assume one opera only, leaving the other gaps to be filled by Knappertsbusch, Karl Böhm, and Vittorio Gui. But Furtwängler was not about to let the Festival or the Philharmonic off without some reminder of exactly whom they were dealing with. He agreed to conduct *Meistersinger*, providing the redoubtable Walter Grossmann, a Jew, understudied the role of Hans Sachs.[24] The demand inflicted whiplash on the Festival administration, but they nodded stiffly. As it turned out, Grossmann sang on the gala Opening Night because Karl Kamann, the announced singer, was ill. A glittering crowd headed by Joseph Goebbels and his entourage sat dutifully enthralled through the Führer's favorite opera while Grossmann brought Nürnberg's most German hero to life. However coincidentally, Furtwängler had made his point delectably, whereupon he fulfilled his contract for the remaining three performances

21. 22 December 1937, p. 33. Otto Strasser, who was Business Manager of the Orchestra at the time, avers that such a statement would have been impossible because it simply was not true. Strasser was in charge of making such applications and he says that Furtwängler had always been so much in demand in Austria that such procedures were never required. "To the best of my knowledge, and I would have known about such things, Toscanini never issued an ultimatum about Furtwängler. Furtwängler postponed his engagement so that Toscanini could conduct his concerts and leave in time for his other engagements." Telephone conversation with the author, 5 May 1991.

22. See Gallup, p. 101.

23. *Tannhäuser, Meistersinger, Fidelio, The Magic Flute,* and *Falstaff.*

24. Grossman was a first-class artist if not a world-class baritone. He sang a leading role in Pfitzner's *Das Herz* at Furtwängler's debut at the Berlin Staatsoper.

and left Salzburg for the remainder of the Third Reich, except for a special hastily arranged concert in 1944 just before Goebbels ordered all theaters in the Reich closed.[25]

If it were not infuriating enough to be portrayed cowering before the livid Titan Toscanini while despairing over his dwindling box office receipts, Furtwängler had again and again to endure accusations of remaining in Germany for personal gain, of making a self-serving deal with the government. He could do little about proving these rumors wrong. After all, he had remained voluntarily in a country where thousands were now trying to escape. What is more, he had important and lucrative offers from abroad. He also knew he was being used by the Nazis as a façade, and he expressed his pain in being caught in such a dilemma to Maria Daelen, a young doctor in Berlin with whom he was having a prolonged relationship:[26]

> It is a great joy to receive a letter or card from you every day and remember that there is something better than the work to which I am obliged whether I like it or not. I must confess that conducting the Ninth and *Walküre* are unbearable to me in the midst of being caught up in the politics going on, as if it all is proof of Toscanini's accusation: but see how he lets himself be used as a political functionary. An artist should be independent! *Paris, (no date), 1937*[27]

Yet, he resolved that he must remain in Germany come what may and share his nation's fate, what ever that was to be. He thought of Goethe's line, "Wherever I may be useful, that is my home." Furtwängler clearly felt he could not be as "useful" abroad as he could at home, even though the Nazis were shamelessly using him to their own ends. He now became aware that his destiny as a musician was indeed political. It was his lot to continue resisting the Nazis in what ever way he could. That struggle was to become increasingly bitter.

Decades later, Elisabeth Furtwängler said, "It may be hard for many people to understand this position because it is not based simply on an opposition of black and white. The easy way out was to go . . . to get out of Germany. But the easy way was never Furtwängler's way.

---

25. In fact, the performance of Bruckner's Eighth Symphony on 14 August was the only full-fledged event that year. The single performance of Strauss' *Liebe der Danaë* (16 August) was a general dress rehearsal. See Kaut, p. 297–298.

26. Furtwängler ultimately married Daelen's younger half-sister Elisabeth *née* Albert. See Chapter 15.

27. Cited in Peter Cahn, "Wilhelm Furtwängler im Spiegel unbekannter Briefe," *NZ (Neue Zeitschrift für Musik)*, January 1986, p. 9.

Even with music he had conducted a hundred times, he always searched and approached it like a beginner, starting all over again each time. In staying in Germany, he took the harder road, and he stayed on that road because he was convinced at the time that it was only course for *him* to take."[28]

Earlier in the year, Furtwängler lost a close kindred spirit if not necessarily an ally. Ernst Hanfstängl, who had groomed Hitler and had put one good face after another on the egregious policies of the Nazis, fell from favor. He had become increasingly horrified at Hitler's growing megalomania and with the associates around him who fed it. He was always convinced that he could soothe the Führer into normal conduct, but his sarcastic wit had made him many enemies. The Gestapo was now after him. Nonetheless, he viewed himself as a German, and his recollections of this period in his life are no less poignant than those of Thomas Mann:

> During the afternoon I wandered around disconsolately. Clearly it had reached the point of no return. My last illusions were shattered. Instead of regenerating Germany, we had brought to power a bunch of dangerous gangsters who now only survive by maintaining the momentum of their ceaseless radical agitation. What on earth were people like me to do? I was a German. My family and my whole life were bound up in my country's future fate. Did the solution lie in exile or must I stick with this thing? (Remember that the worst of Hitler's Germany still lay in the future, the concentration camps in the sense in which we now talk of them, the systematic decimation of the Jews and the plans for armed aggression. In the end every restraining hand was swept aside by this criminal little inner group of narrow-minded fanatics.) It is given to no man to foresee the future in its full dimension and I, who bore my small personal share for what had happened, thought, erroneously, that there must still be opportunities for influencing the course of events towards more respectable channels.[29]

Hanfstängl was not alone in this delusion.

But he, like many others, took action. He narrowly escaped a Gestapo plot to kill him, fled to England, and was put into a detention camp. Later he was shipped to a military stockade in Canada. He got word of his situation to President Roosevelt—his old classmate from Harvard. Despite the protests of the British, he was called to Washington while still officially incarcerated and served as an adviser to the

---

28. Personal conversation with the author, Paris, 22 April 1989.
29. *Unheard Witness*, pp. 265–266.

War Department. After the war, he returned to Munich to live tranquilly in the same house that 20 years earlier had frequently echoed with the shrill oratory and abrasive laughter of a house painter who had stirring ideas about reviving Germany.

Furtwängler's fortunes were to be almost as peripatetic, but not nearly as far-flung.

14

Devilish Duties—I

Furtwängler's accord with the Nazis in 1935 had allowed him to remain in Germany as a free lance, supposedly enabling him to do as much or little conducting as he liked. The comparative latitude he enjoyed convinced those outside Germany that he had made some kind of special deal that brought all sorts of perquisites with it. Except for free rail travel, under the terms of his title as State Councilor, quite the contrary was the case. Virtually from the moment Furtwängler made his uneasy peace, Goebbels had tried assiduously to nullify the accord. Furtwängler's exemption from performing at official or state-sponsored events was the most irritating term of the reconciliation, as far as Goebbels and the rest of the Nazi hierarchy were concerned, and he was determined to make Furtwängler conduct for his supper. As Poland, France, Belgium, Holland, and Norway fell under Nazi domination, Goebbels stepped up his efforts to make Furtwängler take his share in promoting the cultural prestige of the Third Reich. Furtwängler steadfastly refused, writing to Goebbels that he had "no desire to follow tanks into countries where I had formerly been an invited guest."[1] Goebbels retorted to aides, "I don't care if Furtwängler is a National Socialist or not. As far as I am concerned, he can criticize us

1. Riess, p. 246.

as much as he likes. Right now, he is worth the trouble, He may not be a political official, but he must give us a façade."[2]

Furtwängler kept his word. He accepted only personal invitations to conduct abroad. After France had fallen, the Nazis there "asked" Charles Munch to write to Furtwängler personally and persuade him to conduct in France. Munch had been Furtwängler's concertmaster when he was the conductor of the Leipzig Gewandhaus during the 1920s, and they were good friends. Munch later was to become the venerated music director of the Boston Symphony. He wrote the letter as the Nazis had dictated but managed to scribble the words "in agreement with the German occupation authorities" before the letter was sent. Furtwängler replied that he would accept the invitation as long as the German occupation authorities had nothing to do with the concert.[3] Ultimately, he did not go to France.

It was a narrow escape from the embarrassment the Nazis were determined to cause him. But he could not elude them indefinitely. In 1938 he was cornered into conducting a gala performance of *Meistersinger* at Nürnberg on the eve of the annual rally on 5 September. It was not officially part of the rally, but the situation was virtually the same as 1935, when he conducted the same opera in the same city on the same date. This time, however, the production, singers, and orchestra came from the Vienna Staatsoper. The event was broadcast, and large sections of it have survived on acetate recordings.[4] Though neither Furtwängler nor any of the officials in attendance that night would have viewed it as an oracular occasion, the progress of the performance turned out to be something of an omen for the Third Reich and the fortunes of its Führer, who esteemed this opera above all others.

It starts off grandly with the Vienna Philharmonic in glowing form. Furtwängler's majestic view of the work in this performance reveals itself in his traversal of the prelude. It is broadly scaled, and by turns energetic and rhapsodic, giving the brass their head in the processional, drawing a sweet intimacy from the strings in the exposition of the Prize Song theme, and striding toward an epic denouement. The surviving fragments from each of the three acts document a tightly disciplined performance with Tiana Lemnitz as a refulgent Eva, despite a marked inclination toward portamento and moments of under-the-note intonation in the Quintet, Eyvind Lahlom as a beefy

2. Riess, p. 245.
3. Riess, p. 246.
4. Several pressings have been issued, but the inveterate record collector evidently had a copy of the original acetates. It appeared under one of his labels Golden Age of Opera UROC-224.

but impassioned Walter, and Erich Zimmermann and Eugen Fuchs serviceable as David and Beckmesser respectively. But it is Rudolf Bockelmann as Hans Sachs who goes from victory to victory to utter vocal defeat, walking the line from a solid technical footing in the first act, to some tightness at the top of the staff in his two set pieces in the second act. His vocal problems descend into his line notes and trip him occasionally throughout his carefully nursed contribution to the Quintet, but they ultimately conspire with encroaching fatigue to overwhelm him long before Act III has ended. In the declamations of the final scene, tightness gives way to rhythmic insecurity, shortness of breath and pronounced hoarseness. Bockelmann barks his final peroration rather than singing it, an intimation of what the most distinguished member of the audience that night might have sounded like in the bath. Only the unstinting generosity of the Staatsoper chorus, the consistently inspired Philharmonic, and Furtwängler's magisterial hand save the finale from disaster.

The Nazis scored a major coup in bringing Furtwängler within a goose-step of an official Party event, and Goebbels and Göring immediately sought ways to present him more often at close proximity to such gatherings. But Furtwängler managed successfully to sidestep them most of the time. After the war started, he performed three times in occupied countries. Two of those occasions took place in Copenhagen, first in 1942 with the Berlin Philharmonic and second in 1943 when he took the Vienna Philharmonic on tour through Scandinavia.[5] Otto Strasser, the General Manager of the Philharmonic, informed him that the tour would ruin the orchestra financially if it passed up the receipts they expected in Copenhagen. The third and fourth occasions both took place in Prague; first in 1942, a small concert he presented before an invited audience in Prague while he was staying in the Czech capital on his way to Budapest and second, a concert with the Berlin Philharmonic on 16 March 1944.

Perhaps the blessing that truly cursed Furtwängler during the Third Reich was the relentless admiration Adolf Hitler heaped on him throughout the regime. In 1941 the Führer came up with a grand scheme in which an entire ship would be given to Furtwängler so that he could sail around the world with or without his orchestras to conduct concerts in the handful of countries with which Germany still had cordial relations. Goebbels also created on Hitler's orders a massive public relations campaign around Furtwängler, photographing him in every conceivable location, usually with the image of Hitler or a Swastika somewhere within the frame.

5. February 1942 and May 1943.

These blandishments, of course, concealed other dark motives. Even at this stage of the war in 1941 Goebbels was preparing to mobilize every part of German life, especially cultural activities, for quasi-military purposes. Music was to play an integral part in Germany's eventual campaign of Total War, and Goebbels intended that Furtwängler take his place at the head of this massive military offensive. But if Winifred Wagner once despaired because Furtwängler seemed like a sponge that leaked water from all sides the moment he was seized, a conjunction of ill-luck and Furtwängler's maddening unreliability prevented Goebbels from being any more successful in containing him.

Furtwängler was an avid skier and highly skilled for a man of his age. When the Ministry of Propaganda learned that he was in St. Anton, the *Berliner Illustrierte Zeitung* sent a photographer to take shots of Furtwängler on the slopes. The paper got their pictures and a message from the photographer. "This might be Furtwängler's last adventure on skies." Furtwängler had skidded down a dangerous slope, lost his balance and tumbled down the grade. He sustained a broken arm, a concussion, and sixteen other injuries—mostly bruises, and was in critical condition for several days. The doctors also found nerve damage in his right arm and predicted that he would not be able to conduct if he survived.[6]

All this did not stop him from leaving the hospital to hear a radio transmission of a recording he recently had made of Bruckner's Seventh Symphony. He had to go on foot to a tavern in a nearby village, which had the only radio powerful enough to receive the transmission. Usually the radio played dance music, but Furtwängler told the proprietor who he was and asked him to tune to his broadcast. Despite complaints from customers, the tavern resounded with Bruckner. While he listened, Furtwängler realized that he might never have another chance to perform this great work, and he wept. He reconciled himself to the only option he felt he had left: composing.[7]

Eight painful months later, he was back on the podium. "I hoped to cancel a few concerts to be free for a few months, even a year," he told Curt Riess. "But that was impossible. If one is involved in the musical world, one is eaten up by it. A drastic decision would be required to leave it. Liszt, for example, declared from one day to the next: 'from now on, I will not play the piano.'" Furtwängler already had made one binding decision: to stay in Germany to make German music in his own way. When he returned to his first rehearsal after the

6. Riess, p. 247.
7. Riess, pp. 248–250.

accident, his arms caused him so much pain that he had to stop after a few minutes. His doctors advised him to cancel the concert. He refused. They predicted he would have to stop in the middle of the concert, but he completed it. He was exhausted from the pain, but he knew now that he could still conduct. Within a year, the arm was back to normal.[8] Nonetheless, his malady enabled him to evade engagements he did not want to accept and provided him, with a handy means of excusing himself from appearing at politically oriented events.

But Goebbels was just as persistent in pursuing Furtwängler for propaganda purposes as Furtwängler was wily in avoiding him. Now that he was able again to make music, Goebbels was anxious to see to it that Furtwängler made more music in the service of the Third Reich. His new project for promoting the cultural glory of the Nazis was *Symphony and Love*, a film directed by Paul Verhoeven, recounting the achievements of the Berlin Philharmonic.[9] He made numerous offers to Furtwängler to appear in the film and have a say in its production. Furtwängler hated the blatant Nazified bias in the script.[10] It made no mention of any of the Jews who had been connected with the orchestra (Walter, Klemperer, etc.), barely acknowledged Nikisch's contribution to it, and interpolated a ridiculous love story. Furtwängler firmly refused to have anything to do with it. Goebbels could easily have gone to dozens of other conductors who had worked with the orchestra and could not have been more cooperative in this period. For example, Clemens Krauss, Karl Böhm, Hermann Abendroth, Robert Heger, Hans Knappertsbusch, and others took the Berlin Philharmonic on tours to occupied countries, appeared as guest conductors in those states, and took part in domestic propaganda projects. But only the apostate Furtwängler could give the film the stamp of legitimacy it needed.

The film was a masterful example of Nazi public relations in its clever distortion of facts and wholesale untruths. According to the

8. Riess, p. 251.
9. The film was also released under the title "Philharmonic." See *Kraftprobe*, p. 419.
10. Paul Verhoeven's son, Michael, won acclaim in 1990 for his film *The Nasty Girl*, a story about a young girl in Germany of the 1970s who explores the behavior of the people in her home town during the Third Reich. In a lengthy interview in the *New York Times* (8 October 1990), the younger Verhoeven apparently gave no inkling of his own father's behavior as it palpably was documented in *Symphony and Love*. The *Times* article also states that the elder Verhoeven spent the war as a film and stage director of "apolitical light comedies" (p. C14). So "apolitical" was *Symphony and Love* that Verhoeven demanded the arrest of Werner Fiedler, a critic who panned the film. Fiedler's arrest almost certainly would have led to his liquidation. See below, Chapter 18 and Gillis, *Furtwängler and America*, p. 82.

script, the Nazis alone had made the Berlin Philharmonic the great orchestra it had become over the years. The concert agency of Wolff and Sachs, which was largely responsible for marketing the orchestra everywhere, was left unmentioned. Louise Wolff and Bruno Walter never existed.

After it looked as though Furtwängler's refusal to have anything to do with the film was final, Goebbels fingered his only remaining trump card. Richard Strauss was all too happy to make a brief appearance. He was seen conducting a few bars from his *Festival Overture* before the cameras. A stand-in conducted the rest of the segment.[11]

Goebbels had no idea how difficult *Symphony and Love* would be to make, and when it looked as though its completion was far into the future, he ordered a treatment for a film about Beethoven, to star the well-known German actor Gustav Fröhlich. He wanted Furtwängler to supervise the soundtrack. Furtwängler was anxious to humor the Propaganda Minister at this point in 1941, because he needed his help to get more money for the Philharmonic and enlist him in his battle against some virulent enemies who were threatening him at the Berlin Philharmonic, so he did not decline immediately. Eventually, they talked seriously about the film, but Goebbels' arrogant manner collided with Furtwängler's propensity for long-windedness. An argument erupted. Furtwängler stood up and told the Minister, "You are mistaken, Herr Minister, if you think you can exploit Beethoven in a film" and stormed out. Goebbels shelved his plans for immortalizing Beethoven on celluloid.[12]

Symphony and Love, however, kept stewing on ProMi's back burner. When it was finally completed and released in 1944, it nauseated the critic Werner Fiedler, and he said as much in a review. Its director Paul Verhoeven was so angry that he demanded that Fiedler, who was already on Goebbels' blacklist, be apprehended. Furtwängler, on the other hand, was so delighted with the review that he met with Fiedler in one of his rare encounters with critics for an amiable discussion on the nature of criticism. Goebbels had his hands so full with the Allies closing in on Germany that he never got around to ordering Fiedler's arrest.[13]

At the Staatsoper, Göring was also determined to put Furtwängler on a leash and make him conduct more frequently at his musical palace, but he too found himself frustrated. He tried persuasion rather than subterfuge. As far back as 1937, he had arranged for Furtwängler

11. Riess, pp. 252–253.
12. Riess, p. 253.
13. Gillis, p. 82.

to conduct a spectacular production of *Tannhäuser* in Berlin,[14] and he once again asked him to resume his position as Music Director at the Staatsoper.[15] But at that time, Furtwängler was still smarting from Göring's most recent intrigues that had forced him into declining the invitation from the New York Philharmonic. He not only refused to take up his post again at the Staatsoper but asked Göring to release him from his guest conducting arrangement there. Predictably, Göring was furious and insisted that Furtwängler fulfill his guest commitments at the Staatsoper to the absolute letter.[16] But such threats had no teeth; if Furtwängler did not wish to conduct, he was under no obligation because he was a free lance and had no contract.

Furtwängler was Germany's finest conductor, but it galled both Goebbels and Göring to know that Furtwängler could get away with his insubordinance simply because he had no real rivals anywhere in the Reich. They also realized that the racial policies of their own regime had backed them into a desolate corner: the pool of first-class German talent was rapidly thinning out. While Göring once boasted that he alone would decide who was Aryan and who was not at the Staatsoper, Jews were unable to perform there by 1938. It would be only a matter of months before the veteran Leo Blech would have to be dismissed. Blech was probably the only full Jewish conductor still employed at a Reichs institution.[17] The other prominent conductors—Klemperer, Busch, Kleiber, Scherchen, Jascha Horenstein, Fritz Zweig, Fritz Stiedry, William Steinberg, Joseph Rosenstock—all were gone now.[18]

Erich Kleiber ultimately retired to Austria on resigning his position at the Staatsoper in Berlin, this as a sympathy protest when Furtwängler quit all his posts following the Hindemith Scandal in 1934.

14. Premiere: 10 November 1937. Lorenz took the title part in a production designed by Emil Preetorius and directed by Tietjen. Tiana Lemnitz and Heinrich Schlusnus sang Elisabeth and Wolfram respectively. The fascinating switch in casting was Frida Leider, singing Venus for the first time. It was a turning point in her career. She had been the reigning Elisabeth up until that time and still had several seasons of impassioned Isoldes and Brünnhildes left. But she clearly was moving toward the twilight of her singing career.

15. The position of Music Director at the Staatsoper was one of the appointments Furtwängler resigned in 1934 in the wake of the Hindemith Scandal.

16. Riess, p. 229.

17. Göring got special dispensation for Blech, one of the finest opera conductors Germany produced in this century, who remained unmolested and kept his title of Generalmusikdirector until the end of 1937; Prieberg, *Musik im N-S Staat*, p. 45. He emigrated to Sweden and led a successful career during the war at the Royal Opera Stockholm and was influential in developing the early careers of several singers who gained lasting fame in the postwar era. Most notable among them was Birgit Nilsson.

18. For chilling accounts of the talent drain perpetrated by the Nazis, see Prieberg, *Musik im N-S Staat*, pp. 34–62, and Wulf, Chapter I.

Later he conducted in Fascist Italy in 1936 but resigned again when he learned that Jews were not permitted to be subscribers at La Scala Milan. Kleiber eventually emigrated to Latin America, leaving behind countless artists and intellectuals who entered a phase that became known as the "inner emigration." They were not forced to leave Germany, but they had neither the desire nor the hardy temperament to emigrate. At the same time, they had neither the stomach to go along with the Nazis nor the courage to defy them openly. They remained in Germany or what became the Reich, but they were virtually inactive in the darker days to come.[19]

Fritz Busch was also a leading conductor in Germany, and his case demonstrates the frequently confused attitude the Nazis evinced toward their best-known artists. They tried to keep him in Germany even while they caused him untold aggravation. For his part, Busch evidently was willing to remain, at least at first, despite the trouble the Nazis caused him. Busch had maintained Dresden's exceptional 200-year-old musical heritage since he had become General Music Director for Saxony in 1922. His accomplishments included the world premieres of two works by Richard Strauss,[20] On the night of 7 March 1933, his tenure came to an abrupt end. A violent Nazi-backed demonstration broke up a performance of *Rigoletto* Busch was conducting at the Semper Oper.[21] The fighting in the audience caused such an uproar that Busch finally left the pit. Before long, his second Kapellmeister Kurt Striegler entered the pit to shrill, Nazi-inspired applause and completed the performance. According to his autobiography, the fracas was caused by his refusal to join the Nazi Party and give money to its solicitors, but his reluctance to join the Party was irrelevant to his departure.[22] Busch was loathed by members of the Semper com-

---

19. Shortly after Kleiber died in 1956, the sagacious critic Jacques Barzun, who was personally acquainted with Kleiber, wrote a penetrating essay on the conductor's political choices in "The Passing of a Free Mind—Erich Kleiber." It can be found in his collection of essays *Critical Questions*, ed. Bea Friedland, (Chicago) 1982, pp. 39–47. " . . . The public's judgment" he concluded, "should be tempered by the sobering thought, 'What could I do in such perplexities?' A mind like Kleiber's, tracing out consequences in imagination, is strong in the belief that by reasserting the independence of art, its independence both from political direction and from public clamor, he contributes most to the ultimate virtues of civilization" (p. 46).

20. *Intermezzo*, 1924; *Die aegyptische Helena*, 1928.

21. The Semper Opera House (completed in 1841) was named after its original architect, Gottfried Semper (1803–1879). A fire damaged the original building in 1869, and it was rebuilt by Semper's son Manfred nine years later. Weber and Wagner were among its distinguished line of music directors, and before the Second World War, the Semper had a long and impressive record of presenting new works. Three of Wagner's early operas (*Rienzi*, *Der fliegende Holländer*, and *Tannhäuser*) and many of Richard Strauss' works (including *Elektra* and *Der Rosenkavalier*) received their premieres there.

22. *Pages from a Musician's Life*, (Westport) 1971, pp. 195–196. (Published originally in London, 1953). Hereafter referred to as Busch.

pany for a variety of reasons they were all too pleased to make public in an affidavit.[23] Ultimately a convergence of rabble-rousing Nazis infiltrating the opera house with malcontent company members made his continued survival in Dresden highly doubtful. Göring personally tried to convince Busch to stay in Germany if not in Dresden, and Busch was willing at first, but no suitable position seemed to be available for him at that moment.[24]

Emmy Sonnemann, the vivacious actress whom Göring was later to marry, knew Busch and his wife well and arranged for him to meet with the Feldmarschall shortly after the demonstration at the opera house. Busch later recalled one of those encounters:

> I told Göring that at no price would I return to work at Dresden. He made an angry contemptuous gesture.
>
> "That's not the question. Just wait a fortnight till I am president of the Cabinet. You know quite well that we should like to have you here."
>
> I said I would not turn any Jewish colleague out of his position, and used the expression, "I can't collaborate in that."
>
> Göring spoke of legal dismissals and monetary compensation. As I was still obstinate he became more vehement. "Well, my dear friend, you know we have means at hand to compel you!"
>
> "Just try it, Herr Minister," I burst out. "A compulsory performance of *Tannhäuser* conducted by me would be no pleasure to you. You will never in your life have heard anything that would be so stinkingly boring."
>
> The strong expression only resulted in a cynically amused smile from Göring.[25]

Göring left no record of his view of this meeting, but, according to Busch, Göring and Heinz Tietjen—Director of the Prussian State Theaters—offered Busch something of a carrot around this time, and a

23. A resolution dated 12 March 1933 by the artistic management with supporting signatures from 29 members of the company (including Paul Schöffler, Kurt Böhme, Maria Cebotari, Tino Pattiera, and Robert Burg) cited a hefty litany of complaints against him and was prefaced with a statement whose point would be hard to misconstrue: "We regard Herr Busch neither musically nor personally qualified to work at the Staatsoper [of Dresden]. His return would be disruptive and will seriously endanger artistic work at the Opera." Source: Berlin Document Center.

24. While the enmity toward Busch on professional and political grounds was swelling, the demonstration in the opera house that precipitated his ouster was evidently a coincidence and strictly a local development, a case of overzealous Nazi rednecks in Dresden getting out of hand. Fritz Busch had both the racial and musical qualifications attractive to top-ranking Nazis in the cultural sector in Berlin. But neither Busch's pedigree nor his formidable contributions to Dresden's prestige prompted tears backstage over the demonstration and his abrupt departure. It speaks for Busch's strength of character that he refused to step into the vacancy created at the Leipzig Gewandhaus when Bruno Walter, who had succeeded Furtwängler there as Music Director in 1928, fled Germany.

25. Busch, pp. 208–209.

very tempting one: The Wagner Festival at Bayreuth. They had anticipated Toscanini's refusal to return to Bayreuth after quitting in a fury
in 1931 and now invited Busch to replace him. It was an intoxicating
offer, for it would catapult Busch into the very forefront of German
musical circles and crown a distinguished career still in mid-flight.
When Busch met with Toscanini at the maestro's house in the Borro-
mean Islands, he was shown a letter from Hitler inviting Toscanini to
conduct at Bayreuth. Busch told him that he had been offered Bayreuth in the event that Toscanini did not accept the invitation. Toscanini was visibly shocked. Busch promised that under no circumstances would he accept the offer.

Busch was also reportedly offered the Music Director's job at the
Berlin Staatsoper because Göring wanted him in that position and
thought he was under no obligation to Furtwängler, who had signed a
contract with the Weimar regime in 1932 before the Nazis seized
power. Göring learned that he had to honor the contract Furtwängler
had signed, but he apparently asked Busch to wait while he showed
Furtwängler the door.[26]

In the meantime, the Nazis hastily arranged and financed a goodwill operatic guest engagement at the Teatro Colón in Buenos Aires in
late spring and summer 1933, led by Busch and featuring Jews such as
Walter Grossman and some distinguished anti-Nazis of a later day,
notably Lauritz Melchior.[27] The tour was an obvious and expensive
ploy to keep Busch busy and buy the new regime time in the first turbulent months after the Nazi takeover.[28] Busch could hardly believe
such an undertaking would be possible to assemble on such short
notice and declined.[29] But Hinkel personally assured him that everything had been arranged (and Hinkel for once was telling the truth),
and Busch accepted.[30] But after this highly successful tour, the only

26. Riess, p. 160. See Chapter 10.
27. While Melchior was later a vociferous anti-Nazi, even refusing to sing with
Kirsten Flagstad after the war because she returned to her husband's side in Nazi-occupied Norway, his political views evidently underwent some "development" between
1933 and 1951. See Chapter 21. Erich Kleiber originally was engaged for the tour but
cancelled. Others in the distinguished array of singers assembled for the tour included
Anny Konetzni, Kersten Thorborg, Paul Seider, Michael Bohnen and Edith Fleischer.
Carl Ebert was the producer.
28. While Busch suggests for some reason in his memoir that the engagement at
the Teatro Colón was initiated and therefore organized in Buenos Aires, there is compelling evidence to demonstrate, as we see here, that after the invitation was brought
from South America by the Swiss conductor Ernest Ansermet, the tour itself was produced and financed largely if not solely under the auspices of the Third Reich. See also
Busch, p. 211, below, and *Kraftprobe*, pp. 110–114.
29. Letter to Hans Hinkel Kultusministerium, 12 April 1933. Source: Berlin Document Center.
30. Letter to Hans Hinkel Kultusministerium, 26 April 1933. Source: Berlin Document Center.

music directorship that had become available at home in the interim was in Hamburg, a position Busch apparently felt beneath his worth.[31] Furtwängler not only wrote to Busch in Buenos Aires offering to share some of his concerts with the Berlin Philharmonic for the following season but also intervened in his behalf to top Nazi officials. Busch had to turn him down because he now had accepted other attractive invitations.[32] The Dresden affair had brought him both celebrity as a martyr of fascism—even while he was representing Hitler and the Nazi regime in a showboat engagement in South America—and cachet as a box-office draw. As a result, he was getting more offers than he could accept. The following year, he took charge of musical direction at Glyndebourne in England, established it quickly as one of Europe's major summer music festivals and duly became a vociferous anti-Nazi. Meanwhile, always ready to save the show, Richard Strauss filled the vacancy created by Toscanini and Busch at Bayreuth.

By 1939 the number of émigrés had grown astronomically, and it became all but impossible to leave Germany. Of those who fled, the largest group went to the United States. Recent statistics show that America took in 132,000 refugees from Nazi Germany and Austria between 1933 and 1944—the greatest number of these before 1940. Latin America as a whole took about 85,000; Great Britain, 72,000 including Czechs; Palestine, 56,000 including 1,800 illegal immigrants. France accepted about 30,000 permanent refugees and many more transient individuals on their way to other destinations. Shanghai took 17,000; Czechoslovakia accepted 6,500. Switzerland and Holland protected over 30,000 each. South Africa, Australia, and Canada each took only a few thousand. These figures are vague because some of them include transients, and others do not.[33] Some include persons counted twice, while others indicate large omissions. As historian Peter Gay has aptly stated, "the émigrés Hitler made were the greatest collection of transplanted intellect, talent, and scholarship the world has ever seen."[34] Whatever the number of those who fled, the rest ultimately perished.

31. Furtwängler was instrumental in making this position available to Busch. In her memoir, however, Busch's widow, evidently perceived Furtwängler's part in opening up Hamburg for her husband as a contemptuous, crumb-throwing gesture. Grete Busch, *Fritz Busch, Dirigent*, (Frankfurt) 1970, pp. 64–65.

32. See Chapter 19 for a further discussion of this episode and evidence of Furtwängler's assistance to Busch and other beleaguered musicians at this time.

33. See *The Muses Flee Hitler*, (Washington) 1983, pp. 49–53. Also Hartmut Lehmann and James J. Sheehan, eds., *An Interrupted Past: German-Speaking Refugee Historians in the United States after 1933*, (Cambridge) 1991. These valuable collections of lectures and essays both offer diverse perspectives on this harrowing episode in German history.

34. *Weimar Culture*, pp. xiii–xiv.

The exact number of German and Austrian émigrés also cannot be determined with certainty. According to historian Herbert A. Strauss, fewer than 500,000 left Germany during the Nazi era. Unlike the trend in most immigration policies today, intellectuals and professionals were not given preference:

> Quite the contrary: unless they were widely recognized, prestigious figures or useful for some national purpose, intellectual emigrés were unwelcome in many countries around the globe, as were physicians, lawyers, or other professionals. Their migration thus reflected the economic or ideological barriers erected at the time to protect national or economic group interests. And, although many of the victims had only a tenacious connection with Judaism, they also faced in many countries prejudice against Jewish professionals, or, ironically, on account of their German background, against foreigners.[35]

The most fortunate among the victims of the Nazi terrors as well as those who could help them were now gone. Included in these droves were the extraordinary minds that the culture of Weimar had produced.

Despite this exodus of gifted individuals, the pool of talent was not entirely emptied. Several exceptional and Aryan conductors were making their way through the pits of provincial German opera houses in the mid-'30s. One of them was Eugen Jochum. Born in 1902, he had made his way to the podium of the Berlin Philharmonic and Staatsoper by the time the Nazis came to power. On Furtwängler's recommendation, he was appointed music director of the Mannheim Orchestra in 1929 and later went to Hamburg. The Nazis courted him and gave him an enormous public relations campaign, declaring through Party-paid critics that he was a "cannon" who would soon eclipse Furtwängler. He was not, however, one of the boys, so to speak, and he never joined the Nazi party. While he enjoyed esteem during the Third Reich, he was shunted to the back bench when an even younger, gifted, Aryan and Nazi conductor came to the attention of Hermann Göring.

In good time, this new "wonder" also came to the attention of the Berlin Staatsoper's General Intendant, Heinz Tietjen, who had no one of Furtwängler's stature waiting in the wings after he resigned in the wake of the Hindemith Scandal. At the beginning of 1938 Herbert von Karajan was the musical director of the Opera in Aachen and had already made an auspicious debut guest conducting the Berlin Philharmonic. Born in Salzburg in 1905, he was the second son of his fa-

35. "The Movement of People in a Time of Crisis," *The Muses Flee Hitler*, p. 55.

ther's second marriage. The elder Karajan's family came to Austria from Greece by way of Turkey. Ernst von Karajan was a highly respected physician and a senior registrar at St. Johann's Hospital. Heribert, as he was christened, first studied piano at the Academy of Music in Vienna and at the Mozarteum in Salzburg, but he soon turned to conducting, taking classes with Clemens Krauss and Alexander Wunderer. He won his first major engagement conducting *Figaro* in Ulm in 1929 and ascended to the post of its music director in short order. By 1935, he was in charge of a more important opera house in Aachen. He was 30, Germany's youngest *Generalmusikdirector*, and well on his way to even better fortunes. Three years later came the sensational debut with the Berlin Philharmonic on 8 April 1938. Tietjen instantly saw in Karajan the ace he could play against Furtwängler but for the moment only threw a crumb to the junior maestro by offering him a premiere production of Rudolf Wagner-Regegny's *Die Bürger von Calais*, a musically conservative work quite acceptable to the Nazis. Karajan shocked Tietjen by proposing instead three other operas: *Fidelio*, *Tristan*, and *Die Meistersinger*. These were operas Tietjen conducted himself exclusively, now that Furtwängler was gone. Karajan finally met with Tietjen, who found him charming. When Karajan repeated his demands for the three operas, he added that it was not a condition, just a request. Tietjen replied, "You are right, I was in error."[36]

Karajan got most of what he wanted. He led *Fidelio*, *Tristan*, and *The Magic Flute* between September and December of 1938 at the Berlin Staatsoper. He also accepted the original offer for his engagement—*Die Bürger von Calais*. At the first rehearsal of *Fidelio*, Tietjen called him aside and said, "You are a great meteor. Keep conducting as you have. I have heard your rehearsal, and we don't need to discuss these things anymore."[37]

The two men had a symbiotic relationship based on mutual professional dependence, but their egos could never permit them to become friends. Karajan later told his biographer Roger Vaughan, "He was selfish. He couldn't stand other opinions. And I knew that I had not been born to obey others. We had terrible fights. But Tietjen was at odds with Furtwängler, who had left him because of the Hindemith controversy. I was the tool of Tietjen to be used against Furtwängler."[38]

Karajan was also used by Göring to fuel Furtwängler's jealousy,

36. Roger Vaughan, *Karajan*, (New York) 1986, p. 125. Hereafter referred to as Vaughan.
37. Vaughan, pp. 125–126.
38. Vaughan, p. 126.

and the ploy ultimately worked. A massive campaign in the press vaunted the young conductor as *"Das Wunder Karajan,"* a carefully worded echo of the spontaneous reception Furtwängler got in 1922. It was intended to injure Furtwängler, and it made its mark. But if Furtwängler went directly to Göring to raise objections about the handsome new discovery, there is no record of it to date. Göring hoped that Karajan's talent would be titanic enough to eclipse Furtwängler, while Goebbels watched the newcomer carefully. Göring spent extravagantly to tout Karajan as the up-and-coming Aryan conductor, the musician of the present, the miraculous Wunderkind of German music.

Göring and Tietjen personally used every available opportunity to deploy Karajan against Furtwängler, and their efforts were lubriciously abetted by one of the most sinister characters to find a place for himself in the cultural sector of the Third Reich. Rudolf Vedder was one of those fetid personalities for whom the Reich offered unique opportunities to develop and profit. Born in Dortmund in 1895, he was one of nine children of a factory owner. After serving in Siberia and southern Russia during World War I, Vedder went into the retail bookselling business as an apprentice. He then became involved with a concert agency in his native city and soon left bookselling.[39] Some well-supressed notoriety in 1927 attended him when he embezzled 10,200 RM from Steinway and Sons while in charge of their concert direction department. He was caught but never went to jail because the prestigious maker of pianos and concert careers had no desire to publicize the issue and knew that Vedder could not pay them back if he was in prison. Vedder left Steinway by mutual agreement, agreeing to repay the money in monthly installments—but not before he obtained letters of recommendation from the firm.

Over the next two years, Vedder formed his own agency and proceeded to collect a stable of top artists. First, he vigorously pursued the most desirable of them all: Wilhelm Furtwängler. He discovered that Furtwängler had the best agent any artist could ask for. Berta Geissmar handled all his contract negotiations and scheduled all his professional (and personal) engagements. What is more, her salary was paid by the Berlin Philharmonic. Furtwängler may well have awarded her a lagniappe now and then, but Geissmar was independently wealthy anyway. Best of all, her only "client" was Furtwängler, and few artists of that or any other time were so fortunate.

If Vedder could not get Furtwängler, then he would snatch the Berlin Philharmonic. But there again, the Philharmonic had a long and

39. From a curriculum vitae dated 9 August 1944 submitted to the SS by Vedder. Source: Berlin Document Center.

tight relationship with Wolff and Sachs, run by Queen Louise, and had no need or inclination to alter that arrangement. If Vedder could not have either Furtwängler or the Berlin Philharmonic, then he, like Milton's Lucifer, would make Heaven of his Hell. Accordingly, an attempt to ruin Furtwängler became something of a career goal for this unctuous scoundrel, for his true aim was absolute power over concert life in Germany, and, perhaps, beyond its ever widening borders.

He realized he needed four weapons to fulfill his mission, and went about obtaining them with deadly proficiency. First, he needed guns behind him to get himself into a position of sufficient power. To that end, he informally had already become a part of Heinrich Himmler's inner circle at the Schutzstaffel—the Nazi Secret Police—before Hitler seized power in January 1933.[40] Himmler, of course, had come out on top only a few months earlier in the deadly internal power struggle with Roehm, and his SS now was gripping Germany with intimidation and fear. Himmler never forgot Furtwängler after a shouting match he had with him over the telephone during the first months of the new regime. He had begun a file on him, and by 1938 it had grown into a formidable sheaf. But he knew he had to bide his time patiently because Hitler admired Furtwängler and refused all petitions from Himmler to have him arrested. In Vedder, he saw immediately a very useful means toward that end.

A year after the Nazis came to power, Vedder got himself placed as the director of the Concert Affairs Department of the Reichsmusik-kamerschaft (RMK). This department was officially in charge of all concert bookings in the Reich. Vedder's first step once installed was to "de-Judify" the department simply by not booking Jewish musicians. This action directly contravened the decree Furtwängler was instrumental in formulating a few months earlier, but it did not prevent Vedder from seeking an interview with Berta Geissmar and impressing her with his well-known and vast knowledge of the music business in Germany.[41] Next, Vedder needed a pipeline to the public, and he wasted no time in buying off members of the press from the beginning of his career. Having once been a secretary to the pianist Edwin Fischer and the violinist Georg Kulenkampff during his apprenticeship in the agency business, he understood very well the

40. The operative word here is "informal." Vedder had close ties to the SS even before the Nazis took over in 1933, but he did not actually become a member of the SS (with an officer's rank) until 1942. Source: Berlin Document Center.

41. Geissmar, who was well aware of Vedder's role in de-Judifying the RMK, nonetheless wrote to Furtwängler on 22 March 1934 praising Vedder and advising Furtwängler to talk to him. Her motive for having anything to do with him in this early phase of the Third Reich was based on the ill-founded hope that contact and negotiation could somehow make Vedder less virulent.

value of touting his clients in the media. Such measures were superfluous in the cases of Fischer and Kulenkampff, but Vedder went one
better. He also planted vicious implications about the capabilities of
the competition and engendered spurious parables about the extra-
musical activities of rival musicians.

Finally, Vedder knew that if his stable could produce a conducting
talent who would effectively challenge Furtwängler's supremacy, he
not only could supplant his nemesis, but gain his ultimate objective:
absolute control of all concert and operatic activity in the Reich.

There was a need now to consolidate his power, and the opportunity came along just before he joined the RMK. The concert agency
Wolff and Sachs had been running in the red after the ban on Jewish
musicians. The firm was 4,000 marks in debt, and it was, as parlance
of a later decade would put it, ripe for a takeover. The very picture of
a White Knight, Vedder charged into Louise Wolff's office and made
her an offer she was in no position to refuse.

By the end of the year, Rudolf Vedder had virtually appropriated
Wolff and Sachs. Queen Louise abdicated her throne as the doyenne
of Berlin's concert life and closed the firm. She died not long afterward, a lonely and forgotten woman. Vedder took most of her clients
and brought them with him when he took charge of the concert
department of the RMK.

Now that he had the backing of the SS, the press in his pocket, and
the concert agency that operated the Berlin Philharmonic in his portfolio, Vedder was ready to go after Furtwängler.[42] But he was beset
with a momentary inconvenience when one of his arch-rivals in the
agency business, Max R. Müller, brought a suit against him at the
RMK for unfair business practices. The evidence against Vedder—
despite perjured statements attesting to his professional character—
was overwhelming. He was denounced and resigned from the RMK,
leaving it all but defunct, since he had most of its artists also under
personal contract and took them with him. The RMK was not about
to pay him severance, but he pleaded hardship to Steinway And
Sons—to whom he still owed money from the funds embezzled in
1927—and signed over his "severance" from the RMK to ease his
debt load. Steinway sued the RMK for the money and, in an effort to
avoid a long and costly legal battle, the RMK paid Steinway the so-
called severance.

Vedder immediately fired up his own agency. Most of his artists,
for some reason, made no effort to take his ouster from the RMK as
an opportunity to leave him. Could they have been paid visits by

---

42. For several perspectives on Vedder's climb to virtually absolute power, see
Chapter 18.

"insurance agents" from the SS, regaling them with visions of shattered larynxes and fractured fingers? In any event, Vedder now set about trying to produce a conducting personality whose charisma if not talent could challenge Furtwängler. He already had tried with one of the first "sensations" of his career. But only decades of maturation would give Eugen Jochum the kind of patina Furtwängler exuded from the moment he came to Berlin.

Herbert von Karajan, however, was another matter.

When he made his debut at the Staatsoper in Berlin on 30 September 1938 with a performance of *Fidelio* there was a half-empty house. On 21 October he conducted *Tristan und Isolde*, and it became the musical event of the season. One critic—with Göring's encouragement—called him *"Das Wunder Karajan"*—the Miracle Karajan— echoing the phrase that had been coined to describe Furtwängler's debut with the Berlin Philharmonic 16 years earlier.[43] Shortly afterward, Karajan was appointed Music Director of the Berlin Staatsoper and took charge of the eight annual concerts given by the Staatsoper orchestra. He had just turned 30 years old. Between 1938 and 1942, he shuttled between Berlin and Aachen, where he had been General Music Director since 1934.

Karajan's success was buttressed by the writer who had lauded him at Göring's instigation. Edwin von der Null[44] was an ambitious critic trying to ingratiate himself with the Party, a fact that neither escaped Furtwängler's attention nor eluded his anger. Von der Null produced numerous obsequious reviews of Karajan's concerts and suggested that certain "50-year old conductors could learn a few lessons from him."[45] The hype was manufactured, but Karajan's talent and the charisma were genuine, and these attributes were taking him upward far and fast. What is more, Karajan was a full-fledged, card-carrying member of the Nazi Party, having joined twice inside the space of one month, first on 8 April 1933 in Salzburg (Austria, Party Number: 1 607 525) and again on 1 May in Ulm (Germany, Party Number: 3 430 914), long before membership became "strongly advised" for aspiring new arrivals in any field. Göring and Vedder indeed had themselves a winner who could challenge Furtwängler. And Karajan, aided and promoted by Vedder, wasted no time in going after his quarry.

While the extent of his naivete in such worldly matters as politics and totalitarianism bordered on the cretinous, Furtwängler was

43. *Berliner Börser Zeitung am Mittag (BZ am Mittag)*, 22 October 1938.
44. While von der Null was also known as van der Null, he was listed in the Berlin telephone book under "von." He later became a subject of contention at Furtwängler's denazification trial. See Chapter 18.
45. *BZ am Mittag*, 22 October 1938.

always sensitive to a professional threat, and he knew without doubt that there was now a fox in his coop. Elisabeth Furtwängler recalled to me, "Wilhelm was hurt and offended that Karajan never came to see him. That was really the start of the trouble. He felt Karajan was working to undermine him behind his back." For Karajan's part, he never was able to break free from the feeling that Furtwängler was hindering his career and preventing him from performing in Berlin. But he may have resented also the sheer power that Furtwängler's mere presence exerted. Tietjen was heard to say to him more than once, "If Furtwängler comes through the front door, you go out the back door."

There was no doubt in Furtwängler's mind that Karajan and Vedder, with a helping hand from Tietjen, had formed an unholy alliance against him, but he cast Karajan as the instigator and eyed him with particular suspicion. As he saw the alliance becoming more of a menace, he decided he must placate Goebbels because he knew he could not fight Vedder, Karajan, *and* Tietjen without his support. Although he really had much more to fear from Vedder than from Goebbels, Furtwängler regarded the agent as a matter to be dealt with through the bureaucratic channels available to him, even though the balance of favor in the Nazi hierarchy was now undoubtedly against him. Karajan, on the other hand, was gaining popularity and accruing extravagant totemic value in the public imagination, and that was a realm Furtwängler could not prevent him from invading. Furtwängler appealed to Goebbels, complaining about the abuse he had been receiving in the press and got protection. Goebbels noted in his diary on 14 December 1940:[46]

> Furtwängler has objections about Karajan, who is getting too much coverage in the press. I put a stop to this. In other respects, Furtwängler is behaving very decently. And when all is said, he is our greatest conductor.

And again on 22 December:

> Row between Furtwängler and Karajan. Karajan is getting himself feted in the press. Furtwängler is right. He is, after all, a world figure. I put a stop to it.

Part of Furtwängler "behaving decently" not only meant appearing simpatico with Goebbels but rendering certain favors. While he remained firm about not conducting at official Nazi state events, he conducted concerts for charities, workers, students, and youth that were under sponsorship of various departments in the Reich. He also

46. The two passages from Goebbels' daybook are quoted from *The Goebbels' Diaries*, trans. & ed. by Fred Taylor, (New York) 1984, pp. 205 and 213.

stooped to a personal propitiation: he played a brief piano recital at a Christmas reception in the Reichs Chancellery in Hitler's presence.[47]

Furtwängler could take grim solace in receiving a Christmas gift of coffee (which he rarely drank) from Hitler accompanied by a brief note explaining that the packet of African coffee (very hard to obtain after the war started) came from a large shipment sent to him personally from abroad.[48]

When Allied bombing destroyed the Staatsoper on 10 April 1941, however, Karajan demanded and got the right to perform his concerts with the Staatsoper orchestra in the Philharmonie, the home of the Berlin Philharmonic in Bernburgerstrasse near the Potsdamerplatz. Karajan had mounted his very podium. The Nazi-guided critics had long played Furtwängler and Karajan off each other, but now that they were both regularly playing in the same hall, they had a field day comparing the two conductors. The papers always made sure Furtwängler got less space and appeared inferior.[49] Despite their transparency, these reviews produced Furtwängler and Karajan factions who argued the merits of their respective idols in cafes all over Berlin.

He could take cold comfort in knowing that he had not been preempted only because Hitler had despised Karajan ever since the young "Miracle" had presided over a disastrous performance of *Meistersinger* in 1938 in Berlin at which the Führer was present. But Furtwängler knew he alone would have to deal with Karajan if he ultimately was to prevent himself from being pushed aside. Finally, in 1942, the right moment materialized to dispatch both Karajan and Vedder.

That time arrived when Vedder went a step too far in his quest to take full control of the Reich's concert life. Along the way, he continued to pocket his clients' fees and blocked artists who tried to circumvent him or whom he simply did not like.[50] By 1941 he personally represented virtually all the leading conductors and soloists left in the

47. *Kraftprobe*, p. 336.
48. Source: Wilhelm Furtwängler Private Archive, Clarens. According to Prieberg (*Kraftprobe*, p. 334), the coffee was sent by the Imam of Yemen whose ships brought it through an Allied blockade.
49. For a fuller discussion of how the press was manipulated by the authorities during the Third Reich, see Chapter 18. For a fascinating account of the foot-dragging and sheer numbskullery of the American press in recognizing the Nazi menace and in acknowledging the persecution of the Jews, see Deborah E. Lipstadt's *Beyond Belief: The American Press and the Coming of the Holocaust, 1933–1945*, (New York) 1986.
50. Vedder behaved with typical ruthlessness in family matters. His wife evidently disagreed violently with him over their 16-year-old son's involvement with the Hitler Youth Movement. Prompted no doubt by the compassionate propensities he inherited from his father, the son denounced his mother as an enemy of the state. The denunciation cleared the way for divorce. Only a quick remarriage to a younger woman ameliorated Vedder's profound distress over this domestic tragedy. Source: Berlin Document Center. See also *Kraftprobe*, p. 328.

Third Reich. Besides Karajan, the conductors in the Vedder stable included Paul van Kempen, Clemens Krauss, Willem Mengelberg, Hans von Benda, Hans Swarowsky, Gustav König, Eugen Jochum, and Ferdinand Leitner.[51]

After the war began, Vedder took a somewhat superfluous step, given his behavior up to this point. He joined the Nazi Party. He also started a sideline: arranging entertainment events for the SS. This widened his powers to the provinces and to the military as well. He was but one man away from attaining the highest power.

And that man was Wilhelm Furtwängler.

Vedder eventually became a victim of his own unchecked arrogance. He already had come close to the limit at least once. In 1931 Vedder had promised Furtwängler that one of his clients, the soprano Mia Peltenberg, would be available for an orchestra rehearsal of Haydn's *Creation*.[52] When she did not appear, Vedder feigned dismay, wringing his hands and saying, "It is incredible that this woman does not come!" The next day, Peltenberg appeared but behaved as though nothing was wrong. Furtwängler asked her why she had not attended the previous night's rehearsal, and she replied that Vedder had engaged her for another performance and never mentioned the rehearsal she was supposed to attend.[53] Furtwängler confronted Vedder and told him he never wanted to work with him again.[54] Of course, he had to; Vedder had too many clients he needed. Over the next ten years, he watched warily as Vedder's power and empire grew. But Vedder tangled with him again in 1942, and Furtwängler decided enough was enough.

After the exodus of talent in the '30s, top caliber musicians were hard to come by, and violinists capable of solo careers especially were a rare breed in Germany. But Furtwängler had discovered a brilliant 18-year-old violinist named Gerhard Taschner and appointed him second concert master.[55] Always looking out for Karajan's interests, Vedder tried to persuade Taschner to leave the Philharmonic and join Karajan at the Staatsoper. Vedder conjured up a vision of more money

51. Leitner was a recital accompanist at that time. Source: Berlin Document Center.

52. Furtwängler recalled this incident at his denazification proceedings (17 December 1946).

53. The special performance of *The Creation* took place in Berlin on 19 January 1931. Peltenberg's colleagues included Marcel Wittrisch, Hermann Schey, and the Bruno Kittel Choir.

54. Prieberg gives the background to this incident and delectably details Furtwängler's clashes with Vedder in *Kraftprobe*, pp. 320–332.

55. Erich Röhn was first concert master. The Taschner case was discussed at Furtwängler's denazification trial but its essential details are discussed here. See Chapter 18.

and a glittering solo career under Karajan's guidance. None of that, warned Vedder, would be possible under Furtwängler whom Vedder painted as a washed-up old man whose career was all but finished. The doubts Vedder expressed about Taschner's career if he stayed with Furtwängler must certainly have impressed him, for a virulent campaign against Furtwängler was being led in the press by von der Null at the time. In spite of this, Taschner not only remained loyal to Furtwängler but also informed him of the offer he had received.

Furtwängler took this opportunity to lodge a vigorous protest to ProMi. In a letter to a high official at the ProMi, he declared what amounted to war on Vedder's tyranny over musical life in Germany:

> From: Furtwängler to Professor Hauschild
> Date: 22 April 1942
>
> Last year, I had an unsuccessful legal disagreement with Herr Vedder. The artists who had promised to appear as witnesses in my behalf failed to assist me . . . For years, I have been endeavoring to clarify the Vedder case in the interest of all artists; yet I did not succeed because time and again offices, which might have interfered with effect, failed for fear of Herr Vedder's influence with higher quarters.

Those "higher quarters" included Himmler's close associate Ludolf von Alvensleben, the dreaded leader of a large division of liquidation squads in occupied Poland.[56] Nonetheless, Furtwängler minced no words:

> In the long run, the case of Vedder is not acceptable to the interests of musical life in Germany today. There is no denying that Vedder plays his piano of "connections" like a virtuoso under the protection of the SS he has recently gained.[57]

Vedder deftly tried to talk his way out of it, but he ultimately lost his agency license.

The agent's ouster meant he could no longer represent Karajan, and Karajan in turn lost his power base. To turn the screw delectably tighter, Furtwängler took charge of an opulent new production of *Meistersinger* with Bockelmann, Lorenz, and Müller that heralded the opening of the newly rebuilt Staatsoper on 12 December 1942.[58]

---

56. The letter to Hauschild was submitted as evidence in Furtwängler's behalf at his denazification trial. See Denazification Proceedings, Day Two, p. 41. For more on Alvensleben see Chapter 18.

57. Notes for exposing Vedder. No date. Wilhelm Furtwängler Archives, Zürich. Cited also in *Kraftprobe*, p. 332.

58. The producer was Tietjen, and the designer was Emil Preetorius.

The occasion was especially humiliating for Karajan because it was both *Meistersinger* and a supposedly inebriated Bockelmann that brought him to grief in Hitler's presence two years earlier when he was on the podium for a catastrophic performance of the Führer's favorite opera. But Karajan could not be prevented from conducting three charity concerts with the Berlin Philharmonic during the 1942–1943 season. He got away with it because Furtwängler could not openly protest a series of concerts for wounded soldiers and factory workers. Karajan's career was now at a standstill, though, for no other agent dared touch him. Since he had never even met Furtwängler and never had gone to visit him, the timing to make such an acquaintance now seemed inappropriate. He continued conducting in Berlin until Goebbels closed all theaters in August 1944, but he was now a musician without portfolio. He also put himself in bad odor with the Party in 1942 when he married a partly Jewish woman and promptly lost his post at Aachen.[59] He spent the rest of the war free-lancing.

These were bitter times for Karajan, and his experiences in this period taught him a lesson that may go a long way toward explaining his professional motives later in life.

59. According to his biographers, the primary reason Karajan lost his job in Aachen was because he was spending too little time there. His marriage to Anita Guttermann was simply more fuel in the effort to fire him. Karajan was allowed to marry Guttermann because the racial laws permitted marriages between Aryans and quarter-Jews, providing there were no other intervening circumstances.

15

Devilish Duties—II

Vedder and Karajan were only two of the many battles Furtwängler was fighting. Because he long since had given up all his positions, he had little armor left for those skirmishes. Without the power that his former rank as music director of both the Berlin Philharmonic and the Staatsoper implicitly gave him, his protection became increasingly vitiated, and he fell beholden for anything he wanted to the loathsome bureaucracy at ProMi or to Tietjen at the Staatsoper.

And now that Tietjen had a bona fide foil in Karajan to use against Furtwängler, he was not about to forgo the chance of really putting pressure on him. Furtwängler finally protested to Göring:

> Since you have not given me the opportunity to speak with you directly, I am constrained to take up your time in this manner. First of all, I would like briefly to explain the reasons why I cannot conduct at the Staatsoper, for I personally would disregard whatever Herr Tietjen has to say about me.
>
> Previously, I worked well with Tietjen, in any event, that was my impression. I thought he was of that opinion after I resigned from the Staatsoper as chief conductor and came, at his suggestion to Bayreuth. From that moment on, he regarded me as competition, and because he regarded me as competition, his behavior toward me changed. The Führer heard both our performances of *Lohengrin* and said to me at the time: "You can't compare them in the same breath."

The compliment prompted him to start attacking me systematically, partly through the press and partly through the Wagner family, and so forth. Tietjen also tried in all earnestness to undermine my artistic position in Berlin. When I led a Ring Cycle during the next season, no press was invited, apparently because, as Tietjen explained to me, he simply "forgot" (to invite them). Later, at a performance of *Tannhäuser*, Tietjen had already brought the press so much under his influence that they said my capabilities were not longer in good form.[1] My head reels at these developments.[2]

This turn in Furtwängler's relationship with Tietjen was ironic, for Furtwängler had come to Tietjen's aid when the Nazis were about to oust him from his position as Intendant of the Staatsoper in 1933 because they felt he was hiring too many Jewish artists.

Nonetheless, Furtwängler refused to entertain any notion that he might have lost anything to Tietjen, Goebbels, Göring, or to the rest of the Nazis.[3] That conviction alone was all he really now had to carry him through the maddening chess game he endlessly was playing with them, but it was a certitude that steered him around what now looked like Endgame. Even with Hitler's strongest henchmen against him, he remained an all-powerful figure in the public's mind both at home and abroad, and that position enabled him to make a time-buying move to Vienna. In fact, by the mid-1930s, the Austrian cultural authorities were anxious to have him come to Vienna permanently. Furtwängler had become as popular and revered in Vienna as he was in Berlin, and rumors of his impending engagement as music director at the Vienna Staatsoper churned through the gossip mills, even while many of the very artists who had maintained its greatness up to that time were being forced to leave.

Indeed, all of Austria was now subject to the same talent drain that had bled Germany since 1933, for by this time, the Nazi onslaught against the Jews was accelerating, punctuated by the infamous *Kristallnacht* (Night of Broken Glass) of November 1938 when thousands of Jewish synagogues, businesses, and homes were burned and looted. Many Jews who had fled from Germany to Austria in the early days of the Third Reich now were facing the same threat again, and this time it was much more difficult for most of them to emigrate. Richard

1. Tietjen evidently savored such reviews. A news clipping file in the Tietjen Archiv at the Akademie der Künste in Berlin contains a delectable sampler of reviews from the period panning Furtwängler.
2. Excerpt of a draft, letter to Göring, undated, 1939. Source: Wilhelm Furtwängler Archives, Zürich.
3. It should be pointed out that Tietjen never joined the Party, even though he worked closely with Göring and ProMi.

Tauber, Vera Schwarz, Artur Schnabel and many other Jewish musicians were forced out. Göring tried to hold on to the gifted soprano
Lotte Lehmann, a non-Jew, by showering her with lavish gifts, including one of his prize horses. Had she stayed, she could well have been
the queen of the lyric stage in the Reich, but she would have none of it.
She emigrated to the United States and remained there to the end of
her life.

Bruno Walter was typical of Jews who thought they could find safe
haven in Austria, but he was also a Jew who had long been a target of
the SS. Now he was scheduled to be liquidated. But when the police
arrived to arrest him, they learned that he was in Paris. They took his
oldest daughter into custody instead. Walter later recalled the terror
of being stranded abroad while his daughter was being held by the
Nazis:

I met Toscanini in The Hague, where we had moved in the meantime, and
he shared our distress like a true friend. I could not go back to Austria, and
neither could my wife. We might have been permitted to enter, but never
to leave again . . . So we had to rely on our friends in Vienna. All I could do
was to guide their steps from afar. At the same time, I had to attend to my
contractual duties. They took me from the Hague to Monte Carlo and
Nice. My days and nights crawled along in a torment of waiting which
would have been considered exaggerated cruelty even in Dante's infernal
circles. When I returned from an orchestra rehearsal to our hotel in Nice
on March 28, my wife came rushing to me in the street. "I heard her
voice," she called to me from a distance, "she told me on the phone that
she was free." Unceremoniously as she had been arrested, she had been
released from prison. It was now our task to make her departure from
Austria possible.

My son-in-law had been informed that people without tax arrears
were permitted to travel abroad, provided they could prove the professional necessity of their leaving. My daughter's passport still stated her
profession to be that of a singer, and so I asked a concert manager in
Prague with whom I was on friendly terms to engage her for a recital in the
Czech capital. The splendid fellow went so far as to have large placards
announce the fictitious recital in the streets of Prague, so that any possible
German investigation would reveal the professional necessity of my
daughter's journey. I came to a similar conclusion for a somewhat later
date with a Zürich concert manager who was devoted to me. Thus both
frontiers would be open to my daughter. Approval of her exit permit was
delayed. She wrote the agent in Prague that she might be unable to fulfill
her contract. To make the urgency on her petition credible, the agent now
threatened that non-compliance with her obligations would have serious
consequences. Besides, high Czech quarters had let me know that I could
count on their support. I shall never as long as I live forget the Czech
friends' readiness to help. At last, about the middle of April, our daugh-

ter's permit was issued. She chose the Swiss frontier because we were
staying in Lugano at the time.[4]

Ultimately, the family moved to America where Walter led the life of
a successful émigré, his career taking a new and vigorous turn as musical advisor and frequent conductor with the New York Philharmonic.

Walter had enormous prestige, and important people in many
places were more than willing to help him escape to safety, but countless others—both Jews and non-Jews—were not nearly as well-con-
nected. Even cultural institutions feared they were about to become,
in an apt phrase from a later period, zero-based. While most Austrians
welcomed annexation, the *Anschluss* in the spring of 1938 made the
Viennese city elders frantic about keeping the independence and
integrity of their premier orchestra, even though they knew and
approved of what was in store for the country, as German battalions
waving their Nazi banners drove their tanks into Vienna. Goebbels
had made no secret of his desire to co-opt Austrian culture under his
department, and he immediately set out to realize his intentions. The
Vienna Philharmonic soon got a sample of Goebbels' plans for them
when he sent a man who could hardly read music to become their officially sanctioned music director. The musicians could not reject him,
but they relished the opportunity to make life miserable for him. They
improvised on the score, played out of tune, and never looked at him.
He soon left Vienna, but the musicians knew they could not be insub-
ordinate to every hack the Ministry of Propaganda sent them. Vienna's leaders concluded that only Furtwängler could keep the Vienna
Philharmonic out of Nazi clutches. The Mayor, Joseph Bürckel,[5]
approached Furtwängler and asked him to come to Vienna and take
charge of all musical activities there—to become something of a
musical director for the entire city.

Furtwängler already had declined every conceivable post the
Nazis had tried to foist on him, and he was wary of accepting an official appointment in Austria, especially at this time. He also knew that
he could deal with Goebbels and his goon squads only if he had some
sort of authority rendered by the Austrians. There was little time to

4. *Theme and Variations*, (New York) 1946, pp. 324–326.
5. Bürkel was an ambitious and relatively innocuous administrator when Furtwängler encountered him in 1938, but he soon bloomed into a sinister careerist under
the Nazis. After becoming mayor of Vienna after the *Anschluss* that year, Bürkel was
made responsible for organizing scientific and cultural activities in Austria. He soon
went on to bigger things, supervising the deportation of Viennese Jews in 1940 and the
deportation of 6,500 Jews from Baden and Saarpfalz after the Nazis occupied France.
His dubious achievements prompted him to commit suicide on 28 September 1944.

think; the purges of Jewish musicians in the Vienna Philharmonic had already begun, and top-caliber musicians were leaving Austria every day. He saw Austria and Vienna in particular becoming a barren cultural landscape and felt it his duty—now more than ever—to use what was left of his prestige to preserve the culture of Vienna, which had a musical tradition perhaps greater than any other German-speaking city.

So, he reluctantly accepted Bürckel's offer—but only on an informal, honorary basis. There were to be no contracts, no documents. Nor would he receive a salary. But on one issue, he remained adamant. When he learned from the orchestra's General Manager Otto Strasser that Goebbels was attempting to appropriate the Philharmonic and make it into a state orchestra, he sent a stern letter to Strasser, stating he would want nothing to do with the orchestra if it fell into state hands. He also promised to see Goebbels and make his stand clear.[6] His conversation with Goebbels was stormy but ultimately effective. The orchestra had to obtain approval for inviting conductors but otherwise remained independent. "The character of the orchestra would have changed beyond recognition," says Strasser more than 50 years later. "Its traditions would have been lost forever if he had not stepped in and protected us, and we would certainly not have the Vienna Philharmonic we have today."[7] But the continuation of high standards in performance was not Furtwängler's only concern. He also succeeded in keeping Goebbels from plundering the priceless music collection of the Viennese Gesellschaft der Musikfreunde— Society of the Friends of Music.[8] He went further and put the Vienna Staatsoper on firm footing by convincing Hitler and Goebbels to appoint his protegé Karl Böhm as music director of the Vienna State Opera. Böhm was emerging as a fine young conductor who already had a good deal of experience in Dresden where he had conducted the premiere of Strauss' *Daphne*,[9] and while he cooperated with the Nazis, his professional success during the Third Reich proved that Party membership was not a necessary pre-requisite for moving up or around in German musical circles.

The members of the Vienna Philharmonic felt safer now that Furtwängler had come to Vienna, but they felt they ought to make some

    6. The letter is dated 2 August 1939 and addressed to Otto Strasser. Aside from his duties as General Manager at the time, Strasser was also a second violinist and remained with the orchestra until his retirement in 1967. Source: Vienna Philharmonic Archives.
    7. Personal conversation with the author, Vienna, 9 April 1990.
    8. Otto Strasser, personal conversation with the author, Vienna, 9 April 1990.
    9. Premiere: Semper Oper, 15 October 1938. The composer dedicated this work to Böhm.

outward sign of respect to the Nazis. When Furtwängler saw the Swastika banner decorating the hall, he duly informed the administration, "As long as that rag is up there, I will not begin rehearsal." On another occasion soon after his arrival, he noticed that the first clarinetist, Rudolf Jettel, had been replaced. He asked for him, and the personnel manager whispered that "under the circumstances," Jettel had resigned. The "circumstances" were that the clarinetist's wife was a full Jew. Furtwängler roared, "But his wife does not play the clarinet in this orchestra!" At the next rehearsal, Jettel was back at his stand. The incident was but one of countless episodes revealing the most deadly battle line Furtwängler continually fought throughout the Third Reich.

When Furtwängler learned that some of the Jewish members of the orchestra were now finding it impossible to leave Austria, he personally made sure they received exit visas. This, even though he knew full well that he would have to undergo the increasingly difficult task of finding comparably talented replacements. Those for whom he could not get help officially, he assisted covertly in escaping. His generally open efforts to help the Jews in the Vienna Philharmonic was especially dangerous, for many musicians in the orchestra were Nazis. A call to the Gestapo could have put Furtwängler himself into a concentration camp or, at very least, made the escape of the Jews impossible.[10] But the musicians literally turned a deaf ear to Furtwängler's efforts. After all, he also made sure that most members of the orchestra—nearly all of whom were eminently qualified for conscription— were declared unfit for military service.

Helping Jews and other undesirables was becoming all but a fulltime occupation for Furtwängler as the expulsions and persecutions were stepped up following *Kristallnacht*. Furtwängler never hesitated in helping anyone—Jew or otherwise—right up to the end of the war. While some influential persons in English-speaking countries have denied that Furtwängler helped anyone who could not be of use to him in some way,[11] a good deal of evidence shows that simply is not true.

10. Testimony of Mark Hendrik Leuschner, denazification proceedings, 17 December 1946, pp. 88–89. See Chapter 18.

11. "Omnibus," 7 March 1971. In an interview on this British television program, the conductor Jascha Horenstein sneered that Furtwängler only helped Jews and other persecuted people during the Third Reich who were well known, implying that self-interest determined whom he helped. Horenstein should have known better but evidently did not. Nonetheless, Horenstein was furthering one of the nastiest lies that was spread about Furtwängler after the war. The broadcast was produced by Florian Furtwängler for Bavarian Television. English version written by David Bucket for the BBC and narrated by Richard Ebb. The series is not to be confused with the program bearing the same title which ran many years on American television.

He had, for example, protected the full-Jewish musicians in the Berlin Philharmonic until they decided to leave of their own accord.[12] The last to leave the Berlin Philharmonic was Nicolai Graudan. In April 1991, Graudan's widow, Joanna, discussed with me the circumstances of their departure from Berlin at the beginning of 1936:

> My husband was the last full Jew left in the orchestra, and he wanted desperately to leave, but Furtwängler kept begging him to stay because he said my husband, as principal cellist of the Philharmonic, was the only person left who served as an example of resistance against the Nazi racial policy. But finally, one night in 1935, Hitler and all his henchmen came to a concert, and the members of the orchestra were told to give the Nazi salute when they took their seats. My husband could not do it. My husband later told me that when Furtwängler entered, he had his baton in his hand so he did not salute, but only bowed curtly, turned around and started conducting. That very night, we locked our apartment, gave the keys to relatives and left Berlin and Germany for good. We left everything we had—*everything*—behind.[13]

The next group of the Berlin Philharmonic members on the endangered list were three half-Jews: Hans Bottermund (cello), Max Zimolong (violin), and Mark Hendrik Leuschner (violin). Furtwängler obtained special permits for them, and they and their immediate families survived unmolested through 1945.[14] The third group in the Berlin Philharmonic family consisted of three Aryans who were married to full Jews or non-Aryans. This group included the concertmaster Hugo Kolberg, who left the orchestra and Germany (with his wife) in 1938.[15] The musicians in this group and their wives survived unmolested.[16]

12. The full Jews in the Berlin Philharmonic were Szymon Goldberg (first concert master), Joseph Schuster (cello), Gilbert Back (violin), and Nicolai Graudan (cello). Goldberg left Germany in 1934, Back and Schuster in 1935, and Graudan in 1936.

13. Personal conversation with the author, Pacific Palisades, 19 April 1991. Joanna and Nicolai Graudan emigrated to England in 1936 and then to America where they eventually embarked on a successful concert career. Graudan played in the Metropolitan Opera orchestra when he first arrived in the United States and later was appointed principal cello with the Minneapolis Symphony.

14. Some evidence of Furtwängler's help to persecuted persons and their families came to light at his denazification trial in 1946. See Chapter 18. Other evidence of Furtwängler's protection of threatened individuals in the orchestra came from statements made by friends and family members.

15. The other two Aryans in this group were Ernst Fischer, for whom Furtwängler interceded in order to obtain a special permit to marry a full Jewish woman in 1934. Such an occurrence was rare if not unique and demonstrates the influence Furtwängler could frequently bring to bear on individual cases.

16. The names of these Berlin Philharmonic members were provided to the author by Fred K. Prieberg.

Furtwängler had intervened with the authorities to help Jewish artists in general from the moment the exclusionary laws were established in 1933, and hordes of Jewish artists were suddenly tossed out on the streets. Furtwängler formulated a proposal called the Capability Principle *(Leistungsprinzip)* through which he persuaded Goebbels to order state-operated theaters and cultural organizations under his jursidiction to re-hire ousted Jews.[17] The Nazis also permitted Jewish artists and musicians who did not or could not emigrate to form their own alliance. The Nazis allowed this organization to be established because they were convinced it would not survive for the simple reason that Jews were "genetically untalented." The emergent Jewish Cultural Alliance survived fitfully until the Wannsee Conference in January 1941 sealed the fate of all full Jews in the Reich.

By the time Furtwängler assumed his ad hoc position in Vienna in 1938, the full Jews already there had been ousted. The most distinguished among them was Arnold Rosé, who was the husband of Gustav Mahler's daughter Justine and veteran concertmaster of the Vienna Philharmonic. In fact his association with the orchestra went back to 1881. His departure from the orchestra may reflect something of the sentiments prevailing in the Vienna Philharmonic "family" at the time. Shortly after the *Anschluss*, a rehearsal for a concert took place as usual, and Rosé took his seat at the first stand in the usual way. An ambitious colleague approached him and said, "You can't sit there anymore." Before the rehearsal was over, that colleague had taken Rosé's place, at least for the day. Shortly thereafter, Rosé was gone from the orchestra. That summer, Rosé's wife died in Vienna, and he fled to London with his brother Eduard, the eminent cellist. Arnold Rosé died in England in 1946. His daughter Alma perished at Auschwitz. For some reason, Eduard returned to Austria during the war, was arrested, and died of starvation at Theresienstadt at the age of 84.[18]

But there were still nine members of the orchestra who were married to non-Aryans, seven of them to full Jews, and the rest married to half- or part-Jews:[19]

17. Goebbels sent telegrams to the Prussian State Theaters in June and July 1933, strongly urging them, in so many words, to give the broadest possible considerations to all applicants. Source: Bundesarchiv, Koblenz. Fred K. Prieberg gives a fuller discussion of this episode in *Kraftprobe*, pp. 119–121.

18. Coincidentally, Eduard Rosé married Justine Mahler's younger sister Emma (1875). She died in Austria in 1933. Arnold Rosé was ultimately buried next to his wife at Grinzinger Friedhof in Vienna a short distance from Mahler's grave. See Donald Mitchell, *Gustav Mahler: The Early Years*, (Berkeley and Los Angeles) 1980, pp. 231–232, note 39.

19. Source: Vienna Philharmonic Archive.

Married to full Jews:
>Theodor Hess (1st violin)
>Otto Rieger (solo violist)*
>Ernst Moravec (solo violist)*
>Richard Krotschak (solo cellist)
>Rudolf Jettel (1st clarinet)
>Hugo Burghauser (bassoon)
>Josef Hadraba (trombone)

Married to part- or half-Jews:
>Karl Maurer (cellist)
>Gottfried Freiberg (1st horn)

*Served as First Lieutenants *(Oberleutnante)* in military service at the Front.

Quarter- or part-Jews were generally not in danger of deportation, but half-Jews were vulnerable and full Jews all but marked. Furtwängler extracted guarantees from the Austrian authorities that the wives of all these members would never be harmed.[20] All of them survived the Third Reich.

Although it had long been clear that it was very dangerous for German citizens abroad to fraternize with émigrés or Jews, Furtwängler openly met with his younger colleague Issay Dobrowen while he was in Stockholm for a concert in January 1942. Dobrowen was a Russian Jew who had begun to make a name for himself as a conductor in Germany before he was forced to flee. According to an account by Furtwängler's biographer Curt Riess, an aide from the German Embassy met Furtwängler's secretary Fräulein Agathe von Tiedemann in his Swedish hotel lobby to inform her that such meetings were forbidden. Furtwängler overheard the man, and became furious when the aide informed him to "be careful in our associations. Please take note of that."

Furtwängler retorted, "I am in Sweden and not in Germany. Why shouldn't I dine with my friends if I feel like it? You can tell your chief that I intend to do so as often as I wish!"

It was not the last time Furtwängler would be admonished about his associations abroad. Nor would it be the last time he would utter the same reply.[21]

Even when helping Jews became a capital crime, and people were

20. Furtwängler formally requested the so-called *Sonderbewilligung*—Special License—in a letter to the Staatsoper General Manager Erwin Kerber dated 20 April 1938. Source: Vienna Philharmonic Archive.
21. Riess, pp. 253–254.

being publicly hanged on mere suspicion of it, Furtwängler helped or tried to help anyone who asked him. Hundreds whose lives were endangered lined up outside his dressing room after concerts to ask for aid. Furtwängler never turned anybody away and did what he could for each of them directly or indirectly. Fred K. Prieberg has found evidence of his assistance to over 100 people.[22] Furtwängler helped most of these individuals through telephone calls or by arranging assistance through his secretary in Berlin, Freda Winkelmann-von Rechenberg, or his assistant in Vienna, Agathe von Tiedemann. Many of these cases were dealt with over the telephone. Both secretaries were well connected within the Nazi power structure (though neither was a Party member).

Perhaps the most famous of those he already had saved was the eminent German violinist Carl Flesch on the eve of his "removal" to an extermination camp in the East. In 1989, his son Carl Flesch recalled to me:

> My father had left Germany and had taken me with him to England as his so-called personal assistant. I only had a visitor's visa, but he left me there as he and my mother went on to Holland. He was sure that he would be safe there because of the silly pride the Dutch had in their dikes. "Who would dare to sail into those dikes?" they would say. "No, the Germans wouldn't dare do that." Of course, nobody counted on the Luftwaffe, and Holland fell, and my parents were trapped.

Furtwängler's letter of recommendation that Flesch was carrying as part of his identification papers caught the attention of a senior officer just as he and his wife were being "assigned," the dreaded euphemism signaling certain death. They were saved literally at the last moment and were sent to Hungary, Flesch's native country. "They had to ride by train through Germany, which already was showing effects of the bombing, and the sight of all those cities in ruins had a terrible effect on my father. His health started failing, and he developed heart disease."

Eventually, Flesch and his wife escaped to Switzerland, where he died in 1944:

> My father received a letter in the late 1930s from Furtwängler complaining that all his best musicians were Jewish and they were abandoning him!

---

22. See *Kraftprobe*, p. 444, for over eighty names of individuals for whom there is documentation. There are at least twenty more in the forthcoming English edition of the book.

The man was like a child who can only see his own way. He never saw the expulsion of the Jews in the cold political way that the rest of us could. The only thing it meant was that their departure was not only hurting his work but somehow a betrayal of art! No, no. I have thought about Furtwängler many times, and I met him often. But while he was many things one might never like, he was never in any sense a Nazi.[23]

The elder Flesch was a celebrity, but Furtwängler also saved many other musicians with far lesser reputations, even some he never had known, and some, for all he knew, were not even musicians. In 1933 he helped a virtual stranger, an up-and-coming philosophy lecturer at the University of Heidelberg. Raymond Klibansky knew Furtwängler's family, but had barely shaken hands with the conductor once at a reception. When he was dismissed from his post, Furtwängler lodged a protest directly to Goebbels, citing the loss it would mean to Germany.[24] But Klibansky did not hear about it until 1945 when he returned to Berlin as a British military officer and was told of Furtwängler's intercession by the composer Nikolai Nabokov, who was investigating Furtwängler's involvement with the Nazi regime. A Nazi official named Georg Gerullis jotted a remark in the margin: "There is not a Jew left in Germany whom Furtwängler has not helped."[25]

What prompted Furtwängler to write in a stranger's behalf? Almost 60 years later, Klibansky offered me some possible explanations:

1. Furtwängler's mother may have mentioned me to her son. But far more likely is . . .

2. I was very close to Friedrich Gundolf the great historian of German literature and poet (who died in the summer of 1931). Furtwängler knew him and esteemed him highly. He will have heard Gundolf telling him about me. Furtwängler may have felt he owed it to Gundolf's memory to do something or he may have been impressed by what Gundolf told him or both.[26]

In any event, Furtwängler had plenty to lose and nothing to profit from making the protest. Klibansky left Germany and ultimately set-

23. Personal conversation with the author, London, 5 April 1989.
24. The letter is on file in the Bundesarchiv.
25. Goebbels is erroneously credited with writing this statement, though the thought at some point may well have crossed his mind. Gerullis was Under Secretary of Culture and closely connected with Bernhard Rust, the Minister of Science, Education, and Cultural Affairs.
26. Letter to the author, 20 June 1990.

tled in Canada, where he still (as of 1990) teaches philosophy at McGill University.

While there may have been a tenuous connection through his family or probably Gundolf that prompted Furtwängler to help Klibansky, there were many complete strangers who benefited from Furtwängler's intervention. One of them was Hugo Strelitzer, a teacher in the opera department at the Hochschule für Musik in Berlin. Following the Nazi Takeover *(Machtübernahme)*, he was one of thousands of Jews thrown out of work with no notice. He found occasional work conducting workers' choruses, some of which apparently had political coloring offensive to the Nazis. Strelitzer never had any political affiliations and worked with these choruses because they were the only opportunities available to him at the time. In August, one of his rehearsals was interrupted by storm troopers. He was arrested with several "Jewish-looking" members of the chorus and thrown into Columbia House, the infamous prison where the treatment of inmates was particularly barbaric.[27] At this point, it looked as though Strelitzer would join those thousands who were disappearing without a trace never to be heard from again. Strelitzer's sister learned of his whereabouts through one of his Aryan pupils, but there was nothing they or any of his friends could do for him.

A group of Jewish musicians decided that the only resort left to them was to appeal to Furtwängler. A committee sought an appointment with Berta Geissmar, who promised immediately that Furtwängler would help. Furtwängler personally went to see Bernhard Rust, the Minister of Culture at the time, and a certain von Levetzov, the Police Commissar of Berlin to plead Strelitzer's case. They promised his immediate release, but many years later, Strelitzer recalled that he remained at Columbia House for six weeks:

> . . . only because it took this long for my wounds and scars to heal, received from a brutal and merciless beating the night of my capture. At this time, the Nazis did not release any prisoner unless he looked like a halfway decent human being again.
>
> After my release, I . . . asked [Berta Geissmar] to see Dr. Furtwängler personally to thank him for what he had done for me. Miss Geissmar answered me, emphasizing that the fact of my release was a greater satisfaction to Furtwängler than any words of mine could express, and that his heavy schedule did not permit him to see all those he had helped and whose cause he had championed.
>
> If I am alive today (1965), I owe it to this great man . . .[28]

27. This chilling story is taken from Strelitzer's contribution to a collection of remembrances edited by Daniel Gillis in *Furtwängler Recalled*, (Zürich) 1965, p. 98. Hereafter referred to as *Furtwängler Recalled*.
28. See note above.

In another incident where Furtwängler helped a stranger, he was told about a "poor Jewish youth" in Berlin who reportedly possessed an enormous vocal talent and was about to be arrested by the Gestapo. He was a pupil of Walla Hess (who taught Konetzni among many others). Furtwängler agreed to hear him at a secret rendezvous. He was deeply impressed and helped them both to escape to England with the support of the British conductor Sir Adrian Boult. Frau Hess lived through the war. Presumably the boy also survived, but his destiny is not known.[29]

Furtwängler even intervened directly for relatives of people he had no cause to like. Arnold Klatte, for example, was a law clerk and son of the critic and musicologist Wilhelm Klatte. Although the younger Klatte was a quarter-Jew and technically acceptable to the Nazis, he was abruptly dismissed from his job in the District Court Section III of Berlin in the racial purge of the legal system of 1933. He may have been dismissed for other reasons since only full and half-Jews were vulnerable to the new legal obscenities. On 1 July his mother wrote Furtwängler asking assistance for her son, imploring him to include Arnold among the many persecuted people he was helping. (Source: Berlin Document Center.) Furtwängler had little reason to take an interest in the case because he had little regard for the profession of Arnold's late father. Nonetheless, he promptly spoke with Hinkel about the case, and it ultimately was referred to the "appropriate authority" Bureau of the State Secretary. Unfortunately, the man in charge of the Bureau at the time was the notorious Roland Freisler, a rabid Nazi who later presided over the trials of the July 20th Plot to kill Hitler in 1944. Klatte evidently survived the war; Freisler did not.[30]

For some of those he knew personally, such as Heinrich Wollheim, he made an arrangement with the Nazis. Wollheim was half Jewish and a former member of the Berlin Staatsoper orchestra. He lived near the Swiss border and easily managed to get his endangered friends out of the country. When the Nazis caught up with him, he was sent to the concentration camp at Dachau. His wife contacted Furtwängler, who arranged directly with Himmler and Goebbels for Wollheim to be his copyist and also to do similar work for the publisher Bote und Bock. Himmler agreed, but his acquiescence was mor-

29. Information for this anecdote, which took place in 1939, comes from a letter written to the London *Times* by F. L. Kerran, who stated that he, presumably a British subject, acted as an intermediary and carried Furtwängler's letters of recommendation to Boult. Kerran astutely points out: "Dr. Furtwängler took a grave personal risk in the service of these two Jewish refugees" while modestly refraining from giving any suggestion of the acute danger he himself invited by being in possession of such letters. 21 December 1946, p. 5.

30. See *Kraftprobe*, p. 126.

dant. "Well, Herr Staatsrat," he said icily, "we know you like to help criminals." Wollheim remained at Dachau but got better treatment in the camp than most of the other inmates. In a statement he made after the war, Wollheim said:

> If Furtwängler had not stood so steadfastly by my side during my imprisonment, I certainly would not have come out of it with my life. In my situation, I surely would have been consigned to a "commando" unit, which would not have done my health any good.[31]

In yet another instance, Furtwängler insisted that only one doctor—a man named Johannes Ludwig Schmitt—was skillful enough to relieve the pain he had long suffered from spondylitis, a muscular condition peculiar to conductors, which afflicts the neck and shoulder muscles.[32] Schmitt had been put in a concentration camp because he had been caught in seditious activities with one of Hitler's most virulent adversaries, Otto Strasser.[33] But Furtwängler insisted on having Schmitt supervise his treatment. The doctor was released to treat him at regular intervals.

Furtwängler went so far as helping Nazis whom the Party turned against, such as Heinrich Boell, who was General Music Director in Cologne before he fell out of favor with the Nazis,[34] and Karl Straube, the Thomascantor in Leipzig.[35] A few people, such as Margaret Kolmar, a friend of the Furtwängler family,[36] actually declined his help. Most of these cases will now remain forever undocumented because

31. 19 November 1946. This statement appears in an affidavit Wollheim submitted to the Denazification Tribunal when Furtwängler was tried after the war. It was one of numerous such affidavits, none of which was permitted to be read into the record.

32. This case and the context in which it became public are discussed in Chapter 19.

33. Evidence on deposit at the Bavarian Staatsarchiv in Munich strongly suggests that Schmitt and Strasser shared the same mistress, who passed subversive information between them and possibly to others. MA File 107,597. Note: The Otto Strasser mentioned here is not to be confused with the violinist and high-ranking member of the Vienna Philharmonic.

34. Heinrich Boell lost his position for internal political reasons, even though he was a Nazi in apparently good standing. He was sent to Breslau, where he remained as director of the Opera despite Furtwängler's attempt to obtain a better position for him in a musically more important city. Calendar notation.

35. Karl Straube too was a Nazi, but he was concerned about the increased efforts to bring Protestant church music under political domination after the Nazis seized power. He wrote to Furtwängler for help. It is not clear whether Furtwängler was successful in helping him, but it is clear that Straube quickly took a pragmatic view of his problem. He not only got himself appointed to lead the Church Music Section of the newly formed Reichsmusikkammer, but became president of the Reichs Society for Evangelic Music.

36. Margaret Kolmar was a friend of Furtwängler's mother. She declined Furtwängler's help because she did not want to get him into trouble. She emigrated with her husband and son. Gillis, p. 41.

Furtwängler or his secretaries negotiated them in telephone conversations and in meetings with officials, and many people have died without officially acknowledging his help. He was not always successful in his efforts, and occasionally, as in the case of Elsa Bienenfeld,[37] his supplicants ultimately compromised themselves. The passage of time has rendered documentation of Furtwängler's assistance (personal testimony, accounts of friends or relatives, or notations for writing letters or calling authorities made on Furtwängler's calendar) fragmentary, but the fact remains that he helped many people, most of whom were of little or no professional value to him:

HERMANN ABENDROTH was ousted from his position as General Music Director at Cologne. Through Furtwängler's intervention, he was appointed conductor of the Leipzig Gewandhaus Orchestra.[38]

ANNA BAHR-MILDENBURG gained fame as an opera singer in the early part of the century, and her most famous pupil was Lauritz Melchior. She was known to have had a close professional and personal connection with Bruno Walter, a fact she had little reason to conceal until 1933. The Nazis harassed her, and Furtwängler intervened to have her left alone. She survived the Third Reich and died in Vienna in 1947.[39]

WALTER BRAUNFELS had several of his works performed by the Berlin Philharmonic under Furtwängler. He was half Jewish. Furtwängler intervened for him when he was ousted from Cologne Music High-School.[40]

HUGO BURGHAUSER doubled as bassoonist and President of the Vienna Philharmonic Orchestra Committee until 1938. When the Nazis took over Austria, Burghauser found himself in double difficulties. He was Aryan, but he was married, unhappily, it seems, to a Jew. He promptly divorced her, even though Furtwängler had already obtained special permission for all members of the orchestra who were married to Jews. But his troubles did not end there because he also had been a member of the Austrian *Heimwehr*, an anti-Nazi political group. Furtwängler tried to help him again but was unsuccessful. Burghauser fled in 1939, first to Hungary, and then to Paris, where he met with Toscanini, who helped him emigrate to the United States. Burghauser eventually joined the Metropolitan Opera Orchestra in 1942 and retired in 1964. His Jewish ex-wife did not suffer long. She was Margherita Wallman, a well-known dancer who later became a successful stage director.[41]

37. Elsa Bienenfeld, an elderly Viennese music critic and full Jew for whom Furtwängler arranged smooth passage to Switzerland in 1942, at a time when such an act was all but a capital crime. She was caught at the border with gold coins sewn into her coat and was deported to the East. See Gillis, p. 40.
38. Gillis, p. 38.
39. Calendar notation.
40. Calendar notation.
41. Personal conversation between Otto Strasser and the author, 22 May 1991. Also see *Kraftprobe*, p. 306; Otto Burghauser, *Philharmonische Begegnungen*, (Zürich) 1980; Margherita Wallman, *Les Balcons du ciel*, (Paris) 1976.

SIEGMUND VON HAUSEGGER conducted many orchestras, principally the Kaim Orchestra which eventually became the Munich Philharmonic. He was under fire for liberal sympathies, and Furtwängler interceded for him.[42]

FRIEDRICH HERZFELD wrote a biography of Furtwängler during the Nazi period, and re-wrote it in a "de-nazified" version after the war. He was a quarter Jewish *and* a member of the Nazi Party, but even writing anti-Semitic articles were of little avail in keeping him out of trouble with the Nazis. More on this pathetic but not unusual individual later.[43]

JOSEF KRIPS survived the Third Reich to become one of the most distinguished conductors of the post war era. He was a full Jew and his ultimate destiny may have been somewhat more difficult to achieve if Furtwängler had been unable to help him get to Belgrade in 1938 where he spent the war.

FELIX LEDERER turned up like a leitmotif throughout Furtwängler's life. His friendship with Furtwängler went back to their years in Mannheim, when Lederer was second Kappelmeister after Furtwängler. He was first conductor in Saarbrücken at the time he was ousted for internal political reasons after the Nazi take-over. He was partly Jewish, and the fact only worsened his situation. Furtwängler talked with Goebbels to have him left alone and later gave him financial assistance. He wrote a letter acknowledging Furtwängler's help to the Chicago Symphony dated 14 January 1949.[44]

FRIDA LEIDER may have been the world's reigning Wagnerian soprano when the Nazis took over, but the fact did not prevent them from harassing her because her husband was a full Jew. A notebook entry (unpublished) on 3 June 1933 suggests that Furtwängler interceded for her and she appeared with him both at home and abroad throughout the Third Reich in direct contravention to the racial laws. Both she and her husband survived the Holocaust.[45]

ERICH LEIST was another harassed individual from whom Furtwängler could expect little for the help he gave him. He was a ministerial counselor in the Weimar Republic, and Aryan, and a non-musician. He was ousted in 1933. Furtwängler helped him get a partnership in a banking firm.[46]

HERMANN LÜDDECKE was also an Aryan and a choir director in Berlin. He was dismissed because of personality conflicts with the authorities. Furtwängler intervened successfully for him, and Lüddecke was reinstated.[47]

42. Gillis, p. 39.
43. See Chapter 18.
44. See Chapters 13 and 19.
45. Source: Wilhelm Furtwängler Archives, Zürich.
46. *Briefe*, p. 76.
47. Calendar notation.

LUDWIG MISCH was a full Jew, which certainly qualified him for help from Furtwängler. He was also a music critic, which would have given Furtwängler good reason for turning his back. Just as Misch was about to be sent to the East, Furtwängler interceded for him. Misch was re-routed to work in a munitions factory outside Berlin. He survived the war and wrote to Furtwängler acknowledging his help.[48]

HANS-JOACHIM MOSER could have gone far in his career had it not been for the Nazis. He was ousted in 1933 from his position as the Director of State Church Music. He also lost his professorship at the University of Berlin a year later. He was not Jewish, but was *verdächtig* (heritage doubted). He later was reinstated in ProMi through Furtwängler's help. Moser acknowledged his help in one of his books after the war.

HANS PFITZNER could easily have counted on his position as one of Germany's leading composers to keep him in good odor with the Nazis. What is more, he was a real Aryan. But for some reason zealous Nazis made trouble for him and tried to eliminate his pension. Furtwängler talked to Goebbels and succeeded in having Pfitzner's pension guaranteed.[49]

GÜNTER RAFAEL was a composer and half-Jew. He was ousted from the Reichsmusikkammer in 1939. Furtwängler could not succeed in helping him, even though he tried several times to assist him.[50]

CURT SACHS enjoyed a highly successful career as a musicologist and critic after he came to the United States during the talent drain of the 1930s. He went on to become first Adjunct (1947) and later Visiting Professor (1954–1959) of Music at Columbia University. The Nazis tried to seize his papers after he left Germany, but Furtwängler intervened successfully in keeping them intact.[51]

HERMANN SAMUEL was another victim of the Nazis' war on their own culture. Samuel was a student of Leschetizky and a successful concert pianist. He was a full Jew and remained in Vienna even though he could have emigrated to England with his brother. He was deported in 1944. Furtwängler attempted to intervene but did not succeed in getting him released. Hermann Samuel was murdered by the Nazis.[52]

ARNOLD SCHÖNBERG received money from Furtwängler in Paris after the composer fled from Germany. Furtwängler tried to have him come back to Germany and discussed it with Rust. He was unsuccessful.[53]

HANS SCHWIEGER could probably have become a leading conductor in Germany had it not been for his choice of wife. She was Jewish, he was not. After he lost his job as Kleiber's assistant conductor, Furtwängler invited

48. Source: Wilhelm Furtwängler Archives, Zürich.
49. Source: Berlin Document Center.
50. *Briefe*, pp. 68, 143f. 299, 307.
51. A calendar notation to write a memorandum about the papers.
52. See *Kraftprobe*, pp. 406–407.
53. Calendar notation and several acknowledgments by Schönberg and his second wife, Gertrude.

him to conduct the Berlin Philharmonic. He soon emigrated to the United States where he was conductor of the Kansas City Symphony for many years.[54]

H. H. STUCKENSCHMIDT, a musicologist who was as facile with English as he was perceptive in his own language, was expelled at the end of 1934 from the Nazi-established Writer's Guild (Reichsschriftumskammer) after he was attacked from the far right and by musicians he had panned. A year later, he applied for re-admission to the Writers' Union, and Furtwängler intervened in his behalf, even though he had some reason to bear a grudge against Stuckenschmidt because the latter occasionally was critical of his performances. The letter was written to Hinkel 12 February 1936 from Vienna.[55]

JANI SZANTO is remembered today as a footnote in music history. But this presumably Hungarian Jew was a music professor in Munich, who was important enough to be mentioned in Furtwängler's notes for his meeting with Hitler and Goebbels in 1933.[56]

MAX TRAPP was a composer and Professor at the Hochschule für Musik whose libido was almost as compulsive as Furtwängler's. In 1933–1934 Furtwängler interceded for him when he was caught having an affair with one of his students.[57]

A nephew of conductor Fritz Zweig obtained his release from Dachau concentration camp in 1938 after Furtwängler intervened for him. Fritz Zweig was one of Furtwängler's junior colleagues at Mannheim, and he wrote a letter to *Life* mentioning Furtwängler's help.[58]

Furtwängler's record for flagrantly assisting persecuted individuals inside the Third Reich is probably as unequaled as it is astonishing. His estranged first wife Zitla also helped people harassed by the regime, and she intervened independently of Furtwängler, though little is known about how she went about it. One person she helped secretly was the conductor Rudolf Schwarz. He was the leading conductor of the Jüdischer Kulturbund Orchestra in Berlin, one of several orchestras formed after Goebbels reversed the Nazis' racial policy forbidding Jews to perform in the arts. After the Wannsee conference sealed the fate of Jews remaining in Germany in 1941, he was sent to Poland. He gained a somewhat easier regimen at Auschwitz and ultimately was suddenly released in 1944, but the guards at the death camp broke both his arms at the shoulders before they let him go.

54. Personal conversation with the author, 9 June 1990.
55. Source: Berlin Document Center. See *Kraftprobe*, pp. 252–253.
56. Source: Wilhelm Furtwängler Archives, Zürich.
57. The issue of Trapp's improprieties is discussed in an internal memorandum to Reichskulturminister Hans Hinkel from Hubsch, one of his assistants, dated 26 February 1936. File 111, Bundesarchiv, Koblenz. Furtwängler's assistance is mentioned in several calendar notations and memoranda. Wilhelm Furtwängler Archives, Zürich.
58. See Gillis, p. 69.

After the war, Schwarz learned that his release was obtained through Zitla Furtwängler, who had personal connections with the family of Himmler's wife. When he tried to thank Zitla personally for her efforts in his behalf, she reacted somewhat peculiarly. On the one hand, she denied ever having done anything to help him. On the other, she asked him for a testimony averring that she always was sympathetic to the Jews throughout the Third Reich.[59]

While Thomas Mann and others, despite their bouts of anti-Semitic rage, continue to be vaunted as true heroes of anti-fascism, their actions took the form of high-sounding rhetoric uttered from a safe distance far away from the maelstrom.[60] After the war many émigrés such as Bruno Walter, were contemptuous: so Furtwängler saved a few Jews, went the line, it still did not excuse lending his prestige to the Devil's Reich.[61] Wolfgang Stresemann concurred. He was the son of Gustav Stresemann, the first President of the Weimar Republic, and he too had emigrated in 1939. In his capacity as music critic for the American German-language newspaper *New York Staats-Zeitung und Herald*, he deemed Furtwängler's protests against the Nazis would have been far more effective if he had expressed them by leaving Germany.[62] But how effective would Furtwängler have been from abroad in saving those people whose sole chance of survival was the assistance only he had the courage to render them? The obvious answer was beside the point: the right thing for any "decent" German of that day to do was to emigrate.[63]

It was all tiresome and nerve-wracking, and it filled him with a sense of *déjà-vu*. Worse, the Nazis were accelerating their pursuit of partially Jewish, Jewish-related, and Jewish-wedded individuals. Hardly a day went by without Furtwängler having to help at least three people who were begging him for aid in getting out. He always

59. Source: Letters to the author, 27 April and 11 June 1990. I am also indebted to Christabel Bielenberg and Dame Ruth King for their assistance in directing me to this information. Frau Bielenberg's memoir, *Christabel*, was adapted into a television miniseries, and Dame Ruth was founder and for many years chief mainstay of the National Youth Orchestra of Great Britain.

60. At the entrance to an exhibition entitled "Degenerate Art" in Los Angeles in spring 1991, a larger than life poster of Mann ranked first among other artists persecuted by the Nazis. In 1990, long after Mann's diaries were published, I received a letter extoling Mann as a model anti-Nazi from a well-known historian who had taught for many years at a university in New York.

61. See Chapter 19 for a fuller discussion of Walter's attitude toward Furtwängler after the war.

62. 2 December 1945, p. 6B. Stresemann was music critic of *New York Staats-Zeitung und Herald*, from 1945 until 1949.

63. Many years later, Stresemann somewhat revised his attitude toward Furtwängler in his memoirs. He admitted that Furtwängler's efforts in Germany during the Third Reich effectively prevented the Nazis from destroying the Berlin Philharmonic. . . . *Und Abends in die Philharmonie* . . . pp. 47–53.

did what he could and was astonishingly successful, but he reaped no pleasure from knowing that many of the people he was helping to escape persecution were those he needed most to maintain the very standards he was trying to uphold.

Nonetheless, Furtwängler's stand against the Nazis did not go entirely unrecognized. In the summer of 1939, for example, the French government canceled his annual appearance in Paris but gave him a decoration. The world knew that war was about to break out, but the French understood exactly where they stood as far as Furtwängler was concerned. The government named him a Commandant of the Legion of Honor, the most prestigious honor that nation could give an artist. It was the French government's way of informing the world that it distinguished Furtwängler from the political powers that had taken over Germany. No mention of the honor was made in German newspapers.

In 1940 he renewed his acquaintance with Friedelind Wagner, Richard Wagner's granddaughter. Among all of Wagner's descendants at the time, she was the only member of the family who was avowedly anti-Nazi. She had grown into an independent and strong-willed young woman of 22 and had emigrated from Germany to Paris where Toscanini unofficially made her his ward. Her departure from the Third Reich was every bit as sensational as Svetlana Stalin's defection from Soviet Russia thirty years later, and Goebbels made sure the Nazi press gave it the same amount of coverage: none.

Friedelind happened to be in Switzerland while Furtwängler was there for a conducting engagement. They met for lunch in Zurich.

"Was the decision to leave difficult?" asked Furtwängler.

"I did not have to make a decision," she replied. "Hitler made it for me."

Furtwängler now asked this woman who was young enough to be his daughter what he should do. Friedelind leaped at the opening. "It is quite simple," she said. "You are abroad now. Destroy your return ticket!"[64]

But Furtwängler went back.

Shortly before she died in 1991, Frau Wagner recalled her meeting with Furtwängler to me. "Furtwängler thought it was too late for him to get out of Germany even if he wanted to. He had responsibilities there—both professional and philosophical. I was just coming of age and was a free agent. It was easy enough for me to tell him to tear up

64. Both Riess (p. 238) and F. Wagner (p. 215) place the conversation in Paris in 1938. Frau Wagner confirmed the content of her talk with Furtwängler to me, but "It took place after the war began—in 1940," over lunch at a hotel in Zürich. Personal conversation with the author, Mainz, 6 October 1990.

his return ticket at that time. With the distance of 50 years and the perspective it gives you, I now can understand the dilemma he faced."[65]

For all the help he gave and was to continue giving Jews and the other dispossessed of the Third Reich, Furtwängler regarded this time-devouring and exhausting activity as an inconvenient routine. Nowhere in his writings or in any of the recollections by his associates is there any evidence that he had ulterior motives for the estimable danger into which he was putting himself. Nor is there a self-congratulatory word about what he was doing for the cultural enemies of his employers. Music remained his highest and only mission. In pursuing that mission, Furtwängler became tragic in the Aristotelian sense of that word. His was not merely an unfortunate situation nor was he a victim of catastrophic events. For all his unwillingness to participate in the political tide that was engulfing Germany, he felt compelled to articulate and act as a German. At the same time, he was infused with an irascible stubbornness to have his own way. However altruistic or untainted by greed or self-gain, his confidence in the rightness of his actions constituted that unforgivable offense to the gods of antiquity: *Hubris*—overweening pride. And both the mortal and divine powers that were challenged by Furtwängler's hubris were not about to deal with him kindly. For they had given him numerous opportunities to extricate himself from the increasingly heinous position in which he found himself, but he chose instead to remain loyal to the dictates of his truest feelings.

In that determination to stand firmly by his deepest instincts, he made a concession that was to affect him forever: he acknowledged Hitler as the supreme arbiter of cultural matters for Germany. In even entertaining such a notion, not to mention declaring it—no matter how mendaciously uttered or expedient in purpose or, for that matter, how true it may have been in Nazi Germany at the time—Furtwängler made an error that was pathetic in the short run and tragic in the long. Furtwängler now became something of a Steppenwolf manqué, the eponymous hero of the novel by Hermann Hesse, a writer Furtwängler deeply admired.[66]

65. Personal conversation with the author, Mainz, 6 October 1990.
66. In the interpolated essay in the middle of Hermann Hesse's novel, it becomes clear that Steppenwolf has passed beyond bourgeois thinking and reached the "second level." This is the realm to which most intellectuals and artists belong, according to Hesse's system of thought. "Only the strongest of them force their way through the atmosphere of the bourgeois world and arrive in the cosmos [the "third level"]; all others resign themselves and make compromises," says the author of the essay. Such individuals simply do not possess the cosmic strength and transcendent resolution of will to dwell constantly within the third level. They have enough strength in their individual

Naively, he thought he could get around the Nazis and simply envelop himself within his work and his music. His music, though, gradually became an anesthetic rather than the sole source of fulfillment it always had been; and work, as the sign over Himmler's death mills menacingly promised, would not make him free.

Worst of all, the Nazis were making free use of his name for their own purposes. In 1940 he was reported to have sent a printed message to the Berlin Philharmonic before they embarked on a tour of occupied countries. In it, he was quoted equating the musical mission of the Philharmonic with Germany's military mission:

> So one can say there is a common mandate binding the great masters and those who have the hardest mission and the decisive role in the present construction of the New Germany: the champions of our incomparable Wehrmacht.[67]

Goebbels' fingerprints are all over this statement, but it convinced the writer Uwe Sass that Furtwängler was indeed making a nefarious connection between music and war and throwing in his lot with the Nazis.[68] Sass and other un-informed journalists apparently were unaware that Furtwängler had long since quit his musical directorship and was only a free-lance conductor at this time. Consequently, he was not in charge of tours other conductors led with the Berlin Philharmonic and did not have the right—much less the inclination—to

---

identities to contest prevailing mores openly, but the struggle is tortuous and makes them wretched. Three alternatives are open to such individuals, according to the tract (and Hesse's thought):

> Either he will obtain one of our little mirrors, or he will encounter the Immortals, or perhaps will find in one of our Magic Theaters whatever he needs for the liberation of his ravaged soul.

The "magic mirror" is the means by which he can look into the chaos of his miserable soul. The Immortals reside in a realm of permanent and absolute value outside time and space. It can be achieved only through death, but we can occasionally find glimpses of it if we are receptive to the experience. The Magic Theater houses the entire scope of possibilities inherent in human experience within the framework of the present moment. These three alternatives are avenues to the third level, but few are capable of following through completely to experience that cosmic level at all times.

Could Furtwängler fight his way through to that third level? Certainly he looked deeply into the magic mirror, had intimate contact with the Immortals—Beethoven, Mozart—and he indeed found a measure of solace in the Magic Theater of unlimited possibilities. But he had decided to concede to the Nazis for the sake of grasping a tactical advantage in the real world. The moral issues raised by this decision continue to be hotly debated.

67. See Uwe Sass's article on two concerts in Lille by the Berlin Philharmonic under Eugen Jochum quoted in Muck, Vol. II, pp. 153–154.

68. Muck, Vol. II, p. 153.

write drivel such as this. Years later, though, Karajan's biographer Robert C. Bachmann singled out the quote as something of a "smoking gun" on Furtwängler's "real" political sympathies. To add misinformation to false deduction, the word *"Geleitwort"* (preface, prefatory word), which was used both by Sass in his report and by Bachmann in his description of the incident, turned up in the otherwise excellent English translation of Bachmann's book as "speech," as if Furtwängler stood before the orchestra haranguing them with a pep talk extoling the Wehrmacht.[69]

There was, of course, another option available to Furtwängler, but it was one he found basically inimical to his personality. He could have withdrawn into an "inner emigration," joining many artists and intellectuals who hated the Nazis but remained in Germany, and waited out the burgeoning holocaust. That would have been one kind of resistance. But Furtwängler had grown up with the conviction that belief must give rise to action, that ideas are nothing more than that unless manifested through purposeful response. In acting on that belief, he found himself the unofficial leader of the "inner emigration" anyway.[70] He was also committed to that quasi-Platonic and peculiarly German ideal of productively making temporal reality a reflection of a higher, greater, and eternal one. He resolved to remain firm in the faith that such an ideal was possible. To achieve it, he would have to give new meaning through his actions to Nietzsche's exhortation: live dangerously. And in his writings of 1937 he found strength in reflecting upon the German philosopher:

> It is easy to say the right thing. It is hard to do the right thing. It is dangerous to believe that saying and doing are the same thing. It can intermittently mean practical power, and that is what it was for Nietzsche . . . The older I become, the more I comprehend that envy from others is sufficient reason for a "work ethic."

69. See Bachmann German version, (Düsseldorf) 1983, pp. 139–140; English version, Shaun Whiteside, (London) 1990, p. 123.

70. See Allen Welsh Dulles, *Germany's Underground*, (New York) 1947, p. 120. In an editorial/review following the publication of the book, the American German-language newspapers for emigrants *Aufbau* flatly rejected Dulles' mere mention of Furtwängler as having anything to do with the "inner emigration," 2 May 1947, p. 5. But Dulles was probably the one American at the time to speak authoritatively about the roles prominent Germans played in the Third Reich. Dulles was the brother of John Foster Dulles (Secretary of State in the Eisenhower administration) and a partner in the prestigious international law firm Sullivan and Cromwell. He went to Switzerland in 1942 to head the Office of Strategic Services (OSS) mission there. He and his assistant Gero v. S. Gävernitz were highly instrumental in arranging the negotiations resulting in the defeat of the Third Reich. Later, during the Cold War, Dulles served as chief of the Central Intelligence Agency (CIA) whose forerunner was the OSS.

Certainly the sort of loneliness he experienced is difficult to bear, as he says himself, and I do not think he exaggerates. His frailty lies in cultivating that loneliness. But in that loneliness lies the beginning of true heroism. Nietzsche speaks of his "spiritual sleeplessness." How appropriate from someone whom the world views merely as a critical moralist.   *Aufzeichnungen, pp. 148–149*

16

The Devil's Birthday

Gestapo eyes and ears were everywhere. People were disappearing. What could Furtwängler do about the hell into which his country was now sliding? If the true realm of music is above politics, he reasoned, then someone must keep that realm open to those for whom every other means of redemption has been denied. He was not about to join a resistance movement, but music making itself now became a symbol of his own kind of opposition to Hitler and totalitarianism, and Furtwängler saw that this was his destiny.

This form of insurgency dwelt beyond the Gestapo's terrain; there was no concrete means of identifying it and so it could not be easily terminated. And here, perhaps, lay the secret to Furtwängler's phenomenal longevity throughout his peculiar kind of defiance against the regime right up to the end: Furtwängler's realm was in the aural, the suggestive, the intangible, and the very impalpability of music shielded his unique style of sedition. While evidence could easily be produced against writers and visual artists from their own work, it was all but impossible to catch Furtwängler *in flagrante delicto* in his.[1]

1. For example, the artist Emil Nolde, was an ardent Nazi from the 1920s. He was also a vociferous anti-Semite and the Nazis used many of his words in their invectives against Jews in the arts. But after the Brownshirts came to power, they turned Nolde's words against his own work. Nolde suffered the crushing humiliation of having over a thousand of his paintings displayed at the first exhibit of Degenerate Art *(Entartete Kunst)* in Munich in 1937.

Goebbels was well aware of how Furtwängler was exploiting this chink in Party dogma and set about filling it by making the Nazi ideal of acceptable music both explicit and tangible under his ongoing program of Total Conformity *(Gleichschaltung)*. He long since had succeeded in bringing to heel everything relating to literature, film, the visual arts, and the press.[2] And now, in 1938, he set his target on music by sponsoring a festival of German Music Days in Düsseldorf in conjunction with the city's 650th anniversary celebration.

The week-long *Musikfest* lasted from 22 May until 29 May and included more than two dozen events involving the Berlin Philharmonic under Hermann Abendroth, the Düsseldorf Municipal Orchestra, endless parades utilizing army units, the Hitler Youth, labor groups, music students, and a variety of amateur instrumental and choral clubs. Strauss' opera *Arabella*, Pfitzner's cantata *Of the German Soul*, and Beethoven's Ninth Symphony were among the large-scale musical offerings trotted out during that week to affirm German identity at its highest and best. Musicologists from all parts of Germany were brought in for lectures, seminars, and panels to discuss the nature of German music.

Throughout the festivities, a sideshow called "Degenerate Music" was put on to demonstrate how savagely certain "elements" had ravaged German music. The idea first occurred to Hans Severus Ziegler, State Commissar of the Thüringian Theaters, when he saw the huge success accorded the exposition of "Degenerate Art" *(Entartete Kunst)* held in Munich a year earlier in 1937. In that infamous exhibit, the works of such reprehensible artists as Pablo Picasso, Oskar Kokoschka, Vassily Kandinsky, Paul Klee, Emil Nolde, Ernst Ludwig Kirchner, Max Beckmann and many others were held up for ridicule in one building, while the works of artists acceptable to the Reich, such as Adolf Ziegler, who supervised the exposition, Arno Breker, Richard Scheibe, and Sepp Hilz were displayed for adulation in another.[3] (Adolf Ziegler, incidentally, was no relation to Hans Severus Ziegler.) The latter readily saw how a corresponding exposition of "degenerate" music could serve a number of purposes—especially his own—and he recruited the help of three friends from Weimar: Otto zur Nedden, Chief Dramaturg at the Deutsches Nationaltheater, Paul Sixt, a young conductor, and Ernst Nobbe, the General Intendant in Weimar.

2. For fuller information in these areas, see Joseph Wulf, released in five volumes under the title *Kultur im dritten Reich*, (Berlin) 1990. Each volume is devoted to documents relating to the relationship between the Third Reich and film, literature and poetry, the visual arts, and music.
3. About 20,000 people attended the exhibit of acceptable artists. Over two million flocked to the degenerates (purportedly to ridicule).

This lubricious quartet started their project without prompting from any government authority, but their ultimate aim was to gain Berlin's assent in more ways than one. Their overt intention was simply to heap scorn on Jews in music, although such Aryans as Paul Hindemith and Alban Berg were not to be spared. No "superior" Aryan musicians, however, were produced for contrast. Jazz and blacks were also special targets of the exhibit, and the cover of the exhibition booklet showed a thick-lipped, wide-eyed black man playing a saxophone with a flat carnation shaped as a Star of David stuck to his tuxedo lapel.[4]

The covert and primary intention of the show, however, was to produce a "trading card" for its organizers that could be used in their tenuous dealings with the government. Ziegler took the lead in bringing the project to fruition because it was his idea and he had the most at stake. He had long been widely suspected of being homosexual, and "certain rumors" about his conduct in Weimar had brought about an official investigation in January 1935. Such proclivities were a grave and frequently capital offense in the Third Reich, and the grounds for the inquiry were sufficiently serious for him to be suspended from his duties as Commissar.[5] Ziegler appealed to the highest levels of the Reich in Berlin. A few weeks later, the press reported that charges against him had been dropped.[6] Such an abrupt halt in official proceedings of this sort could have been authorized only at the very top. Indeed, Ziegler had many friends in the highest echelons of the Nazi hierarchy, and he had known Hitler since 1925. And while the soles of his libido may have traversed the gutter from time to time, both his pedigree and his qualifications were far from down at the cuff. Born in Eisenach in 1893, his father was a banker, and his maternal grandfather had founded one of the most prestigious and enduring music publishing houses in the United States, G. Schirmer and Sons.[7] Ziegler apparently inherited his musical gifts from his mother's side and developed them through advanced studies in organ at Cambridge, England, and in cultural history in Weimar and at Greifswald University. He had been active in editing Nazi publications since 1924 and rapidly moved up through various capacities in theatrical production and administration until his loyal work for the Brownshirts was

4. While the Third Reich officially condemned jazz, it was too popular to destroy altogether. It frequently was used for propaganda purposes.
5. The news of Ziegler's suspension from his position at the Nationaltheater until the inquiry into his conduct was completed was reported in the *Frankfurter Zeitung*, Nr. 58, 1 February 1935, p. 2.
6. *Frankfurter Zeitung*, Nr. 128, 10 March 1935, p. 2.
7. See the biographical sketch in Ziegler's memoir *Adolf Hitler aus dem Erleben dargestellt*, (Göttingen) 1964, p. 291.

rewarded with the leading position in the Thüringian theaters in 1933.

Ziegler received a stern warning for his peccadillos and kept his job, but he apparently felt that his personal ties in Berlin could continue to exempt his drives from prosecution. Nonetheless, the pursuit of the love that dared not speak its name at that time was fast becoming more dangerous than exciting, and he realized his position was weakening. So the idea of an anti-Semitic and anti-Black music exhibit flowered into a means of ingratiating himself and his cronies with top-level authorities.

A few months before the festival was to take place, Ziegler presented the project to Goebbels and chief Nazi ideologue Alfred Rosenberg. They both expressed great interest.[8] Since the German Music Days were set to begin 22 May, they had to act quickly. In a rare moment of amicable collaboration, they agreed to include it as part of the festivities. Scores, posters, and other "proofs" of degenerate music were displayed in vitrines and along the walls of the exhibition, and visitors could enter private booths equipped with speakers to hear recordings of such worthless composers as Arnold Schönberg, Gustav Mahler, Felix Mendelssohn, Ernst Krenek, and Paul Hindemith performed by such talentless artists as Fritz Kreisler, Emanuel Feuermann, Bruno Walter, and Otto Klemperer. The exhibit went on tour from Düsseldorf to Munich and Vienna, but Goebbels forbade further press coverage when he foresaw its popularity and began to suspect Ziegler's real motive in producing it.[9]

The German Music Days Festival was an unqualified success as a Party event, and the Degenerate Music sideshow was well attended. But their long-range impact on Germany's populace was at best dubious. The Degenerate Music exhibition in particular represented little more than a contemptible joke among the informed and a repository of noisy curiosities to the ignorant. Nonetheless, what was indubitably odious to those who knew of Ziegler and his friends was the shameless spectacle this exhibit produced of one persecuted minority cynically flailing another with utter impunity. Furtwängler was invited to participate, but he and most of the other leading musical figures left in Germany steered clear of having anything to do with it.

8. Rosenberg's interest led him to send an inquiring letter to Ziegler on 25 October 1937. Source: Bundesarchiv, Koblenz, File #NS15/162A.

9. The directive to stop further press coverage is contained in *Vertrauliche Information*, Reichspropaganda Amt, File #114/38, 24 May 1938. Source: Bundesarchiv, Koblenz, R 55/446, p. 83. All the perpetrators of this exhibit except Nobbe survived the war. Nobbe died later in 1938 of apparently natural causes at the age of 44. Ziegler later wrote several books, including a fascinating memoir about Hitler in which he defends the intervention of the Nazis in musical affairs. See note above.

Absence, however, could not mitigate the pernicious enormity of what Furtwängler alone was now up against. The circus in Düsseldorf may merely have been hoopla, but he could not ignore the fact that the intellectual forces behind it and the exhibit could no longer be dismissed as Brownshirt rabble-rousers. Intelligent, cultured individuals such as Hans Severus Ziegler and his friends not only were boarding the Nazi bandwagon but were now helping drive it. The very plexus of musical culture in Germany was becoming palpably degenerate.

Later that year, Furtwängler expressed how he felt about the Degenerate Music project and the base intentions of its creators by boldly presenting the German premiere of the suite from *The Fairy's Kiss* by Stravinsky.[10] He got away with it because music remained a somewhat murky area in Nazi ideology, despite the enormous expense both Goebbels and Rosenberg lavished on proving otherwise, and it resisted codification and made strict enforcement of policy rules almost impossible. This circumstance was peculiar to music alone in the Third Reich, and it further enabled Furtwängler to zigzag through that narrow gray zone with his own line of defense, always a whiff beyond Himmler's Dobermans. But Furtwängler's performance of Stravinsky's bittersweet ballet music was the last time this "Bolshevist noise-maker" was heard in Germany until after World War II.

While Furtwängler went to great lengths to avoid Goebbels' plans for his active involvement with political events, his form of musical resistance was not merely evasive. The very act of performing music—especially the works of the German masters—expressed his opposition to the regime, and the insurgent motive behind his concerts was not lost on his audience. Much later, the German author Rudolf Pechel told him, "In the resistance movement we agreed that you were the only musician truly resisting Hitler, and that you belonged to us." Count Gerd Kanitz, another member of the resistance, frequently said, "At Furtwängler's concerts we all become one family of resistance fighters."[11] Indeed, each time Furtwängler conducted, he drew his audience into his brand of opposition. After the war, he stated the firmness of his conviction at the time in a widely distributed declaration:

> I defended the superior intellectual life of Germany against the Nazi ideology. I did not directly oppose the Party, because I told myself, this was not my job. I should have benefitted no one by active resistance. But I never concealed my opinions. As an artist, I was determined that my

10. 11, 12, 13 December 1938. Berlin Philharmonic.
11. Riess, p. 241.

music, at least, should remain untouched. If I had taken an active part in politics I could not have remained in Germany. I knew that a single performance of a great German masterpiece was a stronger and more vital negation of the spirit of Buchenwald or Auschwitz than words. Please understand me correctly: an artist cannot be entirely unpolitical. He must have some political convictions, because, he is, after all a Human being. As a citizen, it is an artist's duty to express these convictions. But as a musician, I am more than a citizen. I am a German in that eternal sense to which the genius of great music testifies.[12]

But Furtwängler's form of resistance did not prompt physically overt opposition to the regime. At their weakest, the would-be insurgents simply lost themselves in the pervasive musical womb he was famous for creating at his concerts. At best, his audiences dwelled in the hope his performing offered. But they were unable to actualize its secret message through action. Now that nearly all the other serious intellectuals left in Germany had withdrawn into private pursuits of what came to be known as the "inner emigration," Furtwängler was again virtually alone in his crusade.

By the end of 1942 Germany's victory was still nowhere in sight. The Battle of Britain two years earlier had been a disaster for the Nazis, and recent developments in Africa were not encouraging. To make matters worse, Hitler had opened up a second front in the East, his target Moscow. Most Germans knew instinctively that this, 1942, would be a decisive year in its history, and throughout the nation the anticipation was electric.

Projecting an image of a victorious and virile Third Reich was always uppermost among Goebbels' priorities, and pageantry invariably played a big part in his designs for keeping up the people's morale.[13] No occasion was celebrated with greater splendor than 20 April, Hitler's birthday. Royalty from foreign countries sent him elaborate gifts. The most celebrated individuals in the Reich to the most common man on the street sent presents to their Führer according to

12. This statement was part of a brief summarizing Furtwängler's anti-Nazi activities during the Third Reich. He made it public following his denazification trial, and parts of it were published in *Aufbau*, the German-language newspaper for émigrés. The abridged statements were juxtaposed with a protracted reply by writer Fritz von Unruh. In it, he sneered at Furtwängler for "entertaining" Hitler with the very music he was trying to protect. 18 April 1947, p. 1. Furtwängler also released the statement during the scandal resulting from his aborted engagement as guest conductor of the Chicago Symphony in 1948–1949 and sent copies of it to friends in America. Source: Suzanne Bloch archives.

13. See Robert Herzstein, *The War that Hitler Won*, (New York) 1978, for a stimulating survey of Goebbels' manipulation of public opinion in the Third Reich. While most of his assertions are largely well documented, Herzstein contends without providing evidence that Furtwängler was "a favorite of the Propaganda Minister" (p. 88).

their means. The wealthy and the famous sent works of art. Peasant boys picked and delivered enormous bouquets of edelweiss. Old women knitted socks or embroidered curtains and tablecloths.

Goebbels orchestrated these celebrations months in advance so that all the people could do their part for the Great Day. As it approached, the Nazi radio network revved up public anticipation, while the Nazi press churned out sheaves of copy describing preparations for the events celebrating the day, making every effort to ensure that this year's celebration would look better, greater, and more powerful than any before.

For nine years, Furtwängler had successfully managed to evade performing at official Nazi functions. Now, in 1942, Goebbels was determined that Furtwängler make his debut at an official Party event.[14] Furtwängler was all too aware that Goebbels might ask him to conduct the customary concert on the eve of the Day itself. So he not only made sure he was not in Berlin but that he could not return. He already had cancelled many performances because of "illness," and he went to Vienna a week before Hitler's birthday to conduct the Vienna Philharmonic. Without permission from the Gauleiter of Vienna, who was the nominal head of the Vienna Philharmonic, Furtwängler could not leave the city, much less the country. The Gauleiter was Baldur von Schirach, who had succeeded Bürckel.[15] He loathed Goebbels as much as his predecessor did, and he readily agreed to refuse Furtwängler permission to leave Vienna.

Furtwängler was in the midst of rehearsals for Beethoven's Ninth in Vienna when Goebbels telephoned. He so intimidated von Schirach that he caved in. Now Furtwängler had little choice but to conduct at the birthday celebrations concert. The program was to include an Air from Suite no. 3 by Bach and the Beethoven Ninth. Furtwängler had created a sensation with the work in Berlin only a few weeks earlier (21–24 March), and the Führer wanted it performed especially for

14. Furtwängler has been frequently and erroneously cited as conducting at the Nürnberg Rally of 1938. He conducted the Vienna Philharmonic in a performance of *Die Meistersinger* preceding the rally, but it was not part of the official agenda. Nonetheless, the Nazis succeeded in making it look that way.

15. Schirach was named Gauleiter of Vienna on 7 August 1940. He had been a driving force behind the Hitler Youth Movement, lived extravagantly, and was sneered at for his effeminate tastes. During his tenure in Vienna, he supported the Vienna Philharmonic and other cultural institutions, kept them free of Goebbels' covetous tentacles, and enabled them to flourish until a few weeks before the end of the war. However, 185,000 Jews were deported to Poland during his period of leadership. At the Nürnberg Trials, he admitted that he supported the "resettlement" of Jews but denied knowing anything about mass murders. For his professed ignorance of the crimes against humanity to which he indubitably contributed, he was sentenced to 20 years at Spandau. He died in 1974.

him. Under these circumstances, he could not plead insufficient rehearsal time. He finally returned to Berlin, and quickly rehearsed the soloists and the Berlin Philharmonic.[16] All the Party officials were in attendance at the Philharmonie on the evening of 19 April. Newsreel cameras rolled as Furtwängler entered the hall, mounted the podium, bowed curtly without giving the Nazi salute, and began conducting. It was a spectacular performance in spite of himself, and the final moments of the Ninth were edited into every German and some foreign newsreels for weeks to come. Furtwängler returned immediately to Vienna to complete preparations on the Ninth from which he had been abruptly taken.[17] He resolved never to conduct at a Party event no matter what the cost. But he already had broken his word to himself.

The concert left an impression on Hitler and moved him to talk about it. He had mentioned Furtwängler occasionally in his conversations, which were dutifully recorded under the supervision of Martin Bormann between 1941 and 1944. Ten days after the concert on 30 April, Hitler expanded on musical conditions in Germany at the time during a supper at the Berghof:

> Great conductors are as important as great singers. Had there been a sufficiency of good conductors during the time of the Weimar Republic, we should have been saved the ridiculous spectacle of the rise to eminence of a man like Bruno Walter, who in Vienna was regarded as a complete nonentity. It was the Jewish press of Munich, which was echoed by its Viennese counterpart, that drew attention to the man and suddenly proclaimed him to be the greatest conductor in Germany. But the last laugh was against Vienna; for when he was engaged as conductor of the superb Viennese orchestra, all he could produce was beer-hall music. He was dismissed, of course, and with his dismissal Vienna began to realize what a dearth there was of good conductors, and sent for Knappertsbusch.
>
> He with his blond hair and blue eyes, was certainly a German, but unfortunately he believed that, even with no ear, he could, with his temperament, still produce good music. To attend the Opera when he was conducting was a real penance; the orchestra played too loud, the violins were blanketed by the brass, and the voices of the singers were stifled. Instead of melody one was treated to a series of intermittent shrieks, and the wretched soloists looked just like a lot of tadpoles, the conductor him-

---

16. All the soloists raised for this dreaded one-night stand—Erna Berger, Gertrude Pitzinger, Helge Roswänge, and Rudolf Watzke—had sung the Choral Ode with him previously, though only Watzke sang in the concerts Furtwängler conducted in March. His colleagues on those occasions were Tilla Briem, Elisabeth Höngen, and Peter Anders, and tapes of those concerts fully justify the sensation Furtwängler aroused. Hitler's Birthday Concert was an important moment in Berger's career, but she seems to have forgotten to mention it in her memoir *Auf Flügeln des Gesanges*, (Zurich) 1988.

17. 21, 22, 23, 24 April. Soloists: Rokyta, Schürhoff, and Herbert Alsen.

self indulged in such an extravaganza of gesture that it was better to avoid looking at him at all.

The only conductor whose gestures do not appear ridiculous is Furt-wängler. His movements are inspired from the depths of his being. In spite of the meagre financial support he received, he succeeded in turning the Berlin Philharmonic into an ensemble far superior to that of Vienna, and that is greatly to his credit.[18]

Hitler could swing with alarming ease from pure drivel—as in his account of Bruno Walter's tenure in Vienna—to some arguable, though opinionated, perceptions about artists such as Hans Knap-pertsbusch and Furtwängler. The comments here are especially illu-minating because Hitler admits in no uncertain terms that Aryan breeding and superior talent do not necessarily go hand in hand.

As Hitler's birthday approached the following year, 1943, Furt-wängler went to his physician Professor Dr. Ferdinand Sauerbruch and pleaded for a medical excuse. He had cancelled many concerts in the intervening months because of spondylitis, a neuromuscular affliction affecting the neck and upper arms and common to many conductors.

His doctor complained that he had written so many medical excuses for Furtwängler that the authorities were becoming suspi-cious. Furtwängler threatened to jump out the window if he did not receive another excuse: "At any rate that would be better than con-ducting for the man who has thrown Germany and the rest of the world into such a horrible state!"[19]

Furtwängler got his certificate and went again to Vienna. Goeb-bels knew that Furtwängler was a relatively robust specimen and decided to call his bluff. He phoned him in Vienna and informed him that a private plane would be sent for him. "Surely you could stand up for the hour that it takes to conduct the *Eroica*," he chided. "Espe-cially for such an important occasion as Hitler's birthday."

Furtwängler told Goebbels he would be pleased to conduct the concert but reminded him that his appearance in Berlin might offend the Spanish.[20] By "the Spanish," Furtwängler meant the dictator Franco with whom the Nazis were treading upon eggs. Furtwängler recently had cancelled an engagement in Spain. Goebbels had to agree that Furtwängler's appearance in Berlin could offend Franco. It was a close call in every respect, but Goebbels finally excused him.

Military fortunes now had turned decisively against the Third

18. *Hitler's Secret Conversations*, No. 202, p. 364.
19. Riess, p. 257. See also *Kraftprobe*, p. 382.
20. Riess, p. 257.

Reich, and Germany was at Total War. Goebbels had his hands full keeping up the morale of the people, which he did brilliantly. The weary nation fell somnolently under the spell of his harangues. He warned them they would have to sacrifice everything for ultimate victory. But for all his growing problems in keeping the people hypnotized and jockeying all the while to increase his own influence with Hitler, Goebbels always had time to make another attempt at sucking Furtwängler into the Nazi propaganda machine. Furtwängler was slowly becoming aware of how deadly the dance he was engaging with Goebbels was getting, and he continued trying to remain on good terms with Goebbels, who had become the only shield he had left against the growing forces working against him. Goebbels was apparently convinced, as his diary from 1942 reveals

> Furtwängler paid me a visit. He has just made a tour of Sweden and Denmark and is full of high National Socialist spirits. This man has undergone a transformation, which makes me exceedingly happy. I have struggled with him for a long time, and I now see success with him. He approves perfectly my radio and film policies and is putting himself at my service. His judgment of Karajan has become more mature; he is no longer interested in public quarrels, but regards them with sovereign, matured confidence.[21]

Goebbels may have thought he had broken Furtwängler, but an entry two years later in Furtwängler's own *Notebooks* indicates that he believed he continued to represent the resistance of what he felt was the "real" Germany against the plague that had overcome it:

> I am one of the most convincing proofs that the real Germany is alive and will remain alive. The will to live and work in me is, however critically I view myself, that of a completely unbroken nation.   *1944*

Nonetheless, Goebbels tried to exploit that new "matured confidence" he perceived in Furtwängler. Shortly after the failed attempt on Hitler's life on 20 July 1944 he issued a pamphlet entitled, "We stand and fall with Adolf Hitler." Actors and artists were asked to write articles on this theme. Only Furtwängler refused.

How could Furtwängler get away with such insolence? To this day, many are convinced that his evasion of punishment for such audacity is proof enough that he made some kind of self-serving deal

21. 28 February 1942, NL 118. Source: Bundesarchiv, Koblenz.

with the Nazis or was a ruthless opportunist.[22] But the truth is perhaps more mundane. Furtwängler himself was a superb propaganda tool, and both Hitler and Goebbels hoped to the very end that either vanity or intimidation would ultimately bring him to their side. He was also an icon of the Old Order of Germany, and he had legions of admirers. Goebbels had tirelessly touted him as the symbol of how the Old Order had been absorbed into the New Order. As events made the future ever bleaker for the New Order, it became more dangerous to attempt liquidating him. Elimination would imply that the New Order was not working out successfully after all.

As Germany entered the darkest days of the war, Allied bombs hammered German cities day and night. Homes, factories, concert halls and opera houses all over Germany were turning to rubble and cinder. The visible signs of German culture as it had developed since the 14th century vanished. In Dresden, Baroque cathedrals attesting to faith in benevolent Christianity disappeared overnight. Most demoralizing of all, private houses were being destroyed at an alarming rate. Furtwängler lived in Potsdam, a short distance from Berlin. It had not yet been bombed, but he was obliged frequently to go to the underground shelter. He usually was the only adult male among scores of women and children. Invariably, he had music with him. Once he started reading, he was lost to his surroundings.

Never an easy conversationalist, he once said to a child sitting next to him, "This must be a serious attack today. Perhaps we should have a man here."

The boy looked up at him in surprise. "But you are a man, uncle!"

"I am only an artist," said Furtwängler.[23]

So it had come to this. An aging musician—not even a man by his own estimation—who had tried to make people forget the oppressive realities of the here and now, sitting in a bomb shelter being shown the "real" truth by a child.

As the bombs came closer to Potsdam, Furtwängler started looking for another house. He recently had been married a second time to Elisabeth Albert Ackermann, a considerably younger woman. Furtwängler met Elisabeth through her half-sister Maria Daelen, with whom he had been having a relationship since 1935. The mother of Elisabeth and Maria had been a member of the conservative Deutsche

---

22. The view of Furtwängler as a ruthless *intriguant*, who hatched unseemly plots against Karajan and even conspired to have a thorny critic sent to the front, is pressed by Berndt W. Wessling in his *Furtwängler: Ein kritische Biographie*, (Stuttgart) 1985. Voluminous and overwhelming evidence indicates quite the contrary.

23. Riess, p. 259.

Volkspartei, whose leader was Gustav Stresemann. Katarina von Oheimb was elected to the Reichstag between 1920 and 1924. Elisabeth's father was Katarina's third husband, a wealthy tile manufacturer. Elisabeth's aunt on her mother's side was Elisabeth van Endert-Böhm, a well-known principal singer with the Royal Opera Dresden (1909–1911) and in Berlin (until 1923).[24]

While Furtwängler's new wife was every bit as intelligent as Maria, who was a successful internist, she opted for family and children, and now had four children by a former marriage. Her first husband was a lawyer, who had joined the German army, and was killed in 1940 in a shooting accident in Paris. Furtwängler had many long-term relationships with countless women, and the reasons why he lost interest in Maria remains a mystery, but he found himself smitten with Elisabeth shortly after they met in 1940. No one, least of all Elisabeth, suspected that he would be interested in marrying her, for she was a widow with four children in tow. But she was still at 32 a woman of radiant beauty whose past personal misfortunes had imbued her with the kind of wisdom and generosity he would depend upon in the next few years.

"I remember it was New Years Day, 1942," she recalls. "It was in Vienna, and I came to see him with some friends in Vienna just before one of his concerts. The way he looked up at me . . . I knew then that I was in love with him. But he had been with Maria for so long, and even after we both knew we loved each other, I begged him to marry her."[25] For once, though, Furtwängler did not hesitate.

Goebbels took the marriage as an opportunity to try to "help" Furtwängler, for he was convinced that the new husband's protective instincts toward his acquired family would prevent him from refusing an offer of new and safe accommodation. All he had to do was tell him where he wanted to live. Goebbels said the Führer himself had ordered that Furtwängler be given whatever housing he wanted. Furtwängler was too shocked even to reply. All around him women, children, the old, and the infirm were wandering the streets in search of warmth and safety. Eventually, several emissaries from Hitler came to see him about new housing. Furtwängler finally wrote to Hitler, "I cannot

24. Van Endert-Böhm emigrated to England in 1933 because her second husband, Leo Curth, was Jewish. Curth was director of the Electrola Phonograph Corporation before the Nazi racial policies brought about his ouster. He died in London in 1935, and his widow ultimately settled in the United States where she died in 1956. Frau Furtwängler says her husband never worked with van Endert, but he never forgot seeing her Octavian at the Berlin Staatsoper and gave her the highest compliment he could give an artist of van Endert's stature: "I don't remember much about the voice, but her legs were pitched perfectly." Personal conversation with the author, Clarens, 6 December 1989.

25. Personal conversation with the author, Paris, 22 April 1989.

accept a house at a time when so many people in Germany are home-less." Perhaps the message never reached the Führer, for aides again visited the Furtwänglers to ask where they wanted to move and offered to build a bomb shelter in the basement of his home in Pots-dam.[26] Finally, he wrote to Hitler on 21 May 1944 from Achleiten near Linz, Austria:

> At a time when it is the duty of each German to bear a share of burden of the war—which I neither want nor will evade—such a great architectural project is unjustified simply for me and my family . . .[27]

Despite his continued refusals, Goebbels leaked word that Hitler indeed had presented Furtwängler with a fortified house. Eventually, Furtwängler moved with his family to Achleiten where he rented an apartment from friends there and commuted to Vienna, Munich, and Berlin.

Elisabeth Furtwängler recalled this period to me in 1989:

> Wilhelm never thought the war would go on as long as it did. He thought the war would end with Germany's loss as soon as the Nazis invaded Rus-sia. He said it was foolish and hopeless. Once the United States came into the war, he thought it would be a matter of weeks. He felt terrible con-flicts inside him, for it is no easy thing to want your own country to lose, but he thought it was a quick way for Germany to be rid of the Nazis. But it didn't happen that way, of course.
>
> I think the only time Wilhelm cursed the Allies was when they bombed the cities, especially Dresden. "Why?" he cried to me. "It is so unnecessary. They will close in on us on both sides soon anyway. Why destroy such a beautiful city like Dresden?"[28]

Despite the havoc wrought on Germany when the war turned decisively, cultural life continued much as it had before the war, and audiences attended theatrical and musical events in droves, fre-quently at considerable risk from ever more frequent air strikes. Furt-

---

26. As late as 1986, conservative German periodicals cited Hitler's offer as indis-putable proof that Furtwängler was coddled by the Nazi hierarchy. See Rolf Ringguth's review of Fred K. Prieberg's *Kraftprobe* in *Der Spiegel*, "Odem des Allerhöchsten," Nr. 12, 17 March 1986, pp. 249–254. See note below.

27. Source: Bundesarchiv, Koblenz, R3/1578, pp. 242–243. When the popular Ger-man magazine *Der Spiegel* reviewed Prieberg's *Kraftprobe*, it mentioned Hitler's offer to build a bunker for Furtwängler in a manner that diminished Prieberg's exhaustively documented contention that Furtwängler was never cozy with the Third Reich or its leadership. While the reviewer may have been aware of Furtwängler's letter of firm refusal on p. 404 of the book, he made no mention of the fact in his review. See Rolf Ringguth, "Odem des Allerhöchsten," Nr. 12, 17 March 1986, pp. 249–254.

28. Personal conversation with the author, Paris, 22 April 1989.

wängler continued to take the Berlin and Vienna Philharmonics on tours, and obtaining tickets for his concerts became an obsession with his public. Notices in the agony columns offered cigarettes, coffee and other rare commodities in exchange for tickets.

And when he returned to the Staatsoper in Vienna, he for once used art as a means for making a political statement. The occasion was a revised production of *Tristan* in which he doubled as producer and conductor. According to Wagner's stage directions, the lovers are pulled apart at the end of Act I in a tempest of dismay, but Furtwängler left them clinging tenaciously to each other as the curtain fell.[29] In his view of the dramatic situation, the lovers had to remain *physically* as well as emotionally constant throughout the storm in which they have caught themselves. Here, Furtwängler the producer was sending a message to his audiences: they must remain constant to each other in the maelstrom of the real world that now was raining terror over all their lives. Furtwängler acted as he counseled. He himself had several chances to escape at this time, but he rejected them all. On one tour through Scandinavia later in 1943, Otto Strasser and other members of the Vienna Philharmonic saw his distress over the direction Germany was sliding and advised him to remain in Sweden or Norway. "He shook his head," says Strasser. "I can't leave the German people now when they need me most."[30]

When he returned to Berlin in November 1943, he learned that the Allies had bombed the Philharmonie. The interior was still intact but the façade had been badly damaged and fire had destroyed almost the entire library containing precious scores, priceless manuscripts, and most of Furtwängler's personal and professional files. Enough of the rubble was cleared out to present a few concerts, but the Berlin Philharmonic gave its final performance there on 12 January 1944. Two weeks later, on 30 January, eleven years after the Nazis seized power, bombs fell again on the Philharmonie. This time it was destroyed forever.

Shortly afterward, Furtwängler viewed the ruins. The hall had been more of a home to him than any house he had ever lived in. For the first time in his life, he felt old, for here was irrefutable proof that the only part of his life which meant anything to him was gone.

29. Premiere: 2 January 1943. Furtwängler's changes in the stage direction was mentioned in several reviews. He conducted seven performances of the this production in Vienna. It was the opera in which he made his last appearance at the Vienna Staatsoper (20 February 1944) before the end of the war.
30. Personal conversation with the author, Vienna, 9 April 1990. Strasser has also recorded this recollection several times in lectures and various articles he has written on Furtwängler.

Nonetheless, the loss of the building itself was no great loss to him. He never had cared much for its parody of classical Greek architecture, and his new wife recalled his reaction. "Wilhelm was capable of wit and humor at the most unusual moments, and this was one of them. When he phoned me, I was in Austria, and he said to me, 'it looks better as a ruin than it did as a complete building.'"[31] What is more, he now had the unplanned pleasure of colonizing Herbert von Karajan's professional domicile, a delectable rejoinder to a Karajan ploy a year earlier. After the Staatsoper was destroyed by Allied bombing on the night of 9–10 April 1941 Karajan insisted on and got permission to conduct his concerts with the Staatsoper Orchestra in the Berlin Philharmonic's hall, the Philharmonie near Potsdamerplatz. Now that the Philharmonie was gone, Furtwängler promptly moved his orchestra to the lavishly rebuilt Staatsoper. Karajan was in no position to object, for his power base was gone after Furtwängler sued to have Rudolf Vedder's concert agency license revoked. Furtwängler's tenancy there was a short one, however. The saturation bombings destroyed the opera house again on 3 February 1945, and it was not reopened until 1955.

Day by day, Berlin was pounded by Allied bombs and pummeled into rubble, ash and smoke. Furtwängler knew, as most Germans knew by now, that the war was lost. He was happy that it was all coming to an end, but the sight of Berlin, its history, its culture disappearing before his eyes enraged him, and he became increasingly outspoken and open in his criticism of the Nazis, despite the warnings of his new wife and close friends. He openly taunted Baldur von Schirach, the Gauleiter of Vienna who was in charge of the Vienna Philharmonic.

"What happens to the Jews who are transported?"

"What is going on in the concentration camps?

"What really happened at the Battle of Stalingrad?"[32]

Baldur von Schirach was a Nazi, but he was also cultivated and educated. Furtwängler liked him because of the latter qualities, but he also expected him to know these answers. Furtwängler reasoned that if von Schirach had sided with the Nazis despite the qualifications that would have enabled him to know better, he must know what the government was doing to justify his choice.[33] The truth, of course, was that Schirach mostly likely knew exactly what was happening in the

31. Personal conversation with the author, Paris, 22 April 1989.
32. Riess, p. 262.
33. Elisabeth Furtwängler. Personal conversation with the author, 4 December 1989.

East and what was becoming of the Jews. But like most Germans, he also didn't care to contemplate their fate. He had enough problems worrying about his own survival, especially with an albatross like Furtwängler around his neck. According to Elisabeth Furtwängler, they were as aware as most Germans that thousands were being sent to camps in the East, "but we did not, and I swear this to you, we did not know about the gas chambers."[34]

A sophisticated spy network like the Gestapo was hardly necessary to monitor Furtwängler's open challenges to the regime. Himmler, who headed the Gestapo, had long been nursing a grudge against Furtwängler. Now, he saw his chance for revenge approaching.

In the meantime, Richard Strauss asked Furtwängler to intervene with the Nazis on two matters. First, his villa in Garmisch-Partenkirchen had been billeted to house refugees who had lost their homes in the bombings. He complained that he could not get to his piano. The Gauleiter of the area reported him for disloyalty. Hitler, still remembering Strauss' indiscreet letter to Stefan Zweig in which he demeaned top-ranking Nazis, personally ordered that the composer's 80th birthday on 11 June 1944 should not be officially celebrated.

Strauss, of course, had asked his close friends Clemens Krauss and Baldur von Schirach to help, for they were on good terms with Berlin, but they declined. Furtwängler did not hesitate. He was already the "friend of criminals," so what was there to lose in helping an infamous composer-felon?

"We Germans," he wrote to Goebbels, "will make ourselves ridiculous in the eyes of the rest of the world if we neglect to honor the birthday of our greatest living composer."[35] To the end of his dealings with the Nazis, Furtwängler appealed to the sense of national image in foreign relations, no matter how absurd the approach may have become at this point in the war: *We* Germans . . . make *ourselves* . . . if *we* neglected . . . *our* greatest composer.[36] Goebbels and Hitler agreed with Furtwängler and permission was soon issued for the premiere of *Die Liebe der Danaë.* The acceleration in saturation bombing, however, was reaching its zenith in the summer of 1944, and Goebbels ordered all theaters closed before the work could be presented.

Richard Strauss was a major celebrity despite his bad odor with the Nazis, and it was only "good business" for him that Furtwängler

34. Personal conversation with the author, Paris, 22 April 1989.
35. Source: Furtwängler File, Berlin Document Center.
36. See *Kraftprobe*, pp. 85–143, for a fuller discussion of Furtwängler's numerous and complicated attempts to salvage what was left of German culture after the Nazi takeover of 1933.

should help him, for any attempt meant headaches for the Nazi propaganda machine. What was truly "bad business" for Furtwängler at this time was to help persecuted people who no longer meant anything to him professionally. But Furtwängler continued to help as many people as he could even if he had disagreements with them, and he never forgot a friend. In 1942, in the midst of his own problems, a member of the Nationaltheater in Mannheim wrote to him about the illness of his old colleague Felix Lederer. Lederer had been second Kapellmeister at the Opera House under Furtwängler and occasionally conducted the Berlin Philharmonic in the 1920s at Furtwängler's invitation, but Furtwängler had not worked with him directly since he left Mannheim in 1920. In fact, he had not seen Lederer in many years. Lederer had now fallen on especially hard times. He was partly Jewish and had Jewish relatives whom he managed to protect through Furtwängler's intervention, but now he was ailing from heart disease and had entered a sanatorium for treatment and recuperation.

On 29 September 1942 Furtwängler replied:

Dear Herr Heimerich,

I am so pleased to hear from you after such a long time. How times have changed.

What you write about the fate of Lederer is very sad indeed. I want to contribute something toward his sanatorium bill and have instructed my secretary Frau von Rechenberg to phone you in order to learn where she should send my contribution of 300 RM.

With best wishes,[37]

This amount was no mean handout. It was worth more than a month's wages for a mid-level civil servant and certainly enough to cover a lengthy stay in the hospital at that time. Lederer recovered, survived the war, and taught at the Hochschule für Musik in Berlin until his death in 1957.

Furtwängler was not always as successful in helping people in trouble with the authorities. One of his saddest failures late in the war involved a brilliant young pianist named Karlrobert Kreiten, who had made disparaging remarks about the Nazis early in 1943 and had gotten himself arrested. Kreiten was a student of Claudio Arrau, and he was well on his way to a great concert career.[38] Up to the time he was arrested, he had made several recital tours and had appeared twice with the Berlin Philharmonic.[39] But Kreiten had a mouth almost as

37. Source: Mannheim Staatarchiv.
38. Evidence of his formative but formidable pianistic gifts can be heard on an album entitled *Karlrobert Kreiten: In Memoriam*, Thorofon Alternum ATH 259.
39. 14 March 1939 and 25 June 1941.

large as his talent. He argued with a friend of his mother's that he could not see how a "carpet biter" like Hitler could possibly win the war. That woman carelessly repeated the remark to two rabid Nazi supporters, Annmarie Windmöller and Tiny von Passevant who were educational supervisors in the Party.[40] Determined to bring the young man to justice, their repeated invectives finally got the Gestapo to act. After his arrest, Goebbels seized upon this opportunity to serve notice on all artists in the Reich. Kreiten was arrested and ultimately sentenced by the notorious president of the People's Tribunal, Dr. Roland Freisler[41] on 3 September 1943:

> Such a man [as Kreiten] has dishonored himself irrevocably. In spite of his professional achievements as an artist, he is a danger to our victory in our present struggle. He must be sentenced to death. Only then will our people be strong and united and undisturbed in pursuing victory.[42]

Kreiten's parents tried to have the sentence commuted, and Furtwängler personally got a senior security officer interested in the case. He was reassured that the whole matter would blow over in a few weeks. Indeed it did. Kreiten was beheaded on 7 September. He was 27 years old. A month later, Kreiten's parents received a bill from the Berlin Court Accountant for 639.20 Reichsmarks to cover the expenses for the execution.[43]

Goebbels used Kreiten to show everyone, including Furtwängler, that the government was not permitting special status to anyone, particularly artists. The wages of blaspheming, even a little, was now death. Had the young man uttered these remarks even a year earlier, he might have been given only a prison term. But Germany was losing the war by the summer of 1943. The worse the war became for Germany, the more intensely Goebbels persisted in whipping up the German people into a frenzy of false hope that left no room for negativity.

Was Kreiten's execution ordered out of spite for Furtwängler personally? Possibly. Nobody else in the Third Reich at this point was taking any kind of stand against the Nazis except Furtwängler.

40. Riess, p. 266.

41. Freisler presided over the trial of the accused in the July 20th Plot to assassinate Hitler. He died during an air raid in 1945.

42. Cited in *Kraftprobe*, p. 389.

43. Forty years later, Kreiten's ghost came back to haunt a Nazi journalist who had written an article applauding his execution. Werner Höfer became a famous and highly respected television commentator in Germany after the war, but his career ended in scandal in 1987, when he was accused of being the author of the article. The memoir Kreiten's father, Theo, published in 1945 *(Wen der Götter lieben . . .)* and a fascinating account of the decline and fall of Werner Höfer are both documented in *Tod eines Pianisten: Karlrobert Kreiten*, (Berlin) 1988.

Nobody who was even suspected of sedition escaped severe and sometimes mortal punishment—except Furtwängler.

Around the same time he was trying to help Kreiten in 1943, he
embarked upon another failed effort to save a blacklisted artist. Furtwängler heard that a gifted young composer named Richard Geyer
was being sent to the front as the Nazis mounted their last-ditch
attempt to stanch the Allied onslaught. Geyer was the son a of a poor
violin maker, but he had written some astonishingly mature pieces,
some of which Furtwängler had seen. After sending a written petition
on Geyer's behalf to the Propaganda Ministry, he tried to contact
Goebbels himself. But by this time, the German armies had been
beaten back from Stalingrad and the Axis powers had lost North
Africa. The Americans were in the war now, and rumors of a full-scale
land invasion of Europe by the Allies were rife in Germany. Goebbels
was frantically trying to get his futile Total War program into action
and had little time to pay attention to anything else.

The official who took Furtwängler's call told him that Goebbels
would be furious if he heard about the request to spare the boy and
hung up. Furtwängler personally went to the director of the musical
section at the Ministry, where he was similarly received. In fact, the
official was shocked that Furtwängler had dared to meddle in *Wehrmacht* affairs. Geyer went to the front to be used as cannon fodder.
Within a week, he was dead.[44]

Furtwängler wrote another letter to Goebbels:

> The most promising of Germany's musical resources are dying on the
> front while hundreds of cheap tunesmiths are doing what ever they want
> in their homes.[45]

This was vintage Furtwängler, blunt and to the point. But it was
also 1944. Himmler saw the letter and personally tried to persuade
Hitler to allow him to send Furtwängler to a concentration camp. Fury
quenched his bewilderment at Hitler's refusal, and he swiftly moved
Furtwängler's name to the top of his private blacklist.

For a long time, Hitler's Aryan master architect and close friend
Albert Speer had been an admirer of Furtwängler. He enjoyed a father-
son relationship with the Führer and built superb roads, public works
and buildings for the Nazis before the war. It was he who made
Hitler's vision of an Hellenic Germany into reality. While some of his
buildings were crassly mock-classical, a number of his architectural

44. Riess, pp. 267–268.
45. Riess, p. 268.

concepts remain imposing to this day as sleek inflations of Greek designs. His stadium for the 1936 Berlin Olympics certainly is one of them. Although he had turned against Hitler personally after 1941, he remained at his post as Hitler's munitions executive to the end of the war in order to prevent the wholesale destruction the Nazis planned after the inevitable surrender. After the failed July 20th Plot to kill Hitler, he devised his own assassination plan on Hitler, but Speer never put it into action.[46]

Since Speer was close to the lines of communications that revised the blacklist from day to day, he knew the Gestapo was after Furtwängler. According to Furtwängler's widow Elisabeth and his biographer Curt Riess, Speer's admiration for Furtwängler saved his life.[47]

During a concert in January 1945, a power failure interrupted the program for more than an hour. The Philharmonic had moved to Blüthner Hall near Potsdamerplatz now that the Philharmonie and the Staatsoper both had been destroyed, and Speer contrived to talk to Furtwängler casually during this interval. He asked him about his immediate concert plans. Furtwängler told him he was going to conduct in Switzerland soon. Speer nonchalantly suggested that he might want to remain abroad for a while. "After all, you look so very tired, Maestro." Furtwängler immediately understood what he meant.

Speer ultimately sent Furtwängler two more veiled warning messages, but they never reached their destination.[48] In the meantime, a woman connected with the Himmler household secretly told Furtwängler in March 1944 that Himmler did not intend to allow Furtwängler to survive the regime. In a short but harrowing meeting, she told him how Himmler had devised a plan to destroy what still remained of Germany after the surrender. The Nazis' Total War would ultimately be turned upon Germany itself. It then finally became clear to Furtwängler that a "traitor" to the Party like himself might soon be liquidated. The woman later came to his house in the early morning and told him he already had been outlawed by the Party because he had been implicated in the bungled July 20th Plot on Hitler's life. This meant that no one in Germany would be allowed to speak to him or have anything to do with him. Himmler's revenge was at hand.

46. See Albert Speer's account of his life *Inside the Third Reich*, translated by Richard and Clara Winston, (New York) 1970, pp. 429–431. Speer was the only defendant at the Nürnberg Trials to admit his guilt in the crimes perpetrated by the Third Reich and stated that he was probably as close as anyone had come to being a friend of Adolf Hitler. He was sentenced to twenty years at Spandau.

47. Elisabeth Furtwängler, personal conversation with the author, Paris, 22 April 1989; Riess, 268–271.

48. Riess, p. 272.

By this time, though, Furtwängler had moved Elisabeth and his family to Switzerland. She was pregnant and he wanted her to have the child with proper medical care. "All of a sudden, he seemed to wake from a dream," she recalled to me. "We were living outside Linz in Austria at the time, and he suddenly told me we should move to Switzerland. He knew that the Gestapo was after him, and he finally took all the warnings seriously."[49]

Furtwängler still had a few concerts in Vienna before his engagements in Switzerland, and he travelled to Vienna with his friend and sound engineer Friedrich Schnapp. They left Berlin on the night train on 24 January, arriving the next day in Vienna. When they got to the Hotel Imperial, a suite for Furtwängler had been reserved but there was no room available for Schnapp. Furtwängler protested vigorously, but to no avail, and Schnapp eventually found accommodation at the Bristol located across the street. When he returned to the Imperial, he found Furtwängler in the bathroom sitting next to the bathtub filled with hot water. The weather was frigid and there was no heat in the Imperial, but there was plenty of hot water. Furtwängler was warming his hands over the tub. The covered toilet seat supported a fine set of china, and Furtwängler asked Schnapp to bring in a box from the sitting room. It turned out to be a buttercream birthday cake sent by the Gauleiter of Vienna, Baldur von Schirach. Such a delicacy was all but impossible to obtain at this point in the war, but Schirach was nothing if not a gentleman who prided himself on remembering such occasions. So Furtwängler celebrated his 59th birthday over the toilet seat of his suite, as Schnapp demanded to know why newsreel cameras had not yet arrived to record the event.[50]

The next three days were taken up with rehearsals, concerts and a recording session with the Vienna Philharmonic. The program consisted of The Brahms Second, Beethoven's *Third Leonore Overture*, and a new work Furtwängler was adding to his repertoire at Schnapp's suggestion: the Symphony in D minor by César Franck. On the day of his first Vienna concert, he slipped on the ice, fell, and sustained a concussion. Nonetheless, he conducted the concert. It looked as though Furtwängler might not be able to return to Berlin, but he told Schnapp several times that he would be going back to conduct scheduled concerts with the Berlin Philharmonic scheduled for 4 and 5 February.

49. Personal conversation with the author, Paris, 23 April 1989.
50. Schnapp gave Gert Fischer this account of Furtwängler's birthday. The full story appears in the liner notes of the Société Wilhelm Furtwängler CD release of Furtwängler's last concert in Vienna before the end of the war, which Schnapp supervised. SWF 902. The recording was made during the concert in the Gesellschaft der Musikfreunde on 28 February.

Schnapp thought it peculiar that Furtwängler would mention such a detail to him so many times. Finally, Schnapp went back to Berlin alone. Just before he left, Furtwängler embraced him and said, "We shall meet again in better times."

Meanwhile, the Russians were advancing into Austria and soon would arrive in Vienna. Panic was besetting the city. Furtwängler called aside Otto Strasser, the General Manager of the orchestra, and counseled him to advise the orchestra to stay calm and *together*. Regardless of what might happen, the Vienna Philharmonic must remain a group. Under no conditions should its members scatter and flee. He believed that the Soviets had an appreciation of cultural matters and would not harm them.[51] The events of the following weeks proved his advice sage. The Philharmonic, its members, and their concert hall—the Musikverein—survived the heavy Allied air strikes in the coming weeks. But saturation bombing levelled many parts of the city, and the Staatsoper fell to cinder and ashes on Black Monday, 12 March 1945.

Furtwängler left Vienna before the worst attacks damaged the Imperial and destroyed the inner city, but he was almost prevented from leaving because he slipped on an ice patch the day before his intended departure and suffered a concussion. As the hour approached for his journey to Switzerland, his secretary received a telephone call in the middle of the night from the Foreign Office in Berlin. A certain Dr. Schatz demanded to know who had given Furtwängler an exit visa. All such passes were to be cleared through his office. Furtwängler's secretary Agathe von Tiedemann told Schatz he was in bed sleeping off a concussion. Schatz slammed the phone down.[52] The Swiss consul general in Vienna understood the situation and gave Furtwängler an exit visa on his own authority. Furtwängler then left the Hotel Imperial through the service entrance in Dumba-

---

51. Personal conversation with the author, Vienna, 9 April 1990. See also Strasser, p. 192. Furtwängler's advice turned out to be prescient. The Soviets had the Philharmonic performing even before the surrender. Furtwängler was not so sure they would treat him as kindly, a sobering thought that may have contributed to his decision to escape to Switzerland. In the 1960s, however, the Soviets released a recording of a concert in which Furtwängler supposedly conducts the Vienna Philharmonic in Glazunov's symphonic poem *Stenka Razin*, Op. 13 presumably on 2 February. (Melodya M10 46683 000.) Furtwängler left Vienna on 31 January, and Otto Strasser does not recall the Vienna Philharmonic performing that work at any time during this period. This bogus release bears grim testimony to the kind of works Furtwängler almost certainly would have been forced to add to his repertoire had he remained and survived the contract the Gestapo now had put out on his life. Witness the liner notes: "This was the only work by Glazunov that the great musician chose [italics mine] to conduct, and it is especially significant that the performance took place not long before the Austrian capital was liberated by the Soviet army."

52. Riess, p. 271.

strasse during the early hours of the morning, boarded a milk train going west, made several changes, and finally disembarked at Dornbirn near the Swiss border. Here he stayed with strangers who had been recommended to him by friends in Vienna.

Shortly after his arrival at Dornbirn, Furtwängler sent a telegram to von Tiedemann, asking her to call a Dornbirn number, signing it "Wilhelm." Miraculously, the Gestapo overlooked the telegram. He told her where he was and what he was about to do. When he got to the border, he noticed that all other passports had been stamped. He asked the official at the barrier why his had not been stamped. The man looked at the document for a long time. Finally, he decided that it must have been an oversight, stamped the visa, and waved Furtwängler along. A few minutes later, he was in Switzerland.[53]

He later told his wife, "'That man at the border saved my life. I don't know if he recognized me or not. He kept looking at the passport and then up at me, and he finally said nothing and motioned me along.' Wilhelm never saw him again."[54]

53. Riess, p. 272.
54. Personal conversation with the author, Paris, 22 April 1989.

17

Trial by
Patience

Furtwängler learned later that Swiss immigration offices at every border entry had been alerted to his arrival. He was to be allowed into the country even if he arrived on skis. The general populace, however, was not nearly as accommodating when they learned he was to conduct in Zürich and Winterthur. On one hand, the small nation was sharply divided about harboring a "Nazi propagandist," as he was frequently called in the Swiss press.[1] On the other hand, Switzerland had long been a democracy, and many of the Swiss were wary about the consequences of suppressing anybody, even an alleged Nazi. Furtwängler, of course, had been no stranger to Switzerland as a non-political individual in recent years when its neutrality was respected by both Nazi Germany and the Allied powers. He had taken numerous tours there with the Berlin and Vienna Philharmonics, conducted several guest engagements with Swiss orchestras, and gave Zürich memorable performances of *Fidelio*, *Walküre*, and *Meistersinger* in 1939, *Götterdämmerung* in 1942, and *Siegfried* as recently as 1944. Now that Germany was moribund, however, Furtwängler the "Staatsrat"—the State Councilor—suddenly was regarded as a leading member of the Third Reich, a figure whose presence might compromise Switzerland's purity as a neutral country in the eyes of the victorious Allies. This, at any rate, was the line of reasoning several politicians

1. Riess, pp. 273–274.

seized to further their own ends. One member of the Workers Party introduced a proposal in the Municipal Council on 12 February to ban Furtwängler from performing on the grounds that it would threaten Switzerland's foreign policy.[2] Not to be outdone by their political rivals, the Social Democrats issued a statement in the *Volksrecht* four days later, calling for a ban on Furtwängler "because of the man himself and his political frame of mind." An editorial in one of the papers wondered what exactly that meant.[3]

Despite demands from other council members for an explanation, Furtwängler's first concert in Zürich scheduled for 20 February was summarily canceled by the Municipal and State Councils.[4] Most of the local papers vigorously protested this blatant show of fear and hypocrisy:

> If the City Council were to cancel the concert because it was pressured by threats that rabble-rousers would interrupt it or injure the audience, we could understand its action to some extent. But its decision shows they feel it is not worth risking such an incident.[5]

The *Neue Zürcher Zeitung* warned the Swiss not to repeat Germany's mistakes in 1933:

> The "Furtwängler Case" really should be called the "Case of The Zürich City Council." It is unseemly not only in a cultural respect, but is serious enough politically to warrant the cry: Beware the beginnings! Such actions cannot and will not get us anywhere at a time when the war strives against the urge to seize the "politics of the streets" as a means of arousing passion.[6]

Angry demonstrations followed. One was staged by the students of Zürich University, who felt the cancellation endangered the principles of academic freedom. Furtwängler was allowed to conduct at Winterthur a few days later, but hecklers there staged a demonstration against him and threw stink bombs. Ultimately, the crowd had to be dispersed by police using water hoses. Swiss musicians also entered

2. The Councilor was Dr. Harry Gmur (Partei der Arbeit), representing a district of Zürich.

3. "Wer regiert Zürich? Skandal um Furtwängler," *Die Tat*, 21 February 1945.

4. Wilhelm Vontebel, the representative to the Municipal Council from Landesring, led the protest: "Is the State Council prepared to give a full explanation of the compelling reasons why Dr. Furtwängler has been forbidden to appear?" *Tages-Anzeiger*, 21 February 1945.

5. *Die Tat*, 21 February 1945.

6. 22 February 1945.

the fray, deploring the fact that politicians were using music for their political power plays.

Meanwhile, Furtwängler visited his wife Elisabeth in Zürich, where she had given birth to their son Andreas in November 1944. Friends advised him to leave public life for a while. For once, he willingly took their advice, primarily because he was still suffering residual effects from the concussion sustained during his fall in Vienna. What is more, his life was now in danger, both from his own exhaustion and from Nazi agents out to liquidate him. Ironically, he now found himself outlawed in Switzerland as a representative of the very government that was putting a contract out on him. He entered a nursing home at Clarens in February 1945 where he recuperated and waited for the collapse of the Thousand Year Reich.

The inevitable came on 30 April 1945 as Hitler's death was announced over the Nazi radio network. It was ten days after Hitler's 54th birthday. Recordings of the slow movement of Bruckner's Seventh Symphony and Siegfried's Funeral March from *Götterdämmerung* and other appropriately solemn music followed the announcement. Ironically again, most of the selections were conducted by the fugitive Furtwängler, enemy of the Third Reich, now convalescing in a Swiss nursing home.

As soon as the end came, however, Furtwängler found himself a criminal yet again, this time in the eyes of the victorious Allied forces, and though he had no way of knowing it at the time, he was now in very serious trouble indeed. His status as a Staatsrat—State Councilor, the position Göring had thrust upon him and had refused him permission to resign—was now the incriminating mark that made him "a danger to public security." His name was placed on a list of 327 persons in the arts, all of whom were under suspicion for their part in upholding the Third Reich. These cases were, of course, but a tiny fraction of the total number of individuals screened between 1945 and 1949. In all, over 12.4 million individuals were placed under suspicion and brought before 450 tribunals throughout Germany.[7] Reports abounded that Furtwängler would be extradited and tried as a war criminal; this at the very time when *Symphony and Love*, the film about the Berlin Philharmonic by Goebbels' devoted director Paul Verhoeven, was playing to packed houses all over Switzerland. Nobody seemed to notice the lies, the distortions of facts, or the curious absence in the film of the conductor most closely connected with the orchestra. If nothing else, Goebbels' propaganda films were solid entertainment.

7. Almost four million cases were reviewed in the American sector alone. See John D. Montgomery, *Forced to Be Free*, (Chicago) 1957, pp. 26–27, and Fitzgibbon, p. 164.

In the meantime, the Soviets entered Vienna, and the Russian Commandant promptly produced the first postwar concert by the Vienna Philharmonic. None other than Clemens Krauss was awarded the distinction of conducting it. No one had forgotten that Krauss had been a willing Nazi collaborator, and the chaos at the end of the war had not retarded the rate gossip always traveled in Vienna. It was not long before Krauss disappeared for a while.

In Berlin, the Philharmonic had given concerts right up to the end of the war in Blüthner Hall off Potsdamerplatz. On the morning the Germans surrendered to the Allies, the orchestra was in the midst of a rehearsal. Many musicians escaped Berlin. Others simply went home. Their instruments were taken to Plessenburg, not far from Kulmbach, so that they would not be plundered or confiscated by the Allies. But they disappeared anyway.

Furtwängler's apartment in Potsdam was occupied by several Russians, one of them a captain in the Soviet army. He had been well-educated, and he knew of Furtwängler. After a group of marauding Russian soldiers came to take Furtwängler's grand piano away, he wrote a note and gave it to the man sharing part of the apartment. When more soldiers came to take other things away, they were shown the note. They left immediately, and the piano was returned promptly.[8]

Throughout this time, Furtwängler remained in Switzerland. Ernest Ansermet asked him to conduct his orchestra in Geneva, L'Orchestre de la Suisse Romande. An oboist protested that he should be barred from conducting because he had performed in occupied France during the war. He produced a female journalist who was prepared to testify under oath that she had seen him appear in Lyons. Ansermet asked her to describe Furtwängler. She described him as "stout with mutton chop whiskers." She was, of course, describing Clemens Krauss.

Rumors and prevarications about Furtwängler proliferated. It was impossible to deny each one because there were so many of them, and simply refuting each of them might only have imputed credence to them. He was, for example, reported to have been a frequent guest at Hitler's home. He allegedly took Gestapo agents with the Berlin Philharmonic and the Vienna Philharmonic on their tours abroad. Worst and most persistent of all, he was supposed to have fired all the Jews in the Berlin Philharmonic and personally selected Jewish musicians to be sent to concentration camps.[9]

All these stories gained credibility primarily because of two unde-

8. Riess, pp. 276–277.
9. As late as 1983, Ira Hirschmann made this allegation in the *New York Times* (30 September).

niably damning circumstances. First, Furtwängler remained in Germany when he could have gone into exile. Second, he simply was guilty by association. If the great Furtwängler had *anything* to do with the Nazis, his political and criminal involvement with them must have been just as great. While many prominent German artists abroad were astonished by Furtwängler's gall in standing up to the Nazis, they were embarrassed by it too. A good many of them, indeed, some of whom he had helped escape, declared that Furtwängler stayed behind because the Nazis gave him the run of German musical affairs and lavish blandishments.

In any event, the Austrians made an inquiry at the instigation of the Allies that resulted on 9 March 1946 in a "denazification" hearing.

Denazification was a rubric referring to a policy formulated by the Allies even before the war ended. The concept was also the most obvious by-product of the philosophical objectives fostered by the Allies as the war entered the phase known as Endgame. As the victors entered Germany to implement their philosophy, denazification became a means of proving that the war had been an ideological conflict, a sort of a Holy War against the evil of Nazism. The war with Germany, in other words, had really been waged against Nazism, not the German people. Thus, the rationale behind such events as the Nürnberg War Crimes Tribunal and countless other less spectacular trials amounted to a process of exorcism to purge the vanquished Third Reich from its Nazi past by trying those who aided and abetted it.

But the Allies faced several peculiar problems in putting denazification into practice after Germany of the Third Reich surrendered unconditionally. In order to denazify Germany, they first had to determine what Nazism was and who indeed was a Nazi. They then had to decide the degree to which those accused were involved in carrying out or supporting Nazism. With the exception of obvious criminal acts—murder, vandalism, physical violence, etc.—less demonstrable acts such as collusion, "service," and some culpable nonviolent acts such as dismissals carried out under orders of Nazi supervision frequently could not fit neatly into formulated definitions of Nazism.

The notion of Nazism was complicated further by the fact that the defeated nation was now split into four parts or sectors. The Soviet Union took supervision of the eastern Sector, the British occupied the northwest, the French moved into the Rhineland-Palatinate, Saar, Baden and Württemberg in the southwest, and the Americans took most of southern Germany. Although Berlin was located in the Soviet zone, it became a microcosm of the current state of Germany at that time. It also was split up into four areas, one for each of the conquering nations. The Soviets took advantage of having Berlin in their sector, and ultimately East Berlin became the capital of a new Soviet East Germany, while Bonn became the seat of government in West Germany. Although the four victorious powers were in complete agreement about vanquishing the Nazis and the evil they represented through military means, they each had their own agendas for liberating the survivors of that regime from "Nazism." To standardize their prosecution of Nazism, the Allies ultimately passed *Control Council Law No. 10: Punishment of Persons Guilty of War Crimes, Crimes against Peace and Against Humanity*.[10] Under this policy directive, those ultimately deemed to be "Nazis" in one way or another were divided into two large and amorphous groups: Criminals and Accomplices or Big Nazis and Little Nazis. For some reason, the Americans in particular appeared to be making assiduous attempts to characterize Furtwängler as a "big" Nazi, but his record clearly showed that he could at best be accused of being a "little" Nazi who had acted in a big way by giving the Nazis a respectable gloss. But did Furtwängler give the Nazis that gloss willingly? The Americans were determined to prove it beyond a shadow.

Now that Furtwängler was deemed suspicious, he could be charged under any or all of three headings:

1. War Crimes or violations of customs of war such as ill treatment or enslavement of prisoners of war or civilian populations
2. Crimes against peace or invasions of countries in violation of international law or treaties
3. Crimes Against Humanity or atrocities committed on political, racial, or religious grounds

It was also clear, as we will soon see, that only the second of these categories could barely accommodate the charges about to be brought against him. But as a celebrity, Furtwängler's inclusion among those suspected made him a symbol of the entire German nation and identified his name and face with those now culpable *en masse* of "crimes against peace." While nearly 17 million people, collectively or individually, could hardly be put on trial, the logic behind nailing Furtwängler was quite clear: Convicting a non-military luminary like Furtwängler of something—*anything*—might go a long way toward satisfying the punitive motive that lay beneath all the cant about denazification as a means of liberating the entire German population from its Nazi past.

So putting Furtwängler on trial advanced still another notion at

10. *Official Gazette* of the Control Council, 31 January 1946.

the root of this policy: the concept of "collective guilt." This principle stemmed in part from a pre-medieval dictum that led to justifying a wide variety of mayhem such as the persecution of all Jews for killing Christ and legitimizing wholesale destruction by the British in their colonial wars against insurgents in India and in the Middle East during the 19th century. Now, in the middle of the 20th century, all Germans were held culpable, whether or not they had been Nazi Party members, all Germans were viewed as party to the horrors of Auschwitz and Theresienstadt, and so on. This philosophical stance taken by the Allies deeply embittered Germans who already were enduring the hell of annihilation and who now were witnessing former Nazis, many of whom had committed no offense except joining the Party, being summarily dismissed from their jobs and replaced by so-called non-Nazis while others who had committed crimes were going free with little more than token punishments. Why, went the vanquished German line of reasoning, should certain individuals be "tried" if every individual—Nazi or non-Nazi—was guilty in the first place? This contradiction remains a source of rancor for many Germans even 50 years later.[11]

There was no doubt that the Allies were trying to heap such guilt onto Furtwängler. During his proscription, he reflected on the concept, and his *Notebooks* show that he rejected it:[12]

> I have never understood collective responsibility . . . Contrary to all reason . . . realistic feeling . . . all Christian principle, all justice, an entire people was made responsible for all the transgressions committed by a criminal clique and its organs, using all the means of terror and lies and provocation at its disposal.
>
> Those outside have no idea of the hatred that this system has long provoked among upright Germans . . .   *1945, p. 156*

The military branches of the occupying forces were supposed to start the trials off and phase them into German civilian courts as soon as possible, so that denazification could become a *German* process rather than an externally imposed procedure. But the Allies found the project as troubling to put into practice as the Germans found it philosophically controversial. The defeated were fully expecting harsh justice to be meted out to them. But what they got instead was humbug and pseudo-legal bureaucracy, made all the worse by their own people

11. It is an issue raised in Michael Verhoeven's film *The Nasty Girl*. See Chapter 14.

12. To his wife, however, Furtwängler confided that all Germans would be blamed anyway for the atrocities the Nazis had committed. Personal conversation with the author, Paris, 22 April 1989.

increasingly absorbing this bogus operation from the Allies, creating an acrimonious climate of confrontation in which "cleared" non-Nazis were sitting in judgment of their unwashed Nazi peers.[13]

The practicality of this objective to prosecute the collective malfeasance of all Germans may have been questionable, but all adult Germans became subject anyway to filling out questionnaires known as *Fragebogen*, and Furtwängler was no exception. If enough suspicion could be raised from the answers in these questionnaires or through denunciations by other Germans, an individual could be brought before a denazification tribunal. Persons ultimately found guilty could face:

1. Death
2. Imprisonment up to life, with or without hard labor
3. Fine with or without imprisonment or hard labor
4. Restitution of property wrongfully acquired
5. Deprivation of all or some civil rights

If Furtwängler was found guilty of anything, he would almost certainly be fined, imprisoned and/or deprived even further of his civil rights.

As the denazification proceedings began throughout Germany, most Germans felt that much of the tribunal process was hardly a legal procedure in the cause of justice or even of purging an evil ideology. Instead, they viewed these investigations as vehicles for legalizing revenge against the Nazi leaders and others whom the Allies simply wished to punish.[14] Regardless of what their real purpose may have been, Control Council Law No. 10 became the major instrument by which each of the four victorious Allied powers separately and—for the most part—independently set out to cleanse Germany of its evil past, bring to justice those whom they deemed culpable in participating in that evil, denazify what was left of the German nation, and cultivate a resurgence of morality based on Judaeo-Christian principles. By and large, they were quite successful in weeding out the worst offenders.

13. John Gimbel in *The American Occupation of Germany: Politics and the Military 1945–1949*, (Stanford) 1968, argues vigorously that denazification policies, at least those formulated by the Americans, were much more clear-sighted and mindful of revitalizing Germany than prevailing opinion suggests.

14. But eyewitnesses who were in Germany at the time also reported that a good number of those same Germans could not or would not say what ought to be done to those who committed the atrocities that were being reported over the radio in an endless nightmarish litany. See James Stern, *The Hidden Damage*, (New York) 1947, pp. 79–81.

This policy (at least for the United States, Britain, and France), also contained a not so covert intention: inculcating a revolution among the defeated masses against the old order, namely totalitarianism.[15] This aim was not lost upon the Germans, but in viewing some of these tribunals, they felt more revulsion than an impulse for revolution. In their eyes, it was bad enough to have so-called non-Nazis judging their bona fide Nazi peers. But the mechanics of these civilian tribunals— more often than not—were farcical: poorly organized, incompetently run, and lacking a clear-cut forensic or prosecutorial focus. With the exception of the Nürnberg War Crimes Trials, in which the remnants of the top Nazi echelon were fully and justifiably tried, they could see all too clearly that many "trials" of lesser Nazis, or even suspected wrong-doers were punishments in themselves, latter-day *autos-da-fé* that luridly flexed the conquerors' moral machismo.

In Austria, however, the denazification process flowed fairly smoothly, as the authorities there promptly proceeded to set up a Commission to study the political background of prospective artists, producers, conductors, and stage personnel for the newly reorganized Vienna Staatsoper and the Burgtheater. Furtwängler's history under the Nazis was carefully reviewed. On 9 March 1946 the Commission came to two conclusions:[16]

> 1. Furtwängler was never a member of the Nazi Party or any of the organizations subsidiary to the Party. In a number of instances he proved himself to be a definite opponent of the Nazi philosophy of life and cultural policy, and he took this stand regardless of personal and professional disadvantages to himself.
> 2. The resumption of Furtwängler's activities would contribute greatly to the reconstruction of musical life in Austria.

But the Allied Commandatura in Germany rejected the Austrian commission's findings and decided that Furtwängler would also have to prove himself guiltless in Berlin. This development followed word reaching the Americans that the Austrians were lenient with Furtwängler because he had made some sort of deal with them in order to become an Austrian citizen. A switch in citizenship would certainly have made everything easier for Furtwängler in his present situation, but he later said, "I always regarded myself as a German and an international representative of German music, and I am regarded as such now." Had he been deprived of his German citizenship, as Bruno Wal-

15. The Soviets were interested only in absorbing Germany into *their* totalitarian empire, and they pursued that policy aggressively.
16. Riess, p. 278.

ter and Thomas Mann had been, he would have seriously considered the passport the Austrians were offering him. But he had remained in Germany on firm convictions about his German identity when expedient options were open to him. Now that the integrity of that identity was being challenged, he was determined to remain a German while he was under fire.

If Furtwängler was not going to take the easy way out, he had no idea how arduous the path left to him would be. Now that the Allies had rejected the Austrian Commission's findings about his innocence of any culpability in the Third Reich, his status was still that of a suspected war criminal. Under no circumstances could Furtwängler resume his activities as a musician in Germany until his case was acted upon by the Allied Commandatura in Berlin.

Early in April 1946, the Allies started legal proceedings against him in Berlin. He received a message ordering him to submit a memorandum about himself to the Denazification Tribunal for Artists located in Schlütterstrasse off the Kurfürstendamm. He also received the *Fragebogen*, an extensive questionnaire that everybody was required to fill out.

Furtwängler complied immediately and submitted both the completed questionnaire and the memorandum about himself, but he was unable to learn when his case would be heard. General John McClure, who was in charge of the Information Control Service for the Allies, informed Curt Riess that "a mistake" had been made in Furtwängler's case. McClure promised Riess that Furtwängler would be able to work again "in about four weeks."[17]

Four weeks came and went with no word about the date of his trial. Furtwängler remained in Clarens and used the time to take his first unfettered rest since before the war. During this period he completed his Second Symphony in E minor. It became his most enduring work to date, far more mature and inspired than his earlier pieces. Written in the tonal style of the late 19th century, harmonically inventive, wide in dynamic scope, the work evolved into a highly personal statement of loneliness in a world in which he was out of tune in more ways than he ever could have imagined. As a musical extension of Furtwängler's persona, this symphony and his other works have been almost as much a source of controversy as Furtwängler himself.

While he was busily composing, the Soviets approached him about taking over the Staatsoper Unter den Linden, which now was located in the sector of Berlin controlled by them. According to Curt

17. Riess, p. 282.

Riess, the British expressed hopes that Furtwängler could take up his post with the Berlin Philharmonic which was situated in their section of the city. The Soviets were the most forthcoming in their offers, but the Americans opposed Furtwängler having anything to do with them. He followed the advice of friends and put the Russians off, hoping his case would be settled quickly. For some reason, the British could not match their hopes about Furtwängler resuming his podium with any effective action, so he was obliged to remain inactive.

Furtwängler had many sympathizers abroad, especially in America, but only two of them spoke up for him in public. The most vocal was the violinist Yehudi Menuhin. He was Jewish and had no reason to support Furtwängler, but numerous inquiries he made convinced him that Furtwängler was no Nazi. Friedelind Wagner, the composer's granddaughter, was virtually the only other person besides Menuhin actively to take Furtwängler's part. She had emigrated to the United States in 1941 because she was disgusted with Nazi Germany and had become an American citizen four years later.[18] While most other émigrés from Nazi Germany were forced out or left when they had no other recourse, Friedelind was one of the very few who left voluntarily out of political conviction.[19] But she also had a unique understanding of the dilemma faced by Furtwängler and the other artists and intellectuals who hated the regime. In an article published in the American periodical *Musical Courier* on 15 March 1945, she defended Furtwängler's decision to remain in Germany:

> . . . In sticking it out, his life between 1933 and 1945 was like walking a tightrope between exile and the gallows. I do hope that nobody will now start blaming him for not getting hanged voluntarily and joyfully!
>
> The other day somebody attacked Furtwängler with this most ethical argument: "Besides, he could have made more money if he had left Germany!" Certainly he could have, but he obviously felt that art was more important than a fat bank account.

Later in the article, she recalled with an eyewitness account how the Nazis treated him while she was still living in Germany:

> The Nazis kicked and wooed him in succession—disliking and distrusting him on one hand, on the other trying so hard to keep up a front of

18. Frau Wagner lived in Switzerland until her death on 8 May 1991, but she retained her American citizenship to the end.

19. For a moving narrative of one such émigré who made every effort to remain in Germany despite his enormous difficulties with the Nazis, see Elaine Hochman's life of Mies van der Rohe, *Architects of Fortune*, (New York) 1989.

"business as usual" towards the world. They tried to threaten him into again accepting an official position, to no avail.

In 1936, during a big reception in our house, Goebbels, Göring, and Hitler cornered him and tried everything to make him accept, climaxing in Hitler's shrill threat that he would send him to a concentration camp— and Furtwängler's calm answer: "Herr Reichskanzler, I will find myself there only in the very best company!" This so surprised Hitler that he couldn't answer, but vanished from the room.

In another part of the article, she referred to the rivalry between Furtwängler and Toscanini, and Toscanini felt traduced.

"When Toscanini saw the article, he rang me up in a fury," Frau Wagner recalled to me. "'What interest do you have in this affair?' He demanded to know. I simply told him '*La verità*.'" He slammed the phone down and didn't speak to me for months.

"But I can say this much," she continued. "I can't tell you how many people pushed me into dark corners of Carnegie Hall and all along 57th Street in New York, whispering how grateful they were that I wrote the article. They said I spoke for them because they couldn't say anything in favor of Furtwängler. The big agents and the musicians union were against Furtwängler."[20]

Among those who thanked her was the conductor Fritz Stiedry who later headed the German wing at the Metropolitan Opera. While he could do little for Furtwängler in New York, he wrote a letter to Ernst Lothar, an Austrian-Jewish theater critic and formerly an assistant to Max Reinhardt, who had emigrated to the United States and had returned to Vienna to head the Cultural Affairs Section of the Occupation Forces. He apprised Lothar of Furtwängler's stand against the Nazis and admonished him "not to touch one hair on Furtwängler's head."[21]

Even if Furtwängler had been able to conduct freely during this time, he would have had a most difficult time getting an engagement outside Germany. His decision to remain in the Third Reich had "tainted" him, and none of his colleagues, especially in America, wanted to be contaminated through being associated with him. Bruno Walter was among those who understandably wanted to avoid having

20. Personal conversation with the author, Mainz, 6 October 1990. As we will see later, the Musicians' Union Local 802 as well as the most powerful of the artists' representatives of that time were indeed against Furtwängler.

21. Lothar discovered that Stiedry's defense of Furtwängler was well-founded when he researched Furtwängler's file and heard the testimony of others. Everyone defended Furtwängler vehemently. Lothar subsequently met with Furtwängler in Zürich, and they formed a lasting friendship. See his memoir *Das Wunder des Ueberlebens*, (Vienna) 1960, pp. 322–323.

anything to do with him. Having emigrated to America after being terrorized by the Nazis, Walter probably gained more than any other German-speaking conductor through his expulsion. After Furtwängler, he, Klemperer and Kleiber were Germany's foremost conductors, but Walter had the most success during and after the war, even though Walter's career in Germany had already seen its best days in 1933. There were really no new challenges left for him.[22]

But America presented him with numerous opportunities and he made the most of them at the Metropolitan Opera and later with the New York Philharmonic. Walter knew that Furtwängler was no Nazi and firmly withstood all attempts by anti-Nazi groups in the United States to make him join the cabal against his younger colleague, but he also wanted to avoid having to stand next to him or defend him openly in public. The distasteful prospect of having to submit himself to such an indignity became all but probable when he was invited to conduct at the Edinburgh Festival in September 1947. It was with no little consternation that he reacted to reports that Furtwängler had also been invited.[23] The Festival was still over a year away, but on 26 March 1946 Walter set about making the conditions of his acceptance quite clear in a letter to the Festival's director, Rudolf Bing:

> I do not want to come into contact with any Nazis or find myself "in the same boat" with them. So I must know, who besides myself, will conduct concerts of the Vienna Philharmonic in Edinburgh or in London. *There was a rumor that Furtwängler would be invited. In no way do I want to protest against any colleague's activity. So, if Furtwängler should come, I have nothing to say to that. But I want you to know and you can keep this confidential, that in this case, I would not conduct at the Festival. And, of course, my position would be the same if another conductor with Nazi affiliations would appear with the orchestra in England.* Can you give me any information about this point?[24]

Two days later, he drafted another version of this letter deleting the sentences in italics (which are mine). But it is not clear which version of the paragraph he sent. In any event, Walter had little to fear. Furtwängler did not appear at all in Edinburgh until 1948.

22. Aside from their musical gifts, Walter and Kleiber were among Germany's foremost conductors until 1933 because they held the most prestigious positions in German musical life except for Furtwängler's. Walter headed the Municipal Opera in Berlin and the Gewandhaus in Leipzig, and Kleiber was chief conductor at the Berlin Staatsoper.

23. Furtwängler was in no position to accept or reject such offers at the time because of the Allied ban on his activity pending his denazification.

24. Bruno Walter to Rudolf Bing, Edinburgh Festival, 26 and 28 March 1946. Source: Bruno Walter Collection, Lincoln Center Library for the Performing Arts, New York.

The entire summer of 1946 had passed as Furtwängler patiently waited for the Allies to set the trial date. But the long waiting period was not without its surprises. The war had left the major cities in both Germany and Austria devastated, thousands of people were still homeless, and those who were fortunate in having a roof over their heads were vulnerable to robberies and vandalism. The apartment of a singer named Augusta Kraft-Bella was burglarized during this time and its contents strewn about. She was a divorcee and living in the small flat with her daughter, a 25-year-old pianist and student of Emil von Sauer, whose budding concert career had been cut short by the turn in Germany's fortunes. Dagmar helped her mother tidy the mess, and, while she was cleaning up, she found a series of letters addressed to her mother, all in the same hand. One of the letters had fallen out of the envelope and she read it. And then another. They all were from Furtwängler. She showed them to her mother.

"She looked at them," recalls Dagmar Bella-Sturli, "and she finally said to me, 'Without Furtwängler, you would not have been born.'"[25]

Furtwängler had adopted two of his four acknowledged illegitimate children—Wilhelm and Fredericka—but he learned about the latest addition to his "family" in an unusual way. Many years later, Bella-Sturli recounted the incident to me:

> I wrote him a letter that began, "Dear Father . . ." He may have been a little surprised to read that. After that we became very close, but I must say that was primarily because Elisabeth encouraged him to be closer to all of us. She was a wonderful wife to him. She heard me play, and Furtwängler then arranged several recitals and concerts for me in Germany and in Austria. I also played with the Berlin Philharmonic, but he did not conduct. I played the E minor of Chopin.
>
> He told me when I played the Opus 31 no. 2, the 17th sonata ["Tempest"] of Beethoven, that he thought I played it better than Kempff! He was very sweet. I took that as a real compliment.[26]

In the autumn, Furtwängler became increasingly restive, for he had run out of money and was living in Switzerland on the generosity of friends. Dr. Werner Reinhard was an old friend who helped them find a home and obtain a residence permit. For all the periods of inac-

25. Personal conversation with the author, Vienna, 9 April 1990.

26. Bella-Sturli later played with Furtwängler and the Vienna Philharmonic in the Mozart Concerto for Two Pianos No. 10, KV 365, on 8 February 1949. Her colleague was Paul Badura-Skoda. This lively, idiomatic performance was preserved on tape. Société Wilhelm Furtwängler released it on LP: SWF 8401–8402. She also performed an abbreviated version of her father's Symphonie Concertante in Turin under Pietro Argento. She retired with the rank of Professor from the Conservatorium of the City of Vienna in 1988.

tivity he had lived through during the war, Furtwängler had never really been penniless, and his bourgeois background prevented him from living like a Bohemian. It now embarrassed him no end to have to count on friends for financial support when he had offers to work—especially from the Soviets—coming in all the time. The Furtwänglers lived in Clarens for almost two years without any income. In the meantime, his name was dragged through the mud in the press and the ubiquitous international rumor mill. Furtwängler had to keep himself muzzled because his promise to say nothing publicly about his rehabilitation or anything relating to it was one of the conditions the Swiss authorities placed on his residence permit.[27]

During this period, Furtwängler made a note in his diary:

> I have tried to analyze myself closely. I am no better than anybody else. I must always say what my instincts are. And there are two things: the love of my country and my people, who are a body-and-soul matter, and to have the strength of spirit for this challenge and ameliorate injustice.
>
> *Vermächtnis, p. 40*

In November Curt Riess went to Berlin and asked the staff of the Allied Commandatura when Furtwängler's case would be heard. When he was told that it might take up to a year, he informed them that he would advise Furtwängler to accept the post at the Berlin Staatsoper the Russians had been nagging him to take. Forty-eight hours later, an American officer telephoned him. Furtwängler's case was next on the Denazification Tribunal's docket in Berlin.[28]

27. Elisabeth Furtwängler gives a moving account of this period in her memoir *Über Wilhelm Furtwängler,* (Wiesbaden) 1979, pp. 114–141.
28. Riess, p. 286.

18

Day of Reckoning

The Tribunal for Artists in the case of Wilhelm Furtwängler assembled in Schlütterstrasse on 11 December 1946. Prominent people in the arts, the foreign press corps, musicians of the Berlin Philharmonic, clutches of photographers, radio engineers laying down wire and microphones, singers, actors, and a few of the general public who managed to obtain passes packed the small trial chamber. Outside, people unable to get in assembled and muttered to each other. Most of them felt the denazification process was stupid and insulting. Others complained bitterly that Furtwangler's trial (though it officially was never called a "trial") had been played up while the inquiries into other artists who had been extremely cooperative with the Nazis were being virtually ignored by the press.

Whether or not he had been a Nazi to any degree, Furtwängler's trial certainly was bound to be a public burning. And yet, he was oddly oblivious of that prospect, even though he wondered aloud why his day in court was being delayed for so long while bona fide Party members such as von Karajan had been walked through the process and were already working again.

We may never know *exactly* why it took a year and a half for Furtwängler's case to be scheduled, but there may be some simple explanations. In the first place, American officials were trying very hard to build a legitimate case against him, so they could hand the evidence over to his German peers who would try him. That took time because his record contained no evidence of specific crimes nor even connections to crimes. Secondly, the Americans supervising his trial may merely have wanted to postpone his trial because the war crimes trials at Nürnberg were in full swing from 20 November 1945 to 6 September 1946, and nothing could or should deflect attention from those events. Since the Allies viewed Furtwängler as a major celebrity of the Third Reich, however, the public the world over would be ready for the trial of Hitler's band leader by December. Such a plan would enable his anticipated conviction to reap the kind of attention from the media that the Americans surely felt it deserved. Finally, the Allies (i.e., Americans) gradually became aware that they had virtually nothing they could use to "get" Furtwängler, so the best they could do was detain him as long as possible.

In any event, Furtwängler set out for Wiesbaden early in November 1946 when he learned that his case might really be scheduled soon. He went there to discuss and prepare his case with the American Occupation Authorities. "The weather was frightfully cold," recalls Frau Furtwängler. "He told me there was no heat in the house where he stayed with friends, and he had to sleep with his overcoat and several blankets. He was lucky he did not catch influenza or something like that because he was prone to such illness. But some of the American authorities charged with assisting him for his day in court—as distinguished from those who were charged with building a case against him—were very helpful, and there were several people high up on the American staff who knew about his case and wanted to help him."[1] Helpful as he may have thought these Americans had been, they were not nearly helpful enough. What is more, he was soon to learn that the sympathetic treatment he received from those he met in Wiesbaden was hardly being imparted by some of their colleagues in Berlin where the trial would take place.

Just before it was to begin, one member of the Tribunal suddenly resigned.[2] The withdrawal was discreetly mentioned in *Der Kurier* while the trial was in progress, and it prompted a scandal that threatened to disrupt the proceedings.[3] Evidently, Karl Fischer-Walden's resignation was prompted by what he perceived to be unethical behavior on the part of the Allies:

1. Personal telephone conversation with the author, 29 November 1990.
2. See Prieberg, *Kraftprobe*, p. 43.
3. *Der Kurier* was one of the newspapers to be started in the French sector of Berlin at the end of the war. Fischer-Walden's resignation was also mentioned in America in the *Christian Science Monitor*, 19 December 1946, p. 13. In fact, it was about the only paper in the United States that reported the trial objectively and questioned the irregularities in the proceedings. For further reading on the denazification trial process, see Constantine Fitzgibbon's *Denazification*, (New York) 1969, to which I owe much of the background information used here and elsewhere.

[Fischer-Walden] based his decision [to resign from the Tribunal] as a protest against the composition of the Commission, which must deal with Furtwängler's case. On December 10th, Fischer-Walden claimed that the Commission was being convened for a preliminary discussion, whose purpose was to influence the Commission unilaterally. It is customary to give members of the Commission a few days before the proceedings to examine information about a case. In Furtwängler's case, there has [apparently] been a departure from this practice.[4]

In other words, the Commission was being denied the information it needed to conduct a thorough investigation of Furtwängler's case. If they could not induce him to be hoist by his own petard, could the Americans have wanted to "frame" Furtwängler? Fischer-Walden's resignation left little doubt about it among Germans, and it gave the circus atmosphere of the trial an added gist of imposture. But the potential conflagration was quickly quashed: someone else was hastily summoned to join the Tribunal and it convened promptly on the morning of 11 December with five men, two women, and the chairman, a communist named Alex Vogel.[5]

Calling for order in the crowded overheated room—Americans were the first to restore heating and plumbing after the war—Vogel read a short summary of Furtwängler's case:

> The investigations showed that Furtwängler had not been a member of any National Socialist organization, that he tried to help people persecuted because of their race, and that he also avoided certain outward formalities, such as giving the Hitler salute after concerts attended by Hitler.

But Furtwängler was being tried as a Nazi anyway:

> In the first place . . . in his musical activities, he had served the Nazi regime; in the second place, during a dispute with another German composer, he was reported to have said, "Sabata, the Jew, couldn't play Brahms;" in the third place, at a National Socialist Party Rally in Nürnberg, he conducted the opening overture; and in the fourth place, he was a member of the Prussian State Council.

In short, Furtwängler was accused of four transgressions:

1. "Serving" the Nazi regime
2. Uttering an anti-Semitic slur

4. 16 September 1946, p. 6.
5. The members are listed on the transcripts of the Tribunal proceedings as Messrs. Alex Vogel, Chairman, Mr. Wolfgang Schmidt, referent; Messrs. Loewe, Mühlmann, Neumann, Rosen, Dr. Mrs. Flöhren, and Mrs. Müller-Ness.

3. Performing at *one* official Nazi Party function

4. Membership in the Prussian State Council

Furtwängler declared, perhaps ironically: "I am here today not so much because of my desire to conduct again, as by my desire for the truth."[6]

While the trial bore some resemblance to a genuine legal proceeding of the sort found in Western Europe, it was typical of other such denazification trials, especially in lacking a clear focus in the prosecution. The line of interrogation meandered in and out of a wide range of issues: from Furtwängler's activities in various Nazi-established organizations such as the Reichsmusikkammer and the State Council to queries on books written about him by his former secretary Berta Geissmar and by one of his biographers Friedrich Herzfeld; from his alleged anti-Semitic slurs to his arguments with various individuals, including the nefarious concert agent Rudolf Vedder, the music critic Edwin von der Nüll, and Herbert von Karajan. What relevance such issues bore to the charges and to the concept of denazification will probably never be known.

Nonetheless, the Tribunal sought to cast Furtwängler in the worst possible light throughout the proceedings, and they nearly succeeded in "nailing" him because Furtwängler was so poorly prepared that he did not even have an attorney with him. The Commission succeeded in making him look ludicrous because several witnesses gave "damaging" testimony and because he did not have notes or documents to assist his memory in making answers or refutations. The chairman finally halted the proceedings and gave Furtwängler a few days to prepare his defense more adequately. But throughout both days of the trial (11 and 17 December), the Commission itself seemed ill-prepared to pin hard evidence on Furtwängler as it shifted and slid, making it all the more difficult for Furtwängler to defend himself.

Serving the Nazi regime, of course, was the first and most serious charge, but it was also the most vague. The Commission interrogated Furtwängler on his involvement with five areas between 1933 and 1945:

6. This quote is taken from Margaret Goldsmith's translation of Riess' biography, (London) 1955, pp. 218–219. The rest of the translations of the proceedings are taken directly from the English-language transcripts of the trial. Note: The transcript for Day One appears to be a summary, while the transcript for Day Two looks like a verbatim record of that day's proceedings. References to the first are therefore cited as Summary Proceedings, Day One; references to the second day are cited as Denazification Proceedings, Day Two.

1. the State Council

2. the Propaganda Ministry

3. the Reichsmusikkamer

4. the Berlin Philharmonic

5. the Nazi press

Furtwängler's position as State Councilor or Staatsrat was the most highly publicized of his alleged crimes because the title indicated that he was a ranking official of the regime. Göring conferred the title on Furtwängler by telegram on 8 July 1933 when he was trying to form a prestigious showcase or a sort of National Academy to give the regime a glamorous profile. Furtwängler explained that it was an honorary title and a bogus one at that:

> At that time, I did not intend to reject it, inasmuch as I tried first of all to cooperate loyally with them. Soon after my appointment, I ascertained that I only received the title of a Staatsrat but not the office. I attended only one meeting.[7]

Furtwängler went on to survey his conflicts with the Nazis as soon as they took over. The clerk of the court read aloud the letter he wrote to Goebbels concerning his objection to the discrimination against certain (mostly Jewish) artists that Goebbels had published in the *Vossische Zeitung* on 11 April 1933.

Vogel questioned Furtwängler's motivations for writing the letter to Goebbels. Furtwängler explained that he wanted to extract concessions from the Nazis in the cultural areas—at least in music:

> The fact that I had no idea of politics induced me to concentrate my efforts in the musical sphere. I only wanted to create something practical in this sphere.

Vogel remained unconvinced.

> What were your aims?
>
> *Furtwängler:* The maintenance of liberty, humanity, and justice in human life.
>
> But are you conscious that you, making such concessions, gave up a deal of this liberty, aren't you?

7. Summary Proceedings, Day One, p. 2.

Furtwängler: Yes, but I tried to accomplish my purpose. Later on the methods against the Jews, the whole thing was a demogogical development and there was only the hope that this affair would come to nothing and that the Nazis would lose their power. Everything I did until 1934— accepting the title of Staatsrat, Vice-President of the Reichsmusikkammer and so on, must be considered under this point of view.[8]

Vogel then cross-examined Furtwängler on his functions as Vice-President of the Reichsmusikkammer. Furtwängler replied that his most frequent duty was one that was entirely contradictory to his job. As discrimination against the Jews intensified, he had to settle disputes involving greedy Nazi conductors who tried to take work away from Jews. After some prodding, he mentioned the names of the composer and musician Gustav Havemann and the notorious concert agent Rudolf Vedder as two of the worst offenders. He also said he frequently had arguments on the issue with the President of the Reichsmusikkammer—none other than Richard Strauss. The working atmosphere became so untenable that he finally quit.[9]

Angry cries of protest against the Tribunal's line of questioning erupted, and Vogel threatened to remove noisy spectators.

On Furtwängler's relationship to the Propaganda Ministry, Furtwängler stated he had no direct relationship with ProMi, even though the Berlin Philharmonic was eventually taken over as a "Reich orchestra." But Vogel wanted to know if the tours of the Berlin Philharmonic to such places as England in the mid-1930s were part of ProMi's scheme to spread Nazi ideology? Furtwängler explained that most of the tours between 1922, when he took over the orchestra, and 1937, the last time he took the orchestra to England before the war, were made before Hitler came to power.[10] On all its tours abroad, the Berlin Philharmonic under Furtwängler performed strictly as a private ensemble. It never *officially* represented the Third Reich when they toured with Furtwängler, and he remained a free-lance conductor throughout the regime, even foregoing hefty pension benefits the Nazis offered him on several occasions:[11]

Vogel: But after 1933 such tours could be considered political ones.

8. Summary Proceedings, Day One, pp. 3–4.
9. He also mentioned that Strauss quit but for different reasons.
10. Summary Proceedings, Day One, p. 7
11. In negotiating what was to be Furtwängler's last contract with the Berlin Philharmonic in 1952, his business manager Albert Ostoff noted that Furtwängler had refused a pension during the Third Reich because he did not wish to feel he was obliged to the regime. Source: Wilhelm Furtwängler Private Archives, Clarens.

Furtwängler: It was my intention—and this is the reason I did not leave Germany—to prove that art means more than politics.[12]

For some reason, it did not occur to Furtwängler at this time to mention that he canceled a lucrative tour of Great Britain in 1935 with the Berlin Philharmonic that ProMi was trying to promote as a "cultural" event. Furtwängler was all but unemployed at this time, and he certainly had good reason to take on the tour. But he did tell the Tribunal what was common knowledge in musical circles in Germany at the time: he would not come back to the Philharmonic if it meant he was to be designated the official baton twirler for the Nazi government.[13] Furtwängler also testified that his resignation from the Berlin Philharmonic after the Hindemith Scandal was a clear vote against the Nazis, as far as he was concerned.

A bit later in the trial, Vogel returned to Furtwängler's relationship with Goebbels' Propaganda Ministry. He started off with questions about the dates Furtwängler conducted the Berlin Philharmonic at the Nürnberg Rallies. Furtwängler denied ever conducting the Berlin Philharmonic at the Rallies. But he volunteered that it was the Vienna Philharmonic he conducted at Nürnberg in September 1938. This performance, he said, was not officially a state occasion even though Hitler attended it. The opera performance *(Die Meistersinger)* took place *before* the official celebrations began, but the Nazis portrayed it as official in both its own and in the foreign press.

Schmidt swerved into a broader discussion about Furtwängler's use as a propaganda tool outside Germany:

. . . You must have been aware of the fact that your profession was a cultural-political one, and by that created some political effects, that you know about that is clearly seen in the remark in your letter to Funk where you stated: "I am sure that by performing, this wonderful orchestra will make the German name famous and honorable again in the eyes of the world."

Furtwängler: The name of Germany, YES! But not the name of the Nazi government. When I say I was active abroad for the German name as a German musician, I did not mean the name of the Nazi government.[14]

Regardless of whom he thought he was representing, the Tribunal could not make an issue of Furtwängler's performance record outside

12. Summary Proceedings, Day One, p. 7.
13. Summary Proceedings, Day One, p. 7.
14. Summary Proceedings, Day One, pp. 12–13.

Germany.[15] He conducted only three times in occupied countries: twice in Denmark and once in Prague during the war. Otherwise, Furtwängler remained firm by his declaration that he would not follow German tanks into Nazi-occupied countries.

If it could not trap Furtwängler as a tool for foreign propaganda, it would try cornering him again on a well-known incident in which he seemed to be serving as Hitler's personal music master: the concert he conducted for Hitler's birthday celebration on 19 April 1942. This concert was indeed the only bona fide *official* public appearance Furtwängler made at a state event during the Third Reich, but it was a sufficiently grave offense in the view of the Tribunal. Furtwängler explained that he had managed to get himself excused from performing at all other state occasions, but this birthday concert was the first and only such event from which he could not extricate himself.[16] Agathe von Tiedemann, Furtwängler's secretary in Vienna at the time, took the stand and explained he was cornered into performing Beethoven's Ninth by Goebbels; even the Gauleiter (mayor) of Vienna could not get him excused from returning to Berlin for the one night.[17] Again, the Tribunal could not uncover a sinister or incriminating intent on Furtwängler's part in this incident.

The proceedings at this juncture were not entirely bereft of humor, though none of it was intended. Vogel, for example, wanted to know why Furtwängler remained in Germany after 1936 when the situation was getting worse both for him and for the country. Furtwängler told him Goebbels warned him that if he left Germany it would be forever, a prospect he could not countenance. Vogel pursued that line of thought:

So you gave the Nazi regime a considerably long duration . . .

The courtroom erupted in laughter.

When the laughter subsided, Furtwängler told him that Goebbels earlier, in 1935, offered him an arrangement, though it hardly merited the term. Furtwängler could return and conduct as before if he signed a two-point declaration:

1. Acknowledge that Hitler was the master of German cultural policy.

2. To submit to putting himself entirely under Hitler's command

15. Denazification Proceedings, Day Two, pp. 103–105.
16. Denazification Proceedings, Day Two, p. 101.
17. Denazification Proceedings, Day Two, pp. 105–106.

When Furtwängler refused and was about to leave Goebbels' office, he recalled that Goebbels called him back and asked if he did not agree that it was a fact that Hitler ran cultural life in Germany whether he cared to acknowledge it publicly or not. Furtwängler had to agree that it was indeed a fact. Would Furtwängler then agree to making such a statement since he just agreed it was already a fact? Schmidt read the declaration to the court, which omitted Furtwängler's insistence that he would stay in Germany only if he remained an absolute unpolitical artist with the understanding that he would not be used for propaganda purposes:

> Goebbels replied that he was ready to give such a promise to me, since Hitler and he were very interested in maintaining my performing qualities for the German people.[18]

Schmidt pursued the issue tirelessly, and he ultimately harassed Furtwängler into "admitting" that staying in Germany implicitly meant that he had also "accepted" Hitler's racial policies:

> *Schmidt:* Today, are you aware [of] the fact that by recognizing Hitler as the leader of cultural policy, you acknowledged at the same time this racial part of the program?
>
> *Furtwängler:* Of course, it is quite obvious that certain principles could not be changed. I had to make up my mind and decide whether I should remain in Germany and play music for the German people or not. If I did not want to acknowledge the prevailing conditions of life, I would have to leave Germany. If I wanted to stay, I could be compelled to consent to compromises.[19]

Vogel acknowledged that Furtwängler in 1933 could not have foreseen the atrocities the Nazis would perpetrate, but by 1935, he could surely have seen how the racial situation had worsened. Furtwängler replied that was exactly what he saw and chose to do what he could against the Nazis from inside the system:

> My actions at that point might be compared with the doctrine of the Underground Movement: "One has to cooperate with the government in order to be able to work against it." I intended to do just that.

Furtwängler had taken the Underground doctrine literally by staying inside Germany. In doing so, he felt he was infinitely more effec-

18. Summary Proceedings, Day One, p. 14.
19. Summary Proceedings, Day One, pp. 14–15.

tive in contravening its policies. But for some reason, Furtwängler did not exploit this fact, and the committee remained incredulous. Given that Furtwängler received many offers to conduct abroad, could it not have been his "impulse" to remain in Germany? Furtwängler's voice broke as he replied:

> Yes. What you call impulse was my feeling for being German. I have been active in the German Empire, the Weimar government, and later the Nazi state, and I do hope to be able to resume my activities now and in the future.
>
> *Schmidt:* But did you consider the Nazis to be a bearable form of government?
>
> *Furtwängler:* In 1935, I realized that the respective hope went below zero. I also realized that if I left Germany, I would lose my inward human relations to Germany. This feeling had nothing to do with Naziism. May I add that I lived in an atmosphere where people would say, "2 percent of the German people are anti-Nazis, and yet everybody you met belonged to that 2 percent."

The Commission sought to contradict Furtwängler's motives on this issue by reading into the record a portion of Furtwängler's biography by Friedrich Herzfeld written in 1941 at the instigation of the Nazis. It described a concert which Hitler attended:

> The Führer approached Furtwängler and shook hands with him, a symbol of an unbreakable bond between him and Nazi Germany. Furtwängler disclosed a submissiveness towards the grandeur of historical change (which the Italian Toscanini is still denying).[20]

Furtwängler declared that the book was not objective and that the handshake was merely an unavoidable concession. He could not prevent Hitler from making a surprise appearance at that concert. Nor could he prevent him from coming to the edge of the platform and extending his hand. Furtwängler recalled that he was in the midst of taking his call at the end of the performance and was caught off guard.

The Tribunal summoned Herzfeld and asked him to explain his description of the scene in his book:

> *Schmidt:* What about the term "grandeur of historical change"?
>
> *Herzfeld:* It meant that it referred only to his task on behalf of German art.

20. Denazification Proceedings, Day Two, p. 96.

Schmidt: And submissiveness to art or what else? Will you explain that?

Herzfeld: Submissiveness to art and Germany. I wanted to say that Nazi Germany was a given fact. I myself was unable to emigrate and had to stay here.[21]

Herzfeld, of course, was scraping the very limits of probity during his testimony. He was never a Party member because his genetic origins were uncertain, not because he was an anti-Nazi as he claimed. In fact, Herzfeld was one of those pitiable individuals trapped in the Third Reich, who simply did whatever he had to do for the sake of self-preservation and, where possible, self-advancement. To those ends, Herzfeld had published a number of anti-Semitic articles in the 1930s, even though he was partly Jewish himself. During the course of an article reviewing an opera guide in 1935, Herzfeld went on a tirade about its editor for surveying the works of blacklisted composers:

> There are discussion of works by Krenek, Korngold, Milhaud, Berg, Stravinsky, and Schönberg. [Such discussions] attack the Führer in the back, and one can only conclude that [the author] is writing for the Jewish Cultural Alliance [Kulturbund der deutscher Juden]. These works should by all means be taken away from that writer.[22]

In a further effort to show good faith to the Brownshirts, Herzfeld omitted mention of all Jewish composers Furtwängler had ever performed in the first two editions of his biography. Nor was any mention of them made in the appended list of Furtwängler's repertoire in these editions.[23] But such devoted service was insufficient to preserve him from the humiliation of being classed a Person of Mixed Blood *(Mischling)* in the Yellow Book, also known as the *Lexicon of Jews in*

21. Denazification Proceedings, Day Two, pp. 19–20.
22. Review, *Meyers Opernführer* by Otto Schumann, Bibliographisches Institut (Leipzig). *Allgemeine Musikzeitung,* December 1935, p. 785. The tirade was also aimed indirectly at Furtwängler, for the survival of the Jewish Cultural Alliance (Kulturbund der deutscher Juden) was made possible partly through his efforts to institute the Capability Principle *(Leistungsprinzip)* on behalf of Jewish performers in 1933. The adoption of that Principle enabled Jewish performers to keep working in the realm of the Prussian State Theaters, on the orders of its chief, none other than Joseph Goebbels. Furtwängler, however, had no direct connection with the Kulturbund. Herzfeld obviously had no idea at the time that he would be writing Furtwängler's biography five years later. See also Chapter 9.
23. Both editions of *Furtwängler: Weg und Wesen* were published by Wilhelm Goldmann Verlag, (Leipzig) 1941 and 1942. The edition quoted at the Tribunal appeared in 1941 and in a second edition the following year. The third and vastly revised edition was published in Munich in 1950. In that "denazified" version, the passage relating the attendance of Hitler and his minions at this concert was deleted.

Music.[24] Furtwängler, however, protected him from certain annihilation.

The Tribunal turned to Furtwängler's relationship with the Nazi press and spent a substantial portion of the trial trying to make Furtwängler an accessory to the "induction" into the army of a music critic about whom Furtwängler frequently complained. Presumably, he had done this because he held a personal grudge against Edwin von der Nüll even though he knew the reviews published under von der Nüll's by-line were guided by ProMi. Von der Nüll had been senior music critic of the *Berliner Zeitung*—also referred to as *BZ*. From 1938 onwards, he had taken the lead in writing reviews denigrating Furtwängler and extoling Karajan. Furtwängler lodged protests because he felt such criticism was the result of an anti-Furtwängler policy dictated by Göring. The Commission wanted to know if Furtwängler had been engaging in his own brand of influencing the press by somehow "arranging" to have von der Nüll drafted into military service. The question raised sinister issues because von der Nüll had been reported missing in action since the last days of the war. Vogel suggested that it was strange that a man in such a prestigious position would be sent to the front when he could easily have gotten himself exempted. Furtwängler expressed shock at the implication. Perhaps, then, von der Nüll was not guided by the Nazis but instead came up with his anti-Furtwängler reviews himself. Furtwängler hotly denied both allegations. He pointed to the reviews of his appearance at Bayreuth in 1936. During that season, he said, he suddenly was compared unfavorably to Tietjen, who also was conducting there that summer.[25] Schmidt hammered away at the possibility that Furtwängler was merely piqued because he was not getting good reviews and that he himself was trying to influence the press. These harassing remarks brought jeers and laughter from the courtroom.[26]

The Tribunal called two witnesses to testify for the prosecution. The first was Hans von Benda, the orchestra's business manager from

24. *Lexikon der Juden in der Musik* was published by the NSDAP Institute for Research on Jewish Matters in 1942 and 1943. Advertisements boasted "3000 Namen." Josef Wulf mentions Herzfeld's ethnic "demotion" while discussing this rebarbative monument to anti-Semitic scholarship in *Musik im dritten Reich*, (Frankfurt and Berlin) 1983 (abridged version), p. 428.

25. Furtwängler had complained to Göring that Tietjen had turned against him because he was within earshot when Hitler, who attended performances by both conductors, told Furtwängler Tietjen's interpretation of the opera could not be mentioned "in the same breath" as Furtwängler's. Undated letter to Göring, 1939. Source: Wilhelm Furtwängler Archives, Zürich. For more on Furtwängler's stormy relationship with Tietjen, see Chapter 14.

26. Summary Proceedings, Day One, p. 28.

1935 to 1939. He testified that Furtwängler "expected" him to have von der Nüll fired:

> *Vogel:* There is a great difference between order and expectation. What did Furtwängler really say to you?
>
> *Benda:* That it was my task to prevent von der Nüll to continue working.
>
> *Furtwängler:* That is not true!
>
> *Benda:* I only know that your distrust arose out of the fact that your expectation was not fulfilled, Herr Furtwängler.
>
> *Furtwängler:* I absolutely reject this!
>
> *Benda:* My power was not great enough at the time. I know that von der Nüll did not write any more reviews later on.
>
> *Vogel:* Immediately afterwards?
>
> *Benda:* No. I think a considerable time later.[27]

After Vogel dismissed Benda, he admitted that the Tribunal was aware of bad feelings between Furtwängler and Benda, but he also reminded the court that Benda's statement was made under oath and would be regarded as such. He then called Furtwängler's duplicitous old colleague Heinz Tietjen.

Tietjen appeared and testified that he indeed had summoned von der Nüll to get him to explain why he had written such an exaggerated review and used the word "miracle" in the headline:

> *Tietjen:* Von der Nüll replied that he was not responsible for the headline above his article. This was picked out by the editors.

The audience muttered, "Aha."

> *Tietjen:* But he stood for the content of his review, which was nothing but an absolute lauding of Karajan. He refused to be made responsible for the headline.
>
> *Vogel:* Do you know if this criticism was not written voluntarily, but "guided" by a certain side with certain intentions?
>
> *Tietjen:* By no means! I had the impression that this criticism was made personally.[28]

27. Summary Proceedings, Day One, p. 31.
28. Summary Proceedings, Day One, p. 32.

Of course, there was no way to verify if he did summon von der Nüll; nor was there any way to prove what he actually said to him. Finally, it was Tietjen's opinion that von der Nüll was *not* told what to write:

> So . . . you did not have the impression of a "guided campaign" at this time?
>
> *Tietjen:* No.[29]

Tietjen was excused, and the courtroom remained silent at his departure.

Vogel asked Furtwängler if he would care for an adjournment until he could produce more witnesses in his own behalf. Furtwängler had no idea just how badly he had fared and replied, "If you think what has been presented today is not favorable to me."

Furtwängler was depressed and angry. "I don't want to stay in Germany. Perhaps it would have been better if, in 1934, I had left Germany," he muttered.[30] He could not understand why he was being treated like a criminal when it was self-evident—to him at least—that he was innocent of all the absurd accusations and innuendoes that were being treated seriously that day.

The next day, the newspapers—all vehemently anti-Nazi now—agreed that "men like Furtwängler" should not be branded as war criminals. They failed to mention, however, who else had been "like Furtwängler."

On 17 December the Tribunal assembled again to hear the rest of Furtwängler's case. During the intervening week, many people prevailed upon Furtwängler to strengthen his defense. This time, about 25 witnesses came forward in his behalf. Julius Kapp, the archivist for the Berliner Staatsoper, confirmed several important points:

1. The regime did indeed carefully control the press
2. ProMi held weekly meetings to give instructions about who was in favor with the regime and who was not; publicity and favorable reviews would be proportioned accordingly
3. Göring alone decided policy at the Staatsoper

And was von der Nüll's review influenced by the Nazis?

---

29. Summary Proceedings, Day One, p. 33.
30. Riess, p. 290.

Kapp: This criticism in my opinion was absolutely influenced by a higher office, since it was intended to make a conductor prominent in Berlin, who might be played off against Herr Furtwängler.

Vogel: And which was the higher office?

Kapp: It could only have been Göring, who was master of the house. Goebbels could not have done it . . . It was clear to everyone who read the review that it was an attack on Herr Furtwängler.[31]

Kapp added that von der Nüll was also publicly reprimanded for his obsequious paean by another critic at the same newspaper. Without mentioning von der Nüll's name, Wilhelm Matthes wrote an editorial with the headline "Tact in Praise and Blame." Nonetheless, von der Nüll's reviews extoling Karajan continued unabated and stoked a Furtwängler-Karajan rivalry.

Furtwängler now called another witness to speak of conditions inside the newspaper itself. Frau Annaliese Theiler wrote under her maiden name Wiener and joined the BZ in 1937, as third music critic after von der Nüll and Walther Steinhauer. She took her position just after the "Wunder Karajan" review had appeared.[32] She submitted a lengthy written statement prepared in advance for the tribunal.

In it, Theiler-Wiener stated that von der Nüll's part in the rivalry between Furtwängler and Karajan resulted from a couple of factors converging neatly:

1. Von der Nüll said he truly and sincerely admired Karajan

2. Göring wanted to exploit that admiration because Furtwängler had quit once too often, and he needed a "star" to take his place

She also stated that von der Nüll confided something else to her: that he saw the chance of becoming an important critic by supporting Karajan against Furtwängler in behalf of the regime:

Von der Nüll thus held an unrivalled advantage compared with all his other colleagues who did not share his opinion of Furtwängler. He used the advantage of being "guided" to its full extent. He had to admit to himself that . . . he found himself in the position of a mouthpiece for Göring's ministry . . . The guidance and the subjective opinion of the guided were completely identical. These facts do not alter the reality of influence

31. Denazification Proceedings, Day Two, p. 4.
32. Gillis, pp. 76–79.

here. . . . The fact became clear to all of us that Dr. von der Nüll let himself be guided and liked it.[33]

Theiler-Wiener stated emphatically, too, that von der Nüll explicitly told her his "Wunder" review of Karajan was a direct attack on Furtwängler and that he meant every word of it.[34] But he also told her that he wanted to exploit his genuine admiration of Karajan's work as a means of advancing himself as a critic. Finally, she stated what Furtwängler wanted most for the court to hear from a witness with no special axe to grind:

> Reducing a critic to silence was nothing that [Furtwängler], with his international reputation, wanted. He did not need it. Yet, here it was not a matter of the criticism, but of the campaign of a dictatorial power group against him.[35]

Furtwängler called for Dr. Kurt Westphal, a personal acquaintance of von der Nüll from their student days at the University of Berlin. He testified that Wilhelm Matthes, the senior music critic at the *BZ* who wrote the article urging tact in praising artists, was fired after the article was published. He said further that von der Nüll told him personally that he had appealed to Göring's ministry to have Matthes dismissed:

> *Furtwängler:* He told you himself?
>
> *Westphal:* He did. I was in frequent touch with him at that time, and he told me all these details because I was a very good friend of his.[36]

In having Matthes fired, said Westphal, von der Nüll accomplished two purposes. First, he silenced opposition, and second, he took Matthes' place as senior music critic. But Westphal readily admitted he had no hard evidence to prove von der Nüll moved to get Matthes fired.

Later in the day, Edwin von der Nüll's wife was located and brought to the Tribunal, and it asked her if Furtwängler could have arranged her husband's conscription into the army in 1940. Frau von der Nüll said she did not believe so. Nor did she have any reason to believe that her husband thought there was any sinister movement

33. Denazification Proceedings, Day Two, p. 9.
34. Denazification Proceedings, Day Two, pp. 8–9.
35. Denazification Proceedings, Day Two, p. 12
36. Denazification Proceedings, Day Two, p. 14.

behind his conscription. Although the war had been over for more than a year and a half, she had not heard from him. As far as she knew, he was in an internment camp in Belgium.[37]

If Furtwängler had not done in von der Null, suspicions still remained that he had demanded the conscription of another critic at the *BZ*, Walter Steinhauer. A telephoned statement from Steinhauer's widow, Marie-Luise, was read into the court. It was well known that Furtwängler frequently had arguments with Steinhauer over the years because Steinhauer derided him for not performing enough contemporary music. Furtwängler always replied that he would gladly perform modern music, as long as it was *quality* modern music. Their disagreements were entirely professional, however, and they respected each other. In fact, they had shared opinions on an important issue: Steinhauer was an anti-Fascist and had never joined the Nazi Party.[38] In 1943 Steinhauer was drafted into military service, and Furtwängler was rumored (never charged) to have arranged for his conscription. Frau Steinhauer rejected the allegation that Furtwängler had anything to do with it:

> The direct cause of his being drafted was the closing down of the paper *BZ am Mittag*. That Wilhelm Furtwängler is said to have caused my husband's conscription I believe is impossible. It was the time following the Battle of Leningrad, and very many other papers and periodicals were shut down too. For two years, my husband had been deferred. If Furtwängler had wanted to push his conscription, he might have done so before . . . After the revolution in 1933, many adversaries of the Nationalist Socialist Regime placed all their hopes in Wilhelm Furtwängler. Furtwängler was ready time and again to help these cases involving political charges.[39]

Furtwängler's next witness was a film critic. Werner Fiedler spoke about Furtwängler's refusal to appear in Goebbels' propaganda film on the Berlin Philharmonic in 1944 directed by Paul Verhoeven. Fiedler panned *Symphony and Love*, which featured Richard Strauss leading a parade of conductors including Karl Böhm, Hans Knappertsbusch, and Eugen Jochum.[40] Fiedler said he narrowly missed being liquidated for criticizing the film after Verhoeven demanded his

37. Denazification Proceedings, Day Two, pp. 32–33. Von der Null was in fact killed during the last days of the war.
38. Denazification Proceedings, Day Two, p. 21.
39. Denazification Proceedings, Day Two, p. 20.
40. The film was produced by Goebbels and ProMi, and it was directed by the late Paul Verhoeven. Verhoeven is not to be confused with the younger Dutch film director of the same name whose films include *Robocop*. The deceased (1974) Paul Verhoeven's son, Michael, however, is also a filmmaker, who directed *The Nasty Girl*. See Chapter 14.

arrest.[41] When a member of the Tribunal belittled the degree of pressure brought to bear on the press in such matters, Fiedler retorted:

> That is not so! Each time anybody gave a contrary opinion, he risked his very existence.[42]

Furtwängler thoroughly enjoyed the review and immediately contacted Fielder to make his acquaintance. Fiedler related the gist of their conversations:

> One thing was clear. Dr. Furtwängler was very touchy about anything that could be regarded as a misuse of art for cultural-political purposes, and secondly, he got together with a critic in ill-favor (me) who in case of a reprimand (which actually happened later) might refer to Furtwängler's attitude to clear himself. This, of course, I did not do.[43]

Fiedler also recalled that Furtwängler wholeheartedly approved of the hissing and booing that attended the premiere of Theodor Berger's *Ballad* at the Philharmonic in the 1941–42 season.[44] That approval, of course, ran in the face of ProMi's policy against audience disapproval:

> Dr. Furtwängler's attitude caused great anger at the Propaganda Ministry because they were of the opinion that art was to be directed and supervised by the state, and any sign of displeasure was therefore regarded as a criticism of the state.[45]

The Tribunal finally was convinced that the Nazi press was controlled as a matter of policy and specifically guided against him.[46] They were willing to let it go at that, but Furtwängler wanted to clarify his integrity in the face of the conspiracy that was trying to undermine him during the Third Reich. He called another witness to testify how furious Goebbels was with him for being recalcitrant. Eduard Lucas was summoned.

Until 1934 Lucas was production manager of Telefunken, a recording company that eventually evolved into a subsidiary of Polydor/Deutsche Grammophon. He became a successful music publisher and was on friendly terms with both managements and artists during the Third Reich. During his testimony, he made several important dis-

41. See also Gillis, p. 82.
42. Denazification Proceedings, Day Two, p. 26.
43. Denazification Proceedings, Day Two, pp. 24–25.
44. Premiere: 2, 3, 4 November 1941, Berlin. Furtwängler also performed the work on 5 November in Leipzig with the Berlin Philharmonic.
45. Denazification Proceedings, Day Two, p. 25.
46. Denazification Proceedings, Day Two, p. 37.

closures that demonstrated that Furtwängler was anything but "cozy" with the Nazis. He pointed out, for example, that Rudolf Vedder, the notorious concert agent, worked with the Nazis to foist on the public a new conducting personality strong enough to supplant Furtwängler:

> Vedder was not fussy about the methods he used, and I know for sure that he used, above all, his connections with the SS in Karajan's behalf. In particular he exploited his tie with Herr Ludolf von Alvensleben,[47] who, I think, was the personal adjutant at the time to Himmler. I saw them together many times. I am convinced von Alvensleben used his influence with the press.[48]

Lucas went on to say that Vedder several times boasted that Karajan's success would soon make Furtwängler a distant memory. But Vedder's infamous underhanded dealings eventually caught up with him, and he became an embarrassment to the SS. Furtwängler confirmed Lucas' testimony by recounting at length various difficulties he had encountered with Vedder.[49]

The Tribunal eventually reached a cul-de-sac in trying to impute selfish motives to Furtwängler's dealings with Vedder, Karajan, and von der Nüll and the press, and it moved on to another potentially damaging subject. Vogel prefaced the inquiry into an anti-Semitic remark Furtwängler was alleged to have made by assuring him the Tribunal was well aware of Furtwängler's assistance to Jews and other persecuted people. "Yet," he insisted, "we must deal with single points resulting from the preliminary investigation."[50]

The issue stemmed from a memo dating from 1939 stating that Furtwängler had used the phrase, "the Jew de Sabata" in an implicitly derogatory way in referring to his colleague and friend from Milan.[51]

---

47. Von Alvensleben led the so-called self-defense organization of the dreaded SS in West Prussia from the autumn of 1939 onwards. While Himmler dispatched the organization to occupied Poland in order to stop the wholesale murder of the German minority by Polish nationalists, this highly efficient organization quickly evolved into a network of liquidation squads. Von Alvensleben was a rabid Nazi devoted to purifying the "German Race," and he instituted a reign of terror in West Prussia in which thousands of Poles were arbitrarily executed. See Louis de Jong, *Die deutsche fünfte Kolonne im Zweitenweltkrieg*, (Stuttgart) 1959, p. 61, and Heinz Höhne (trans. by Richard Barry), *The Order of the Death's Head*, (London) 1959, p. 341.

48. Denazification Proceedings, Day Two, p. 41.

49. These included several instances of double-dealing involving the soprano Mia Peltenberg and the violinist Gerhard Taschner. Gerhard von Westerman, one of the Philharmonic's business managers during this period testified to Furtwängler's forthrightness in these incidents. For more on the Vedder affair, see Chapter 14 and Denazification Proceedings, Day Two, pp. 37–59.

50. Denazification Proceedings, Day Two, p. 68.

51. Victor de Sabata was one of the major conductors of this century, and Italy's leading conductor in the generation that followed Toscanini. In the postwar years, he became a champion of Maria Callas. Together they ultimately recorded for EMI in 1953 a *Tosca* seething with excitement.

Furtwängler was incredulous, for he had invited Sabata on many occasions to conduct the Berlin Philharmonic. Sabata was also one of the few people from any walk of life whom Furtwängler regarded as a friend. Schmidt read the letter into the record:

> What should I do when Dr. Furtwängler declared to me that it is a piece of impudence that the Jew Sabata . . . since the day when Sabata performed *Tristan* in Bayreuth, Furtwängler speaks only of "Jew Sabata."[52]

Furtwängler demanded to know who wrote the letter. Schmidt would not tell him. He admitted that Furtwängler's attitude toward Jews was well known and was not an issue in the trial. Nonetheless, individual "incidents" known to the Tribunal had to be investigated, and this was one of them. Furtwängler was now reduced to denying that he was an anti-Semite:

> There is only one thing I can say. I did not say anything that went counter to my convictions and cannot have said anything that did. Quite apart from the instances when I had to speak with specific Nazis and to use their language, as one had to say Heil Hitler,—quite apart from these instances, I did not make any compromises by saying things other than what I believed. And I have always been frank in my attitude toward the Jews.[53]

Two witnesses were called to support the contents of the letter, but neither of them could be concrete about the place and context of the remark. The first witness was Lorenz Höber, a violist in the Berlin Philharmonic, who had been called earlier to testify whether the orchestra had performed at the official portions of the Nürnberg Rally in 1938 under Furtwängler, and he testified correctly that it had not. He presumably was the author of the letter. Höber averred on the witness stand that Furtwängler used the phrase "Sabata the Jew " or "the Jew Sabata." The best he could recall was that the incident in which the remark was supposedly made occurred in the conductor's room after a concert. Vogel suggested perhaps it might have been something to do with the way Sabata had conducted Brahms' Fourth Symphony, which the Italian conductor had just performed with the orchestra. Höber replied that it might have had something to do with it.

Furtwängler, however, would not call Höber an out-and-out liar. Naively, he much preferred, even on this critical point, to have a

52. Denazification Proceedings, Day Two, p. 67.
53. Denazification Proceedings, Day Two, p. 73.

quasi-semantic/philosophical discussion about modes of verbal expression. He insisted that if indeed he referred to Sabata bearing Jewish blood, he had not done so in a derogatory manner. Nor did he have any recollection of being angry with Sabata or with what Sabata may have done interpretively.

Schmidt called Hans von Benda again as the second witness on the issue. Benda recalled that Furtwängler was angry once after Sabata conducted the Brahms Fourth Symphony and exclaimed Sabata had "once been a Jew." He guessed that Furtwängler did not like they way he conducted Brahms.[54] Furtwängler dignified Benda's statement with a rebuttal, only to make himself appear ludicrous:

> I discussed the programs myself with Sabata. We discussed everything. I invited him myself!
>
> *Vogel:* Dr. Furtwängler. Will you please ask real questions and not give explanations.
>
> *Furtwängler:* I don't know what real questions I can ask in this case.[55]

Vogel turned to Furtwängler's assistance to the Jews.

> Did you know that Furtwängler assisted Jews and other people who were persecuted?

Here, at least, Benda was truthful.

> *Benda:* I not only heard about it, he actually did it. If Herr Furtwängler had intended something serious when he made the statement that Sabata was a Jew, he would have had the means to take serious measures against him, provided he had a good reason.
>
> *Vogel:* Do you wish to state that you considered the utterance anti-Semitic?
>
> *Benda:* No, I do not. It just slipped from him. Furtwängler has never been an anti-Semite. When the Nazis fired Jews from all orchestras, sometimes in a most disgraceful way, they all came to him. There is the case of one a Jewish violinist. I think Bax was his name. He was given an indemnity of 18,000 marks, much of it in foreign currency. This may have been a special case, but if it is true, only Dr. Furtwängler could have sponsored him.[56]

54. Denazification Proceedings, Day Two, p. 74
55. Denazification Proceedings, Day Two, pp. 74–75.
56. Denazification Proceedings, Day Two, pp. 75–76.

Schmidt pursued the subject further with Furtwängler:

> Is it possible that without being an anti-Semite, you nonetheless believe that certain things should not be executed by a Jew?
>
> *Furtwängler:* That is ridiculous.

The courtroom erupted with gales of jeers and laughter.

Schmidt continued harassing Furtwängler toward admitting that he really meant the "Jew" remark derogatorily in a moment of anger. But Furtwängler steadfastly denied the possibility:

> An attitude must exist in ourselves to make this outburst possible. And this is what I deny. I have no basic attitude that could have caused me to link the statement and my mood together in a disparaging manner. Even in the greatest anger, I could not have said it. I may have been upset with one thing or the other. I do not know. But I deem it impossible that I said anything in the connection you are suggesting.[57]

Ultimately, the Tribunal heard again from Westermann, the Business Manager of the Berlin Philharmonic. He testified that Furtwängler invited Sabata to conduct the Philharmonic every year and even suggested that Westermann go to Italy to pay him a visit of respect when he stayed away from Germany after 1940.[58]

If the remark Furtwängler was supposed to have made about Sabata could not be proved, then perhaps Furtwängler could be found to have manifested an anti-Semitic "attitude." To support that possibility, Schmidt produced a letter regarding the composer Arnold Schönberg dated 4 June 1933 that Furtwängler wrote to the former Cultural Minister Rust and read part of it to the court:

> Arnold Schönberg is considered by the Jewish International as the most significant musician of the present. It must be recommended that he not be made a martyr. And if he is suspended now—I would not indeed consider this right—to treat the question of indemnity with generosity.[59]

The letter clearly showed Furtwängler interceding for a proscribed individual, but that was hardly the issue here. Schmidt wanted to know what Furtwängler meant by the term "Jewish International." Furtwängler explained that Schönberg was a great figure in music who was held in special esteem by the Jewish and cosmopolitan commu-

57. Denazification Proceedings, Day Two, p. 79.
58. Denazification Proceedings, Day Two, p. 86.
59. Denazification Proceedings, Day Two, p. 80.

nities of large cities. Those groups, which were by no means exclusively Jewish, constituted the "Jewish International." What is more, he used the term so that he could communicate with the Nazis on the matter using their own terms:

> To a certain degree, I had to fight with their weapons, otherwise I could not have achieved anything.[60]

But Schmidt tried to widen a fissure by suggesting that Furtwängler only helped a few outstanding and well-known musicians but let lesser musicians be removed without mercy. Furtwängler countered with promises to provide letters and affidavits from less notable figures whom he helped, adding that he was not always successful on behalf of the persecuted. Vogel wanted testimony from just one. The spectators began to shout names. Wollheim! Waldner! Fritz Zweig![61] The name heard loudest was Mark Leuschner. Furtwängler explained that Leuschner's father Karl was a bassoon player in the Berlin Philharmonic who was married to a Jew. Consequently, their son, Mark, who was a violinist, had encountered great difficulty because he was half Jewish.

Mark Hendricks Leuschner took the stand and got right to the point:

> Dr. Furtwängler . . . pleaded for me even at a time when he did not know anything of my work as a violinist.
> What is more, Furtwängler had no special reason to plead my case because there had been a certain friction between him and my father, who is a member of the Berlin Philharmonic. In spite of this tension, he backed me in 1940. Earlier, Dr. Furtwängler tried to help me when I attempted to get a temporary permit to give concerts in 1935. He tried for the next four years, and he succeeded in 1939 through his intervention with the authorities to assure my survival as an artist.

> *Schmidt:* Dr. Furtwängler gave you a letter . . . an all-purpose letter of recommendation which was not restricted to any special purpose?

> *Leuschner:* Dr. Furtwängler finally gave me a letter of blank power, the original of which I submitted to the board. One last thing I want to add. After each rehearsal, after each concert, Dr. Furtwängler was besieged by people who were in the same position as I. He never refused to listen to anyone. I personally saw him in this situation at least 20 times. In his

60. Denazification Proceedings, Day Two, p. 82.
61. Zweig was one of Furtwängler's associate Kapellmeisters during his years in Mannheim (1915–1920). He emigrated to the United States where he had a successful career as a conductor and coach. He is no relation to the author Stefan Zweig.

exposed position and prominence as a member of musical life, it was certainly very dangerous for Dr. Furtwängler to talk to people like me, especially since there was a group in the Philharmonic in touch with the Gestapo. The Gestapo watched Furtwängler very closely and worked to remove anti-Nazi individuals.[62]

Furtwängler called Clemens Herzberg for further testimony on the Jewish question, although the need for it was beginning to diminish at this point. Herzberg was business manager for stage director Max Reinhardt. Herzberg said Reinhardt told him in Paris in 1933:

> I hope Furtwängler will stay in Germany since such people must stay there. I would have stayed there myself if I had not been forced to leave. What Furtwängler has done or not done is of no importance. The courage he had to write open letters of protest to Goebbels speaks for the man, and I must tell you: wherever you meet him, remember me to him and tell him what I said.[63]

Vogel was manifestly irritated by this testimony and asked Herzberg whether he had ever been a Nazi. Herzberg pointed to his nose and said, "I don't think you have looked too closely at my nose."

Schmidt also read into the record a letter from Reinhardt to Furtwängler dated 18 April 1933 following the publication of Furtwängler's letters to Goebbels:

> The noble free words you have dared to utter as one of the servants of art have moved me deeply. It behooves those who are concerned to be quiet today. I only wish to thank you and to finish up with the untimely sigh: Oh, Friends, not such a sound!"[64] Whether and where we may meet again in a better and happier spirit, I do not know.

The committee had long run out of witnesses to be brought against Furtwängler, and it also came to the conclusion that it had run out of issues that could be brought against him. Vogel formally cleared Furtwängler of suspicion as an anti-Semite:

> For the third time, I declare that the board is aware from the files of the preliminary investigation that you, Herr Furtwängler, often assisted Jews and people persecuted for racial reasons and even risked a great deal, so that anti-Semitism is not part of the accusations made against you here or elsewhere.[65]

62. Denazification Proceedings, Day Two, pp. 88–89.
63. Denazification Proceedings, Day Two, p. 91.
64. From Schiller's "Ode to Joy," which constitutes the choral movement of Beethoven's Ninth Symphony.
65. Denazification Proceedings, Day Two, pp. 93–94.

The Tribunal was slowly becoming more sympathetic to Furt-wängler. It read a note written by an official at ProMi to Secretary Hin-kel in the margin of an application Furtwängler had made in behalf of Raymond Klibansky,[66] a philosopher who was making a brilliant career at the University of Heidelberg, someone whom Furtwängler hardly knew:

> Can you give me the name of a Jew who is not backed by Furtwängler?[67] But seriously, even if I wanted to, I could not do anything for Dr. Ray-mond Klibansky, since he does not come under the suspicion of my department. Heil Hitler![68]

It also allowed him to call several more character witnesses. Jas-trau, the servant at the Philharmonie, also testified and recalled how Furtwängler avoided the Nazi salute when Hitler suddenly showed up at a concert. He also ventured, "It seems to me those war criminals who are still at liberty should be treated like Dr. Furtwängler is being treated."

But it was Boleslav Barlog who gave the most moving testimony. He had been the first stage director to be denazified and had been head of the Schlosspark Theater in Berlin-Stieglitz since the end of the war. "Furtwängler gave me a reason for living during the Third Reich," he said. "If every four weeks there was a Furtwängler concert, one did not utterly despair." On this utterance alone, Furtwängler felt vindi-cated.

The Tribunal adjourned for two hours and returned with a decla-ration which amounted to acquittal. It announced that Furtwängler's appeal to resume his musical activities was to be forwarded to the Allied Commandatura for approval. Furtwängler read a short speech. In it, he restated his motives for remaining in Nazi Germany:

> The fear of being misused for propaganda purposes was wiped out by the greater concern for preserving German music as far as this was possi-ble . . .
> I could not leave Germany in her deepest misery. To get out at that moment would have been a shameful flight, After all, I am a German,

---

66. See Chapter 15 for more on Furtwängler's assistance to Klibansky.

67. The remark in the letter later became transformed into "There is not a dirty Jew left in Germany that Furtwängler has not helped!" and attributed to Goebbels. However, the letter was signed by Georg Gerullis, the Under Secretary of Culture and one of Rust's closest colleagues. Part of the confusion about the author of the original statement arose from the similarity between the signatures of Gerullis, the true author of the sentiment, and Goebbels who surely must have shared exactly the same thought. Also see Chapter 14 and *Kraftprobe*, pp. 131–132.

68. Denazification Proceedings, Day Two, p. 94.

whatever may be thought of that abroad, and I do not regret having done it for the German people.[69]

The packed hall burst into applause. Vogel motioned for quiet. Furtwängler bowed with a slight nod.

If Furtwängler's denazification proceedings bore the air of a kangaroo court, the treatment of the trial by some American newspapers gave new dimensions to biased reporting. Perhaps the most egregious account was given by the *New York Times*, made all the worse because other papers around the country picked it up from the *Times'* wire service.[70] The reporter Delbert Clark recited three "proved charges":

1. That Furtwängler was the president of the Berlin Music Chamber.

[However: No such organization as the "Berlin Music Chamber" ever existed. Furtwängler was vice-president of the Reichsmusikkammer from 1933 until he resigned in 1934, again in the wake of the Hindemith Scandal. He did not resign because he had quarreled with the regime about its attitude toward the Jews. His membership in the Reichsmusikkammer was never an issue in the denazification proceedings, although he was questioned about it.]

2. That Furtwängler had been "director" of the Berlin Philharmonic during the Third Reich.

[However: Furtwängler was never indicted for being the "director" of the Berlin Philharmonic—which he led only as a guest after he resigned his directorship following the Hindemith Scandal. Nor was his relationship with the Berlin Philharmonic as a free-lance conductor ever held against him.]

3. That Furtwängler was a Staatsrat or State Councilor.

[However: This was a meaningless title which Göring conferred upon him, which he tried to abrogate, but Göring would not so allow him, saying it was a lifetime title. The Councilors convened only once in 1934. This was the so-called "high office" to which the American papers referred in his obituaries .]

Clark called the quickly discredited Hans von Benda a "defense witness" and an example of Furtwängler's "deceit." Benda—a Nazi— was in fact a well-prepared key witness for the prosecution. Clark also mentioned Furtwängler's assistance to Jews, but he questioned his motives, implying that he helped only famous musicians—a long-

69. Denazification Proceedings, Day Two, p. 127.
70. Daniel Gillis has given a detailed analysis of the distortion in Delbert Clark's reporting in his excellent *Furtwängler and America*, and he calls him to task for generally biased reporting.

belabored issue in the proceedings that finally was put to rest. Many lesser known, even obscure Jewish musicians and members of their families came forward and testified in Furtwängler's behalf, but Clark does not mention the fact.

In the matter of "punishing" the critic von der Nüll for writing hymns of praise to von Karajan and appealing to the State Opera to get rid of Karajan, Clark omitted saying that several witnesses, including the Indendant of the Staatsoper, its press chief, and one of von der Nüll's fellow critics testified that the press was controlled by the Nazis. Nor did he report that witnesses testified that von der Nüll himself had declared he was out to get Furtwängler. Clark also wrote that von der Nüll could not be found to testify on the matter himself when, in fact, it was being widely reported in the German newspapers that von der Nüll had died in the last days of the war at Potsdam.

In addition, Clark said that Furtwängler called Werner Fiedler to discuss the necessity of criticism after the critic had given a scathing review to *Symphony and Love,* Goebbels' propaganda film about the Berlin Philharmonic in 1944, implying that Furtwängler called him to rake him over the coals. Furtwängler did quite the opposite, and Fiedler told the court of the fact.

Quite apart from what Clark's article may have had to do with accuracy or truth, there were a number of other omissions in his coverage that only exacerbated the distortions of his report. He made no mention either of Clemens Herzfeld's testimony or Max Reinhardt's letter. Neither did he mention further supportive testimony from other witnesses such as Boleslav Barlog, Franz Jastrau, and members of the Berlin Philharmonic who gave repetition after repetition of Furtwängler's unyielding protection throughout the regime.

How could a reporter representing one of the world's most respected papers, especially at that time, have been possessed to write a dispatch that appears to be so patently and willfully distorted? Perhaps his copy was poorly edited after it arrived in the United States. Unlikely. A corresponding tone and similar disregard for facts pervades his account of the trial in *Again the Goosestep: The Lost Fruits of Victory.*[71]

Furtwängler was shocked when he saw the report, but instead of sending a litany of inaccuracies and distortions to the *New York Times,* he sent a letter to his friend Carleton Smith:

> I was astonished to see that though the trial had cleared every single detail in my favor, the *New York Times* brought an account of it which was

71. (New York) 1949.

forged in large parts, and the account of it which was in the American-controlled press in Germany were not objective either. This is one of the reasons why it is absolutely necessary that the public should be informed of the facts about me.[72]

Here again Furtwängler's astounding naivete was crushing any hope that he might wipe the tar from his name. It may not have done any good anyway; Professor Victor Zuckerkandl, a musicologist whose life Furtwängler had saved before the war, sent a letter to the *Times* defending him, and the paper did not publish it.

"I also took papers and evidence to one of the most influential music critics in New York," recalls Friedelind Wagner. But he just said, 'I can't publish any of it.' No one wanted to hear Furtwängler's side of the story."[73]

So the vast majority of the American public was left with the impressions that Delbert Clark had presented to it. We may never know why he distorted the facts. Possibly it was an equally distorted sense of righteousness. Perhaps it was sheer maliciousness. More than likely, his apparent nastiness was a concomitant of the delusion that good was being done for a cause, justifying any means used in that service. It all might not have been so odious had his brand of journalistic justice not been blessed by the inviolable prestige of the *New York Times*. His report prompted heinous embellishments that eventually evolved into received knowledge, and ultimately into truth.

The energy spent in the Tribunal's attempt to nail Furtwängler for supposedly using the Nazi government to further own his career and suppress Karajan's produced an irony, for Karajan's flagrant use of every means the Nazis readily made available to him not only to further himself but to do it at Furtwängler's expense never became an issue. That a ruthless neophyte would use his avowed membership in the Nazi Party to further his career seemed irrelevant to this Tribunal and the forces behind it. On the other hand, it was implicitly criminal for an established artist to defend his position, a position he gained long before the Nazis came to power, even though he demonstrably tried to oppose, limit, and undermine the cultural devastations of the regime.

If Furtwängler was culpable of anything it was hubris, that overweening pride that was the undoing of all the protagonists in Greek tragedy. But Furtwängler's hubris was grounded in the belief that he, one man, could prevail, not over the gods, but merely over the dep-

---

72. Source: Wilhelm Furtwängler Archives, Zürich. Cited in Gillis, p. 86.
73. Personal conversation with the author, Mainz, 6 October 1990.

redations of fellow mortals. For that temerity, there was punishment still to come. But in one objective, he had succeeded, at least for the moment. He had kept German music from being irrevocably befouled; he had kept the orchestras of Berlin and Vienna from losing their identities forever. In the coming years of reconstruction, however, that arcane victory would be cold comfort indeed.

But for the moment, Furtwängler was finally on his way back to resuming his conducting career. At least it looked that way.

19

Trial by Endurance

Once the Tribunal cleared those under suspicion, each case proceeded to the final step of normalization, a "rubber stamp" approval by the Allied Commandatura. It was all to be routine. Furtwängler would be free to work again in a few days. But nothing, it seems, was ever routine for Furtwängler. Weeks passed. Curt Riess reports that his friends made frequent inquiries at the Tribunal and were met with hostility. The office staff at the Tribunal could not understand the uproar. Furtwängler simply would have to wait his turn for clearance. His friend Boleslav Barlog, who had testified so movingly for him, persisted daily and was finally told the case could not be processed because the Tribunal had run out of typing paper. He personally placed an advertisement imploring donations in one of the Berlin newspapers. The Tribunal was besieged with hundreds of reams of paper—a precious commodity immediately after the war. The paper was all sent to Barlog with a warning not to make any more attempts at "bribing" the Commission.[1]

As the weeks dragged into months, Furtwängler again became the center of controversy. The well-known journalist Erik Reger wrote an article in the *Tageszeitung* describing the bitter condemnation still cast on Furtwängler. Reger was a scrupulous anti-Fascist and the edi-

1. Riess, p. 293.

tor of the *Tageszeitung*. Obviously referring to Furtwängler, he observed:

> It is a strange kind of compassion that prompts certain people to look kindly upon men who had served the Nazi criminals, but who realized their 'true sentiments' as soon as they realized that things were going badly for the regime. It was the kind of compassion that caused some people to put music ahead of politics . . . Such musicians, offered no assurance that, if a new Hitler appeared, they would not place their art, which they claimed to be above it all, at his disposal . . .[2]

Boleslav Barlog responded to the article in an essay entitled "For Furtwängler" in the *Kurier*, a paper licensed by the French. Barlog again repeated what he had told the Tribunal:

> . . . For me and for many others, Furtwängler's concerts were an indispensable source of strength during the Nazi regime . . . Therefore, duty and justice demand that everyone aware of what he did should enlighten people who know nothing about his case or do not wish to know anything about it.[3]

While the controversy coursed through the newspapers, the Tribunal continued to keep Furtwängler's file buried in its slush pile. In March, however, Furtwängler received unexpected news. Enrico Mainardi, the gifted Italian cellist and a longtime friend, brought an offer for an engagement with the Santa Cecilia Orchestra in Rome from a concert agency there. Furtwängler replied immediately that he would accept if he could get permission from the Tribunal. The agency promptly informed him that the Allies could not prevent him from accepting this invitation because the scope of the Tribunal's jurisdiction did not extend to Italy. They also extended an invitation from the Teatro Communale Orchestra in Florence, and Furtwängler promptly went to Rome to conduct his first concert after the war on 6 April in a program that included Beethoven's *Third Leonore Overture*, Schubert's Eighth ("Unfinished") Symphony, and Brahms' Second Symphony, the last work he performed with the Vienna Philharmonic in January 1945 just before he fled to Switzerland.[4]

News of the offer put the Allied Commandatura in Berlin in an awkward situation. They would look foolish if Furtwängler con-

2. Riess, pp. 223–224.
3. Riess, p. 224.
4. Furtwängler also conducted in Rome on 9 April 1947. He conducted in Florence on 13 and 20 April.

ducted in another defeated country before he had been officially denazified. The bureaucratic wheels churned out his "rubber stamp" for
complete acquittal in a few days. Almost two years after Germany surrendered and after numerous willing and avowed Nazi collaborators
had resumed their careers, Furtwängler—whom Himmler described
as that "friend of criminals" and whom the Allies had tried to brand a
danger to public safety—was free again to make music.

On 25 May 1947 Furtwängler conducted the Berlin Philharmonic
for the first time since the end of the war. The event took place at the
Titania Palast, an enormous cinema theater that had survived the
bombing. Berlin had hardly begun its arduous reconstruction, and
thousands were still homeless. But the concert sold out so quickly that
a second concert was scheduled, which also "went clean" within
hours after the box office opened. When Furtwängler appeared on
stage to begin the concert, the audience rose to their feet and cheered
wildly, shouting "Stay here! Stay here!" in rhythmic unison. The
orchestra joined in the ovation. The program was German music—all
Beethoven. The Overture to *Egmont*, the *Pastorale* Symphony, and
the Fifth. The audience cheered for 15 minutes at the end of the concert, and Furtwängler was recalled many times.

News of Furtwängler's triumph at his first concert in Berlin made
headlines around the world. The report of the event in the European
edition of the *New York Herald-Tribune* prompted Erika Mann,
Thomas Mann's daughter, to ask the editor if the concert was merely
the occasion for exploiting music to make "a political demonstration?" Erika, an author who had gained something of a reputation in
cabaret during the Weimar period, had followed her father, uncle, and
brothers into exile, and her statement amounted to a nasty chorus of
disapproval from the émigrés who believed that Furtwängler should
have joined them. What is more, she claimed its success, if indeed it
was one, owed its supposed excellence to a "minor miracle," for the
concert was put together in "one or two" rehearsals with a "makeshift
ensemble," two-thirds of which had not played with Furtwängler at
his last concert in Berlin in 1945.[5]

Furtwängler, for some reason, did not reply to Erika Mann but
instead wrote to her father inviting him to a dialogue about the current state of Germany.[6] The tone of the letter suggests that the two
men knew each other personally before 1933, possibly in Munich
where Furtwängler grew up or during the time he was a rehearsal assistant at the Court Opera between 1907 and 1909. Mann had spent most

5. The letter was dated 31 May from Zürich. It was published 5 June 1947, p. 4.
6. Undated, probably the end of June 1947. *Briefe*, p. 165.

of the war in America and had been an active anti-Nazi crusader in the war, even though his attitude toward National Socialism was at best equivocal before he was forced to leave and his view of Jews in Germany anything but sympathetic.[7] He was in Switzerland when Furtwängler wrote to him. Furtwängler knew the family of Mann's wife, the Pringsheims, and was trying to help them enter Switzerland around that time. Furtwängler wrote to Mann on their behalf and took the opportunity to make a proposal:

> Clarens, 29 June 1947
>
> I have just arrived from Munich. There I talked briefly to Frau Pringsheim. She and her husband still have difficulties with travel to Switzerland. Frau Pringsheim said the best arrangement would be for your daughter, as an American, to come and pick up the Pringsheims in Munich with her car. Frau Pringsheim asked me to ask you this, which I am now doing. Some time ago, I had written a reply to your publication "Germany and the Germans." But it was not originally my intention to send it you. Nevertheless, I would be very happy if the prospect arose to discuss questions relating to Germany with you. (My own case, which now has been settled, would play a very small part.) I do not know how or what position those around you would take with respect to me, or how you would react to such a proposal, and I would not want to receive "no" for an answer. I also don't know how long you will be in Switzerland. Should you not answer this letter, I will assume that you would think it better that we do not meet.

Mann was not about to get into a "discussion" about Germany, for he already had said all he had to say on the matter (at least at the time) in an essay called "Germany and the Germans." It originated as an address to members of the Library of Congress in Washington, delivered on 29 May 1945 shortly after Germany's surrender. It later was published in Germany where Furtwängler read it and disliked it intensely. The crux of the disagreement between Furtwängler and Mann lay in their divergent views on the number of Germanys. Furtwängler steadfastly believed the Nazis had split Germany into two irreconcilable camps: the "real" Germany that produced the Titans of its culture, and the false, evil Germany represented by Hitler and Himmler which had vanquished this true Germany. While Mann believed there was something frighteningly schizoid about the Ger-

---

7. In Mann's Diaries, he remarked on 10 April 1933 that the expulsion of the "Nietzsche-baiting" Jewish critic Alfred Kerr and the "de-Judification" of the German legal system were no misfortunes. *Thomas Manns Tagebücher*, (Frankfurt) 1977, p. 46. Mann also railed against Jews on 15 July 1934, calling them pathbreakers for the anti-liberal turn Germany had taken (pp. 473–474). See Chapter 5.

man psyche that produced its glorious cultural heritage on one hand and the death camps on the other, he ultimately felt the concept of two Germanys was poppycock:[8]

> There are *not* two Germanys, a good one and a bad one, but only one, whose best turned into evil through devilish cunning. Wicked Germany is merely good Germany gone astray, good Germany in misfortune, in guilt, and ruin. For that reason it is quite impossible for one born there simply to renounce the wicked, guilty Germany and to declare: "I am the good, the noble Germany in the white robe; I leave it to you to exterminate the wicked one." Not a word of all that I have just told you about Germany or tried to indicate to you, came out of alien, cool, objective knowledge, it is all within me, I have been through it all."

He replied to Furtwängler immediately on 1 July:

> I would consider it improper if I left unanswered a handwritten note by a man whom I consider the greatest conductor of our time—as you say, I would not give you "no" for an answer. Of this there will be no further discussion. But a discussion about Germany, which would also be about yourself, a case I consider in no way finished, would actually make little sense, and would offer an inferior prospect for understanding. I approve as little of your defense, which Alma Mahler-Werfel sent me to read, as I do of the 15 minute demonstration which gave you 16 curtain calls. I am better informed about the present mood and circumstances in Germany than those who stayed behind, those who call for silence from me, but who encourage me to come back to be "tactfully informed." (Thus it was printed.) As far as the past is concerned, "Germany and the Germans" was an attempt to explain to a friendly American public how it could all have happened in Germany. I suppose you argued against what you may think was wrong with it, although I am inclined to suspect that your true disapproval was directed more against what really went on. On the whole, we are not very truth-loving people and hate psychology probably because our own is so peculiar.
>   There is still difficulty with respect to the emigration of my relatives. At least we could greet my younger brother at the border and even take him for one day to Zürich.[9]

So Mann, at least in private, was acknowledging that Furtwängler was not sympathetic to the Nazis, even though he remained behind, even though Mann believed that the ovation for Furtwängler on his return to the podium was a political demonstration in which the

8. Unpublished address delivered at Library of Congress, 29 May 1945.
9. This handwritten letter from Mann is unpublished, and is translated by me from a typed transcript of it. It also appears in translation in Gillis, pp. 92–93. Source: Wilhelm Furtwängler Private Archives, Clarens.

applause symbolized a cheer for Nazi Germany rather than the "true Germany" for which Furtwängler believed he remained the most intrepid symbol. But Mann also reveals something about his own status among Germans at the time. Like many of those non-Jews who fled or left of their own accord, Mann was among those the Germans did not relish welcoming back. As far as the Germans were concerned, he had traduced them, even though he was forced to leave. His low esteem among many Germans was not helped by his active role on the Allied side in the war effort, which included a series of messages to the Germans broadcast over the BBC and Swedish Radio encouraging them to sedition. The price Mann and other non-Jews would pay for openly siding with the Allies, however right they may ultimately have been, was exile, now and forever. It was a condition Furtwängler simply could not countenance when Goebbels presented him with it at the time he told him he could never return if he left.[10]

To this letter, Furtwängler in turn made swift reply. After assuring Mann at some length that he had prepared his concert with more than one or two rehearsals (referring to Erika's snide remarks), he went after Mann's well-publicized statement before the war that no Beethoven—the Beethoven that is the quintessence of the finest instincts of German and western culture—should be played in Nazi Germany. He concluded:

> I believe—as I write [this letter] to you without actually sending it yet— that it is necessary to distinguish between expressions which are born from the heat of the moment and those which presently come to mind. If you really said that Beethoven's *Fidelio* should not be played in Himmler's Germany, then you will not receive this letter. For *Fidelio* never has been presented in the Germany of Himmler, only in a Germany raped by Himmler. It is more than just mindless to insist that such a work that is so essentially German should not be played here, simply because

10. Both Carl Flesch, Jr., and Friedelind Wagner agree that Germans would never have forgiven Furtwängler if he had left. Frau Wagner said, "Many people went back after the war, but the only ones who were welcomed were the Jews. Those like me, who left on principle, were shunned." She added that life became so unbearable for her when she returned to live in Bayreuth after 1953, that she ultimately settled in Switzerland. "I feel at home almost anywhere in the world except Germany," she said matter-of-factly. Some of those who did befriend her after she returned, however, say she was shunned only in Bayreuth and only because she had written a book *(Heritage of Fire)* in which the general populace of Bayreuth felt she treated her mother Winifred unfairly. Frau Wagner clearly had no regrets about what she did, though she waxed choleric with regard to the injustice she has borne. When she drove me from Mainz to Wiesbaden and left me at the Casino, she eyed my camera and advised me, "If you're looking around to take pictures, take a good look at some of the old men walking around on crutches and canes. You can bet a good lot of them are war criminals living here on their fat pensions." Personal conversation with the author, Wiesbaden, 6 October 1990.

another nation is furious with its real inner possibilities. Such an attitude can be changed with your efforts to explain Germans psychologically. Precisely because we both are Germans and agree on many matters, I believe a personal meeting would be productive. You hold the possibility and to a certain extent the obligation to help Germany . . .

And if I must infer from your letter, that there is a division between us now that is too much in the foreground, I am still hoping that will one day change. *Clarens, 4 July 1947*[11]

Mann did say that Beethoven should not be played in Himmler's Germany and meant it, but Furtwängler had sent his letter anyway. Mann apparently did not feel a face-to-face meeting would be productive after receiving Furtwängler's second letter. The correspondence stopped here, and the two men were never to meet, even though they later planned to participate together in a symposium on the arts some years later.[12]

The Philharmonic meanwhile had not remained idle during Furtwängler's enforced hiatus. In a proverbial case of being in the right place at the right time, a young Roumanian named Sergiu Celibidache was appointed to lead the orchestra through its first two postwar seasons.[13] After Furtwängler returned to the orchestra, Celibidache remained as his chief assistant until 1952. He went on to earn a reputation as a gifted but temperamental maestro, leading several German radio orchestras, but making few studio recordings over the years. He made his first appearance in the United States in 1984 conducting the concert orchestra of the Curtis Institute of Music at the Academy of Music in Philadelphia and at Carnegie Hall. He returned to make a nationwide tour in 1989 with the Munich Philharmonic.

I wrote to him prior to the 1989 tour asking to talk with him about Furtwängler. He did not reply. I tried to get through to him via intermediaries during the tour, but could not reach him. Finally, I went backstage after the last concert of the tour on April 26 at the Kennedy Center in Washington, and asked him directly if he would speak to me.

"Yes, I remember your letter," said the aging rotund man, seated in an armchair in the conductor's dressing room. "They wrote a book

11. *Briefe,* pp. 168–169. Furtwängler also expressed his resentment at Erika's deprecating remarks about the length of the ovation he received at his first postwar concert in Berlin.

12. The symposium was scheduled to take place in Munich in December 1954 and was to have included Martin Buber. Furtwängler died on 30 November 1954.

13. Leo Borchard was Music Director briefly but was killed by an American patrol guard on 23 August 1945 when he was returning from a dinner party after the curfew.

about me, and I refused to let them publish my correspondence with Furtwängler. I am sorry but I do not wish to collaborate with you."

"But I only want to ask you about your impressions of him after the war when you took over the Berlin Philharmonic."

"That is exactly what I don't wish to discuss."

"May I ask why?"

"My reaction to Furtwängler is a big secret."[14]

What is no secret is that Celibidache and Furtwängler admired each other, and Furtwängler was pleased that the orchestra had come into such capable hands. Despite a financial shortfall for the first time in his life and his frustration at being hindered from working until he could be cleared through a denazification proceeding, Furtwängler was really in no hurry to return to the Berlin Philharmonic. He had now acquired four children through his second marriage, and his wife had borne him a son during the last year of the war. The infant Andreas became his first and only legitimate child.[15] He also saw the enforced hiatus as a real opportunity to devote himself to composition, and he set to work on several projects, most notably the completion of his Second Symphony.[16]

What is also no secret is that Celibidache's contentious relationship with the Philharmonic deteriorated precipitously over the next five years, a tortuous rending played behind the scenes and even in public performances. This unfortunate situation led to frequent appeals from the Philharmonic for Furtwängler to take a more active role with the orchestra. Furtwängler was eager to continue as a guest with the orchestra, but he had little desire to take it over again. Over these five years, it became clearer to Furtwängler that he might again have to choose between composition and a full commitment to the orchestra. But that choice was still in the future.

Meanwhile, Furtwängler resumed conducting as a much sought-after guest conductor. On 10 August 1947, three months after he made his triumphant return to the Berlin Philharmonic, he returned to the Salzburg Festival and conducted the Vienna Philharmonic in two

14. Klaus Lang, *Lieber Herr Celibidache . . .* , (Zürich) 1988, presents a thorough exploration of the relationship by examining their correspondence. Unfortunately, Celibidache refused to grant permission for the letters he wrote to Furtwängler to be quoted directly, and so Lang was forced to paraphrase them. Hereafter referred to as Lang.

15. Furtwängler had four known illegitimate children, and it was rumored that he had even more.

16. The Second Symphony is actually Furtwängler's third work in the symphonic form. The First Symphony—dating from 1941—did not receive its world premiere until 1991. That work was preceded by an unnumbered symphony composed during his youth.

concerts. The soloist for the second concert was Yehudi Menuhin in Brahms' Violin Concerto. Menuhin, of course, was one of the artists who had refused to perform with him 14 years earlier, but he now was the first Jewish soloist to perform with Furtwängler after the war, a distinction that earned him few friends.[17] During the war, he had heard many contradictory reports about Furtwängler, most of them negative and fostered by the American press. Since he was of Russian-Jewish background, Menuhin had little reason for being kindly disposed toward Furtwängler. He became convinced of Furtwängler's integrity only when he went to Germany immediately after the war to play concerts and perform for the displaced and the survivors of Hitler's death camps. After he arrived in Germany, he listened closely to countless people—many of whom had survived the concentration camps—who had witnessed the events in Germany first hand. He returned to America and announced publicly that Furtwängler had been misjudged. He was everything contrary to a Nazi, said Menuhin.

The statement caused a furor, especially among certain prominent American Jews. They were led by Ira A. Hirschmann, a department store executive, who declared he was "horror-stricken" at Menuhin for "attempting to whitewash the official music director of the Third Reich."[18] Hirschmann had led the fight against Furtwängler's appointment as Music Director of the New York Philharmonic in 1936, and he now was determined to use every means at his disposal—and they were considerable—to maintain his view of Furtwängler as a rabid Nazi. For the rest of his life, Hirschmann remained convinced that Furtwängler had been involved with the worst possible activities regarding the Jews in Germany and attacked him whenever he got the opportunity. When he attacked Menuhin in 1945 for defending Furtwängler's character during the Third Reich, Menuhin retorted:

> Even those beasts on trial at Nürnberg are getting a fair democratic trial. Surely it is wrong to condemn Furtwängler, about whom there are divided opinions, without a fair trial.[19]

Menuhin returned to Europe a few months later and was introduced to Furtwängler by his second wife, Diana. She was an Englishwoman who had known Furtwängler before the war. Their conversation made Furtwängler feel as though he had known Menuhin for a

17. See Chapter 17.
18. Robert Magidoff, *Yehudi Menuhin: The Story of the Man and the Musician,* (London) 1956, p. 245.
19. Quoted from Gillis, pp. 61–62.

long time, and they played many concerts and recitals together over the next few years.[20]

After Menuhin performed with Furtwängler for the first time at Salzburg on 13 August 1947 playing the Brahms Violin Concerto, they went to Switzerland later in the month and performed together again with the Lucerne Festival Orchestra on 30 August. Menuhin played the Beethoven Violin Concerto and it was recorded in a studio session by HMV under the supervision of Walter Legge, a brilliant producer from England who was becoming a figure to be reckoned with in musical circles.[21] Legge and Furtwängler, of course, had been acquainted with each other since 1937, when Legge had engaged Furtwängler for the *Ring* at Covent Garden, but this was their first collaboration on a recording, and, as we will soon see, the beginning of a difficult association, redolent with mistrust, jealousy, and anger.

In Vienna, Furtwängler conducted his first concert after the war with the Vienna Philharmonic's concertmaster Wolfgang Schneiderhan as soloist in an all-Mendelssohn program in the Musikvereinsaal on 8 November. He had been the only conductor in Germany to continue playing this Jewish composer's works after the Nazis took over, and he was among the first to resume performing them in Austria after the war. At the second concert, a group of 150 concentration camp survivors picketed the entrance to the Musikverein, refusing to let the audience past them.[22] They had been protesting the concert for weeks, refusing to accept the Austrian government's warrant that Furtwängler was not a Nazi. When Furtwängler arrived with Baron Mayer, the pack assaulted them. Furtwängler escaped, but Mayer was badly injured. The audience gained entry to the hall by way of the Gallery stairs and chanted in unison, urging Furtwängler to begin the concert. Outside, the police had arrived but were loath to use force in dispersing the protestors, many of whom clearly bore evidence of the treatment they had received in the camps. One of the City Councilors finally addressed the crowd, calmed them down, and dispersed them. Throughout the fracas, Furtwängler sat in the green room reading a piano score of *The Magic Flute*. When the disruption ceased, Furtwängler went ahead with the concert.

Virtually everywhere he went, he was called a "Nazi conductor" who had been "made" by Hitler. The French, however, were well aware of his stand against the Nazis and received him warmly. As

20. See Menuhin's memoir *Unfinished Journey* for his own account of his relationship with Furtwängler, (New York) 1977, pp. 220–224.

21. See Chapter 20.

22. Riess, p. 298.

early as 1939 they had inducted him into the *Légion d'Honneur* to show their support of his opposition to the Nazis. Furtwängler withstood the initial hostility greeting him in most other cities, and audiences soon warmed up after hearing him make music. Within the 18 months following his denazification trial, Furtwängler made up for some of the performances the public had lost during the ban on his activity, and Munich, Hamburg, Leipzig, Stockholm, Geneva, Schaffhausen, Winterthur, Paris, Birmingham, Edinburgh, and London all witnessed his return to the international music scene, primarily with the Berlin or Vienna Philharmonic. His return to England at the end of February 1948 was marked by eleven concerts with the London Philharmonic and a studio recording of the Brahms Second.[23] After some hesitancy, British audiences welcomed him and arrangements were set in motion for his concerts to be broadcast. However, the BBC was in no hurry to engage him to conduct their orchestra—on or off the air.[24] In April, he went to Buenos Aires to make his South American debut in eight concerts with the Teatro Colon Orchestra.

Furtwängler also returned to the opera podium during this period, making his first postwar appearance in the pit of the Berlin Staatsoper on 3 October 1947 in a new production of *Tristan* with Ludwig Suthaus, Josef Greindl, Margarete Klose, and Erna Schlüter in the first cast.[25] It was produced by Furtwängler's Isolde of many triumphs before the war, Frida Leider.

He made his first postwar appearance at Salzburg the following summer, performing *Fidelio* with Schlüter, Lisa Della Casa, Julius Patzak as Florestan, Rudolf Schock, and Ferdinand Frantz. Furtwängler performed Beethoven's only opera more frequently than any other work for the stage, and he was to return again in 1949 and 1950 to repeat his success with Kirsten Flagstad in the title role.[26]

By 1950 he was in full stride again, making his debut in the pit of La Scala. His association with Italy's first opera house went back to 1923 when he conducted the Scala Orchestra for the first time in two concerts. Now he was making his first opera appearance with a new production of the *Ring*, again with Kirsten Flagstad as Brünnhilde.

23. This recording is one of Furtwängler's oddest performances and about as close to a disaster as he left for posterity.
24. The government-owned broadcasting Leviathan apparently became more enthusiastic about permitting Furtwängler to conduct its symphony orchestra only in 1953. See John Squire and John Hunt, *Furtwängler and Great Britain*, 2d ed., (London) 1985, p. 37.
25. Paula Büchner sang Isolde in the second performance on 30 October.
26. See Chapter 21 for a fuller discussion of the surviving tapes from these performances.

Flagstad was also his partner in probably the most important addition to his repertoire after the war—Strauss' *Four Last Songs.*

Furtwängler's rate of giving first performances of contemporary works in this period was no different from most other conductors entering the late summer of their middle years; it was slowing down markedly. But if quality is any compensation for quantity, the premiere of the *Four Last Songs* alone in Furtwängler's hands put him at the forefront of contemporary music. The world premiere was originally set for Paris, but it ultimately took place at the Royal Albert Hall with the Philharmonia Orchestra in London on 22 May 1950, almost nine months after Strauss' death.

The composer had designated Flagstad as his choice for the premiere, but he stipulated that her conductor should be "first class."[27] While such a stipulation might have seemed superfluous under the circumstances, Strauss probably spelled it out because he was aware that Flagstad frequently insisted on collaborating with her accompanist, close friend, and biographer Edwin MacArthur as her conductor.[28] This demand fouled several interesting offers she received from various recording companies.[29] But being chosen for such an honor was, of course, every singer's dream, and Flagstad was not about to pass it up. She had not forgotten that she had done extremely well by Furtwängler before the war, and her vote went to him.[30]

The *Ring* in Milan presented an additional challenge for Furtwängler because it had not been performed there since the 1920s. Most of the musicians had never played it, and Furtwängler was put in a position of teaching them the music while forging a cohesive interpretation on the entire production at the same time. During his rehearsals, a young music student was permitted to watch and listen. "I remember clearly," he recalled 40 years later:

> Even when Furtwängler was walking into the pit, there was tension around him—like electricity. In the rehearsals, he would go over certain

27. The phrase "first-class" issues replete with quotation marks from Edwin MacArthur, *Flagstad: A Personal Memoir,* (New York) 1965, p. 289.

28. MacArthur also became a loyal friend to Furtwängler and acted as an informal go-between with American concert agents in trying to find ways of bringing Furtwängler to America with either the Berlin or Vienna Philharmonics.

29. See John Culshaw, *Ring Resounding,* (New York) 1965, pp. 43–44, for a fuller discussion of Flagstad's relationship with various recording companies.

30. Strauss' choice of Flagstad was also revealing because she had never sung any of his operas on stage and had performed with him only once. That was in Bayreuth in the summer of 1933, when she was singing relatively minor roles—Gutrune and the Third Norn. Strauss plucked her from the ranks and appointed her as soloist at the Festival's performance of Beethoven's Ninth that year. The political catastrophes of the years following their collaboration separated them forever, but Strauss never forgot nor ceased loving her voice to the end of his life.

parts again and again, patiently explaining what he wanted . . . patiently, everything patiently. And slowly, this wonderful warm sound came out of the orchestra, and the tension, always this wonderful *tension* from beginning to end. He was one of the few musicians who could create tension even in the pauses when there was nothing but silence. That continuity, that *flow* . . . was something I will never forget. Those rehearsals and the performances were something very special for me.

That music student was Claudio Abbado.[31] He had no idea that one day he would be appointed Music Director of the Berlin Philharmonic.

Furtwängler's progress in reclaiming his old audiences and conquering new ones had now extended through most of Europe. But the United States was a different story. Furtwängler had not appeared in the United States since 1927. He had come close to succeeding Toscanini as chief conductor of the New York Philharmonic in 1936, but it never came to pass because of Göring's intrigues.[32] He also had earned Toscanini's undying enmity when he refused to leave Germany during the Nazi regime. And now there were new enemies among the intellectual and artistic community who had fled Germany and had started over again in America.

Toscanini had come to America as the specter of Fascism crossed Italy, but he was not a refugee in the sense that Thomas Mann or Arnold Schönberg were. They could not go back to Germany; he could and did return to Italy for summer vacations until the war broke out. He had been known in the United States since the turn of the century and became its undisputed king of conductors in 1937 when the NBC Radio Network gave him his own orchestra and access to millions through regular weekly broadcasts. To the end, he never really admired any of his contemporaries and was quite candid about it. He loathed Bruno Walter as a "weak artist, a weak man" whose fame rested far less on his talent than the pity of influential people who were appalled at his treatment by the Nazis.[33] He dismissed Stokowski as a "genial dilettante." Nonetheless, he was intelligent enough to keep politics apart from his true feelings about talent. When pressed at a social gathering in New York in 1948 about whom he felt was the finest conductor in the world apart from himself, he finally blurted out "Furtwängler!" and stormed away.

Now, as the spring of 1948 approached, the board of the Chicago Symphony fired its chief conductor Artur Rodzinski. Twelve years before, Rodzinski had been one of the conductors whom the New

31. Personal conversation with the author, Vienna, 24 October 1990.
32. See Chapter 11.
33. Gallup, p. 100.

York Philharmonic engaged for the season that would have marked Furtwängler's inaugural appearance as music director. The Chicago board sent out feelers to learn if Furtwängler would be interested in becoming its music director. Furtwängler was interested, but he was not sure if he would be welcomed. Chicago had always had a large German population and its cultural life had traditionally been run by Germans and other middle Europeans. Furtwängler's stand against the Nazis was well known there, and the board felt he would be the ideal choice to make their exceptionally fine orchestra a great one. They assured him that he would have no difficulty gaining entry into the United States. Furtwängler wanted to come to Chicago, but he proposed an extended guest conducting arrangement instead of a more involved commitment. The board wanted Furtwängler on any terms, and he signed a contract for an eight-week engagement during the 1949–1950 season.

When the news of the agreement hit the papers, all hell broke loose.[34] The board received telegrams from various prominent artists stating they would not appear with the orchestra if Furtwängler was engaged. The protestors included pianists Vladimir Horowitz, Arthur Rubinstein, and Alexander Brailowsky; French soprano Lily Pons and her conductor-husband André Kostelanetz, Fritz Busch, Gregor Piatigorsky (who had been Furtwängler's first cellist in Berlin), and violinists Nathan Milstein and Jascha Heifetz. In reports of these protests, Furtwängler was mentioned in the same breath as pianist Walter Gieseking, who was returning for a tour of the United States for the first time in over a decade just as the Furtwängler scandal was brewing. Gieseking never had been enthusiastic about the Nazis but evidently had been most obliging of their requests. The outcry against him led to his arrest by immigration officials shortly after his arrival in New York early at the end of January 1949. He voluntarily went back to Germany immediately. Later, reporters quoted him as saying, "[The Americans] evidently believe 70 million Germans should have evacuated Germany and left Hitler there alone."[35]

In his telegram, Rubinstein expressed the feelings of many at the time who had no empathy with Furtwängler's situation: anyone who didn't leave Germany *had* to be a Nazi:

I refuse to be associated with anyone who sympathized with Hitler, Göring, or Goebbels. Had Furtwängler been a good democrat, he would have turned his back on Germany, as, for example, Thomas Mann did.

34. See *Furtwängler and America* for a detailed account of Furtwängler's controversy in Chicago, pp. 97–126.
35. This statement appeared in several papers. The *Chicago Daily Tribune* reported it on 27 January 1949.

Furtwängler remained because he assumed that Germany would win the war. Gieseking behaved in a similar manner. It is said that Furtwängler rescued some people from the Nazis' clutches. This has not been confirmed. At present, he is seeking dollars and prestige in America, and he deserves neither.[36]

Horowitz also made it plain that he would not appear with any orchestra that engaged either Furtwängler or Gieseking. From another corner of this fray, a man from New York anonymously telephoned other artists and spoke of blacklists for those who declined.[37]

Horowitz would probably not have appeared with Furtwängler under the best of circumstances, for he had long harbored a dislike for his "ignorant" German colleague. Back in 1929, during a rehearsal of the Brahms Piano Concerto in B flat in Berlin, Furtwängler made a remark to Horowitz that the pianist never forgot or forgave. As Horowitz recalled it to his biographer Glenn Plaskin: "Unlike America," said Furtwängler during a break, "we don't play like such virtuosos here."[38]

Furtwängler had earlier observed that Horowitz's playing was "definitely not my type," and Horowitz regarded the virtuoso remark as a slur on his phenomenal success in America. To add palpable professional injury to desultory insult, Horowitz claimed Furtwängler began the concert by performing Bruckner's Eighth Symphony, which lasts at least 80 minutes. At the end of the concerto, only a handful of people were left in a hall that had started off packed to the rafters. Horowitz vowed never to appear with Furtwängler again, and he was keeping his word.[39]

By this time Horowitz was also Toscanini's son-in-law, and the tacit message to those thinking of refusing to sign the petition was

36. This telegram was released to the press and appeared in virtually every news report about Rubinstein's protest. See *Time*, 17 January 1949.
37. Riess, p. 302.
38. *Horowitz*, p. 129.
39. While Horowitz's memory for music was considered infallible to the end of his life, the programs of the Berlin Philharmonic for that 1929 season list Bruckner's Third Symphony—not the Eighth—as the opening work for that performance. The Third Symphony is almost half the length of the Eighth. Three seasons earlier, actually, Furtwängler played the Bruckner Ninth Symphony (another long work) as the opening work when they appeared together in Leipzig and in Berlin within the space of 10 days. Horowitz played Liszt's Second Piano Concerto on those occasions. Bruckner's Ninth takes almost 90 minutes to complete if played without cuts, and the audience must surely have become a bit restive by the time Horowitz forged into the slow section in the Liszt. Horowitz's story seems to make more sense in that 1926 context, though it does not explain why he appeared with Furtwängler again in 1929 if the first collaboration was so sour. In any event, Horowitz recalled that by the time he started the slow section of his piece in 1929, people were going home. The handful of people left at the end were rewarded for their patience with an account of Tchaikovsky's *Overture-Fantasia, Romeo and Juliet.*

clear: if Horowitz couldn't apply sanctions against them, his father-in-law certainly would.[40] Few artists dared to decline signing a petition protesting Furtwängler's engagement. Among this minority, Yehudi Menuhin was again the most vociferous.[41] The Associated Press ran an excerpt from Menuhin's telegram to the Chicago Symphony:

> I shall have to give up the pleasure of playing with the Chicago Symphony Orchestra until this affair has been clarified. . . . Furtwängler showed firm resistance to the Nazis; he kept as many Jews as possible in the Berlin Philharmonic Orchestra, never undertook propaganda tours, was never a member of the Nazi Party . . . He has been denazified by those responsible for clarifying his case, and it is not for us to question their judgment.[42]

The Chicago Symphony needed the signers of the petition more than they, as a bloc, needed the Chicago Symphony. What is more, a nightmare loomed menacingly before the board: the legendary father-in-law of one of the greatest pianists before the public becoming personally involved in the scandal. Among the performers who had their careers at stake in this controversy, Menuhin alone published a statement condemning the cabal against Furtwängler:

> I have never encountered a more brazen attitude than that of three or four ringleaders in the frantic and obvious efforts to exclude an illustrious colleague from their happy hunting grounds. I consider their behavior beneath contempt.[43]

Menuhin's musical colleagues could say little in response to this charge without making themselves look defensive, but the venom from the publicity they generated with their protest took swift effect on the Jewish population. An acrimonious report promptly appeared in *Der Tag* (usually referred to as the "Jewish Day"), a Yiddish language newspaper based in New York and widely read by Jewish émigrés. The piece lambasted Menuhin for playing with Furtwängler only because he "loves to play with the murderers of his people."[44] None-

40. Horowitz married Toscanini's daughter Wanda in 1933.
41. Friedelind Wagner had voiced her support of Furtwängler earlier in 1946. See Chapter 17.
42. 13 January 1949.
43. See *New York Times*, 6 January 1949, p. 20; *Chicago Daily Tribune*, 6 January 1949, p. 25 (same *New York Times* wire story).
44. "While Menuhin Fiddled," by Mordechai Danzis, 6 December 1949, p. 4. Menuhin's father, Moshe, fired off an open letter (in English) to the editor dated 12 January 1949. The typed, six-page, single-spaced missive began by suggesting that Danzis "consult a good psychiatrist" and closed with Balaam's words from the Old Testament: "Oh, how shall I curse whom God hath not cursed? Or shall I defy whom the Lord hath not defied? Let me die the death of the righteous, and let my end be like his."

theless, it was only Menuhin, of all the top-flight musicians involved in this affair, who remained steadfast in his support of Furtwängler, and his public stand throughout this period made him few friends. He was almost mobbed when he went to Israel for concert performances a year earlier in 1948.[45] After a grueling news conference and a frank conference with Israeli leaders, Menuhin convinced his attackers of Furtwängler's integrity, and the storm blew over quickly. But that harrowing experience did not diminish his support for Furtwängler when the controversy in Chicago erupted. In 1989 Menuhin recalled that scandal to me:

> I received calls from various Jews—I've forgotten their names, though Ira Hirschmann was certainly one of them—who applied strong pressure on me to dissociate myself from Furtwängler. Although they didn't say it in so many words, their meaning was clear: if I persisted in backing Furtwängler, I would never play with any of the major orchestras and certainly never again with any of the people who were against Furtwängler. Of course, I did play with the major orchestras again and frequently, but it was a time of hysterical emotions. But I'll tell you one thing, Sam. I would do exactly the same thing if I had the chance to do it over again.[46]

Over the years, Menuhin has played with every well-known conductor—as well as many not so well known. His eyes glaze over as he recalls his work with Furtwängler:

> Of all the great conductors I played with, only Furtwängler made one look into the music to search for a truth within it. He was grateful to me for what I did, but he never articulated it in words. The only time Furtwängler said anything remotely hostile about the Allies was when he could not rehearse with me at the time he wanted because of some military bureaucratic procedure. He just sighed and said, "So this is what Germany has come to."[47]

Of the musicians whose names did appear on the list of protesters, Furtwängler was especially hurt by Piatigorsky.[48] The cellist owed his

---

45. Robert Magidoff presents a comprehensive account of the attacks on Menuhin in Israel in *Yehudi Menuhin: The Man and His Story*, (London) 1956, pp. 252–254.

46. Personal conversation with the author, London, 18 April 1989.

47. Personal conversation with the author, 18 April 1989.

48. See the notable critic Claudia Cassidy's summary of her conversation with Furtwängler while she was in Salzburg during the summer of 1949, *Chicago Daily Tribune*, 4 September 1949, Part 7, p. 8. While Cassidy was convinced that Furtwängler was no Nazi, she apparently based her decision about him entirely on her personal reaction to his performances rather than an intensive interview with him about his activities during the Third Reich: "I knew to my own satisfaction when I heard his Beethoven that a small man could not make such music." An account of Furtwängler's reaction to

start to Furtwängler and must have known exactly where Furtwängler stood with regard to the Nazis. It later came to light that the names of several artists were used in the protest without their permission, and Piatigorsky always categorically denied that he had joined the protest.

Nathan Milstein volunteered his name but eventually withdrew from the group of protestors. Milstein told the press that he saw a parallel between the Furtwängler case and the Nazi scientists the United States was importing at the time:

> We brought those scientists presumably to benefit us by giving us their know-how. Well, maybe we can obtain some of those benefits from the musical skills of persons like Furtwängler.[49]

Milstein's statement brought an angry public retort from Rubinstein, who had lost most of his family in the Holocaust:

> German scientists may be considered in the category of spoils of war that belong to the victor. Those who have been imported are being used by our government for specific purposes within laboratory walls. If Gieseking and Furtwängler were brought here on this same basis, I would say use them, not for public appearances where they may exert some influence [as Nazis] . . . but in institutions experimenting with musical therapy and other humanitarian projects. The comparison with scientists would then be analogous.[50]

Fritz Busch found himself more radically involved in the controversy. He was quoted in the United Press calling Furtwängler

> . . . a man without character, and I don't think that a man without character should be allowed to conduct Beethoven, Mozart and Haydn. They were men of character.[51]

Busch, of course, specialized in these composers "of character." Six weeks later, Busch suddenly contested the veracity of the statements that had been alleged to him. Where had Busch been all this time? It was mid-February by now, the proverbial barn door had long been

---

Cassidy's inquisition might well have settled doubts about his reputation more decisively. When I reached Miss Cassidy by telephone on 17 April 1991 in an effort to discuss the Chicago scandal and other matters relating to Furtwängler, she politely but firmly declined to comment, whereupon the connection was terminated.

49. See "Kup's Column," *Chicago Sun*, 17 January 1949. Note: Page numbers are omitted in some citations of Chicago newspapers because they were taken from the clippings file of the Chicago Symphony Archives. I am deeply indebted to Ms. Brenda Nelson-Strauss and the staff of the Archives for assisting me in gathering these clippings.

50. *Chicago Daily Tribune*, 20 February 1949.

51. Report dated 6 January 1949.

closed on the controversy, and echoes of Busch's imputed stand on the matter were peeling off green room walls throughout the world. Nonetheless, he enlisted the influence of the Chicago Symphony's president to issue a belated rebuttal. Edward L. Ryerson planted a telegram from Busch in a story bearing the headline "Fritz Busch Denies He Opposed Furtwängler's Coming Here" under the by-line of William Leonard, a music critic for the *Journal of Commerce:*

> Just learned about statement which I am said to have made in the Furt- wängler case. I herewith declare that I never since at least 1932 met Furt- wängler, nor have I been in contact with him. Second, that he, however, contacted me in July 1933, while I was conducting in Buenos Aires and proposed that I share with him Berlin Philharmonic concerts that follow- ing winter which I did not accept. Third, that since the Furtwängler case came up towards the end of the last war, I strictly refused to give infor- mation to the press or to organizations in public, as I was asked, because I consider the average man unable to make appropriate distinction between a person's moral viewpoint or mere jealous rivalry. Fourth, all other information is erroneous. Regards.[52]

The cable glistened with whitewash, and the headline ("Fritz Busch Denies He Opposed Furtwängler . . .") asserted far more than anything he said in his telegram. In fact, Busch merely denied that he made *any* statements about Furtwängler, not that he opposed or approved of his appearance in America. Busch probably never cast aspersions on Furtwängler publicly, but the telegram really never addressed that issue either. Instead, its wording succeeded only in betraying a defensive hauteur regarding the "average man" and his capacity to discern "jealous rivalry."

Busch's telegram may have been mostly blather under pressure, but it divulged a fact that implicitly spoke volumes for Furtwängler's character under duress: Furtwängler had indeed invited Busch to share his subscription concerts at the Berlin Philharmonic (no paltry honor) in the 1933–1934 season even though Busch posed a palpable threat to his professional longevity. What is more, Furtwängler even inter- vened to get Busch his own series, pressing him on Bernhard Rust, the Nazi Minister of Science, Art and National Education at the time:

> It goes without saying that Busch could work in Berlin. In any event, he can certainly lead a series of concerts as guest with the [Berlin] Philhar- monic in the Philharmonie (such as the one Bruno Walter had) . . .[53]

52. Dated 18 February 1949.
53. 4 June 1933, pp. 3–4. Furtwängler also pleaded for composer Arnold Schönberg and musicians Robert Hernreid and Karl Straube in this letter. Source: Furtwängler File, Berlin Document Center.

These few lines also go far in contradicting the image of Furt-wängler as a ruthless opportunist that his harsher critics try to maintain.[54] Furtwängler tried actively to help Busch, even though he had good reason to turn his back: Göring had recently tried to tear up Furtwängler's contract as Music Director of the Staatsoper in Berlin so that he could give the job to Busch. Much later, Furtwängler recalled the controversy over his contract in a letter to former Berlin Philharmonic member Gilbert Back dated 12 March 1949:

> General Intendant Tietjen had already signed a contract with me at the Staatsoper in the winter of 1932 before the Nazis took over. When Göring presented Tietjen with his wish to make Busch Music Director, Tietjen told him he would have to be careful since a contract with Furtwängler already existed. I remember very well how this fact upset Göring, and in his first meeting with Tietjen and me in Spring 1933, he said bluntly that he would really have preferred it otherwise.[55]

In the wake of such a bruise to his ego, Furtwängler's generosity to his colleague indicates just how threatened *he* felt, despite the calibre of "gun" backing Busch. Never one to fish for gratitude, Furtwängler did not inform Busch of what he had done in his behalf, and he was now— in 1949—paying dearly for that restraint.

The maelstrom surrounding his engagement in Chicago made Furtwängler all the more determined to conduct there. He felt that once he confronted his detractors and enemies, he could set them straight about what he had done in Germany during the war. Similarly, he felt that backing off without a fight would lend credence to the condemnation being heaped on him. Letters and cables between the Board of the Chicago Symphony and Furtwängler containing proposals and counter-proposals crossed the Atlantic.

Newspapers and magazines across the nation blew up the controversy into an international media brouhaha with an unlikely set of cross-currents: musical, political, religious, intellectual, and ethnic. Hugo Kolberg, a former concertmaster of the Berlin Philharmonic who was forced to emigrate because he was married to a Jew, Friedelind Wagner, and many others who knew Furtwängler was no Nazi wrote letters to the editor of the *Chicago Daily Tribune*. One of the most notable of the letter writers was Louis P. Lochner, who later edited Goebbels' diaries and wrote a biography of the violinist Fritz

---

54. Wessling, for example, portrays Furtwängler as little more than a ruthless careerist.

55. Wilhelm Furtwängler Archives, Zürich. Busch himself refers vaguely to a "contract to go to Berlin" in *Pages from a Musician's Life*, p. 210. See also *Kraftprobe*, p. 63, and Riess, p. 160.

Kreisler. He had been the Associated Press' Bureau Chief in Berlin before the war and knew Furtwängler's situation first hand. A *Tribune* correspondent named Sigrid Schmidt who had been based in Berlin during the regime recalled a personal incident in an article at the height of the controversy:

> While I was in Germany, Furtwängler had a well-known German doctor, Johannes Ludwig Schmitt[56] who was a glowing anti-Nazi and whom, to my personal knowledge, the Gestapo had twice tried to kill in 1939 and 1940. Later Schmidt was arrested and thrown into a concentration camp. When Furtwängler became ill, he complained to the authorities that he would not be able to conduct unless his doctor could treat him. Schmitt then was released for a few hours to treat Furtwängler.
>
> To Americans who do not know terror, a conductor who asked for treatment from a doctor under Nazi arrest might not seem brave, but in Germany people hastened to forget victims of Nazis because it was dangerous to know anyone in a concentration camp.[57]

Schmidt also added, however, that the Nazis were displeased with his "unenthusiastic Nazi salute." He stated too that the Nazis gave Furtwängler a new limousine as a birthday gift when he never received anything of the sort.

The credentials of Furtwängler's supporters were flawless, but Jewish groups headed by the Chicago chief of the American Jewish Congress mounted an attack on Furtwängler anyway. Rabbi Morton Berman stated the attitude not only of the Jewish community, but those who remained "neutral" in the controversy:

> Furtwängler attributes the protest principally to Jewish Organizations, while claiming that the American public itself disapproves of such a protest. This is a Nazi method.
>
> Furtwängler preferred to swear fealty to Hitler. He accepted at Hitler's hands his reappointment as Director of the Berlin Philharmonic Orchestra. He was unfailing in his service to Goebbels' ministry of culture and propaganda.
>
> With reference to Furtwängler's claim that he had helped individual Jews, it was my experience in Germany last summer, in listening to those who were being tried in Nürnberg, that every Nazi seeks to make the same claim. The token saving of a few Jewish lives does not excuse Mr. Furtwängler from official, active, participation in a regime which mur-

56. Johannes Ludwig Schmitt's name is spelled incorrectly on the published copy. Possibly a copy-editing error. I have corrected it. See Chapter 15 for a fuller account of this physician.
57. *Chicago Daily Tribune*, 7 January 1949, Part 2, p. 1.

dered six million Jews and millions of non-Jews. Furtwängler is a symbol of all those hateful things for the defeat of which the youth of our city and nation paid an ineffable price.

Berman was joined by such diverse groups as the American Veterans' Committee; The Pioneer Women, an arm of the Women's Labor Zionist organization of America; and the Society for the Prevention of World War III, Inc., headed by historian Mark van Doren.

While the papers published well-screened letters from their readers, *Nation*, an intellectual, somewhat leftish periodical, published an editorial on a similar scandal that occurred around the same the time: Walter Gieseking's aborted concert tour of America. It advised its readers to stay away from concerts by suspected Nazi collaborators—and almost anyone coming from Germany at this time was highly suspect. Perhaps the most cogent articulation of the dilemma faced by the public in contemplating both the Furtwängler and Gieseking controversies was put into a letter from a Harvard philosophy professor responding to the editorial in *Nation*:[58]

> . . . I keep away from performances by collaborators; I don't want to go. Then, what is all the arguing about, you might ask. The point is that while my *feelings* point one way, my reason points another way, and this sort of schizophrenia is not very agreeable.[59]

In the meantime, the Chicago Symphony also received sheaves of opinions from a wide variety of parties with equally as many diverse motivations. There were no conflicts between feelings and reason expressed in most of these letters, and they presented a much more visceral barometer of cultural and ethnic attitudes in middle America at that time. The reactions included notes from subscribers, and there were many like this one:[60]

> Should Wilhelm Furtwängler come to Chicago . . . I shall boycott all . . . performances and urge all my friends to do the same.[61]

But Furtwängler also received support from unlikely sources such as individual veterans:

58. The editorial appeared in *Nation* on 4 December 1948. Demos' letter appeared 18 December 1948, pp. 708–709.
59. Raphael Demos, Cambridge, Mass. This letter was but one of many reactions *Nation* published over several issues. Delbert Clark, who covered Furtwängler's denazification trial for the *New York Times*, was among the correspondents.
60. Source for all the following letters: Chicago Symphony Archives.
61. S.Z.D., 9 January 1949.

Should we throw aside the fine leadership and training received from a
great musician for a slander-fear?[62]

He also was championed by ethnocentrics:

... If these people do not like [Furtwängler's engagement], let them
return to Poland or France, the land of their birth, and dictate to the people over there.[63]

A legendary retired opera diva who had sung frequently with Caruso
came forward on condition that her remarks be withheld from the
press:

Most of these complaining musicians have learned everything they know
in Germany. They have no right to make one Individual responsible for
things that have happened.[64]

Finally, the aphoristic man on the street sent in a form he received
from a protest group, scratched out the text, and typed in a vote in
favor of Furtwängler:

These bums talk about racial discrimination. Wow!! Get Furtwängler. I'm
all for it.[65]

News of the scandal spread through Europe, and the Board of
Directors also received telegrams of support from the Berlin Philharmonic and the Vienna Philharmonic, as well as letters from individual
parties who were well acquainted with Furtwängler's relationship to
the Third Reich. Serena Krafft was a Holocaust survivor and the wife
of Anthony Krafft, once a musician in the Berlin Philharmonic who
died at Auschwitz:

Dr. Furtwängler did his best to carry through that the Jewish musicians
could stay in their jobs, and he especially defended Mr. Gilbert Back.
    After the Jewish members had left the orchestra, Dr. Furtwängler
kept on trying to get at least some material help for them. I do not believe
that Dr. Furtwängler changed his standpoint and behavior during the
time I was in the concentration camp.[66]

62. V.P.S., U.S. Marines.
63. M. DuE., Seymour, Connecticut, no date.
64. F.H., New York, 8 January 1949.
65. No date, R.H.
66. 15 January 1949, Helgicka, Czechoslovakia.

But the most moving of these letters came from Felix Lederer, Furtwängler's colleague during his Mannheim years, now Professor of Music at the famous High School for Music in Berlin, whom he had helped through a particularly difficult health crisis during the war:[67]

> It is *incomprehensible* to me that *Furtwängler* should be tainted with an anti-Semitic attitude. I am Jewish and was associated with Furtwängler in Mannheim (1915–1920) and in Berlin during the Nazi period. He always wholeheartedly supported Jewish artists with his whole being. He remained loyal to me in spite of being watched by the Gestapo, and always addressed me as "my very dear friend" in his letters even at a time when such familiarity [with a Jew] could have cost him his head. Only those artists who are falsely informed could refuse to play under his leadership. Anybody who endured the terrible Nazi period knows how bravely and selflessly Furtwängler intervened in behalf of Jewish artists. I hope that these lines will therefore contribute to opening the path for Furtwängler to America, where my son lives in San Francisco.[68]

Unfortunately, these letters arrived after the affair was long over. To add an extra measure of ugliness to it all, Furtwängler himself received a telegram from a certain "Israel Stern," threatening him with physical harm if he came to Chicago.[69]

In the middle of this fracas, an artist who may well have wished to be in any other city on the planet at that moment arrived in Chicago for a recital.[70] Kirsten Flagstad already had faced an angry press and public on two previous occasions: first, over her decision in 1941 to return to Nazi-occupied Norway to be with her husband, who later was accused of being a collaborator; second, over her temerity in returning to concertize in the United States after the war. But she captivated her audiences, and the headline for one review of her recital in Chicago trumpeted: "Flagstad Triumph Bears Augury for Furtwängler Return,"[71] a banner that undoubtedly sent chills through the corps of opposition lined up against Furtwängler. Flagstad rarely gave interviews, and her availability to the press during this visit was particularly restricted.[72]

The sheer weight of the controversy was becoming too much for the board of the Symphony to withstand, even though the public

67. See Chapter 14.
68. 14 January 1949, Berlin.
69. Source: Wilhelm Furtwängler Private Archives, Clarens.
70. 7 January 1949, Orchestra Hall.
71. (Chicago) *Journal of Commerce*, 8 January 1949.
72. See Chapter 21 for more on Flagstad's political travails.

slowly was learning more about Furtwängler's political stance during the Third Reich. A decision for or against Furtwängler was now academic. The row was promptly settled by the musicians' union. President James C. Petrillo announced that Furtwängler would probably not be allowed a union work permit. This meant, in the words of a union spokesman, "Furtwängler is not coming to Chicago. He won't have an orchestra to conduct." Finally, the orchestra directors asked him to withdraw, offering full payment of the salary stipulated in the contract. Furtwängler obliged but refused payment of any sort, even though he was still in difficult financial straits and could easily have demanded a hefty settlement on top of the salary offer. In the end, the Chicago Symphony got off cheap: the board generously arranged to send him $900 to cover the cost of cable and telephone charges.[73]

Bruno Walter, meanwhile, was one of the few prominent musicians who had openly refused to join the boycott against Furtwängler and had managed to keep his name from being used without his consent. But neither was Walter inclined to speak openly in support of Furtwängler; he simply wanted to stay out of the mess altogether. Nonetheless, involvement was unavoidable, for the anti-Furtwängler feeling had long passed the point of hysteria. Sol Hurok had emerged as one of the most powerful impresarios in America at the time and wrote to Walter after he supposedly misread a blurb about Walter and Furtwängler in the *New York Post* by gossip columnist Elsa Maxwell.[74] In this letter, he supposedly confused the name Furtwängler with Lion Feuchtwanger, the Jewish émigré writer and author of *Jew Süss*. While Hurok was purportedly asking Walter to clarify his position regarding Furtwängler, he also made it clear that his concern stemmed from being a "member of several anti-Nazi organizations" who opposed Furtwängler coming to America.[75] Walter sensed muscle being applied, and he reacted accordingly. On 25 November, he replied curtly to Hurok:

> I am not in the habit of rectifying incorrect statements of this kind. However, your letter is so completely erroneous that I feel I should set things right:
> Lion Feuchtwanger, the author of world-wide reputation, has been living in California for many years as a refugee from Nazi persecution, as everybody knows.
> Anyway, how wrong your quotation of Miss Maxwell's statement, or

73. Source: Minutes, Meeting of Trustees of the Orchestral Association, Finance Committee transactions, 16 May 1949, Chicago Symphony Archives.
74. 17 November 1948, p. 12.
75. The letter from Hurok to Walter is dated 22 November 1948. Source: Bruno Walter Collection, Lincoln Center Library for the Performing Arts, New York.

Miss Maxwell's quotation of whatever I said, may be, you are insinuating a tendency on my part to favor the admission of Nazis to this country, an insinuation which is utterly unfounded. I refer in this connection to page 263 of my autobiography "Theme and Variations" where my clearly defined view on this subject is expressed in a way very much compatible with your attitude.

Two days later, Hurok sent him an obsequious note of regret over the confusion in names and enclosed a copy of Maxwell's column in the *Post*. But the apology was actually a "thank you" note, for Hurok now had in his hands what he wanted all along: a signed affidavit stating Walter's "clearly defined view on this subject . . . expressed in a way very much compatible with your attitude."

The Chicago scandal both confused and unnerved Furtwängler. He simply could not understand the rabid hostility against him alone when others who were avowed Nazis met little or no resistance as they continued their postwar careers. Bruno Walter had been something of a mentor to Furtwängler since the turn of the century, and Furtwängler turned again to him:[76]

I received your telegram in which you disclose that you would never have declared either publicly or privately that you would decline to appear wherever I might be engaged.

The whole matter was so unexpected and shocking that I spontaneously sent you this telegram, since I knew for a fact that you had been there as a guest conductor last year. My colleague Ansermet told me over the phone that [the boycott] was a nefarious agitation, pressure brought to bear by a few isolated conductors who risked nothing in withdrawing or making the situation difficult for the Chicago Symphony. I freely acknowledge that I can make no sense out of this matter. I believe they are all in collaboration with a threatening telegram I recently received signed "Israel Stern." I can only repeat my great astonishment at what is being said against me, for of all the musicians in the Third Reich, I took up the position of the Jews more than anybody else.

Today, four years after the horrible war, we all stand before a new and different problem, and I believe it would be good for all concerned if all of us who spring from the same culture and who ultimately have the same attitude toward art and its mission were all aware as a community of how different the world is now. In any case, your telegram made a deep impression on my soul.

Permit me to say something here. I presently face many problems of the practical world which will be hard to shake free. If it would be possible that I might be permitted to approach you now and then with a question

76. The source for this correspondence is the Bruno Walter Collection, Lincoln Center Library for the Performing Arts, New York. Walter's letters to Furtwängler are included in an edition of his correspondence, *Briefe*, Frankfurt, 1962.

or a request about advice in remembrance of earlier times of friendly and amicable relations between us, I would be so grateful. I ask you however to write to me openly, unless you think for whatever reasons that it is not permissible.   *1 January 1949*[77]

While Walter never made his feelings about the Furtwängler matter public, he was privately furious that Furtwängler had remained in Germany regardless of his motivations.[78] Walter replied promptly from Beverly Hills in a tone whose anger was hardly disguised:

You write that the "whole matter was unexpected and shocking." Please consider thus: Throughout the years [of the Nazi regime], your art was used as a conspicuously effective means of propaganda for the Regime of the Devil, that you performed high service to this regime through your prominent image and great talent, that the presence and performance of an artist of your stature abetted every horrible crime against culture and morality, or at least, gave considerable support to them. Consider too that you ultimately have lived for twelve years in the Nazi Empire without terror, or fear of it, of what was happening there, and you were never forced into extremity, and that you carried your title and positions during this time. In light of all that, of what significance is your assistance in the isolated cases of a few Jews?

The general public knows nothing about your conflicts, problems, or depressions. Few know about your opposition and protests and they remain skeptical about your denazification. The world judges by "how it seems," not "what it is."

I was sure that you could not be a Nazi. I considered the suffering, conflicts, and daily hardships in connection with my basic repugnance to such a tyranny, and it was clear to me and remains a fact to me that finally anger and resentment of internal feelings must lead to reconciliation, as long as one does not look with equanimity upon unquestionable criminality.

Coming to your request to counsel you now and then in the solution of the problems of the practical world, I simply have no credentials to advise you in such matters. The "practical world" is chaotic, and every piece of advice carries a burden of responsibility which oppresses me. I believe in any case that I must communicate this thought with you. We should hope that the chaotic conditions may take a turn for the better before our next meeting this summer in Salzburg!   *13 January 1949*[79]

77. Source: Bruno Walter Collection, Lincoln Center Library for the Performing Arts, New York.

78. Walter drafted a letter to Rudolf Bing on 26 March 1946 informing him that he would not conduct at the Edinburgh Festival in 1947 if Furtwängler also was invited, but two days later, he wrote another version of it omitting Furtwängler's name but leaving no doubt to whom he was referring. See Chapter 17.

79. Source: Bruno Walter Collection, Lincoln Center Library for the Performing Arts, New York.

But Furtwängler was not about to let the matter go at that:

> I have always believed that the Third Reich passed on false statements by
> or about me—as I have experienced in several instances throughout my
> career—and I wish to ask you to point out briefly how my behavior is per-
> ceived, how my conduct is regarded in your own thoughts.
>
> What you write about the boycott against me seems to represent the
> prevailing attitude toward Germany and, at very least, shows a sickness
> in the very great lack in the capacity of others to understand the condi-
> tions and circumstances in a totalitarian country . . . Since the Nazis used
> my art for their propaganda wagon, my reputation was injured far more
> than I could possibly exploit the Nazis for my own profit. I feel the whole
> affair is a slanderous steam roller, grossly unfair, and it is deeply upsetting
> for me to see that genuine artists share these impressions without making
> an effort to inform themselves properly.
>
> . . . I can thoroughly understand the feelings of the Jews against the
> German people, particularly those who suffered at the hands of the Nazis.
> But is it not more frightful to suppress your own people in so terrorizing
> and detestable a manner, terroristic, and placing us with impunity on the
> pillory in the same way the Germans were pilloried previously? Why does
> no one seek to put themselves in the place of those who were born in Ger-
> many and detested everything that happened there as much as those on
> the outside did? Don't these people deserve respect because they stayed
> out of love for Germany?   *22 January 1949*[80]

Walter carefully told Furtwängler off again:

> Your letter of the 22d shows how divergent our views are with respect to
> important questions, and my experience in the fruitlessness of debating
> opposing convictions leads me to believe that we should not continue our
> discussion. Yet, I don't want my silence to be construed as ill will or as an
> assent to your views. I therefore will at least indicate the differences of
> our viewpoints without further discussing them with you . . . You write
> that the boycott shows a sickness that incapacitates the ability of those
> demonstrating against you to empathize with your situation. This sick-
> ness is a world epidemic, against which only a firm and sincerely pains-
> taking good will can be immune. And I must say respectfully that you
> exhibit the symptoms of this illness in your attitude toward the partici-
> pants in the boycott.
>
> You "understand the feelings of the Jews"!—as if the great number
> of demonstrators were non-Jews. As if it were a matter of national feeling
> and not essentially about abhorrence against German criminals! I don't
> subscribe to a collective judgment if it is a matter of "Germans," "Jews,"
> "French," "musicians," etc.

80. Source: Bruno Walter Collection, Lincoln Center Library for the Performing
Arts, New York.

But most of all our views diverge if you speak of "true Germans." A True German is always in possession of that praiseworthy frame of mind. But from it comes the sound of nationalism, patriotism, and out of that grows the sound and fury of catastrophe. I believe that only through the overcoming of this kind of nationalism, through developing a feeling of a world community can an improvement in the situation be reached.

Let me now reply to your question in the earlier part of your letter. I say, only that the basis of our relationship in those earlier times had nothing to do with musical matters. It all seems insignificant after the tragedies and everything else that has happened that I should want to devote only a word about them to you.

I am sorry if these lines should burden you again after all that you have endured . . . But I feel that my readiness to forgive does not prevent me from being completely sincere in my statements.   *10 February 1949*[81]

This extraordinary correspondence was articulated in the courtly literary style common to German intellectuals grounded in the manners and expressive embellishments of the 19th century. Nonetheless, Walter not only hit the mark in his replies, but he expressed the feelings of most people in America who had direct experience with the Nazi terrors. They, like Walter, simply could not understand why a man of Furtwängler's background—which Walter shared even though he was his senior by 15 years—either could not or, worse, would not leave *Nazi* Germany—a Germany that had turned the culture from which they all sprang into a pustulating disease. For his part, Furtwängler maintained that he remained in Germany to do what he could to check that disease. But Walter and other émigrés would have none of that line of reasoning, and they now were exasperated and incensed that Furtwängler could not or would not see that he had made what they felt was the wrong decision. Even feigning a little remorse would surely have brought a fair number of his howling enemies running to proffer reconciliation. But hypocrisy was simply not a word in Furtwängler's behavioral lexicon.

Fred K. Prieberg, whose monumental book on Furtwängler's excruciating relationship with the Third Reich *(Kraftprobe)* carefully documents how Furtwängler fought the Nazis "within the system," becomes especially distressed at Walter and others belittling Furtwängler's efforts to "save a few Jews."

"What is the value of the life of a Jew?" he asks. "How many Jews would Furtwängler have had to save? If he saved the life of only one Jew, *one single Jew* . . . it would have justified his decision to remain in Germany. And Furtwängler saved many lives, not only Jews."[82]

81. Source: Bruno Walter Collection, Lincoln Center Library for the Performing Arts, New York.

82. Personal conversation with the author, Diersheim, 1 April 1990.

Nonetheless, the discomfort in these letters to Walter is real. The embarrassment and anguish are genuine. But the conviction in the rightness of his decision remains unwavering. However errant they may seem to some in hindsight, these letters show the runes of a true believer. This correspondence comes as close as any man of Furtwängler's stature in this century has come to that tragic paradox of being right in what many still believe was the wrong way.

For once, Furtwängler appears to have been at a loss for words, for their correspondence on the subject ended there. But the friendship continued to the end of their lives—though it was haunted with the queasy feeling that nothing could ever be quite the same again.

Several months later, he seemed resigned to being alienated forever from America, as he wrote to Suzanne Bloch:

> I was at first very distraught at the outcome of the Chicago Affair, for I was under the impression that the Chicago Symphony would have stood by my engagement. I was convinced that if they had let me come to America just to conduct just one beat that all the difficulties would be overcome. It has turned out otherwise, and perhaps it is all just as well. The fact is, the rest of the world remains open to me even if I am shunned in America. I do not know if the matter in America will ever be straightened out. *24 June 1949*[83]

Many years later, one of the ring leaders in the cabal against Furtwängler wrote a letter to the *New York Times* claiming he had "proof" that Furtwängler had fired Jewish musicians and was indeed a Nazi collaborator. Ira Hirschmann had led the opposition against his appointment to the New York Philharmonic in 1936, and his letter was published under the two-column headline "Setting the Record Straight on Furtwängler," a damning rubric that left no doubt about the *Times'* opinion of the letter's contents. It had been touched off by a previous letter sent by Richard H. Goldstone, who lamented the scorn the public still heaped on Furtwängler, whom he knew from personal experience was never a Nazi.[84] Although Hirschmann's irresponsible statements hardly merit a full recitation, the letter serves to show the hysterical cant that was still being aired as late as 1983.

> A letter from Richard H. Goldstone (Sept. 11) contains a dangerous distortion of history on a sensitive matter that demands correction. His statement that the late German conductor Wilhelm Furtwängler "did whatever he could to protect and shield Jewish musicians" is a blatant twisting of the facts.

83. Source: Suzanne Bloch.
84. Dated 31 August 1983.

The incontrovertible truth is that Furtwängler as conductor of the Berlin Philharmonic yielded to Hitler's anti-Semitic demands and fired the Jewish members of his orchestra. Some of them fled to Ankara, Turkey, where I was serving at the time as a member of the U.S. diplomatic corps.

Furtwängler remained at his post in Germany while most of his colleagues including Artur Schnabel, Adolf Busch and Bronislaw Hubermann left the country in a public act of defiance. A photograph was published in The New York Times showing Furtwängler bowing from the podium of the Berlin Philharmonic to Hitler and his gang seated in the first row of the orchestra.

Furtwängler was the subject of an international scandal in 1936 when the board of the New York Philharmonic Orchestra engaged him to supplant the peerless Arturo Toscanini, who had defied Mussolini. I personally led a public protest against his appointment which was supported by the press and succeeded in keeping Furtwängler out of the country.

After the war, while on a Government mission to Germany, I was given access to the official U.S. records in Berlin where I located documentary evidence (now in my possession) of Furtwängler's collaboration with the Nazi regime.

Mr. Goldstone also states that: "Menuhin came to Vienna on Furtwängler's behalf." The famous violinist's defense of his conductor-friend is a blot on his record. Details of Furtwängler's perfidy are revealed in my forthcoming book, "Obbligato."[85]

Despite this clever advertising ploy, "Obbligato" has never been published, but Hirschmann contributed his manuscript of the book (spelled "Obligato" on the title page) to the New York Public Library. In it, he attacks Furtwängler tirelessly, but it contains no evidence, tangible or in testimony, that Furtwängler fired Jews or sent them to camps.

If there was indeed a coordinated force in the American music world that spearheaded and organized the cabal against Furtwängler coming to America again, its brain was surely Ira Hirschmann and its muscle was the impresario Sol Hurok. Hurok may have really been convinced that Furtwängler was a Nazi, but he also had the most to lose if Furtwängler appeared in America. Having declared a boycott on Furtwängler, he had boxed himself in by denying his stable of artists appearances with any orchestra that engaged Furtwängler. If they honored his ban, it would mean fewer engagements for them and bad business for him. If they did not, it would imply impotence. Hirschmann had the closest contact with Jewish groups and was in a position to manipulate and mobilize their sentiments against the supposed

85. 21 September 1983.

Devil's music master. Hurok's alliance with Hirschmann made them so influential that few dared to go against them. But if Jewish interest groups were the most vehement in attacking Furtwängler, it was also individual Jews who were the most vociferous in defending him. Later, Moshe Menuhin, Yehudi's father, minced no words about the scandal:

> Wilhelm Furtwängler was a victim of envious and jealous rivals who had to resort to publicity, to smear, to calumny, in order to keep him out of America so it could remain their private bailiwick. He was the victim of the small fry and puny souls among concert artists, who, in order to get a bit of national publicity, joined the bandwagon of the professional ideal ists, the professional Jews and the hired hands who irresponsibly assaulted an innocent and humane and broad-minded man . . .[86]

20

Autumn Fires

By the time Furtwängler resumed conducting after the war, he was 61 years old, and he now experienced something he never had known before: domestic tranquility. He made his home in a chalet in Clarens, Switzerland, where the four children from his wife's previous marriage and his own young son Andreas were growing up. Much as he tried to devote more of his time to composition, he was constantly being called to conduct everywhere. Differences between Celibidache and the Berlin Philharmonic were growing critical, and Furtwängler finally found that he had little choice but to take a bigger role in the orchestra's affairs. Celibidache and Furtwängler got along personally, but Furtwängler could not prevent the eccentricities that were beginning to sour the brilliant young conductor's relationship with the orchestra. At one point, for example, Celibidache wanted to fire the entire Berlin Philharmonic. He then agreed to continue conducting only if he got 1500 marks per musician at each performance for his trouble.

Furtwängler also knew that there was another conductor more than willing to take over if he did not step in, and he never had gotten over the bruising he took from Herbert von Karajan and his allies during the Third Reich.[1] Furtwängler felt that Karajan not only had used

1. For that matter, Karajan never got over the "persecution" he felt from Furtwängler for the rest of *his* life. More about that later.

all the means the Nazis gave him to further his own career but also had done it at Furtwängler's expense. Furtwängler was not about to forgive or forget. After all, even the notorious Rudolf Vedder, who had gone to such nefarious lengths to strengthen Karajan's position, had survived the war and the mock tribunals of the denazification proceedings and was now running his own agency again in Vienna. Tietjen had cleverly managed to get by, too, and he still was in charge of the Berlin Staatsoper.[2] But it was the specter of Karajan that worried and haunted Furtwängler, and Karajan, for his part, was all too willing to do so.

What alarmed Furtwängler most about Karajan was not his talent necessarily—though he was well aware of its magnitude—but what Karajan had chillingly demonstrated during the Third Reich: his steam-rolling drive for power. If Karajan were to succeed Celibidache at Berlin, he would have an impregnable power base, at least in Europe. Furtwängler himself was never interested in music as a means of gaining personal power, and he viewed Karajan's lust for it with the same consternation with which he regarded the relentless drive by the Nazis toward using music for political ends. Furtwängler was not without power even in the darkest days of his dealings with the Nazis. But that power derived from the totemic magnetism that had accrued to him naturally over his first decade as director of the Berlin Philharmonic. It was this unquantifiable quality that Karajan desperately wanted to obtain.[3]

Furtwängler was determined to prevent these power drives from being realized. The opportunity to make sure he could achieve that objective materialized in 1952 when the Berlin Philharmonic offered him a Contract for Life. Although he kept protesting that he wanted no binding contract to any orchestra, his business manager Albert Ostoff sternly warned him that he no longer was a young man and the orchestra might be forced to choose someone *younger* for its music director if Furtwängler kept refusing. What is more, the Berlin Philharmonic was proving its faith by offering him not only a pension but something no other musician ever had before in writing; the *Verwaltungsordnung*. While a single-word translation of this term is as impossible as it would be misleading, what it meant for Furtwängler

2. "Tietjen was too smart to ever join the Nazis," said Friedelind Wagner. "I remember him administering the Nazi oath to the whole company at Bayreuth, but he didn't take the oath himself. No one ever bothered to ask, 'What about Tietjen?' There were no limits to his cleverness." Personal conversation with the author, Mainz, 6 October 1990. Tietjen remained at the Staatsoper in Berlin until 1954 and rounded out his versatile career as the Intendant of the Hamburg Oper from 1954 to 1959.
3. See conversation with Griffith below.

was absolute and irrevocable power of approval and veto in the affairs of the Berlin Philharmonic. Although he long had tacitly held these powers anyway before the Nazis took over, the management of the orchestra and the Senate of Berlin were now putting the fact in his contract. For reasons we may never know, Furtwängler was at first indifferent to these blandishments.

While he was all too well aware that Karajan's image was mushrooming into a major musical figure who could make his old age even more miserable than the Third Reich had made his middle years, the notion of being bound to the orchestra by contract was somehow more onerous than the renewed menace that Karajan was presenting. Ultimately, he virtually had to be shoved to the table to sign it at the beginning of January.[4] It was the first legal document binding him to the Berlin Philharmonic since he resigned in the wake of the Hindemith Scandal in 1934. In total, Furtwängler held the position of Music Director of the Berlin Philharmonic from 1922 to 1934, and from 1952 to his death in November 1954—a total of fourteen years.

Meanwhile, Furtwängler continued to be pursued by factions in the English-speaking world who reviled him for his decision to remain in Nazi Germany. In 1951 the Metropolitan Opera approached him about leading a new production of *Lohengrin, Meistersinger* or *Tristan und Isolde.* Rudolf Bing had recently become General Manager, and he was anxious to rebuild the German wing of the company. In mid-summer 1951 he met and discussed plans with Furtwängler in Salzburg, where Furtwängler was conducting *Otello* and his third and last revival of *The Magic Flute.* They agreed in principle that Furtwängler would open the 1952 season with *Lohengrin* in a new production staged by Herbert Graf. Furtwängler was concerned about the political repercussions of this invitation, and Bing gave him a progress report about the matter when he asked for a definite commitment from Furtwängler on 8 November 1952:

> . . . My board in principle welcomes the idea of inviting you. We are still making one or two inquiries of important personalities and leaders of

4. The exact date when Furtwängler signed the contract is not clear. The *Berliner Tagesspiegel* announced that he signed on 8 January, but a letter written by Furtwängler on 2 January suggests that he signed it earlier, possibly before the Christmas holidays in 1951. See Lang, pp. 150–151. Also personal conversation between Lang and the author, Berlin, 9 October 1990. Frau Furtwängler confirmed her husband's reluctance to take a life contract. "Both the Berlin Philharmonic administration and his legal representatives had to spend a long time trying to make him understand that he had to take the contract in order to protect himself and to insure a pension for himself." (Telephone conversation with the author, 30 November 1990.) Karajan evidently was not the only one who wanted the job, but his covetousness was the substantive issue in solidifying Furtwängler's position for life at the Berlin Philharmonic.

public opinion after which I will know definitely whether or not an official invitation on behalf of the Metropolitan Opera can be extended to you.[5]

The following week, Bing wrote Furtwängler again:

> The information reports we have gathered from really important persons in public life—four or five are in the highest government and press circles—were all unanimous, that it would be a most unfavorable time for your coming right now; however, they were of the opinion that things would be quite different a year from now . . . I am deeply disappointed, but as a foreigner I am myself too new here to challenge such advice. I will try again next year and hope that you personally are not angry with me—these problems are beyond my control and exceed my power.[6]

By this time, of course, Gestapo sadists had been freed. Top aides to Goebbels at the Propaganda Ministry were let go unimpugned. Even Hans Hinkel, the cultural chief at the Propaganda Office who drove Bruno Walter out of Germany and committed numerous offenses that were severely punishable by the Allies was on his way back to prosperity. Richard Strauss had died on 12 September 1949. A resplendent funeral was given him in Munich. The obituaries barely mentioned his cozy relationship with the Nazis.

While traveling in America in 1952, Furtwängler's biographer Curt Riess asked a well known musician why so much antagonism was being heaped on Furtwängler in America. The musician replied, "People are afraid of him. Everyone knows that when he returns to America, he will receive wonderful offers. Other conductors are convinced that his return would be to their disadvantage."[7]

Much as Furtwängler wanted to face down his enemies in America, he could not help but feel a gnawing sense of irrelevance in continuing to argue his point. Although he never really gave into it until the incursions of age and ill health overwhelmed him, he found it extremely difficult to resist the feeling that something had gone terribly out of kilter with both the world and the world of music since the end of the war. The entire nature of music had been changing gradually throughout the first four decades of the century, and that development accelerated in the wake of the war, gaining further momentum with the advent of the long-play record. "Classical" music, as Furtwängler's brand of art was now called, was becoming as much of a business as the extremely lucrative "popular" side of the industry. But

5. Source: Wilhelm Furtwängler Archives, Zürich.
6. Source: Wilhelm Furtwängler Archives, Zürich.
7. Riess, p. 304.

Furtwängler was never at ease in the studio. His clashes with a brilliant recording producer, who was emerging at the British-owned recording leviathan EMI (Electrical & Musical Industries, Ltd.) and its subsidiary HMV (His Master's Voice), resulted in limiting his studio activity at a time when the power base for conductors was shifting from the concert hall to record shops around the world.

That producer was Walter Legge.[8] The son of a tailor, he was born on 1 June 1906 in the Shepherds Bush section of London. His parents were both English. Many of those who came to know him after he became an internationally famous record producer thought of him more as a European because he was so fluent in languages and was associated primarily with non-British artists. They even pronounced his name "Legguh." But Legge was as middle-class British as most Londoners of his generation, and the correct pronunciation of his name is "leg." After their relationship soured, Furtwängler frequently referred to him as "His Master's Leg[ge]." Highly intelligent and precocious, he received a disciplined secondary education. But his great love was music, and early on his ambition set its sights on becoming an important figure in music without being a musician, for he realized that he really had no specific musical talent. Indeed he had taught himself how to read music.

Like many frustrated musicians, he developed mental images of ideal performances of all the scores he borrowed from libraries. Unlike many would-be musicians, however, he decided on finding a way to bring his aural images into reality. At twenty, Legge joined HMV as a sort of public relations lecturer, going around England giving talks on the content of the company's latest releases. But he was shortly dismissed because he was considered too critical of his employers' recording policies. In less than a year he was back again and put in charge of the firm's house organ, The Voice. He also was required to write program notes for all the company's classical releases. His literary talents led to a part-time position as music critic for the *Manchester Guardian*, which he held from 1931 to 1937.

Legge's ambition to influence recording policy, however, remained unfulfilled. He saw many composers and artists being neglected, and his suggestions to redress those omissions were met with scorn. Eventually, he came up with an inspiration that he knew the company would find hard to turn down. The idea was to create subscription audiences for the works of various composers, many of

8. This summary of Legge's career is based in part on Elisabeth Schwarzkopf's memoir of her husband: *On and Off the Record: A Memoir of Walter Legge*, (New York) 1982.

whom had rarely or never been recorded before. By collecting money for recordings in advance, the company's risk and initial expenses for less than sure-fire projects would be virtually eliminated.

One composer, in particular, was high on his list for recognition: Hugo Wolf. Elena Gerhardt, probably the finest Lieder singer of the inter-war years, was engaged to record the first volume of twelve sides. The idea was a success. More than five hundred subscriptions (mostly from Japan) turned up almost at once. Legge quickly followed this bonanza by forming The HMV Beethoven Society, and Artur Schnabel sallied into his historic set of Beethoven's complete piano sonatas.

Legge's career as a recording impresario was safely launched. His circle of intimate professional contacts now included not only the internationally known artists he had secured, but such pillars of English cultural life as Ernest Newman, the British music critic of the London *Times*, whose books on Wagner did more to enlarge the musician's and layman's understanding of that composer than any other writer in the 20th century. Newman wrote the notes for the Society releases, and those essays have become almost as celebrated as the recordings for which they were written.

Newman, as we have seen, was no admirer of Furtwängler. As a champion of "objectivity," he wrote a steady stream of negative notices on Furtwängler's performances whenever he conducted in England. But Newman's tastes did not stop Legge from engaging Furtwängler to conduct the *Ring* as part of Sir Thomas Beecham's Coronation Season of opera at Covent Garden in 1937. It was a relatively felicitous first meeting, for Legge knew that Beecham wanted Furtwängler, and Beecham himself dealt directly with Furtwängler after the negotiations were completed.[9]

The onset of hostilities after 1939 prevented further contact with Furtwängler until after the war, but Legge kept in touch with German colleagues throughout those years. Within weeks of the Nazi surrender, he was busily pursuing German artists and signing them up to exclusive contracts. Furtwängler was high on his list. For his part, Furtwängler was reluctant to sign any contract in a medium he viewed with suspicion, but Legge dangled a tempting carrot in front of him. During the war years, HMV had impounded Furtwängler's royalties from his 1938 recording of Tchaikovsky's *Pathétique* Symphony, and they now amounted to about 80,000 Swiss francs. Furtwängler was

9. By 1937 Berta Geissmar, Furtwängler's friend and secretary since 1915, had been forced out by the Nazis and had become Beecham's assistant. See Geissmar, *Two Worlds of Music*, pp. 165f.

deeply in debt like many other Germans at the end of the war, and the promise of an instant windfall caused him, probably for only the second time in his life to make a decision for financial reasons.[10] He signed a contract in 1946 with HMV but did not make his first recording until the summer of the following year, three months after he resumed conducting.

The first session was held in Lucerne. Furtwängler had been invited to conduct two performances there, and one of the programs included the Beethoven Violin Concerto with Yehudi Menuhin. The occasion engendered some sense of vindication for both artists. Furtwängler had finally been cleared of complicity with the Nazis, though he had been prevented from resuming work far longer than a number of prominent Nazi conductors.[11]

In the meantime, however, Legge was indeed occupied. Not only did he move swiftly in signing artists, especially conductors, but he realized a long-held dream to create a new orchestra, whose members would be the finest players in England. It was called the Philharmonia, and Sir Thomas Beecham conducted its first performance on 25 October 1945.[12] Legge wanted Beecham to be its music director, but Beecham wanted final authority. Legge, of course, was not about to give that to him. Several conductors, including Furtwängler, performed with the orchestra and honed it into a major ensemble, but Paul Kletzki was its first principal conductor.[13] At first, there was some confusion whether the Philharmonia was strictly a recording entity rather than a bona fide concert hall ensemble because it immediately became resident at HMV. But Legge always had conceived of it as a full-service concert orchestra. Within three years of its founding, the Philharmonia was touring the continent and being lauded as world-class.

Legge's tireless enterprise got the Philharmonia under way as he was scooping up the cream of Europe's musicians for HMV: pianist Dinu Lipatti, composer Francis Poulenc, singers Hans Hotter, Pierre Bernac, Irmgard Seefried, and Elisabeth Schwarzkopf (whom he later married), were only a few of the current and future stars he signed up before the end of 1946. No sooner had Legge brought Furtwängler

10. Furtwängler first turned to conducting in 1907 in order to support himself and his family after the death of his father.
11. Among them, Clemens Krauss, Hermann Abendroth, Robert Heger, and Herbert von Karajan.
12. Stephen J. Pettitt's comprehensive history of the *Philharmonia Orchestra: A Record of Achievement, 1945–1985*, (London) 1985.
13. Kletzki was also a composer. Furtwängler performed his *Overture to a Tragedy* with the Gewandhaus Orchestra in 1925 and *Orchestral Variations* in Berlin five years later.

into the HMV stable than he signed Herbert von Karajan, too. Had Legge known something about the intensity of bad blood between the two conductors, he might have thought twice about signing Karajan or would have chosen between them. But Legge's sole aim at this point was empire: to build up HMV's repertoire performed by as many of the leading musicians in Europe as he could find before rival companies caught them. Furtwängler, always suspicious to the point of paranoia, not only was livid but felt betrayed that Legge had signed Karajan. He had barely survived the nightmare of being played off against the younger, rabidly ambitious conductor by the hands of two Machiavellian masters during the Third Reich. But for all their invidiousness, Göring and Tietjen were small scale in comparison to Legge, who easily outmatched both masters for cunning manipulation and was far more influential on the international music scene than they had ever been. And now Furtwängler looked grimly at the prospect of having to defend his preeminence as Germany's leading conductor all over again with yet another power broker, this one a good deal more dangerous to his future. The thought chilled him all the more, for the battle would be waged primarily in the recording studio, a terrain both alien and uncomfortable to him.

Nonetheless, the first sessions with Menuhin were a success, and Furtwängler completed six projects with Legge by the end of 1947; a symphony each by Beethoven (the Third) and Brahms (the First), a Mozart symphony (the 40th) and a Serenade, and two shorter works by Wagner and Beethoven.[14]

Between 1947 and 1952 Legge brought Furtwängler to the microphone over forty times in Lucerne, London and Vienna. Theirs was an exceedingly difficult collaboration. Furtwängler loathed the idea of recording in snippets of four minute takes, re-recording to correct tiny flaws, or just re-recording for the hope of a "better" take, and he especially hated recording those snippets out of sequence. Legge, in turn, found the association trying in several ways, especially along technical lines. Anthony C. Griffith was the sound engineer on many of the early Legge-Furtwängler sessions and recalled them to me in 1989 during a series of conversations at his home in Newton Abbot, England:

> I remember once when we recorded *Eine kleine Nachtmusik*, and I think I never heard a more lovely sound from a string orchestra than those here in front of me now. It always worried me because one could never get that sound on records. There was a warmth and glow to it that was just fan-

14. The Act I Prelude from *Lohengrin* and the *Coriolan Overture*, respectively.

tastic. But I think Legge was right about him. Furtwängler was much more effective in the flesh than he was on records.

I think Furtwängler and Beecham had a lot in common. The maximum playing time on a 12-inch 78 was 4 minutes and 50 seconds. They both got slower on retakes. The first take might take 4.10. The second 4.15 and so on. If they did it more than six times, they couldn't make it through before the record side ran out.

The variance in tempo between takes made continuity from one side of a 78 record to the next difficult to adjust. Although Furtwängler later acknowledged Legge as the first in his field, Legge must also have found it frustrating to work with an autocratic conductor who was sometimes loath to take suggestions from someone who was not a professional musician. Furtwängler's well-known indecision on committing himself to engagements and dates also frayed Legge's nerves, which were proverbial if not legendary for their resilience. While Furtwängler was clearly worth the trouble he created willy-nilly, Legge made no secret of finding Karajan infinitely easier to work with. As a result, Legge recorded far more with Karajan than he did with Furtwängler, and all but broadcast his preference for the younger conductor.

Griffith had a unique opportunity to view Legge's relationship with both conductors because he also worked on Legge's sessions with Karajan. We discussed his experiences with all three figures when I visited with him at Newton Abbot:[15]

Legge was a frustrated musician. He could not play any instrument. But his knowledge of music was fantastic, no doubt about it—all types of music. He liked to get hold of these young budding conductors. Here I'm thinking of people like Alceo Galliera, Igor Markevitch, and others who hadn't yet got big names but had good command of the orchestra. I think he decided that they would be his hands. He used to tell them, "do this, that . . ." and so forth. And they had to do whatever he said because there was no chance for them to get on in the world unless they made records. And he also did that for a time with Karajan—hard as that may be to even imagine now—but the time came when Karajan was getting bigger than Legge, and Legge didn't have that influence over him any longer.

Furtwängler didn't like to take direction from a producer. Perhaps that is why Legge turned away from him.

I think you may well have something there. I remember distinctly . . . we recorded the Beethoven 4th, and Furtwängler's interpretation did not

15. 12 December 1989.

please Legge. But there was little he could do about it. So he didn't have quite the personal interest in a Furtwängler recording session as he did at sessions with other conductors, especially Karajan.

Did Furtwängler take any interest in the technical side of the recording process?

I don't think so, and that may have annoyed Walter. For example, when we came to record the Siegfried Funeral March, EMI had given us two new microphones, so I thought recording a large work like that would be a good way to test them out. So I asked Legge if I might place them farther out in the hall for a natural balance, and he agreed. Furtwängler arrived and was about to conduct when he saw that the microphones were not in their usual places. So he complained to Legge, who asked him just to try it. Furtwängler refused to conduct. So Legge turned to me and asked me to put out the microphones in their usual places, but not to connect them. So we did this. Furtwängler started the orchestra and we recorded on the distant microphones. Furtwängler listened to the playback, and it eventually became a demonstration record of our new microphone technique.

Karajan, on the other hand, always was fascinated with the hardware, though maybe too interested for Walter's taste. I remember once we developed a crackle in one of our microphones, and our maintenance engineers cut off the amplifier to try and fix it. And Karajan was watching closely as he opened the equipment and suddenly said, "I think it's there," and he touched one of the components. Of course, he immediately got a violent shock. He didn't do that again.

How did the Vienna Philharmonic react to Furtwängler and Karajan during recording sessions?

Without doubt, the orchestra adored Furtwängler. The great thing about him that impressed me tremendously, was that he would always bring a few of the musicians into the control booth to listen to playbacks. He always brought anyone who had played a solo. They would sit down and listen as Furtwängler followed along with the score. The musicians would sometimes make a suggestion about re-doing a passage this way or that. Furtwängler might say, "That's an excellent idea. We'll go out and do it that way." Or he would say, "Yes, I see what you mean, but I want you to play it exactly the way you did, and I will give you more support from the basses . . ." or something to that effect. Furtwängler would always discuss what he was doing.

Karajan almost never came to listen to a playback with any of the musicians. He would come in with one or two of his friends, but never with a player. He never said anything after the playback. He just went out and told the orchestra what he wanted for the re-take.

And I'll tell you something else about Karajan in those early days. We recorded a Mozart symphony . . . the 39th. And he had a little portable record player in the control room of the recording studio with the Beecham recording, and he kept referring to it.

Were there any visible signs of friction between Furtwängler and Legge during your time with them?

Occasionally Legge would say, "Tomorrow, we'll do this and that," and Furtwängler would reply, "I'm not doing that. I'm doing something else." Furtwängler was very much the dominant person, so I think Legge rather enjoyed pulling a few fast ones on him. One got the feeling that he really was waiting for Karajan to come up in the world so that he could ditch Furtwängler. It was not easy to tell Furtwängler what to do, and Legge was very frustrated by that.

Griffith was by no means the only person who came in close contact with Furtwängler, Legge, and Karajan. Elisabeth Schwarzkopf, who married Legge in 1953, had a fruitful professional relationship with both Furtwängler and Karajan. In fact, she candidly credits Furtwängler with starting off her international career, and discussed him at length with me at her home in Switzerland:[16]

I was in awe of him all my life. A super musician whose ideal was not to impose himself on the music or the limelight . . . ever. He wasn't concerned with himself; he was only concerned about the piece of music at hand. He was not concerned with stage so much as he was concerned with the overall music on the stage. That changed a little bit over the years because he became a little deaf and so the tempi became a little slower. It was really quite disconcerting for all of us and we really had to labor to be in tempo with him. But never mind, with other conductors you were afraid of them because they would have discarded you . . . and they have . . . other famous conductors could just squash you, but not Furtwängler.

Did Furtwängler ever refer to Karajan in your presence?

I had been singing Donna Elvira almost everywhere, and I had been singing the La Scala production under Karajan. That production went to Munich, and one night, I sang Elvira there under Karajan and the next night at Salzburg under Furtwängler. The Salzburg performance especially went very well. But at the very end when we were coming away from the last curtain call, Furtwängler took my arm and said, "Whose version have we sung tonight? That of K? or mine?" I replied, "Herr Doktor, you know that my greatest pleasure is to give every great conductor their version. That is the greatest pleasure I have in life. It's a great challenge, and you know perfectly well that I was singing your version tonight." He said, "Ach, but I just wanted to test you, you know." And he laughed and patted me on the back. But it was a moment that could have turned . . . ughrrrah."

But *listen* to the pirate disc from Salzburg with Furtwängler. It's quite a wonderful thing. It is very free. But that indicates Furtwängler's dramatic sense of something that is very different from any other conductor.

16. 4 April 1990.

I have been asked to do it many different ways, but I think it is the best way I ever did it. I found it was musically and dramatically the most convincing way.

Did Furtwängler use his insecurities about Karajan or anything else against his colleagues?

We who knew Karajan intimately know that he often said how he envied Furtwängler for what he could achieve. Not that I like Karajan. I have no reason to like him at all, but I must grant him that. He always listened to Furtwängler's way and to Toscanini's way and many other conductors. There must have been some kind of love-hate on Karajan's part toward Furtwängler. And enormous admiration.

Whereas Furtwängler . . . ?

. . . Did not so much as pronounce the word. He just said "K." Karajan never, never, ever said anything negative about Furtwängler. And I say that even though I have no reason to say a good word about Karajan. I have to say the truth. He *never said a bad word* about Furtwängler. He admired him. About Furtwängler I can say only good things because he was the first one to really help me in my career. Karajan and I did marvelous work together. I must give him his due, but I do have to say, Karajan was an utterly bad character. In my case and in the case of my husband, it was so utterly awful. Although he was a great conductor, the behavior of Karajan was such that we have no reason, even after his death, to say he was a great man. He was not. He was somebody who wielded his might over everybody else. He was really a *Macht* possessor, and he used that power in a very, very awful way. But we are talking about Furtwängler, aren't we?

Tensions came to a head in late 1950, after Furtwängler had prepared and conducted all the performances of *The Magic Flute* at Salzburg for the second year in a row. In early November, Legge supervised a recording of the opera in Vienna with the same principals and orchestra—Seefried, Lipp, Dermota, the Vienna Philharmonic. The conductor, however, was Herbert von Karajan. Almost everyone was taken by surprise. In a city where nothing is more open than a secret about cultural affairs, Legge had managed to make arrangements for the recording under Karajan without Furtwängler knowing about it. His own secrets for accomplishing this covert feat were timing and technology. The world knew that Karajan was to record *Le Nozze di Figaro*, beginning on 23 October 1950. What the world did not know was that Legge added extra recording sessions, presumably for that project, extending far into November. The *Figaro* sessions had virtually the same cast of principals as *The Magic Flute* project. One project flowed into the other, and before even Vienna was aware of it, both *Figaro* and *The Magic Flute* were recorded by 21 November, *Figaro* hastily completed in six marathon sessions and *The Magic Flute* finished in twelve days. Legge's technological secret was magnetic tape. The entire industry was shifting in those years from 78-rpm shellac recordings to the long-play—LP—format, and Legge was at the forefront in implementing these advances. Instead of using the cumbersome method of recording directly onto a wax master that was used for recording 78s, Legge used reel-to-reel magnetic tape, which vastly facilitated editing and post-production procedures.

Shortly before the surreptitious sessions for *The Magic Flute*, Legge and his administrative superior David Bicknell had proposed recording *Fidelio* to Furtwängler, but Furtwängler felt it pointless to record it without the only clear choice for the eponymous role—Kirsten Flagstad. Even while *The Magic Flute* sessions were in progress under Karajan in Vienna, Bicknell again proposed recording it, probably to use it as a bargaining chip to compensate Furtwängler after he learned *The Magic Flute* was not his to record.[17] When Furtwängler finally learned he had been stabbed in the back for all posterity to see, he sent a note to Legge addressed to his house in London:

> I understand you have recorded the Salzburg *Magic Flute* with Karajan without my knowledge. Apart from the fact that this indicates an *outrageous personal breach of trust* [Furtwängler's italics]—about which I shall return in due course—I must perceive in the release of this recording a most flagrant public humiliation and personal affront, for *The Magic Flute* at Salzburg has been connected to my name in the past several years. What is more, I am scheduled to conduct it there again next year. Furthermore, we have already made a recording of the Queen of the Night aria with [Wilma] Lipp (which, of course, you have never brought to me). In any case, if it cannot be released, it makes no difference to me.
>
> I must therefore remain adamant in my proposal to record the Salzburg *Magic Flute* with HMV. The projected *Fidelio* would not be well executed in my opinion if Flagstad is omitted.   *29 November 1950*[18]

The company was now faced with the specter of having two recordings of the same opera with the same cast and different conductors. Legge and his administrative superior David Bicknell had to scramble long and deftly to convince Furtwängler that such a course would be neither wise nor profitable for anybody concerned, least of all HMV.

Schwarzkopf was not involved in *The Magic Flute* controversy, but she defends her husband's actions:

17. Letter Bicknell to Furtwängler, 16 October 1950. Source: Wilhelm Furtwängler Private Archives, Clarens.

18. Source: Wilhelm Furtwängler Private Archives, Clarens.

The cast for *The Magic Flute* happened to be *the* cast at the time. It was neither Karajan's nor Furtwängler's. They both had the same cast all the time. Krips had the same cast too. It simply was the best cast to have.

But Furtwängler evidently felt that Legge had promised the recording to him.

But it was mentioned to many people . . . I would like to stress here . . . nothing like this is anybody's property. Nobody can say, "This is my opera . . ." or whatever. Please clarify that to the public. It has to be stressed.

I will be delighted to quote you on that.

I hope you are behind that opinion. The idea that my husband gave the cast that "belonged" to Furtwängler to another conductor is really dotty. It was the great cast, the number one cast in the world at the time. And besides, where is the contract for Furtwängler to record *The Magic Flute*?

And there, as future generations would put it, was the bottom line. There was no contract for Furtwängler to conduct a recording of *The Magic Flute* with anybody, only what he felt was an agreement, presumably between gentlemen. There was, in fact, nothing legal to bind Legge to keep what Furtwängler regarded as a promise.

Anthony Griffith was closely associated with Legge at the time. I asked him if there might be an element of fable in Legge's apparently unseemly behavior:

> Legge was certainly covert and would stab you in the back, if it suited his purpose. I wouldn't trust Legge a yard. He was the rudest man I have ever come across, although I must say I generally got along very nicely with him, but from a distance. He would be absolutely charming if you could be of use to him. Once you ceased being of use, he would turn on you and do anything . . .[19]

Furtwängler considered severing his relationship with EMI/HMV altogether, but if he did that, he knew he would only be conforming to Legge's plans for Karajan. He also had a number of important engagements in London coming up with the Philharmonia that he did not want to let go, including a performance of the Beethoven Fifth Piano Concerto with Edwin Fischer as soloist. A recording of that performance was also scheduled, and it was one he wanted to make with his old friend.

Over the next two weeks, Furtwängler reconciled himself to the

19. Personal conversation with the author, Newton Abbot, 12 December 1989.

The Magic Flute affair as a fait accompli, but he was not about to let the injury done to him go. EMI was negotiating for a new contract with him at this time, and it was a grim Christmas Eve in Clarens when he fired off another letter to Legge:

> . . . You have deliberately concealed behind my back the *The Magic Flute* you recorded with someone else, which, for some years I prepared and conducted [at Salzburg] . . . I feel that I am not being treated by your firm as a first Kapellmeister, but as some sort of rehearsal assistant.

Later in the letter, he demanded to know exactly where he stood with Legge and his firm:

> At the beginning of our contract four years ago, you suggested I record *Tristan* and *Meistersinger*. Now you have cancelled these works. Naturally, these works will be a significant factor in my new contract, and I must ask you as representative of your firm to answer the following questions clearly and explicitly:
> Have you already entered into agreements elsewhere with respect to any of the major classical and romantic vocal works, especially the operas of Mozart and Wagner? If so, specifically which works?
> *24 December 1950*

Furtwängler received several letters from Bicknell assuring him that all his demands would be met, that he was a valued artist at EMI, and that any misunderstandings between Furtwängler and the firm could easily be resolved. Bandaging his devastated pride, Furtwängler resolved to keep his commitments to EMI but demanded another producer for all his future recordings. Bicknell granted him his wish immediately. Lawrence Collingwood, a well-known and respected British conductor who was on the recording staff of HMV, became Furtwängler's producer. But there were still three sets of recording dates that Collingwood was not able to produce. The first was a series of shorter works such as the *Rosamunde* Overture and Cherubini's Overture to *Anacreon*, capped off by the recording of the Beethoven "Emperor" Concerto with Furtwängler and Fischer. Legge took these sessions. It was a tense series of encounters, but the sessions went well. In the summer of 1951 Furtwängler conducted two performances of the Beethoven Ninth at the re-opening of Bayreuth which had been closed since 1944.[20] Legge was present, but had no direct involvement with Furtwängler on this occasion because he was going to record the symphony, presumably with Furtwängler, later in Lon-

20. See Chapter 26 for a fuller discussion of the Bayreuth Ninth.

don. Although neither of them knew it at the time, they ultimately would collaborate on this work in a most unusual way.

In the meantime, Furtwängler moved on to Salzburg where he conducted what turned out to be his last revival of *The Magic Flute.* The commercial recording of the work with the same cast Furtwängler had prepared and conducted the previous summer had been released on EMI/Columbia, and the world now could compare what Furtwängler was doing with the cast in the wake of Karajan's recording sessions during the previous winter.

The critic John Ardoin has rightly described Furtwängler's Salzburg performances of Mozart as "theater on an epic, yet always human level."[21] What is most striking about the tape from this revival of *The Magic Flute*, though, is the overwhelming sense of the work as an organism emerging from nature rather than merely a genially crafted stage piece. Karajan made good use of Furtwängler as a rehearsal assistant in the recording, for his interpretation fully highlighted the attention to detail Furtwängler put into it. Although it was the first full-length *Magic Flute* on records, it came close to achieving a perfection of technique and unity of ensemble that since has been equalled but rarely surpassed. But Karajan's attitude toward the opera and particularly toward the cast was quite different from Furtwängler's. Karajan illuminated the singers with his slick though undeniable brilliance; Furtwängler now was conjuring an incandescence of spirit from within the same vocalists.[22] Furtwängler's performance breathed with a continual sense of emergence; Karajan's responded unceasingly to his effectively calculated applications.

Furtwängler also conducted the only performances of an Italian romantic opera he performed between the end of the war and his death. The work was Verdi's *Otello*. It was received with both surprise and elation, for only those who had known Furtwängler from his Mannheim days before 1922 had any idea what to expect. Otto Strasser recalls playing in those Salzburg performances: "Furtwängler gave it wonderful power. His *Otello* was not an 'Italianate' performance, but it was convincing because Furtwängler's personality made it immense and tremendously exciting."[23]

21. "Furtwängler and Opera, Part Two, Mozart," *Opera Quarterly*, Autumn 1984, p. 70.
22. The performance of Furtwängler's view of *The Magic Flute* most frequently released on a variety of pirate CDs and records comes from 1 and/or 6 August 1951. The production was performed also on 10, 17, and 29 August.
23. Personal conversation with the author, Vienna, 9 April 1990. See Chapter 24 for a fuller discussion of these performances.

It was Furtwängler's most successful year since the war, and he was rapidly re-establishing his career in France, England and Italy and enhancing the prestige of the Berlin and Vienna Philharmonics with extensive tours through those countries. He was now also recording regularly with the Vienna Philharmonic. As 1952 approached, the idea of recording *Tristan* for EMI came up again. Furtwängler wanted to do it, and he was animated by EMI's promise that Kirsten Flagstad was to be Isolde. But he now was leery of promises made by EMI, especially since Legge was still very powerful there and was painstakingly advancing Karajan's career with one challenging recording opportunity after another. Both Furtwängler and Legge wanted to make *Tristan*, but each wanted to make it on his own terms.

21

The Tristan Recording

The terms on which Furtwängler and Legge were willing to make *Tristan* were inimical, primarily because they no longer wanted to work with each other. Furtwängler came to the project still injured and angered from *The Magic Flute* scandal. Less than three weeks before the sessions were to begin, there was grave doubt whether he would conduct *Tristan* at all. Furtwängler now viewed Walter Legge as an enemy and the bickering between them became the table talk of every rehearsal break at all the major musical institutions in Europe. Legge, after all, had turned from him and gone after a younger conductor who could give EMI an image of up-and-coming pep and pragmatism. And by 1952 Herbert von Karajan was indeed the very paragon of the New Conductor. Never mind that he had been a Nazi from the outset of the Third Reich. Forgotten was the fact that he had been the model of the Aryan musician—the conductor of the future—under the care and protection of Göring and Rudolf Vedder. While many people— important people—refused to "forgive" Furtwängler for remaining in Nazi Germany though he was never a Nazi, all was quietly swept under the carpet for Karajan as Legge carefully groomed him, making sure he got the right engagements and carefully selecting the repertoire he recorded.

While others watched Karajan with one eye on their own backs, Furtwängler's gaze turned from suspicion to loathing, for Legge made no secret of his intentions to prime the young conductor as Furtwängler's probable successor. Legge took up Göring's old cry about Furtwängler representing the old and outmoded and Karajan symbolizing the new, the current, the next stage of musical interpretive genius. Barely a month before the *Tristan* sessions were to begin in June 1952, Furtwängler heard that Legge was making disparaging remarks about him, and he was not about to enter another collaboration with Legge in such an atmosphere of disharmony. In a letter written in English, he informed Bernard Mittell, a senior executive at EMI, that he was ready to cancel his contract:

> I have told Mr. Bicknell [another EMI executive] before witnesses that I shall withdraw my signature under my contract if the firm does not prohibit that Mr. Legge is acting in words or deeds against me while he is an employee of H.M.V.
>
> The firm cannot require me to conclude an exclusive agreement with it if it is doing everything to make such situations in the future impossible.
>
> In my contract exists a clause which entitles me to withdraw from it as soon as the contract is violated in any way.
>
> I consider the propaganda of Mr. Legge to be such a violation of my contract. Just at the beginning of our new agreement, I do want to make this explicitly clear.
>
> I suppose the firm is sharing my point of view in respect to Mr. Legge to its fullest extent. I told Mr. Bicknell before signing that this was to be the condition on which I would give my signature.   *25 April 1952*[1]

A flurry of placating notes descended upon Clarens from senior EMI officials frantically trying to soothe Furtwängler. Legge himself sent him a letter expressing regret that remarks "alleged" to have been made by him had caused the maestro hurt. He appealed to Furtwängler to forget the remarks "reported" to him and assured him that his admiration had been revealed in "the most concrete terms" in the invitations he had extended to Furtwängler to conduct the Philharmonia Orchestra in what programs he wished.[2]

Furtwängler could probably have eliminated Legge from the project had it not been for the intervention of an indispensable constituent to the success of the recording. Despite her 57 years, Kirsten Flagstad was still the reigning Isolde of mid-century, and without her a recording of the opera would be a most precarious investment. Furt-

1. Source: Wilhelm Furtwängler Private Archives, Clarens.
2. Letter Legge to Furtwängler, 10 May 1952. Mittel followed up with a shoulder-massaging message on 15 May 1952. Source: Wilhelm Furtwängler Private Archives, Clarens.

wängler tried to convince her to have another producer, preferably
Lawrence Collingwood, and Legge reportedly tried to sell her Karajan
as conductor. But even if she fully understood the atavistic nature of
the enmity between Furtwängler and Legge (she probably did not), she
apparently could not have cared less. She knew this recording of her
Isolde would be what posterity would remember her by, and she
promptly made it quite clear that she wanted Furtwängler to conduct
and Legge to produce.[3]

The project was also threatened by the difficulties in engaging a
Brangaene of international class with whom all parties could be satisfied. Several possibilities had been mentioned—Inge Borkh, Margarete Klose, a few others—but the first choice was Martha Mödl. The
offer may well have struck her as a giant step back in her development,
for Brangaene is a hefty but secondary role and usually assigned to a
mezzo-soprano. She had fought her way long and hard out of the
mezzo *Fach* where she started her career so that she could sing parts in
which she was waited upon rather than waiting for the first ladies of
her evenings to meet calamity. Mödl already was making a name for
herself as Isolde in various German houses, but her recording career
had not taken a leap into the league where her voice palpably was taking her. The idea of being in the sovereign light shed by such distinguished company as Furtwängler, Flagstad, and HMV obviously
appealed to her sufficiently to accept the invitation.

News of Mödl's casting brought tremors of consternation to Bayreuth, where she was scheduled to sing Isolde less than a month after
committing Brangaene to record in London. Wieland Wagner now
was in charge of safeguarding Bayreuth's artistic welfare, and he was
not about to have the second fiddle on a June recording of his grandfather's opera sully the stage of the composer's shrine by attempting a
star turn on it in July. He promptly told her that if she sang Brangaene
on the recording, she could abandon all hope of ever singing Isolde at
Bayreuth.[4] On one face of the situation, Wieland had good reason to be
concerned. After all, Bayreuth would have to cope with whatever rav-
ages Mödl might incur after singing a heavy mezzo role in June, as she
shifted a few weeks later to taking on one of the most taxing soprano
parts ever composed. He simply could not risk that liability in a production that purported to be given under festival conditions. On the

3. Elisabeth Schwarzkopf: "Furtwängler said, 'if that man Legge is in the studio, I
will not conduct.' Flagstad said, that without Legge she would not sing." Personal conversation with the author, Zürich, 4 April 1990.
4. Legge cabled Furtwängler of the fact on 16 April 1952. Source: Wilhelm Furtwängler Private Archives, Clarens.

other face, Wieland was engaging in a futile attempt to make Bayreuth the exclusive recording center for all Wagner operas. The notion of a competent *Tristan* recording, much less a recording of the calibre promised by Furtwängler, Flagstad, and Legge stuck in his craw, and if all he could do to delay the inevitable was deprive the enterprise of his star Isolde, he would do it.

Furtwängler now turned to Margarete Klose, aging but still eminently serviceable. She, however, had tied herself to a contract with the Staatsoper in East Berlin, and the Cold War froze her application for a visa. May was almost over by now, and HMV had neither a Brangaene nor a conductor firmly committed. It was at this point that Furtwängler finally agreed to conduct the project with Legge as producer. It was at this point, too, that Flagstad suggested Blanche Thebom as Brangaene.

There were better Brangaenes than Blanche Thebom at the time of the recording. Indeed there were better mezzos within flying distance of London who could easily have learned the role. But the American Thebom was a fellow Scandinavian (of Swedish stock) and had befriended Flagstad on her stormy return to the United States after the war. Flagstad did not forget Thebom's kindness toward her.[5] Furtwängler loved the voice and the firm musicianship behind it. Thebom was cast.

Furtwängler re-studied the score for hours on end, as he always did no matter what work or how many times he had conducted it. And he was no stranger to *Tristan*. Although he had conducted the opera on many occasions during his apprenticeship days,[6] his first major traversal of the work took place at Bayreuth in 1931, and he later performed it at the Berlin Staatsoper, London, Zürich, and in Paris throughout the 1930s, and even doubled as producer for what amounted to a new production in Vienna in 1943.[7] In 1947 *Tristan* was also his first operatic performance after the war when the great Isolde Frida Leider produced it in Berlin.[8]

Furtwängler conducted many Isoldes,[9] and they all were distinctive if not uniformly great. But Flagstad and Leider were the only sopranos in this group that made the whole world take notice. Many

5. One version of the saga behind her engagement in the role is that Flagstad tied Thebom to her contract with EMI, and Legge was all too willing to accommodate her.
6. Furtwängler conducted *Tristan* nine times during his tenure at Mannheim.
7. Furtwängler conducted *Tristan* fourteen times in Vienna between 6 November 1929 and 20 February 1944, his last performance in the house before the end of the war.
8. See Chapter 19.
9. Including Hermine Rabl, Dorothea Manski, Helene Wildbrunn, Anny Konetzni, Germaine Lubin, Nanny Larsen-Todsen, Kirsten Flagstad, and Frida Leider.

of those who heard Leider insisted that she was the greatest Isolde in the first half of the 20th century, and Leider's recordings go a long way toward validating such hyperbole.[10] Leider's instinct for projecting Teutonic *morbidezza* (passion) made her an ideal collaborator for Furtwängler, and she speaks fondly of him in her memoir *Playing My Part*.[11] With his childlike willingness to take chances during a performance, he marshaled her white-hot passion into performances that drove audiences to the point where Wagner wanted to drive them: madness and delirium. When partnered with a Melchior in an attentive mood (he could frequently be sloppy and slipshod), the three could make magic of the sort operagoers always hope for, but too rarely find. Though we have no sustained sampling of their collaboration in *Tristan*, the volatility of their chemistry together can still be heard in a sizable stretch of the *Ring* at Covent Garden in 1938.[12]

Leider's intensity and dramatic instinct notwithstanding, though, Furtwängler fell in love with Kirsten Flagstad's voice when he first worked with her in the Coronation Season *Ring* cycle at Covent Garden in 1937. He simply could not get over the lambent majesty of this voice, which literally had come out of nowhere only two seasons before. Flagstad, in fact, was preparing for retirement when she auditioned for Artur Bodansky in Switzerland in 1934.[13] He had tried to get Leider to go to the Metropolitan Opera for a number of years, and she finally went for two brief, uneventful seasons. After 1934 she called it quits and returned to Germany, and the Met frantically looked for a replacement. At the audition, the choice became a tossup between Flagstad and Elisabeth Delius. When Flagstad heard Delius, she was intimidated because Delius knew everything in German. Flagstad knew hardly any of the repertoire for which the Metropolitan

10. Some of them made the statement after hearing such mere also-rans as Olive Fremstad, Johanna Gadski, Elisabeth Ohms, Gertrude Kappel, Florence Easton, and, of course, Flagstad. There is no complete performance of Leider in a Wagner opera, but the "bleeding chunks" of the second act duet from *Tristan* with Lauritz Melchior and at least two conductors and two different orchestras made for EMI at various sessions were recorded between 1928 and 1932. This agglomeration was skillfully sewn together on an LP in EMI's Great Recordings of the Century series COLH 132. An acoustic "Dich teure Halle" from 1924 (Polydor 65627 matrix Nr: 598.as) has been regarded by some as Leider's most impressive disc in the dramatic soprano *Fach*. Other chunks of Wagner live from London between 1936 and 1938, and a sizable canon of studio-made 78s form a montage of an intense, larger-than-life singing actress whose forte is heartbreak and suffering.
11. Translated by Charles Osborne, (reprinted New York) 1978.
12. Incorrectly pitched (sharp), but nonetheless available on Pearl GEMM CD 9331.
13. Bodansky, of course, had been Furtwängler's predecessor at Mannheim until he left to take over the Metropolitan opera's German wing in 1915. See Chapter 2.

wanted her, and she was used to singing the roles she did know in Norwegian. What is more, Delius had a superb, abundant voice. Unfortunately she also was abundantly corpulent. Bodansky offered Flagstad the contract, warning her not to put on weight.[14]

Flagstad's flight to stardom at the Met is the stuff of American storybooks. She made her debut at the Metropolitan with no ballyhoo at a Saturday matinee (2 February 1935) as Sieglinde in *Die Walküre*, and the performance happened to be broadcast on the radio.[15] Millions of listeners across the United States and Canada discovered Flagstad for themselves.[16] It might be safe in one sense to say Flagstad never looked back after that, but her personal destiny ultimately proved otherwise. She did look back; back at her home and husband in Norway. All very understandable, except for timing: 1941 was the year she looked over her shoulder. Her husband Henry Johansen was connected with the Nazi-imposed Norwegian government, and the United States was about to take on Nazi Germany. Friends and fans pleaded with her not to go back. But she went.

Her career at this point began to parallel Furtwängler's. She rarely performed in public during the war years, and she never performed officially for the Nazi regime. But her return to her husband's side was betrayal enough for the American public. It would be six years before she set foot on American soil again, and a decade before she reappeared at the Metropolitan. Johansen, her husband, was arrested at the end of the war and charged with profiteering during the Nazi regime as a member of Quisling's party. Flagstad always defended her husband's innocence, claiming that he was singled out for punishment—not for what he might have done, but for being Flagstad's husband. Johansen became ill in prison and died in 1946 before being brought to trial.

When Flagstad returned to the United States in 1947, her welcome was anything but warm. During a recital tour in Philadelphia, she was greeted with a stink bomb as she launched into her program on stage at the Academy of Music, and protestors carried placards outside Carnegie Hall and other auditoriums where she appeared. She had a better time of it in England. While there were grumblings about her decision

14. Two similar accounts of this incident can be found in Howard Vogt's demurely titled biography *Kirsten Flagstad: Singer of the Century*, (London) 1987, pp. 100–101, and Louis Biancolli's *Flagstad Manuscript*, (New York) 1952, pp. 64–68.

15. Act I of this extraordinary performance is available on several pirate issues, notably The Golden Age of Opera EJS 200.

16. The intermission commentator on this broadcast happened to be no less than Geraldine Farrar, who threw away her script and extolled the beauties of this new artist for a good portion of the interval.

to stand by her Nazi, the nation that certainly had just cause in making her into a scapegoat welcomed her with open arms.

The Metropolitan invited Flagstad back in 1950 for the 1951–1952 season. Melchior was still singing there with great success, usually partnered by Helen Traubel, who had become Flagstad's successor in the big Wagnerian roles. Neither of them were elated at rumors that Flagstad would be returning. Melchior apparently never condemned Flagstad in public for leaving America at the beginning of the war, but it was an open secret that he had no desire to sing with her because of the political turpitude implied by her return to Norway.[17]

Melchior's public silence on Flagstad's return was certainly circumspect, but his private agitation against her so-called "politics" smacks of the proverbial pot calling the kettle *schwarz.* After all, he evidently painted his own political views a different color *after* the Nazis occupied Denmark. In 1933, for example, he gladly joined a spectacular Nazi-sponsored opera tour of Argentina that was hastily arranged and closely supervised by Goebbels' Propaganda Ministry. It was no secret that the tour was nothing short of a political showboat whose purpose was to promote the Nazi government and ameliorate its neo-Neanderthal image. It was led by Fritz Busch and included some of the best known names in the German lyric theater at that time: Kerstin Thorborg, Edith Fleischer, Anny Konetzni, Carl Ebert (stage director), Walter Grossmann, Karl Wiedemann, Paul Seider, Walter Laufkötter, Michael Bohnen, and, of course, Melchior. Even though the anti-Semitic policies of the Nazis were already in place, Jews such as Grossmann were prominently displayed on the cast lists of an ambitious repertory of operas including *Parsifal, Meistersinger, Tristan, Rosenkavalier,* and *Fidelio.*

Everyone on the tour was well aware of exactly what and whom he or she were representing, even though Fritz Busch apparently forgot to make mention of the fact in his memoirs.[18] Some of the artists enthusiastically supported the political nature of the tour, while others simply did not care who was sending them abroad at great expense. Nor were they concerned about who was aware of their indifference. That apathy toward Hitler and the Nazis as the benevolent sponsors of the tour became a focal point of a contretemps, and a ProMi represen-

17. See Eammons, *Tristanissimo,* (New York) 1990, p. 254.
18. See *Pages from a Musician's Life,* p. 214. Busch had a short but successful stay on the conducting roster of the Metropolitan beginning with the Opening Night *Lohengrin* on 26 September 1945. A reviewer described him as a "self-dictated wanderer from the Hitler Scourge" (*New York Times,* 27 September). He departed in 1949, two seasons before Bing arrived.

tative who was assigned to the tour promptly reported it to headquarters in detail:

> Unfortunately, there were a few very unpleasant encounters in which Herr General Music Director Busch . . . and also the tenor Lauritz Melchior were involved. I would like especially to bring up the last named because of a particular incident: When Melchior broke the silence with the words, "Be aware that you are representing Hitler here," the Tenor Seider answered: "That does not matter to me." Melchior replied: "It is indeed unfortunate that it is all the same to you, a German. For me, as a Dane, who has been active in the service of German art for 20 years, it certainly matters to me!"[19]

Condemned though she may have been for returning to her husband's side, Flagstad herself never at any time represented Hitler, much less took pride in such a fact.

Her cause ultimately was taken up by the new General Manager of the Metropolitan. By 1950 Rudolf Bing had been appointed. He was a part-Jewish German who had fled the Nazis, and he knew exactly who had done what. He knew Flagstad was no Nazi. He also knew that he had no taste for Melchior's continued presence at the Metropolitan. Why? He later said he let Melchior go for artistic and policy reasons. But his attitude toward him may well have been influenced by the discrepancy he saw between Melchior's private grumbling about Flagstad's politics and his own recollection of Melchior's well-publicized participation in Goebbels' extravagant South American tour 17 years before.

In any event, Melchior left the Metropolitan a year shy of his 25th season, a milestone he was eagerly anticipating. Bing was severely criticized in the press for denying the Danish Bear his silver anniversary celebration. But a cunning sense of poetic justice rather than mere nastiness may have accounted more for the style with which he eliminated the aging but still dependable trouper. Melchior left the Metropolitan with leonine dignity and ultimately went to Hollywood, radio, and television. Traubel eventually moved on to nightclub work.

If Melchior was not to sing Tristan on the recording, who then? Several tenors were mentioned, but Ludwig Suthaus was chosen. There will be more about him later.

With or without Melchior, Flagstad now was at the threshold of her twilight years, but it was to be a long summer sunset with frequent

19. The incident was recorded in a transcript of a report about the tour to ProMi sent from South America to the Office of Hans Hinkel, Prussian Ministry for Science, Art, and People's Education. Covering note dated 12 October 1933. Source: Busch File, Berlin Document Center.

streams of glory that would flow for at least four years to come. She wanted to make her return as Elisabeth in *Tannhäuser,* possibly as an operatic *apologia* for remaining faithful to her husband in spite of everything. But her first performance turned out to be Isolde on 22 January 1951, and with it she was on her way to reclaiming her audiences. But it had not been easy.

Once the war was behind her—at least as far as she was concerned—Flagstad's most significant triumphs were in Europe, and a number of them were with Furtwängler, with whom she shared a mutually abiding respect and admiration. Early in 1950, they worked together in a complete *Ring* cycle at La Scala in Milan—the first in many years at Italy's leading opera house.[20] And now, he set to work on *Tristan* with a British orchestra. But this time, Furtwängler had several factors going in his favor from the outset. The Philharmonia of London was no stranger to Furtwängler either in the concert hall or the recording studio. Nor was it a stranger to Furtwängler's way with Wagner. He already had recorded one version of the Immolation Scene from *Götterdämmerung* with the orchestra, and he would soon record another one. Kirsten Flagstad was the vocalist in both. The first version was recorded in the electrical 78-rpm format in 1948. The second version was taped for long-play release in 1952 following the *Tristan* sessions. The Philharmonia had also been the orchestra of choice in the world premiere of Richard Strauss' valedictory *Four Last Songs* at the Royal Albert Hall on 22 May 1950, also with Kirsten Flagstad.

The war had taken its toll on every European orchestra, but the Philharmonia was an exception. Although it would take years before Otto Klemperer would take over and forge it into an even greater ensemble in the 1960s and 1970s, it already had achieved recognition as a major orchestra within two seasons after Legge had formed it in 1945.[21] Most of the players had a deep affection for Furtwängler, and they looked forward to making the first major, complete studio recording of *Tristan* with a great conductor and, for the most part, a tantalizing cast.[22]

The recording was "modern" to the extent that it later caused something of a scandal. At this late stage of her career, Flagstad was still in full possession of her immense luminous voice, but her top had

20. See Chapter 19 for Claudio Abbado's eyewitness account of the rehearsals for the Milan *Ring.*
21. See Chapter 20 and also Stephen J. Pettitt, *The Philharmonia Orchestra,* (London) 1985.
22. Another quickly forgotten recording of the opera was made and released on the Urania label in 1952.

never been secure even in her prime. She was never comfortable above B flat, and even that note occasionally gave her a challenge. Her high Cs sound arbitrary in the Ho-jo-to-ho from a *Walküre* excerpt she recorded in 1935, and her top sounds a trifle squeezed in the Prologue from *Götterdämmerung* made in 1937.[23] She rarely sang the note after 1938, and this *Götterdämmerung* excerpt tells why.[24] The rest of the voice was still molten gold, cooled by a relatively placid temperament, and it remained so right up to her death in 1962.

When the problem of the two top Cs in Act II of *Tristan* came up for the complete recording, Legge solved it neatly by offering his soon-to-be wife Elisabeth Schwarzkopf a cameo appearance just for the two notes.[25] When word of the substitution leaked out, Flagstad was furious, and she blamed EMI, ultimately breaking her ties with the company altogether. "That story should never have been told . . . never!" says Schwarzkopf, still bristling more than 38 years later:

> I did it out of admiration of Flagstad and also to save that performance. Otherwise it would not have been put on records. She said to me at the time, "I can still sing those high notes in a performance, but I can't sing them five or six times again and again for a recording." So it was the most natural thing for me to do. In my husband's obituary, Irving Kolodin said my husband cheated by cutting those high notes in. Nobody cut anything in. I stood behind her and crept into the two high notes and sang them. You would never have noticed it. Top notes among all sopranos are usually similar. It is under the top notes where the timbre begins. So anybody could have done it. Even I cannot discern it.[26]

Furtwängler always thought the idea of recording little phrases separately and pasting them together electronically was dishonest, and he was basically indifferent to the financial gain and personal fame that making records might bring. But if two notes were the only obstacles in the way of making a recording he really wanted to make with a cast he approved of and on conditions (except for Legge as producer) he set, Furtwängler did not view them as a fraudulent compromise at the time of the decision. By and large, the recording went smoothly.

23. The War Cry was made on 9 October 1935 with Hans Lange conducting an unnamed orchestra. The Immolation Scene was made with Eugene Ormandy and the Philadelphia Orchestra on 17 October 1937. Both items have been re-issued on various RCA catalog numbers.

24. But a recently unearthed recording of the Duet dating from 1951 for EMI, with Set Svanholm as her Siegfried under Georges Sébastian leading the Philharmonia exhibits a cautious but creditable high C, proving that fear rather than time had withered her capacity to produce this note. EMI (US) IB 6158.

25. Legge married Schwarzkopf in 1953.

26. Personal conversation with the author, Zürich, 4 April 1990.

Furtwängler and the Philharmonia players got through it on excellent terms, and he was pleased with the playbacks after each session.[27]

What makes this *Tristan* so special to many listeners is that it reveals Furtwängler's peculiar paradox as a conductor, for he was at once the most Germanic and, at the same time, the most un-German of all conductors. The chief characteristic that marked the German conductors of his generation and those who preceded him was the projection of the architectonic features in the works of the great Romantic masters with obsessive care for minute details, threading them all together with a basic, governing tempo. But Furtwängler brought something else to his performances. Some call it spirit, others call it spirituality, and still others name it an improvisational impulse. He was not content to purvey each note of a score slavishly according to the instructions printed above the staff. Rather, he wanted to find some essential mystery, truth, or nexus in every work he approached, even in such trifles as overtures which other conductors fobbed off with little or no regard. Nowhere in his commercially recorded output is he more intent upon discovering the spirit of the work than in this *Tristan.*

That search can be heard from the very outset of the prelude: cellos in hushed ascent, swelling into a sigh, violins taking up the glance motive after the airless pause. The basic tempo Furtwängler sets here varies little throughout the rest of the introduction. A quickening here and there, a sagely judged broadening at surprising but somehow inevitable junctures—all poised on a propulsive, vaguely felt carpet, evoking cosmic yearning and tragic destiny. While some conductors barrel their way into canyons of loudness, and others resort to coy understatement, Furtwängler seems to be withstanding that inexorable force driving the music toward the edge of the abyss, at once longed for and yet dreaded. When that chasm looms before him, Furtwängler gives in to it as to the orgasm that passage may well describe.

If Wagner had the least intention of making the Love Duet into an operatic representation of sexual intercourse (which he evidently did), Furtwängler vivifies it to the fullest. Blessedly unlike a number of later recordings of this scene, Furtwängler's lovers neither thump nor shriek in primal lust while they claw and hump toward orgasm. What best characterizes Flagstad and Ludwig Suthaus as the lovers consummating their passion here is tenderness. Theirs is a couple who have

27. In 1990 the popular rock duo Milli Vanilli were shamed into returning their Grammy after they had been caught out for not singing a single note on their prize-winning recording. One British newspaper likened the scandal to the two notes Schwarzkopf contributed to Furtwängler's recording of *Tristan.*

done it before, but they hardly take each other for granted. After a fair dose of lung-busting declamation, it comes almost as a surprise to hear them singing quietly, not *mezzo voce*, and certainly not *halbstimme*, just softly; exchanging confidences, wondering who they each are, searching for one other and ultimately finding reality in themselves at the very moment they are discovered by the real world.

For all the encomia extoling the febrile excitement Furtwängler generates in the Duet, the distinguishing virtue of his account is spontaneity. The singers and orchestra react to each other as much as they respond to the music and Furtwängler's conjuring gifts. Even for the seasoned listener, this Duet no longer is a set of notes, words, and dynamic markings. Furtwängler does not observe all of them anyway, but it somehow does not matter. What matters is how Furtwängler unleashes the spirit of the scene; trajecting the lovers' ascent above the merely physical into the realm of *"hold Umnachten"* and *"übersel'ges Träumen . . ."*—"blessed darkness" and "rapturous dreams." At the same time, though, he imbues it all with an aching, pulsative sensuality.

The challenge for the bass who sings King Marke, of course, is to enliven a set-piece whose very essence is soporific. And Josef Greindl is at his best when articulating his profound grief at having his trust in Tristan abused. But his Marke is also a bit of a whiner, and Greindl begins to hamper what little sympathy the monarch's protestations can muster by projecting most of the monologue through his resonant but dichromatic nasal cavity. What saves the day (or the millennium it always takes to get through this portion of the opera) is Greindl's dramatic conviction in the rightness of Marke's complaints and Furt-wängler's generous care in allowing a prosaic point to be made in its own much deserved time and tempo. Under Furtwängler's hand, this scene rewards patient, concentrated re-savoring. Like good Bordeaux of controversial vintage, though, it should not be imbibed too steadily or too often.

Act III begins with Cimmerian basses, winds, and horns throbbing with Tristan's wound. 1952 was the year Furtwängler's health precipitously declined. He was an acutely saddened if not embittered man at this point in his life, and the funereal droning from the outset of this act seems prescient of more than just Tristan's death. The shepherd's pipe only underscores the charnel mood. It is also here, more than anywhere else in the recording, that it becomes unquestionably evident that Walter Legge produced the recording with Bayreuth and its unique acoustics in mind, though he flatly denied such intentions on several occasions.

The aural experience of listening to a performance at the Bayreuth Festspielhaus is very much like listening to music in a perpendicular or even late Baroque period church. There is a "bloom" on the sound along the entire range of the scale. Sound technicians call it "reverb." Laymen might call it a slight echo. Such an acoustic environment is particularly hospitable to singers. The orchestra pit is much deeper than in most other opera houses, tucked beneath the stage apron (an architectural feature Furtwängler did not care much for because he believed sound balance was the conductor's job), and all but concealed by a shell-like barrier around the perimeter that arches just above the conductor's head. This guard not only serves to hide the orchestra and reduce the spill from the lights on the music stands, but acts as a reflective wall—bouncing the orchestral sound onto the stage rather than directly into the house. Even at full tilt, the orchestral sound never overpowers the singers, but serves as a cushion for them. Only at certain spots along the outermost sides of the fan-shaped auditorium is the balance between pit and stage off kilter. By and large, though, this virtually unique architectural arrangement—which Wagner himself helped design—creates a clean, "open" aural effect. Even recordings made in the Festspielhaus during the electrical period—a *Tristan* from 1928 and several extended tapings from the mid-1930s—give a good impression of the Bayreuth sound. And later recordings made in the house during the stereo period communicate the dynamic with astonishing effectiveness. That Legge was able to create a sense of the Bayreuth "reverb" so naturally with audio equipment that was paleolithic by today's standards is a mark of his brilliance as a producer. Coincidentally, Kingsway Hall—where the recording was made— was originally built as a church along latter-day Protestant designs and is still used by both recording companies and worshippers today.

The final act belongs to Tristan and Kurwenal, though Isolde claims the show just before the tale ends. The young Dietrich Fischer-Dieskau offers a Kurwenal in Act III that is very much a prospectus outlining the rest of his long career. He was 27 at the time of the recording and had worked with Furtwängler at Salzburg a year before the *Tristan* recording in a remarkable performance of Mahler's *Songs of a Wayfarer*. Here was prime vocal real estate being ripely developed. It started off as a voice in peak form, and it only got better as the years went by. Intelligently managed and never forced out of proportion, his Kurwenal is clever, arrogant, and blindly loyal. Some Kurwenals are ruffians in breastplates. Not Fischer-Dieskau. An idealistic and ideal squire.

For all that, Kurwenal is something of a Teutonic Suzuki. If in *Madama Butterfly* she is opera's highest-paid housekeeper, he in *Tristan* must surely be the lyric theater's best-known male nurse. They both must stand by in hand-wringing concern while passion unhinges their employers. They both must also dress the psychic and physical wounds and find other employers after the depredations of the inevitable leave their pensions in doubt. But they also are called on to do a fair amount of singing for their suppers, and Fischer-Dieskau more than earns his meals. In fact, his singing is as imaginative as he himself seems inexhaustible. It is not easy to play off Suthaus' stolid Tristan, but Fischer-Dieskau will not be worn down. The relentlessness of his ardent composure, in fact, is what gives credibility and life to Suthaus' deeply felt, carefully sung, but not always soaring Tristan in this act.

The problem with Suthaus, this hard-working and frequently stimulating singer, is comparative: he simply is not stimulating as frequently as Lauritz Melchior, who has—to this day—no serious rivals among Heldentenors. The Danish Bear could be sloppy and distracted sometimes, but for sheer, raw power only Paul Franz came close. Even Melchior's third-rate recordings of the Love Duet and other Wagner snippets he made with Flagstad in the 1930s for Victor easily demonstrate a Tristan for all time as well as a vocal match made in heaven. But it is fruitless to lash out at Suthaus for falling below the ideal set by Melchior, or just for being an interloper.

Taken on his own merits, Suthaus performs an affecting and sometimes heartbreaking Tristan in this recording despite the limits of his vocal equipment: he simply was not a true Heldentenor. The twilight of heroic tenors was darkening the operatic landscape after the war, and Suthaus was just about first among several equals in 1952.[28] But Suthaus had the most satisfactory package of requisites (except being a true Heldentenor) in recondite proportions.

For all that, Suthaus' voice still ascends only to sub-celestial heights. Perhaps its most serious problem is that it lacks that gripping stentorian timbre that is the provenance of the ideal Wagnerian tenor. It simply fails to trumpet out in that burst of animal virility when it climbs above the staff. Listen to some other tenors active around this time,[29] and you will hear that unmistakable ring always right there. The true benison in Suthaus' voice is its relative consistency from top to bottom, but that is also its curse. It remains maddeningly bogged down in baritonality, even when it hits its ceiling. Nowhere is this more evident than in the throes of Tristan's madness in Act III.[30]

But there are compensations in possessing a voice so evenly dis-

28. Ramón Vinay may have been more lyrical, Set Svanholm more energetic, Wolfgang Windgassen a tad more musical. He might also have been given a run for his money by Karl Liebl, Fritz Uhl, Brian Sullivan, and a number of other up-and-comers who are hardly remembered today.

29. Max Lorenz, Ramón Vinay, or even Wolfgang Windgassen.

30. The excerpts of Melchior, Max Lorenz, Fritz Soot, and, more recently, Jon Vickers, Jess Thomas, René Kollo—all communicate that terror and agony in the "wounded animal" sound that Wagner gives Tristan a marathon chance to exploit in the protracted passage beginning with *"Mein Kurwenal, du trauter Freund!"*

tributed, and Furtwängler helps Suthaus make the most of them. He does so quite simply. Rather than bullying the tempo, Furtwängler maintains a flexible, pulsating cadence on a long, tightly strung out leash while Suthaus' Tristan writhes fitfully about through his mad scene. What emerges is a man articulating profound sorrow at a life ill-spent instead of the more histrionic gesticulations expressed by some other Tristans. Almost imperceptibly, the tension grows from paragraph to paragraph, generating an excitement that springs from a collective volition rather than coming from a haranguing baton. Suthaus is at his best in the swifter moving passages; the voice, the temperament, and the cosmic regret in Tristan's lot all pouring out in opulent despair.

For some reason, he is at less than his best at the crucial moments where the heat remains feverish but the dynamic takes on tense quietude. Even though Tristan is suffering from an abdominal or peritoneal wound at this point and clearly would have trouble breathing, it is hard to fathom what Suthaus had in mind, or why Furtwängler let him virtually ruin Tristan's vision of Isolde (*"Und darauf Isolde . . ."*) by breaking up words and phrases with breaths and intrusive vowel aspirations. After singing in tightly arched phrases for far longer than might reasonably be expected from a victim sustaining such a wound, Suthaus takes no less than three breaks within the phrase: *"Wie sie selig, hehr und milde wandelt durch des Meer's Gefilde?"* Aspirations on both vowels in *"milde"* and a breath after *"wandelt"* split the phrase into jagged fragments. The next phrase, *" . . . Blumen lichten Wogen kommt . . ."* receives another aspiration in the middle of *"Wogen."*

Several other phrases are broken up in a similar manner to the one in these lines, and they do nothing to enhance this scene, perhaps the most poignant in the whole opera. This may seem to be nitpicking, but these offenses occur at a critical moment in the opera and deserve attention. Perhaps the intent was to convey a manly grief, but it does not work. Suthaus merely sounds short of breath here and somewhat at a loss for how to sing. Many who heard Suthaus perform Tristan live in the opera house say audiences were spellbound and heartbroken by his breathlessness at these critical points, but what was affecting in the theater in the late '40s has turned to tawdry affectation for posterity. These curious moments, however, are the only blemish— though a serious one—within a lengthy passage where Suthaus maintains ever mounting excitement, and Furtwängler marshals all his forces into a thrilling ferocity as Isolde's ship draws closer to Tristan's paroxysms of demented anguish.

The Liebestod that closes the recording of the opera was among the very last Flagstad was to sing in her long career. Her version under

Furtwängler is something akin to ecstatic keening, and her vocalism soars incandescently. Here is Flagstad at her majestic apogee, lifted and carried above the vast surges of elemental sound with which Furtwängler supports her. Even at the sunset of her career, she could still summon the magic that made her the icon of Isoldes in the middle years of this century: warm in tone, generous in musicality, effulgent in soul, and irresistibly moving.

If comparisons are ultimately odious, juxtaposing this *Tristan* against the others which have been produced on records after it is futile. It was the original studio recording of *Tristan und Isolde* in the long-play era, and it set the standard not only for later recorded *Tristans*, but for recording all classical music, especially opera. It is for those recordings to be compared to this *Tristan*, not vice versa. Contrasting it to the chunks of live performances of Furtwängler conducting in the theater that have come to light or referring to the complete live performances in Berlin from 1947 with Paula Büchner in one performance and Erna Schlüter in the other does not make much sense either. What is remarkable about the commercial recording is that it has the "feel" of a live performance, even though it was recorded in sections and snippets—a practice Furtwängler loathed to no end. It has even more excitement than the 1947 live performance, primarily because the sound naturally is superior, and because Paula Büchner and Erna Schlüter are simply not in Flagstad's league. Pitting the commercial set against other live performances presided over by other conductors is even more odious. What would those other fellows have done if they had been able to correct mistakes, set better balances, and obtain different singers?

This recording is also one of the few made by Furtwängler that bears close scrutiny. Few of his recordings survive the kind of analysis that almost any Toscanini, Knappertsbusch, or Kleiber recording thrives upon. Furtwängler was a communicator, not a documentarian. His art lay in the inspiration of the moment, and the inherent unpredictability of this approach is always a mixed blessing for the listener who was not present at the moment of inspiration. More often than not, Furtwängler's inspiration created architectonic vistas worthy of the Renaissance masters or the inspired quietude distilled by the Dutch landscapers of the 17th century. Occasionally, his stimulating faculties misfired, producing intensely interesting but inappropriate post-cubist fragments out of the Romantic masters he sought single-mindedly to serve.[31] This *Tristan*, however, is both inspired and care-

31. The Brahms Second on Decca/London is a noteworthy example of Furtwängler misfiring in a most interesting way.

fully thought out, exploiting the finer qualities of the vocalists while redressing their limitations. It is a recording that was made for *listening* without attempting aurally to simulate a stage performance replete with stage movements, as John Culshaw managed (quite successfully) in a number of operatic stereo recordings he produced for Decca/London. In this *Tristan* Furtwängler demonstrates how viscerally influenced he was by Heinrich Schenker's view of form: in its beginning Furtwängler conjures a sense of its end. In drawing the first expectant A natural from the cellos, he intimates its ultimate cluster of B major fading into the ether at the other end of a vast cosmic arc. Its glory for the attentive listener lies not in measuring the geometric intricacies of that arc, but simply in experiencing the cumulative excitement of its totality.

The reviews of the original release were mostly ecstatic. *The Gramophone*, the British journal of record on classical music, gave it two reviews in March and April of 1953. Said Alec Robertson:

> This fine recording has the great merit of suggesting a performance in the house without the corresponding drawback of extraneous noises, and the balance between voices and orchestra seems to me as good as anything we have yet had, and in the last act, even better than that.[32]

Gushed Desmond Shawe-Taylor a month later:

> After Wagner himself, Furtwängler is the hero of the occasion: he has inspired both players and singers to give of their best. At Covent Garden, I thought better of Ludwig Suthaus' Tristan than did some of my colleagues; but I hardly believed him capable of rising to the heights he here attains in the last act. Incidentally, the joy of playing this marvellous act all by itself on the gramophone is intense: in the theatre we come to it tired—and so does the tenor![33]

In America, *High Fidelity* magazine advised the consumer:

> If you want a full-length *Tristan und Isolde*, this is the one to buy. Some millennial day someone may record a performance that is its equal in sum of merits; but there are elements here that are not likely to fade with the passage of years, and the total accomplishment, if not unexceptionally perfect, is tremendously valuable.[34]

32. P. 246.
33. P. 277.
34. J. H. Jr., November–December 1953, p. 84.

That "millennial day" appears to be yet in the future, though two subsequent recordings came very close—The DGG "live" version at Bayreuth with Birgit Nilsson under Karl Böhm (released in 1967) and the Decca/London version under Reginald Goodall (released in 1981).

The Furtwängler-Legge *Tristan* is at once the most modern and the most antiquated of all long-play opera recordings because it straddles the great watershed in the history of commercial recording in almost every way. All the artists were schooled in performing exclusively for the stage. They all made 78-rpm recordings as well as long-play albums. But recording horns and microphones were largely intrusive inconveniences to most of these artists rather than vehicles to be pursued in lust of wealth and fame. Hence, their prevailing attitude while they joined forces under a galvanizing producer was quite different from the disposition of recording personalities entering the studio today.

This does not mean that they were entirely innocent of ego. For all the complaints he raised about the dishonesty of recording in bits and pieces, Furtwängler knew full well at this stage of the game that if his name outlasted his life it would be partly because he conducted this recording. As the cast and orchestra gathered in Kingsway Hall for the last time, he probably understood that much more than an era in music may already have come to an end. He would make two more opera recordings in the studio and would still commit many orchestral works for documentation, but making music was now becoming an industry, a money machine based on profit projections and public relations. And he saw it all too clearly:

> We live in a time thoroughly characterized by our stepping back from questions about genuine worth. Our ability to measure the individuality and intrinsic worth (of Beethoven or Bellini) becomes lost, and institutions, maneuvers, and trends alienate our power to be and stymie all things that spring from our volition. It is a period of inflation in music— and if it goes on like that—it will be the beginning of the end.
>
> *Aufzeichnungen, 1953, p. 336*

Here, then, is perhaps the last recording to be made whose artists participated primarily and simply to document their gifts, to demonstrate their way of collaborating on a work of musical art. It also became the first operatic recording to prove once and for all that classical recordings were an industry, a money machine, a sound investment whose multiple meanings could be only dimly imagined during those warm sunny weeks in London of June, 1952.[35]

The *Tristan* was one of the great achievements in Legge's extensive career. He, too, had made recordings in the 78 period, and he was to make thousands of long-play recordings in the years to come and set the standard for younger producers. He lured such quixotic personalities as Victor de Sabata into the studio and documented their finest performances. He supervised some of the best his protegé Karajan was ever to make—and Karajan made hundreds of them—and kicked off the recording careers of many future stars, Birgit Nilsson and Maria Callas being just two of them. But if fame ever fell upon a classical recording producer, it immortalized Walter Legge for this *Tristan.* Toward the end of the sessions, he and Furtwängler evidently thawed out their mutual antagonism—for a moment. After the final playback, Furtwängler put his arm around Legge's shoulder and said, "My name will be remembered for this, but yours should be."[36]

No sooner had Furtwängler made this remark in the control booth, which Legge later said was the only compliment Furtwängler ever gave him, when Legge pointed out that the orchestra was engaged for another two hours. Furtwängler and Flagstad had just completed several takes of the Immolation Scene from *Götterdämmerung,* which they both were contracted to do at the end of the *Tristan* sessions, but they had gone so well that extra time with the orchestra was left over. Furtwängler and Fischer-Dieskau had agreed to record Mahler's *Songs of a Wayfarer* together at some time, and now seemed to be as good a time as any to do it. Legge was visibly thrilled to be able to record Mahler with Furtwängler, and Furtwängler in turn was finally getting to record repertoire that Legge had been passing out to other

35. Since 1950, there have been no less than six studio recordings of *Tristan und Isolde* on the market. Furtwängler's account is the only monaural version that never has been deleted from the catalogue. For that matter, it is the only recording in the entire EMI catalogue that never has been deleted. In 1988 EMI lovingly transferred the masters to compact disc format, making the voices sound more forward than they had projected on LP and giving greater clarity to the orchestral choirs in some of the louder passages while maintaining the "Bayreuth bloom" from the original tapes. [U.S.A.] CDCD 47321.

36. The Furtwängler *Tristan* was originally recorded in England on the HMV label, though the parent company was EMI, frequently called The Gramophone Company too, and released on six discs with manual couplings which could be bought record by record. It originally was released in the United States on the RCA Victor label as a set of five records with automatic couplings and later re-released in America under Angel/EMI in the same five-disc format after an epic lawsuit over the ownership of the HMV logo (Nipper) and other disputes. I have avoided recounting the details of these changes of labels and couplings because they are as complicated as they are irrelevant to this discussion.

conductors. But as Legge called for the music to be brought out, Furt-wängler turned to him and said, "I promised you *Tristan* and that is all you are getting. Send me Collingwood."

Nearly two years after he suffered the brutal public humiliation of having the Salzburg cast of *The Magic Flute* handed over in secret by Legge to Karajan for a recording, Furtwängler now had the private bit-tersweet pleasure of banishing the Czar of the Turntable from his own recording booth. Collingwood was promptly summoned, and to-gether with Fischer-Dieskau they turned out one of the most moving recordings of the work yet made.

It surprised no one that Furtwängler and Legge never worked together again. Nonetheless, they had completed over forty projects during the six wintry seasons of their mutual discontent, many of which have re-appeared in the catalogue in various formats over the years. But Walter Legge would ultimately have two final words on Furtwängler's recording career at HMV—one false, the other an ever-lasting compliment. Those utterances, however, would come more than two years later.

Tristan was not the only extraordinary recording Furtwängler made, nor was Legge the only producer with whom he worked. It is to his fitful but frequently triumphant forays into those projects that we now turn.

22

The Studio Recordings

Furtwängler's recorded legacy is almost as badly confused as many issues relating to his life.[1] The misunderstandings stem primarily from the mistaken presumption that every recording with Furtwängler's name on it was made under studio-controlled conditions, and, for that matter, was actually made by Furtwängler. Fakes abound. Furtwängler made comparatively few "studio" recordings for a conductor of his stature. After a handful of such records made before and during the war, he visited the sound studio for little more than sixty projects in the postwar and long-play periods.

Most of his performances released on commercial and pirate recordings are really "live" performances. Some of these "live" performances have been so well engineered that they are regarded as studio enterprises. Other so-called "live" performances were recorded in the concert hall without stopping for corrections but with no audience

---

1. The most up-to-date Furtwängler discography (as of 1991) is to be found in *The Furtwängler Sound*, 3d edition, edited by John Hunt, (London) 1989. It is compiled by Hans Hubert Schönzeler from an earlier discography by Henning Smidth Olsen (San Francisco), 1973. The facts and data on Furtwängler's recordings reveal as much about the recording industry in the first half of this century as they do about Furtwängler's uncomfortable relationship with the medium. Both subjects merit more extensive investigation.

present to mar the ambience with coughs and shuffling. A further misunderstanding about Furtwängler himself arises from a quick look at the recorded canon. Yards of Wagner, barrels of Beethoven and Bruckner, heaps of fascinating collaborations with eminent soloists in Brahms, Mozart, and Schumann. It all suggests that Furtwängler conducted little else, making it easy to forget that Furtwängler conducted more than his share of contemporary composers.[2] Unfortunately, surviving documents of his readings of contemporary composers are few and far between. While several examples of Furtwängler's way with Stravinsky have surfaced in the 1980s, there is no *Rite of Spring*, a work he performed with tremendous success in Berlin and introduced to the New York Philharmonic during his first American season.[3] Most sadly, we have no account of the suite from Hindemith's *Mathis der Maler*—the work that embroiled him in his most famous public contretemps with the Nazis—though there are several other performances of Hindemith that have been released as recordings.[4] But the challenge in making a survey and some sort of assessment of what *is* available is frequently dazzling and occasionally frustrating.

In an attempt to avoid further confusion, I am first discussing Furtwängler's studio-made recordings in roughly chronological order. I then will survey the "live" recordings or those recordings that were *not* made in the studio.

Furtwängler's *studio* recording career can be divided into two broad groups:

1. The recordings he made with Walter Legge as producer, 1947–1952

2. Everything else

Since Furtwängler's career with Legge already has been surveyed, the discussion here addresses the rest of his studio output. That group of recordings can also be split into two batches:

---

2. Furtwängler gave more than 1,000 performances of 180 composers living during his lifetime. He could have given far more if he had conducted "acceptable" composers the Nazis tried to foist on him.

3. Furtwängler first conducted *Rite* at the Leipzig Gewandhaus on 1 November 1923 and later with the Berlin Philharmonic on 7 January 1924. The following season, he gave the first of three performances of this work on 22 January 1925 with the New York Philharmonic. For a fuller discussion of the scandalous New York Philharmonic premiere, see Chapter 4.

4. For more on this incident, see Chapter 11.

1. Prewar and wartime 78-rpm recordings 1926–1944
2. Postwar long-play recordings with Lawrence Collingwood as producer, 1952–1954

Furtwängler recorded for only three companies in his studio career: Polydor (later to become Deutsche Grammophon), Telefunken (later associated with Decca), and the Electrola-HMV-EMI consortium. Taking a chronological view of these recordings can be rewarding, for such an approach reveals much of the characteristics one might expect from it: development of technique, style, idiosyncrasies, and so on. In the beginnings, we can hear some evidence of the end. So that is what I am going to do.

Polydor (1926–1935)

A selection of recordings Furtwängler made for Polydor (later to become Deutsche Grammophon Gesellschaft or DG) and German EMI (Electrola) between 1926 and 1935 has been released on Compact Disc.[5] One disc was made in cooperation with the Furtwängler Society of Great Britain, and apparently is made from relatively high quality copies rather than from the original masters. As of late 1991, at least two other issues comprising most of Furtwängler's early recordings are also available.[6] These collections present a virtually complete sampling of Furtwängler's work in the studio with the Berlin Philharmonic during that golden decade that bridged the latter part of the Weimar Republic (1918–1933) and the first years of the Third Reich (1933–1945), years in which he came into his own as Germany's foremost conductor. Despite a good deal of hiss and surface noise (which could probably have been reduced by using more appropriate styli),

---

5. Symposium 1043 (1988).
6. Koch Legacy 3-7059-2 K2 and 3 7073-2 K2 consists of recordings he made for both Polydor and EMI up to 1937; a Japanese Deutsche Grammophone release (POCG-2342/4) contains his recordings for Polydor up to that time. Furtwängler also made Tchaikovsky's Violin Concerto with the Berlin Philharmonic and the American violinist Eddie Brown during this period, but the recording company is unclear. It has never been released. In the 1970s, a private release of Mendelssohn's Violin Concerto claiming Furtwängler conducting Brown and the Berlin Philharmonic got into circulation before Tom Clear, the producer, became aware that Friedrich Weissman was actually the conductor. Clear immediately issued a statement to his subscribers correcting details. Nonetheless, a dealer in New York in 1990 unknowingly offered a mint copy of the record with Furtwängler identified as conductor and fetched $600 for it. (Brown outlined the corrections relating to his recordings in a letter to Clear dated 16 January 1973.)

the sound spectrum is generally of sufficient quality to appeal to listeners seriously interested in Furtwängler's art. They were made in the first stage of the electrical period which began in 1926, and they provide immense, though occasionally disconcerting pleasure.[7] They also purvey a wordless lesson in the history of performing traditions.

Furtwängler made his first known gramophone recording in 1926, and it is the first of ten selections on this disc. The piece was the Overture to Weber's *Der Freischütz*.[8] Furtwängler revered this opera, and his affection for the work shows in the care with which he draws some impassioned playing from the orchestra. The strings are full and buoyant, but there is relatively little portamenti—the practice of sliding from one note to the other—that was both accepted and encouraged at the time.[9]

The second item can be both pleasurable and confounding to ears conditioned by performing customs of the 1980s. The *Brandenburg Concerto No. 3* from 1930[10] is performed very much in the Romantic style prevalent before our contemporary trend toward recreating the original style. It is large scale and mighty in weight, boldly dispensing with a harpsichord continuo altogether. For Furtwängler, Bach not only anticipates Beethoven but is almost his contemporary. The epic clashes of thematic conflicts in Beethoven are presaged by the heated contrapuntal arguments in Furtwängler's view of Bach.[11] Those clashes in Beethoven are set off a few tracks later in Furtwängler's only studio-made account of the Overture to *Egmont*.[12] This recording has all the antagonistic tension in Beethoven that Furtwängler always drew from the Berlin Philharmonic in live performances, but it lacks some of the fleet charm and tripping joy that he elicited in the allegro section of later documented performances. The texture of the string

7. The electrical period is generally regarded as the second of three phases in the history of recording thus far. It was preceded by the acoustic method in which sound was transmitted to a wax master through a large acoustic horn. The advances made in this method of recording became so refined by the mid-1920s that many late acoustic recordings were far superior to early electrics. The electrical period began at the end of 1925 with experiments by Victor in the United States and continued with innumerable technological improvements until the beginning of the long-play period at the end of World War II. For the purposes of this discussion, I include the digital technology within the long-play period.

8. Polydor 66466 Matrices 172, 173bm.

9. Compare Furtwängler's recordings of Bach with those of Beecham and Stokowski. Listen then to more recent accounts by Roger Norrington.

10. Polydor 95417-8 Matrices 1104, 1105½, 1106½, BI I.

11. Furtwängler once told the French critic Bernard Gavoty, " . . . Both composers seek the same objective, the liberation of mysterious forces and the cleansing of the natural instincts." (*Wilhelm Furtwängler*, Great Concert Artists, translated by F. E. Richardson, [Geneva] 1956.) A number of musicologists, of course, disagree. See, for example, Peter J. Pirie, *Furtwängler and the Art of Conducting*, p. 25. Hereafter cited as Pirie.

12. Polydor 67055 Matrices 735, 736, BE I (1933).

sound also seems a bit more transparent in this recording than in his subsequent accounts with the Berliners.

His view of the Overture to *The Marriage of Figaro* reflects a muscular texture in the winds that may strike present-day listeners on first hearing as muscle-bound.[13] But the agility of movement and sprightly transitions in moods and colors contradict such an impression and show Furtwängler's acute appreciation of both the piece and the work it prefaces. This again is the only known studio recording Furtwängler made of the overture. It gives us a glimpse of how thoroughly he understood the underlying structure of the piece and indicates his appreciation of this opera's serious side, an insight he later realized in a production at Salzburg in 1953.

Perhaps the most interesting selection on this CD is Furtwängler's reading of the Overture to *The Barber of Seville*.[14] Again, the performance can hardly be called idiomatic. To some ears today, it amounts to a prime example of a Furtwängler disaster. But on its own terms it is a glowing testament of viewing Italian works according to the Teutonic tradition from which Furtwängler and his contemporaries emerged. Furtwängler might be taken to task here for taking Rossini too seriously, for present-day readings rarely see the overture as a series of provocative musical statements set in opposition to each other, punching themselves out into rowdy, even violent, *stretti.* The current preference, of course, leans instead toward a linear approach in which one idea leads into another, ultimately accelerating toward a prescribed resolution. Furtwängler's reading may not be "right" by standards we have learned long after this recording was made. But he induces the orchestra to catch its infectious good spirits in an unusual and stirring way and thereby serves Rossini more faithfully perhaps than some more devotedly idiomatic interpretations.

The most technically ambitious track among these selections is Siegfried's Funeral March from *Götterdämmerung*.[15] Made in 1933, it shows the technical brilliance of the Berlin Philharmonic at that time, the technical improvements in recording equipment, as well as Furtwängler's maturing sense of this music as the true climax of the *Ring* tetralogy.[16] We take such gifted ensemble work and solo playing for granted today, but this track alone shows why the Berlin Philharmonic more than deserved its reputation as Europe's finest orchestra even at that time. Listen to the ever-cumulative sense of epic grief Furtwäng-

---

13. Polydor 35013 Matrix 737, BE I (1933).
14. Polydor 35028 Matrices 526½, 527½, GS (1935).
15. Polydor 67054 Matrices 733, 734½, BE I.
16. This recording was used, among other Furtwängler recordings, to provide continuity in the radio announcements of Hitler's death on 30 April 1945.

ler draws from the orchestra, topped off by a commanding trumpet solo swelling from fully centered *piano* to riveting *fortissimo*. Even though the recording had to be made in two parts, Furtwängler amplifies the mounting paragraphs of sorrow into a single, self-contained, cathartic apostrophe.

The collection also includes music from Schubert's *Rosamunde* and two Hungarian Dances by Brahms.[17] He recorded these again after the war with the Vienna Philharmonic. More about these selections later.

In the fall of 1926, Furtwängler committed his first account of a full-length symphony to record. It was the first of three studio versions he was to make of Beethoven's Fifth Symphony.[18] Produced by Polydor in Berlin with the Berlin Philharmonic over three sessions, it was released before the end of the year. It was made at the very beginning of the electrical recording period, and the technique was called "beam of light," a primitive method of transferring sound onto shellac. Ultimately, it proved unsatisfactory and major advances soon were invented to take its place. Furtwängler's first recording of the Fifth turned out to be a test piece for future ventures in Germany, so it was essentially an experiment rather than a polished presentation of a new technique. Bruno Seidler-Winkler, Toscanini, and Felix Weingartner in their documented versions of the symphony benefited from the technological improvements following Furtwängler's experiment with the new process.

Much as a Furtwängler partisan might like to rave about the marvels of his first recording of Beethoven's most popular symphony, there really is not much to stand in awe of. Its importance is very much akin to Artur Nikisch's pioneering enterprise with the same symphony made in 1913, also with the Berlin Philharmonic. They are both far more significant as historical artifacts than as models of their conductors' interpretive powers. Furtwängler's primal reading appears more elementary than elemental.

A nervous stiffness permeates Furtwängler's reading, and it probably stems as much from his life-long unease with the sound technology as it does from the dry acoustics of Polydor's studio and a pronounced flatness in bass response throughout the whole recording. What is peculiar, even disturbing about it, though, is the lack of a driving point of view. If nothing else, nearly every other documented per-

17. Schubert, *Rosamunde*, Overture, Brunswick 90147 (1930), Entracte, Polydor 95458 (1929), and Ballet Music in G, Polydor 66935 (1929).
18. Polydor 69855-9 Matrices 174bm, 175bm, 216bm, 218bm, 179bm, 330½bm, 214bm, 215bm.

formance of Furtwängler in Beethoven is livid with conflict. Here, the focal point seems to be upon correctness. Only in the final movement does any sense of the ecstatic abandon that characterized Furtwängler at his inspired best emerge.

Electrola and Telefunken (1935–1945)

During the Nazi regime before 1940, Furtwängler conducted infrequently and completed only two major projects in the studio. Electrola and Telefunken vied for his services after he left Polydor, where he apparently was dissatisfied with their techniques. Telefunken tried to lure Furtwängler to its camp by promising the capability of recording in long takes rather than the five-minute snippets that Furtwängler considered disruptive to the flow of the music and somehow dishonest. Ultimately, Electrola won out, but it managed to get him into the studio for only two projects. He also reserved the right to record with any company that used the long-play system, but Telefunken never succeeded in importing the new technology before the outbreak of the war. However, it released one record with Furtwängler: the Adagio from a live performance of Bruckner's Seventh Symphony given in 1942.[19]

The two major projects for Electrola during this period were a second version of the Beethoven Fifth and what turned out to be the only Tchaikovsky *Pathétique* Furtwängler made in the studio, both with the Berlin Philharmonic.[20] These recordings were the first to bring a substantial facsimile of Furtwängler's art to a public beyond the concert hall. For most listeners who have encountered the 1938 *Pathétique* recording over the years, it comes as no surprise to find it continually available despite a plethora of more recent recordings made with the most advanced techniques. Furtwängler made it during one of the most difficult periods in his life, and some critics have found it as much an expression of his personal trauma at the time as it is an interpretation of the pathos in Tchaikovsky's symphony. The world was girding itself for war, and the Nazis appeared to have put Germany firmly under their control. A number of critics hear the anguish of the age palpably expressed in this recording. André Tubeuf even hears a switch of identities between Furtwängler and Tchaikovsky in this recording, but he finds Furtwängler's anguish at the time more vicarious than directly personal:

19. Performance date: 28 October 1942. The recording has been released on CD by DG: CD 427 774-2 (1989).
20. Original issue: HMV DB 4609-14/8600-5.

... The two men exchanged their destinies, giving one another all they knew, all they had. Lucid, increasingly laconic [sic], as the Pathetic draws to an end, Tchaikovsky approaches his own end. Furtwängler sees the approach of chaos [of world war]. Both men experience the abyss. And, both surpass and sublimate it in the only possible way—through Art, from whose heights, they view the world and the abyss.[21]

What is more significant about this recording, perhaps, is that it presented Furtwängler with the sort of challenge he had never really encountered before. For example, 1938 was undoubtedly one of the worst years of his career. He was merely a free-lance conductor at this point, having given up all his titles and positions. Göring was supervising a massive talent hunt for a cooperative conductor who could take Furtwängler's place. And Furtwängler knew by the autumn of 1938 when this recording was made that a young Aryan wonder boy was threatening to usurp his position as Germany's foremost conductor. Indeed, Herbert von Karajan had already made a sensational debut with the Berlin Philharmonic and had just made his first appearance at the Staatsoper.[22]

Because of all the traumatic circumstances under which this *Pathétique* was made, or perhaps in spite of them, it remains one of Furtwängler's most remarkable studio recordings. The characteristics that became typical of Furtwängler at his best are in clear evidence here, even though the record was made in six separate blocks over two months (October and November) between concerts and engagements. The account smoulders with intensity, the tempo changes are seamless and organic, and the musical narrative gains epic resonance as it moves forward.

What perhaps makes this recording so special among *Pathétique*s recorded at any time before or after 1938, however, is the absence of pity, or worse, the sort of self-indulgence a number of reputable conductors use as an excuse to demonstrate the basic "feeling" of the work. Furtwängler instead purveys its emotional scope by imbuing it with a vast range of tonal colors on one hand, and propulsively driving it toward the outer limits of joy or dark pathos on the other. He imparts the intimations of catastrophe in the first movement with a gnawing anxiety. The worried vibrato in the strings plays off mourning woodwinds against the interplay of violent pronouncements in the brass in that peculiarly recondite way that became an instantly recognizable mark of Furtwängler's style. In the next movement, the

21. Sleeve note, EMI Pathé 1008371 PM 322. Translation: Ira Gardner-Smith.
22. See Chapter 14.

mood shifts from an anxious cold twilight to a warmer, hazy afternoon. A thin cloud veiling the sun, with charm dancing lightly around the thematic exchanges among the strings and winds. Furtwängler was one of the few conductors bequeathing documents of his work who fully understood that tonal mass was the clay and mortar of his art, and he expresses whatever programmatic intent Tchaikovsky communicates through his instrumentation by molding the possibilities inherent in the tonal capabilities of each instrument.

Not to be outdone, Karajan documented *his* view of the *Pathétique* for Polydor also with the Berlin Philharmonic in April, 1939. To appreciate this venture with the benefit of fifty years' hindsight is to learn how far Karajan progressed as an orchestral master in the intervening years. While the recording techniques on Karajan's version are inferior to those on Furtwängler's for EMI, it is difficult to believe that Karajan is conducting the same orchestra.

Furtwängler made the Beethoven Fifth in 1937, and many listeners consider it their favorite Furtwängler recording. Listening to it on LP, it comes across as a fascinating document, seamless and of a whole despite the "bleeding chunks" of the 78-rpm format under which it was made. It inspired the French critic André Tubeuf to proclaim:

Listen to this Beethoven, it will remain the only one you will ever hear.[23]

Many share this sentiment. But such gavel pounding deprives the listener of later perspectives Furtwängler brought to bear on the work that some may find even more compelling, especially the resounding breadth of vision and tragic conjunction of solemnity and joy he reveals in the studio performance he made with the Vienna Philharmonic seventeen years later, only a few months before he died.

Heretical though it may seem to some, Furtwängler's account of the *Pathétique* was probably a finer accomplishment at that stage of his career than his account of the Beethoven, if only because his interpretation puts Tchaikovsky in a bolder, more individual perspective than any of his performances that survive from this time. By the standards of Furtwängler's development, it is a mature and finished vision of the work, whereas his statement in the 1937 Fifth, while complete and presaging the profundity he essayed in his later live performances, is an expression of the work's mysteries rather than a pulsating fulcrum of them. What is more, there were at least ten recordings of the

23. Record Sleeve PM322 2C 051-03587.

Fifth available in 1937 in the United States alone.[24] Furtwängler's is better recorded than most of them, but he was still developing his life-long grasp of the nine symphonies, and it does not necessarily outclass such great conductors of the period as Serge Koussevitsky or Richard Strauss by the sheer force of its weight or commitment to a vision of this symphony. It would be five years hence before his Beethoven readings would begin to reveal his visionary command of the tonal mass Beethoven creates through his ineluctable instrumentation, dynamics, and contrapuntal vistas.[25]

When Furtwängler recorded the *Pathétique* in 1938, at least five other recordings were available in both Europe and America. Furtwängler's account clearly outclasses the competition on several counts.[26] None of them is as well recorded or as deeply felt as Furtwängler's. While the other orchestras play well for standards of that time, none of them purveys the dexterity of ensemble the Berlin Philharmonic possesses. Only Koussevitzky and the Boston Symphony begin to match them in the minuscule fluctuations in tempo and variants in tonal shading both as an instrumental collective as well as within each choir. Perhaps for the first time on records up to that period, Furtwängler makes the music say something of a world beyond sound alone. Those who want a *Pathétique* rooted firmly in this world would probably find the other contemporary recordings of it much more satisfactory. But for those who seek a *Pathétique* that clearly strives toward the visionary, this recording is probably the first of his commercial records to give indisputable evidence of what had been known only to those who were hearing him "live" at the time: that Wilhelm Furtwängler was not merely a world-class conductor but indeed becoming a unique artist whose work might endure beyond him.

Wartime Studio Recordings

The fact that a large number of recordings by Furtwängler during the period 1940–45 are available might suggest that he virtually lived in the sound studios during those years. The truth is that Furtwängler made only four studio recordings during the war. Many projects were planned, but Furtwängler always managed to delay them indefinitely or simply refused to make them. What we have from that period represent, with these four exceptions, tapes of live concerts or broadcasts that were relayed live or recorded for later transmission. Some of the

24. R. D. Darrell, *The Gramophone Record Shop Record Catalogue*, (New York) 1936, p. 46.
25. See Chapter 23.
26. Koussevitsky, Fried, and Coates were among the competitors at the time.

recorded broadcasts were played before an audience. The latter frequently became quasi-recording sessions immediately after certain concerts in which mistakes and faulty ensemble were corrected. The ultimate composite from edited takes served as the broadcast master.[27] In at least two instances—performances of the Beethoven Sixth and Brahms First with the Vienna Philharmonic—it is not clear if the recordings were made for broadcast or made exclusively for commercial release.

Of the four studio projects, three were made for Telefunken and one for Electrola/HMV. Only the Telefunken recordings were released during the war. The Electrola project remained in storage until it was released privately in 1976 by the Société Wilhelm Furtwängler of France.

Perhaps the most remarkable feature of the Telefunken releases is their relative randomness:

> 15 October 1940, Beethoven, arrangement of the Cavatina, String Quartet No. 13, op. 130, Berlin Philharmonic, Telefunken SK 3104.

Furtwängler rarely performed the Cavatina from Beethoven's late quartet, though he was intensely influenced by the last four quartets in his chamber compositions.

> 7 April 1942, Bruckner, Adagio from Symphony No. 7, Berlin Philharmonic, Telefunken 3230-2.

Bruckner, of course, was the single most important influence in Furtwängler's composition, and the Adagio became distinguished more as an historic artifact than a key item in Furtwängler's recorded oeuvre: It was one of the two recordings the Reich Radio played when Hitler's death was announced on 30 April 1945. The other was Siegfried's Funeral March, also conducted by Furtwängler.

> 29 October 1942, Gluck, Overture to *Alceste*, Berlin Philharmonic, Telefunken SK 3266.

The Overture to *Alceste* is a curious item. Furtwängler always admired Gluck's classical austerity and recorded him throughout his career, but the reason behind the choice of this particular item during wartime is a matter of speculation. Perhaps Furtwängler identified

---

27. A number of these broadcasts were eventually released as edited recordings, parts of which were taken from performances with an audience and parts of which were performed without. A survey of these "semi-recordings" follows later.

with the unwavering loyalty of the eponymous character as he came to realize his own loyalty to the "true Germany" being tested to the limits.

> 18–23 December 1943, Brahms, Variations on St. Anthony Chorale, Vienna Philharmonic, HMV.[28]

For some reason, Furtwängler was taken with the Brahms Variations throughout his life, and he recorded it in the studio twice. Echoes of it run in and out of several of his compositions.[29] While many of Furtwängler's performances during the war take on a percusive quality, this one revels in a dance-like sparkle caught all too rarely by the microphone in his other performances of the work.

The end of the war signaled the beginning of a new and more abundant era of recordings by Furtwängler. That era also turned out to be the final phase of his career. Although he was not permitted to perform for more than two years after Germany's surrender, Furtwängler resumed recording only a few months after his first postwar performance in Berlin on 25 May 1947. But this new period in the studio was marked with the same kind of strife that characterized virtually anything he encountered. The conflict focussed primarily upon Furtwängler's relationship with Walter Legge, the man who came to dominate the shape and course of the classical recording industry as no one had before and whose tenacity and talent brought Furtwängler's vision of *Tristan* to a life that endured beyond them both. Furtwängler's stormy dealings with this czar took a heavy toll on his energies and ultimately taxed his formidable will to its outermost limits. But from this maelstrom emerged some of the most important documents by which posterity has come to view Wilhelm Furtwängler.

Postwar Studio Recordings (1952–1954)

The studio recording of *Tristan* in 1952 marked not only the end of Furtwängler's collaboration with Walter Legge but the beginning of his own demise. The years after the end of World War II were both physically and emotionally difficult for him. Pragmatic, go-getting times were rearing up to taint the sacred values he had sought to preserve by remaining in Germany. He was getting older but keeping up

---

28. This recording was never issued on 78 rpm but first released privately on long-play format by the Société Wilhelm Furtwängler in 1976: SWF 7602. This issue included rejected takes. The approved take was later released commercially in 1986: EMI ED 29 06661.
29. Notably his Second Symphony.

an even more hectic schedule than he had followed thirty years before. Ultimately, the reservoir of nerves on which he was living drained away. Less than a month after he completed recording *Tristan* in London, he fell ill with double pneumonia in July 1952. He collapsed during a rehearsal for the Salzburg Festival. For some reason, the illness dragged on. Furtwängler was never a good patient, and his fever persisted. He was living in Switzerland now with his second wife and their five children.

"I did not know at first that he was ill," recalls Andreas, "but later I saw him trying all kinds of different cures. He wanted a very quick recovery, so he listened to all kinds of advice and took bad advice. His cousin was a doctor in Switzerland and was always calling him about one kind of specialist or another. But someone else would come along and give him other ideas which he followed. So it was very difficult for the doctors to follow his condition because he was trying all kinds of treatments. The real problem was that he was taking such heavy doses of tetracyclin."[30]

One or a combination of the drugs Furtwängler took to accelerate his recovery damaged the hearing in his right ear. It was particularly aggravating because the loss of audibility came and went unpredictably but was almost certain after air travel. This produced bouts of mounting depression.

Nonetheless, he began recording a Beethoven Cycle with the Vienna Philharmonic in late November. Between 27 November and 3 December he completed recording the First, Third, and Fourth Symphonies in rapid succession with Collingwood producing. In addition, he recorded the Overture to the Dresden version of *Tannhäuser*. HMV had completed its switch from the 78 format to LP, and magnetic tape was now used exclusively for all recordings, as it had been done at the *Tristan* sessions. This new technique allowed long stretches of music to be recorded without interruption, and Furtwängler now finally saw the possibilities inherent in the medium for documenting work that he felt had been impossible previously. The longer takes permitted by the tape process also facilitated the recording of larger paragraphs of music at one time and made editing far easier than it ever had been with the 78 format. Furtwängler got along well with Collingwood and Collingwood proved to be a politic and clever midwife, insinuating suggestions and manoeuvering Furtwängler into making certain changes without challenging his sovereignty.

Furtwängler's new contract enabled him to record with other

---

30. Personal conversation with the author, Saarbrücken, 29 March 1990.

companies now, and he made one studio recording with Decca/London—the Franck D Minor Symphony with the Vienna Philharmonic—and made several more with Deutsche Grammophon, all of them with the Berlin Philharmonic. After he died, DG issued many recordings by Furtwängler from the final phase of his career, but the vast majority of them were taken from live concerts and broadcasts intended for commercial release rather than from the studio.

In the spring of the following year, Collingwood produced Furtwängler's second recording with Yehudi Menuhin of the Beethoven Violin Concerto, this time with the Philharmonia Orchestra, and the *Romances for Violin and Orchestra* also with the Philharmonia. They all met again in September of 1953 to record the Bartók Second Violin Concerto.

The big project of that season, however, was to be *Fidelio* in Vienna. Furtwängler and HMV had been discussing a recording of the opera since the end of the war, and Furtwängler almost did it in 1950. But he rejected the idea if Flagstad was not going to take the title role. What is more, he was furious that the offer of a *Fidelio* (without Flagstad) had been used as a decoy to lure him away from his desire to record the Salzburg *Magic Flute*, which Legge handed over to Karajan. Now, in 1953, however, Furtwängler's ongoing problems stemming from recent illness had given him a stern intimation of his own mortality, and he wanted very much to document this work he loved more, perhaps, than any other opera with the possible exception of *Freischütz*. What is more, an American tour with either the Berlin Philharmonic or the Vienna Philharmonic was being negotiated for 1954 or 1955, and Furtwängler wisely took heed of the advice that there was no better way to send an advance calling card to the American public than records made with the most advanced techniques of that time.

A stellar cast was assembled for *Fidelio:* Mödl as Leonore, Wolfgang Windgassen as Florestan, and Otto Edelmann, Alfred Poell, Sena Jurinac, and Rudolf Schock taking the other principal parts. And yet, it is quite possibly the least satisfying commercial opera recording Furtwängler made. It is bereft of nearly all the dialogue, and the singers sound at less than peak form.

There is good reason for the palpable fatigue that at times infects both cast and orchestra. HMV/EMI was never enthusiastic about producing it, citing lack of public interest and the expense involved. To make it cost-effective and to satisfy Furtwängler's demands to record it in the first place, a penny-wise/pound-foolish schedule was devised. A single session was scheduled toward the end of a string of *Fidelio* performances at the Vienna Staatsoper, and it was held in the middle of the night following a performance. *Fidelio* is not lengthy by operatic standards, but it is no less demanding than any other Beethoven score; two performances of any opera on one night by the same cast is bound to exact a toll, and that toll is in abundant evidence on the recording. Its major asset is not the singing but the orchestra, which plays spectacularly for Furtwängler despite an occasional frayed woodwind and a wearied second trumpet.

Otherwise, it amounts to a program of extensive highlights, rendering most of the music, but none of the drama that informs it. Perhaps its most grievous flaw is the absence of Kirsten Flagstad, with whom Furtwängler prepared the opera twice at Salzburg in 1949 and 1950. Mödl may have been an effective Leonore in the theater, but she simply is no substitute for Flagstad in a recording of this opera, especially under such trying circumstances which she cannot entirely surmount. The less said about her and the rest of the cast the better.[31]

During late October and November 1953 Furtwängler went to Rome to conduct a series of concert performances of the *Ring* cycle. These events were broadcast and were meant to serve as "dress rehearsals" for a complete studio-made recording on EMI.[32] Early the following year, he returned to the studios in Vienna to record Beethoven's Fifth and several shorter pieces. By this time, the first test pressings of *Tristan* had come out, and Furtwängler and HMV moved toward finalizing a "Vienna *Ring*," to be made with the Vienna Philharmonic.

On 28 September 1954 Furtwängler began recording the first project in the series. *Die Walküre* was completed in nine days, finishing up on 6 October. The project was not plagued with the difficulties that had attended the *Tristan*, though there was initially some doubt if Mödl would be able to sing Brünnhilde, since she was still very much contracted to Bayreuth where Wieland Wagner continued his futile efforts to keep Wagner recordings the exclusive franchise of the Wagner family. The cast, which included Ferdinand Frantz as Wotan, worked quickly and well. The orchestra knew that Furtwängler was being plagued with health problems and played as much with their telepathic instincts as with their unique technical polish.

A young up-and-coming singer was chosen for Sieglinde, and it was her first major recording project. Leonie Rysanek had grown up in Austria worshiping Furtwängler, and she suddenly found herself not only singing but recording under his direction. Born in 1926, she

---

31. Several pirate editions of Furtwängler's production of *Fidelio* at Salzburg with Flagstad are on the market. For more about Mödl, see the section on *Walküre* later in this chapter, and the discussion of the "Rome *Ring*" in Chapter 24.

32. For a fuller discussion of the "Rome *Ring*," see Chapter 24.

had made her debut at Innsbruck in 1949, only five years prior to the *Walküre* recording. But her progress was swift, and according to her, Furtwängler chose her for the part without an audition, basing his decision on the strength of her success in the role at Bayreuth:

> When I sang the first big phrases . . . he stopped the orchestra at the rehearsal, and he said to the orchestra, "Who ever kept this gorgeous voice from me?" And he wanted to do everything with me. Brünnhilde, Isolde, and other recordings. But maybe it was lucky for me that he died, because it would have been much to early for me to do those roles, and the temptation would have been very great if he offered those roles to me at that point.
>
> We were of one mind when we first met. I liked him, and he liked me. We had piano rehearsals, of course, but he was so pleased with me that he never really "corrected" me. It was more like . . . "a littler faster here, a little slower there"—that kind of thing. It was so long ago, but I will say this. It was like a dream working with him. So extraordinary a man and musician. When I finished my part and left the studio, the last thing he said to me was "you will hear from me, and we will work together again soon." But I never heard from him again.

Rysanek was aware of Furtwängler's hearing problems before she came to the recording:

> He was already hard of hearing when I made the recording. I knew he was hard of hearing because people told me. But I really became aware of it only when we listened to the playback in the control booth. They always had to turn the playbacks on very loud. But I also got the feeling that it was not so important for him to have full hearing in the recording studio because they could check balances electronically.

Since Rysanek had never met Furtwängler before she could not detect any general breakdown in his health. However:

> To me he always looked a little fragile, never robust—at least when I knew him. But I didn't think of any of that when I worked with him. Of his music, his way, I never ever again experienced anything so . . . so romantic . . . so different in sound from all the others.[33]

On 6 November, less than two weeks after he had completed the last take of *Walküre* in Vienna, Furtwängler fell ill under another attack of double pneumonia. He died on 30 November before hearing the final edited master of his last recording project.

No sooner had he been buried when *Walküre* was released to

33. Personal conversation, 11 January 1990.

ecstatic notices in early 1955. Its instant success was marred only by a rumor, which took fast hold and gained credence as fact, suggesting that Karajan was called in to re-record Wotan's Farewell and the closing scene because Ferdinand Frantz had not been in good voice.[34] However, there is no evidence that HMV was dissatisfied with any part of the recording.[35] Bicknell, in fact, sent Furtwängler a congratulatory note on November 1st:

> On Friday Mr. Collingwood and I heard a large part of the 1st Act of "Die Walküre" and the end of the 3d Act and found the recording even better than I expected. In fact, in every way it was quite outstanding. We were both greatly moved by your unique interpretation and certainly you have inspired the singers to give their best.[36]

Perhaps the most notable feature of this *Walküre* is the resplendent playing of the Vienna Philharmonic. Here is a great orchestra responding with unfailing concentration, giving itself over completely to the conductor with whom it had undergone and survived the depredations of the worst decades of the century. Rysanek is probably right in saying that it really did not matter if Furtwängler's hearing was failing precipitously at the time of the recording. The players knew their parts almost from memory and could dedicate themselves entirely to his rapt vision of the music.

The vocal end is dominated by the Wotan of Ferdinand Frantz. It was the third recorded *Walküre* he sang under Furtwängler, and it is a masterful performance indeed. By 1954 his voice had palpably darkened, and his Wotan is more deeply shaded than his performance at La Scala in 1950, and his command of the great paragraphs in his narrative of Act Two is firmer than his reading three years later in Rome. Born in Kassel in 1906, his only real vocal training was in the local choir. He made his debut as a bass in 1930 and switched to baritone roles in 1943. The darkly luminous lower end of his voice endows his Wotan with a formidable brooding timbre that he uses to widen the spectrum of his character. The amplitude of his upper register, pro-

---

34. Pirie, p. 93, simply states that Karajan recorded the last side, implying Furtwängler either did not finish the recording or that it required re-recording.

35. Almost 5 years later, Frau Furtwängler's eyes blaze with anger in recalling the rumor: "I even asked several members of the Vienna Philharmonic who were at the recording sessions if Karajan was called in later. They all laughed at the idea—'Karajan help finish a Furtwängler recording? Ha!' I checked further and learned that 'Legge's people,' whoever they were, started the rumor." Personal conversation with the author, Clarens, 9 December 1989. Otto Strasser, a violinist in the Vienna Philharmonic and a member of its management was present at all the sessions for *Walküre*. He flatly denies Karajan having anything to do with the recording: "I would have certainly remembered something like that. No." Personal conversation with the author, Vienna, 9 April 1990.

36. Italics mine. Source: Wilhelm Furtwängler Private Archives, Clarens.

duced here with greater ease than previously, makes his fury at his encounter with his daughters in Act III especially powerful. The age of heroic baritones had all but passed when this recording was made, but Frantz is a genuine example of that dying breed. He, too, would be dead five years later in 1959, at the pinnacle of a career that seemed sure of bringing him the recognition he steadily had been accumulating.

While the baritonal timbre of Ludwig Suthaus might make him a strange choice for the hapless Siegmund, he turns out to be surprisingly sympathetic, both to listen to and to follow as a character. His is a Siegmund staving off his destiny with as much tenderness as the text and music allow, and it is with that heartfelt commitment to his sister and bride that he wins his encounter with Brünnhilde and makes the scene known as the Todesverkündigung (warning of death) an inevitable pivot in the drama rather than a mere twist of plot.

Gottlob Frick produces a nasty, menacing Hunding, whose offer to Siegmund of bed and breakfast before he certainly will die is aptly resistible. Though he articulates the role with greater hostility in the Rome *Ring*, he is in better vocal form here. That form proved consistent for the next two decades. His career extended well into the 1970s in major Wagnerian bass roles. Born in 1908, and making his debut at Coburg in 1936, Frick appeared frequently with Furtwängler after the war. He had already had a great success at the Metropolitan four years before he made this recording, which sealed his international reputation.

Furtwängler's guiding hand over Frantz and Suthaus and Frick is unmistakable here, if only by the absence of any palpable intrusion. Just as the unique timbre of his orchestral sound emerges from a fundamental bass, the baritonal weight of their voices seems an integral part of that fundamental line, flexing its limits and extending its range.

Margarete Klose's Fricka is an excellent example of what makes the art of singing so fragile and frequently tragic. Here is one of the great mezzo-sopranos leaving posterity the best recorded sample of her voice and interpretive powers. Unlike instrumentalists who can switch instruments at will if one or another does not serve them well anymore, the singer has only one instrument subject at any moment to a plethora of depredations. By 1954, Klose was near the end of her long and illustrious career, which started at Ulm in 1926. She appeared many times with Furtwängler, most notably at his debut at the Berlin Staatsoper in 1932 in the premiere of Pfitzner's *Das Herz*. Her voice had long since taken a downturn before she made the *Wal-*

küre recording, but the heights from which it declined enabled her to sing thrillingly for many years after the bloom of its prime had faded.[37] While her voice diminished, her interpretive powers kept evolving, and it is those powers that make her Fricka perhaps the most penetrating essay of the role on commercial records up to 1990. Unfortunately, the power of the voice—never a blazing phenomenon, but from beginning to end an uncommon vessel of evenness, flexibility and warmth—no longer can articulate her insights with the kind of ease that once came so naturally. Consequently, her Fricka has effortful moments, but it is richly complicated—part harridan, part grimalkin, part wounded wife at long last getting even. Klose's is not a pretty consort, but her intrepid will to maintain dignity drenches every syllable and colors every note of her protracted encounter with her beleaguered husband, despite a bad marriage where divorce is inconceivable. She entreats even as she reprimands, leaving a sad sense of love proffered in the face of love bitterly scorned.

Now for the most problematic casting: Leonie Rysanek's Sieglinde and Martha Mödl's Brünnhilde. Among those who have admired the work of these two artists in live performances, it is almost a capital crime to utter a dissenting syllable about either of them. Rysanek in particular engenders the sort of loyalty commanded by those few singers whose careers have lasted a long time. And in the last decade of this century, Rysanek's sounds as if it may last well into the next millennium. Like her work or loathe it, though, the recordings she has made—both commercial and pirated—say much for the argument that the microphone does not love her voice. The experience of hearing her voice electronically reproduced rarely induces the kind of *frisson* it elicits more often than not in the theater, where the combined force of her personality, stage demeanor, and mere *presence* conspire to make some peculiarities in the voice and in its delivery— the recurring whiteness at the top, a sharpening of notes here and there, the occasional unsteadiness—all the more forgivable and even irresistible. Except for some pressure toward the top in loud passages, she sings Sieglinde here radiantly indeed. But that imponderable thrill she certainly must have incited in Furtwängler and anyone else within earshot of the studio fizzles out somewhere between her microphone and the speakers reproducing it. That Leonie Rysanek may well be the greatest Sieglinde the lyric theater has heard in the second half of this

---

37. For the bloom of Klose's prime, listen to some of her records from the 1930s. They are well produced and reveal a the full amplitude of the musicality and warmth she radiated.

century, there is little doubt. Unfortunately, this *Walküre* simply does not prove it.

Martha Mödl is a similar case of vocal wine that does not travel well through an electronic medium. Legions of those who heard Mödl live during her glory days swear by her. Some of those who know her only through recordings are apt to swear at her. The rich claret texture and abundant warmth of her voice are undeniable. But they are offset by an edge—especially above the staff—that such detractors are wont to call harsh. It certainly is not a voice for those preferring the rubescence of Flagstad. She also has a frequent tendency to scoop up or down onto a note, again a convention very much a part of the Wagner vocal tradition and one that Flagstad, Elisabeth Ohms, and others used most effectively. In Mödl's palate, however, the effect occasionally becomes tiresome. The biggest problem with this voice as a vehicle for a Brünnhilde for the ages, however, is its general unease. What strikes many listeners as basic discomfort, especially where pressure is applied above the staff, is apparent at the very outset. Mödl's traversal of the Valkyrie's calling card, Ho-jo-to-ho, is nothing if not effortful. From the first note, we are confronted not with an Olympian Brünnhilde, but with a very human one, subject to the fits and pitfalls to which all mortal singers are heir. That is just fine for the listener who has acquired a first-hand taste for this artist, but the top Bs and Cs, reportedly thrilling in the opera house, are simply toe-curling to some who may not have had the pleasure of that aural experience live. Nonetheless, Mödl generates a depth of feeling in her exchange with Siegmund that is quite beyond the imperious dignity purveyed by some other well-known sopranos who have gained fame in the role, including Flagstad in her later years, and Mödl's final plea to her father is an essay in desperation that bears echoes of her remarkable performances as Kundry.

That this *Walküre* recording manages to hold its own in record stores around the world against more recent competition from complete sets led by Solti, Karajan, Böhm, Janowski, Levine, Haitink and others may say something about its solid virtues: a sense of the excitement generated in a soaring "live" performance presented through sound technology that is up-to-date even by today's standards; superlative orchestral playing under a conductor whose approach encompasses its dramatic, philosophical, and musical values; and the experience of that sensation of "flow" that Furtwängler constantly strove for in his studio recordings. Unlike his *Tristan* recording, however, there are some arid patches. The tension in Wotan's narrative in Act II, for example, nearly dissipates, as Ferdinand Frantz tries to ration his breath under Furtwängler's tempo. But Frantz's was an achieve-

ment to reckon with, and neither time nor better-publicized inter-
preters have withered its power.

During the last ten years of his life, Furtwängler made the recordings to which critics and listeners most often refer when discussing his
art. While these constitute his final accounts of the works he cared
about most throughout his life, they do not always represent him in
top form. Nonetheless, taken as a group, these studio efforts reveal a
different kind of musical experience, one that could only be achieved
through this medium. Perhaps what bothers most people about these
late recordings is their peculiarities of tempo. A frequently voiced
criticism is that they are too slow. As Furtwängler often stated,
though, the matter of correct tempo is defined within the performance
itself. By the time he came to the last phase of his career, he had finally
arrived at an appreciation of the possibilities in long-play records, and
in them he sets about making all the music clearly heard in a forward-
moving continuum. The slower tempos in many of these recordings
allow notes, phrases, and details to be heard that are frequently passed
over in the heat and headier speeds of live performances. What
emerges is an effort to create a different kind of musical experience,
one that could never be achieved in a concert hall; a listening experience in which it would be possible to hear all the notes and yet perceive the greater structural outlines of a work. Otto Klemperer later
developed this concept in his own way, but some of his tempos are so
slow that the structure of the work dissipates—especially in his commercially recorded Beethoven cycle, and vitiates whatever semblance
of performance immediacy there may be. By and large, Furtwängler's
tempos are slow only to those used to hearing them taken faster.
While the external momentum sometimes languishes, a sense mate-
rializes of experiencing the music internally, from *inside*. Concomitantly, the structure and spirit of the work take on a new and unexpected perspective. Nowhere is this ever-evolving spirit more evident
than in the final recording Furtwängler made of the Beethoven Fifth
on 28 February and 1 March 1954, just eight months before he died.

If running times are at all relevant to the spirit and force of a work,
the Fifth with the Vienna Philharmonic recorded for HMV runs the
longest of the three studio versions: 34:50. It is exceeded in length
only by a live performance with the RAI orchestra in Rome in 1952
(36:00). Furtwängler usually took about 32 minutes to finish the Fifth.
Speed is mentioned here because Furtwängler's tempos in his last
recordings are frequently criticized as being slow, while Toscanini,
say, is lauded for his energetic briskness. The cumulative time for this
reading, in fact, is only ten seconds slower than Toscanini's with the
NBC Symphony in 1939. What makes the difference in the general

impression rendered in these two recordings (and all of Toscanini's readings of this symphony) are the variances in rhythmic punctuation. Toscanini always articulated his view of music by bringing a sense of rhythmic inflection into bold relief—chipping, striking, and hammering away until a monumental effigy materialized. Furtwängler, too, took this approach in several of his readings, especially in the live performances from 1943 and 1947 (with the Berlin Philharmonic) and 1950 (in Stockholm with the Vienna Philharmonic). But in the final studio recording in Vienna, he imbues his interpretation with a majestic confidence, made palpable through a grand but never grandiose refusal to be hurried. That exalted forward thrust characterizing most of his other performances is replaced by a tension arising from the sheer act of divaricating the tempo with nothing short of empyrean certitude. The Vienna Philharmonic responds by dwelling within this music they know so well rather than by simply executing it, and the development and finale of the first movement thus become a series of noble statements responding to one another, culminating in the challenge set forth by the final chords.

The second movement transforms the nobility characterizing the preceding movement into a stately but curiously delicate meditation full of elegiac thoughts sung out on the upper strings. It finishes without quite coming to a conclusion; there is more to be said, perhaps for another time. That sense of expectation in the third movement is picked up and continued. Horns intimate the imminence of a fatalistic change as the woodwinds and strings amuse themselves on the subject of imminence. When the main subject finally arrives, it is not in glory but in moderation. This reading of the Fifth differs from virtually all the others Furtwängler had led before, for it generates a sense of abstinence in the principal theme of the last movement. Only in the final pages is there any perceptible quickening of tempo. At that point, the release of accumulated tension leads to a exalted vision, rather than the simply joyous one he conjures up in his previous studio recording of 1937 and in his live performances of 1943 and 1947. What he generates is virtually a psychological view of the finale rather than the theatrical or rhetorical view that informs most documented performances of this work by other conductors.

Was this what Beethoven was trying to achieve? Furtwängler spent his life thinking and rethinking the works he conducted so that he might come into direct contact with their composers. "Correct expression," he was fond of saying, can only be achieved in correct context, and this can result only from a "vision of the whole" reflecting the one imagined by the work's creator. "This is the place where creator and interpreter meet, and where the interpreter has to subor-

dinate himself completely to the composer."[38] In the final movement
of this recording, Furtwängler seems to make one more attempt at
encountering Beethoven in the creative process. But the gravity of the
coda and the virtual reluctance to let the music rush forward to its end
until the last rapturous fifty bars, suggests that he was conducting the
music as he heard it in his mind's ears instead of a strictly presenta-
tional context.

There is no doubt that this interpretation may strike some as odd,
but for those seeking to hear this oft-played war-horse anew, it discovers the spirit of Beethoven in an unexpected and riveting way. We
may never know how many splices were made to produce the final
master, but the result was, in its own place and terms, one of the few
late studio productions taking the kind of soaring wing that invariably
informed his live performances.

Furtwängler's late studio output is a very strange bag of blessings,
for it can strike those used to hearing other recordings of the same
works as most peculiar indeed. The most significant flaw that will
haunt some of these recordings forever is the very complaint Furtwängler leveled against the studio recording process in the first place.
Furtwängler always sought to convey the sense of any work he conducted, as a living, kinetic experience. It was generated by the adren-
alin driving a group of musicians through a series of critical junctures
in the music and is, alas, palpably missing in a number of the studio
recordings. While they all evince a musical standard and a sound signature that are unmistakably Furtwängler's, the technical precision
they purvey frequently flattens that "edge of the ledge" *frisson* so frequently an inseparable part of his best work in the concert hall. Some
of the recordings from this period are also described as sounding tired,
and some of them, such as the Beethoven Sixth from 1952, occasionally lapse into lethargy.

In place of that sometimes missing immediacy, however, there
emerges a new perspective, a sense of experiencing the music from
within; the listener is drawn into an active participation in the aural
experience rather than merely "hearing" the music passively. Furtwängler evokes a mystical sense of the work's inner structure and
spirit through a widening of the tempo's spatial spectrum. Among the
large-scale works Furtwängler recorded, that euphoric, forward-mov-
ing sensation he achieved in his live performances is best heard in the

38. Quoted in the sleeve notes to the three-record commemorative set issued on
Deutsche Grammophon, *In Memoriam*, KL27-32. The booklet also contains a thoughtful essay on Furtwängler by K. H. Ruppel, "A Commemoration of Wilhelm Furtwängler," originally a broadcast over West German Radio Cologne on 25 January 1961 on
the anniversary of Furtwängler's 75th birthday.

Tristan from 1952, whose success he willingly credited to Walter Legge. But the better part of the most rewarding work with Legge was the smaller pieces, such as the overtures, where there were at most only one or two side breaks in the 78 format to interrupt the flow of the music. With Collingwood, his finest efforts certainly were the recordings of *Walküre* and the third (and final) studio recording of Beethoven's Fifth Symphony, both made with the Vienna Philharmonic.

While the charges that these recordings give a somewhat "manufactured" sense of Furtwängler's art rather than a natural, inevitable one, cannot be entirely dismissed, such cavils can be leveled at virtually any studio-made recording. What Furtwängler searches for in these recordings is something quite new and different from the expectations his live performances aroused, and from the expectations aroused by other studio recordings. While discovery is not always the corollary of that search, a sense of ongoing revelation remains at the heart of his best work in this last period. For a sense, however, of what made so many among his audiences rate him the finest conductor this century has produced, we turn now to the "live" performances.

23

The Live
Recordings I:
The War
Recordings

In late 1989 Deutsche Grammophon released 19 of the broadcast recordings Furtwängler made with the Berlin Philharmonic during the darkest days of the war (1942–1944), appropriately dubbed "The War Recordings." Their appearance evoked sharp and divided reactions, but many of those responses had nothing to do with music. From a musical standpoint, however, there has been virtual consensus ever since they came out. Few will say they are worthless—and that is all the more infuriating to those who still condemn Furtwängler. For how, the oft-repeated argument runs, could a man of such supernal gifts be conducting such sublime music for a nation at a time when its government was exterminating several races of people and attempting to submerge the world in totalitarianism?[1]

These broadcasts are not the earliest documents of Furtwängler performing live, but they are the first surviving live performances with superior sound quality, and that quality is astonishingly good for the period. A scherzo from the Beethoven Ninth with the Berlin Philharmonic apparently exists from 1930, and truncated excerpts of *Tristan* with Nanny Larsen-Todsen and Gotthelf Pistor from Furtwängler's debut at Bayreuth in 1931 have been widely circulated.

---

1. See Fritz von Unruh's intemperate but point-making reaction to Furtwängler's decision to remain in Germany during the Third Reich, *Aufbau*, 18 April 1947, p. 5.

There is a riveting BBC broadcast performance of Beethoven's Ninth also available in wretched sound taken during the Berlin Philharmonic's visit to London during the Coronation Season of 1937. The performance was relayed live from Queens Hall and included Erna Berger, Gertrude Pitzinger, Walter Ludwig, and Rudolf Watzke as vocal soloists. There also are pirated tapes of Furtwängler leading tantalizing slices of *Walküre* and *Götterdämmerung* at Covent Garden during that same season. Furtwängler collaborated with the two reigning Wagnerian sopranos during the middle third of the century, and while his work with Frida Leider here suggests a match that may not have reflected the vocal felicities evident in his collaboration with Flagstad, it shows an affinity of temperaments rarely equaled in surviving documents of his other operatic collaborations.

For the earliest evidence of Furtwängler at work in relatively good sound, though, we turn to the war recordings. Political hostilities curtailed Furtwängler's international career severely between 1941 and 1945, and he recorded almost exclusively with two orchestras during this time—the Vienna Philharmonic and the Berlin Philharmonic. But it is only with the latter that we have a generous sampling of his work under consistent acoustic conditions. Many occasions on which he conducted the Berlin Philharmonic were caught for posterity, and the release of these 19 performances on ten compact discs fills a major gap in Furtwängler's recorded legacy. These CDs also appear at a time when Furtwängler is beginning to be re-valued both as a musician and as an historical figure. On the one hand, we can hear Furtwängler coming to what turned out to be the apogee of his career in these live performances. While his interpretive instincts continued to grow after the war, the concentration of his finest qualities—so omnipresent in these war recordings—was sometimes diluted during that last period, owing to increasing health problems and the accumulation of the psychic burdens his decision to stay in Nazi Germany brought upon him. On the other hand, these performances constitute a political statement of a most unusual sort, in spite of Furtwängler's muddled-headed insistence that art and politics should have nothing to do with one another.

Looked at as events in the history of recorded sound, these represent the cream skimmed from an incredible number of recordings—both studio-made and broadcast relays—that were produced throughout a Germany lurching toward the abyss. Little attention has been paid to the near-pathological interest the Germans took in music during the Third Reich, but it evidently was everywhere. Even concentration camps had their orchestras, and more than a few musicians played for time to survive (as Arthur Miller has dramatized on television). The notorious Dr. Mengele reportedly conducted his heinous medical experiments with recordings of Wagner playing continuously in counterpoint to the screaming of his human guinea pigs.

As the tide of war turned against Germany, the number of concerts, broadcasts and recordings multiplied in almost astronomical proportions. Between 1943 and early 1945, literally thousands of concerts, musicals, ice shows, marching bands, folk groups, and other forms of musical entertainment were broadcast and recorded on wire or magnetic tape. A good portion of recordings from that period have survived, but they have never, for various inexplicable reasons, been re-released.

The phenomenon of this craze for music has been explained in a number of ways. These broadcasts meant more than wallpaper music to the beleaguered German populace. As the End approached, it seems all Germany was engulfing itself in a womb of music. It was certainly a clever way for Goebbels' propaganda machine to prop up the sagging spirits of *Das Volk* as Allied bombing challenged national morale. There may also have been a collective urge to preserve the remnants of a culture that was rapidly disintegrating in the face of a war indubitably lost. The Austrian music critic Clemens Höslinger suggests a purely practical explanation:

> At the end of August 1944, theaters throughout the Reich were closed because of the danger in the state of war. As a substitute for the cancelled 1944–45 season, and to keep employed those artists who had been excused from military service or the war industry, there was an enormous increase in radio recordings.[2]

After the collapse of Nazi resistance in spring of 1945, the Soviets occupied Berlin and found broadcast tapes of Furtwängler and the Berlin Philharmonic made during the war. They were among the earliest magnetic tape recordings ever made of complete concert broadcasts in Germany. Despite the scarcity of top flight artists in this period, Walter Gieseking, Edwin Fischer, and Peter Anders were among the soloists. Even the most jaded listener at that time (or any other) might call the find sensational.

They were shipped to Moscow and released on long-play discs beginning in the 1960s. But they were put out sporadically and with little publicity. Nonetheless, Furtwängler fans in the West grabbed them up hungrily during the intermittent periods of thaw in the cold war. Few of them knew exactly how much material had been taken or

2. Sleeve note, *Walküre* Act I, Preiser 90015.

how much remained to be released. Finally, the fruits of Glasnost produced an agreement by the Soviets to return the tapes they had taken to Moscow, and they arrived in Berlin in October 1987.

The return of Furtwängler's war recordings came at a time when Furtwängler—long a pariah in some parts of the musical world even three decades after his death—was coming full circle to the position of world eminence he had lost after he decided to remain in Germany. Coincidentally, the Berlin Wall came down shortly after the recordings were released on Deutsche Grammophon. The interest these recordings generated stems primarily from their contents, but they are also exciting because they represent recording techniques far in advance of their time.

Throughout the 1930s something of a quiet race was taking place between English and German recording companies. The goal of both contestants was to eliminate the four-minute limitations of the shellac 78-rpm disc so that whole movements of symphonies and entire acts of operas could be recorded without interruption. To this end, English companies experimented with the optical process. This technique was used in sound film from the virtual inception of talking films right up through the 1950s. In fact, it is still used in 16-mm films. The Germans, on the other hand, experimented with wire magnetic tape techniques. From the outset, this was far superior to the optical process, even though it was slower in gaining acceptance. Ultimately, its quarter-inch wide, reel-to-reel descendant became the medium of choice, especially in recent years. The British almost won out, EMI having succeeded in recording such lengthy ventures as a complete *Tristan* at Covent Garden in 1936 under Fritz Reiner with Kirsten Flagstad and Lauritz Melchior. But neither singer was entirely happy with the performance, and efforts to produce it commercially were eventually abandoned.

Germany forged ahead with magnetic wire tape, and by 1940 the Reichs-Rundfunks-Gesellschaft was regularly recording complete operas and symphonies. Since there were no adequate facilities for recording in the Philharmonie, Helmut Kruger and Dr. Friedrich Schnapp, who was both the first recording supervisor with RRF and Furtwängler's personal "Tonmeister" since 1939, had to improvise a sound booth. They started off with a small room in the Philharmonie building and set up transmission operations for broadcasts and recordings. Since the tape machines were too cumbersome to bring to the Philharmonie, land line connections were established with a telephone link between the concert hall and the broadcasting headquarters where the tape machines were located. Most of these events were broadcast live and taped at the same time with a view toward broadcasting them again or turning them into commercial recordings.

Other performances were recorded with the same intentions in exactly the same way, but they were made without an audience and broadcast at a later date.[3]

Deutsche Grammophon has lovingly cleaned and spruced up these documents, though finicky audiophiles may carp here and there. While they are accurately called "War Recordings," they are by no means a complete set of broadcasts or recordings Furtwängler made between 1942 and the end of the war. An absent gem, for example, is an astonishing Beethoven Ninth with Anders, Tilla Briem, Elisabeth Höngen, and Rudolf Watzke from March 1942. That broadcast tape was among those taken by the Soviets and is currently available on several labels, widely varying in sound quality and pitch.[4]

For decades, many people, especially in America, simply could not understand or refused to believe Furtwängler's claim that he stayed behind in Germany to be the sole guardian of what was worthwhile in German culture and to give solace through his concerts to "real Germans," most of whom he strongly believed were not sympathetic to the Nazis. Despite his antipathy to the regime, Furtwängler's concerts were always sold out during the war years, evidence, perhaps, that he was not entirely wrong about where the Germans secretly stood vis-à-vis the Nazis. These concerts provided a sanctuary for the German people as the war came closer to home. The Germany they were always being told was invincible crumbled before their eyes and from under their feet. Even historian William Shirer admitted in his memoirs *The Nightmare Years* that attending a Furtwängler concert gave him respite from the daily routine of enduring the war.[5] According to leaders of resistance groups, what intellectual opposition there was to

3. The Bruckner Ninth from 1944 is a superb example.

4. *Caveat emptor:* Finding a Furtwängler performance properly produced on CDs can be highly problematic. If the sound is superior, it is sometimes offset by inaccurate pitching. If the pitching is correct, the sound production can occasionally be mediocre. The now defunct Price-less (D13256) had the cheapest version and the worst sound on CDs of the 1942 Ninth, but it preserved the best performance and is pitched accurately. The French Furtwängler Society Edition (SWF 891) has the best over-all sound but is pitched a half step flat at the beginning of the third movement. It moves up to about a quartertone under by the end of the movement. Most Japanese releases of Furtwängler are well worth their astronomic prices. But in 1991 Japanese EMI released a surprisingly sub-standard CD set of this performance, coupled with a wretchedly produced Fifth dating from 27 or 30 June 1943 (CE28-5748-49). Despite a marked lack of crispness in the sound reproduction, the transfer of the Ninth is at least pitched properly in all four movements. The last three movements of the Fifth, however, not only are haphazardly dubbed but are pitched a half step flat. This masterful performance of the Fifth is produced accurately and lovingly on DG 427 775-2.

5. A television documentary based on Shirer's survey of the Third Reich, shown on PBS in America, shows a film of Furtwängler conducting in 1942, and appears to imply that he was positively disposed to contributing toward the war effort through such activities. But Shirer's recollections of his experiences attending Furtwängler's concerts at the beginning of the war in *The Nightmare Years* are more sympathetic to Furtwängler; (Boston and Toronto) 1984, pp. 157–159.

speak of attended his concerts regularly.[6] The conspirators in the July 20th Plot to assassinate Hitler used the intervals at these concerts during late 1943 and early 1944 to hatch their ill-fated coup. But also in attendance were some few who must have known what was going on at places like Auschwitz even as these concerts yielded up their musical balm. While Furtwängler indubitably was performing for "true Germans," he also had to play for *all* Germans at these concerts, even Hitler on a few unavoidable occasions. In the ghostly coughing that punctuates a soft passage here and there, the breath of history heaves a shiver upon more than just the sanctity of German culture.

Furtwängler's Berlin war concerts were gala events, even as the war made it more difficult for the public to attend. They were always sold out within hours after tickets went on sale, and the beleaguered citizens of Berlin sacrificed their increasingly strained budgets in order to attend. Furtwängler's concerts became such an obsession for Berliners that their ticket demands eventually elicited as many as four concerts of the same program, sometimes twice on the same day.[7]

To some listeners, these recordings might at first appear to be quaint relics of a bygone master, but their ongoing value to the public is as much an object lesson in supernal grace under supreme pressure as it is a model of superb orchestral playing of the sort too rarely heard in concert halls today. For while the Berlin Philharmonic is always alert to the expectant urgency of an attending audience, its members also play from one concert to the next with consistent discipline of ensemble and intonation, even as their homes are going up in flames, their loved ones dying at the front or from the bombings, and food and basic necessities—even strings and reeds—are becoming increasingly scarce.

The selections traverse virtually the whole of Furtwängler's scope, running from Handel to Beethoven and then to Richard Strauss, and several works not normally associated with him, such as a wide-canvassed view of Sibelius' *En Saga* and a swirling account of the Second Suite from Ravel's *Daphnis et Chloë*. For whatever reason, there is no Wagner. Some of the soloists are better known than others. Edwin Fischer plays the Brahms Second Piano Concerto replete with bushels of wrong notes, while Walter Gieseking traverses the Schumann Piano Concerto in A Minor with the same heartfelt involvement that characterizes nearly all his documented performances. Tibor de Machula was the orchestra's first cellist during those years, and Erich

6. See remarks of Rudolf Pechel and Count Gert Kanitz about Furtwängler as an inspiration to resistance fighters. Riess, p. 241, and Chapter 16.
7. For example, 8 February 1944, 11 a.m. and 3 p.m., and 21 March 1944, 11 a.m. and 4 p.m.

Röhn one of several concertmasters. They play the Schumann and the Beethoven concertos respectively and expressively. These performances demonstrate Furtwängler's gifts as an accompanist, a talent such enemies as Horowitz derided.

The majority of the works played are from the Austro-German Romantic repertoire, and they range from Mozart to Richard Strauss. Critics have noted that at least one performance—Mozart's Symphony No. 39—is not done by Furtwängler, though there is some disagreement as to who exactly might be on the podium. It is indeed the weakest of all the performances. Dating from August 1944, it was performed at the Staatsoper Unter den Linden where some of the Philharmonic concerts were held after the old Philharmonie was bombed in January of that year. Despite the change of ambience, though, the famous "Furtwängler Sound" remains intact in the five performances of other works played at the Staatsoper before it too was destroyed by Allied bombing in 1945.

It is indeed unfortunate that Deutsche Grammophon did not (for obvious practical reasons) arrange this group of concerts in sequence, for if they are heard in chronological order, the performances gain perceptibly in intensity and deeply felt refinement. This is not to say that the performances get better and better. To speak of Furtwängler performances in qualitative terms of good or bad is usually unproductive. These performances have no more or fewer mistakes and ambivalences than any other live performance of its standard.

In listening to these performances, though, a sense of giddy finality seeps into phrase upon phrase with intensifying imminence at each succeeding concert that is at once thrilling and vaguely morbid. Indeed, neither players nor conductors knew if there would be another performance after the one they happened to be playing, and interruptions from air-raid sirens were coming with increasing frequency after 1942. In the midst of these worsening conditions, these performances reflect the very real specter of inevitable catastrophe and the orgasmic euphoria felt by the audience hearing them. But there still are some phenomenal moments that are as thrilling as they are troubling.

Take, for example, two Beethoven symphonies given within five months of each other in the second half of 1943. Listen to the final movement of the Fifth, given on 30 June 1943. From a strictly interpretive point of view, Furtwängler accumulates the statements in the first paragraphs of the movement, imperceptibly building them into an almost hysterical stretto. What is remarkable about this movement in Furtwängler's hands is that its momentum is unpremeditated. Furtwängler is not calculating the increments; it is all happening naturally, spontaneously. Nowhere, perhaps, is there more palpable evidence of what Furtwängler meant when he said over and over that he strove to "re-create" the music than in this finale.

Listen also to the second and fourth movements of the Beethoven Seventh from November 1943, just before the war was going into what is called Endgame, its final and worst phase. In the former, Furtwängler conjures a stoic grief from the upper strings and woodwinds that swells into a seamless sigh arching over the rest of the movement. Furtwängler gave some fabulous accounts of this symphony after the war, but he never again so caught the elegiac sublimity that is at the heart of this Allegretto. In the final movement of this performance, the ecstatic abandonment toward which each succeeding paragraph inexorably strides may make some sense of the seeming poppycock that some Germans of the time secretly referred to as "the true German spirit," a spirit that in this performance transcends national and ethnic lines.

After the war, Furtwängler reflected on this period of terror among the German people:

> The other development which finally led to war with the whole world was something quite separate. Here the German people did not follow [Hitler], and he needed all his set pieces of lies and distortions to convince them that only the wicked Jews, only the wicked English, Russians, etc., were repeatedly to blame [for the degradation Germany suffered after the Treaty of Versailles]. This can only really be judged by someone who has lived in Germany [throughout the regime]. For Hitler's propaganda increasingly silenced the real Germany. The terror is the *sign* of this. It was necessary, it was imperative. I would like to know how any other people would have behaved under this cross fire of terror and the most skillful lies.   *Notebooks, pp. 156–157*[8]

Furtwängler has been condemned, especially in America, for continuing to bolster the spirits of his fellow Germans, most of whom got churned up in the monstrous machine that was National Socialism. That he never issued a truly comprehensive defense of his position, or at least one that non-Germans could understand at the time his intentions were called into question, suggests that he tacitly accepted that condemnation. The contrary, in fact, is the case. As the war moved toward Endgame, he reflected in 1943 on his mission as an artist and his duty to his people, regardless of the political circumstances in which they now were trapped:

---

8. Brackets added for clarity.

I am—in Germany and elsewhere a German artist, a representative of Germany who re-creates himself in German music. One can reject and boycott German music as "made in Germany"—but one cannot play Mozart and Beethoven and turn away from those who live and die for them.

But the message Beethoven gave mankind in his works and particularly in the Ninth Symphony, the message of goodness, of trust, of unity before God, seems to me never to have been more urgent than it is today.

Aufzeichnungen, p. 236

That urgency permeates two performances of marked contrast during this period. The first took place in Berlin on 21 and 24 March 1942. While some commentators prefer to dwell on the glories of the first three movements, it is Furtwängler's traversal of the last movement that illuminates his view of Beethoven as a tragedian in whose works the ineluctable conflicts of human nature are played out with harsh Senecan violence, ultimately resolving in a vision of unearthly joy.

Nowhere is that vision borne out more fully than in this Berlin performance. The chorus and orchestra cry out the theme carrying Schiller's text exhorting peace and joy, more in anguish than in elation, playing with almost manic concentration and singing with such declamatory power that the text becomes transformed into a *Dies Irae*, whose strength quite palpably comes from a demonic source. Critics and colleagues alike have remarked on Furtwängler's capacity to inspire those who came under his baton, but whether or not you care for such a seething, white-hot realization of Beethoven's valedictory symphony, the awesome faculty with which Furtwängler imbues it in this performance is undeniable.

More than a year later, on 12 December 1943, he performed the work with the Stockholm Music Society Choir and Orchestra in Stockholm. While many critics have remarked how much more relaxed this performance seems compared to the terror-laden performance of the previous year, possibly because Furtwängler was experiencing his first real encounter with a non-totalitarian environment since his visit to England in 1938, it is not relaxation that informs this performance, but longing. Again, it is the fourth movement, in which the vocal line predominates, that Furtwängler elicits the kind of rapturous yearning from his players and soloists that was an inexplicable aspect of his talent.

Taken as a group, these recordings can offer easy proof to some ears of what was called the "prostitution of [Furtwängler's] art before the Nazi regime." But they show him—for better or for worse, right or wrong—putting his belief in "another, true Germany" into action, and what emerges from these war recordings is an Aeschylean conflict of ideologies in which Furtwängler's notion of patriotism is played off against the Nazis' concept of nationalism. The setting of this ongoing drama is the concert hall, and the protagonist is Furtwängler himself. On one side of this conflict, *Patriotism*, as Furtwängler viewed it, refers to loyalty to his country and love for his country while permitting individual liberty. On the other side of this battle of wills, *Nationalism*, as the Nazis conceived of it, refers to mass suppression, reinforced not only by the abrogation of individual liberty, but through the violent exclusion of all that is not strictly within its prescribed doctrines.[9]

Ironically, the Nazis could not see what Furtwängler believed he was doing, or simply chose to ignore it because they had no consistent policy about what constituted Nazi music. These recordings go a long way toward demonstrating how much Furtwängler got away with. There is no doubt that Furtwängler's musical activity was indeed misused by the Nazis, but the subversive message in his live performances during that grim period rings more clearly as the years of nightmare in Germany begin to merge into the dark sad spectrum of contemporary history. Furtwängler was the unsung hero of the German resistance.

For all his stubborn labors to keep art apart from politics during those twelve years, however, Furtwängler ultimately admitted in 1945 that his mission may have been hopeless, although he never conceded that he had failed in his attempt to keep them separate:

> Apart from the fact that art basically served only as a supplement to politics, here the whole movement was one of comfortable mediocrity, a true re-action, a renunciation of any advance.   *Notebooks, p. 164*

While Furtwängler lashed out at the idea of a collective guilt,[10] he personally felt tormented by the proof of the atrocities committed by the Nazis. He also never felt that what he personally had done for individual Jews in any way ameliorated or put him above those Germans who had done nothing or who had actively participated in the genocide of millions of Jews, Poles, gypsies, and others. This perhaps may

---

9. See Louis L. Snyder, *The Roots of German Nationalism*, (Bloomington and London) 1978. See also George Mosse, *The Crisis of German Ideology*, (New York) 1964 and 1981; *Masses and Man*, (New York) 1980; and *The Nationalization of the Masses*, (New York) 1975; as well as Chapter 7.

10. See Chapter 17.

explain why he never personally advertised how much he had done for the persecuted in the Third Reich.

"I remember him taking my hand after the descriptions of the atrocities came out," Frau Furtwängler recalled to me. "He said, 'we Germans will never be free of this as long as we live. Generations to come will bear the burden of what has happened.'"[11]

11. Personal conversation with the author, Paris, 22 April 1989.

24

The Live Recordings II: Ring Cycles and Cyclical Issues

If Furtwängler's wartime recordings with the Berlin Philharmonic reveal his ever-growing mastery over orchestral works, there is also a wide body of evidence contradicting assertions that he was less than masterful in the opera house.[1] In any event, Furtwängler's gifts as an opera conductor emerge from tapes of two traversals he made of the *Ring* in 1950 and 1953. Both performances were broadcast, but they were relayed under very different conditions. The *Ring* from 1950 consisted of edited tapes from two cycles Furtwängler conducted at La Scala with Kirsten Flagstad as Brünnhilde and Ferdinand Frantz as Wotan. The second *Ring* was given under broadcast conditions before invited studio audiences in Rome in autumn 1953. The four operas were presented and taped over ten nights, one act at a time, between 26 October and 27 November.[2] Dress rehearsals were also taped to increase the number of options from which the broadcast master could be made. The best sections from all the tapings were then edited

---

1. Otto Klemperer and others have felt Furtwängler's true métier was the concert hall. See Peter Heyworth, ed., *Conversations with Klemperer*, p. 119. In a personal conversation with the author in April 1989 Sir Reginald Goodall said he was inclined to agree with Klemperer, though he stressed that his opinion derived from his own preference rather than any defect he detected in Furtwängler as an opera conductor.

2. *Rheingold*, 26 October. *Walküre*, 29 October, 3 and 6 November. *Siegfried*, 10, 13, and 17 November. *Götterdämmerung*, 20, 24, and 27 November 1953.

together and broadcast to Italian audiences, one complete opera a night over four days. *Rheingold*, of course, was performed in its entirety, edited, and broadcast complete. The logic behind this procedure was incontestable: singers and orchestra came to each succeeding act with the benefit of both rest and up-to-the-minute rehearsal. Neither *Ring* was ever meant to be released on commercial discs, but the Rome *Ring* was discussed as a "rehearsal" for a complete studio *Ring* led by Furtwängler. In fact, Furtwängler's decision to renew his contract with HMV/EMI in 1952 was largely consummated on this understanding, though the enmity that had developed in his relationship with Walter Legge almost terminated his dealings with the company.[3]

During Furtwängler's engagement at La Scala conducting *Meistersinger* that year, he concluded his new contract with David Bicknell, Head of the International Division of HMV/EMI. The major project of this new arrangement was to be a complete *Ring*, beginning with *Walküre* recorded in the studio with the Vienna Philharmonic. Within eight weeks of finishing *Walküre* in October 1954, Furtwängler was dead. EMI's hopes for a complete *Ring* came to a sudden and shocking halt, at least for the moment, a long moment lasting 17 years.[4]

As it turned out, both Italian *Rings* eventually were released on records long after Furtwängler's death, the Scala cycle on pirate vinyl records and CDs, and the Rome broadcasts on HMV/EMI, though wretchedly produced pirates of substantial sections from what has come to be known as "the Rome *Ring*" circulated privately before it was released commercially. The latter turned out to be a labor of tribulations. The primary bugaboo was the presence of two singers on the broadcasts who were signed exclusively to Polydor. Bicknell and HMV/EMI tried on several occasions in the late 1950s and 1960s to wrest exemptions for Wolfgang Windgassen and Josef Greindl, but Polydor was not about to be moved. Eventually, Frau Furtwängler personally besought Polydor to allow the recording to be released. When HMV/EMI finally got clearance for Windgassen and Greindl, the project again appeared to become permanently stalled in one bureaucratic

3. See Chapter 21.
4. Ultimately the Rome *Ring* was released in the United States under Angel AB 9601-18 and in Britain under HMV RLS 702. The British and European editions contained informative notes in English, German, French, and Italian. The American boxed set of the four operas contained no introductory notes in the libretto booklet. A CD produced from remastering the original tapes was released in 1991: CZS 7671232. Evidence of how perfunctorily EMI continues to treat Furtwängler is to be seen in this CD release. The edition released in America is bereft of those valuable essays contained in the British and European sets of the LPs as well as libretti for the operas.

delay after another. In the meantime, Philips became interested in the project and decided to do it. When EMI got wind of it, the project suddenly moved swiftly to completion. Frau Furtwängler recalled those tense moments in late 1971:

> It was only after Philips decided to do it that EMI finally decided to do it. There was no publicity on the release because Electrola, the German branch of EMI/HMV, did not want complications. That, of course, meant trouble with Karajan, who was still signed to them and had his own *Ring* cycle out by then [on DG]. But the newspapers started talking about it anyway, and suddenly it had a life of its own and sold very, very well. This surprised me because it came out last. Solti first, then Karajan, and then Furtwängler."[5]

On one hand, the release of a third *Ring* on the market at a time when two spectacularly produced studio *Rings* by Solti (1958–1966) and Karajan (1967–1971) were selling like rock albums was a risky venture indeed. Furtwängler's version could not begin to compete with either of them on recording quality standards, and the critics almost unanimously began their reviews with this cavil. On the other hand, a recording of the *Ring* without the benefit of mistakes corrected, but imbued with the organic ebb and flow of the total work and fired by the now-or-never tensions generated in a live performance looked like a good gamble. What HMV/EMI did, possibly without knowing it, was to offer the record buyer a clear choice between the technical felicities guaranteed in the Solti and Karajan sets and the raw excitement promised by Furtwängler. Whether out of curiosity or from a need for something the studio-made sets did not offer, the public rushed to buy it. The records sold at approximately two-thirds the cost of the studio *Rings,* and the combined incentive proved to be irresistible. In any event, the absence of anything resembling the costly advertising campaigns that attended both the Solti and Karajan versions made the success of the Furtwängler set all the more surprising to HMV/EMI executives—and more profitable to their accountants.

When the reviews of the Rome *Ring* came out, *The Gramophone*'s critic, David Cairns, wrote a penetrating analysis of Furtwängler's view of the tetralogy as a "stark, heavy, brooding work, a profound tragedy set in an ancient Teutonic world of gods and heroes, to whom every action is of the utmost existential importance."[6] While critics by no means said Furtwängler's recording could, with its inferior sound quality, supplant Decca/London's phenomenally popular ver-

5. Personal conversation with the author, Clarens, 8 December 1989.
6. David Cairns, September 1972.

sion under Georg Solti or Herbert von Karajan's rival version on Deutsche Grammophon, they all, virtually to a man, put it in a venerable class by itself. *The Gramophone* went so far as to call it the "gramophone *event* of the century," distinguishing it from the gramophone *achievements* of the century the studio versions had attained. In a two-part essay in the *New York Times*, Harvey Philips was distraught by the sound quality on the first two operas, but he admitted that he ultimately fell under Furtwängler's spell anyway. He concluded that it was Martha Mödl's flawed but exquisitely powerful Brünnhilde, "risking all for the sake of communication." that brought the tetralogy to life under Furtwängler's inspiring hand.[7]

The Scala *Ring* came out on a pirate label in late 1976.[8] Though parts of it had circulated among collectors for years, its appearance as a complete entity caught everyone by surprise. Furtwängler performed a great deal in Italy after the war, and La Scala became the stage for a good part of his major operatic triumphs in the last period of his life. Although he had first appeared at Italy's leading opera house as early as 1923 with the Scala Orchestra, he made his operatic debut there conducting the *Ring* in 1950 and returned there for *Parsifal* in 1951 and for *Meistersinger* in 1952. Unlike so many of his contracts, his agreement with La Scala was a happy one, and he frequently remarked how quickly the Italians on both sides of the orchestra pit absorbed the subtleties of Wagner.[9]

Though the Murray Hill release of the Scala *Ring* was technically a pirate, it appeared openly in record shops in America and Europe. The poor sound quality was further aggravated by squeezing the entire cycle on eleven records. Some sides on this release run for more than forty minutes. Nonetheless, British critic Alan Blyth began his review in *The Gramophone* by calling it "the greatest performance of the whole cycle I have ever heard."[10] He spent the rest of the review carefully justifying the gauntlet he had thrown down. What impressed him most about Furtwängler in this set was a more complete sense of the cycle as a single unit than he perceived in the Rome *Ring:*

> [Furtwängler's] command of Wagner's *unendliche melodie*, heard at its most potent throughout the first act and final scene of *Die Walküre*, are the crux of Furtwängler's art. They are enhanced by the wonderfully refulgent sound he seemed able to draw from any orchestra. The Scala

7. 17 September 1972.
8. Murray Hill 944 477.
9. Claudio Abbado was a music student in Milan in 1950 and attended Furtwängler's rehearsals. See Chapter 20.
10. October 1976.

players, much more accomplished than their colleagues of Rome Radio, enable him to knit together scenes with unerring breadth at fundamentally fast speeds, here quicker than those in either the Rome performance or in the Bayreuth *Ring* of 1936.[11]

What may be most remarkable about both *Rings* is that they both originated in Italy with Italian orchestras, a fact remarked upon by most of the critics. Neither La Scala's orchestra nor the Rome Radio's musicians could play with the weight of tradition and certainty of style that would have come naturally to even a second-rate Germanic orchestra. But the absence of that burden of authenticity is perhaps the peculiar blessing alighting upon these performances, for they document not only two sets of the *Ring*, but also two first-class orchestras discovering and experiencing the first blush of understanding this music as ensembles. Critics often have remarked how Furtwängler made whatever music he was conducting sound as though it were coming into being for the first time. Nowhere is that more in evidence than in the Scala and Rome *Rings*, where it was indeed the first time for most of the musicians.

Perhaps the most telling examples of this sense of discovery occur in the same places in both performances: the last scene of Act I of *Walküre*. The woodwinds begin the scene tentatively in both performances, giving no hint of what is in store. As Sieglinde nears the end of her sad narrative ["O, *fänd ich ihm heut* . . ."] and sparks the first pangs of sympathy from Siegmund, the strings well up and fold into the winds and brass, as Furtwängler draws that peculiarly intense sound from the orchestra that is at once passionate, inimitably Furt-wängler, and thoroughly "Wagnerian." But in both performances, the pulsating sweep of this scene reveals not professional passion and knowing Wagnerism but that genuine *feel* for the inner flow of the music sometimes encountered in superb amateur ensembles. Such an achievement could not be accomplished through hectoring, intimidation, or mere repetition at rehearsal. While a non-German orchestra sympathetic to Wagner might have given a good imitation of style on the first go-around, only Furtwängler's telepathic musicality induced what comes across so powerfully as real and essentially Wagnerian, a sound surge coming forth up from an intuitive source of understanding. The Scala orchestra plays a tad more expressively here and there, for they are, player for player, a more gifted group. But the Rome ensemble plays with more raw excitement and note-for-note accuracy.

11. P. 654, October 1976.

Vocally, the two sets are a series of trade-offs. The Scala performance has the name-brand cast for any *Ring* produced in the first decade after the war, but it also reveals that cast laboring under the rigors
of continuous live performing. It also switches from Set Svanholm, as
the hero in *Siegfried*, to Max Lorenz in *Götterdämmerung*, while the
Rome set has Ludwig Suthaus in both operas. Svanholm is a weary and
occasionally wearying hero in *Siegfried* by the time he encounters a
well-rested Kirsten Flagstad in the third act, after singing out his lungs
for four hours. But he is a more vocally attractive Siegfried than Ludwig Suthaus on the Rome set.

Nonetheless, Suthaus delivers a surprisingly tender hero in Act
Two of *Siegfried*, appealingly vulnerable when he tries to communicate with the comely Forest Bird of Rita Streich. The *Götterdämmerung* Siegfrieds pit the artistic experience of Max Lorenz at La Scala
against the vocal ripeness of Suthaus at Rome. Lorenz was almost 60
by the time he encountered Flagstad's Brünnhilde in Milan, and he
was coming to the end of a glorious career that had survived not only
the adoration of high-ranking Nazis but their lethal attitude toward
his sexual proclivities. Lorenz is perhaps more remarkable, for he
arrives at the final act without the benefit of the few days' respite
afforded to Suthaus. He is also a hero more confident in meeting his
death in the final pages of the hunting scene. His vision of the awaken-
ing Brünnhilde is ecstatic, while Suthaus seems to wonder why it all
happened to *him*.

The Siegmunds of Günther Treptow (Scala) and Wolfgang Windgassen (Rome) offer a clear choice between talents. Treptow was a
highly successful postwar dramatic tenor, but his hectoring delivery is
an acquired taste indeed. Windgassen gives no impression of having
ever thought about the words he is singing, but he is an ardent and
sympathetic brother to his sister. For voice and passion Windgassen
wins hands down.

Both sets are dominated by the Wotan of Ferdinand Frantz,
though Josef Hermann replaces him capably as the Wanderer in *Siegfried* at La Scala. Critics sometimes carp that they would prefer hearing Hans Hotter's Wotan more than anyone else's, but Frantz is by
turns far angrier and more mournful than the stoic Hotter later proved
to be in the Solti studio version, though Hotter was born with a better
instrument.

The Frickas of Elisabeth Höngen in both *Rheingold* and *Walküre*
in the Scala set far out sing those of Ira Malaniuk *(Rheingold)* and Elsa
Calveti *(Walküre)* on EMI, but the redoubtable Margarete Klose gives
her heated competition as Erda in *Siegfried*. Hilde Konetzni sings an
effectively distraught Sieglinde in both sets of *Walküres*, but there are

some signs of fraying in the Rome recording, especially in the desperate moments in Act II where she cries out for Siegmund. Konetzni, Höngen, and Klose, incidentally, were among the finest singers in the world in the late 1930s and 1940s, and they were among that generation of superlative singers, including Helge Roswänge, Franz Völker, Tiana Lemnitz, Marcel Wittrisch, and Margarete Teschemacher, who all had the misfortune of coming to the heights of their careers in Nazi Germany.[12] The war and its aftermath destroyed their chances at international fame, but Konetzni, Höngen, and Klose were among the few to regain a measure of the success their talents warranted. Fine as their performances are in these *Rings*, they regrettably represent valedictory rather than introductory essays of their gifts.

If a choice must be made among *Rings* based on who is singing Brünnhilde, the competition against Kirsten Flagstad runs thin in any age. Few indeed are the Wagner sopranos of this century who can come close to her for that complete palette of power, size, beauty, heart, and range. Some may have equalled or surpassed her in several of these qualities, but few sopranos can compete with her on all these counts. Unfortunately Marta Mödl's palpable sincerity is no substitute for the effort she must exert to squeeze out those notes above the staff. To be fair, Flagstad was no longer at her peak when she went to La Scala, but enough voice and energy were left to deliver a Brünnhilde to reckon with. True, she omits the final high C on the last page of the score, but listen to Mödl in the same passage at Rome. She omits it, too. Listen also to the end of the Todesverkündigung (warning of death) in *Walküre* in both sets. There is no doubt that Flagstad's Valkyrie will make good her promise to Siegmund. Mödl promises to do the best she can. Flagstad subdues her listener by the consummate power of her vocal presence; she inspires awe. Mödl captivates her auditor by the very frailties of her vocal condition; she arouses empathy.

What Furtwängler brings to all these performances that sets them apart from traversals of the *Ring* by other conductors is his sagacious capacity to vivify the endless series of transitions within the tetralogy. Frau Furtwängler recalls how frequently Furtwängler used the term "flow" when referring to Wagner, and it is that sense of inexorable surge that enlivens both *Rings*. The Milan performances gain nothing

12. Konetzni sang Sieglinde in the first of two cycles under Furtwängler at Covent Garden on 20 May 1938. Her sister Anny Konetzni sang Brünnhilde. Tiana Lemnitz sang Sieglinde with Frida Leider as the Valkyrie in the second cycle. Furtwängler never conducted opera again at Covent Garden, though he conducted his first concerts in England after the war in 1948 with the London Philharmonic.

from several massive cuts, notably in Wotan's narrative in Act Two of *Walküre* and in the exchange between Wotan/Wanderer and Siegfried, but Furtwängler never compromises the dark and inexorably *disturbing* vision he draws of the work as whole. If Furtwängler accomplished such feats with non-German orchestras and choruses, it is a sadly compelling impulse to consider what he might have wrought had he lived to document a complete cycle entirely with orchestral forces weaned upon this music.

Making a choice between the Milan and Rome *Rings* may be analogous to Paris awarding the golden apple. No one will be entirely satisfied by either recording, and everybody will be offended in some way. What is important to decide is which priority ranks first and foremost to the listener. For sheer vocalism, the presence of Flagstad alone on the Milan set outweighs all other considerations. For technological clarity, EMI's sound engineers have performed a yeoman job on cleaning up the masters in their CD release of the Rome set. For sweep and excitement, there is more white heat in the Milan set than in the Rome. For musical probity, Rome wins hands down: there are far fewer mistakes and the character of the orchestral sound is more idiomatic and unstintingly compelling. If you want to hear it just once or twice, the Milan set offers the once-in-a-lifetime opportunity of hearing Flagstad and Furtwängler in volant ascent during a live performance. If you want to hear it more frequently, the Rome set is the choice for lasting dependability.

Furtwängler's posthumous reputation rests primarily with recordings of his live performances because they evince a sense of his powers of presentation that his studio recordings rarely reflected. There are several more live performances buttressing that reputation, and they have become inseparably associated with his "recorded" legacy not only because they are singular for one reason or another in connection with Furtwängler's career, but because of the historical circumstances under which they took place. It is to those recordings we turn now.

Had he said as much about modern music in documented performances as he theorized about it in his writings, we might have a better idea of Furtwängler's practical attitudes as a conductor of 20th-century music. What little evidence we have indicates he was both astute and imaginative in these works, even though he made no secret of his aversion to the atonal directions his contemporaries were taking. He always regarded conducting their music as his sacred responsibility, and he was always interested in any kind of music by living composers. Frau Furtwängler recalls:

Whenever he heard the announcement over the radio of a new piece by a new or contemporary composer, he always dropped everything to listen to it. That always surprised me because he would always do that no matter how busy he was. He was very interested in what directions music was taking, and he took every chance to hear the latest step.[13]

Furtwängler regarded Paul Hindemith as first among several leaders in the development of music in Germany. "In Hindemith . . . we ultimately come face to face with our own culture of German music," he declares in *Ton und Wort*.[14] We have no Furtwängler recording of the suite from Hindemith's *Mathis der Maler*, but he did conduct performances of *Harmonie der Welt* and the *Concerto for Orchestra* after the war.[15] What is striking even to those who find Hindemith less than sublime, is the drive and dash with which Furtwängler energizes both pieces. He also reflects a sympathetic understanding of how this kind of music "goes." Many conductors can bring astonishing knowledge to this kind of music, but few indeed can find warmth in it. Furtwängler endows not only Hindemith, but his readings of Bartók and Stravinsky with as much heart as their geometric dissonances can bear.

Furtwängler's only commercial recording of a "modern" composer was Béla Bartók's Second Violin Concerto with Yehudi Menuhin for HMV/EMI in 1953. Menuhin has frequently remarked on Furtwängler's capacity to accompany by keeping him "afloat" upon the music, and that feat is palpable in every note of this recording.[16] But what makes this recording remarkable is the musky sensuousness Furtwängler culls out of the orchestral support in the slow movement. While he draws out the tension, he keeps the legato line undulating and twining about Menuhin's visionary incantations.

Although Furtwängler presented the German premieres of several works by Igor Stravinsky and was among the first to program his pieces regularly in Leipzig and Berlin during the 1920s, he was not especially fond of his music:

13. Personal conversation with the author, Clarens, 9 December 1989.
14. P. 44. He also includes Ernst Krenek, Bruno Walter, Otto Klemperer and Fritz Kreisler among the group whom he considered had remained essentially German even though they had emigrated.
15. *Concerto for Orchestra* was performed in Berlin on 20 June 1950 with the Berlin Philharmonic. *Harmonie der Welt* was performed by the Vienna Philharmonic on 30 August 1953 in Salzburg. Both live performances were released on Fonit-Cetra FE 22.
16. "It was the way he made you feel as though you were on a marvelous cushion that always moved with you . . ." is how he put it to me in my conversation with him in April 1989.

Stravinsky does not take the living as his point of origin, as he has usually stated, but rather the artificial organism of the doll, the machine. The Russian revolutionary devotion to the machine finds a voice in him. Germany has got beyond this. Germany is struggling from the machine to life, and therefore it much prefers Bruckner's "stupid" music to the "clever" music of Stravinsky. *Notebooks, p. 146*

What is startling about this statement is its shameless nationalist bias. Furtwängler cannot help restraining himself from making a crack about Soviet Bolshevism and its mechanical, heartless associations, a profoundly dreaded theme deeply ingrained in most Germans between the wars. Furtwängler was not exempt from these fears, but the perspective on which he based these and other nationalist-biased statements was always personal preference rather than ideological cant. But a dislike of Stravinsky or other music to which he had an aversion never meant that they should not be performed, and he performed Stravinsky as late as 1938 when it had become all but a capital crime in Nazi Germany. And when he came to conduct Stravinsky and other "Bolsheviks" in performances that have survived on tape, he betrays an abiding sympathy for both Stravinsky's music and its stylistic ambience.

The only surviving evidence of his way with Stravinsky are live performances of the Suite from *The Fairy's Kiss* and the Symphony in Three Movements, both in wretched sound. But a wary ear would find it difficult indeed to find a trace of condescension in either performance. The lingering effect is of the music taking flight with the natural inevitability he brings to composers of whom he is more fond. *The Fairy's Kiss* was broadcast and recorded during a performance by the Berlin Philharmonic on 15 May 1953. The Symphony was performed at the Salzburg Festival with the Vienna Philharmonic on 15 August 1950. The former is one of Stravinsky's more sentient works, and Furtwängler brings a lustral tenderness to the slow movement quite free of the restless anxiety heard in the other movements. In the Symphony, the strings occasionally lack unison at the outset of the first movement, but the Vienna Philharmonic bounce along with Furtwängler in a sprightly amble that is at once exhilarating and almost jocular.

While Furtwängler may have met Mahler in Vienna, there is no evidence of it. He admired his compositions, but he was at best ambivalent about their intrinsic worth:

In Mahler, Reger, Strauss, Debussy, technique begins to distance itself from experience, to become high-handed. The disappearance of substance, an aesthetic formed by the age and also the form of the audience, is characteristic. (1939)   *Notebooks, p. 114*

He appreciated the alienation with which Mahler's songs are filled, but he found more longing in them than genuine substance:

> Mahler used the folk song as something alien, as wish fulfillment, a yearning to be confronted, so to speak. For him it was the sheltered haven, for which his restless soul longed. He seized it [as a concept] and produced a "synthetic" folk song. (1931)   *Ton und Wort, p. 51*

By the time he came to performing and recording *Songs of a Wayfarer* in 1952, he may well have warmed to them a bit more than these thoughts might indicate.[17] Made with Dietrich Fischer-Dieskau immediately after the *Tristan* sessions on 23 June 1952, the recording has come to be regarded as one of Fischer-Dieskau's finest in a career that has made him the second most recorded singer in history thus far.[18] Though the set is frequently sung by a female voice, Fischer-Dieskau deepens the changing moods of the lovelorn wanderer with his youthful elegiac baritone—he was 27 at the time. Furtwängler, however, kneads the four songs into a cohesive whole, suffusing it with profound sadness. One influential critic found the final song ("*Die zwei blauen Augen von meinem Schatz . . .*") so shattering, that he privately once remarked (and with dead seriousness) that it ought to be ranked with Billy Holiday's rendition of "Good Morning, Heartache," a record several American radio stations once banned during the hours of 6 and 11 a.m. because of the number of suicides it supposedly prompted. Perhaps it is fortunate Furtwängler never recorded *Songs on the Death of Children (Kindertotenlieder).*

Furtwängler's recording of *Songs of a Wayfarer* offers evidence of why so many soloists enjoyed working with him. He is a consummate accompanist because he can "breathe" with a soloist. He was also an accomplished pianist, but evidence of his skill is meager: a *Brandenburg Concerto* in which he plays the continuo on a piano and a recital of Hugo Wolf songs with Schwarzkopf are among the few examples. The recital with Schwarzkopf came about almost by coincidence. At a dinner party in Turin following a performance of the Beethoven Ninth, the table talk turned to the upcoming Wolf celebration at Salzburg. Furtwängler meekly asked Schwarzkopf if he might be her accompanist if one had not yet been chosen. Probably for the first and only time in her long career, Schwarzkopf suffered a lapse in breath

---

17. See Chapter 21 for more about the tensions surrounding the recording.
18. As of 1990, the most recorded singer in history was reportedly Nicolai Gedda.

control. Furtwängler as piano accompanist? Despite uncertain health and increasingly intermittent hearing difficulties, Furtwängler practised daily for weeks before the recital between rehearsals and performances he was conducting.

"The problem was that he could not play the fast tempi," says Schwarzkopf candidly, "but you couldn't say that to Furtwängler and you had to accommodate him. And accommodate him I did. The end result is valid. You can't take it as a model, but the expression is right. That recital is a very valid exposition of what Hugo Wolf can be . . . wrong tempi and all."

Wrong tempi and all, they performed twenty songs by Wolf at the Mozarteum on 13 August 1953 in a recital commemorating the 50th anniversary of the composer's death. The recital was sort of an oddity at the time, for Wolf had not yet become a popular composer even a half-century after his death. If there was one event that turned the tide in favor of his popularity, however, it was this recital. Schwarzkopf's husband Walter Legge had been championing Wolf for more than 20 years since he had founded the Wolf Society in 1931. He had recorded a series of seven albums over the years featuring the finest singers of that age, beginning with Elena Gerhardt, and continuing with Herbert Janssen, John McCormack, Alexander Kipnis, Gerhard Hüsch, and Elisabeth Rethberg. These albums sold well, especially in Japan for some reason.[19]

The recital of Wolf songs at Salzburg was also a risky venture for the Festival. It was the first Lieder Evening of its kind since the war, and it caught attention primarily because Furtwängler was lending his name to it. The success of this recital led to *Liederabende* as a featured staple of the Festival from 1956 onwards. Schwarzkopf in 1953 was a fast-rising star, but she had a tough road yet to travel before she became the legend to which a recital such as this one gave luster. The event was, of course, broadcast and recorded, but the master tape was mislaid. Parts of it turned up in 1968, and it was released forthwith. Ultimately, a well-preserved tape of the rest of the recital was found, re-engineered, and released by EMI in 1983.[20]

What is perhaps most remarkable about the recital, aside from the range and plenitude of Schwarzkopf's generosity, is Furtwängler's instincts at work in giving her creative support. "You always felt as though you were borne on salt water with him," she says. "One didn't think about breathing. And you were not afraid of him. You were in awe of him, but never afraid."

19. See *On and Off the Record*, pp. 214–216, and also Chapter 20.
20. It has been released on several pressings. The most widely distributed is EMI/Pathé 1435491/PM 322.

Despite the keyboard technical limitations to which he was subject at this time of his life, his accompaniment is indeed like salt water. Listening to the recital after having had the benefit of hearing Schwarzkopf perform many of these songs often throughout her career, it is the opening number, "Lebewohl," which is most surprising. Schwarzkopf recorded it later with Geoffrey Parsons, and rarely did she purvey such a polarity of moods with one piece. With Furtwängler her goodbye is animated with the anticipation of return. Its rhetoric radiates enthusiastic hope. With Parsons, her apostrophe bidding farewell is wracked with sadness and no little foreboding.[21] Both views are deeply moving, but with Furtwängler she broaches a more difficult approach. The deftness with which she succeeds at turning away from morbidity makes it perhaps the more astonishing accomplishment.

For all the unwholesome sentiments uttered by the Moor in *Otello*, Furtwängler's only surviving encounter with Verdi in 1951 at Salzburg is anything but dismal.[22] The critic John Ardoin has depicted Furtwängler's view of the work as a vast tone poem, and the description is apt, at least as far as the orchestra (the Vienna Philharmonic) is concerned.[23] But the vocalists at Salzburg are by no means mere adjuncts of the orchestral sonorities. Furtwängler had conducted *Otello* and *Aida* during his tenure at Mannheim and fully realized that Verdi was a true man of the theater, uncluttered by the philosophical baggage that Wagner carried with him. More here perhaps than in any other work he conducted in the pit, Furtwängler focuses upon the full range of raw human emotions that bristles throughout this tragedy. Under Furtwängler, the tragic elements are played out as a synthesis of what is going on between stage and pit, but he never fails to give the singers their head. Nor does he fail to realize fully that only through the text and the voices giving utterance to it can the opera take on dramatic life.

Furtwängler invariably shapes Verdi's sonorities to support that text and give breath and breadth to his singers. Ramón Vinay was the reigning Otello of the day, and he brings all the raging passion of the Moor to his portrayal that Verdi and his librettist Arrigio Boito distilled from Shakespeare. Paul Schöffler is unctuously malevolent as his trusted Iago. Dragica Martinis was a strange choice for Desdemona, for she simply is not, at least in the performance preserved on records, quite up to the vocal and musical standard of her colleagues. None-

21. The recording has been released in several pressings. *Elisabeth Schwarzkopf Songbook*, Vol. 2, is one of them. EMI (Japanese) EAC 60168
22. Both Turnabout and Fonit-Cetra have released it on long-play records.
23. See *Opera Quarterly*, Winter 1984/85, pp. 32–34.

theless, she projects a nervous discomfort that evinces an arcane fear of Otello, and her portrayal endows this miscegenetic union with a dimension of dread that Shakespeare and Boito may not have entirely intended.

Furtwängler's *Otello* is a far cry from the idiomatic, "Italianate" interpretations that would soon become the international norm in the late 1950s and onwards, but its essentially Germanic attitude brings to bear a peculiar authenticity of its own, for the orchestra, singers, and Furtwängler all collectively and individually serve the music in a manner entirely natural to them. There is mercifully no attempt to ape the Mediterranean cut and thrust of dynamics and phrasing that mark the genuine Made-in-Italy Verdi line. Within the parameters of what they all bring to the work from their respective cultural backgrounds, this performance strikes at the listener with far more visceral force than many a later festival performance reduced to mimicking standards of "authentic style."

While Furtwängler is not widely known as a "Mozart conductor," through a quirk of fate, Mozart is the composer he left the most complete documentation of in a live performance. Shortly before he died, he conducted *Don Giovanni*, which was filmed by Paul Czinner at Salzburg. It is one of the several extant films where he can be seen conducting.[24] After the war, he led extraordinary productions of three of the five great Mozart operas at Salzburg between 1949 and 1953: *The Magic Flute* three times—1950, 1951, and 1952; *Giovanni* also three times—in 1950, 1953 and 1954—when it was filmed. In 1953 he conducted his only surviving account of *The Marriage of Figaro*. John Ardoin has written a perceptive survey of these performances, though a couple of his judgments on the singers might be open to challenge.[25] What makes these performances special and peculiarly Furtwängler is the "human" touch he gives them. Although he revered *The Marriage of Figaro* and *Don Giovanni*, He was especially fond of *The Magic Flute*, and he regarded it as an entity quite apart from the rest of Mozart's canon:

> All classifications, all attempts at typification break down in the face of a work like *The Magic Flute*. It is neither one thing nor the other, neither light nor serious, neither tragedy nor comedy, it is—so to speak—all these things at once, all these things in one. Our urge to classify might have tried to recognize a new 'type' here, if the work had not remained on

24. The others include a newsreel from 1948, excerpts of the Beethoven Ninth in 1942, a complete *Till Eulenspiegel*, and the opening bars of the Prelude from *Die Meistersinger* in 1951 *(Botschafter der Musik)*.
25. See *Opera Quarterly*, Autumn 1984, pp. 69–76.

> its own *entirely sui generis* as a type and work of art in the history of the opera. *The Magic Flute* is life itself; all classification breaks down here.
>
> *Notebooks, 1950, p. 195*

Instead of following the trend toward "classification," which he finds so unhelpful in coming to grips with this work, Furtwängler's focal point throughout the three years he led the opera at Salzburg is much more elemental and natural. Since he regarded Mozart as one of the most generously spirited composers of all time, it is the nature of that expansive spirit he pursues. Throughout the rites of passage Papageno undergoes, Furtwängler imbues that search for the elusive human element, the basic need to find trust, companionship, and love with an ever regenerating sense of life itself unfolding. This capacity to distill extra-musical values from a performance while remaining entirely within the realm of musical values boggles many listeners, especially critics enslaved to classification as the basis of praise or condemnation. More perhaps in Mozart's music than in any other composer's, Furtwängler evokes the heart of the creator simply by letting his music flow along its course. It is almost by chance that he finds its infinite variety of colors, moods, and lyrical riches along the way. And yet, he encounters and takes that chance virtually every time.

Don Giovanni and *The Marriage of Figaro* were also extraordinary accomplishments because he had perhaps the finest singers in this repertory available at the time at his disposal and an intelligent unobtrusive producer in Herbert Graf. *Giovanni* had several cast variances[26] in those three years, but Furtwängler's view of the opera as something of a picaresque tragedy never changed, it only deepened. He had two of the finest Dons of the mid-century: Tito Gobbi and Cesare Siepi. Siepi ultimately was featured in the film, but Gobbi's interpretation is preserved on records pirated from tapes. Siepi is a traditional dashing Don, charming and at a loss to resist or explain his destructive libido. Gobbi's view is more modern, a touch of sadism at the root of his insatiable conquests. As Ardoin rightly points out, he rather enjoys the suffering he inflicts.[27] Given these divergent views of this enigmatic character, Furtwängler frames a tragedy of Christian morality around Siepi's Don. In meeting the Commendatore, the Don meets his Maker, having been finally caught out. The wages of lust

26. There were five performances of *Giovanni* in 1950 beginning 27 July. The cast included Tito Gobbi, Ljuba Welitsch (Küpper 29 August), Elisabeth Schwarzkopf (Esther Rethy 29 August), Irmgard Seefried, Anton Dermota, Erich Kunz, and Josef Greindl. In 1953 and 1954, there were again five performances each summer with virtually the same cast: Cesare Siepi, Elisabeth Grümmer, Schwarzkopf, Erna Berger, Otto Edelmann, and Raffaele Arié (Dezsö Ernster in 1954).

27. *Opera Quarterly*, Autumn 1984, p. 75.

here is death. Around Gobbi, he builds a social tragedy, and the final scene with the Commendatore takes on a more secular kind of inevitability. The wages of unrepentant sociopathic behavior in this context is the hellfire of eternal repression.

In each instance, Furtwängler drives the musical line in the same direction, but the extraordinary gift he reveals in that drive is twofold. First, it can both harness and liberate interpretations, relating them to the larger structure of the opera. Second, it is possessed of the uncanny knack of accommodating the interpretive imponderables in any given cast, while imbuing them with cogency and a fine sense of Mozart's benevolent spirit informing this work. The achievement is remarkable, for it represents quite the antithesis of most opera productions, especially "festival productions" in the latter half of the 20th century. Rarely do they take their inspiration from a process of collaboration, compromise, and collective devotion to the work at hand. Instead, the germ of inspiration is imposed from outside, frequently by a producer or stage director with questionable musical and dramatic instincts. Furtwängler took the riches he had before him and forged an overall musical interpretation that a producer like Herbert Graf enhanced, not dominated; an interpretation that grew spontaneously from within all the assembled participants.

If Furtwängler is not widely known as a "Mozart conductor," he is all but unknown for his way with Gluck. Yet, from the runes he left in several recorded overtures and a complete *Orfeo ed Euridice* from La Scala in 1951, a tantalizing image emerges of what he might have done with some of his other works. The governing mood of the *Orfeo* is restrained passion. Furtwängler always keeps pushing the pace and texture of the performance against the limits of Gluck's stately framework, creating multiple tensions that reinforce the various conflicts within both the libretto and the music. Despite a general ignorance of "authentic" performance traditions that are virtually mandatory today, Furtwängler is always mindful of the contrasts in Gluck's setting of the great Greek myth of love lost and found, faith tested and renewed, and the vindication of sacrifice, endurance and perseverance.

Taking the score in his own way, he casts a veil of enchantment over proceedings that far too often sound artificial in purportedly idiomatic readings. Essentially, he trimmed Gluck's Paris edition dating from 1774 and made a few additions from the Vienna premiere twelve years earlier. Conforming to the ongoing practice of using a mezzo instead of a male voice to sing Orfeo, the performance is sung in Italian with a reduced orchestra and harpsichord continuum and is shorn of most of the ballet music.

Fedora Barbieri is a robust Orfeo, perhaps too full of *morbidezza* (passion) for the hero's chaste line, but she sings musically and with intense involvement. Hilde Gueden is hardly a natural Euridice, but she exudes helpless charm. The Amor of Magda Gabory is more effortful than effective, but she too sings with a commitment that deflates her considerable flaws. The sum of their parts under Furtwängler's flexible direction totals far more than the deficits of their individual quirks might portend. Here is a prime example of a Furtwängler performance where you can endlessly carp about holes and gaffes (especially in the choral singing). But only if you can withstand the radiant spell he weaves around his cast and musicians.

While Furtwängler revered Beethoven, his love of Brahms was of a more secular nature. He frequently mentions Brahms in his *Notebooks*, but his two essays in *Ton und Wort* reveal the best written and thought-through descriptions of what he saw in Brahms and what he tried to translate into interpretive terms. On the one hand, he notes that Brahms carries on a peculiarly Germanic tradition of music:

> I have always regarded him as a descendant of those old German and Dutch painters, such as Van Dyck and Rembrandt, etc., whose works combine profound feeling, imagination, and persuasive power that is often impetuous, and are united with a wonderful sense of form. In certain works by Brahms, in the great cycles of variations, for instance, his relationship to the sensibility of the old German artists is particularly evident. His exceptional capacity to realize form expresses itself in everything he has left, from his most modest correspondence to his symphonies and lieder. The form Brahms possesses is a peculiarly German species, a form that never appears to be an end in itself, but is merely a function of "content" which is integrated with harmony of proportion and graceful clarity.　　　　　　　　　*"Brahms," Ton und Wort, p. 48*

On the other, Furtwängler sees Brahms as far more modern an artist than, say, Wagner or Debussy. For Brahms, in Furtwängler's view, was an artist alienated from his time:

> Brahms is the first great musician in whom historical significance and artistic significance no longer converge as one and the same. He was not to blame for this. Rather it was the fault of his times. Even Beethoven's most abnormal conceptions were born of the demands of his time and derived from the linguistic and expressive possibilities of that time. Although Beethoven's will, a creative will so timeless and touched with insight into the future, was somehow in complete accordance with the will of his time; Beethoven was "sustained" by his time. Wagner's boldest and most coherent works not only articulated the powerful personality of their creator, they revealed the will and possibilities of his time. There is

a consonance between personal will and the general will of the time in Beethoven and Wagner, and later in Strauss, Reger, Debussy and Stravinsky. In Brahms, for the first time, these wills become separated; not because Brahms was most profoundly a man of his time, but because the musical possibilities of his time had taken a different direction from his own inclinations, and did not satisfy him. He is the first artist and creator who transcends his historical and musical function.

Ton und Wort,[28] *pp. 88–89*

Furtwängler rightly saw Brahms as an artist alienated from the prevailing musical cross-currents of his time, but the musical by-product of that alienation in itself expressed the will of his time every bit as much as anything Wagner or Beethoven produced.[29] Brahms was one of scores of sensitive individuals who felt at overwhelming odds with the accepted social, religious, and philosophical truths of the late eighteenth and nineteenth centuries, not the least of whom were Baudelaire, de Sade, Berlioz, Swinburne, Melville, and Hawthorne. Goethe and Byron were probably the spiritual fathers of them all, even though they were not necessarily among the first generation of artists who might fall under the vast and unwieldy rubric, "romantic." Nonetheless, the impact of such personalities as Byron and Goethe was all but thermonuclear upon the thinking and attitudes developing throughout not only the nineteenth century but the twentieth as well.

The various ideas these disaffected artists and thinkers articulated had an inestimable effect upon all the individuals who ultimately shaped European history and culture including Wilhelm Furtwängler. For all these artists, many of whom never met or even knew of each other, were tough-minded and determined to create both value and order as a means of both asserting their identities and coming to grips with their respective realities; realities that for many of them were becoming chaotic and impossible to share, simply because each beheld a different view of his reality. But a general agreement was becoming increasingly prevalent that externally imposed reality simply bore too many contradictions and inconsistencies to be trusted as the source of

28. "Brahms and the Crisis of Our Time."
29. The mid-nineteenth century was the period when the great givens of the past nine centuries were beginning to disintegrate irrevocably; when the medieval view of the universe as a static mechanism based on a hierarchy with God at the top, man in the middle, and nothingness at the bottom, began to dissolve into an organic mind-frame, a view of the universe as a constantly evolving process devoid of top or bottom and replaced by development, growth, and process; when the image of the universe as a perfectly operating machine or clock that was so popular during the Enlightenment of the previous century gave way to the tree or flower as the prevailing image of the cosmos. See Arthur O. Lovejoy, *The Great Chain of Being,* (Cambridge) 1936, for a vigorous and lucid exploration of this transformation.

truth. For such individuals, reality now was beginning to shift away from imposed, universally accepted truths existing independently from men's minds. Instead, the locus of reality shifted to the mind of the individual. By the time Brahms was composing his mature works, the mind indeed was becoming its own time and place.[30]

Furtwängler also correctly distinguished Brahms from most other composers of his time on an important issue. Brahms did not search for new realities by following the route taken by Wagner and Baudelaire, for example. Nor was he subject to the lure of drugs and flagrantly promiscuous sex to which so many artists classed as "romantic" were given.[31] Brahms may have been alienated from what was becoming the prevailing musical trend toward "Wagnerism" during his life, but he was never alienated from his own musical environment. While Bach and the contrapuntal complexities of his music became the foundation for the "revolutionary" and "progressive" direction taken by Wagner, Brahms looked for inspiration to the earlier Baroque period for technical inspiration and to popular German tunes and folk songs for melodic stimulation, and Furtwängler admired him especially for searching in this direction.[32] If ever a composer went back, not just to basics, but to *nationalistic* basics in a time of cultural and personal crisis, it was Johannes Brahms, and Furtwängler never fails to remind his reader of the fact, especially in his essay "Johannes Brahms."[33]

30. Byron, *Manfred*, Act III, Scene 4 (1817):
The mind which is immortal makes itself
Requital for its good and evil thoughts,—
Is its own origin of ill and end—
And its own place and time: its innate sense,
When stripped of this mortality, derives
No color from the fleeting things without,
But is absorbed in sufferance or in joy,
Born from the knowledge of its own desert.
31. See Peckham, *The Triumph of Romanticism*, pp. 14–35. He sees two major components in the romantic period, which he describes respectively as positive romanticism and negative romanticism. In the former, the universe is seen as an organism: possibilities are endless, and coherence can be created through the imagination. In the latter, the individual has become alienated from his environment and has not yet reintegrated his thought and art through the *self* as the center of order and value.
32. See also Morse Peckham, *Beyond the Tragic Vision*, (New York) 1962, for a provocative inquiry into the manner in which Brahms derived his musical esthetic by transforming Baroque counterpoint into a means by which he arrived at a personal style. Paolo Isotta also writes perceptively about "Brahms e Furtwängler" in the program booklet enclosed in the box set containing a vast selection of Furtwängler's recordings of Brahms—*Wilhelm Furtwängler, Volume II*—released by Italian EMI in its Discoteca Classica Series 3C 153 53661/69M.
33. See *Ton und Wort*, pp. 48f. In both essays in this book, Furtwängler constantly lauds Brahms for finding solutions to his musical problems from German culture, the culture of the folk and so on.

While Furtwängler as interpreter worshiped Beethoven, he gave his greatest affection as conductor and composer to Brahms.[34] The key to Furtwängler's Brahms is his mastery over that restless chain of transformations where the tragic element he saw in nearly all the composer's works becomes apparent. For the resolution of one set of musical problems only folds into another set of frustrations. Even where resolutions seem absolute, they are somehow incomplete and unfulfilled. Furtwängler works through this undulating series of transformations fully cognizant of Brahms' awareness that inevitability no longer lies in a breakthrough to a new reality but only within the realm of what already exists. So the truth that gives Furtwängler's readings of the symphonies a special depth of understanding is his keen appreciation of Brahms' own realization that there are no new truths. That is the tragedy of Brahms as Furtwängler sees him, and it in turn is the tragedy of Furtwängler's own condition, both as composer and man. But Furtwängler's Brahms does not project a catastrophic tragedy. Rather, both he and Brahms find a cathartic exhilaration in contemplating the known, in making the forms of the past live again in the present.

What makes them live again is neither rote repetition nor superficial disguises concealing their origins, but *style*. Brahms contemplates the masters of the past and makes them resound again through his imagination, his unique and individual manner of reworking the materials and forms of Handel, Bach, Haydn and Mozart. Furtwängler continually rediscovers Brahms' mystic enthusiasm and his way with those forms, for they are the very materials he saw as his own when he composed. His empathy for the works of Brahms could not have been more profound, for he saw his own condition in Brahms' alienation from his own time. Brahms also created something of a problem for him, for without actually setting out to do so, Furtwängler ended up in his own compositions trying to outdo both Brahms and Bruckner, to take their quasi-mannerist view of music and charge it with life through his own imaginative gifts. Whether he succeeded is another question, and it will be addressed later.[35]

Although Furtwängler made eloquent statements about Brahms in print, he never recorded a complete cycle of Brahms' symphonies in the studio. In fact, he made studio recordings of only the First and Second Symphonies—two of the First for HMV and one of the Second for Decca/London. Even at that, only one recording of the First Sym-

---

34. See Furtwängler's essay "Johannes Brahms" (1931) in *Ton und Wort*, pp. 40–52.
35. See Chapter 25.

phony (from 1947 with the Vienna Philharmonic) was officially released. An earlier wartime recording (whose exact date is uncertain) was released on HMV exclusively in Japan.

The First Symphony was his favorite, and he programmed it frequently. In fact, it was the major work at his American debut in New York on 3 January 1925. The studio version was made in the 78-rpm format with the Vienna Philharmonic in slabs of four-minute sides. Despite the side breaks, its transfer to the long-play medium bears out an uninterrupted arclike structure, and sounds surprisingly like a live performance in its palpable unbroken tension.

While the specific emotional experiences behind Brahms' work are not clear, Furtwängler rightly found his mature works engulfed with emotional torment. In all his documented performances of the Second, Third, and Fourth Symphonies, Furtwängler evokes that torment, galvanizing its surges of terror, drifts of elegy, and that bloom of peace brought about by persevering through to new understanding. What keeps Furtwängler's performances from disintegrating into bathos, of course, is his keen awareness of the forms Brahms uses. The peculiar tension in Brahms arises from the double purpose of any form he employs. On one hand, the formal dams he erects around his streams of melody are always close to bursting from the rich flow of musical ideas he pours into them. On the other, the coherence these forms exert upon the music becomes transformed into another kind of dam: a highly individual style that is at once continent and liberating. At his best, Furtwängler maintains the tension from the former and the ecstatic drive of the latter. Nowhere is his best revealed in Brahms than in a performance of the Third Symphony given in Berlin with the Berlin Philharmonic on 27 April 1954, only seven months before he died.

Commercially released in 1989 by Deutsche Grammophon, it is a very different kind of performance from the Beethoven he was committing to disc in the studio around this time.[36] If you come to it after hearing performances by other conductors, it can be a little unsettling at first. The fluctuations in tempo are almost too many to enumerate. But close listening reveal Furtwängler responding to what the critic David Cairns calls:

> . . . a carefully pondered idea of the work which does equal justice to the music's two aspects, the monumental and the lyrical, the dramatic and the intimate, and which brings out its wealth of color and richness of inner parts with inspired fidelity.[37]

36. DG 423572-2.
37. Sleeve note.

Just as Furtwängler perceives Brahms signaling the end of musical development, the orchestra plays on this occasion with a sense of an end at hand. What Furtwängler performs here has little of the inward-looking mood of his studio recordings in this period. To the contrary, it is a public rite, and he performs his musical ablutions by evoking a sense of song and of singing from the innermost depths of the orchestra as a collective organism. The tragedy inherent in Brahms' lamentations over the end of musical tradition is transformed here into a celebration of existing musical possibilities newly discovered. The finale ascends to the peculiar state of transcendence Furtwängler always educes when he is at his most inspired, and he is indeed inspired here. Furtwängler follows Brahms as he passes beyond his simple enthusiasm in contemplating great formal structures at work throughout the symphony toward a transcendent peace that comes from having striven through the travails presented by those structures.

What may be most remarkable about this recording simply as a fulcrum of musical rewards, however, is the consummate responsiveness of the Berlin Philharmonic. Furtwängler's health had long been a widely discussed issue, and it is difficult to say what the state of his hearing may have been at this concert. But the orchestra plays with an intensity and telepathic unity of ensemble that is astonishing even for the Berlin Philharmonic. Nuance after nuance, grades of dynamics flow into each other with inexorable inevitability, intonation unfailingly precise. The performance bristles with a feeling of occasion and destiny as few other performances by the Berlin Philharmonic under Furtwängler were marked. Indeed, the performance turned out to be one of his last concerts in Berlin.[38]

But if Furtwängler was close to Brahms, he was closer still to Anton Bruckner. In a stroke of reckless devotion, he programmed the Ninth Symphony in the first public orchestral concert he conducted in Munich in 1910. For a time, he even was president of the International Bruckner Society. In fact, it is almost impossible to speak of his view of Bruckner without avoiding his view of himself as a composer. The Swiss critic Günther Birkner has perceptively noted that what Furtwängler says about Bruckner in his writings could well be said about his own work:

> Furtwängler regarded Bruckner, to whom he here assigned a central position, as marking a turning point in the development of music, at which the roads diverged: "until Brahms, Bruckner and Wagner music devel-

---

38. Furtwängler's last performance in Berlin was 20 September 1954. The program included his Second Symphony and the Beethoven First.

oped. What appeared to be further outward development was [actually] inflation (Strauss, Reger, Mahler) . . . the tendency of the age is toward even greater complication. Until Schumann, Wagner, and Bruckner there were natural phenomena within the complication. The generation of Reger and Strauss went further . . . with Mahler, Reger, Strauss and Debussy technique began to move away from experience, to become autocratic. Evaporation of the substance . . . Since Reger, Strauss, Mahler, etc., there has blossomed the art of creating an effervescent surface, giving the appearance of something which is not there."[39]

Furtwängler grouped Bruckner with Brahms and Wagner as one of the three most powerful voices in the musical history of the late 19th century, but he placed Bruckner quite apart if not above the other two. It is difficult to say what he most admired about Bruckner, but his genuine piety and determined individualism in the face of the crosscurrents and vogues besetting new music of his time affected Furtwängler deeply. What is more, Furtwängler saw Bruckner as anything but a composer out for quick recognition or financial return. His aim in all his works and even in his life was toward the infinite, the universal, and the all-encompassing. The ongoing struggle he underwent to attain it appealed greatly to Furtwängler. While Bach humbly dedicated his works to "the Glory of God," Bruckner, this devout Catholic organist, sought with equal humility to reflect that glory in all his compositions. Consequently, his major works, particularly the symphonies, are immense constructs, cathedrals of sound with soaring spires, colossal domes, and catacombs full of intricate, if occasionally crudely designed passages.

Perhaps the Fourth Symphony is the most accessible among the symphonies of Bruckner's maturity, and it now is possible to hear Furtwängler give two performances of it with the Vienna Philharmonic within ten days in October 1951. The first was given at Stuttgart on October 22d, the second on October 29th in Munich at the Deutsches Museum. Both were preserved on tape.[40] Although they were given at a close interval, the character of Furtwängler's interpretation varies widely from one to the other. Bruckner dubbed the symphony "Romantic," and the symphony does indeed work through the psychic frustrations of the romantic artist. Bruckner struggles to find value, truth, and the voice of God in the universe he reflects in his work. It is a long and taxing struggle, an almost interminable series of frustrations marked by sudden stops, leaping starts, repetitions in

39. Günther Birkner, "Wilhelm Furtwängler and Anton Bruckner," translation: John Coombs. Sleeve note, DG 2740 201.
40. They have been released on both vinyl and CD formats under various numbers. As of 1990, The performance of 22 October 1951 is on Deutsche Grammophon DG 415 664-2. The performance of 29 October 1951 is on Crown Record PAL 1074 (Japan).

related keys, and climaxes seemingly leading nowhere. In the final pages of the symphony, he at last arrives at the pinnacle of the mountain and faces the infinite expanses of heaven above and earth below.

In both performances, Furtwängler follows Bruckner's simple but iron faith that binds each frustrating turn and strengthens him to persevere until he finally arrives at his destiny. But in the earlier performance, Furtwängler colors the journey with a dark, sombre hue, casting ineluctable sadness over the basic tempo (marked *andante quasi allegretto*) in the second movement, and striding with emboldened gait toward the climax of the last movement. Here is a fearsome longing to aspire to the Almighty, requited only after profound travail. In the second performance, taken at a generally faster pace both in actual time and in psychic attitude, Furtwängler imparts an ecstatic sweep to the climb from earthly disquiet to transcendent reassurance. In this performance the work also evolves as more of a whole, its end intimated in its beginnings, its convolutions dimly revealing the great resolution toward which Bruckner ascends. Unfortunately, coughs, wheezes, and scuffling feet badly mar the recording of the performance in Munich. It seems the audience is either creating a flu epidemic or is succumbing to one.

The three works in Bruckner's canon that adumbrate his quest for the Almighty at its most eloquent are undoubtedly his Seventh, Eighth, and Ninth Symphonies. At present, there are three known complete and one incomplete documentations by Furtwängler in live performances of the Seventh, and one studio account of the Adagio from 1942, all with the Berlin Philharmonic.[41] Four complete live performances of the Eighth are extant: two with Vienna, two with Berlin. Only one performance of the Ninth has been unearthed.[42] Except for one performance of the Eighth, Furtwängler uses the editions by Robert Haas, the eminent musicologist who published editions of 22 Bruckner scores between 1930 and 1944.[43] Another musicologist, Leopold Nowak, continued his work after 1951, and produced a revised edition of the Eighth which Furtwängler conducted shortly before his death.[44] All three works are epic in scope, monumental in

---

41. Complete Performances: 18 October 1949, Berlin-Dahlem; 23 April 1951, Cairo; and 1 May 1951, Rome. Incomplete: 2–4 February 1941, Berlin. Studio recording of Adagio: Telefunken SK 3230-1. All these performances have been commercially available from time to time.

42. 7 October 1944, Berlin, (Haas Edition, Berlin Philharmonic).

43. 17 October 1944, Vienna, (Haas Edition, Vienna Philharmonic); 14 March 1949, Berlin-Dahlem, (Haas Edition, Berlin Philharmonic); 15 March 1949, Berlin, (Berlin Philharmonic); 10 April 1954, Vienna, (Nowak Edition, Vienna Philharmonic).

44. Some arguments have been raised on the authenticity of the performance on 10 April 1954, but it has been verified by Frau Elisabeth Furtwängler. The performance took place before the edition of Nowak's score was published, but Furtwängler received a galley of the proofs to examine, and used it on that date.

design, and mystical in content. They test the mettle of any conductor and most approach them through one of these access points, inevitably the one most compatible with their personalities. Furtwängler has a peculiar advantage over Brucknerians close to or among his generation because he was gifted with a master builder's recondite sense of proportion. Consequently, his interpretations ride the epic crests of these scores, arch across their monumental terrains, and vivify Bruckner's mystical contemplations with rapture. Heard in chronological order, Furtwängler's interpretations seems to progress from an acute preoccupation with structural tension, especially in his earlier explorations of the Seventh and Eighth Symphonies, toward a liberation of that tension in unearthly rapture in the later performances.

Oddly enough, the most moving episode in all these experiences is not from a live performance, for a change, but the studio recording of the Adagio from Bruckner's Seventh Symphony, made in 1942. It heaves and rocks with deep, abiding sorrow, but remains remarkably free of bathos. Even at this point in the war Furtwängler was transforming this movement into a requiem for a culture about to be annihilated. Ironically, it was this recording that was played over the Reichs radio when Hitler's death was announced. In the later performances from 1951 his characterization of this movement is quite something else, its eloquence different but no less puissant. The agony becomes supplanted by an amplitude of mind in a calmly exalted mood.

In his writings on Bruckner, Furtwängler fully appreciates his faults, but he also points out that the grand scale on which Bruckner pitches his works cannot free them of faults and are all the more interesting because of them:

> . . . There are—and Bruckner, like Beethoven is an example of this— works of such vast stature that they cannot be, in the customary sense of the word, faultless.   1939[45]

Nonetheless, Furtwängler does not regard Bruckner's faults necessarily as virtues:

> One should not present faults as though they were virtues, and Bruckner has faults. It is a piece of philistinism to believe that the absence of faults (i.e., unevenness and rough patches) produces greatness. On the contrary, the greatness of Bruckner is all the more impressive by virtue of the fact

---

45. ". . . Es gibt—und Bruckner, auch Beethoven, ist dafür Beispiel—Werke von solcher übergemessener Gestalt, dass sie gar nichts im land läufigen Sinn tadellos sein können."

that it overcomes his faults and makes them important. Undoubtedly, he was not always able to keep up an entire movement on the high level of the beginning—but where else are such beginnings to be found? The same is true of his formal structures—flawed in small details, in their entirety they are wonderful. Bruckner is said to have remarked of Brahms that he could achieve a great deal but had no ideas; Brahms is supposed to have commented that Bruckner had plenty of ideas but could achieve nothing. A kernel of truth: Brahms with his powerful concentration of creative abilities, felt repelled by Bruckner's signs of carelessness and his use of stereotyped formulae. Bruckner on the other hand, felt the lack of breadth and stature in Brahms' principal ideas.[46]

The heart of both Brahms and Bruckner, of course, lies in their use of the sonata or sonata-allegro form, which constituted the very backbone of serious music in Europe, especially in Germany, from the 17th century onwards. While it underwent an evolution far too prolix even to begin outlining here, its essentials consist to this day of two separate melodies placed in conflict with each other. The nature of this conflict is something akin to the struggle between protagonist and antagonist in Aristotle's view of dramatic tragedy:

> [The sonata and fugue] are forms which possess depth of proportion. Something happens, something is transformed, something manifests itself; the music is plastic—it is not a mood but an event . . .
> *Aufzeichnungen, 1939, p. 182*

Although the basic rules of the sonata form are fairly simple, Beethoven added innovations of such overwhelming magnitude that further development seemed both extremely difficult and somewhat pointless. The crisis this impasse created for composers of succeeding generations began to rupture European musical tradition. Furtwängler was but one composer who was subject to the chaos this rupture was producing. Part of the problem inherent in the sonata as a viable form for all composers after Beethoven was the issue of tonality, which declined as the central feature of music after Wagner. Furtwängler was never in doubt about where he stood regarding tonality. He felt strongly that music was taking a turn in the wrong direction by moving toward atonality:

> Today, there is good reason why no symphonies are being composed any more. Writing a symphony makes sense only if, as in the case of Bruckner in his free manner, the entire form can be realized tonally—that is—everything has its place tonally in the structural scheme. This has long

46. 1939, translation: John Coombs.

been abrogated in modern music regardless of how it may otherwise
relate to tonality.   *Aufzeichnungen, 1940, pp. 212–213*

But he also felt that atonality was something of an aberrant phase
through which European culture had to pass before returning to tonality, for as far as he could determine, tonality was the only viable path
for the future of music. The current direction of serious music appears
to be bearing out his belief.

While Furtwängler left far more thoughts about modern music in
writing than in recorded performances of the composers about whom
he at best felt ambivalent, he actualized his attitude toward tonality
in his own compositions. They are clearly realized in five of his own
major compositions: his three full-length symphonies and the *Symphonie Concertante for Piano and Orchestra*. They are beginning to
be performed with greater frequency by major orchestras, and his own
accounts of the Second Symphony and the *Concertante* have been preserved on tape.

The *Symphonie Concertante* was composed in 1937, and it was
the first of his larger works to be performed in public. It is epic in scale,
tortuously convoluted, and "old-fashioned" to ears accustomed to
atonality. It is cast in the traditional forms to which Furtwängler was
devoted. In fact, virtually all of Furtwängler's works are based on principles found in chamber music, but his chamber music is characterized by symphonic elements.[47] The three movements of the *Concertante* are each dominated by a prevailing mood: passion in the first,
fitful tranquility in the second, and triumph in the third, ending in
hard-won repose.

Perhaps the most interesting of the movements is the second, for
it bridges the moods of the outer movements with its somber eloquence. In it Furtwängler goes a long way toward reconciling the
romantic's longing for the realm of the boundless and the classicist's
observance of form. A melody evoking serene tranquility opens the
movement. The piano takes up an ascending line, developing a melody characterized by triplets. Gradually, the orchestra and piano play
off each other, developing an extended and powerful crescendo.
Ultimately, the crescendo shatters into a distended climax. The
piano repeats the theme suggesting renunciation and spiritual bliss,
losing itself amid the underlying murmuring of strings and clarinet
solo.

Until recently, only the adagio from his *Concertante* was available
in a commercial recording made by Edwin Fischer and the Berlin Phil-

47. See Birkner, sleeve note Bruckner Symphonies DG 2740 201.

harmonic from August 1939. A tape from a radio archive in East Germany of a performance dated 19 January 1939 surfaced in 1989, and the entire live performance can now be heard on a German-made CD.[48]

Furtwängler and Edwin Fischer played the *Concertante* in several cities during 1939, and it was enthusiastically received by the press and public. Furtwängler himself copied each orchestral part himself— about 85 items. Just as Bruckner was constantly revising his works, Furtwängler revised his compositions too. Those revisions can be heard in a performance on a pirate disc by Daniel Barenboim with Zubin Mehta conducting the Los Angeles Philharmonic in 1971. Barenboim and Mehta earlier did it with the Berlin Philharmonic in 1965 in a concert commemorating the tenth anniversary of Furtwängler's death. The alterations are of minor character.

Furtwängler also started work on a symphony while he was composing the *Concertante*, and he completed it in 1941. The work was never performed during his lifetime because he abandoned it after several rehearsals. (He frequently said that performing his own works made him feel like a virgin doing a strip-tease before a horde of lascivious men.) It is called the First Symphony in B Minor and received its world premiere on 27 April 1991 in Marl, Germany, in a performance by Alfred Walter and the Philharmonia Hungarica.[49] Parts of this work derive from sketches of an unnumbered symphony dating from 1903 also in B minor. The critic Bruno d'Heudières rightly sees a greater affinity to Bruckner than to Brahms in this and all of Furtwängler's symphonies.[50] In fact, the reprise that brings the first movement to its close is highly reminiscent of Bruckner. But Furtwängler's fundamental approach to his musical tasks is quite different from the way Brahms and Bruckner address theirs. Both Brahms and Bruckner strive *outward* to reconcile the unprecedented musical crisis in which they have found themselves. Furtwängler searches for his solutions by moving in the opposite direction. It seems he already is driving *inward* at the very outset of the Largo that opens the First Symphony. The harmonic convolutions become progressively complicated and push him further into the darker regions of his self.

Despite wide-ranging changes of rhythmic moods in the succeeding three movements—a scherzo, an adagio, and a contemplative finale, the basic thrust of the symphony pushes inexorably inward.

48. Pilz Media 78 004.
49. Walter recorded the symphony with the Czecho-Slovak State Philharmonic in May 1989. CD Marco Polo 8.223295.
50. Program note, world premiere First Symphony, Marl, Germany, 27 April 1991.

The scherzo in A-B-A form furthers the mounting tension of the work despite its sprightly mood. The adagio plays a dreamlike theme in G major against a colorful contrapuntal background but it functions as a transition toward further structural complexities rather than providing a respite from them. Solos by the clarinet and the bassoon look back at a modal phrase presented earlier and foreshadow the coda of the movement. This broad and cumulative coda intimates the transcendent resolution at which he arrives in the final pages of the last movement. That dénouement bears a cathartic ambience common to most works composed in the tonal style of the late Romantics, but it is of quite a different character from Brahms' joy or Bruckner's euphoria. The end of Furtwängler's struggle is characterized by a grand forbearance won from that fortitude of spirit that he accumulates throughout his musical trials. It amounts to a victory that is no less rewarding to Furtwängler than the triumphs Brahms and Bruckner achieve in their own ways.

The Second Symphony was begun in earnest during the last three years of the war and completed between the end of the war in 1945 and 1947 when he was permitted to resume conducting. Furtwängler by this time had undergone many difficult periods, but none was as difficult for him professionally as these two years, for he did not know whether he would ever be able to resume a public career again. The symphony became something of an *apologia pro vita sua*, and he described it to his friend John Knittel as a spiritual testament.[51]

Indeed, that is precisely what it is, even though Furtwängler made a number of significant revisions between the time he completed it and the last performance he gave of it a few months before he died. Every musical turn suggests the romantic wayfarer struggling to find redemption and new understanding in a universe struggling with chaos. The first movement is the largest in scale of the four parts and the most complicated musically. Here the effort to make sense out of chaos takes on an aggressive, outward thrust, driving head-on into the external world. The second movement counterbalances the first in mood and form, becoming introspective and meditative. Frustrations here are on a smaller scale, the basic mood almost liturgical. The tensions, however, are no less compelling. The scherzo links the previous movements with the final part. In it, the main themes introduced in the first movement playfully bounce off each other in a moment of respite before the majestic revelations of the final movement. All the musical problems Furtwängler sets for himself in the first three movements are unraveled and brought to a triumphant resolution in this section.

51. See *Briefe*, 18 October 1945.

Furtwängler's Third Symphony is more explicitly programmatic, its four movements having subtitles: Fate (*Verhängnis*), Life (*Leben*), the World Beyond (*Jenseits*), and The Struggle Continues (*Der Kampf geht weiter*). The themes introduced in the first movement are developed and related to each other throughout the entire work. An epic sadness fills the whole work, eventually finding soaring liberation in the final movement. The first movement hovers between vast stretches of torment and despair and fits of tenuous affirmation. The scherzo is driven by demoniac forces, defying the world and shunning reconciliation. In the adagio, Furtwängler once again enters the world of the boundless in search for the world beyond earthly cares. At its close, a sense of achieving a perfect world in some sphere beyond mortal comprehension settles upon the resolution, but Furtwängler has a surprise for us in the last movement. Subtitled "The Struggle Continues," it marks his return to earth and resumes the conflict he has sought to transcend. But the struggle is now informed by the new level of understanding he has gained in the third movement. It is not clear whether Furtwängler is searching for another kind of Nirvana or is now reconciled to finding a measure of peace simply in engaging with the mortal world.

The fourth movement precipitates an irony, for if the Nirvana Furtwängler achieves in the third movement can be readily abandoned for resuming the conflicts inherent in mortality, where indeed is paradise? What constitutes Nirvana? The inclusion of a fourth movement to this symphony with the subtitle "The Struggle Continues" suggests that for Furtwängler paradise lies in continually engaging in the conflicts of life. If there is any truth in this, it provides a clue to some of the seemingly mad choices he made in his own life, for it suggests that escape from conflict and turmoil was not the ruling motivation of his life. Instead, his ruling need was for an ongoing real life in conflict.

Perhaps the Third Symphony as a whole is Furtwängler's true apologia, for it expresses his penchant for facing headlong the various crises in his life, although the mystery it cannot explain is why he chose antagonizing some of the most sarcomatous individuals the world has yet witnessed in this millennium. Ultimately, it also reveals a personality who viewed himself as tragic in the classical sense of that word, whose life turned into a contemporary tragedy.

The first three movements of the Third Symphony were given their world premiere by Joseph Keilberth and the Berlin Philharmonic on 26 January 1956 to commemorate Furtwängler's 70th birthday.[52] The fourth movement was omitted out of respect for Furtwängler's dissatisfaction with it, but it was completed and copied shortly before

52. Furtwängler's actual birthday is 25 January.

Furtwängler died. The full four-movement version has been performed on several occasions, most notably at its world premiere
broadcast by the BBC Symphony under Brian Wright. It was also commercially recorded by Alfred Walter and the RTBF Symphony Orchestra of Brussels in 1987.[53]

While his compositions have steadily been gaining recognition
more than 30 years after he died, Furtwängler's vast orchestral can-
vases from the First Symphony on are nothing if not *difficult*.
Although he never set out consciously to make them prolix, they are
so large in scope that they require the same kind of devoted concentration demanded by the later symphonies of Bruckner and Mahler.
They also demand that concentration without the acclimating preparation of several formative symphonies. Consequently, their imperfections and difficulties are far more jarring than those infelicities
readily granted as stylistic peculiarities in the late works of Bruckner
and Mahler. What is more, they require a certain amount of non-musical background from the listener because they are as much intense
philosophical meditations as they are epic musical constructs. The
sheer weight of these ruminations occasionally brings these works
perilously close to the point where their philosophical content
becomes more compelling than their musical substance.

Some critics have asked—though none has dared assert it—if
Furtwängler the composer might have been compelled to challenge
Mahler as the last great symphonist in the German tradition of serious
music.[54] Furtwängler never considered Mahler in such extravagant
terms, and it is doubtful whether he ever suspected Mahler would
seize the imagination of the concert-going public the way he has in the
past quarter century. Nonetheless, his major works share one feature
in common with all great composers, especially Mahler. They reveal
the fruition of a supreme act of will, whose force takes utterance in
large-scale musical form. What has yet to be determined is whether
the acts of will that pushed the music of Beethoven, Brahms, Bruckner, and even Mahler to utterances never clearly articulated before
also pushed Furtwängler's inflections to new horizons.

The consensus on Furtwängler the composer in the last years of
the millennium is that he synthesizes and summarizes rather than
strikes out boldly for uncharted realms of expression. Werner Thärichen, who was timpanist with the Berlin Philharmonic from 1948 to

53. CD Marco Polo 8.223105.
54. See K. H. Rappel, Commemorative Lecture on the Anniversary of Furtwängler's Birth, delivered over West German Radio, Cologne, 25 January 1961. The
text appears in the booklet accomanying Deutsche Grammophon's boxed 3-record set
In Memoriam KL27-32.

1987 and also a composer of several large-scale works for timpani and orchestra, takes a sanguine view of Furtwängler's compositions:

> Is he a great composer? I don't know what greatness means in a composer. But Furtwängler had a great love for music, and that is what is communicated in his compositions. There is both great joy and sadness in his works.[55]

Wolfgang Stresemann was Intendant of the Berlin Philharmonic when Barenboim and Mehta played Furtwängler's *Symphonie Concertante* in 1964. He also has had many of his own compositions performed, and he poses a somewhat different view of Furtwängler as composer:

> When Barenboim and Mehta performed the *Concertante* in 1965, it was a tremendous success because they were both young at the time, and they played it with such conviction. And that's what you need for Furtwängler's works: conviction. They will never become part of the regular repertory in my view because they lack that originality that can survive bad or indifferent performances.
>
> The *Te Deum* [1910] is early, short, to the point, and has some beautiful moments. You can concentrate on it. You can't concentrate on the later longer works. They require too much, and they are too long. You eventually give up because in spite of all his skill in working out themes, you feel it's an exercise in music you heard somewhere before.
>
> He always said he was first a composer and second a conductor, but if a man permits himself to do so much conducting instead of composing, especially later when there was no financial need to conduct so much, deep down, he was not a composer in the first place.
>
> If you hear a piece by Mahler—just one theme, you know it's Mahler. With Furtwängler, you're not quite so sure. His works don't have that air of originality that, say, Mahler has. But it is still very good music.[56]

But until very recently, the same observation was regarded as the final pejorative word on Mahler and Bruckner. Only now, almost a century after their works came to pass, are their so-called summations regarded as progressive. Furtwängler's works may have to wait even longer to be assessed. If they bear a mark of truly distinctive originality, which some believe they indubitably do, the collective ear has yet to respond fully to it.

55. Personal conversation with the author, Berlin, 8 October 1990.
56. Personal conversation with the author, Berlin, 9 October 1990.

25

Eroica

Furtwängler completed the recording of *Walküre* for EMI in Vienna on 6 October 1954. He returned to Clarens to finish his Third Symphony. At the end of the month he came down with what seemed like a bad cold. Elisabeth drove him to a clinic in Wiesbaden, where his doctor said he had come down with pneumonia again but would pull through. Furtwängler calmly told his wife he was going to die. When she told the doctors what he had said, they scoffed, showing her x-rays to prove that the damage to his lungs was by no means irreparable. But his condition deteriorated, and his doctors finally shrugged and asked, "How can we save a man who no longer wants to live?"

There was no question but that his health had declined precipitously since 1952, when he came down with an especially virulent bout of pneumonia. The following year, he collapsed on the podium in Vienna during a performance of Beethoven's Ninth.[1] In the last months of his life, his failing hearing could be noticed during performances of *Don Giovanni* at Salzburg when there were pregnant pauses between the end of the harpsichord cadenzas and the cues for the rest of the orchestra to start playing.[2] For what turned out to be his last concert in Berlin, microphones were arranged around the platform during rehearsals so the sound could be amplified into a pair of headphones he wore. It was of no avail. He stopped the orchestra, and

1. 23 January 1953.
2. See Erich Leinsdorf, *Cadenza*, (Boston) 1976, p. 5.

said quietly, "That will be all, gentlemen." The concert came off as though nothing was wrong. Furtwängler never returned to Berlin again.[3]

But the boundless sadness he felt in the way everything was going with his health, in the world, his music, which was his world, never communicated itself to his immediate family. His son by Elisabeth, Andreas, was almost ten now, and he recalls the pleasure father and son gave each other in the few years Andreas was old enough to appreciate his father as a companion.

"With the family, he was very happy," says Andreas over 35 years later. Now a successful classical archaeologist (like his paternal grandfather), he bears a striking resemblance in his mid-forties to his father at a younger age. During a conversation with me in Saarbrücken in spring 1990, Andreas recalled memories of his father:

> He loved to joke and play with the children. He was perhaps a bit of a child himself. But he was a hard worker, and sometimes, he would stay in his studio from morning to night just working, working. Sometimes he would take a short walk—he loved walking, and he would take me with him. He walked very fast, and I had to run to keep up with him. He was doing a lot of composing at this time, and doing a lot of conducting.

Furtwängler spent a good deal of time away from home, but he brought all his children to rehearsal when it was possible for him to do so:

> I never thought it was strange that he was a musician rather than somebody who worked in an office or a factory. Once in Lucerne, he took me to a rehearsal. At one point he called for me from the audience and put me on the podium. I was frightened, and the orchestra had a good laugh. He was always full of music, even when he was driving, he was conducting and singing. He very narrowly escaped a couple of accidents. We all loved him, because he was a little bit crazy.
>
> My father also took me and Thomas [Andreas' half-brother, one of four children from Elisabeth's first marriage] many times to the rehearsals at Lucerne and Salzburg. That was quite a treat for us. It was just important to me that we all be together.

Since they lived in Switzerland where his schooling was in French, they spoke French at home. While Furtwängler loved having children, he had a threshold of tolerance when it came to discipline.

---

3. Curt Riess reports Furtwängler told him at dinner after his last concert that he would never again conduct in Berlin. See "Abschied von Berlin," *Ein Mass, dass Heute fehlt . . .*, (Vienna) 1986, pp. 158–159.

"I remember my father getting really angry at me only once," says Andreas, grinning:

> One time, I was skating with friends on the wooden veranda outside his studio, while he was working. We were making a terrible clatter. But for my father it was nothing. He could concentrate fully even with all that noise.
>
> But once I bragged to a friend who had a very strict father that my father would never yell at me. So I took him into my father's studio where he was working at the piano. I hit the keys a couple of times, and he said, "Stop that." And I did it again. Again he said, "Stop that! I have to work. Go outside with your friend." The third time I did it, he gave me the hardest slap on the behind I ever had. It was very humiliating for me, because he had never done that before.

What Andreas remembers most vividly about his father is his love for nature:

> He would take me for walks and show me details about leaves and flowers and animals. He also liked lizards and snakes. I remember once some boys were trying to kill a snake with stones on the shore of Lake Leman while I was walking with him. He saw them and he became furious. He started yelling at them to stop.[4]

"At the end of Furtwängler's life," says Wolfgang Stresemann, "he felt beaten himself. He felt that he was a remnant of the past and that people had changed. He got very pessimistic about life. You might say that death came to him as a friend."[5]

When the end came on 30 November 1954 Elisabeth was with him. Berta Geissmar's mother sent her a condolence note, and she replied:

> As he would have had it, he was fully conscious before he died, without sorrow, great in his humility. I was alone with him and held his hand until he drew his last breath.[6]

Even in death, Furtwängler could not avoid politics. "Berlin wanted me to let them build a tomb for him there," says Frau Furtwängler, "but quite frankly, I was afraid the Russians would try to take him for themselves. Wilhelm would not have wanted that. So I decided to bury him in the family plot in Heidelberg."

4. Personal conversation with the author, Saarbrücken, 30 March 1990.
5. Personal conversation with the author, Berlin, 9 October 1990.
6. No date. Source: Staatarchiv Mannheim.

His death made headlines in all the newspapers, and in America most published reports described him as a Nazi collaborator whose loss was the world's gain. For those who knew better, though, Furtwängler's passing brought forth some eloquent tributes. Perhaps the most moving of these was offered by Paul Hindemith:

> It was a deep belief in the fundamental truth of the Beautiful, a belief which enabled him to understand how to transform musical experiences into confessions of faith: and whoever can do that is more than a conductor, more than a composer, and more than a pianist. He is simply a truly great musician and a great man. In this form of his being, he was closely related to the medieval masters, who always practiced their art *ad maiorum Dei gloriam* (to the greater glory of God), and in this sense his image will live on in us, to make music for us in the future, as a *scientia bene modulandi* (well modulated skill) again and again to be created, perceived, and experienced.[7]

In his memorial address at Salzburg on 17 August 1955, Bernard Paumgartner concluded:

> It was something divine that spoke through him, an inspiration which we should continue to share as a light and a blessing not to be lost, in this by no means best of worlds.[8]

The first tour of the Berlin Philharmonic through the United States with Furtwängler at its helm had been scheduled for spring 1955.[9] He was reluctant to go on such a mission, for the trip was perforce a political one. Even a letter from the President of West Germany, Konrad Adenauer, pleading with him to take the tour was not sufficient to move him.[10] He was also terrified of the state his hearing would be in after an arduous trans-Atlantic flight.[11] Frau Furtwängler recalls that he was anxious to face down his American audiences, but he was afraid the extent of his hearing loss would be detected:

> He kept saying to me, "If only we were going to Japan or someplace where I would not have to talk directly in German. But all those émigrés in

7. Quoted from *Furtwängler Recalled*, p. 59.
8. *Furtwängler Recalled*, p. 64.
9. The Vienna Philharmonic originally engaged Furtwängler for a tour of the United States in 1954 but he canceled because he wanted to tour first with the Berlin Philharmonic.
10. Adenauer to Furtwängler, 13 July 1953. See Muck, p. 256.
11. See Erich Leinsdorf's *Cadenza*, (Boston) 1976, p. 5.

478 « » The Devil's Music Master

America will start talking to me . . . I won't hear what they are saying . . .
and they'll know . . . they'll *know* . . ." I'm sure his loss of hearing was
what really broke his will to go on living. He wanted to die rather than go
on that tour in his condition.[12]

The tour, of course, was undertaken by Karajan. It caused sensation rather than being sensational. When the orchestra performed in
Carnegie Hall, demonstrators outside picketed and passed out anti-
Nazi pamphlets. A flock of street pigeons was released into the hall
when Karajan entered the stage. But in Pittsburgh on 5 March 1955
Karajan's long-held wish came true. The orchestra voted him Conductor for Life. The Conductor for Life stipulation in his contract meant
that he could not be fired. Karajan always felt that Furtwängler had
persecuted him by keeping his engagements with the Berlin Philharmonic to a minimum, and he was determined to make sure nothing
like that would ever happen to him again. But just as Furtwängler justifiably felt haunted by the specter of the younger, ambitious Karajan
seeking to muscle in on his turf, so Furtwängler haunted Karajan in
death.

"Karajan felt throughout his tenure that he didn't get the Furtwängler contract," says Stresemann, who was Intendant of the Berlin
Philharmonic in two periods between 1957 to 1978:

> In other words, he felt he never got the full extent of the privileges that
> Furtwängler got because Furtwängler had a clause written in his contract
> called the *Verwaltungsordnung* that gave him what amounted to absolute
> power. Karajan felt that he didn't have the full extent of Furtwängler's
> might.
>
> The orchestra did have more rights under Karajan than they had
> under Furtwängler. The issue came to a head with the arrival of Sabine
> Meyer [a solo clarinetist who became a focal point of a protracted and
> divisive controversy between Karajan and the orchestra in 1983]. Tradi-
> tionally, new members were elected to the orchestra through a vote, with
> the conductor as one of the voices. If there was too much resistance, a
> compromise would be reached, and it worked out beautifully. But with
> Meyer, Karajan wanted his way, and the Intendant Peter Girth [Strese-
> mann's successor] took his side against the orchestra.[13]

The controversy spurred seething resentment in many members
of the orchestra, prompting one of them to write a book, whose subtitle, "Furtwängler or Karajan," invoked Karajan's dreaded Ghost of

12. Personal conversation with the author, Clarens, 23 August 1991.
13. Personal conversation with the author, Berlin, 9 October 1991.

Greatness Past.[14] To add insult to detriment, Furtwängler comes out far ahead as both musician and human being. But the author, Werner Thärichen, who was the orchestra's first timpanist from 1948, does credit Karajan with astronomically improving the standard of living of Philharmonic members. In Thärichen's eyes, Karajan was indeed a Greek bearing gifts, for he wanted concessions in exchange for the money he secured for the orchestra. But from a purely musical stand-point, he finds that Karajan never really wanted to communicate with the orchestra as Furtwängler did because he had the irritating habit of keeping his eyes shut tightly while he was conducting.[15] Thärichen also found that Karajan's climaxes were so noisy that he had to stuff his ears with cotton.[16]

Over the following season, Sabine Meyer became the wind that launched a thousand ships, and she ultimately resigned of her own accord. The dispute led to an unhappy end for the long and frequently beautiful marriage between Karajan and the Berlin Philharmonic. He resigned in 1988. By July of the following year he was dead.

No suitable German could be found to succeed him, and Karajan really had groomed no one to take his place. Ultimately, his post was taken by Claudio Abbado, but he has received only a seven-year con-tract, an arrangement with which he is quite comfortable. "I think they picked me because I prefer the human approach to everything I do," he says, getting to the heart of his intentions in leadership style. "I hate dictators because I grew up in Fascist Italy, and in music, I pre-fer the human approach as in chamber music," he adds in a discreet allusion to the approach of his predecessor. "The Berlin Philharmonic is like a family to me, we are wonderful friends and we understand each other. You get the feeling you can fly with them. They give every-thing."[17]

Karajan did not groom a successor possibly because he found the concept almost inconceivable. In a way, that vacuity of foresight was not mere vanity. His way with music and his attitude toward it as a means of acquiring absolute power was becoming passé in his eighth decade. To some, even the importance of music itself in Germany has become an antiquated priority in the closing years of this century.

14. *Paukenschläge: Furtwängler oder Karajan*, (Zürich) 1987. Hereafter referred to as Thärichen. The improvement in standards of living among members of the Berlin Philharmonic under Karajan is indisputable. Thärichen, for example, lives with his fam-ily in a comfortable suburb of Berlin in a spacious home replete with a barn, farm ani-mals, and a pony on the adjoining grounds.

15. Thärichen, p. 39.

16. Thärichen, p. 65.

17. Personal conversation with the author, Vienna, 24 October 1990.

"Germany had a great time being number one in music from Bach to Richard Strauss; now it's over," says Stresemann firmly:

> Germany is just one of several countries producing good musicians, but it's not first. No country is first. You see, music is not important in our age. This is an age of science and technology, and to oversimplify a little, you can't have an Einstein and a Bach at the same time. People are far more interested in technology than they are in the arts. The Himalayas of arts lie in the past . . . at least at the moment. The coming generations are interested in other things. Music now is the most endangered of all the arts because it doesn't exist as a painting, a book, or even a film exists. You can't touch it, and people are interested in tangible things these days. Strauss himself once said that he was the last chapter in the greatness of German music, and he added modestly that it was, for whatever it was worth, a short chapter.[18]

18. Personal conversation with the author, Berlin, 8 October 1990.

26

Coda: A Dominant Ninth

The next chapter in Wilhelm Furtwängler's life began the moment he died. The public all but resurrected him as it flocked to buy a commemorative recording EMI released of his live performance of Beethoven's Ninth at Bayreuth. That event took place on 29 July 1951 to consecrate the re-opening of the Bayreuth Festival for the first time since the end of World War II. Furtwängler had last conducted there the summer of 1944, just before Goebbels closed all German theaters. By the following summer, the theater had been damaged by Allied bombing, and the Americans commandeered it for entertainment purposes after the German surrender in May 1945. Except for occasional use by the GIs, it remained dark until the Wagner family was permitted to resume the yearly festivals. Furtwängler was chosen to conduct what amounted to a re-consecration of the house that Richard Wagner built.

The event received world-wide attention, and nearly every seat in the unique demi-amphitheater was occupied by a recognizable luminary—past or present—from the music, cultural or political world. There were, however, two choice empty seats. Frau Furtwängler and Andreas—then seven years old—were delayed on the highway leading to Bayreuth, and they both missed the performance. They did attend the second one two days later.

The orchestra and chorus were drawn from the best musicians in Germany and Austria, many subordinate positions being taken by artists of first-chair caliber. The soloists were hand-picked by Furtwängler: Elizabeth Schwarzkopf, Elisabeth Höngen, Hans Hopf, and Otto Edelmann. Although he always had maintained that music and politics should be kept apart, this was a performance bearing significance far beyond the mere re-opening of an old theater, and a lot was at stake. It marked the litmus test of whether German culture had indeed survived what Nazis and Allies both had hammered literally into the ground, the emergence of German music from its disastrous immediate past, and the official beginning of normalizing Germany in the emerging scheme of international cultural relations.

The concert was a major test for Furtwängler too, for he had maintained that he remained in Germany during the Third Reich to husband and protect German music from the devils within. This performance would tell a whole world listening with baleful ears, if in fact that guardianship had been in vain, if in fact the Devil had been exorcised. Even more important, perhaps, it would tell millions of Germans, whose national identity was inextricably steeped in the music of its great masters, if they were indeed on the path to recovering their self-respect. Once again, Furtwängler became in spite of himself every bit a political figure as he had been for twenty years, but in a way he probably never imagined. For now, during a concert lasting little more than 80 minutes, he was not merely representing the Germany of his mind and heart. For that brief hour, he was Germany to the whole world.

"It was terrifying," recalls Schwarzkopf. "Really terrifying. *Everybody* was nervous. We rehearsed in the morning, and we had one run-through immediately before the performance. We had three frightful movements waiting outside before the soloists came onto the stage. The soprano part is so fiendishly difficult, and you have an enormous responsibility, so one is always in terror, but especially at that performance."[1]

Fortunately, we do not have to rely on verbal or written accounts of everybody's vindication, at least on purely musical terms. Furtwängler regarded the Ninth and the event at which he was now performing it both as rituals, but in the sense of marking renewal rather than denoting mere solemnity of occasion. He gave 103 performances of the work between 1911 and his death, and at least nine complete recordings of these concerts survive.[2] All these documentations reflect that ongoing labor, and those who have listened carefully to

---

1. Personal conversation with the author, Zürich, 4 April 1990.
2. Furtwängler never made a studio recording of the Ninth, though one was planned with the Philharmonia Orchestra as part of his new contract with HMV/EMI in 1952.

them all have their personal choices for the most extraordinary among them. Furtwängler's habit of reworking every piece he conducted makes each encounter with this valedictory symphony special in one way or another, but this one stands out in bold relief from the rest on interpretive as well as historical grounds. Even for Furtwängler, this Ninth was an extraordinary performance, and like it or not, its power is hard to abjure. It remains at once impulsive and thoughtful, rhetorical and lyrical, dramatic in attitude and epic in scope.

Speed and dynamic shadings do not vary as much in the extant versions of the Ninth as in his performances of the other symphonies—at least in the first three movements. Instead, what distinguishes them from each other are attitude and feeling. The performance from 21– 24 March 1942, for example, is filled with dark foreboding. Even the choral movement reveals a presentiment of *Dies Irae* rather than a vision of Elysium.[3] By contrast, the Bayreuth performance is imbued with a feeling of jubilant celebration in tragedy surmounted. Here great cosmic forces clash for dominance as they always do in Furtwängler's view of Beethoven, but the conflict now is filled with sunlight. Even the scherzo is rescued from being submerged by the conflict, extricated by the imperturbable charm Furtwängler draws from each instrumental section.

Perhaps what makes the slow movement so remarkable is the sustained image of a softly undulating landscape Furtwängler evokes without unduly distending the orchestral line. Ritual here takes on a sense of prayer, as the winds and brass sweeten their tone, dove-tailing into and swelling within the upper strings, only to descend softly onto the recurring bass pedal. The movement is not without flaws; a momentary lapse in a transitional horn solo, for example. Again and again, however, the lapses serve only to underscore the frailty of human chances as each soloist spins out his share of the melodic line.

In the final movement, the ritual turns to the desired consecration. Opposing forces clash again as Furtwängler uses two timpanists to rattle out the clamor introducing the movement. The fitful leaps in the lower strings anticipate the arrival of the main theme of joy as chaos threatens to obliterate it. But Furtwängler endows these troubled passages with a feeling of inevitable triumph. Ultimately, the hushed entry of the choral theme justifies that intimation. Taken slightly faster than some of his other performances, the bass line swells and

3. Beethoven also considered composing a purely orchestral finale before deciding upon the choral movement. The main theme of this discarded concept became the principal theme in the finale of his String Quartet in A Minor, Opus 132. It suggests that Beethoven may well have had a somber, tragic conclusion in mind for the Ninth, rather than the exultant anthem that ultimately crowned the work.

recedes into the repetition of the theme taken up by upper strings and winds, eventually hastening toward still another rehearsal of the theme by the whole orchestra, only to be interrupted by the forces of negativity again. When the arrival of the first vocalist finally calls for an end to disharmony, Furtwängler has already informed the movement with a sense of unifying joy.

The solo singers were all primed for the occasion, and they each respond eagerly to Furtwängler's inspiring hand. Perhaps the most surprising singer in the quartet is Hans Hopf. It is hard to guess why Furtwängler chose this stalwart and not always musical tenor of beefy voice, but Hopf was beginning to make a name for himself as Tristan and Tannhäuser throughout Europe, and, as it turns out, he proves quite nimble in manoeuvering his voice around some extremely difficult music. He also delivers his short solo ("*Froh, wie seine Sonnen fliegen . . .*") with the kind of good-natured gusto that befitted the occasion. Otto Edelmann is neither darker nor heavier than some basses who call the warring elements of the universe to peace ("*O Freunde, nicht diese Töne . . .*"), but he proffers the sort of wise amiability here that eventually made him a fine Hans Sachs. Elisabeth Höngen has lost none of the warmth that characterized her singing during the 1942 performances, and she was on the stage for good reason too. She represented the many German artists active during the Nazi period who now had put the war behind them.

In 1951 Elisabeth Schwarzkopf was coming into the glory period of a career that spanned over three decades. She had worked with Furtwängler since 1949 at Salzburg, and they collaborated on numerous projects right up to his death. By the time she came to Bayreuth, the voice had developed from a light lyric soprano into an agile spinto, and with it she went on to become the quintessential Marschallin and the standard-bearer for post-Elektra Strauss heroines for the next twenty years. While she is not quite possessed of Tilla Briem's ecstatic utterance in 1942, her voice here is a bit more evenly distributed than Briem's in weight from top to bottom, and she peals forth Schiller's text in radiant blush.

Despite the occasional gaffes, the electric tension, exacerbated by what was at stake for everybody on both sides of the footlights, is transmuted into an endless rapturous *frisson*. While the live performance of 1942 amounts to an anguished cry intimating impending cataclysm, the Bayreuth Ninth reveals Furtwängler portraying the work as a manifesto of consolation, renewal, and psychic healing. Even repeated hearings do not dull that attestation; to the contrary, they reinforce it.

In its afterlife on records, the salubrious revels of this Bayreuth

Ninth have extended far beyond the mere specifics of the occasion. The commercial release came out almost immediately after Furtwängler died, and it remains by far his most popular record, outselling even his version of *Tristan*.[4] But its commercial popularity may obscure what is most compelling about this performance, quite apart from its importance as a document of Furtwängler at his most inspired. It survives as incandescent proof that Wilhelm Furtwängler's life, however tragic its course may have been, was not ill-spent.

One final word about what survives of Furtwängler on records. Immortality usually grants but one life to those on whom posthumous fame may fall, but Furtwängler lives on with two: through his studio recordings and in recordings of his live performances. The relays and tapes of the live performances disclose a conductor demonstrating his greatness by grappling, constantly and humbly, with the raw material in the score before him. They bear witness to that ongoing struggle to give music shape, meaning, and a life of its own, as he inspires both players and spectators at each encounter to achieve those objectives with him. In so doing, the live performances are transmuted into communal events in the ancient sense of that concept. They become forums for cleansing the spirit. Apart from his recording of *Tristan*, the studio recordings show Furtwängler fitfully coming to terms with a medium in which he was never comfortable. His objective in his later studio recordings became an exploration into the tonal mass lying at the heart of every composition. In doing so, Furtwängler came full circle back to his primary objective in making music: re-creating the work as it first occurred to the composer as a whole, a unit, something borne from nothing.

In the time that has passed since Furtwängler's death, his musical reputation at least has undergone a quiet renascence and steady revaluation. In the first ten years after his death, Furtwängler's records became almost impossible to find except in second-hand stores. But his recordings of *Tristan* and the Bayreuth Ninth always bore the standard for any new recording of Wagner and Beethoven throughout this time. The classical recording industry was becoming a mighty money machine throughout the 1960s and 1970s, and stocks of recordings by Furtwängler and other conductors of his generation shrank to make room for the glut of new issues by a vast parade of living and younger conductors. Ironically, the variety of new interpretive viewpoints seemed to diminish in direct proportion to their overwhelming numbers. Only the small persistent presence of Furtwängler, the later recordings of Otto Klemperer, and a few conductors from earlier gen-

4. The Bayreuth Ninth has appeared on 40 labels throughout the world.

erations seemed to offer the record buyer compelling alternatives to the ever increasing trend toward glamorous, silken homogeneity of orchestral and vocal sound that became the stock-in-trade of other highly touted conductors.

Many have since pursued beauty of tone virtually as an end in itself, but no conductor in the 20th century made more of a fetish of it than Herbert von Karajan. As reproduction techniques improved and created heightened sonic verisimilitude, the preoccupation with tonal *purity* became one and the same as tonal *beauty* in these recordings. Perhaps the apogee of this pursuit of sonic lucidity ultimately materialized in his digital recording of *Parsifal* dating from 1981 where the sound seems to be emanating from a vacuum in which there is no atmosphere and almost no ambience, just pure sound. Such a feat was rapturously received by many listeners as a triumph in the marriage between music and science. Whether it was also an achievement in musical expression did not seem to matter much at the time. This issue still remains unanswered, and the verdict on technologically produced sonic glamor as a valid component of recorded musical expression has yet to be brought in.

But Karajan always felt cowed by his inner fear that Furtwängler was irrefutably superior, and he turned from merely striving to be the world's greatest conductor to becoming the world's most powerful conductor, and in that objective he attained the highest glory. There may never be another to surpass him in that goal, for few musicians leave an estate worth more than 270 million dollars. But the Alberich within Karajan made him miserable. After an undeniably sensational performance, for example, his own men came up to congratulate him. "*Quatsch!*" he grunted. "Furtwängler would not have liked it." The fear was real for them both, and at least one conductor who knew them both thinks the mutual apprehension was well founded. "Toscanini—you just covered your nose," as Sergiu Celibidache so elegantly put it. "Karajan was Furtwängler's only real rival."[5]

Furtwängler, however, might never have achieved the Olympian interpretive insights at which he arrived in his final years without a nemesis such as Karajan, forever goading and teasing and menacing and eternally *younger*. If Furtwängler believed in a world in which all things have their time and place, and he did, Karajan alternately embodied Aeschylus' Eumenides, pursuing him relentlessly, and Stephen King's obsessively adoring Anne Wilkes, hobbling him to new heights of inspiration. Real or imagined, this sleek incarnation of outrageous fortune prodded Furtwängler ceaselessly forward until he

5. Lang, pp. 211–212.

ultimately found inner understanding and fitful peace in his last recordings and in the final movement of his Third Symphony.

However posterity may ultimately judge Furtwängler morally as a public figure, and he still continues to be viewed harshly by some biographers of his contemporaries[6] and in some areas of the German boulevard press,[7] his most palpable vindication is the ever-increasing number of present and emerging conductors who credit him as a role model in their musical development. They include Claudio Abbado, Daniel Barenboim, Zubin Mehta, and Simon Rattle. Further proof can be seen in the Furtwängler section of many large record stores: the turnover in stock of his recordings now sometimes exceeds those of other far more publicized conductors. The supply confirms the demand. But the key to his growing popularity among new listeners is more than a matter of cyclical recurrence. It lies in his capacity to communicate in his recordings what mattered most to him about his life and life's work:

> To appreciate the greatness of the Masters is to keep faith in the greatness of humanity. To believe in material development is to believe in matter itself. By keeping faith in human greatness, the soul returns once again to the source from which it springs.

6. See Bachmann, *Karajan: Anmerkungen zu eine Karriere*, (Düsseldorf and Vienna) 1983. English version, *Karajan: Notes on a Career*, (London) 1990.

7. See Rolf Ringguth's fascinating review of Fred K. Prieberg's *Kraftprobe* in *Der Spiegel*. "Odem des Allerhöchsten," Nr. 12, 17 March 1986, pp. 249–254. See also Bernd W. Wessling, *Furtwängler: Eine kritische Biographie*, (Stuttgart) 1985, (Munich) 1987.

Index